CORPORATE
SHOWCASE 7
PHOTOGRAPHY, ILLUSTRATION & GRAPHIC DESIGN

President and Publisher
Ira Shapiro

Vice President
Advertising Sales
Julia Martin Morris

Vice-President
Operations
Wendl Kornfeld

Production Director
Kyla Kanz

Marketing Director
Ann Middlebrook

Administration

Controller
Ronald Durr

Executive Assistant
Connie Grunwald

Administrative Assistant
Danell McDowell

Advertising Sales

Sales Manager/Mail Service Manager
Lisa Wilker

Sales Representatives

New York
John Bergstrom
Barbara Preminger
Wendy Saunders
Joe Safferson

Rocky Mountain
Kate Hoffman
(303) 493-1492

West Coast
Robert J. Courtman
(213) 669-8021

Published by
American Showcase, Inc.
724 Fifth Avenue, 10th Floor
New York, New York 10019
Telephone: (212) 245-0981
Telex: 880356 AMSHOW P
Fax: (212) 265-2247

Corporate Showcase 7
Hardback 0931144-54-X
Softback 0931144-53-1

ISSN 0742-9975

Production

Production Manager
Karen Bochow

Grey Pages/Distribution Manager
Scott Holden

Production Coordinator
Chuck Rosenow

Production Coordinator
John D. Jay

Marketing

Promotion/New Projects Manager
Stephanie Whitney

Book Sales Coordinator
Richard Arlauskas

Marketing Assistant
Kate Hobbie

Special Thanks to:
Julia Curry, Matt Dreyer, Thad Grimes-Gruczka,
Leslie Haynes, Tina McKenna, Karen Minster,
Jeff Morgan

Book Design and Mechanical Production
American Showcase Inc.

Grey Pages Mechanical Production
The Mike Saltzman Group, NYC

Typesetting
Ultra Typographic Service, Inc., NYC
**Automatech Graphics
Corporation, NYC**

Color Separation, Printing and Binding
**Dai Nippon Printing Co. Ltd.,
Tokyo, Japan**

U.S. Book Trade Distribution
Watson-Guptill Publications
1515 Broadway, New York, New York 10036
(212) 764-7300
Watson-Guptill ISBN: 8230-0952-1

For Sales Outside U.S.
Rotovision S.A.
9 Route Suisse
1295 Mies Switzerland
Telephone: (22) 553055
Telex: 419246 ROVI

Cover Credits

Front Cover Photograph: © Ken Haas
for Citicorp Investment Bank

Title Page Illustration: Catherine Kanner

F O R E W O R D

Corporations make a statement in many ways—with their products, through their consumer advertising, via transmittal of annual reports to their shareholders. The sum of these, and other parts, translates into corporate image.

The right visual profile can be of tremendous help in maintaining, or even establishing, that corporate image.

The business of business communications—from TV commercials and print ads to annual reports, brochures, corporate identity and logos, packaging and product design—is highly specialized, requiring its own presentation vehicle. So, Corporate Showcase was conceived, as a marketing tool to provide corporate communicators with access to the variety of visual resources available to them.

Each August, just prior to the annual report season, the latest edition of Corporate Showcase

is released, highlighting visual trends in the field of business communications. This is the time of year when corporate executives seek designers, photographers and illustrators. In this seventh edition, more than 200 of those corporate photographers, illustrators and graphic designers from across the country showcase their unique styles. All of these creatives play a key role in making corporations accessible and visible to their audiences. Corporate Showcase presents the visual expertise available to convey the right corporate message.

Inside you'll find:

• More than 1300 photographs and illustrations on 242 full-color art pages.

• Articles by industry leaders providing a fresh viewpoint on the complex world of corporate communications.

• A telephone directory section with thousands of updated phone listings and addresses for photographers, illustrators, graphic designers, reps, stock photo agencies and other production/ support services.

• A listing of the associations, guilds and clubs within the advertising and graphics community.

• Photographers presented by geographic region, and indexed, for quick and easy reference.

Corporate Showcase 7 is an essential sourcebook for graphic designers, corporate communications directors and others involved in corporate advertising and promotion, professional and amateur photographers, illustrators and students in those fields.

I sincerely hope you'll find the range of talent presented in these pages both stimulating and relevant.

Ira B Shapiro

Publisher

American Showcase, Inc.
New York

Contents

Viewpoints

Graphic Arts Organizations

Grey Pages

Indexes

Alphabetical Listing
Illustrators, Photographers & Graphic Designers

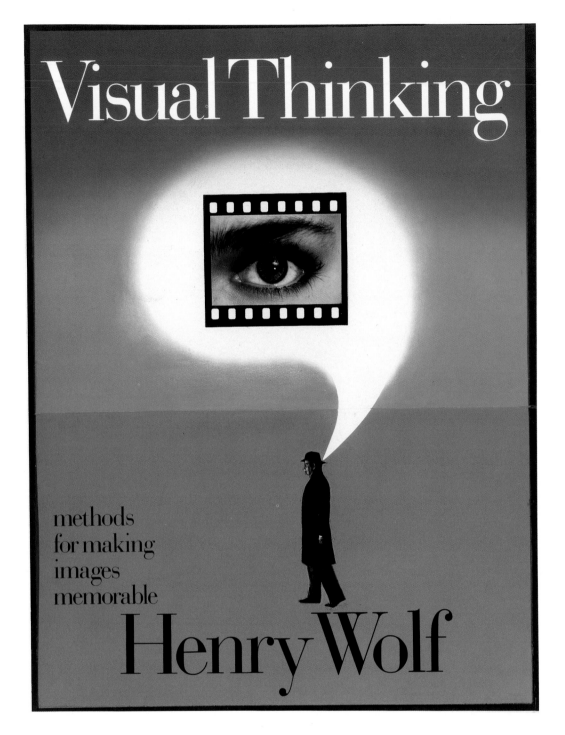

Creation by design, not accident.

Outstanding visual images rarely just happen. They are the result of careful premeditation, planning and design.

This new book by Henry Wolf, one of today's foremost photographers and art directors, examines the many creative methods he employs—from use of strange perspective to settings in improbable places to unexpected combinations.

Here are 17 chapters of techniques for translating words into photographic images that will be more com-pelling, more unique and therefore more memorable.

Any visual communicator will find inspiration in these pages.

Clothbound with hundreds of full-color photographs, as well as reproductions of many classic works of art that have been an influence on them.

184 pages. $45.00. Released in October 1988. Order now! American Showcase, 724 Fifth Avenue, New York, New York 10019, (212) 245-0981.

Illustrators & Graphic Designers

Renard Represents

MICHAEL
SCHWAB

Renard Represents Inc.
501 Fifth Avenue
New York, N.Y. 10017
Tel: 212 490 2450
Fax: 212 697 6828

Renard Represents

BART FORBES

Renard Represents Inc.
501 Fifth Avenue
New York, N.Y. 10017
Tel: 212 490 2450
Fax: 212 697 6828

© 1987 BART FORBES

Renard Represents

RICHARD NEWTON

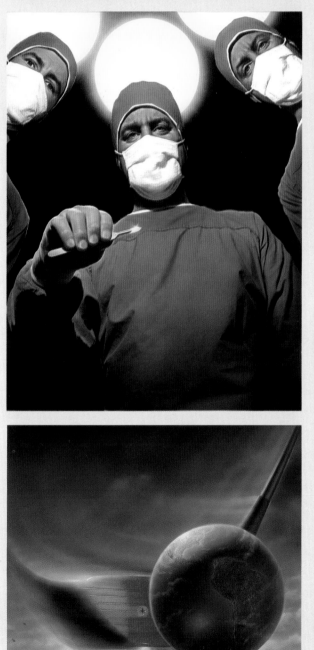

Renard Represents Inc.
501 Fifth Avenue
New York, N.Y. 10017
Tel: 212 490 2450
Fax: 212 697 6828

Renard Represents

JOHN COLLIER

Renard Represents Inc.
501 Fifth Avenue
New York, N.Y. 10017
Tel: 212 490 2450
Fax: 212 697 6828

Renard Represents

JOHN MARTIN

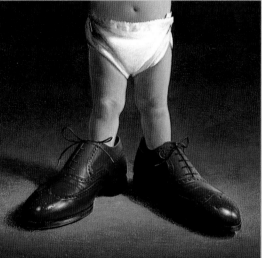

Renard Represents Inc.
501 Fifth Avenue
New York, N.Y. 10017
Tel: 212 490 2450
Fax: 212 697 6828

15

Renard Represents

STEVE BJÖRKMAN

Available for print and film

Renard Represents Inc.
501 Fifth Avenue
New York, N.Y. 10017
Tel: 212 490 2450
Fax: 212 697 6828

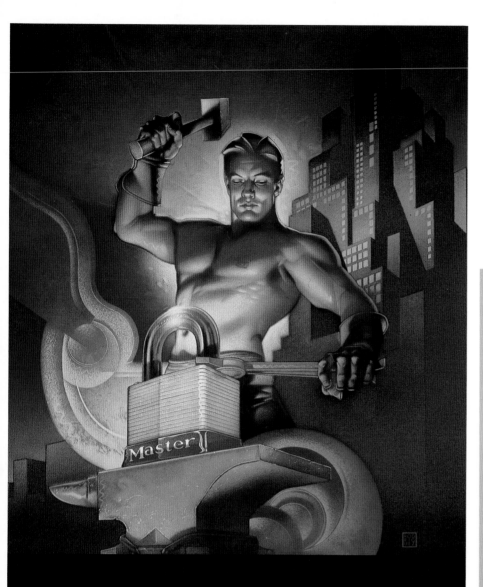

ROBERT RODRIGUEZ

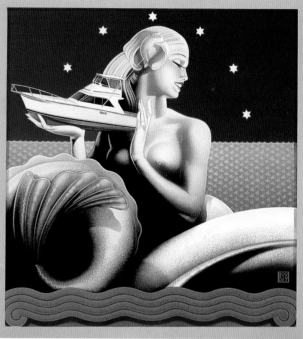

Glenn Dean
R.D. 2 — Box 788
Sussex, New Jersey 07461
(212) 490-2450

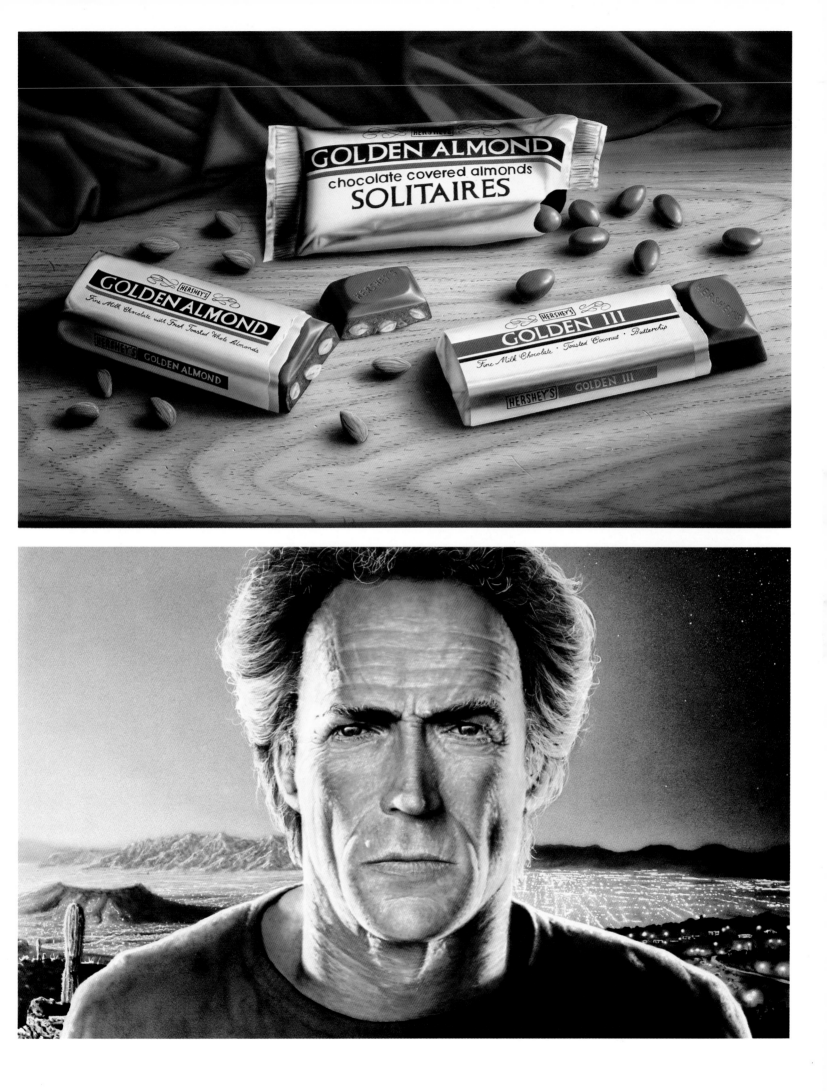

Guy Billout

225 Lafayette Street
Suite 1008
New York, New York 10012
(212) 431-6350

Illustration for "Choices" in Annual Report for
MICOM Systems, Inc.

Roger Boehm
529 South 7th Street
Suite 539
Minneapolis, Minnesota 55415
(612) 332-0787

NORWEST CENTER

SNOW GUY

The Annual Report Team

The designer and photographer have to be involved in almost every phase of annual report planning and production for the report to be a success.

At Singer, we have used the same designer for over ten years, and the same photographer for the past six reports. That is unusual in the industry. The only explanation for it is that an unusual amount of communication takes place between all of us, all the time. That kind of active interchange of ideas keeps us all fresh and keeps original ideas flowing.

Our planning, for a report issued in March covering the calendar year, starts with discussions with the designer in July. It is my job, as Director of Corporate Communications & Advertising, to understand and accurately describe the company's accomplishments for the year that is still in progress. Senior management shifts in goals and direction, reflected in formal speeches or presented in more casual forums, are also discussed. In addition, I describe what is happening within markets, the financial community, and the general economy that is affecting the way we do business, and how these factors might affect our future.

Early on, I suggest several overall themes for the report that will hopefully provide a fresh way for shareholder, financial, political, and customer audiences to favorably view the company's accomplishments and prospects.

Each theme is carefully examined in terms of the way it might influence or open up new design possibilities. Eventually, one theme is chosen and the designer sketches out rough formats for the cover, a special section specifically reflecting the new theme, and the Review of Operations section required every year.

The sketches are discussed within the company, and in late August or early September a full presentation is made to the Chairman and President. This involves a color mock-up, with headlines and general sections typeset, and photographs (from previous years or from stock) placed in the correct order and size for the theme and design format.

The theme and design are usually accepted with suggested improvements or alterations. At this stage, and at all succeeding ones as well, it is an enormous advantage to have a designer who is very familiar with the company and who is a constant source of fresh design concepts. Confidence in his work was long ago established with senior management and they look forward to his presentations.

The choice of a photographer has been discussed with the designer since our first meeting in early summer. Sample reels of slides have been viewed and the final selection is made once the report theme has been established. I feel very strongly that, if at all possible, one photographer should take all the shots for the book (other than those bought from stock of a general subject nature). This gives the report a unified look that cannot be duplicated with the work of several or many photographers knit together, no matter how strong the design.

Again, as with the designer, it is a very real advantage to work with the same photographer year after year. Plans immediately go forward for fall shooting. This means reserving six to nine weeks of time from the last week in September right into December.

By the first week in September, I have received replies from each division president to a memo requesting their suggestions concerning photo subjects for the report. They are asked to recommend products that are market leaders, leading contributors to the bottom line, or are examples of state-of-the-art technology.

Continued on page 44

Andy Buttram

1636 Hickory Glen Drive
Miamisburg, Ohio 45342
(513) 859-7428

Corporate and Advertising Illustrator
Also black and white and line work

Work appearing in Black Book 1985, 86, 87
Society of Illustrators 25

A N D Y · B U T T R A M

Bob Conge

28 Harper Street
Rochester, New York 14607
(716) 473-0291

Telex in Studio

Clients
Allendale Insurance
American Express
Amoco
AMP
Bank of America
Bausch & Lomb
Chase Manhattan Bank
Chicago Bar Association
Citibank
Continental Insurance Co.
Corning Glass Works
Digital Equipment
Eastman Kodak
Gannett Corp.
General Electric
Lapp Insulator Co.
Merrill Lynch
Merchants Insurance Group
Mobil
Nalge
Rochester Philharmonic
Orchestra
R.R. Donnelley
Schering-Plough
State Street Bank & Trust
The New York Times
University of Rochester
U.S. Sprint
Westwood Pharmaceuticals
Xerox Corp

To View More Work:
AR 1986, 1988; ADWEEK
Portfolios 87, 88; American
Illustration Showcase Volumes
8, 9, 10, 11; CA Illustration
Annual 1987; The Clio Book
1987; Society of Illustrators
Annuals 26, 27, 28, 29, 30; Print
Regional Design Annuals 83,
84, 85, 86, 87; Graphis Annual
85, 87; Graphis Poster Annuals
85, 86; New York Art Directors
Annuals 62nd, 64th, 65th, 66th;
Society of Publication Designers
Annuals 20th, 22nd; Print
Magazine article May 1986.

STATE STREET BANK AND TRUST COMPANY

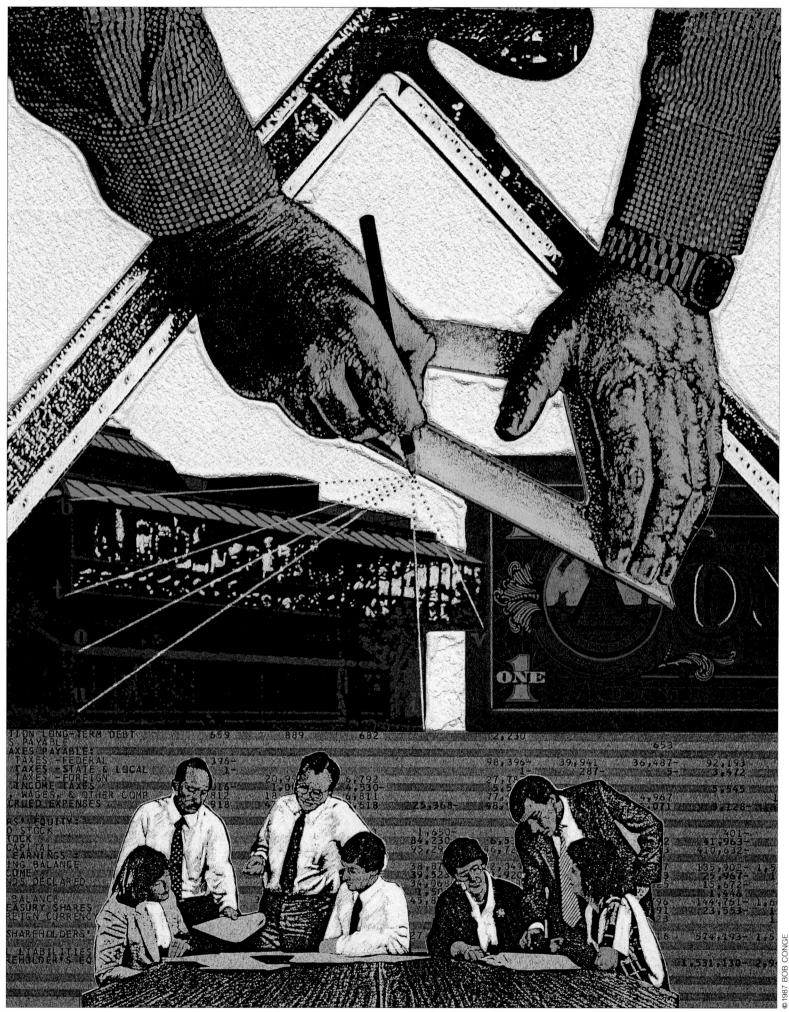

SCHERING-PLOUGH 1986 ANNUAL REPORT

David FeBland
670 West End Avenue
New York, NY 10025
(212) 580-9299

TELECOPIER SERVICE

CLIENTS:
ABC
American Express
AT&T
Atlantic Records
Anheiser-Busch
Avis
Avon Products
Bankers Trust
Bloomingdales
CBS
Celanese
Chase Manhattan Bank
Chicago Marathon
Dancer Fitzgerald Sample
Disneyland
Dutch Tourist Board
Exxon
Filenes
General Foods
HBO
IBM
Intercontinental Hotels
J. Walter Thompson
John Deere Corp.
Lever Bros.
Macy's
Mastercard
Montgomery Ward
Milton Bradley
NBC
N.W. Ayer
Ogilvy & Mather
Prudential Insurance
Revlon
RCA
Sears Roebuck
Scali McCabe Sloves
Sony
Texaco
T.V. Guide
TWA
Vista Hotels
Young & Rubicam

AWARDS & EXHIBITIONS:
Art Directors Annual
Art Direction Creativity
Graphis
Print
Advertising Techniques

Additional Samples Upon
Request

See Also:
American Showcase 7, 8, 9, 10
Corporate Showcase 4, 5, 6

Member Graphic Artists Guild

© David FeBland 1988

STOCK IMAGES AVAILABLE

DAVID
Febland
STUDIO

Jack Graber

Represented by:
Walter Supley, Jr.
The Creative Advantage
707 Union Street
Schenectady, New York 12305
(518) 370-0312

James Ibusuki

2920 Rosanna Street
Los Angeles, CA 90039
(818) 244-1645

Specializing in automotive and product illustration utilizing airbrush, brush, and pencil media.

Member Society of Illustrators of Los Angeles

Clients include:
Robert Abel & Associates
American Sunroof Corp.
Bryant Rubber Corp.
California State Lottery
Disney Channel
Fox Television Stations
KAL Vitamins
Martin Marietta
McDonnell Douglas
New World Pictures
Orion Pictures
Paramount Pictures
Ralphs Grocery Company
Seiniger Advertising
Tri Star Pictures
Vogel Communications Group
Walt Disney Company
Warner Bros.
Wrather Port Properties, Ltd.

Additional work may be seen in The Workbook, California Edition 1987, 1988

© James Ibusuki 1988

JAMES IBUSUKI
Ē · BOO · SUE · KEY

Catherine Kanner

Represented by:

John Locke
Nonnie Locke
John Locke Studios, Inc.
15 East 76th Street
New York, New York 10021
(212) 288-8010

Studio:
717 Hampden Place
Pacific Palisades, California
90272
(213) 454-7675

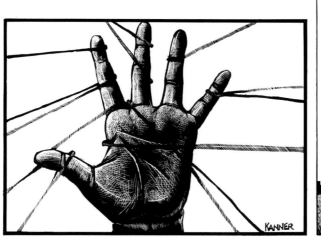

Rip Kastaris

3301 South Jefferson
St. Louis, Missouri 63118
(314) 773-9989

Telecopier in studio

Les Katz

ILLUSTRATION & DESIGN
451 Westminster Road
Brooklyn, New York 11218
(718) 284-4779

Represented by: SHARON DREXLER
110 West 40th Street
Suite 1004
New York, New York 10018

COMPLETE PORTFOLIO AVAILABLE FOR REVIEW

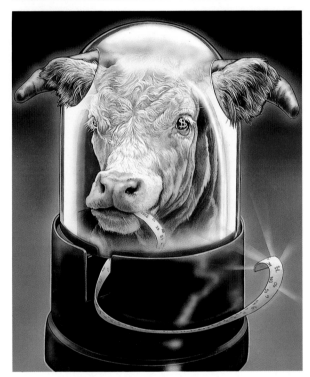

Kauftheil/ Rothschild, Ltd.

Catalog Design and Production

220 West 19th Street
New York, New York 10011
(212) 633-0222
Fax No. (212) 633-0969

We cure headaches. From design, photography, separations and printing, to the impossible deadline.

We create impressions that arrest, influence and encourage. Our graphics establish a dynamic presence for the small business or the major corporation, and persuade audiences consistently. Our catalogs not only create an image, they sell products.

Recently, we were presented with an Echo Award, the Direct Marketing Association's award for creative excellence in direct mail. That, along with frequent attention to our work in major design publications, confirms that Kauftheil/Rothschild catalogs work. Beautifully.

Clients include: ABC Carpet, American Greetings, Bulova Watch, Columbia, Crystal Clear, Hasbro, Lightolier and Olympia & York.

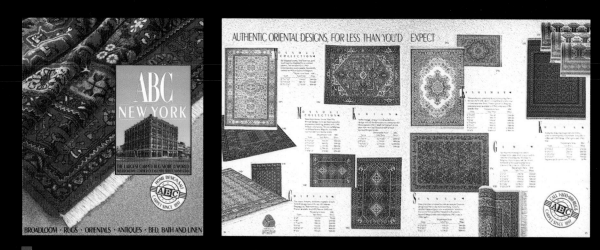

This consumer catalog put ABC carpet, the largest rug and carpet store in the US, in the mail order business. Placed as an insert in The Sunday Times, its cover parallels the style of the The New York Times Magazine, giving it greater visibility and higher readership.

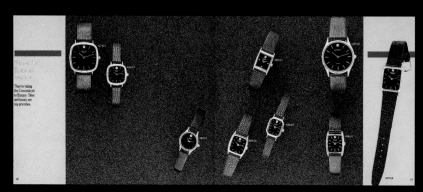

Bulova wanted us to create an image for 1987 that would position it as a leader in quality time pieces. By incorporating the simplicity of Swiss graphics into this trade catalog, these moderately priced watches take on a rich, luxurious look.

Each year, the DMA presents the Echo Award for outstanding creative work in direct mail. In 1987, we were a recipient of this prestigious award for our work on a 9-color direct response piece.

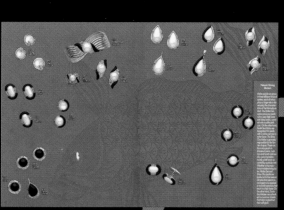

A business catalog that educates as well as sells. With its Japanese theme, it offers a guide to understanding and appreciating the cultured pearl.

The challenge was to create a catalog with color that jumps off the page and texture that can practically be felt — all within six weeks. The result, one of our best catalogs ever.

Classic styling, rich hues and fine crafting define the pages of this catalog. Through exacting production techniques we captured the textures and color combinations of this fine table linen.

Michael McCurdy

66 Lake Buel Road
Great Barrington, Massachusetts 01230-9504
(413) 528-5036 or (413) 528-2749

Wood engraving for distinctive illustration

Partial client list:

Sara Lee Corporation
H.J. Heinz Company
Maxell Corporation
Lincoln Center Theater
Evergreen Memorials

Esquire
Little, Brown and Company
Houghton Mifflin Company
Dodd, Mead, Inc.
Sierra Club Books

Fabian Melgar
14 Clover Drive
Smithtown, New York 11787
(516) 543-7561

Mixed Art/Photo Illustration
Graphic Design
Photography
Illustration

Mark Moscarillo

106 Benefit Street
Providence, Rhode Island 02903
(401) 751-3919
Studio FAX No. (401) 751-9688

Portfolio available upon request
Member Graphic Artists Guild
©1988 Mark Moscarillo

Merle Nacht

374 Main Street
Wethersfield, Connecticut 06109
(203) 563-7993

Clients include:

United Technologies
Xerox Corporation
General Electric
Otis Elevator
Georgia-Pacific
Dayton-Hudson Department
  Stores
Northeast Utilities
Insilco
The Watergate Hotel
  Restaurants
Bay Pacific Health Plan

The New Yorker (covers and
  spot drawings)
Travel and Leisure
New York Magazine
Gourmet
GQ
Vogue
Harvard Business School
  Magazine
Lotus Magazine
Applause Magazine (WHYY,
  Philadelphia)
Technology Review
Harcourt, Brace, Jovanovich
Houghton-Mifflin

The New York Times
The Boston Globe
The Plain Dealer Magazine
The Hartford Courant
Philadelphia Inquirer

HARVARD BUSINESS SCHOOL BULLETIN

XEROX WORLD

HARVARD BUSINESS SCHOOL BULLETIN

XEROX WORLD

TECHNOLOGY REVIEW

PLAIN DEALER MAGAZINE (COVER, SUMMER FICTION ISSUE)

Ken Orvidas
832 Evelyn Avenue
Albany, California 94706
(415) 525-6626

Norman Rainock
Glen Allen, Virginia
(804) 264-8123

Ross Culbert Holland & Lavery

15 West Twentieth Street
New York, New York 10011
(212) 206-0044

Peter Ross
Mecca Culbert
DK Holland
Bud Lavery

When you think of charts and maps, think of RCH&L.

To view more of our work,
see Graphis Diagrams 1988;
AIGA's Graphic Design USA 7;
Communication Arts' CA87
Design Annual; Print's Regional
Design Annual 1986 & 1987;
Corporate Showcase 3, 4, 5,
& 6 and Adweek's Portfolio of
Graphic Design 1985, 1986
& 1987.

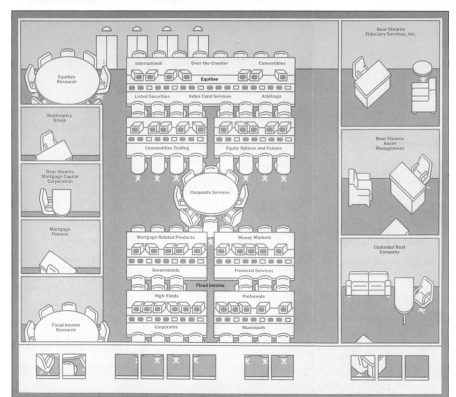

(Top, left) The Bear Stearns 1987 Annual Report explains the organization's internal structure while the cover tells the economic story simply and clearly.

(Below, right) Four charts appearing in *Nation's Business Week* illustrate how small business principals see the economy impacting on their companies.

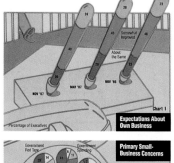

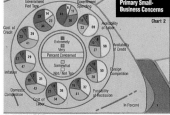

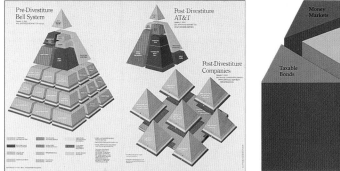

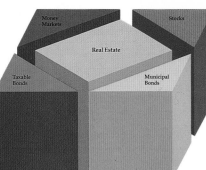

(Far left) Commissioned by AT&T to create charts explaining the corporate break up to their employees, we chose to use a pyramid, the archetypal symbol of the corporation.

(Left) RCH&L created this handsome chart for T. Rowe Price illustrating how their investments support their real estate fund.

(Below) This *Wall Street Journal* poster, which shows the *Journal's* circulation by zip code, offers the advertiser a quick and clear reference to their potential regional markets. The color-coding serves to outline the four regional editions, as well as make an eye-catching promotion piece.

THE WALL STREET JOURNAL.

Midwest Edition		563,652
Sharon, Pennsylvania		87,469
Bowling Green, Ohio		128,610
Naperville, Illinois		161,017
Highland, Illinois		95,178
Des Moines, Iowa		88,378

Eastern Edition		825,376
Chicopee, Massachusetts		199,989
Princeton, New Jersey		267,973
Silver Spring, Maryland		123,708
Charlotte, North Carolina		70,195
LaGrange, Georgia		60,505
Orlando, Florida		103,006

New England Region		152,593
Chicopee, Massachusetts		152,593

Southeast Region		233,706
Charlotte, North Carolina		70,195
LaGrange, Georgia		60,505
Orlando, Florida		103,006

Western Edition		427,799
Seattle, Washington		67,474
Palo Alto, California		119,446
Denver, Colorado		62,249
Riverside, California		178,630

Northern California Region		119,446
Palo Alto, California		119,446

Southern California Region		178,630
Riverside, California		178,630

Southwest Edition		222,427
Dallas, Texas		139,438
Beaumont, Texas		82,989

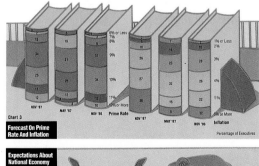

(Above) This map of the world was part of our design for Citicorp's *Chairman's Conference.* The spectrum used in the globe was the color theme used throughout the design for this project.

(Right) RCH&L's map for the new Mellon Bank Center points out the benefits of its easy access location at a glance.

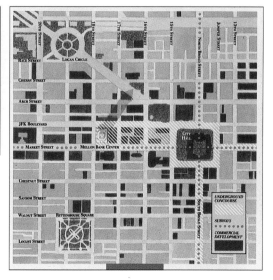

Robert Rubyan

270 Park Avenue South
Apartment 7C
New York, New York 10017
(212) 460-9217

Multi media: Audio-visual and print. Design, illustration, computer graphics, video, animation and calligraphy. Client list available on request.

Unique images created with microcomputers and animation stand photography. Using software for graphics and desk top publishing Rubyan produces high contrast film separations which are then enhanced with optical and motion control effects on the Marron Carrel camera. The final product is a high resolution color transparency ready for print or for your audio-visual or video module.

© R. Rubyan 1988

Richard Sparks

2 West Rocks Road
Norwalk, Connecticut 06851
(203) 866-2002

Clients:
Exxon
Mobil Oil
CIGNA
United States Postal Service
Yale/New Haven Hospital
Sports Illustrated
TIME
New York Magazine
KLM
Encyclopedia Britannica
Johnson & Johnson
DuPont
Book of the Month Club
NBC
CBS
RCA
Audi
Ladies' Home Journal
Redbook
Playboy
Playboy Deutschland
Reader's Digest
Sports Afield
Connecticut National Bank
Heritage Press Limited
    Edition Prints
Boy Scouts of America
McGraw-Hill
Avenue/Netherlands
Denny's
International Wool
Esquire
Rolling Stone
Forbes
Fortune
Money Magazine
Seventeen
TV Guide
Simpson Paper
etc.

Continued from page 22

The initial meeting with the photographer is very important for the success of the entire shooting schedule. A great deal of time is spent explaining not just the theme of the report and specific photographic challenges, but also reviewing the company, how it has changed internally, and how it is being perceived externally. During the past decade, Singer was transformed from a sewing firm to a high-technology company supplying aerospace electronic systems for defense and commercial markets. Each year there were new challenges, as divisions were sold, bought, or brought new products to market.

A photographer is chosen for the individual vision reflected in work he has done in the past. Certainly he could be sent out cold and good work would be accomplished. However, I am convinced that the more the photographer knows about the company, the people who run it and the spirit they inspire throughout its operating units, the better and more unique will be the shots taken. A photographer stated in a previous Showcase that input from outside himself deletes and dilutes his unique way of seeing. I agree if a client messes with lights or angles or composition—that's not his job. But until the photographer really knows why he is at a particular location taking a particular product, how that product works, and why it is important to the company's customer, he should not only listen, but ask questions. The only way to make this happen is constant contact and communication between the company contact, (in this case me), and the photographer.

A photographer has to feel that each subject is unique, and the company he is working for during this particular week is also unique. And the best way to do that is make him an important part of the report team from the start.

I have worked with enough photographers to know why I like the best of them. First, of course, is the portfolio. There is no substitute for proven experience. His curiosity is almost as important. Without it the right questions don't get asked, or explanations listened to. A high energy level has to be there. The company requires a number of set-ups at each location and that takes calories. A sense of humor is vital. Anything and everything can go wrong during the course of a shoot. And finally, a respect for people is essential, and not just for the ones paying the bills.

We go to press with our report in early March, but long before that time I know if the job will be outstanding. In the end, a crucial reason an annual report is looked at, much less read, is the quality of the images used to represent and express the company's people, products and vision.

Bruce Kaukas
Director, Corporate
Communications & Advertising
The Singer Company
Stamford, Connecticut

William & Hinds

2790 Skypark Drive #112
Torrance, California 90505
(213) 539-3259

We're a New Team of
Old Kids on the block.
Each Team Member is
a specialist in the
following fields:

Corporate Identity
Brochures
Calendars
Logo Design
Illustration
Computer Graphics
Video Presentations
Printing
Photography
Copywriting
Strategic Business Plans
Marketing Plans
Project Development
Project Management
Graphic Buying Guides

Our commitment is to
supply you with cost
effective answers to
your Corporate Marketing
Objectives.

A few of
our Team's Clients:

Admar
American Honda Motors
Bank of America
Dancer Fitzgerald
ITT Cannon
J. Walter Thompson
Matlow-Kennedy
Neutrogena
Rockwell International
Xerox Corporation

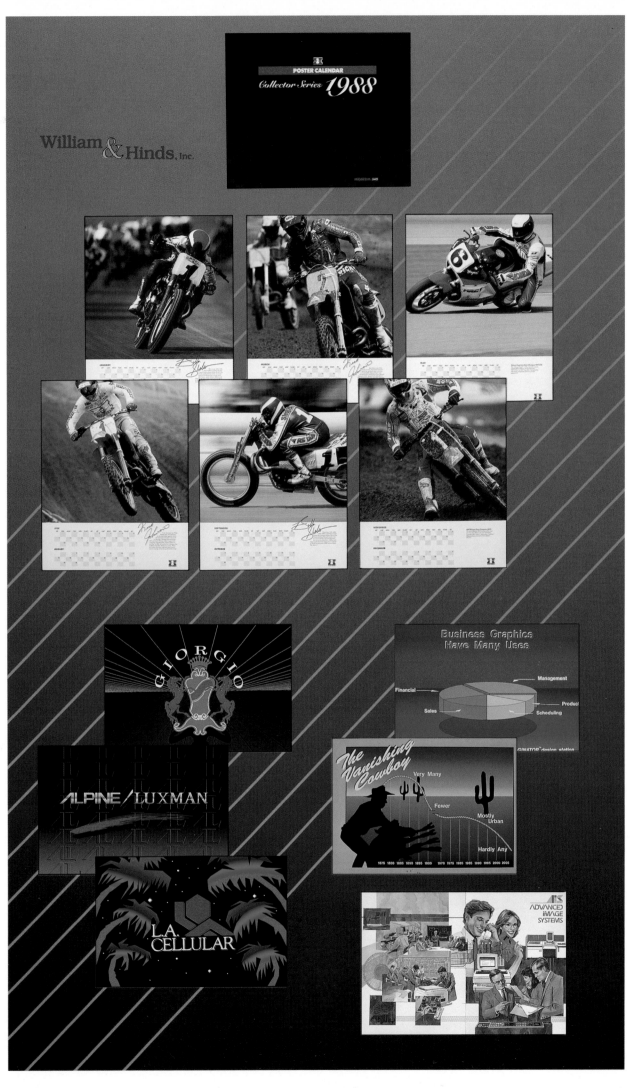

Index Illustrators & Graphic Designers

Photography

New York City

TED HOROWITZ

214 WILTON RD. • WESTPORT, CONNECTICUT • 06880

CORPORATE PHOTOGRAPHY

203 • 454 • 8766

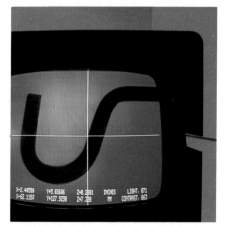

terry
WIER
(212) 685-6021

Randy Duchaine

200 W 18th Street
New York, NY 10011
212 243 4371

Stock Photography
Available

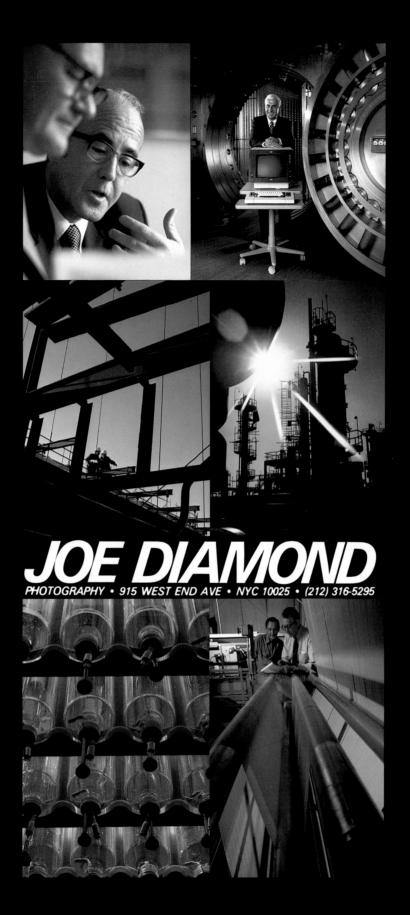

JOE DIAMOND

PHOTOGRAPHY • 915 WEST END AVE • NYC 10025 • (212) 316-5295

ANNUAL REPORTS • CAPABILITY BROCHURES • INSTITUTIONAL ADVERTISING • CORPORATE COMMUNICATIONS

LEV NISNEVICH
Corporate, Advertising and Editorial Photography

133 Mulberry Street
New York, NY 10013
(212) 219-0535

GIORGIO PALMISANO

NEW YORK CITY
212·431·7719

Prudential-Bache
American Express
Eastern Airlines
Warner Brothers
Ogilvy & Mather
Saatchi & Saatchi
Grey Advertising
ELLE
Cosmopolitan
Time
New York
Inc.
Fortune
Money
Forbes
Sports Illustrated
Discover
Institutional Investor
IN Fashion
Opera News

FRANK STELLA

PETER WESTBROOK–OLYMPIC CHAMPION

Mason
PHOTOGRAPHER

Represented by
Kathy Mason

212·675·3809

Ol West 18th St. New York NY 10011

Tornberg·Coghlan

6 EAST 39TH STREET   NEW YORK CITY 10016   685-7333

Corporate, Industrial and Location Photography

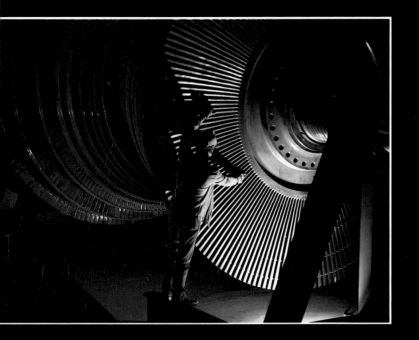

NORTH

Bill
WESTHEIMER   EAST
167 Spring St. New York, NY 10012
212/431-6360

SOUTH

MARK FERRI

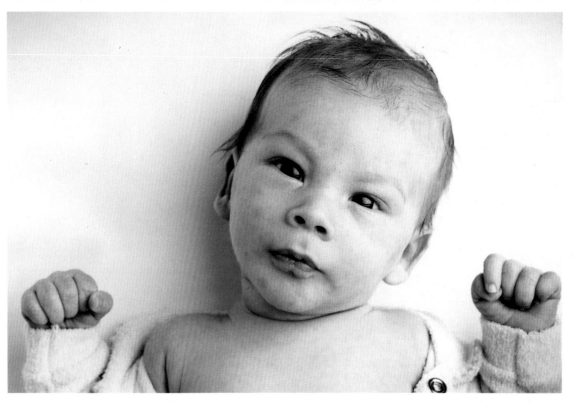

463 BROOME ST. NY, NY 10013 (212) 431-1356

Pobereskin

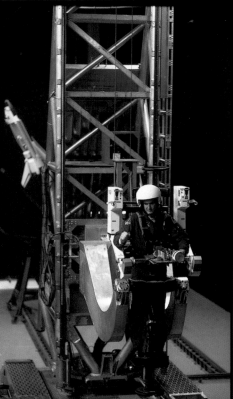

Doug Abdelnour

Represented by:
Bedford Photo-Graphic

The Playhouse
Route 22
P.O. Box 64
Bedford, New York 10506
(914) 234-3123

People & Environments:

Industrial,
Corporate,
Advertising,
Travel,
Editorial,
Multi-Image Specialists.

See Corporate Showcase 6.

Michael Abramson

15 Renwick Street
New York, New York 10013
(212) 941-1970

Location and studio photography: corporate/
industrial, editorial, still life, and travel.

Partial list of clients: Forbes, Fortune, Business Week,
Time, Life, Stern, People, Chase Manhattan Bank,
Seligman Brothers, Sony, New York Life Insurance
Company, Corporate Graphics, Jack Hough, Sheldon
Cotler & Associates, Carbone Smolan, Bloch Graulich
& Whelan, Hill & Knowlton.

Annual Reports worked on: Mead Corporation,
Washington Post Company, W.R. Grace & Company,
Arab-American Bank, Torchmark Corporation,
Comsat, HealthAmerica, New York Life Insurance
Company, Montclair Savings Bank, J.C. Penney.
Member ASMP

PANORAMIC PORTRAIT: NEW YORK LIFE INSURANCE COMPANY

PANORAMIC PORTRAIT: MONTCLAIR SAVINGS BANK

Wendy Barrows
Photography

205 East 22 Street
New York, New York 10010
(212) 685-0799

BOB SCHMIDT, PRESIDENT & CEO LEVINE HUNTLEY SCHMIDT & BEAVER

JAMES D. ROBINSON III, CHAIRMAN OF
THE BOARD AND CEO, AMERICAN EXPRESS

PETER BERLA, SAAB-SCANIA

ARY LEHNES, CHASE MANHATTAN

HERBERT M. BAUM, PRESIDENT, CAMPBELL USA

SUMIKO ITO, NOMURA
SECURITY INTERNATIONAL

Jonathan
Becker

(212) 929-3180

Principal clients:
Town & Country; Vanity Fair;
Manhattan, Inc.; Fortune;
Forbes; Revlon.

Joseph Berger

121 Madison Avenue
New York, New York 10016
(212) 685-7191

People On Location

Represented by Nancy Slome
(212) 685-8185

Clients include: Alexander and Alexander, American Express, Apple Bank For Savings, B. Dalton Bookstores, *Chief Information Officer,* Citibank, Commodore Computer, Dean Witter Reynolds, *Family Computing,*

Forbes, Hattori Corporation, JC Penney, McKinsey and Company, Metropolitan Life, New York Telephone, *Savvy,* Shearson Lehman Brothers, *The Yacht.*

Existing photography available.

More of my work can be seen in Corporate Showcase 4, 5 and 6.

© Joseph Berger 1987

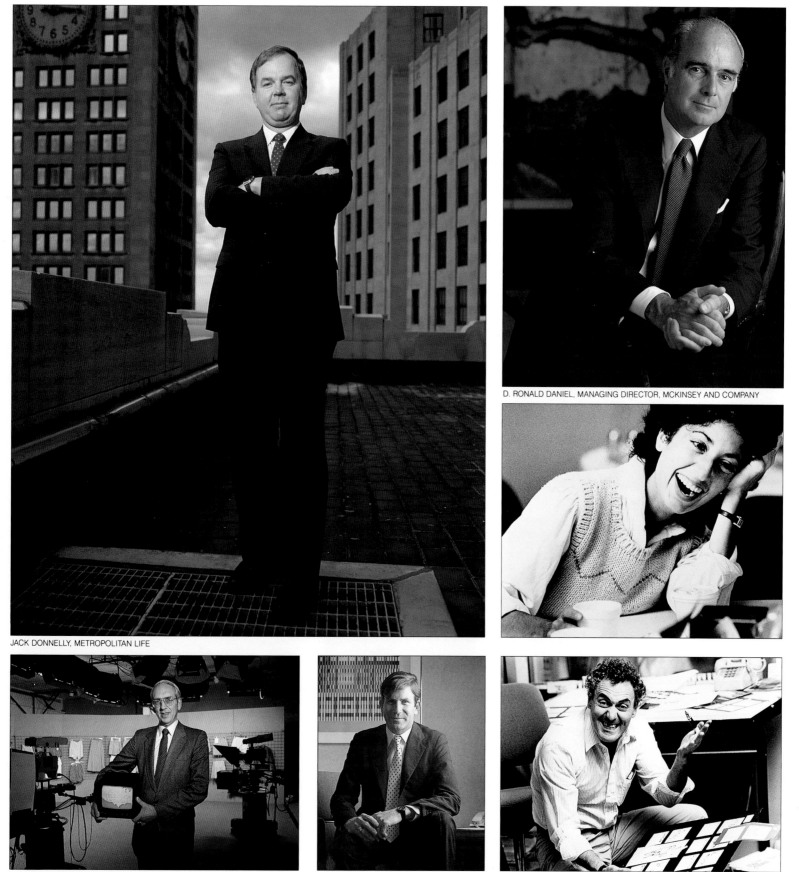

JACK DONNELLY, METROPOLITAN LIFE

D. RONALD DANIEL, MANAGING DIRECTOR, MCKINSEY AND COMPANY

RUSSELL LONGYEAR, JC PENNEY

JOHN CONROY, CRESTVALE INTERNATIONAL

Bezushko
1311 Irving Street
Philadelphia, Pennsylvania
19107
(215) 735-7771

George Bezushko
Bob Bezushko

Representative:
Christine Pierce

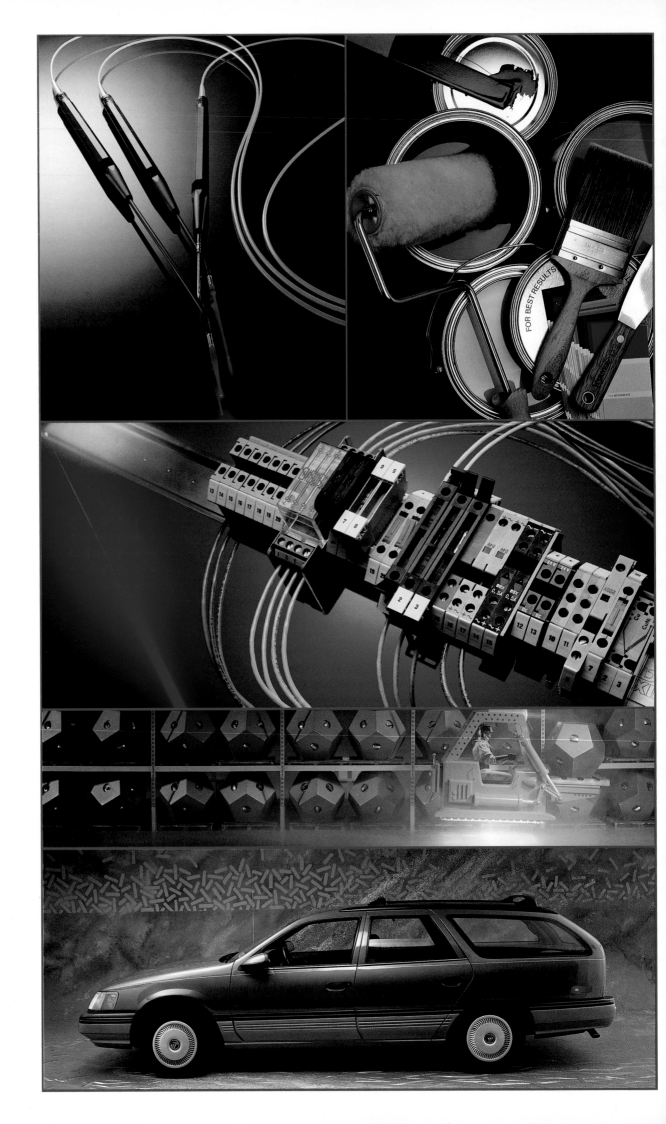

Charles Blecker

380 Bleecker Street
Suite 140
New York, New York 10014
(212) 242-8390

People and location
photography for annual
reports, advertising, corporate
industrial, travel and stock.

Stock available directly.

John Campos
John Campos Studio, Inc.
132 West 21st Street
New York, New York 10011
(212) 675-0601
Fax: (212) 242-5209

David Chalk
157 Hudson Street
New York, New York 10013
(212) 874-9042

PEOPLE PHOTOGRAPHY FOR CREATIVE PEOPLE.

According to public relations literature we are an uncommon profession. We never fail. In the more than three decades that I've been following our trade's exploits I cannot remember reading one case study of a failure, or of a mistake in judgment, or of an unvarnished blooper. Oh yes, they've been chronicled by others reporting on us—but never have we straightforwardly acknowledged such transgressions ourselves. The rationale for such relentless self-glorification, I'm told, is that by sharing our success we help others later facing the same problem.

Well, one can learn from mistakes, too. Probably better. Much of this business of ours is an apprenticeship. Over time you storehouse experiences. And mistakes are a stern, unforgettable teacher.

Well, I've ample inventory to choose from. You don't survive in this business for more than 30 years—as a consultant and as practicing corporate public relations officer—without having your share of failures. I can look back now on many of these and smile, but I can assure you that at the time none of them were funny. But, each taught me a practical lesson.

For example, not to be naive or too trusting.

When General Omar N. Bradley was chairman of Bulova Watch Company, and I its account executive, I arranged an interview with the general to discuss recent Bulova developments. Or so I naively thought. Bear in mind this was early in Bradley's post-Army career and he was copy. But he determinedly avoided all media queries because he didn't want to get entangled in discussing current issues. The first question out of the box from the AP-man was "General Bradley, how would you have handled the Bay of Pigs?" Shooting a laser look at me that would have melted titanium, Bradley stared briefly at the reporter, turned on his heel, and left the room.

This new wisdom was short lived. Some years later, I got burned again. We were going through one of those inevitable executive changes, where "differences of opinion" were legitimate. No heat, no animus. The departing president and I agreed upon a simple straightforward story line. So, when he asked if he should return a Wall Street Journal phone call, I said, "Sure, why not?" Well, he got so carried away with the sound of his voice that the resulting story suggested that there was, at the company, either widespread dissension or a personality clash.

Once I advised the public relations vice president of Republic Aircraft and trustee of Adelphi College (now University) that he certainly could recommend that Adelphi give out a passel of honorary degrees to a group of prominent citizens, including space scientist Werner Von Braun, secure in the knowledge that we—the great Carl Byoir organization—would generate nationwide publicity. On graduation day, the client and I stood at the entrance to Adelphi as the press bus, organized by my firm, drove up. The doors opened and out poured—one man, the Byoir media contact. Later, by assiduous follow-up, writing second-day news leads and personality features, we generated an extraordinary amount of coverage.

Sometimes in sticking your neck out it gets pinched. Back when the foreign corrupt practices act was topic "A," I noticed that buried in torrid legal prose of an Emhart 8K filing was a statement that we had found an unaccountable $3 million charge. Not a big deal but worthy of a small news item. I wrote the piece recognizing that it would be a hard one for conservative Emhart management to swallow. It was. The CEO flinched but said he would pass it along for review to the Board's audit committee. They flatly rejected it.

Continued on page 82

Vincent Colabella
304 East Forty-First Street
New York, New York
(212) 949-7456

Robert Essel

39 West 71st Street
New York, New York 10023
(212) 877-5228

Specialist in world wide location, corporate/industrial and medical photography.

Fortune 500 clients include: New York Telephone, Wall St. Journal, PSE&G, IBM, Celanese, Engelhard, Exxon, Johnson & Johnson, Holly Farms, Salomon Brothers, Irving Trust and others.

Extensive stock photography available.

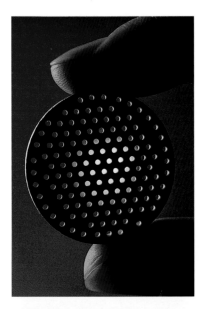

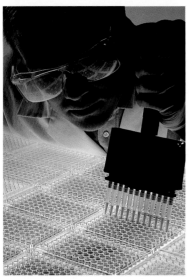

Robert Essel

39 West 71st Street
New York, New York 10023
(212) 877-5228

Specialist in world wide location, corporate/industrial and medical photography.

Fortune 500 clients include: New York Telephone, Wall St. Journal, PSE&G, IBM, Celanese, Engelhard, Exxon, Johnson & Johnson, Holly Farms, Salomon Brothers, Irving Trust and others.

Extensive stock photography available.

Robert I. Faulkner

52 Comstock Street
New Brunswick, New Jersey
08901
(201) 828-6984

Specializing in photography of
architecture and interior design.
Stock available. Portfolio upon
request.

Clients include:

I.M. Pei
Haines Lundberg Waehler
Swanke Hayden Connell
Edward Durell Stone
Spector Group
Grad Partnership
CUH2A
Hillier Group
Rothe-Johnson Associates
Barrett Ginsberg
Duffy Inc.
Armstrong Jordan Pease
Bartos & Rhodes
Johnson & Johnson
Merck Company
General Electric
Prudential
Dun & Bradstreet
New Jersey Bell
Hilton Hotels
Purolator Courier
Revlon
North American Phillips
Carter Wallace
Tishman Construction
Torcon Construction
Mahoney Troast
Sudler Construction
Trammell Crow
Lincoln Properties
Segal & Morel
Cushman Wakefield
Coldwell Banker

Architectural credits:

1. Haines Lundberg Waehler
2. Bartos & Rhodes
3. The Grad Partnership
4. Haines Lundberg Waehler
5. The Grad Partnership
6. Ehrlick Romenger

1

2

3

4

5

6

Abe Frajndlich

30 East 20 #605
New York City, New York 10003
(212) 995-8648

Location and Studio Photography: Advertising,
Corporate/Industrial, Editorial. Stock available. B&W
and Color.

Clients include: American Can, Capitol Records,
*Fortune, Frankfurter Allgemeine Zeitung, Life, London
Observer, Manhattan Inc., Metropolitan Home,
New York Times Magazine,* Progressive Corporation,
Vanity Fair.

Galvin/Europe
Kevin Galvin

Oblatterwallstr 44
8900 Augsburg, Germany
(011 49) 821 156393

Location photography in Europe. Corporate, editorial, sports, travel.

Clients include:
Corporate:
AT&T, Berry & Boyle, Boise Cascade, Digital Equipment Corp., Epsilon, Exxon, Harris Graphics, Sperry, Symbolics, Wang.

Editorial:
ABC, Business Week, Fortune, Houghton Mifflin, Newsweek, New York Times, Parade, Physicians Weekly, The Yacht.

Member ASMP

Garry Geer

Geer Photography
183 Saint Paul Street
Rochester, New York 14604
(212) 819-0808
(716) 232-2393

Specializing in corporate, editorial, and advertising photography. Existing stock photography available upon request.

Fred George

737 Canal Street
Building #35, 2nd Floor
Stamford, Connecticut 06902
(203) 348-7454

Clients include:
American Trading
Champion Paper International
Rreef Corporation
Richardson/Vicks
C.B.S.
The New York Times Company
Rexham Corporation
Skidmore, Owings & Merrill
Connecticut Magazine
Chase Manhattan Bank
Compaq Computer
New England Monthly
Remington Products, Inc.
Hubbell Marine Products, Inc.

Stock available upon request.

Fred George

737 Canal Street
Building #35, 2nd Floor
Stamford, Connecticut 06902
(203) 348-7454

Clients include:
The Pittston Company/
    Pittson Coal
    Brinks Home Security
    Burlington Air Express
Business Express Airlines
3M Scotchguard
UPS/Roadnet
York Research
Pitney Bowes/Dictaphone
Act Media, Inc.
Marketing Corporation of
    America
Allied Bank
Exxon
Ally Gargano/MCA
Tenneco
Hilton
Seven Up
American Speed/Harley
    Davidson

Stock available upon request.

Continued from page 72

I wasn't being naive. I knew that the Wall Street Journal and the AP, to mention two, regularly scanned the 8K's filed with the SEC and put in a daily press rack. So it was inevitable it would be read. I was simply trying to put it in the right context, hoping that by taking the initiative I could minimize, or preclude, overstated reports. As you'd expect, the headlines ran, "Emhart in $3 million dollar Kickback Scheme!" The story—which should have been a one day affair—ran for about four days and forced the CEO to have employee meetings to assure them that Emhart wasn't dishonest. A tough period and, of course, for a while some suspected I should have been able to prevent it. But, in the end, the lesson was made—not to me but to Emhart—and I was never again overruled when disclosures of negative news were in order.

There are a host of other times when I was less than persuasive and I—and my company—received criticism that could have been avoided. One that comes immediately to mind concerns our plans to sell a unit whose ties to its community were unique, going back to the early 1900s. Several generations of family worked in the plant. But, because the sales agreement was so tentative I allowed myself to be persuaded to maintain a low, almost no-comment profile. It

was absolutely the worst course of action. For one thing we did the unpardonable: embarrassed a sitting official, the first selectman (mayor), who didn't know what was going on— and later we needed his support on a down-zoning matter. We also sabotaged our credibility with our employees and the community—and probably with those friends they had elsewhere in the company.

It was a tough reminder that knowing what to do, and, even knowing how to do it, is secondary to the ability to being able to persuade those involved to take your counsel.

Looking back on those experiences, I think an important point to keep in mind is that our business is an imperfect one. We are in constant battle with the status quo and to disturb it is to take risk. If you win, if you're right 60 percent of the time, you are doing all right.

John F. Budd, Jr.
Senior Vice President
Corporate Communications
Emhart Corporation
Farmington, Connecticut

Reprinted with permission from the January 1988 issue of the Public Relations Journal.

Ken Haas, Inc.

15 Sheridan Square
New York, New York 10014
(212) 255-0707

Clients serviced include: AT&T; New York Telephone; Asarco; SCM; Peugeot; Dexter; Cheesebrough-Ponds; 3M; Penntech Paper; NBC; Stanadyne; Panasonic; Holiday Inns; St. Regis Paper; YMCA; Abraham & Strauss; Colgate-Palmolive; Harcourt, Brace, Jovanovich; CPC International; General Instrument; Hongkong Land; The Hongkong & Shanghai Bank; Oscar Mayer; Singer; Chris-Craft; Pinkerton's; Republic Bank of New York; Continental Illinois National Bank; Columbis Line; General Electric; The Commonwealth Fund; Manufacturers Hanover Trust; Merrill Lynch; Dillon Read; The Henry Luce Foundation; Chicago Board Options Exchange; New York City Partnership; Cigna; Reuters; Sloan Kettering; IBM; Citicorp; Mass Transit Railway of Hong Kong; Harvard Medical School; E.F. Hutton; Pacific Telesis, Donaldson Lufkin & Jenrette; U.S. Army; American Brands; St. Luke's Roosevelt; Carteret Savings Bank; Prudential Bache; Chase Manhattan.

Designers serviced include: Applebaum & Curtis; Beau Gardner; Bob Gill; Galen Harley; John Morning; Arnold Saks; Reba Sochis; Henry Steiner; Marco DePlano; Anthony Russell; Graphic Expression; Burson Marsteller; Spence Glassberg; HBM/Creamer; Barton-Gillet; Becker Hockfield; Mayo-Infurna; Robert Miles Runyan, Sherin & Matejka; Page Arbitrio & Resen; Jack Hough Assoc.; Laurel Emery.

Editorial credits include: Bicentennial cover of Newsweek, The New York Times Magazine, Fortune, People, Natural History, Americana, Outdoor Life, Oggi, Bunte.

CLIENT: CITICORP INVESTMENT BANK;

DESIGN: SHERIN & MATEJKA;

EDITOR: PETER CAREY.

George Haling Shoots: Industrial

NYC Photo District
(212) 736-6822

Energy
Esso-Rivista (Italy)
Exxon
Combustion Engineering
Conoco
Consolidated Natural Gas
PSE & G
Schlumberger Ltd.
Sun Company
Texaco

Transportation
American Airlines
Continental Airlines
Sabena
Seatrain

The Orient Express
TWA
United Airlines

Communications
ABC
CBS
IBM
ITT
Metromedia
NBC
New York Telephone
N.Y.C. Post Office
Perkin-Elmer
RCA
Sperry

Xerox
Blair Graphics
Inmont

**Forest Products/
Graphic Arts**
Champion International
Kimberly-Clark
Blair Graphics
Inmont
Sterling Roman Press

Editorial
Advertising Council
Camera Magazine
DU Magazine

Fortune Magazine
Ladies Home Journal
Lamp Magazine
LIFE Magazine
London Daily Telegraph
Money Magazine
Museum of Natural History
N.Y. Times Books
Réalités Magazine
Singer Corporation
Stern Magazine
Time-Life Books
United Fund

George Haling Shoots: Corporate

NYC Photo District
(212) 736-6822

Photobases in New York and Europe.

Twenty-five years of excellence Here and There.

Great stock of Now and Then.

Corporate/Financial
ADT
Alexander & Alexander
American Express
Carteret
Citco
Citibank (N.Y.)
Emery Financial Services
Hartford Group
Manhattan Life
Merrill-Lynch
Mitchell-Hutchins
Mortgage Bankers Assn.
Morgan-Stanley
Salomon Brothers

The Travelers

Industrial
Alcoa
Amerace
American Can
Blount
Celanese
Chrysler Corp.
Fasco
GAF
General Cable
General Electric
Hunt Chemical
IBM

Indian Head
Inmont
ITT
3M
Otis
Perkin-Elmer
PepsiCo
Singer
Sperry Rand
Thomas & Betts
Xerox

Kent Hanson

147 Bleecker Street
New York, New York 10012
(212) 777-2399

Editorial, Advertising, and Corporate photography.
Portfolio available upon request.

Stock Photographs: DOT Picture Agency
(212) 684-3441
Telex 238198 TLXA UR

Brownie Harris

Brownie Harris Productions
New York City
(212) 929-1796
Westchester County, New York
(914) 271-6426

Clients include major Fortune 500 Corporations

Specializing in people worldwide for annual reports, corporate communications, industrial and advertising photography.

Additional work may be seen in
Corporate Showcase Vol. 4 pg. 73 and 5 p. 91
American Showcase 5 pg. 83, 6 pg. 64, 7 pg. 101, 8 pg. 95

Photographs © Brownie Harris 1987

Hashimoto Studio

Photography
153 West 27th Street
Suite 1202
New York, New York 10001
(212) 645-1221

Assignment Photography
Portraits in the studio and on location.
Editorial/Corporate/Interior/
Annual Reports/Advertising.

Credits:
American Red Cross, Executive Self-Defense Center, J.B. Keller Public Relations, M.P.L. Advertising, New York Philharmonic, Philips Records, Ear Magazine, Guitar World Magazine, Interior Magazine, Leaders Magazine, Restaurant and Hotel Magazine, Stereo Review Magazine, and others.

Photos:
Guy-Georges Herregat/
    S.V.P. banker/Credit Du Nord
Sam Lopata/C.E.O./
    conceptual designer/
    Sam Lopata Inc.
W. Boss Inc.

James Joern

125 Fifth Avenue
New York City, New York 10003
(212) 260-8025

PHOTOGRAPHY FOR THE CORPORATE NEEDS,
INDUSTRIAL, ADVERTISING, FEATURE EDITORIAL &
ESSAY, PLUS THE INDIVIDUAL BOOKLET.

YOUR VISUAL PROBLEMS ARE MY PHOTOGRAPHIC
ADVENTURES.

PHOTOGRAPHY CAN ALSO BE SEEN IN AMERICAN
SHOWCASE #7, CORPORATE SHOWCASE #5, AND
SILVER BOOKS 1, 2 & 6.

JJ

Charles W. Kelley, Jr.

649 Second Avenue, #6C-30
New York City, New York 10016
(212) 686-3879

Represented by Marck Smith
(212) 222-4735

Specializing in Location
Photography for Corporate,
Advertising, Industrial and
Architectural.

See Corporate Showcase #5,
also feel free to call for samples
in color or black & white.

Member: APA

Stock Available Direct

Clients Include:
IBM Corporation
F. Schumacher & Sons, Inc.
U.S. Army/West Point
N.Y.S. Bridge Authority
Graham Corporation
Eastman Kodak
Federal Reserve
Tradewell International
N.Y.S. Museum
Allegheny Power Corp.
JG Furniture
Montgomery Hospital
Unicorp American Corporation
Packaging Systems, Inc.
Alan Robert Garry, Architect
SKM & Partners, Architects
MacMillan
US Castings
Oppenheimer Gov't Securities
C.I.T. Financial
Salpeter/Paganucci
Kelley/Kellner Associates

Design:
Kelley/Kellner Associates

All Photography
© C. Kelley 1987

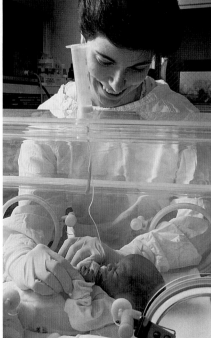

Robert M. Knowles

2 Fordham Hill Oval
Bronx, New York 10468
(212) 367-4430

1. Manhattan Eyelab
2. James T. Cullen, Jr.
3. IMNET
4. IBM
5. Trump Tower

Ed Lederman

166 East 34th Street
New York, New York 10016
(212) 685-8612

Location and studio photography for annual reports,
corporate brochures and advertising.

Portfolio available upon request.

Wide range of stock photography available.

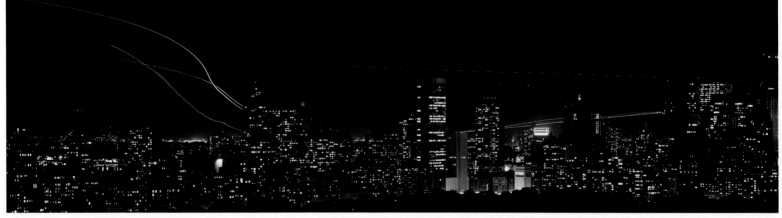

Ed Lederman

166 East 34th Street
New York, New York 10016
(212) 685-8612

Location and studio photography for annual reports,
corporate brochures and advertising.

Portfolio available upon request.

Wide range of stock photography available.

Lester Lefkowitz

370 Lexington Avenue
Suite 2010
New York, New York 10017
(212) 627-8088
(516) 751-5193

PHOTOGRAPHY
FOR SCIENCE
AND TECHNOLOGY

An expert in photographing
high-technology products and
processes, from the ultra-tiny
to the scientifically complex.

A consultant in technical
photography to major
corporations and agencies.

A graduate engineer.

Extensive scientific and medical
photographic experience.

Facilities for studio
and location projects

- 35mm to 8x10
- In-house processing
- High magnification macro
  or micro
- Equipped with lasers,
  microscopes, fiber optics
- Stroboscopic, time-lapse,
  stop-action and special effects
- Extensive state-of-the-art
  lighting equipment
- Vast stock of high-tech props
  and backgrounds

Stock photography available

Photographic clients include:
IBM
Citicorp
Polaroid
CBS
Eastman Kodak
Glenbrook Laboratories
Science Digest
General Electric
Panasonic
European American Bank
NatWest Bank
TDK
Microwave Development
WNYC-TV

CREATIVE SENSIBILITIES
COMBINED WITH
A STRONG UNDERSTANDING
OF SCIENCE AND
TECHNOLOGY

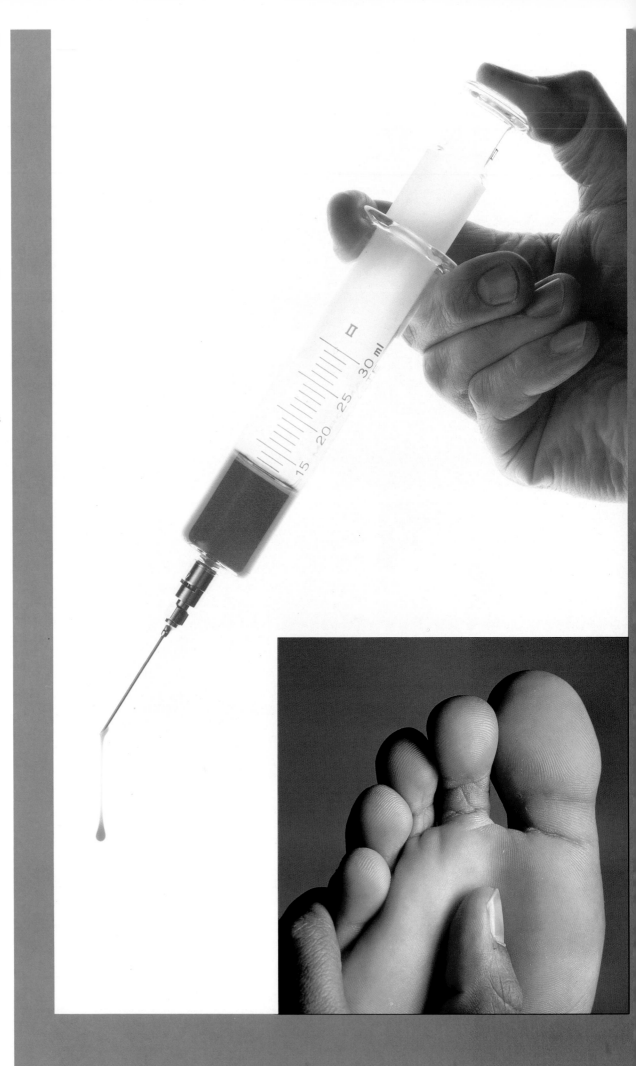

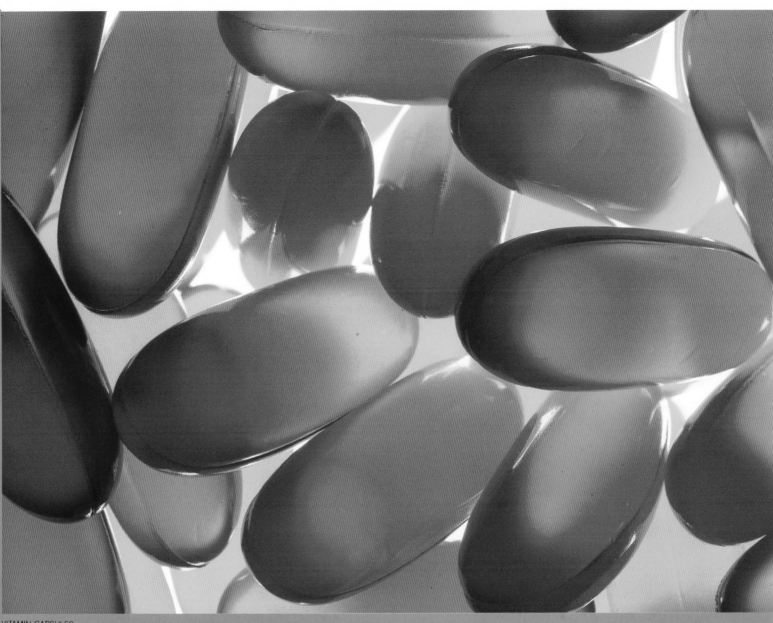

VITAMIN CAPSULES

CRAB (OR PUBIC) LOUSE, 30X

Photos © Lester Lefkowitz 1988

Lester Lefkowitz

*Photography
for Science
and Technology*

(212) 627-8088
(516) 751-5193

MAIN FUEL TANK, SPACE SHUTTLE

Lester Lefkowitz

*Photography
for Science
and Technology*

(212) 627-8088
(516) 751-5193

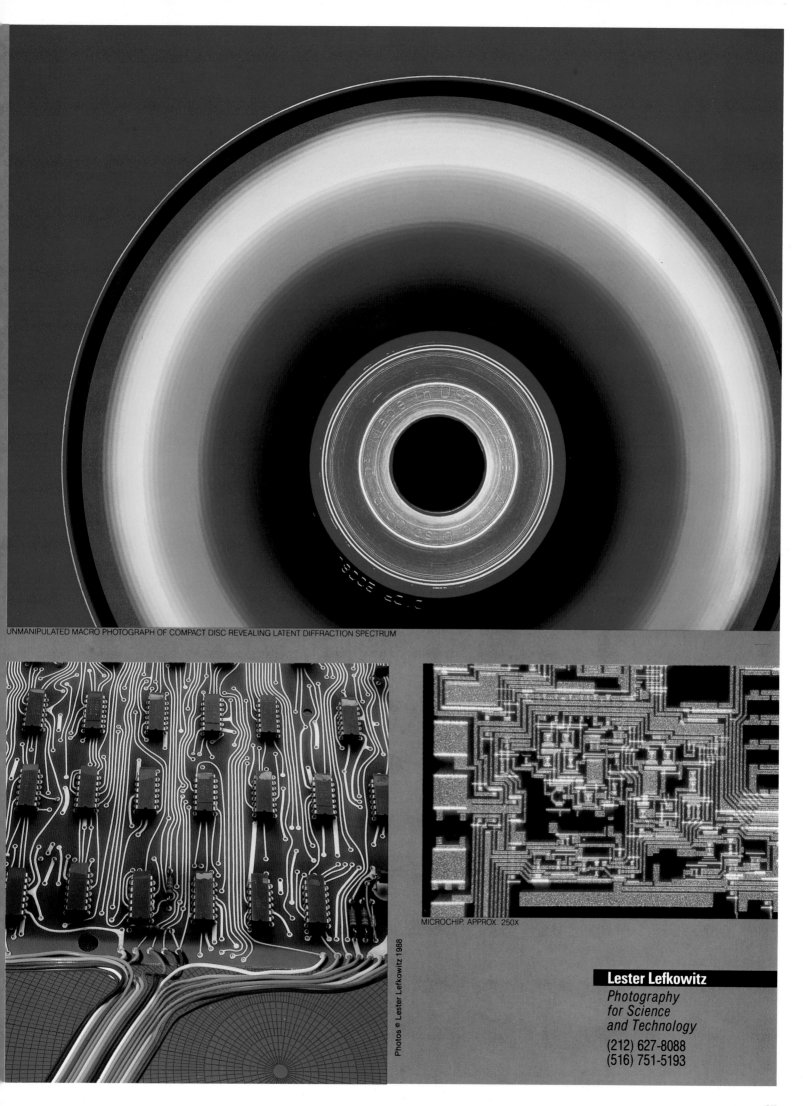

UNMANIPULATED MACRO PHOTOGRAPH OF COMPACT DISC REVEALING LATENT DIFFRACTION SPECTRUM

MICROCHIP, APPROX. 250X

Photos © Lester Lefkowitz 1988

Lester Lefkowitz

Photography
for Science
and Technology

(212) 627-8088
(516) 751-5193

Jim Lennon
Brenner/Lennon
Photo Productions Inc.

24 South Mall
Plainview, New York 11803
(516) 752-0610
FAX: (516) 752-0613

Photography for:

Annual Reports,
Corporate, Industrial,
Advertising, Editorial

Studio & Location

Clients Include:
Audiovox
Bank of Smithtown
Better Health & Living
Bolar Pharmaceutical
Columbia University
Chemtronics
Fortunoffs
Gull Inc.
Harmon Kardon
Hirsch International
Indo-Atlantic Corp.
L.I. Cablevision
MIX Magazine
NEC Computers
North Fork Bancorp
Phoenix Labs
The Royal Bank & Trust Co.
Schaffer, Clarke & Co., Inc.

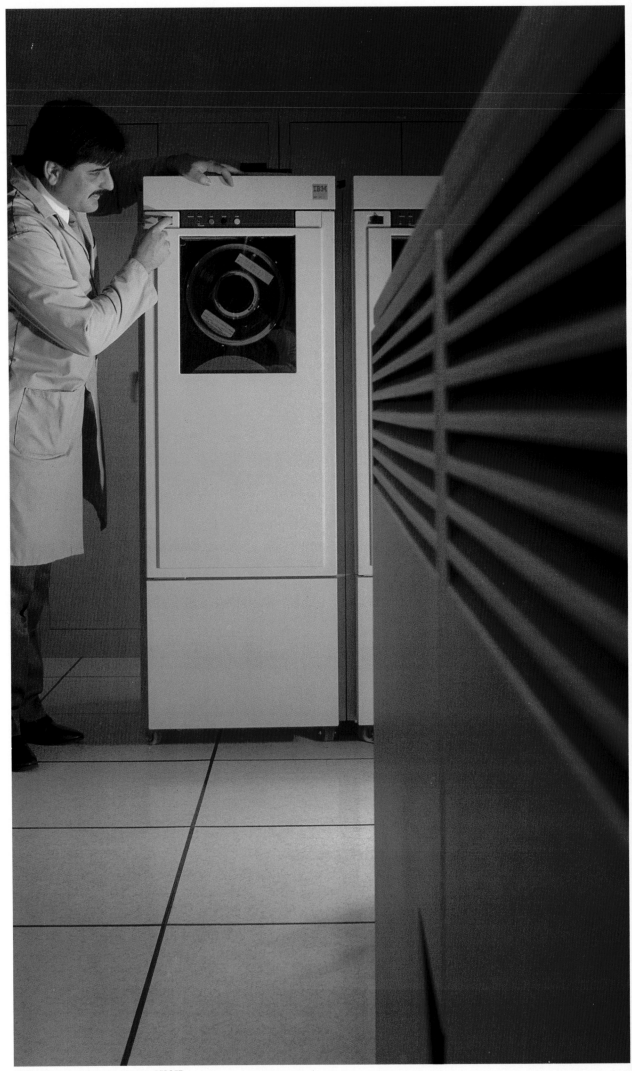

NORTH FORK BANCORP 1987 ANNUAL REPORT

J. Ming Leung
Photography

60 Pineapple Street, Suite 6B
New York, New York 11201
(212) 254-8570
(718) 522-1894

Specializing in:

Annual Reports	Concepts and Effects	Selected Stock Photography and Portfolio available
Corporate/Industrial	Editorial	upon request.
Architectural/Interiors	Travel	
Studio/Location	Advertising	Member ASMP
Photo-Illustrations	People	© J. Ming Leung 1988

Franck Levy
305 East 40th Street
New York City, New York 10016
(212) 557-8256

Brian T. McNally

234 East 81st Street
Suite #1A
New York, New York 10028
N.Y. (212) 744-1263
L.A. (213) 462-6565

On location around the globe for corporate/industrial, advertising, interior design and architecture.

Partial client list includes:

Adjustable Steel, American Standard, Berlitz, Carnegie Hall, C. Itoh, CRS Sirrine, Duffy, E.F. Hutton, Gensler, Grad Partnership, Herzfeld & Stern, IBM, IFA, ILGWU, James Stewart Polshek, Jeffcoat Schoen

Morrell, J. Walter Thompson, Kaplan McLaughlin Diaz, King Features Syndicate, Knoll Intl., Kuhn Smith Harris, Lehrer McGovern Bovis, Leo A. Daly, Lloyds Bank Intl., Lou Hammond & Associates, McGraw Hill/Nikkei, Mead Data Central, Mead Paper, Metromedia, Neville Lewis, Nikon's World, Random House, Ross & Cohen, Scali McCabe Sloves, Seligman & Latz, Sierra Club, Swanke Hayden Connell, The Reef Fund, Time Inc., Tishman Realty & Construction, Walker & Associates, Xerox Corp.

All photos © Brian T. McNally

Donald L. Miller

295 Central Park West
New York, New York 10024
(212) 496-2830

Specializing in C.E.O.s, Chairmen, Presidents,
Directors, and top management.

Donald L. Miller

295 Central Park West
New York, New York 10024
(212) 496-2830

Specializing in C.E.O.s, Chairmen, Presidents,
Directors, and top management.

J.L. Peláez

568 Broadway Suite 103
New York, New York 10012
(212) 995-2283
(212) 925-5149

Location and studio photography for annual reports,
advertising, editorial, and corporate communications.
Stock available.

Randy Plimpton

401 West 48th Street 2W
New York, New York 10036
(212) 603-9338

Location photography worldwide for corporate/
industrial, editorial, and travel clients.

Stock available

How I Would Select an Advertising Agency

When we read in Adweek that a number of advertising agency executives had selected Alvin Achenbaum as one of the most important industry figures in 1987, we asked him to submit his thoughts on how a client and shop can best match their talents. Here's what he had to say.

Viewed superficially, choosing an advertising agency appears like a stimulating, almost exhilarating experience for the advertiser. You get to rub elbows with creative stars, eat lunch in trendy restaurants, and watch some of the world's great advertising agencies perform.

But done properly, more is involved than visiting the latest hot agencies and looking at their carefully culled television reels. Instead, it is a logistical nightmare involving the constant preparation of paperwork; including invitations, agendas, lists of questions to be asked, fact sheets, evaluations, requests for position papers, rejection letters, and more. It includes the irritations that accompany the arrangement and scheduling of countless meetings and the travel plans of busy, often unavailable executives. But perhaps worst of all, it entails considerable uncertainty because there is virtually no assurance that the new agency will be any better than the old one.

Nowadays, with the concentration of advertising agencies into mega-systems, finding an acceptable group of candidate agencies without a conflict is a chore in itself. Compared with ten years ago, your options are quite limited. As a consequence, switching advertising agencies should be avoided unless it is absolutely necessary.

Of course, competing for new business by advertising agencies—the other side of the coin, while challenging and exciting, is also no fun. It is an onerous and expensive process. And if you don't win the account, extremely demoralizing. Thus, agencies should decline the invitation unless they feel that the exercise is worth the candle and that they have some chance of winning. Very few adhere to this dictum.

Actually, very little business changes hands each year. Paradoxically, it is harder to divorce an agency than a wife. For every thousand advertisers, at most one to two percent switch shops each year. That's a loyalty rate higher than found among cigarette brands. It is also not a lot of turnover. Most agency growth comes from existing business; very little from new accounts. The fact is that clients do not like to fire agencies.

Yet, as reluctant as they are to switch, there are circumstances when an advertiser feels it has no alternative, when its trust and confidence in its agency has deteriorated to such a point that it is willing to accept the unpleasantness associated with making a change.

Therefore, I'd like to outline a systematic procedure that will help both large and small budget advertisers select an agency that meets their particular needs.

Step #1: Formulating the Evaluative Criteria

The first step—and the most critical one because it affects everything else in the process—is to determine exactly what the advertiser expects from its agency if the advertiser is to have a satisfactory relationship with it. These expectations become the criteria by which the advertiser evaluates the agencies during the process. They are extremely important in deciding what the candidate agencies are to demonstrate in the various meetings the advertiser has with them.

These criteria are developed by interviewing the people at the client who interface with the agency. Their expectations are then synthesized, committed to writing, reviewed and prioritized.

The aim is to have a very precise written document of what the advertiser expects and one on which the selection committee can sign off. Normally two sets of criteria are developed. One is objective criteria, such as size and location of the agency, conflicts, relationships with other organizations, and experience with similar business. These criteria are usually used in an initial screening of candidates to reduce the group to a reasonable number. The second set of criteria is more qualitative and is the basis for the final evaluation of the candidates. It is concerned with the basic service requirements of the advertiser. Depending on the client, it includes, for example, the ability of the agency to develop strategies and solve marketing problems, the type of account people it wants, the nature of the creative process, media innovativeness, research involvement, and so on. It also deals with such critical relationship issues as responsiveness, sensitivity to people, agency philosophy, attitudes toward compensation, etc.

Step #2: Screening the Initial Candidates

The second step is the initial screening of candidates. In this step we apply the objective screening criteria to all possible candidates. With such criteria, it is quite easy to rather quickly narrow the number of candidates to eight or ten. To see more than this number is unnecessary. Most of the work can be done from published sources. Being familiar with the agencies can help make appropriate choices. It saves a lot of time, money, and effort if this part of the process is carefully done.

Continued on page 114

Bill Ray

350 Central Park West
New York, New York 10025

Represented by Marlys Ray
(212) 222-7680

© Bill Ray, 1988

TIMELESS & DYNAMIC, PORTRAITS & GROUPS, LOCATION & STUDIO; SPECIALIZING IN PEOPLE. For more of my work see Corporate Showcase 3, 4, 5, 6; Black & white samples and portfolio on request.

1. Henry Ford II, with portrait of grandfather, Henry Ford.
2. Edward L. Hennessy, Jr. Chairman, CEO, Allied-Signal Inc.
3. Executives of The Bank of New York.
4. Howard M. Love, Chairman, CEO, National Intergroup, Inc.
5. Thomas F. Donovan, Vice Chairman of the Board, Marine Midland Bank.
6. J. Carter Bacot, Chairman, CEO, Peter Herrick, President, and members of the Steering Committee, The Bank of New York.
7. Donald W. Weber, President, CEO, Charles Wohlstetter, Chairman, Contel Corp.

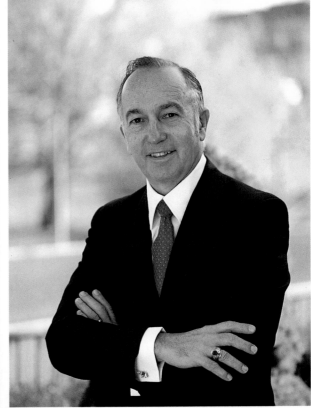

Jon Riley

12 East 37th Street
New York, New York 10016
(212) 532-8326

1. Bankers Trust
2. First American Bank–Tennessee
3. Warner Lambert

And on the eighth day God created . . . executives.

Jon Riley
12 East 37th Street
New York, New York 10016
(212) 532-8326

God created...light.

Bob Sacha

370 Central Park West
New York, New York 10025
(212) 749-4128

Advertising
Annual Reports
Corporate
Industrial
Editorial

NATIONAL GEOGRAPHIC

MERCK, INC.

Jed Share/Tokyo

Sunny Heights Seijo
2-8-8-102 Seijo
Tokyo, Setagaya-Ku. 157. Japan
Telephone 81-3-415-5475 or
Fax 81-3-470-0243

Winner of the two highest
awards for annual report
photography in Japan

Fluent in Japanese, totally
familiar with Japanese customs.

Bridging the international gap
between East and West.

**Representative in the
United States:
Ursula G. Kreis
(212) 562-8931**

代表　株式会社
エイダスインターナショナル
Tel: (03) 478-1715
Fax: (03) 470-0243

**Lewis Skolnik
Photography**
135 West 29th Street
New York, New York 10001
(212) 239-1455

By employing unique design
and high resolution computer
technology, we create a
personalized slide presentation
to fulfill your communication
needs.

Diane M. Specht

167 West 71st Street
New York, New York 10023
(212) 877-8381

Corporate, editorial, advertising and public relations

Location and studio

Clients include: Group W Westinghouse; Burson-Marsteller; Doremus, Porter, Novelli; AT&T; Hearst/ABC/NBC; Merrill Lynch/Teleport Communications; Canadian Imperial Bank; Knapp Communications/Architectural Digest; USA Network

Colorado representative (303) 482-6314

Continued from page 106

Step #3: Designing the Selection Process

The third step is to outline the specific process that the advertiser should follow in making the selection. It includes but is not limited to:

...Indicating all of the steps included in the remainder of the process;

...Delineating the logistics involved;

...Outlining what material is needed to implement the process;

...Preparing the material, announcements, invitations, agendas, etc.;

...Preparing questions to be used in the meetings;

...Deciding what speculative material, if any, should be requested from candidates; and

...Preparing evaluation forms necessary to make a selection.

It is also at this stage in the process that the number of meetings necessary for candidates to demonstrate their ability to meet the client's needs and expectations is determined. Exactly how many meetings are needed and how they should be structured will depend on the advertiser's specific needs and expectations, and whether the advertiser wishes the candidates to do some speculative work. Normally, three meetings of varying length, each with a separate purpose, are required.

A. Meeting With Agency Principals

The first meeting should be with two principals from each of the candidate agencies. The purpose of this meeting is to ascertain whether the agency is in a position to take the business, whether it wants the account, whether the basic philosophy of the agency's management is compatible with the advertiser's, and whether the chemistry at the top is satisfactory. It is amazing what can be learned at such a meeting. We consider it a crucial first step because the agency's management plays a very major role in every client/agency relationship. It also serves as a very effective means for reducing the candidate list still further. On the other hand, it allows the client to describe the process he intends to follow, to set the ground rules of the competition, and to solicit whatever position papers it needs from the agency.

B. Agency Credentials Meetings

This next meeting is what we often call the "credentials meeting." This is when the advertiser spends a substantial amount of time with the candidates. Normally, we suggest spending the better part of a day with each agency to view a formal presentation in which each is expected to demonstrate its ability to meet the client's needs, to tour the agency, to have a meal with the key agency people, to ask questions and to discuss the position papers that were requested by the advertiser.

Basically, in these meetings, the advertiser is evaluating what the agencies have done for their current clients and how they relate that experience to the advertiser's business. We often compare it with interviewing a number of applicants for a key executive position. Before you select one to work with you, you usually have to spend considerable time with him to really gauge his abilities and chemistry. Too much is at stake not to take the necessary time.

In many instances, an advertiser can make its choice after the credentials meetings. This is usually the case for a small budget advertiser or one that is not a very specialized advertiser. In such instances, it is usually a good idea to also give the agencies an assignment to address at the credentials meeting—either a few marketing issues, some strategic questions, or points of view on advertising and media.

But in most cases, advertisers want to see how prospective agencies think and work in their product categories. This being the case, "speculative" presentations are called for.

C. Final Speculative Presentation

If a speculative presentation is deemed necessary, two additional meetings are necessary. The first is an orientation meeting at which time the candidates are told what the advertiser wants prepared and are given the necessary background information for doing an effective job. The second meeting is the final agency presentation where the candidates produce work specifically for the advertiser.

The kind of speculative work requested depends upon what can best help the advertiser make an intelligent choice. If the advertiser seeks to obtain a great campaign that he can use from this speculative material, he might be sorely disappointed. He would also be misusing the real purposes of such a meeting, which are to ascertain how the agency works, thinks, operates under pressure, and presents material.

Continued on page 122

Ken Tannenbaum
16 West 21 Street
New York, New York 10010
(212) 675-2345

Ken's experience is extraordinary. He's been a team player solving problems for fourteen years, working in large and small format, on location and in his drive-in facility in New York City. Give him a tight layout or simply a thought; he'll present a rock-solid analysis, and deliver quality...whether you need it or not. He is a photo-illustrator of people, places and things, having worked for many companies most people know by initials. So whether you're an IBM, an ITT or an I wish I were, the same dedication and careful eye can serve you. And, by the way, he's as comfortable with a nightwatchman waiting for the sun to come up as he is over lunch with the Board. Speaking of which, Ken's on the Board of Directors of the APA, NY Chapter. You don't get there, unless your peers put you there.

Hino Diesel

Somehow, there's always something left on the loading dock.

The new Hino FB: Not too big. Not too small.

Hauling around this much truck half-empty just isn't cost-efficient.

AT&T

Unionmutual

Monsanto

AT&T Infoquest, NYC

Michel Tcherevkoff

873 Broadway
New York, New York 10003
(212) 228-0540

Represented by:

New York City–Fran Black (212) 725-3806
Philadelphia–Deborah Wolfe (215) 232-6666
Chicago–Joni Tuke (312) 787-6826

Call for Michel's mini-portfolio

1. National Geographic A.D. Dave Seager
2. Panasonic A.D. Vasken Kalayjian
3. AT&T A.D. Steve Phillips
4. Metier A.D. Rini Wu
5. Searle A.D. Thom Qualkinbush
6. AT&T A.D. Kevin Drexler
7. Stock Photography A.D. Michel Tcherevkoff
8. National Geographic A.D. Dave Seager
9. S.E.O.P.F. A.D. Kenneth Youngstein
10. Stock Photography A.D. Michel Tcherevkoff

1

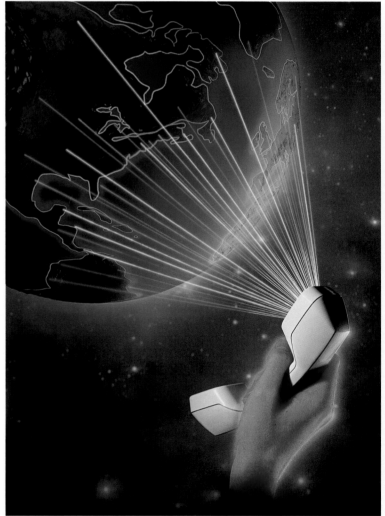

2

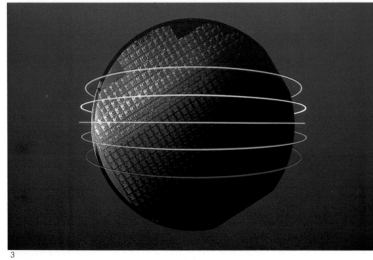

3

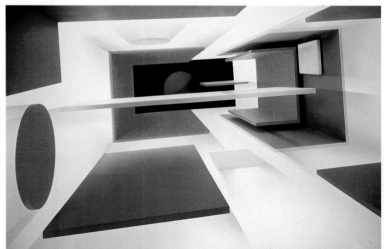

4

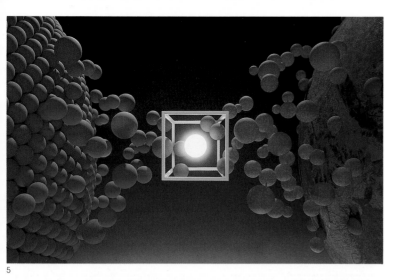

5

6

7

8

9

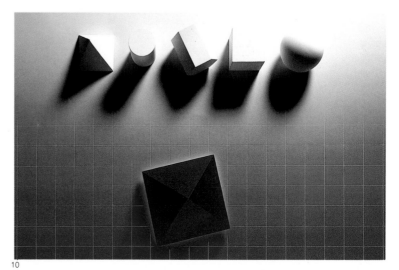

10

Yoav
4523 Broadway
New York, New York 10040
(212) 942-8185

Represented by:
Phototake, The Creative Link
(Ask for Leila)
(212) 942-8185

For Phototake Ad, see also ASMP #6
stock section p. 269.

Northeast

Connecticut
Maine
Massachusetts
New Hampshire
New Jersey
New York
Pennsylvania
Rhode Island
Vermont

SIMMONS

Specializing in location photography for Advertising, Annual Reports, Corporations and Industry. Clients include: Acushnet, Alpha Industries, Analog Devices, Avon, Bank of New England, Bose Corp., Bozell Jacobs Kenyon & Eckhardt, Citibank, Conde Naste Publications, Data Packaging, Digital Equipment Corp., Fairchild, Fidelity, Forbes Magazine, General Electric, Gillette Co., W.R. Grace, Grumman Aerospace, Heublein, Holt Rinehart & Winston, Houghton-Mifflin, IBM, Kimberly-Clark, McGraw-Hill, Microwave Associates, Nashua Corp., Polaroid, Prime Computer, Random House, Rockwell International, Scott Paper, Sola Basic Industries, State Street Bank & Trust, Syncor, Teradyne, 3M, Time Magazine, Touche-Ross, Vogue, S.D. Warren, Young & Rubicam.

ERIK LEIGH SIMMONS
241 'A' Street
Boston, Massachusetts 02210
(617) 482-5325
Represented by Brigitte
(617) 542-6768

SIMMONS

Specializing in location photography for Advertising, Annual Reports, Corporations and Industry. Clients include: *Adage, Amtrak, Apollo Computer, Bank of Boston, Boise-Cascade, The Boston Company, CBS, Commercial Union Assurance, Data General, Deere & Company, EG&G, Ferrofluidics, Foote Cone & Belding, GCA, General Foods Corp., Goodyear, Graylock Industries, Harcourt Brace Jovanovich, HHCC, Horticulture, HBM-Creamer, John Hancock, LTX, Metagraphics, Moore Business Forms, New England Electric, Prentice Hall, Putnam Funds, Raymond Corp., St. Regis, Sheraton Corp., Sonat Inc., Sun Co., TWA, J. Walter Thompson, Time-Life Books, Touch of Class Catalog, Unionmutual, Warner Communications, Westinghouse.*

ERIK LEIGH SIMMONS
241 'A' Street
Boston, Massachusetts 02210
(617) 482-5325
Represented by Brigitte
(617) 542-6768

Continued from page 114

Step #4: Developing the Compensation Arrangement

The fourth step in the process involves designing a compensation arrangement which is equitable to both parties and which accomplishes what the advertiser wants for his money. Unless the compensation arrangement is acceptable to both sides, the relationship is bound to be unsatisfactory in the long run.

As in any transaction, what you pay for a service affects its value. Moreover, not every buyer wants the same quantity or quality of service. The traditional unnegotiated 15% commission system related to billings is an anathema to this kind of thinking. It also is an anachronism in which advertisers see little point. Hence, almost every advertiser we have worked with wanted to have a tailored compensation system that made sense for it.

It has been our experience that small budget brands will often require paying more than the traditional 15% commission to get what they need, and that large budget brands can be handled for substantially less. Until careful analysis is made of agency costs for a particular account, a fair price for the agency's services cannot be determined. But one thing has been clear to us. Compensation has very little to do with the quality of the output.

Step #5: Making the Choice

The final step is deciding which candidate meets the advertiser's needs and expectations best. This is often the most difficult step unless it is done systematically and dispassionately. It is usually best to have evaluation forms that can be referred to during the session.

It would also be a mistake to believe that the selection process is a static one. Additional criteria often enter the picture. Others, that seemed so important before the process began, sometimes become irrelevant. It is, therefore, critical not to be too rigid. An objective moderator can help in making sure that the discussion and evaluations are based on the final criteria for selection rather than extraneous and self-serving issues that are bound to enter the picture.

If there is one lesson to be learned from our experience in selecting agencies, it is that there is a need for a formal, carefully planned competition where a number of people in the client organization are involved in the decision making process. This is the only way to select an agency that will fill their needs and be compatible with their corporate culture.

It is the only way they have a chance to learn the truth about the agency. A new business presentation forces an agency to articulate what it stands for. No matter how it is done, it exposes the agency's true qualities.

Advertisers cannot rely on public images. A declining agency's work has usually begun to slip before clients and prospects are aware of it. Conversely, an agency on the rise has usually begun to solve its problems before this is recognized on the outside. The only way an advertiser can tell where an agency stands at any given time is through a competitive solicitation.

A properly designed agency selection procedure forces the advertiser to make explicit its needs, to carefully take stock of its situation, and to consider its key people who are involved with the agency's output.

Thus, when it finally makes a decision, it knows the real reason for it, and that its own people will be satisfied with the choice. Moreover, it gives the advertiser the basis for evaluating the agency once it is on board and for holding it accountable over time.

And finally, a competitive selection procedure will give the advertiser the basis for deciding on the compensation arrangement it might wish to make with the agency. As I have stated many times before, the traditional, unnegotiated 15 percent commission system is dead. Just about every sophisticated advertiser negotiates a compensation package. Why shouldn't you?

Let me finish with this last thought. Selecting an advertising agency is of critical importance to most marketers. In most instances, the advertising prepared by the agency is usually the only voice the advertiser has with the ultimate consumer. The quality of that advertising, the price the advertiser pays for having it prepared and placed, and the pleasure and respect the advertiser shares with those who are responsible for it have much to do with the health of the advertiser's company. If an advertiser ever becomes dissatisfied with its agency, it owes it to itself—and to those with whom it will eventually work in the agency—to expose the decision to the competitive forces of the marketplace. That is the ethos under which companies sell their products and services. The choice of agency deserves no less.

Alvin A. Achenbaum
Chairman
Canter, Achenbaum, Associates Inc.
Marketing-Management Consultants
New York City

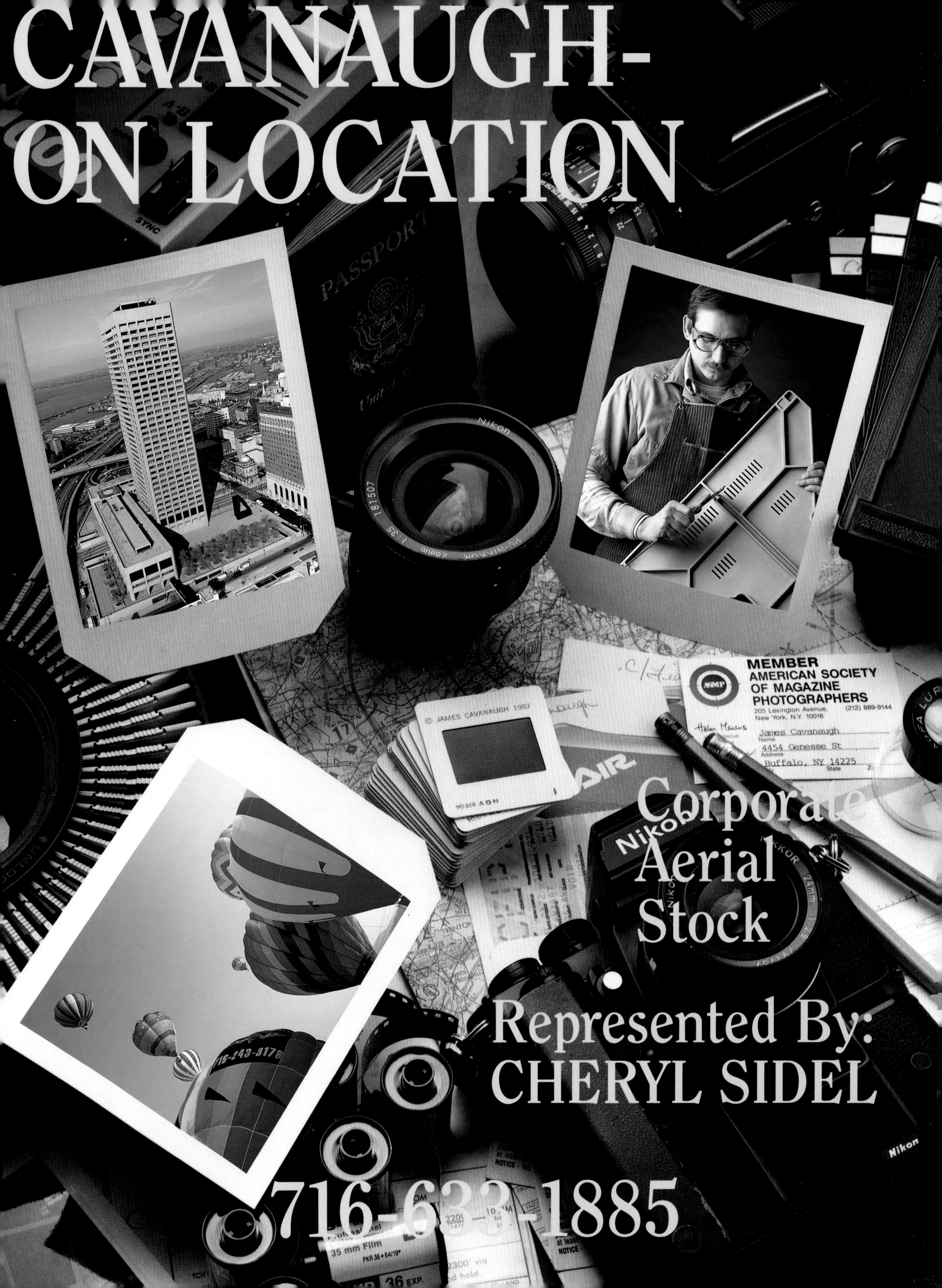
CAVANAUGH-
ON LOCATION
PASSPORT
© JAMES CAVANAUGH 1987
MEMBER
AMERICAN SOCIETY
OF MAGAZINE
PHOTOGRAPHERS
205 Lexington Avenue, New York, N.Y. 10016
(212) 889-9144
James Cavanaugh
4454 Genesse St
Buffalo, NY 14225
Corporate
Aerial
Stock
Represented By:
CHERYL SIDEL
716-633-1885

Mark Bolster/Pittsburgh

1235 Monterey Street
Pittsburgh, Pennsylvania 15212
(412) 231-3757

Specializing in domestic and foreign location
assignments for annual reports, brochures, and
corporate/industrial advertising.

Most recent clients include: Apple Computer,
Aristech, Chambers Development Corporation,
Hardwood Manufacturers Association, Inc., Koppers,
Monsanto, PPG Industries, Sperry, Thermo-King,
University of Pittsburgh, Westinghouse, Westinghouse
Credit Corporation.

Additional work can be seen in:
CORPORATE SHOWCASE 2, 3, 5
PITTSBURGH CREATIVE DIRECTORY 87
A.R. 3
ART DIRECTION—Upcoming Photographer, Dec. 84

EXTENSIVE STOCK AVAILABLE

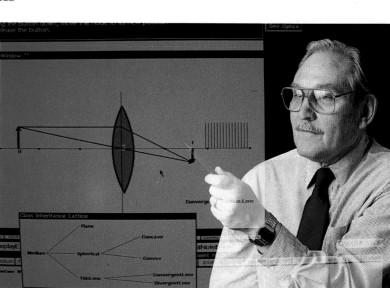

Mark Bolster/Pittsburgh

(412) 231-3757

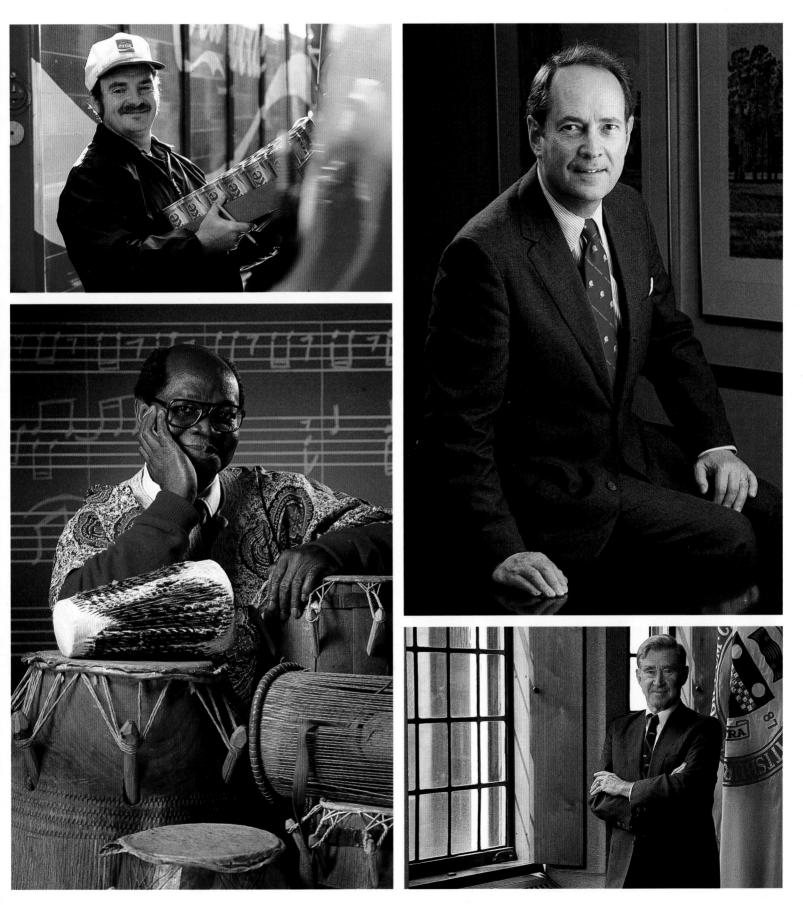

Linc Cornell

107 South Street
Suite 600
Boston, Massachusetts 02111
(617) 423-1511

Location/Studio
Advertising
Annual Reports
Corporate
Editorial
Multi-Media
Travel

Clients include
American Cancer Society
Apollo Computers
Beacon Press
Codex
Computerworld
Dexter Shoe Co.
Digital Review
Footjoy
John Hancock
Herman Boots
McDonalds
Mobil
Newsday
Oxfam America
Reebok
Teledyne Philbrick
Waters/Millipore
W.R. Grace & Co.

Awards include
1st Place, 2nd Place, Distinctive
Merit and Merit Awards from the
Francis W. Hatch Awards, the
Art Directors Club of Boston
Design Show, Graphic Design:
USA's Desi Awards, the New
York Art Directors Club and the
Thomas Edison Award for
Science Advertising.

Stock Available Through:
Stock Boston

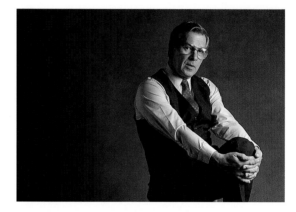

John DeWaele
14 Almy Street
Lincoln, Rhode Island 02865
(401) 726-0084

Photography on location
Corporations and Advertising

JOHN DeWAELE

PHOTOGRAPHY ON LOCATION

401-726-0084

Bryce Flynn Photography

17 Carmine Avenue
Foxboro, Massachusetts 02035
(508) 543-3020

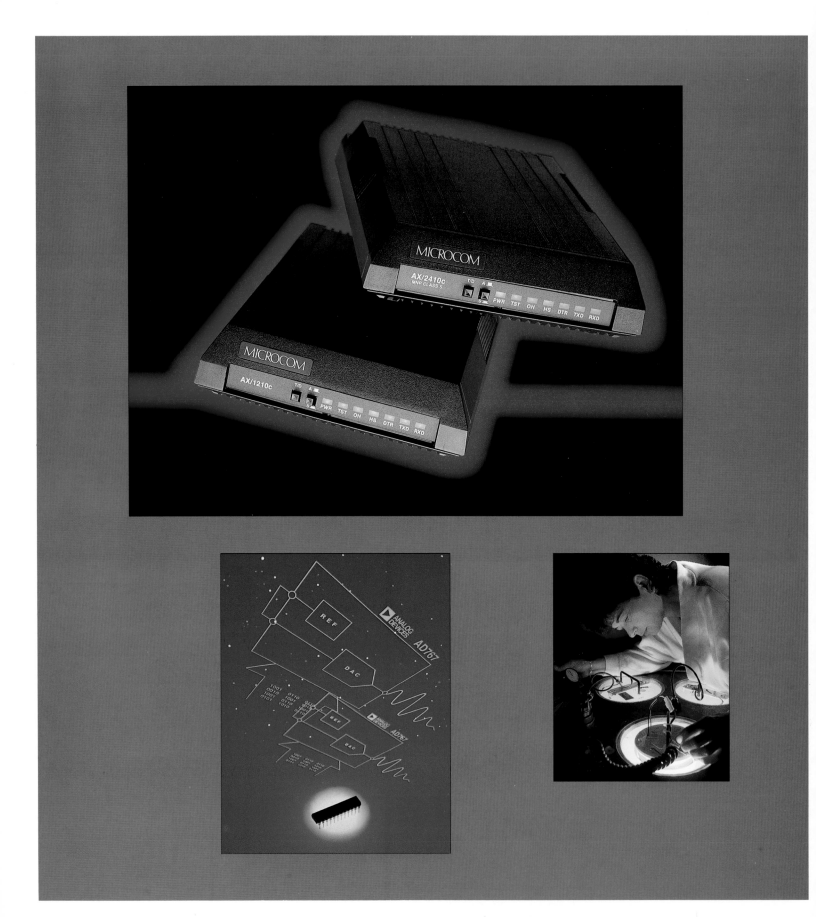

Bryce Flynn Photography

17 Carmine Avenue
Foxboro, Massachusetts 02035
(508) 543-3020

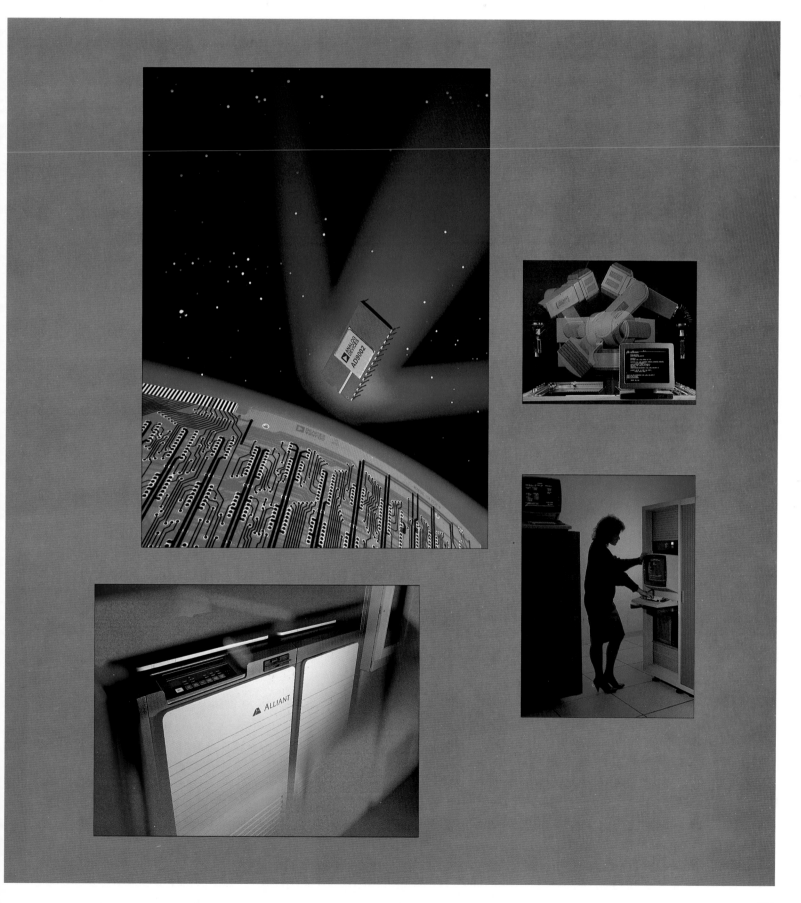

Malcolm Hewitt

179 Massachusetts Avenue
Boston, Massachusetts 02115
(617) 262-7227

In the studio for STILL LIFE, SPECIAL EFFECTS
or PRODUCT. On location for CORPORATE,
INSTITUTIONAL or TRAVEL. Stock available direct
from studio.

Kenneth Kauffman

915 Spring Garden Street
Philadelphia, Pennsylvania 19123
(215) 649-4474

Location and studio photography for annual reports,
corporate/industrial communications, and editorial
assignments.

Ed Malitsky

337 Summer Street
Boston, Massachusetts 02210
(617) 451-0655

On location for annual reports, corporate, industrial,
advertising and editorial assignments, stock.

Member: A.S.M.P.

Phil Matt

Box 10406
Rochester, New York 14610
Office: (716) 461-5977

Studio:
1237 East Main Street
Rochester, New York 14609

Phil specializes in location photography for corporate, editorial, and advertising assignments. His clients rely on Phil's sense of design and wide experience in photographing people from all walks of life. Extensive color and B/W stock. See our ads in American Showcase 8, 9, 10, 11 and in AdIndex 11.

Some recent clients:

(Editorial)—Black Enterprise, Business Week, Cahners Publishing, Changing Times, Connoisseur, Essence, Euromoney, Farm Journal, Financial World, Fortune, GEO, High Technology, Inc., Industry Week, Newsweek, New York Magazine, The New York Times, Time, USA Today, US News & World Report, Venture.

(Corporate & Other)—Cornell University, Corning Glass, Eastman Kodak, Eastman School of Music, Entré Computer, Grolier's, IBM, Monsanto, NY Stock Exchange, Norstar Bancorp, Nutri/System, Nynex, Pillsbury, Rochester Philharmonic Orchestra, Silver Burdett, Simon Graduate School of Business Administration, U.S.I.A., 13-30 Corporation, Xerox.

Member: ASMP NPPA   All Photographs © Phil Matt.

1: Anita Racine, Senior Lecturer in Textiles & Apparel, Cornell University

2: Colby H. Chandler, Chief Executive Officer, Eastman Kodak Company

3: Marshall Hyman, President, Nalge Company

4: Dr. Pamela Powers, D.V.M.

1.

2.

3.

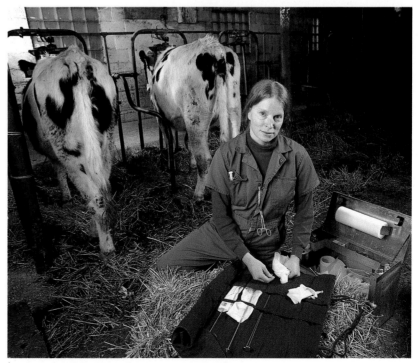

4.

Kevin R. McDonald

319 Newtown Turnpike
Redding, Connecticut 06896
(203) 938-9276

The studio is located in the historical town of Redding and is easily accessible from the Merritt Parkway and I-95. In addition, studios in New York and West Palm Beach are available.

Superb Photography...

...From an award-winning commercial photographer. One who discovers the creative possibilities in every photograph. His talents have covered a wide range of subjects and techniques around the corner and around the world.

...For more than a decade, Kevin has served the needs of international and domestic clients in both the corporate and non-profit sectors. Whether he's photographing fashion for Pierre Cardin, a national ad with coach Mike Ditka of the Chicago Bears or the Board of Directors of Environmental Risk Ltd., Kevin R. McDonald understands color, form, texture and most importantly people.

Partial Client List:
Australian Trade Commission
Pierre Cardin Inc.
Cliff Engle
Connecticut Magazine
Danbury Hospital
Mike Ditka—Chicago Bears
Environmental Risk Ltd.
ESE Electronics
Harris Publications
Jamaica Tourism Council
Jet
Michael Knight—ABC Television
Lee Jeans Corp.
Lego
McCalls Magazine
Roche Pharmaceutical
Starter Co.
Robin Strasser—ABC Television
Darryl Strawberry—N.Y. Mets
Lawrence Taylor—N.Y. Giants
Isiah Thomas—Detroit Pistons
Westwind Aviation
Women's Wear Daily

His work has been seen in such publications as Sports, Inside Sports and Sports Illustrated.

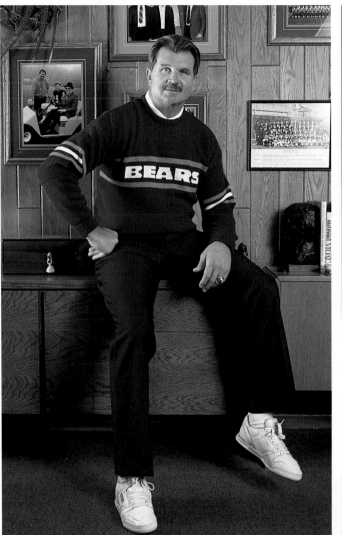

Ralph Mercer

239 A Street
Boston, Massachusetts 02210
(617) 482-2942

Location and studio photography for corporate
advertising, annual report, and collateral usage.
Conceptual special effects photography is a specialty.

HONEYWELL BULL/A.D. ROSE CONROY

FUTURE SOUND/A.D. JUDITH RICHLAND

HONEYWELL BULL/A.D. RANDY SHERMAN

A.D.S./A.D. STUART DARSCH

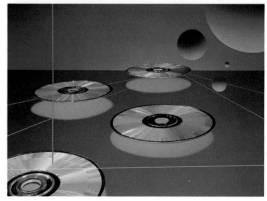

PORTFOLIO/A.D. RALPH MERCER

Mozo

MOZO Photo/Design
282 Shelton Road (Route 110)
Monroe, Connecticut 06468-2529
(203) 261-7400

FAX: (203) 452-7369

Brief descriptions on specialties and services.

BUBBLES – A vast collection in all shapes, colors and sizes. They could be done on commission.

SPECIAL EFFECTS – Altering and enhancing reality through crafted, in-camera or darkroom techniques.

CREATIVITY – The (bottom left) sample is one of 17 variations, from a suggested idea, for a GE cover in Marketing Education. The experience as Designer/Art Director is included with the service.

FAX – For stock or assignment, visualization and estimates. Also for evaluation of work-in-progress, in case you can't be with us.

MAILERS – To include your name in our mailing list, please send a note, in company letterhead, specifying position, department and area of interest.

REFERENCE MATERIALS – American Showcase Vol. 8/206, 9/193, 10/199 and Corporate Showcase Vol. 5/107, 6/127. Reprints, stock and portfolio available upon request.

David Plank
Cherry & Carpenter Streets
Reading, Pennsylvania 19602
(215) 376-3461
FAX (215) 376-8261

David was spending more time trying to make up his mind about which assignment shots to show in this ad than it took to shoot this Porsche. So here's the Porsche:

Seth Resnick

15 Sleeper Street #507
Boston, Massachusetts 02210
(617) 423-7475

Annual Reports
Corporate
Advertising
Editorial
Travel
Stock

Some clients:
American Management Association
Anthony Russell
Apollo Computer
Ciba-Corning
DR Labs
Forbes
Fortune
Harvard Business School
Haystack
Interleaf

Lotus
McGraw-Hill
National Geographic
National Wildlife Federation
Ontario Research
Peat Marwick
Smithsonian
The Boston Company
The New York Times
Tufts
Ziff-Davis

Seth Resnick

15 Sleeper Street #507
Boston, Massachusetts 02210
(617) 423-7475

Annual Reports
Corporate
Advertising
Editorial
Travel
Stock

Some clients:
American Management Association
Anthony Russell
Apollo Computer
Ciba-Corning
DR Labs
Forbes
Fortune
Harvard Business School
Haystack
Interleaf

Lotus
McGraw-Hill
National Geographic
National Wildlife Federation
Ontario Research
Peat Marwick
Smithsonian
The Boston Company
The New York Times
Tufts
Ziff-Davis

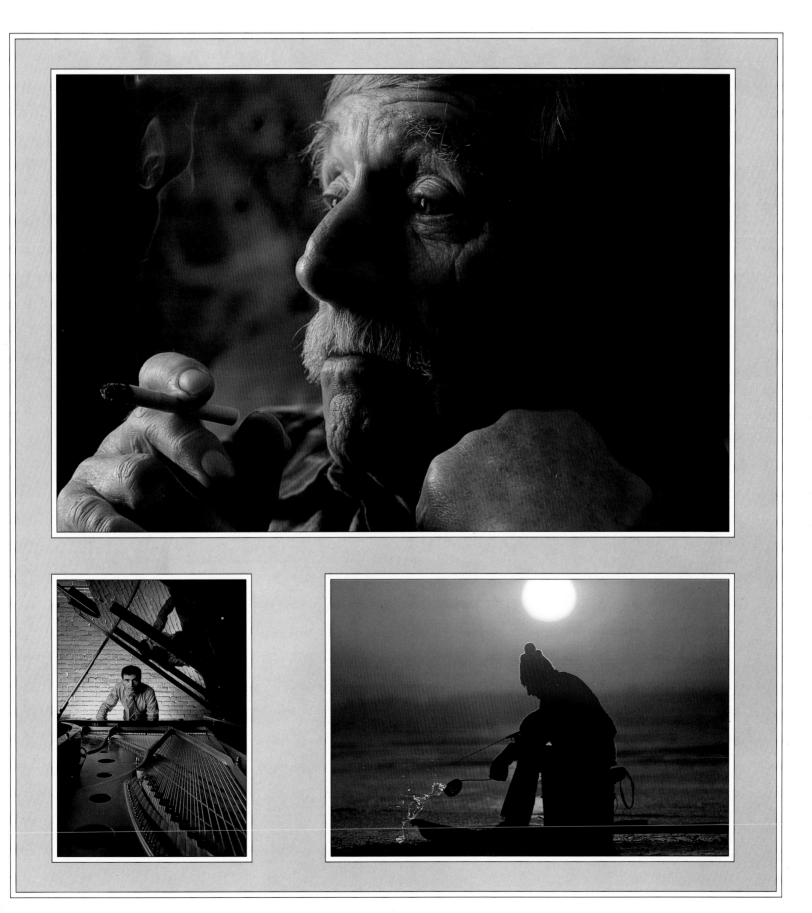

Len Rubenstein
87 Pine Street
Easton, Massachusetts 02375
(617) 238-0744

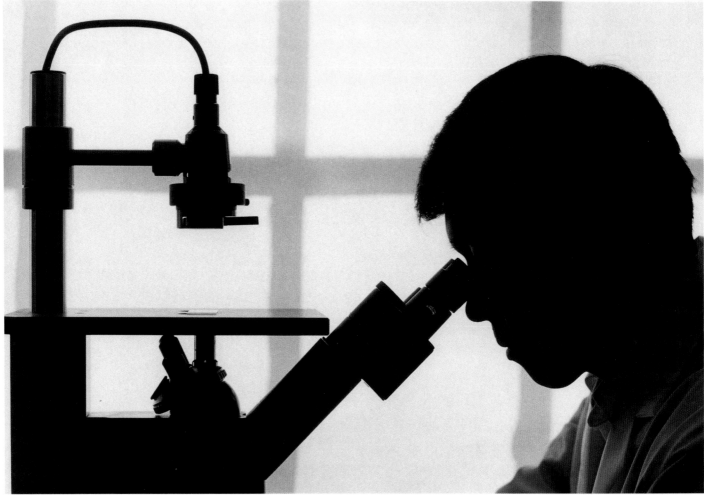

ARTHUR D. LITTLE

ENVIRONMENTAL POWER COMPANY

FIDELITY INVESTMENTS

Russell Schleipman

298A Columbus Avenue
Boston, Massachusetts 02116
(617) 267-1677

AMCA International
Automatix
Bank of New England
Bausch & Lomb
Centocor
Chelsea Industries
Citizen's Bank
Courier Corp.
Cullinet
Digital Equipment Corp.
Dunkin' Donuts
Ernst & Whinney
First NH Banks
Forbes Magazine
Fortune Magazine
Helix Technology Corp.
Integrated Genetics
Life Magazine
Ma/Com Inc.
Money Magazine
New England Electric
Neworld Bank
Omni Flow
Outside Magazine
Pitney Bowes
Polaroid Corp.
Raytheon Corp.
Repligen Corp.
Rockresorts Inc.
Sail Magazine
Shawmut Bank
Tech Ops

Frank Siteman

(617) 729-3747

Select Stock Available

Member ASMP

© 1988 Frank Siteman

John Still Photography

17 Edinboro Street
Boston, Massachusetts 02111
(617) 451-8178
FAX (617) 482-1826

Clients include: Digital Equipment, International Paper,
Polaroid, Monsanto, Lotus Software, BASF, Shawmut
Corp., Teradyne, Bank of New England, Addison/
Wesley Publishing, Times-Mirror Publishing,
McCormack & Dodge, Interleaf.

Awards: Art Directors Club of Boston Design Show
Print's Regional Design Annual
Connecticut Art Directors Annual One Show
Advertising Club of Boston Hatch Awards

CLIENT INSET PHOTO: POLAROID CORP.

Jamey Stillings

87 North Clinton Avenue
Rochester, New York 14604
(716) 232-5296
FAX (716) 232-6443

Represented by Pat Urban

ASMP
Languages:
English, German, Spanish
See also:
Corporate Showcase 5 & 6

Jamey Stillings

87 North Clinton Avenue
Rochester, New York 14604
(716) 232-5296
FAX (716) 232-6443

Represented by Pat Urban

ASMP
Languages:
English, German, Spanish
See also:
Corporate Showcase 5 & 6

Yamil R. Sued/Photographics

P.O. Box 15558
Park Square Station
Stamford, Connecticut 06901-5558
(203) 353-8865

Advertising and editorial photography, studio or location. Specializing in product still-life, fashion and beauty. Extensive stock photography file available. Portfolio available for review upon request.

Member ASMP APA PP of A

Clients Include:

Anderson & Lembke, Comp-U-Card Int., Dow Chemical, Helo Sauna, Hyers Smith, James River Corp., Plus Development Corp.

DOW CHEMICAL

HELO SAUNA

DOW CHEMICAL

Mid-Atlantic

Delaware
Maryland
Virginia
West Virginia
Washington, D.C.
North Carolina

How to Remain Creative in a Commercially Oriented Environment

There's no doubt that we live in a commercially oriented environment. The average supermarket now carries over 19,000 products. Over 10,000 new grocery items were introduced in 1987 vs. 2,600 in 1980. Almost half a million trademarks are now registered and approximately 25,000 new ones are added each year. According to the Thomas Register, there are now 80,000 corporations – all of which bombard the consumer with a multitude of advertising messages. The question is: How do we remain creative in today's marketplace?

Our firm's strategy has always been rather straightforward. Let the designers concentrate on design and the marketing people handle the marketing. We actually have separated the two functions into what we call "church" and "state". The designers are "church," and the marketing people are "state".

In order to avoid conflicts between church and state, we never put a designer over a marketing person, or vice versa, on any project. Everybody is capable of understanding what his or her job is. We don't want the designers to say, "This is going to sell" and we don't want the marketers to say, "I hate orange". With this system, we succeed in answering the marketing objectives, and we answer them in the most creative way possible.

If the design doesn't meet the marketing objectives, it is not a good design. As we answer the marketing objectives, we must also strive to create a solution that evokes emotion. Creativity is the answer for stimulation particularly in an overcrowded supermarket. But to be creative in a commercially oriented environment, one must understand the environment and respond to it.

More than any other graphic medium, a package design must strike a balance between impact and image. To keep our designers fresh, we do not lock them into one area of design, such as corporate identity or package design or even more specifically, packaging for food clients or corporate identity work for banks. We believe designers need change and we rotate our designers to give them different types of projects.

There is no question that there are still antiquated grocery categories that suffer and lack good design. You have more creative expression when working on a package for a new product than on an existing one, which may have numerous equities.

Statistics have shown that it is no longer enough to put the brand name on top in big bold letters and assume the consumer will trust it. In 1986, 80% of every dollar spent in the grocery store resulted from in-store decisions; 60% of consumers bought items they didn't intend to buy and 15% entered the store without a specific brand in mind in a specific category.

We need to "sell hard, tastefully" through the use of appetizing photography, higher quality illustrations and tasteful typography. We hire only the best food photographers who are accustomed to working for advertising agencies and gourmet food magazines. Package design is much more restrictive than other mediums because of the legal limitations. A package design is an advertisement on the shelf and should be treated accordingly – it competes with all the other designs on the shelf. It must compete with hundreds of other images at one time, unlike a poster, an annual report or brochure. This is not to say these graphic mediums are not competitive. They are. But package design is unique in the way that it must grab the consumer and influence a purchase competing with other packages developed to accomplish the same goal at the same time.

Jerry Berman
Principal and Creative Director
Sidjakov Berman Gomez & Partners
San Francisco, California

Maxwell
MacKenzie

2641 Garfield Street, N.W.
Washington, D.C. 20008
(202) 232-6686

Specializing in
Architecture & Interiors
for Advertising, Corporate
& Editorial Clients.

Stock Available from
Photographer and from:
After-Image
Click/Chicago
Uniphoto

For more work see
ASMP Silver Books 2 & 4

Clients include:
American Inst. of Architects
American Iron & Steel Inst.
Artery Organization
Best Products
Better Homes & Gardens
  Magazine
Bomstein-Gura Agency
Boston Properties
Brick Institute of America
CRS Sirrine
Cadillac Fairview
Comsat
Connoisseur Magazine
Corporate Design Magazine
Decorating Magazine
Earle Palmer Brown Advertising
Fed. National Mortgage Assoc.
Firestone Corporation
Fortune Magazine
Four Seasons Hotels
Glen-Gery Brick
Goldman-Sachs & Company
Goldberg-Marchesano
  Advertising
Group Health Association
HOK
Hazel-Peterson Companies
Helmsley-Spear
Hershey Corporation
Home Magazine
IBM
IKEA
Intelsat
Interiors Magazine
Kodak
Leo A. Daly
3M
National Paint & Coatings
  Assoc.
National Park Service
Nat. Trust for Historic
  Preservation
Oliver Carr Company
Radisson Hotels
Regardie's Magazine
Restaurant Business Magazine
Sheraton Hotels
Skidmore, Owings & Merrill
Smithsonian Institution
Spaulding & Slye
Swanke Hayden Connell
TAC
Time-Life Books
Trammell Crow Company
U.S. Information Agency
United Way of America
VVKR
Washingtonian Magazine
Washington Post Company
Western Development
  Corporation
Westin Hotels
World Bank

ASMP

Greg Pease

23 East 22nd Street
Baltimore, Maryland 21218
(301) 332-0583

Studio Manager:
Kelly Baumgartner

Corporate, industrial, editorial,
advertising and stock
photography.

Client list available

Also see:
American Showcase 4, 5, 6, 7,
8, 9, 10, 11
Corporate Showcase 1, 4, 5, 6

1. Alex. Brown
2. Isaly-Klondike
3. Isaly-Klondike
4. NASA

2

3

4

Portrait Alliance

6083 Arlington Boulevard
Falls Church, Virginia 22044
(703) 533-9453

Portrait Alliance specializes in high quality Executive
Portraiture and editorial photography for discerning
corporate clients throughout the Eastern United
States. We respectfully invite your inquiry.

Contact: Suna Lee
(703) 533-9453

Ross Stansfield

4938 D Eisenhower Avenue
Alexandria, Virginia 22304
(703) 370-5142

Studio and location

Clients include: Coca Cola, Marriot Corporation, The Peau Corporation, Future Farmers of America, Fairfax Hospital Association, N V Homes, Metropolitan Office Furniture, The United States Air Force, The United Way, The Washington Post, American Concrete Pressure Pipe Association, Automobile Quarterly, and Rouse Corporation.

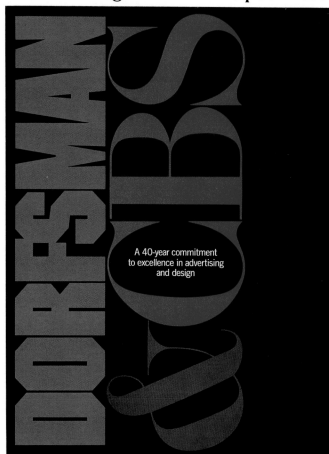

Southeast

Alabama
Florida
Georgia
Kentucky
Louisiana
Mississippi
South Carolina
Tennessee

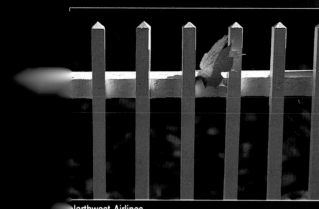

Northwest Airlines

Independent Life Insurance

Jack Daniels Distillery

Richland Cigarettes

Robin Hood

615 / 794-2041

Real Places, Real People... Pulitzer Prize Winning
Photographer Robin Hood Photographs on Location For
Corporate and Advertising. Stock Available.

Location and Studio Photography for Advertising & Annual Reports, and Corporate/Industrial Communications

Clients Include:

American Hospitex
Amoco
Atlanta Magazine
Anaconda Ericsson
Blue Cross & Blue Shield
Budweiser
Burger King
CNN
Coats & Clark
Coca-Cola USA
Georgia Federal Bank
Graphic Industries
Harris-Lanier
HBO & Company
Hitachi
Hyatt Regency Hotels
IBM
Kentucky Fried Chicken
Kimberly-Clark
Marriott Hotels
Milliken Textiles
Mobile
Monsanto
Nissan
Panasonic
Peachtree Software
R.J. Reynolds
Scripto
Sears
Southern Bell
The United Way
Touche Ross
Union Carbide
U.S. Forestry Dept.
WSB-TV
Yamaha

FRED GERLICH

Photographic Illustration and Advertising
1220 Spring Street / Atlanta, Georgia 30309
(404) 872-3487

Bob Gelberg

7035-E Southwest 47th Street
Miami, Florida 33155
(305) 665-3200

Twenty years experience in advertising
and corporate location photography.

Cosby Bowyer, Inc.

209 North Foushee Street
Richmond, Virginia 23220
(804) 643-1100

Operating out of one of the most beautiful and functional advertising photography studios on the eastern seaboard, Herbert Cosby and Sonny Bowyer consistently produce top-notch studio and location work.

With a highly motivated staff of five, the 10,000 sq. ft. facility includes an in-house E-6 lab, a large cyc in the main shooting area and a sophisticated kitchen/shooting space that food stylists *love* to work in.

Additional work can be seen in the 1988 Washington Sourcebook and the 1988 Adweek Portfolio.

Jose A. Fernandez
1011 Valencia Avenue
Coral Gables, Florida 33134
(305) 443-6501

Location photography:
Corporate/Industrial
Technical
Aerial
Environmental portraiture

Based in Miami. Fluent in Spanish & English.

Henderson/Muir Photography

6005 Chapel Hill Road
Raleigh, North Carolina 27607
(919) 851-0458

New 7000 square-foot
studio now available.

See additional work in
American Showcase,
Volumes 8, 9, & 10.

Stock Representation through:
Woodfin Camp & Associates
(212) 750-1020 New York
(202) 638-5705 Washington

Clients include:
Ajinomoto, U.S.A.
Athol Vinyl Fabrics
Bald Head Island
Branch Banking & Trust
Collins & Aikman
Colorcraft Corporation
Data General
Domino's Pizza
General Electric
Hardees Food Systems
Harlon Properties Group
Harris Semi-Conductor
Hilton Hotels
IBM
ITT
Karastan Carpets
Liggett & Myers
Mallinckrodt
McDonalds
Mead CompuChem
Mitsubishi Semi-Conductor
NC Travel & Tourism
NC State Ports
Northern Telecom
Piedmont Airlines
Record Bar, Inc.
Research Triangle Foundation
Sheraton Hotels
The New York Times Magazine
Thurston Trucking Company
Time-Life Books
Union Carbide
U.S. Air
Wachovia Bank & Trust

Advertising,
Business Publications,
Annual Reports,
Corporate/Industrial,
Travel/Personalities

Represented by:
Faithe Benson
(919) 851-0458

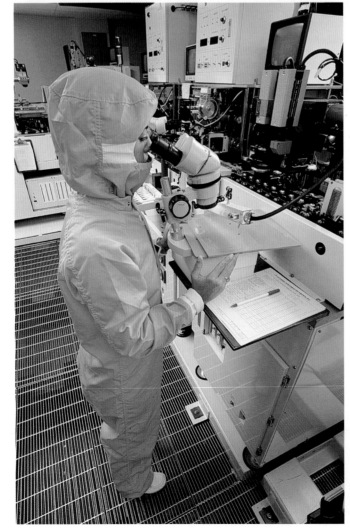

Steve Hogben

ARCHITECTURAL PHOTOGRAPHICS
6269 McDonough Drive
Atlanta, Georgia 30093
(404) 266-2894

Specializing in Architectural and Interior Photography.
Photographer of the best selling book
"Building Atlanta."

Member ASMP

Tom Knibbs

5907 Northeast 27th Avenue
Fort Lauderdale, Florida 33308
(305) 491-6263

Specializing in architectural and interior design photography for more than 13 years in the Southeast. Well published in national and regional magazines including Architectural Digest, Better Homes & Gardens, Southern Accents, South Florida Home & Garden, Designer's Quarterly, Professional Builder, Builder, National Real Estate Investor, Design and Construction and Area Development, his work is welcomed by editors and art directors. Tom has helped earn professionals dozens of architectural and interior design awards in major competitions. Stock photography available through The Image Bank. Portfolio on request.

To view additional work, see Corporate Showcase Volume 6.

Dennis O'Kain

DOK/Lexington Photo Works, Inc.
102 West Main
Lexington, Georgia 30648
(404) 743-3140

Architectural and design photography with an emphasis on the Documentary tradition. Inhouse custom lab specializing in exhibition grade Black & White and Cibachrome printing. No limitations on travel or time.

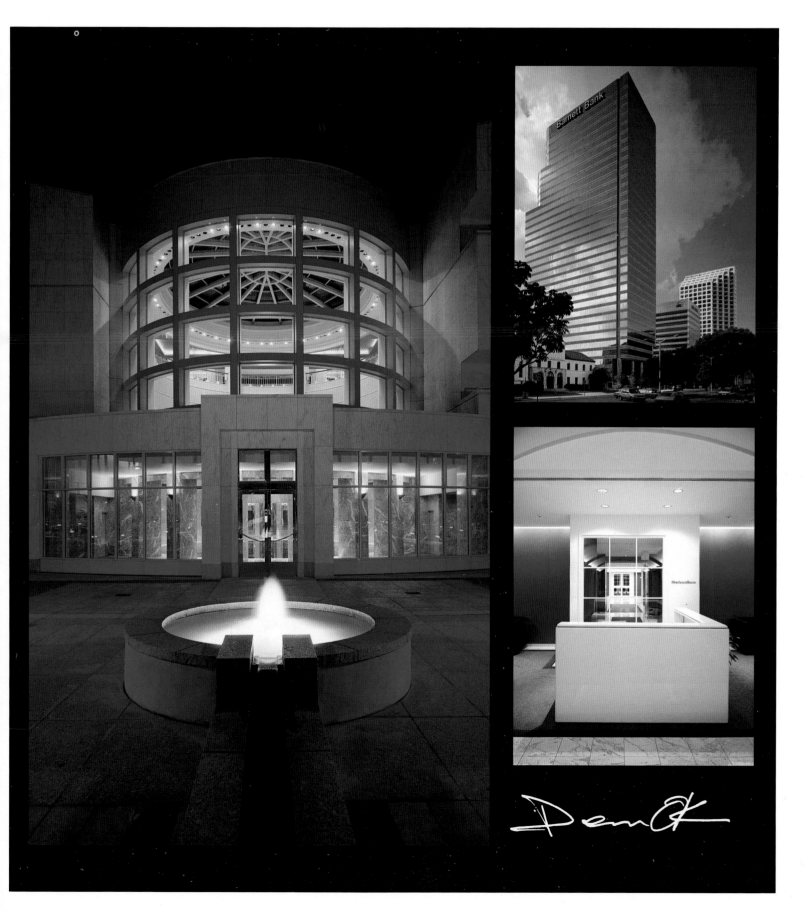

165

Ron Sherman

P.O. Box 28656
Atlanta, Georgia 30328
(404) 993-7197

Representative:
Bruce Wetta, Wooden/Grubbs
& Bate
(404) 892-6303

Location photography for
annual reports, advertising,
corporate, industrial, editorial,
travel and sports assignments.

Stock Photography available.
(404) 993-7197

Also see ads in Corporate
Showcase Volume 3, Volume 4,
Volume 5, Volume 6, American
Showcase Volume 8 and Volume
10 and ASMP BOOK 1981,
Book 2, Book 3 and Book 4.

Member ASMP

© 1988 Ron Sherman

Design: Patt Farrell

Ken Touchton

3011 Northeast 40th Street
Fort Lauderdale, Florida 33308
(305) 566-9756

Location photography for annual reports, advertising, corporation, industrial and editorial assignments. We are located just a little south of New York City and a little north of Rio with our cases packed and film in hand.

Stock photography available
All photographs © 1987
Ken Touchton

See American Showcase 6 & 7 for additional examples of executive portraiture, aerial, telecommunications and medical technology.

Clients include:
AMA
Avitas
Bank of Maryland
BDM Corp
Bell Atlantic
Carter/Cosgrove & Co
Celanese Corp
Changing Times
Coca-Cola USA
CNN
C&P Telephone
Creative Ideas
DuPont Co
Farmers Savings Bank
Horizon
IBM Corp
ITT
MCI
Nations Business
New Jersey Bell
RJ Reynolds
Sheraton
Whittle Comm
Unitec

Design:
    O'Leary/O'Neil Associates

WHO WAS HERB LUBALIN?

THE FACE BEHIND THE FACES.

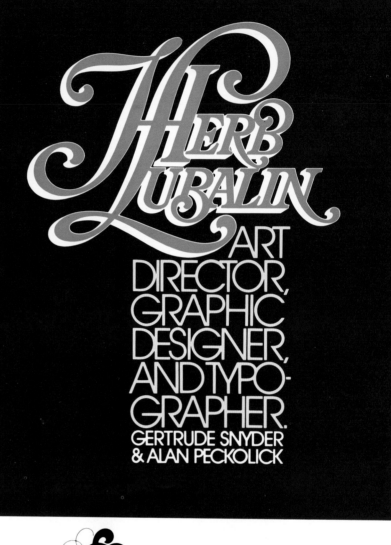

He was a skinny, colorblind, left-handed artist, known to friends and colleagues as a deafeningly silent man. But through his typography-based and editorial designs, he created bold new forms for communication and changed the demensions of advertising and graphics. **Herb Lubalin** is the definitive book about the typographic impresario and design master of our time. It is illustrated with more than 360 extraordinary examples of Lubalin's award-winning work, including: ■ Logos and Letterheads ■ Editorial and Book Design ■ Packaging ■ Advertising and Sales Promotion ■ Annual Reports ■ Best of U&lc, and more.

Now in paperback. 184 pages, Color throughout, 9"x11 7/8". Paperback: $25.00.

Send for your copy of **Herb Lubalin** today. Pay $25.00 plus $3.00 for postage and handling within the US and Canada. To order, call **(212) 245-0981** and charge your AMEX, Visa or Mastercard. Or send your check or money order to: AMERICAN SHOWCASE, INC. 724 Fifth Avenue, New York, NY 10019

*New York residents, please add appropriate sales tax.

More than Tradition...

a legendary and internationally acclaimed Boston landmark where celebrated seafood is the star, and sea and sky, the artful staging.

 IMMY'S HARBORSIDE RESTAURANT

242 Northern Avenue, Boston • (617) 423-1000
en Lunch and Dinner—Monday thru Saturday 11:30 AM to 9:30 PM
Open Sundays—12 noon to 8:00 PM
nited Reservations—Valet Parking—All Major Credit Cards Accepted

PANORAMA

BOSTON'S OFFICIAL BI-WEEKLY VISITOR GUIDE

COMPLETE LISTING OF EVENTS NOVEMBER 26-DECEMBER 9

Midwest

Illinois
Indiana
Iowa
Kansas
Michigan
Minnesota
Missouri
Nebraska
North Dakota
Ohio
South Dakota
Wisconsin

DON GETSUG STUDIOS · 610 FAIRBANKS CT · CHICAGO 60611 · 312 440 1311

DON GETSUG STUDIOS · 610 FAIRBANKS CT · CHICAGO 60611 · 312 440 1311

171

OLAUSEN

J udy Olausen, whose work was selected for

the 1987 Mead Annual Report Show, is combining a fine art background with corporate photography.

Her Address is 213 North Washington Avenue, Minneapolis, Minnesota 55401.

Telephone (612) 332-5009.

Factory worker

DICK REED

1330 Coolidge
Troy, Michigan 48084
(313) 280-0090

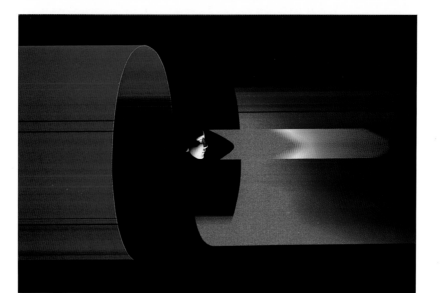

Transforming imagination into image is our specialty. On Location or in the Studio, creative photography is our business.

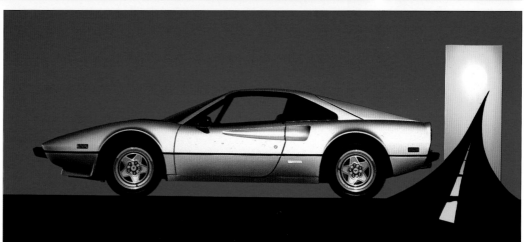

Bob Williams

Bob Williams (signature)

Represented by:

Northlight Studios
32049 Milton Avenue
Madison Heights, Michigan 4807

5635 Melrose Avenue
Hollywood, California 90038

313 · 588 · 6544

213 · 876 · 4370

800 · 248 · 7856
Outside Michigan

519 · 254 · 2197
In Canada

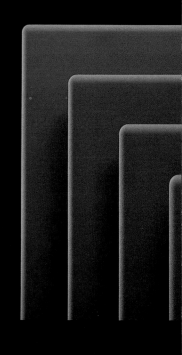

Bob Barrett

3733 Pennsylvania
Kansas City, Missouri 64111
(816) 753-3208 (home)
(816) 842-3833 (studio)

Assignment and Stock

Corporate, Industrial,
Architectural & Editorial

Corporate clients:
Alchem Plastics
Angeles Corporation
Boylan Realty
Chase Manhattan
KC Masterpiece
Kinney Shoes
Mellon Bank
Montgomery-Ward
National Fidelity Life
Pella Windows
Pinkerton Security
Random House
Rival Mfg.
Universal Underwriters
U S Sprint
Yellow Freight

Editorial clients:
American Cities Business
    Journals
Changing Times
Cope Magazine
Eastern Review
Financial Planning
Home Furnishings Daily
Leisureguide
Midwest Living
Midwest Motorist
NY Photo District News
Portal Publications
Scott-Foresman
Step-by-Step Graphics

See additional ads in ASMP
Silver Books 2, 3, 4, 5, & 6

Member: ASMP

National Fidelity Life

Boylan Realty

Chase Manhattan

Gard Oil

Tom Berthiaume Studio

Tom Berthiaume Studio
1008 Nicollet Mall
Minneapolis, Minnesota 55403
(612) 338-1999

Specializing in the corporate portrait in studio and on location. B/W and color.

Clients include: AT&T, Apple Computers, Dayton-Hudson, First Wisconsin, General Mills, H.B. Fuller, Honeywell, Jockey, Lee Jeans, Levis, Monsanto, Northwest Airlines, U.S. West, and Wall Street Journal.

RICHARD J. MAHONEY   CEO   MONSANTO CORPORATION

WALTER CRONKITE

GARRISON KEILLOR   INTERNATIONAL PAPER COMPANY

NORTHWEST AIRLINES

Al Buschauer

11416 South Harlem Avenue
Worth, Illinois 60482
(312) 448-2222

(30 minutes from downtown
Chicago)

Specializing in distinctive
portraits both on location and in
studio.

Corporate and personal.

Photo styling by:
Savannah Walters

CLICK/
Chicago Ltd.

213 West Institute Place
Suite 503
Chicago, Illinois 60610
(312) 787-7880

We are the most creative
and knowledgeable stock/
assignment agency in the
Midwest.

Our 40 assignment
photographers are spread
throughout the U.S.A. and Europe,
with the majority located in the
Midwest. All of our photographers
work both in color and b/w. We
have experts in the following
fields: Advertising, Aerial,
Annual Reports, Architecture,
Audiovisual, Illustration,
Location, Heavy and Light
Industry, Medical, Panoramic,
Photojournalism, Portraiture,
Products, Public Relations and
Still Life. We can show you
portfolios of photographers
whose work is relevant to
your needs.

We also have an extensive library
of current, top-quality stock
photographs and will be happy
to supply stock images where
available budget, season of the
year, or far-flung locations make
an assignment impractical.
Please see our other ad in the
Stock Section.

Joe DeNatale

DeNATALE, INC.
215 West Ohio Street
Chicago, Illinois 60610
(312) 329-0234

Fax your layout.

Mini portfolio available.

Recent clients:

Sara Lee, Mead Johnson, Beatrice, UpJohn, AT&T, Beecham, Masonite Corp., Chi-Chi's Restaurant, Popeye's, Emerson Electric, John Deere, American Dairy Association, Northrop, Henniger, Bristol Laboratories, Dorsey Laboratories, General Mills Corporation, G.D. Searle, Land O'Lakes, Honeywell, Yamaha, Dean Foods, Tobler, McCormick, French's, Chemical Bank, All Steel, Shasta, Kelloggs, Wendy's Morton Thiokol Inc., Hyatt Hotels, Raybestos, Leaf Inc., Baxter Travenol, Swift-Eckrich, Playboy, Stroh Brewery, McDonalds, Alberto Culver, Hartmarx, S.C. Johnson, Prudential, Andes Candies, Gulf & Western Co., Dubuque, Jensen, Northern Telecom, Quaker Oats, Prudential, Dynascan

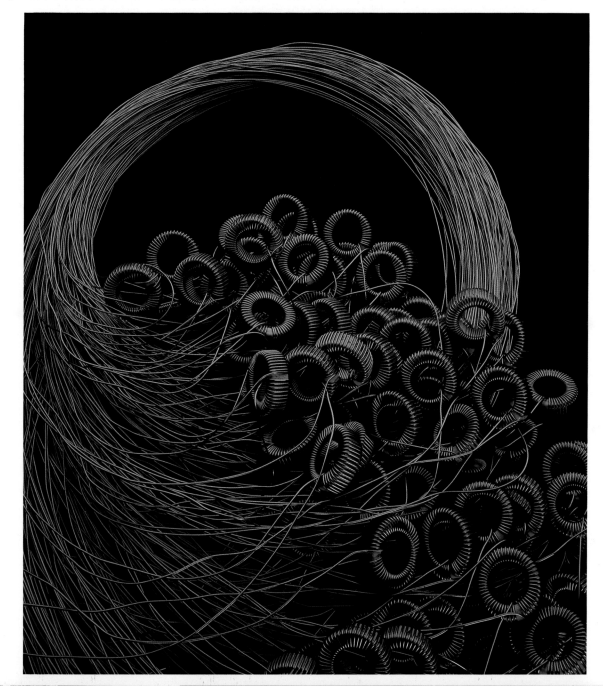

Rick Dieringer

19 West Court Street
Cincinnati, Ohio 45202
(513) 621-2544

Advertising, fashion and
corporate/industrial
photography

A partial list of clients:
Kroger
Clarion Hotels
Harnischfeger Corp.
Monsanto
Belcan Corp.
Formica Corp.
Litton Industries
F&W Publishing
Inc. Magazine
Clippard Instrument
   Laboratory Inc.
Jacor Communications
Prudential Realty Co.
Sheffer Corp.
Hemmer Construction
Cincinnati Electronics

See also Corporate Showcase
Nos. 4 & 6

© 1987 Rick Dieringer

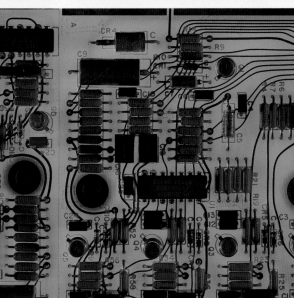

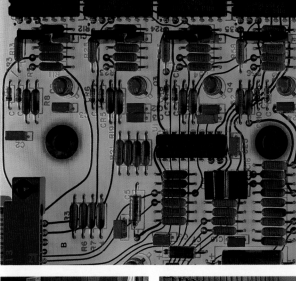

John Gilroy Photography

2407 West Main Street
Kalamazoo, Michigan 49007
(616) 349-6805
(616) 381-8764

Images shown are from: (L-R) The Upjohn Annual
Report (top two photographs), Varbusiness magazine
feature article, Corporate Responsibility Report for
The Dow Chemical Company, audio visual presentation
for the Asgrow/O's Gold Seed Company and annual
report photography for the Brown Paper Company
(now James River Corporation).

For more examples of work, see Corporate Showcase
4, 5 and 6.

Phillip MacMillan James

2300 Hazelwood Avenue
Saint Paul, Minnesota 55109-2649
(612) 777-2303

Member ASMP

Client list includes:

Landor Associates	House Beautiful	Westinghouse Elevators
Vignelli Associates	Cargill	Time-Life Books
Dayton-Hudson	EcoLab Inc.	McGraw-Hill Publications
Honeywell	Andersen Windows	Embassey Suites Hotels
CPT	Ellerbe	McDonalds
Turner Construction	Cold Spring Granite	3M

David Joel Photography Inc.

1342 West Hood Avenue
Chicago, Illinois 60660
(312) 262-0794

Specializing in Multiple Strobe-Light Applications on Location

Corporate
Industrial
Annual Reports
Medical
Education

Partial client list:
Quaker Oats Company
CNA Financial Corporation
Carnegie Council
Gannett Foundation
Chicago Pacific Corporation
University of Chicago
Sara Lee Corporation
Burson Marsteller
United Charities/Catholic Charities

Unisys
Baxter Travenol
William Benton Foundation
Allstate Insurance
Business Week Careers
National Arthritis Foundation
Kraft Inc.
For more samples please see page 211 of Corporate Showcase 5, and page 169 of Corporate Showcase 6.

Dawson Jones
PHOTOJOURNALIST
DAWSON JONES, INC.
44 East Franklin Street
Dayton, Ohio 45459
Telephone (513) 435-1121

CLIENTS INCLUDE
Airborne Express
A.H. Robbins
Accu-Ray
Amcast
Bordens
Cahners Publishing Co.
Codex Corp.
Copeland
Dayco
Digital Equipment
Domino's Pizza
Group 243
INC Magazine
J. Walter Thompson
Kuhn & Wittenborn
Lord Sullivan Yoder
M.A. Hanna Co.
McGraw-Hill
Mead
Mead Data Central
Mosinee Paper
Nations Business
NCR
PennCorp Financial
Polessi Clancy
ProClinica
Reynolds + Reynolds
Robbins & Myers
Scott Foresman
Sonoco Products
Standard Register
Sulzer Escher Wyss
Venture
Wolf Blumberg Krody

STOCK AVAILABLE
Dayton
Afterimage, Los Angeles
Click/Chicago
Gamma Liaison
Stock, Boston
Uniphoto, Washington, DC

© Dawson Jones, Inc. 1988

David Kogan

1242 West Washington
Chicago, Illinois 60607
(312) 243-1929

Location and Studio photography for annual reports, corporate communications, and advertising. Black & White and color.

Recent clients include:
IBM
American Airlines
Frito Lay
Raven Industries
Architex International

Illinois Hospital Assoc.
Blue Cross/Blue Shield
Viskase
American Express
Saatchi & Saatchi
Union Carbide
Wallace Computer Supply
Skidmore, Owings & Merrill
Working Woman Magazine
ECO Labs Inc.

John Lehn & Associates

Advertising Photography, Inc.
2601 East Franklin
Minneapolis, Minnesota 55406
(612) 338-0257

People, Products, Location,
Advertising, Corporate,
Financial, Industrial.

Additional work can be seen in.
Showcase 10 and
Northern Review

Clients include:

3M
Amhoist
B. Dalton
Citicorp
Control Data
County Seat
Dayton Hudson
General Mills
Gimbels Midwest
Great Clips
Homecrest
Honeywell
IBM
Jostens
Levi-Strauss
Litton
Martha White Co.
Mercury & Mercruiser
Pearl Vision
Pillsbury
Radisson Hotel
Rainier Bank
Target Stores
Tonka Toys

© 1988 John Lehn & Associates

Richard Mack

Richard Mack Photography, Ltd.
2119 Lincoln
Evanston, Illinois 60201
(312) 869-7794

Location and studio
photography for annual reports,
advertising, and corporate
communications.

A partial list of clients includes:
ABN/LaSalle Bank Corp.
Alcan Aluminum Corp.
AT&T
Bell & Howell Corp.
Boise Cascade
Dubois Design
Dun & Bradstreet
Dragonette, Inc.
FirstChicago Corp.
GATX Corp.
General Numeric Corp.
Hyatt Hotels Corporation
Lewis University
Lutheran General Hospital
Metropolitan Life Insurance
Metropolitan Structures Corp.
Motorola Corporation
Page Arbitrio & Reasen
Rich Nickel Design
Steelcase, Inc.
Westinghouse Corp.

Member: Advertising
Photographers of America.

© 1988 Richard Mack
Photography, Ltd.

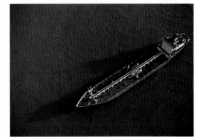

Richard Mack
PHOTOGRAPHY

3 1 2 / 8 6 9 - 7 7 9 4

Robert Mead

Photo Pros
711 Hillgrove Avenue
La Grange, Illinois 60525 (Chicago)

Specializing in corporate brochures, annual reports
and advertising photography—on location or in
studio settings.

What you want
When you want it
How you want it

Steve Niedorf

Niedorf Photography
Suite 304
700 Washington Avenue North
Minneapolis, Minnesota 55401
(612) 332-7124

Clients include:
3M
Honeywell
General Mills
DS/American Express
Control Data Corporation
ATT
Coca-Cola USA
Pillsbury
IBM
Anheuser-Busch
Burlington Northern
Potlatch Paper

Steve has produced
photographs for these and
other corporations throughout
America, Europe, and Asia.

Don O'Barski

The Image Works Incorporated
17239 Parkside Avenue
South Holland, Illinois 60473
(312) 596-0606

Location and aerial photography for annual reports,
advertising, capability brochures, product literature,
and audio-visual presentations.

Eric W. Perry

Charles Schridde Photography Inc.
600 Ajax Drive
Madison Heights (Detroit), Michigan 48071
(313) 589-0111
(313) 535-2926

Stock Representation; Third Coast 1-800-323-9337

Pioneer Hi-Bred
International, Inc.

Curt Maas
5860 Merle Hay Road, Box 127
Johnston, Iowa 50131
(515) 270-3732

Location photography worldwide for corporate,
industrial, agricultural and editorial assignments.

© 1988 Curt Maas

Pioneer Hi-Bred
International, Inc.

Scott Sinklier
5860 Merle Hay Road, Box 127
Johnston, Iowa 50131
(515) 270-3732

Photography for annual reports, corporate
communications and advertising.

r.d. renken

P.O. Box 11010
St. Louis, Missouri 63135
(314) 394-5055

Corporate Communications
Annual Reports
Advertising
Architecture

Andrew Sacks
20727 Scio Church Rd.
Chelsea (Detroit),
Michigan 48118
(313) 475-2310

Location/Studio

Corporate
Editorial
Advertising

Serving major publications and
corporations since 1970.

Portfolio available for overnight
delivery upon request.

Member ASMP.

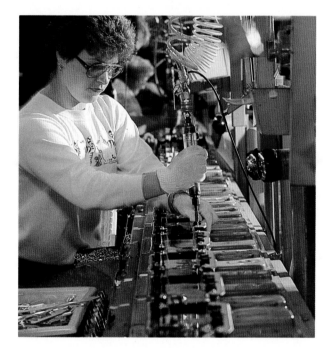

Charles Schabes
Photography

1220 West Grace Street
Chicago, Illinois 60613-2806
(312) 787-2629

Advertising illustration and editorial photography
for domestic and international corporate
communications, publishers, design groups.

Lee Schulman
P.O. Box 09506
Columbus, Ohio 43209
(614) 235-5307

Advertising
Corporate/Industrial
Editorial
Public Relation
Special Effects
Stock

Gary C. Silber

300 Main
Racine, Wisconsin 53403
(414) 637-5097

Mr. Silber specializes in fine executive portraiture
for Fortune 500 corporations and other discerning
corporate clients. Studio work can be done in the
convenience of your facility; Environmental portraiture;
Individuals and especially strong with Groups. Strong
emphasis on developing rapport with subject and
professionalism. Client list and reference upon request.
We respectfully invite your inquiry.

Mike Steinberg
ON LOCATION
633 Huron Road
Cleveland, Ohio 44115
(216) 589-9953

Represented By:
Rick Nicholson
(216) 389-1494

Annual Reports
Corporate Brochures
Industrial Facilities
Medical services

All lighting created
by photographer.

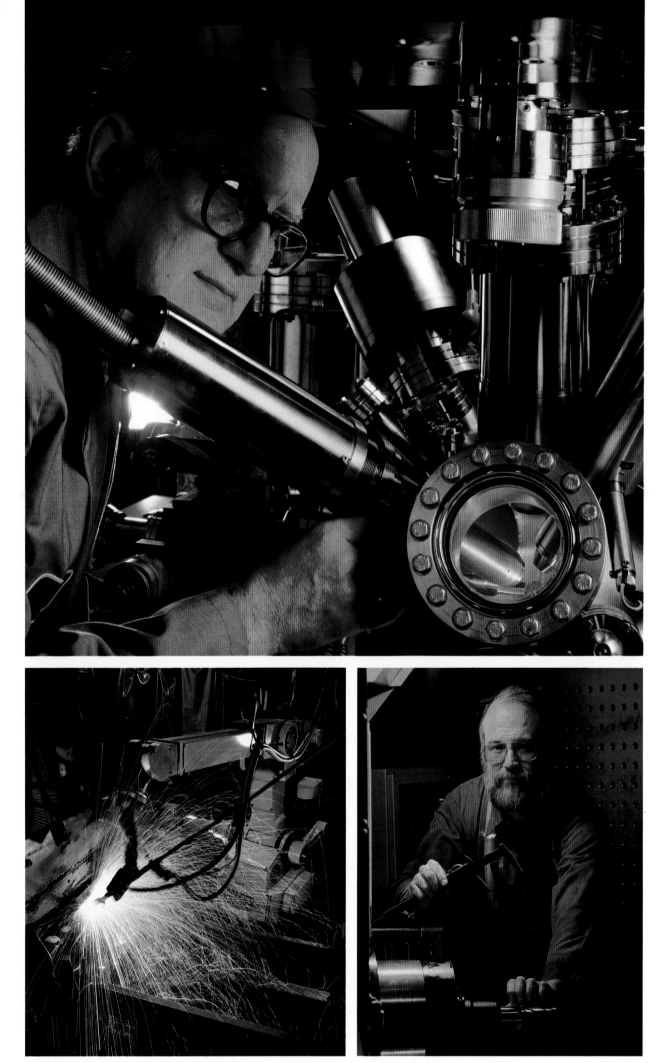

GRAPHIC ARTS ORGANIZATIONS

Arizona:

Phoenix Society of Visual Arts
P.O. Box 469
Phoenix, AZ 85001

California:

Advertising Club of Los Angeles
3600 Wilshire Blvd., Suite 432
Los Angeles, CA 90010
(213) 382-1228

Art Directors and Artists Club
2791 24th St.
Sacramento, CA 95818
(916) 731-8802

Book Club of California
312 Sutter St., Ste. 510
San Francisco, CA 94108
(415) 781-7532

Graphic Artists Guild of Los Angeles
849 S. Broadway
Los Angeles, CA 90014
(213) 933-7199

Los Angeles Advertising Women
5000 Van Nuys Blvd., Suite 400
Sherman Oaks, CA 91403
(818) 995-7338

Los Angeles Chapter of the Graphic Artists Guild
5971 W. 3rd St.
Los Angeles, CA 90036
(213) 938-0009

San Francisco Art Directors Club
2757 16th Street, Box 277
San Francisco, CA 94103
(415) 387-4040

Society of Illustrators of Los Angeles
1258 N. Highland Ave.
Los Angeles, CA 90038

Society of Motion Pictures & TV Art Directors
14724 Ventura Blvd., Penthouse #4
Sherman Oaks, CA 91403
(818) 905-0599

Western Art Directors Club
P.O. Box 996
Palo Alto, CA 94302
(415) 321-4196

Women's Graphic Center
The Woman's Building
1727 N. Spring St.
Los Angeles, CA 90012
(213) 222-5101

Colorado:

Art Directors Club of Denver
1900 Grant St., Suite 1130
Denver, CO 80203
(303) 830-7888

International Design Conference in Aspen
1000 N. 3rd
Aspen, CO 81612
(303) 925-2257

Connecticut:

Connecticut Art Directors Club
P.O. Box 639
Avon, CT 06001
(203) 673-0374

District of Columbia:

American Advertising Federation
1400 K. St. N.W., Ste. 1000
Washington, DC 20005
(202) 898-0089

American Institute of Architects
1735 New York Avenue, N.W.
Washington, DC 20006
(202) 626-7300

Art Directors Club of Washington, DC
1015 20th St., N.W., Suite M100
Washington, DC 20036
(202) 955-5775

Federal Design Council
P.O. Box 7537
Washington, DC 20044

Georgia:

Atlanta Art Papers, Inc.
P.O. Box 77348
Atlanta, GA 30357
(404) 588-1837

Graphic Artists Guild
P.O. Box 8178
Atlanta, GA 30306
(404) 473-8620

Illinois:

Institute of Business Designers
1155 Merchandise Mart
Chicago, IL 60654
(312) 467-1950

STA
233 East Ontario St.
Chicago, IL 60611
(312) 787-2018

Women in Design
2 N. Riverside Plaza, Suite 2400
Chicago, IL 60606
(312) 648-1874

Kansas:

Wichita Art Directors Club
P.O. Box 562
Wichita, KS 67202

Maryland

Council of Communications Societies
P.O. Box 1074
Silver Springs, MD 20910

Continued on page 206

John Sundlof Photography

1324 Isabella Street
Wilmette, Illinois 60091
(312) 256-8877

Location and studio photography in black and white or color of people, places, and things for advertising, editorial, architectural, and corporate/industrial communications.

Conceptually oriented, specialist in black and white photomontage looking for opportunities to seek new solutions to stock visual situations.

Superior communicative ability affords a unique directorial skill with actor/models or "real" people.

Fluent German, passing French, bad Italian, magnificent mime.

Sundlöf

Deborah Van Kirk

855 West Blackhawk
Chicago, Illinois 60622
(312) 642-7766

Precision Photography. Food, Product & Special
Projects emphasizing Fine Detail & Artistry.

References:

Alberto Culver, Allegis, American Hospital Supply,
Brown & Williamson, Brunswick, Burger King, Burry-
Lu, Coca-Cola, Continental Grain, Corning, Dae Julie,
EZ-Pour, Fotomat, Frito Lay, Hart Schaffner & Marx,
Kellogg's, Kraft, LaBatts, LaChoy, LaSalle Bank,
MasterCard, McDonald's, Midway Airlines, Miles Lab,
A.V. Mueller, Parker Pen, Pepsi, Quaker Oats, Rank
Precision Industries, Revere, Searle, Sears, Seven-Up,
Swift, Tombstone, USG, VanCamps, Visa.

Bruce Zake

633 Huron Road
Cleveland, Ohio 44115
(216) 694-3686
(216) 869-6466

Represented by:
Rick Nicholson
(216) 398-1494

Specializing in editorial and
corporate communications
photography on location.

Southwest

**Arizona
Arkansas
New Mexico
Oklahoma
Texas**

GRAPHIC ARTS ORGANIZATIONS

Continued from page 200

Massachusetts:

Creative Club of Boston
155 Massachusetts Ave.
Boston, MA 02115
(617) 536-8999

Center for Design of Industrial Schedules
221 Longwood Ave.
Boston, MA 02115
(617) 734-2163

Graphic Artists Guild
P.O. Box 1454–GMF
Boston, MA 02205
(617) 451-5362

Society of Environmental Graphics Designers
47 Third Street
Cambridge, MA 02141
(617) 577-8225

Michigan:

Creative Advertising Club of Detroit
c/o Rhoda Parkin
30400 Van Dyke
Warren, MI 48093

Minnesota:

Minnesota Graphic Designers Association
P.O. Box 24272
Minneapolis, MN 55424

Missouri:

Advertising Center of Greater St. Louis
440 Mansion House Center
St. Louis, MO 63102
(314) 231-4185

Advertising Club of Kansas City
1 Ward Parkway Center, Ste. 102
Kansas City, MO 64112
(816) 753-4088

New Jersey:

Point-of-Purchase Advertising Institute
66 North Van Brunt Street
Englewood, NJ 07631
(201) 894-8899

New York:

The Advertising Club of New York
155 E. 55th St.
New York, NY 10022
(212) 935-8080

The Advertising Council, Inc.
825 Third Ave.
New York, NY 10022
(212) 758-0400

APA
Advertising Photographers of America, Inc.
45 E. 20th Street
New York, NY 10003
(212) 254-5500

Advertising Typographers Association of America, Inc.
Two Penn Plaza, Suite 1070
New York, NY 10121
(212) 629-3232

Advertising Women of New York Foundation, Inc.
153 E. 57th St.
New York, NY 10022
(212) 593-1950

American Association of Advertising Agencies
666 Third Ave.
New York, NY 10017
(212) 682-2500

American Booksellers Association, Inc.
137 West 25th Street
New York, NY 10001
(212) 463-8450

American Council for the Arts
1285 Ave. of the Americas
Third Floor
New York, NY 10019
(212) 245-4510

The American Institute of Graphic Arts
1059 Third Ave., 3rd Floor
New York, NY 10021
(212) 752-0813

American Society of Interior Designers
National Headquarters
1430 Broadway
New York, NY 10018
(212) 944-9220

New York Chapter
200 Lexington Ave.
New York, NY 10016
(212) 685-3480

American Society of Magazine Photographers
205 Lexington Ave.
New York, NY 10016
(212) 889-9144

Art Directors Club of New York
250 Park Ave. So.
New York, NY 10003
(212) 674-0500

Association of American Publishers
220 E. 23rd St.
New York, NY 10010
(212) 689-8920

Association of the Graphic Arts
5 Penn Plaza
New York, NY 10001
(212) 279-2100

Center for Arts Information
1285 Ave. of the Americas
Third Floor
New York, NY 10019
(212) 977-2544

The Children's Book Council, Inc.
67 Irving Place
New York, NY 10003
(212) 254-2666

CLIO
336 E. 59th St.
New York, NY 10022
(212) 593-1900

Foundation for the Community of Artists
280 Broadway, Ste. 412
New York, NY 10007
(212) 227-3770

Graphic Artists Guild
11 West 20th Street
New York, NY 10011
(212) 463-7730

Guild of Book Workers
521 Fifth Avenue
New York, NY 10175
(212) 757-6454

Institute of Outdoor Advertising
342 Madison Ave.
New York, NY 10173
(212) 986-5920

International Advertising Association, Inc.
342 Madison Ave., Suite 2000
New York, NY 10017
(212) 557-1133

The One Club
3 West 18th Street
New York, NY 10011
(212) 255-7070

Continued on page 220

Wolenski

Stan Wolenski • Photographer • 2919 Canton • Dallas, Texas 75226 • 214-749-0749

Aker/Burnette Studio, Inc.

Joe C. Aker
Raymond V. Burnette III
4710 Lillian
Houston, Texas 77007
(713) 862-6343

Los Angeles
(213) 623-3054

Architectural interior, exterior and model photography.
Model photocompositions and photography a
speciality. Portfolio available upon request.

ARCHITECTURAL MODEL PHOTOGRAPHY AND PHOTOCOMPOSITES

LINCOLN PROPERTY CO., DALLAS

LOHMAN ORGANIZATION INC., NEW YORK

LINCOLN PROPERTY CO., DALLAS

3 D /INTERNATIONAL INC., HOUSTON

ARCHITECTURAL PHOTOGRAPHY

HERITAGE PLAZA, HOUSTON

TRAMMELL CROW CO., DALLAS

SKIDMORE, OWINGS & MERRILL, LOS ANGELES

LASALLE PARTNERS INC., CHICAGO

MORRIS ARCHITECTS, HOUSTON

MORRIS ARCHITECTS, HOUSTON

HERRING DESIGN, HOUSTON

T. L. HORTON DESIGN INC., DALLAS

Jeff Baker

2401 South Ervay #302
Dallas, Texas 75215
(214) 720-0178

PORTRAITS EXPRESSING THE
INTEGRITY OF AMERICA'S
LEADERS.

Annette Strauss
  Mayor of Dallas
  'D' Magazine

Stanley Marcus
  Chairman Emeritus
  Neiman-Marcus
  INC. Magazine

Earl Marshall & Dow Hickam
  C.O.'s   Dow B. Hickam, Inc.
  Tracy-Locke

Recent clients include:
AT&T
Chevron
Dupont
E.D.S.
Ensearch
Lincoln Properties
Mary Kay Cosmetics
Neiman-Marcus
Northern Telecom
PageNet
Specialized Products Company
Tramell Crow Companies
U.S. Life & Title Company
Wang-Intecom

Hill, Holiday, Conners,
  Cosmopolus
Hill & Knowlton
N.W. Ayer
Richards, Brock, Miller, Mitchell
The Richards Group
Tracy-Locke

Business Week International
Changing Times
Esquire
Financial World
Forbes
INC. Magazine
Rolling Stone
Texas Monthly

We are proud to have received
the Dallas Press Club's
KATY award for Magazine
photojournalism and Catalog
Age's American Catalog Award
in the same year. If this seems a
rather diverse set of clients and
awards for a portraitist; check
our ads in the '85 & '86 Black
Book or call, and we'll show you
something really different!

© Jeff Baker, 1988

Scott Baxter

P.O. Box 25041
Phoenix, Arizona 85002
(602) 254-5879

Stock available

America West Airlines
Cathay Pacific Airways
Forbes
Pinnacle West Capital
    Corporation
Polaroid
Princess Cruise Lines

© Scott Baxter 1988

Steve Brady

(713) 660-6663 Houston
(212) 213-6024 New York

Steve Brady thrives in all kinds
of light for a variety of clients
including:
Shearson Lehman
I.B.M.
Mooney Aircraft
Enron
Nations Business
Citibank
Mitsubishi
Centel
The New York Stock Exchange
Exxon
Monsanto
USX
Unisys

Portfolio, stock and color
samples available upon
request.

Jim Caldwell

2422 Quenby
Houston, Texas 77005
(713) 527-9121

Corporate, advertising, industrial, architectural, medical, and theatrical photography.

Location and studio photography in our new, expanded studio, opening Fall, 1987.

Editorial clients include: Compaq Magazine, Dance Magazine, Financial Planning Magazine, Newsweek, Opera News, Signature, Southern Living, Texas Monthly, Time, Travel and Leisure, U.S. News and World Report.

Corporate clients include: Austin Industries, Coca-Cola Foods, Columbia Artists, Coldwell Banker, Continental Can, The Dover Group, Exxon Chemical Americas, Exxon U.S.A., Houghton Mifflin Publ., Houston Ballet, Houston Grand Opera, Humana Hospitals, Kentucky Fried Chicken, Kingdom of Saudi Arabia, MacMillan Publishers, Owens-Corning, Pitney Bowes, Prudential Insurance, Texas Childrens Hospital, Texas Heart Institute, Unisys Corp., Warner Amex Communications.

Photographs © 1987 Jim Caldwell

Tim Fuller

135½ South Sixth Avenue
Tucson, Arizona 85701
(602) 622-3900

Why do corporations that provide care for the elderly spend good money to fly Tim Fuller from Tucson, Az. to shoot in cities all over the United States?

Simple. He solves problems, shoots real people showing real emotions and wins awards. Call and ask him to send examples of his work.

Mark Green
2406 Taft Street
Houston, Texas 77006
(713) 523-6146
Telex: 4997187 GREEN UI

Represented in New York by
John Henry (212) 686-6883.

Corporate/Industrial.
Annual Report.
Advertising.
Architecture.
Travel.
Stock.

For more samples see
Corporate Showcase
Volumes 3, 4, 5, & 6.
ASMP Silver Book 5.

Limited edition Cibachrome
prints available.

Holly Kuper

5522 Anita
Dallas, Texas 75206
(214) 827-4494

CHALLENGE ME!

Still enthusiastic
after 9 years in business.

Reliable quality.
Just ask my clients.

Frito Lay
Farm Journal
Forbes
Business Week
Fortune
Money
Blount, Inc.

IBM
Texas Instruments
my son
Dun & Bradstreet

see page 242,
Corporate Showcase 5

Dennis Meyler

1903 Portsmouth
Suite 25
Houston, Texas 77098-4235
(713) 778-1700

Advertising/Corporate/Editorial/Industrial

For additional work see American Showcase,
Volumes 7, 8, 9 and 10.

Partial client list: 3M, Sperry Computers, Prudential
Insurance, Reed Tool, Schlumberger, Biotx, Anadrill,
Coldwell Banker, Dr. Pepper, Hughes Tool, IBM,
Anderson Clayton Foods, Exxon, Curtin Matheson
Scientific.

GRAPHIC ARTS ORGANIZATIONS

Continued from page 206

The Public Relations Society of America, Inc.
33 Irving Place
New York, NY 10003
(212) 995-2230

Society of Illustrators
128 E. 63rd St.
New York, NY 10021
(212) 838-2560

Society of Photographers and Artists Representatives
1123 Broadway
New York, NY 10010
(212) 924-6023

Society of Publication Designers
60 E. 42nd St., Ste. 1130
New York, NY 10165
(212) 983-8585

Television Bureau of Advertising
477 Madison Ave.
New York, NY 10022
(212) 486-1111

Type Directors Club of New York
60 E. 42nd St., Ste. 1130
New York, NY 10165
(212) 983-6042

U.S. Trademark Association
6 E. 45th St.
New York, NY 10017
(212) 986-5880

Volunteer Lawyers for the Arts
1285 Ave. of the Americas
New York, NY 10019
(212) 977-9270

Women in the Arts
325 Spring St., Room 200
New York, NY 10013
(212) 691-0988

Women in Design
P.O. Box 5315
FDR Station
New York, NY 10022

Ohio:

Advertising Club of Cincinnati
P.O. Box 43252
Cincinnati, OH 45243
(513) 575-9331

Cleveland Society of Communicating Arts
Maggie Moore
P.O. Box 14759
Cleveland, OH 44114
(216) 621-5139

Columbus Society of Communicating Arts
c/o Orby Kelly
1900 Crown Park Court
Columbus, OH 43220
(614) 761-9405

Design Collective
D.F. Cooke
131 North High St.
Columbus, OH 43215
(614) 464-2883

Pennsylvania:

Art Directors Club of Philadelphia
2017 Walnut St.
Philadelphia, PA 19103
(215) 569-3650

Tennessee:

Engraved Stationery Manufacturers Association
c/o Printing Industries Association of the South
1000 17th Ave. South
Nashville, TN 37212
(615) 327-4444

Texas:

Advertising Club of Fort Worth
1801 Oak Knoll
Colleyville, TX 76034
(817) 283-3615

Art Directors Club of Houston
P.O. Box 271137
Houston, TX 77277
(713) 661-7267

Dallas Society of Visual Communications
3530 High Mesa Dr.
Dallas, TX 75234
(214) 241-2017

Print Production Association of Dallas/Fort Worth
P.O. Box 160605
Irving, TX 75016

Virginia:

Industrial Designers Society of America
1142 East Walker Road
Great Falls, VA 22066
(703) 759-0100

Tidewater Society of Communicating Arts
P.O. Box 153
Norfolk, VA 23501

Washington:

Puget Sound Ad Federation
c/o Sylvia Fruichantie
Kraft Smith Advertising
200 1st West St.
Seattle, WA 98119

Seattle Design Association
P.O. Box 1097
Main Office Station
Seattle, WA 98111
(206) 285-6725

Society of Professional Graphic Artists
c/o Steve Chin, Pres.
85 S. Washington Street, Ste. 204
Seattle, WA 98104

Wisconsin:

Illustrators & Designers of Milwaukee
c/o IDM
5600 W. Browndeer Road
Browndeer, WI 53223
(414) 355-1405

Milwaukee Advertising Club
231 W. Wisconsin Avenue
Milwaukee, WI 53203
(414) 271-7351

Michael Norton

Norton Photographic, Inc.
P.O. Box 20807
Phoenix, Arizona 85036
(602) 840-9463

Partial Client List:
American Express
IBM
Talley Industries
Holiday Inns
Embassy Suites
Porsche-Audi
Thunderbird Bank
Chase Bank
Burns International
Coscan
British Leyland

Stock Photography Available:
THE STOCK OPTION
(602) 437-8772

Tomás Pantin

1601 East 7th Street
Suite 100
Austin, Texas 78702
(512) 474-9968

Ready to work on location or create what you need in
our 6,000 square-foot studio.

Fluent in English and Spanish.

Call or write for additional color and B&W sample
sheets.

Reel upon request.

Clients include:

IBM, Motorola, Hyatt, Hertz, Bell Telephone, Deloitte Haskins Sells, Four Seasons Hotel, NY Life, Norwood Properties, L.D. Brinkman, Southwest Airlines, Wide-Lite.

1601 East 7th Street
Suite 100
Austin, Texas 78702
(512) 474-9968

Tomás Pantin

Pfuhl Photographic

P.O. Box 542
Phoenix, Arizona 85001
(602) 253-0525

As a photographer with an eye for design and the unusual, I create images that work to communicate. I like to produce photography as strong as your ideas.

Advertising, design, corporate and editorial. On location or... wherever.

Partial Client List:
America West Airlines
Goldstar
Greyhound
Harcourt Brace Jovanovich
ITT
MeraBank
Motorola

Navistar
United Way
Westin Hotels

All images: © Pfuhl Photographic, 1988

Donovan Reese

3007 Canton
Dallas, Texas 75226
(214) 748-5900

Agent-Rebekah McKinney-Reese
(214) 357-6615

Location Photography for Advertising, Annual Report,
Architectural, Corporate, Industrial & Travel Clients.
Worldwide...

Stock available in US through studio. Stock Agent for
Europe & Asia – TSW/Worldwide, 28 Finchley Rd.,
London NW8 6ES 01-722-9305.

Portfolio upon request.

Additional images: Corp. Showcase 5 pg. 247; Corp.
Showcase 6. pg. 199, Adweek/Ad 11. pg. 294.

Ron Scott

1000 Jackson Boulevard
Houston, Texas 77006
(713) 529-5868

Landscapes or cityscapes, indoors or out, Ron Scott is at home with a range of subjects, whether they wear hard hats or cowboy hats. "Hats say a lot about people. They tell you what they do and that's what I am interested in. People who 'do' something are more interesting than people who 'are' something. Most of my assignments involve real people doing their everyday job. My job is to tell a story about their job."

Ron is also interested in your next 'job'. If you will call or write he will send you a portfolio that you may keep (no deposit, no return!) and of course one of his famous Color Samples books as well.

© 1988 Ron Scott. Member ASMP.

Micheal Simpson

415 North Bishop Avenue
Dallas, Texas 75208
(214) 943-9347

Represented by:
ELIZABETH SIMPSON
(214) 943-9355
THE NEW YORK PORTFOLIO DEPOT
(212) 989-8588

1987 Clients include:

American Airlines, A-R-A, CTI, DSC, Dillards,
E-Systems, 1st Texas Savings, Frito Lay, Genstar
Roofing, Halliburton, J.C. Penney, MCI, PQI, Photon,
QSI, Stepan Chemical, Texas Instruments, VHAE, Varo

Magazine Clients:
AMERICAN WAY, DALLAS MAGAZINE,
HEALTHSENSE, McGRAW HILL, MEETING
MANAGER, OMNI, TRAIL BLAZER

For additional work, please refer to Corporate
Showcase Volumes: 4, 5 & 6.

Stock photography available through the studio or
contact F.P.G. International, New York.

Portfolio available upon request.

© Micheal Simpson

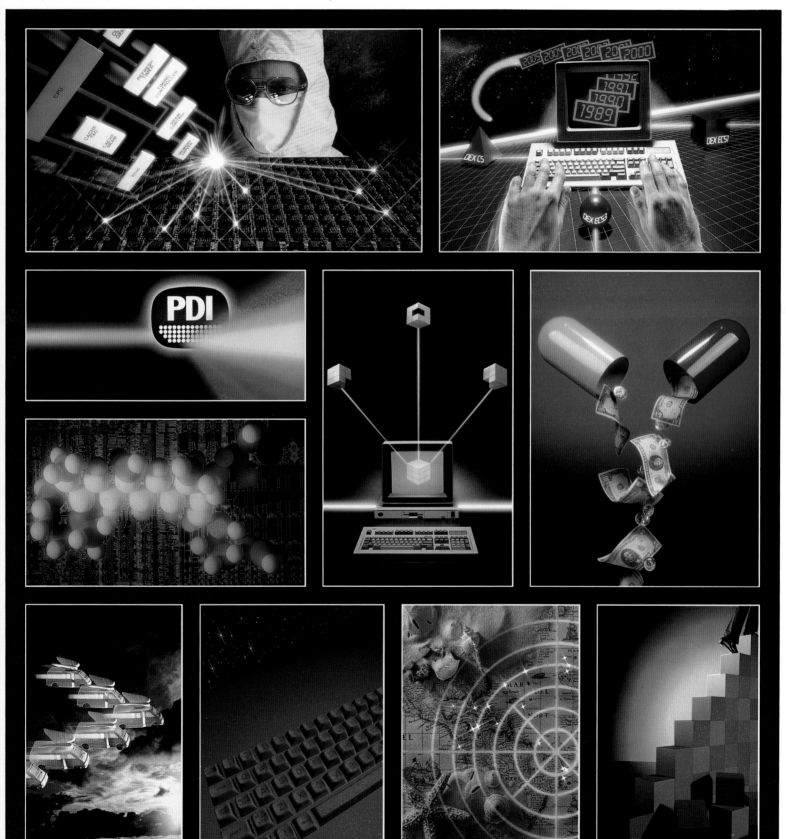

WANTED
Sages. Wits. Philosophers.
Problem-solvers. Boat-rockers.

We hope you've enjoyed reading the **VIEWPOINTS** in this issue. This popular feature is designed to enlighten as well as entertain as it provides unique insights on the current state of corporate communications.

We'd like to take this opportunity to invite you to share your own thoughts, opinions and methods with thousands of your colleagues worldwide.

The average **VIEWPOINT** is 1000 words but we'll consider longer (or shorter) pieces. Have the article titled, typed double-space, and be sure to include your own name, title, company and address. Contributors to the next volume will receive a copy of the book, a small gift, and our eternal gratitude. (Of course, we can't *guarantee* that your article will be published but we do promise to acknowledge and read every submission.)

Go ahead, write down all those things you've always wanted to get off your chest. Speak out to those photographers, illustrators, and designers you

hire…share confidences with your colleagues…tell off your boss. Do it while you're feeling outraged/satisfied/frustrated about the work you create. Do it *today* and mail it to:

Stephanie Whitney
New Projects Manager
American Showcase, Inc.
724 Fifth Avenue—10th Floor
New York, New York 10019

Thanks a lot. We're looking forward to hearing from you and hope to see you in **CORPORATE SHOWCASE VOLUME 8!**

Paul Talley

4756 Algiers Street
Dallas, Texas 75207
(214) 951-0039

Location and studio photography for annual reports, advertising, and corporate communications.

Clients include: Adolphus Hotel, American Heart Association, Central Southwest Services Inc., Crisa Corporation, Dr. Pepper, Fred Joaillier, Gaylord Broadcasting, Gerald D. Hines Interest, HCB, Hogan Systems, Intellicall Inc., John Deere Corporation, Kaiser Foundation, Lowes Anatole, MADD, National FSI Inc., Renolds Penland, Southland Corporation, Trammel Crow Company, Villeroy and Boch, VMX, Welch's, etc.

© PAUL TALLEY 1987

Member ASMP

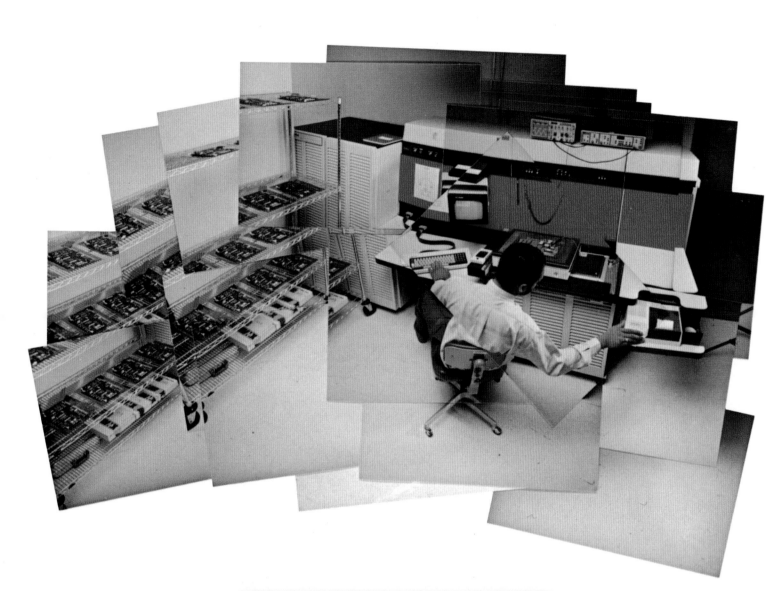

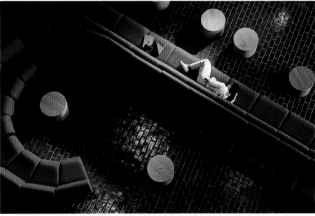

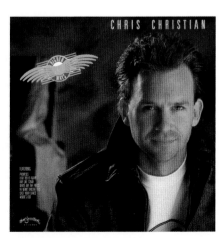

Terry Vine

5455 Dashwood #200
Houston, Texas 77401
(713) 664-2920

Location and studio
assignments for annual reports,
corporate communications,
advertising and travel.

Recent clients include:
American Express
BPI Systems
Continental Airlines
Exxon Chemical
Hertz
Houston Cellular Telephone
Precision Tune
Remco
System One
Roy M. Huffington, Inc
Trammell Crow
Triten Industries
Uncle Ben's Rice
Westin Hotels

Terry Vine
5455 Dashwood #200
Houston, Texas 77401
(713) 664-2920

Location and studio
assignments for annual reports,
corporate communications,
advertising and travel.

Recent clients include:
American Express
BPI Systems
Continental Airlines
Exxon Chemical
Hertz
Houston Cellular Telephone
Precision Tune
Remco
System One
Roy M. Huffington, Inc
Trammell Crow
Triten Industries
Uncle Ben's Rice
Westin Hotels

Bob Werre

2437 Bartlett Street
Houston, Texas 77098
(713) 529-4841

I specialize in working for corporate, medical,
industrial, advertising and architectural clients.

Additional images in Corporate Showcase 6

Member ASMP

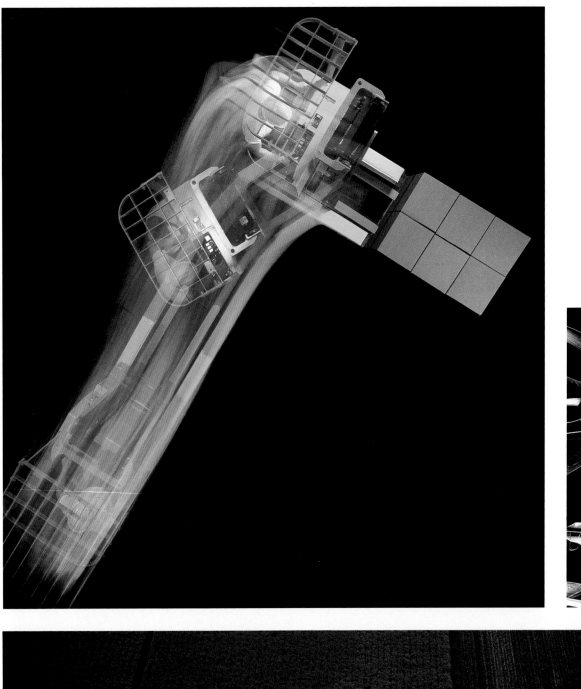

Les Wollam

5215 Goodwin Avenue
Dallas, Texas 75206
(214) 760-7721

Also see my portraiture in Corporate Showcase Vol. 4, page 217 and Vol. 6, page 204. Additional images in Corporate Showcases Volumes 1, 2 & 5.

Recent clients include: AT&T, Central & South West Corp., Erskine House Ltd, Fortune, Frito Lay, IBM, National Intergroup, Occidental Chemical, Price Waterhouse, Southwestern Energy Co, Summit Energy, Texas Utilities, Triton Energy.

Keith Wood Photography, Inc.

1308 Conant
Dallas, Texas 75207
(214) 634-7344

There must be a fine balance between pure creativity and pure business...for neither can exist without the other. Photographer, Keith Wood walks delicately in that balance. A dull Australia mine can be represented with the humor of its workers. An unattractive "oil patch" setting can be represented (saved) with proper visual design. It's a matter of experience and excitement in finding solutions. More importantly, it's a matter of the reliability that maintains professional balance in his work. He is dedicated to the viewers of his images.

M.A.R.C./Marketing
  Corporation
Freeport-McMoRan/Mineral
  Recovery
Diamond Shamrock/Oil &
  Gas
Motorola Corporation
Swearingen/Commercial Real
  Estate
Red Man Tobacco
Surgikos/Medical
Humana Hospital
Redman Industries
Dresser Industries
Ericson Telecommunications
Northern Telecom
Hall Financial
Dallas Symphony
Bay St. Restaurants

Keith Wood Photography, Inc.
1308 Conant
Dallas, Texas 75207
(214) 634-7344

W O O D

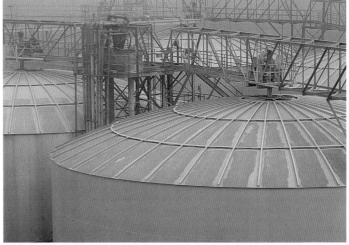

THE GREATEST INTERNATIONAL EXHIBITION OF ADVERTISING

ARCHIVE MAGAZINE

This is the one exhibition you won't want to miss. ARCHIVE brings you the most innovative up-to-date collection of the best in print, poster and T.V. advertising from around the world. Every page is packed with ads appearing exactly as they originally ran—all arranged by subject and all translated into English. Order today and get a full year (6 issues) of ARCHIVE for only $43.97, a savings of 20% off the annual cover price. Call (212) 245-0981 to enter your subscription, or write to: ARCHIVE MAGAZINE, Dept. C, 724 Fifth Ave., New York, NY 10019.

Rocky Mountain

Colorado
Idaho
Montana
Utah
Wyoming

STEVEN HUNT

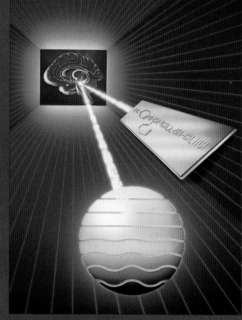

IMAGES THAT
EXPAND TRADITION AND
INVENT THE FUTURE.

801-451-6552

Aiuppy Photographs
(eye-you-pea)

Laurance B. Aiuppy (Assignments)
Janis M. Aiuppy (Stock)
522 West Chinook, P.O. Box 26
Livingston, Montana 59047
(406) 222-7308

Location photography in 35mm, 2¼ and 4 × 5 formats for corporate, industrial, annual report, travel and editorial clients worldwide. Portfolio upon request. Stock list available.

See also: ASMP BOOK 2, ASMP BOOK 4
Member: ASMP, ASPP, OWAA

During fifteen years of professional photography I have shot coast to coast – Alaska to Florida – armadillos to airplanes, beaches to buildings, cars to coal mines, dams to draglines, fiber optics to wool fibers, machine tools to heavy machinery, oil rigs to railroads, talc to trucks, welders to wapiti, and everything in between. Good light makes anything exciting. I do whatever it takes to get that good light.

Some clients who have used my vision: Morrison Knudsen Corporation, Occidental Petroleum, J.P. Stevens Co., Pfizer Chemical, PPG, TRW, GTE, Pontiac, Pentax, Chevrolet, Dana Industrial, Wells-Index Corp., Bostitch, First Bank System, Oldsmobile, Palm Beach, Orvis, Foster Grant, Solarex, Light Publicity Ltd. (Japan), Bozell & Jacobs, D'Arcy

MacManus & Masius, Campbell-Mithun, Campbell/Ewald, Leo Burnett, DDB Needham, Time, Newsweek, U.S. News & World Report, Business Week, Fortune, INC, Smithsonian, National Geographic, Diversion, Changing Times, Friends, Communication Arts, Ford Times, USA Today, USA Weekend, New York Times, American West, Country Journal, Field & Stream, Sports Afield, Outside, Fly Fisherman, Rod & Reel, Fliegenfischen (Germany), Capital (Italy), La Revista (Spain), Aktuelle (Germany), Actuel (France), Wochenend (Germany), Baltic (Sweden), A Rapport (Norway), Stewart Tabori & Chang, World Book, Encyclopaedia Britannica.

Kevin Beebe

2460 Eliot Street
Denver, Colorado 80211
(303) 455-3627

Specializing in location
photography for Corporate/
Healthcare, Advertising, and
Editorial clients.

Selected Clients include:
American Medical International
Combs Gates Learjet
U.S. News & World Report
Conoco Inc.
The Children's Hospital
    of Denver
Vail Valley Medical Center
ALPS Securities Inc.
The Instrumentalist Magazine
Portfolio Management
    Consultants, Inc.
American Water Works
    Association
Rocky Mountain Hospital
Amerabass Realty
    Management Co.
Wang Corporation
Baron Investments, Ltd.
Integrated Medical Campus
Arabian Horse Registry
Senior Corporation
Softsearch, Inc.
Community Hospitals of
    Central California
Borning Corporation
Contemporary Learning, Inc.
Westward Electronics, Inc.
Ciba-Geigy

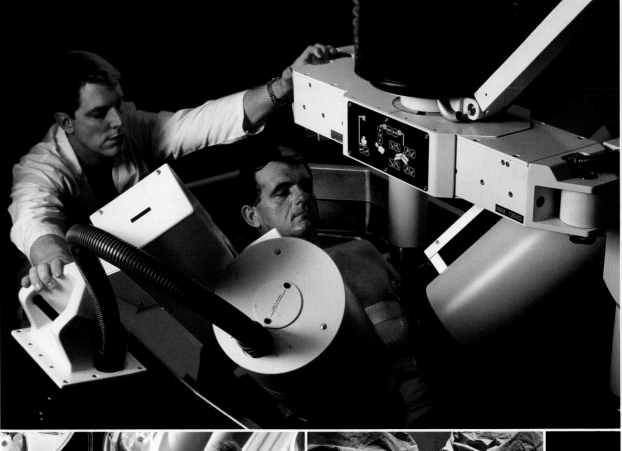

K · E · V · I · N
BEEBE
PHOTOGRAPHY

James H. Berchert

2886 West 119th Avenue
Denver, Colorado 80234
(303) 466-7414

Jim is an experienced location photographer specializing in architectural, corporate/industrial, advertising, and editorial photography. Based in Denver, he travels extensively. Editors, architects, and designers like the emphasis he places on lighting, design, and composition.

**Dirk Douglass
Photography**
2755 South 300 West, Suite D
Salt Lake City, Utah 84115
(801) 485-5691

ON LOCATION IN UTAH
Corporate, editorial and
industrial photography in studio
and on location

Patricia Barry Levy

Denver, Colorado
(303) 458-6692

Has photographed Henry
Bloch, Peter Drucker and Jeff
Coors.

Has worked for U.S. West
International, Forbes, Inc., U.S.
News and World Report and
Gates Rubber Company.

Henry Bloch of H & R Block.

Longin Lonczyna Jr.

(That's Lon...gin...Lon...chan...na...Oh...
on second thought, just call me Lonnie.)

Longin Lonczyna Photography
257-R South Rio Grande Street
Salt Lake City, Utah 84101
(801) 355-7513

In business, too many gray areas usually create problems. The people photographed on this page, however, were enhanced by expanding the gray areas. Longin can solve problems and create beautiful, rich, black and white photographs for his clients. He is proficient at capturing personality as well as mood. Contact Longin for your next project to capture personalities and solve your gray area problems.

Some clients Longin has captured and expanded gray areas for are: Ireco Chemical, American Gilsonite, Boniville Corp., First Interstate Bank, American Savings, Mountain Fuel Supply, KSL-TV 5, Novell Corp., Word Perfect Corp., Iomega, Icon, Cottonwood Medical Center, Research Industries, FHP Health Plan, Magic Mill International.

Kent Miles
Photography

465 East Ninth Avenue
Salt Lake City, Utah 84103
(801) 364-5755
(213) 274-2553

P.O. Box 512
Salt Lake City, Utah 84110-0512

Kent Miles shoots the West and
the World for Advertising,
Corporate and Editorial use.

Specialties include
   Documentary
   Multi-Image
   Performance
   Portraiture
   Travel

Call for samples or client list.
Also see Corporate Showcase 6.

Stock Available
Member ASMP

1. Delicate Arch
   Arches National Park, Utah
2. Flaming Gorge
   Flaming Gorge National
   Recreation Area, Utah
3. Man and Wall Mural
   Salt Lake City, Utah
4. Julius Murray, Medicine Man
   Uintah and Ouray
   Reservation
   Fort Duchesne, Utah

David Quinney Jr.
Photographic Illustration

423 East Broadway
Salt Lake City, Utah 84111
(801) 363-0434

Studio and location capabilities, with emphasis toward advertising, corporate/industrial, and fine art Black & White photographic illustration.

Clients include:
Amax Magnesium, American Barrick Resources, Apple Computer, Axonix Inc, Robert Bosch Corp., Cath-Tech, Commercial Security Bank, Cover Pools Inc., Cura Financial, Deseret Book, Hilton Hotel, Jackson Hole, Jetway Systems, Motion Control, O.C. Tanner, Rockford Fosgate, Speech Plus, Unimobil Systems, United States Film Festival.

EVANS & SUTHERLAND

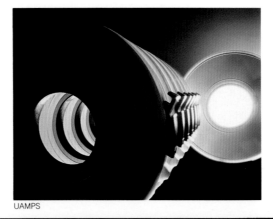
UAMPS

UNIBASE

SALT LAKE AIRPORT AUTHORITY

CURA FINANCIAL

I.C. INDUSTRIES

Doug Stearns

1738 Wynkoop Street
Denver, Colorado 80202
(303) 296-1133

Providing photographic solutions for corporate communications and advertising. On location or in the studio.

Portfolio available upon request.
Also see:
Corporate Showcase #5 pg 265
Corporate Showcase #6 pg 211

Clients include:

AT&T Information Systems
Boeing Computers
Boettcher & Company
Burson-Marsteller, NY
Central Bank of Denver
CH2M Hill
College for Financial Planning
Color Tile
Daniels & Associates
Desks, Inc.
Empire Savings
First Interstate Bank
First Wyoming Bancorporation
Gates Energy Products
General American Insurance
Guaranty National Corporation
Hensel Phelps Corporation
Hyatt Hotels
Integrated Resources, Inc
Masonite Corporation
MDC Capital Investment
Owens-Corning Fiberglass
Pearle Vision
Porter Memorial Hospital
Prudential Insurance Company
Rocky Mountain News
Safeco Insurance Company
Scientech
Scientific Software
Selz, Seabolt & Assoc.
Taco Bell
Trammell Crow Company
United Banks of Colorado
Vari L Company
Wickliff & Company
Writer Corporation

David X. Tejada

1553 Platte Street., Suite 205
Denver, Colorado 80202
(303) 458-1220

Represented in Chicago by:
Munro Goodman Artist Representatives

(312) 528-7056

Specializing in location photography for corporate annual reports, brochures, and advertising clients. Black and white portfolio available upon request.

We truly are a designer's photography studio because we work with designers to incorporate shapes, textures and colors into the photograph which will enhance the design of the printed piece. We also understand the difficulties of producing an annual report or corporate brochure. And our aim is to put an end to at least some of the nail-biting and thumb-chewing that often occurs during such a process. By doing our job in a top-notch and professional manner, we'll make yours a whole lot easier.

Some of the clients working with Tejada Photography are: Anheuser Busch, AT&T, AMI, Inc., Energy Systems, Clarion Hotels, Marriot Hotels, Trusthouse Forte Hotels, Prudential-Bache, Mountain Bell, Wynmark Development, The United Way, etc.

Give us a call or drop us a line to receive a color brochure on Tejada Photography. Additional work can be seen in Corporate Showcase 6.

© DAVID X. TEJADA

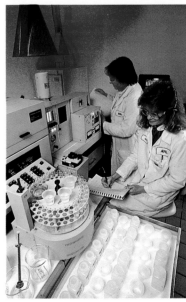

West

Alaska
California
Hawaii
Nevada
Oregon
Washington

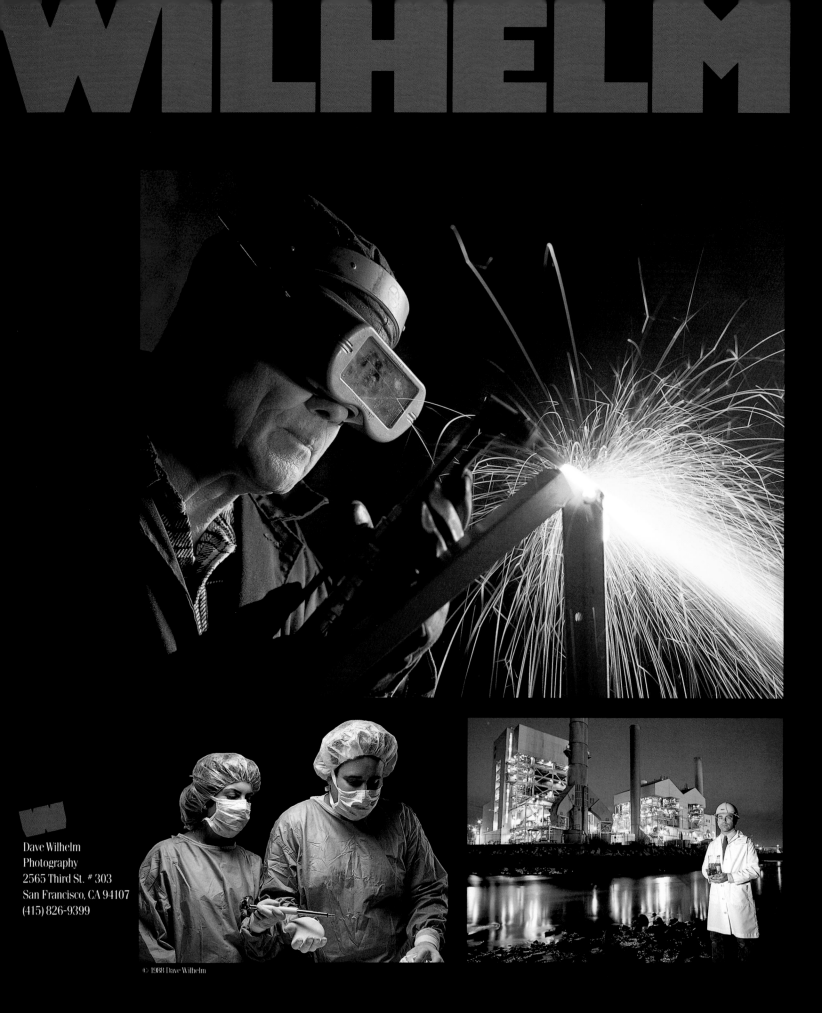

WILHELM

WILHELM

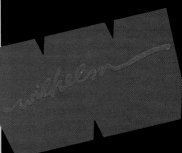

Dave Wilhelm
Photography
2565 Third St. # 303
San Francisco, CA 94107
(415) 826-9399

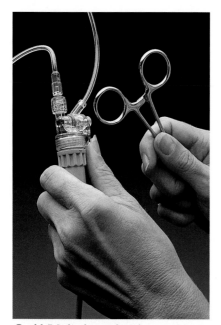

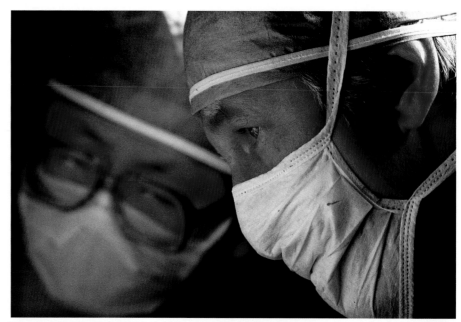

Gould (Medical transducer)

HCA/Los Robles Regional Medical Center (Actual neurosurgery)

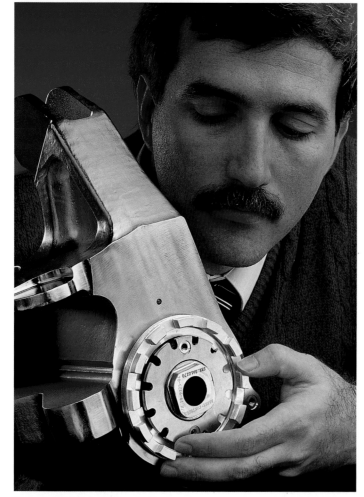

Barry Wright Corp. (Vibration isolator)

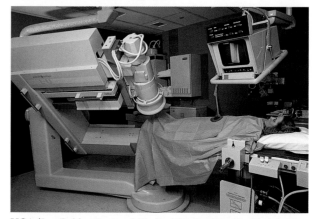

HCA/Los Robles Regional Medical Center (Cardiac Cath Lab)

International Technology (Construction workers)

International Technology (Hazardous waste disposal site)

252

Russell Abraham

17 Brosnan Street
San Francisco, California 94103
(415) 558-9100

Russell Abraham photographs architecture, interiors, building products, furniture. He has worked for most of the West Coast architectural and interior design firms and his work has appeared in all the major trade journals.

Representative Clients:

Architectural Digest
Architectural Record

Avonite Corporation
Bramalea Corporation
Campbell-Mithun
Canteen Corporation
CBS Publications
Coldwell Banker
Designers West Magazine
Dillingham Corporation
Homsey Advertising
Hyatt Hotel Corporation

Interior Design
Japan Airlines
Kerker & Associates
Masonite Corporation
McKone & Company
Nikko Hotels International
Shakertown Corporation
Takenaka International
Wells Fargo Realty Finance
Westin Hotel Corporation

Frank Baker

15031 Parkway Loop, Suite B
Tustin, California 92680
(714) 259-1462

Specializing in business photography for corporate and industrial communications. Conveniently located in the heart of Southern California.

Clients include:
Allergan
American Hospital
AST Research
Avery International
Beatrice
Bevmar Industries
Brock Homes
California Avocado Commission
Carl's Jr.
CMS
Doelz Network
Elco
GTE
O'Keefe Communications
OCTD
Pacificare
Mony Financial Services
Restaurant Business
Shell Oil
Sunshine Makers
Taco Bell
Toshiba
TRW
Winchells Donuts
Yamaha

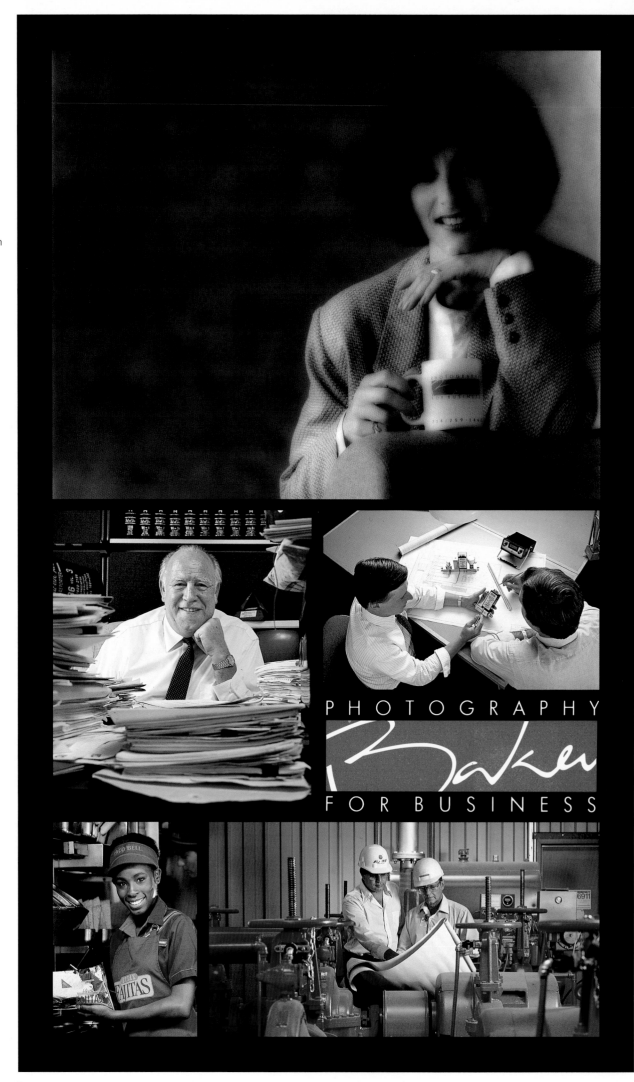

PHOTOGRAPHY
Baker
FOR BUSINESS

Jay Daniel

Jay Daniel Associates
Mail: P.O. Box 1232
San Rafael, California 94915
Studio: 517 Jacoby #11
San Rafael, California 94901
(415) 459-1495

Corporate, advertising and editorial photography
Member ASMP
Portfolio available on request
Stock photography available

Recent clients include:
Firemans Fund
American Express
MicroPro International
Pixar
University of California at San Francisco
Axion
Southmark Foundation
Pacific Medical Center

Hank
deLespinasse

Hank deLespinasse Studio, Inc.
2300 East Patrick Lane #21
Las Vegas, Nevada 89119
(702) 798-6693
(702) 361-6628

Stock: The Image Bank

For additional work see:
American Showcase 3,
page 238
ASMP Book 1, page 408
ADIP 6, page 95

Black Book '77, page 182
Black Book '78, page W26
Corporate Showcase 6,
page 218
or call for samples

© Hank deLespinasse 1987

Dana Edmunds Photography

188 North King Street
Honolulu, Hawaii 96817
(808) 521-7711

Location and studio photography for advertising and corporate communications for clients in Hawaii and points beyond.

Clients include: American Airlines, Amfac Corporation, Bank of Hawaii, Campbell Estate, Central Pacific Bank, First Hawaiian Bank, Halekulani Hotel, Hamakua Sugar, Hawaii Visitors Bureau, Hawaiian Airlines, Hawaiian Regent Hotel, Hawaiian Telephone, Hilton Hotels, Honolulu Federal Savings & Loan, Kaiser Permanente, Liberty House, Mauna Lani Resort, Mid Pacific Airlines, Outrigger Hotels, Pacific Construction Company, Queens Hospital, Toshiba Corporation, United Airlines.

257

Van W. Frazier

2770 South Maryland Parkway
Las Vegas, Nevada 89109
(702) 735-1165

Specializing in Portraiture of Chief Executive Officers,
Directors and top level management. Individuals and
groups, in studio or on location.

Clients include:

Caesar's Palace, Showboat Hotel, Boyd Group, City of
Las Vegas, Osmonds, U.S. Senator Harry Reid, First
Interstate Bank, Southern Utah State College, Boy
Scouts of America, Palace Station Casino, Allstate
Insurance, Duvall Network, Nevada Beverage, Silver
State Disposal, Nevada Federal Credit Union.

Raymond Gendreau

303 Belmont Avenue East
Seattle, Washington 98102
(206) 329-9902

In Dallas:
Represented by
Elizabeth Simpson
(214) 943-9355

In New York:
New York Portfolio Depot
(212) 989-8588

1987 clients include:
American Airlines
Chevron
CTI Ltd.
D-Magazine
Domain
Milton Development
Pacific Northwest Magazine
Simpson Paper
Southern Magazine
TechScape
Texas Monthly
Volunteer Hospitals of America
Wyndham Hotels

Stock Photography Available

The advertising community has faced many challenges over the years. One of the challenges that gives us the most concern today is the move to levy taxes on advertising.

Advertisers already pay a great many taxes—corporate taxes, sales taxes, property taxes, Social Security taxes, just to name a few. In recent years, however, lawmakers have begun to focus on the advertising process as a potential new source of tax revenue. In 1987, 23 states considered advertising taxes, and for the first time in history, one state, Florida, even went so far as to impose—and then repeal—a tax on all national and local advertising within its borders. At the same time, the federal government had before it several proposals to defer or disallow the tax deductibility of advertising expenses. There is little doubt that these proposals and others will be reintroduced in the future. On the surface, advertising taxes can look like a ready source to raise revenue.

Those of us who work with advertising every day recognize its role as a powerful engine driving sales, production, employment and income in our economy. We know also, however, that taxes on advertising will make it more expensive and force businesses to either reduce advertising expenditures or increase product prices.

If this happens, consumer demand will drop, as will the level of overall sales. Fewer sales mean lower production levels, fewer jobs, less personal income and a further drop in consumer demand. The bottom line is that advertising taxes hurt the economy. Our challenge is to help potential supporters of advertising taxes understand the true effects such taxes would produce.

The ad tax proposals, which have surfaced in the past few years, have taken many forms, including taxes on services, production taxes, professional and gross receipts taxes. In some cases, states have even attempted to tax certain aspects of advertising following a so-called "reexamination" and reinterpretation of existing tax law.

At the federal level, Congress has looked at several advertising tax proposals. One such measure would have denied a tax deduction for 20% of a business' advertising costs and required the remaining 80% to be amortized over two years; the estimate of the additional tax revenue generated by this proposal was $37.9 billion by 1990.

With such activity at the federal and state levels, it is very possible that advertising may some day face a double hit from the tax man, with local governments taxing advertising expenditures, while the federal government requires advertisers to defer some portion of their advertising expense deduction until a future year.

There are several steps that we can take now to reach decision makers before advertising taxes become a reality. First, we must monitor the legislatures in every state for proposals of ad tax legislation. The earlier we know about these proposals, the better our chances of influencing their outcome. Second, we need to open channels of communications with key lawmakers and educate them on advertising's contribution to economic growth and expansion. If we want government officials to share our understanding of the advertising process and its importance in generating sales, we have to take the initiative. Third, we need to demonstrate just how broad based a constituency the advertising community really is with large and small businesses, artists, the media, actors, songwriters, photographers, graphic designers and many others depending on advertising for their livelihoods.

Continued on page 268

Ronald R. Johnson

2104 Valley Glen
Orange, California 92667
(714) 637-1145

Location photography worldwide for corporate,
industrial, and editorial assignments

Jim Karageorge

610 22nd Street #309
San Francisco, California 94107
(415) 648-3444

transforming locations with light

all photos on both pages were shot on location

call the studio for a complete portfolio

see previous pages in Corporate Showcase Vols. 1, 2, 3, 4 & 5 and in American Showcase Vols. 9, 10 & 11

stock is available through the studio and through H. Armstrong Roberts, Inc. (215) 386-6300

multiple awards for annual report photography in the AR 100 and in Print magazine

member ASMP

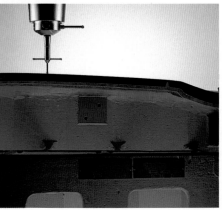

Jim Karageorge

610 22nd Street #309
San Francisco, California 94107
(415) 648-3444

transforming locations with light
all photos on both pages were shot on location
call the studio for a complete portfolio

see previous pages in Corporate Showcase Vols. 1, 2,
3, 4 & 5 and in American Showcase Vols. 9, 10 & 11

stock is available through the studio and through
H. Armstrong Roberts, Inc. (215) 386-6300

member ASMP

Larry Keenan

421 Bryant Street
San Francisco, California 94107
(415) 495-6474

Advertising, annual reports,
corporate/industrial, travel,
conceptual and special effects
photography. International
experience, numerous awards.
Stock photographs available
through The Image Bank
(212) 529-6700

Clients:
Activision
Advanced Micro Devices
Amdahl
Ampex
Apple Computers
Bank of America
Bell + Howell
Broderbund
CBS Records
Clorox
Del Monte
Electronic Arts
Genentech
General Instrument
Hewlett-Packard
Levi-Strauss
Lorimar Productions
Microsoft
Motorola
Omni Magazine
PacBell
Syntex Labs
Tandem Computers

Publicité, Rapports annuels,
Commercial/Industriel,
Reportages, Abstrait/Effets
spéciaux, Une expérience
internationale, Nombreux prix
reçus. Photothèque très
complète, Membre APA.

Fotografie für Werbung,
Jahresberichte, Reise und
Tourismus, Wirtschaft und
Industrie, Konzeption und
Special Effects Fotografie,
Foto Archiev, Internationale
Erfahrung, Mitglied: APA.

宣伝広告、決算報告書、会社案内書、観
光案内、特殊撮影等最も効果的なイメー
ジにてご希望に応じます。世界各国での
仕事経験あります。フィルムライブラリ
ー有ります。ニューヨーク国際広告賞他
多数受賞致しました。APA 会員。

Photographs are not retouched.

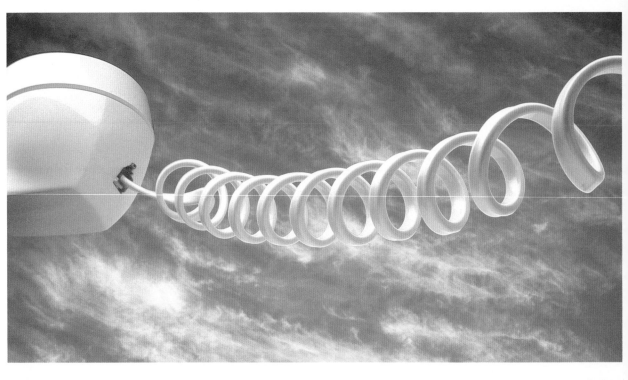

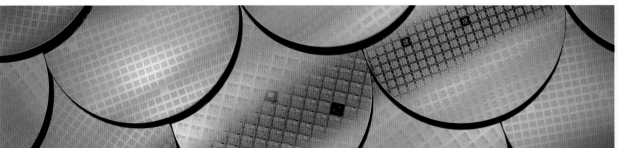

Rob Lewine

8929 Holly Place
Los Angeles, California 90046
(213) 654-0830

Represented in New York by Shelley Spierman:
(212) 749-8911

Client List:

ABC Television, Ashton-Worthington, Bantam Books, Bartel-Werndorf & Associates, BBDO, Bradley-Vale Advertising, Broyles/Garamella/Cavanaugh, California Magazine, Carbone/Smolan Associates, Carnegie Publications, CBS Entertainment, CBS Records, Center Stage Advertising, Channels Magazine, Coast Savings and Loan, Columbia Pictures, Commtek Publishing, Cross Associates, DeLaurentiis Entertainment Group, Deutsch Design, Discover Magazine, DJMC Advertising, Douglas Boyd Design, Dyer-Kahn, East/West Network, Elle Magazine, Emmy Magazine, Esquire Magazine, Flex Magazine, Forbes Magazine, Fortune Magazine, Fox Television, Gateway, General Cinema, GEO, High Technology Magazine, Home Magazine, Interview, Life Magazine, London Sunday Time's Magazine, Lorimar Telepictures, Los Angeles Magazine, Money Magazine, National Geographic, Newsweek, Outside Magazine, Parade, People Magazine, Playgirl, Psychology Today, Rolling Stone, Robert Miles Runyan, Safeco Title Insurance, Schneider/Parker/Jakuc, Scott Mednick & Associates, Seiniger Advertising, Shape Magazine, Smithsonian Magazine, Snyder Advertising, Southern California Edison, Stern Magazine, The Graphic Expression, Time Magazine, Town & Country, Travel & Leisure, T. Rowe Price Associates, Universal Pictures, Us Magazine, Warner Brothers.
Member ASMP

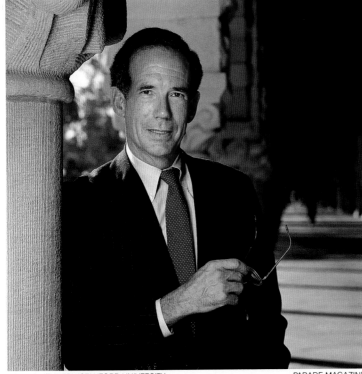

DONALD KENNEDY/STANFORD UNIVERSITY   PARADE MAGAZINE

DR. ROY WALFORD/PATHOLOGIST, UCLA   PARADE MAGAZINE

DR. KURT FORSTER/THE GETTY TRUST   SMITHSONIAN MAGAZINE

RUSTY POWELL/LOS ANGELES COUNTY MUSEUM OF ART   SMITHSONIAN MAGAZINE

DMiller Photo

Dennis Miller
1467 12th Street #C
Manhattan Beach, California 90266
(213) 546-3205

Location
Corporate
Industrial
Stock

Milroy/McAleer Photography

3857 Birch Street, Suite #170
Newport Beach, California 92660
(714) 957-0219

Milroy/McAleer are a team of photographers specializing in architecture, interiors, hotels (working with or without models), furniture and building products.

Our clients include a wide range of design firms, hotel companies, real estate interests, furniture, building and public relations agencies.

Our clients include:
Austin Company
Barry Design
Beckham Eisenham
D.M.J.M.
Di Leonardo International
Four Seasons
Gensler
Haller Systems
Hilton Hotels
Irvine Company
Kimball/Artec International
Lacy Champion Carpets

La Mansion Hotel
Landgon Wilson Mumper
Marriott Host International
Nadel Partnership
Ogden International
Quality Inns
Red Lion Inns
Registry Hotels
Ritz Carlton Hotels
Security Pacific Bank
Sheraton Hotels
Stouffer Hotels
The Biltmore Hotel

Weyerhaeuser
Wrather Corporation

Our work has appeared editorially in the following magazines:
Better Homes and Gardens
Corporate Design and Reality
Designers West
Facilities Design and Management
Interior Design
Interiors
Neiki Architecture
Restaurant and Hotel Design

267

Continued from page 260

Finally, we need to show our government representatives that all businesses rely on advertising. How many realize that even businesses that do little consumer advertising may advertise extensively on a business-to-business basis? How many understand that businesses which do no advertising themselves may depend entirely on the ultimate sale of heavily advertised products to sustain demand for their goods or services?

The advertising community, when united, can be an extremely powerful force. Our experience with Florida's advertising tax in 1987 demonstrates this fact. On July 1, 1987, Florida put in place a five percent tax on all advertising within its borders. Advertising expenditures in the state dropped substantially, with the media feeling the impact most directly and immediately. National spot-TV advertising declined an average of 11.8% in Florida's top six media markets during the third quarter of 1987, versus the same period in 1986. And in two of these markets, the dropoff was almost 20 percent. In addition, many businesses and professional organizations cancelled meetings and conferences in the state to protest the tax, resulting in the loss of some 150,000 room nights.

Lawsuits were filed challenging the constitutionality of the tax, and a strong grass roots movement coalesced behind support for a constitutional amendment prohibiting a tax on services. The public outcry was effective. In just six months, the Florida Legislature voted to remove the tax. By January 1, 1988, the tax was off the books.

The Association of National Advertisers (A.N.A.) was deeply involved in the Florida effort and has been active in working against similar proposals at the federal, state and local levels. As A.N.A.'s chairperson, I fully support the Association's decision to make the ad tax issue our first priority.

To make our efforts successful, all sectors of the advertising community must work together effectively. If even one state successfully implements an ad tax, others are likely to follow its lead. The Florida experience can be a powerful tool to persuade legislators at the state and federal level that ad taxes just don't work. With the support and active involvement of everyone in the advertising community, we can ensure that advertising remains a positive and constructive force in our economy.

Kim Armstrong
Advertising Director
AT&T Communications
Basking Ridge, New Jersey

Marshal Safron

606 South San Vicente Boulevard
Los Angeles, California 90048
(213) 653-1234

Specializing in architecture, interiors, furniture, hotels
and building products on location and in the studio.
My work has appeared in all related national trade and
consumer publications.

Client list available upon request.

Additional work can be seen in American Showcase
Volume 9, page 373.

Marc
Solomon

Ingersoll-Rand
Tishman
Waukesha
Financial Planning
Port Of Los Angeles
Baker Int.
Family Circle
Nabisco
Pfizer
ILFC
Ethyl Corp.
National Medical Ent.
Holt, Rinehart & Winston
First Business Bank
East/West Network
Maxicare
Nikon
Dryden Press
Guestinformant
Celanese
NCR
Personnel Journal
Southern Calif. Edison
Integrated Resources
Neutrogena
Unocal
Ford
Amtrak
First Interstate Bank
APCOA
Institutional Investor
GTE
Sperry
Burlington Ind.
Frito Lay
AFG Ind.
Eastman Chemical
Garrett
AT&T
General Life
Frank B. Hall
Dow Chemicals
TRW
Pier One Imports
Staley Continental
Security Pacific Bank

MARC
BOX 480574, LOS ANGELES, CA 90048 • 213 935 1771
SOLOMON

**MARC
SOLOMON**

BOX 480574, LOS ANGELES, CA 90048 • 213 935 1771

Glenn Steiner Studios

301 Eighth Street #212
San Francisco, California 94103
(415) 863-1214

3102 Moore Street
San Diego, California 92110
(619) 299-0197

New York Representative:
Joan Kramer
Joan Kramer & Associates
(212) 567-5545

Black and white. Pure and simple. Hand printed.
Award winning. Fortune 500 clientele.

GOOD SAMARITAN HOSPITAL, SAN JOSE

Stock

When your image means the world . . . 503/389-7662

Images of Nature®
Thomas D. Mangelsen

Post Office Box 2935
Jackson Hole, Wyoming 83001
(307) 733-6179

Stock Photographs of North American and African
    Wildlife and Landscapes.
Distinctive Limited Edition Photographic Prints.
Free Catalog.

Advertising & Editorial Clients
Amoco International Sales Company
Audubon
CBS Magazines

Chevron Chemical Company
CSX Corporation/Grand Teton Lodge Company
Defenders of Wildlife
Ducks Unlimited
Eastman Kodak Company
Economy Press
Environmental Defense Fund
Freedom Rent-A-Car Systems, Inc.
Hallmark Cards
Honeywell, Inc.
MacMillan Publishing Company
McGraw Hill
National Geographic Society

National Geographic WORLD
National Wildlife Federation
Nature Conservancy
Natural History
Norden Labs
Orion Nature Quarterly
Outdoor Photographer
Princeton University Press
Smithsonian Magazine
Stern Magazine
U.S. Postal Service/Express Mail
Woodmen of the World
Young and Rubicam New York

IMAGES
—OF—
NATURE®

David Muench

David Muench Photography, Inc
P.O. Box 30500
Santa Barbara, California 93130
(805) 967-4488

A Collection of Stock Photography

The American Landscape...North...South...East... West. The wild beauty and presence of mountain, desert, coast, prairie, water, texture and sky...The landscape elements. Specializing in the mysterious moods, natural rhythms, unusual lighting and spacial forms. Over 26 large format books exhibit this original photography on the American landscape.

Photographs are made primarily on large format 4 × 5 film.

Available for advertising, annual reports, books, editorial, calendar, poster and brochures.

Original creative seeing in both black and white and color.

West Stock, Inc.

83 South King Street Suite #520
Seattle, Washington 98104
(206) 621-1611
Call Toll Free 800-821-9600

"Pictures Of Practically Everything"

Dedicated to serving the needs of the communications industry, we take the risk, uncertainty, and high cost out of photography acquisition. West Stock's files contain an enormous variety of topics from an unusually diverse group of professional photographers. These photographers have traveled to all parts of the world,

each has their own special skills, and our files showing that variety. Anywhere in the United States, we can have photographs on your desk tomorrow, if not sooner.

To view more of our photographer's work see: American Showcase 10, 11, Adweek Portfolio 10, 11, 12, 13. Call or write for our complete catalog.

WEST STOCK

RICK MORLEY

RICK MORLEY

BRYAN F. PETERSON

PHIL SCHOFIELD

JEFF GNASS

TAYLOR CAMPBELL

DAVID STOECKLEIN

Neither a borrower nor a lender be.

Borrowing someone else's Showcase is like living on borrowed time.

Creatives hate to lend you their copies of Illustration and Photography Showcase. That's because while you're benefiting from all the dynamic talent and thought-provoking images you find in each edition, they're wasting time looking for *you.*

So, if you're getting a little unpopular around the office, here's some advice: buy your own Showcase. Illustration Showcase 11 gives you nearly 800 full-color pages containing 4500 works by this country's best commercial illustrators for only $45.00. For just $35.00, Photography Showcase 11 brings you almost 350 color pages with 1700 innovative images by today's top commercial photographers. Both

softcover volumes have an oversized page format with superior color reproduction.

Once you get your own copies of Showcase, you can relax with your private source of talent and inspiration. And if a friend wants to borrow them... lend him your ears, but not your Showcase.

To order, send your check to American Showcase, 724 Fifth Avenue, New York, NY 10019. Postage and handling are free. (NY residents please add sales tax.) Or call (212) 245-0981 for even faster service.

IndexPhotographers

Continued on next page.

IndexPhotographers

Continued from previous page.

Phone Listings & Addresses of Representatives, Visual Artists & Suppliers

Contents

Regions

New York City

Northeast
Connecticut
Delaware
Maine
Maryland
Massachusetts
New Hampshire
New Jersey
New York State
Pennsylvania
Rhode Island
Vermont
Washington, D.C.
West Virginia

Southeast
Alabama
Florida
Georgia
Kentucky
Louisiana
Mississippi
North Carolina
South Carolina
Tennessee
Virginia

Midwest
Illinois
Indiana
Iowa
Kansas
Michigan
Minnesota
Missouri
Nebraska
North Dakota
Ohio
South Dakota
Wisconsin

Southwest
Arizona
Arkansas
New Mexico
Oklahoma
Texas

Rocky Mountain
Colorado
Idaho
Montana
Utah
Wyoming

West Coast
Alaska
British Columbia
California
Hawaii
Nevada
Oregon
Washington

Grey Pages

Representatives

Legend
A = Animator
AV = Audio Visual
C = Cartoonist
D = Director
F = Film
G = Graphic Designer
H & MU = Hair & Make-up
I = Illustrator
L = Lettering
M = Music
P = Photographer
R = Retoucher
TV = Television

New York City

A

Abbey, Ken & Assoc/421 Seventh Ave, New York, NY — 212-947-7577
Edmund Goldsphink, (P), David Greenberg, (P), Hal Oringer, (P), Ted Pobiner, (P)

Adler, Phil/18 E 16th St, New York, NY — 212-627-8448
Walter Auster, (P)

Altamore, Bob/237 W 54th St 4th Fl, New York, NY — 212-977-4300
Cailor/Resnick, (P)

American Artists/353 W 53rd St #1W, New York, NY — 212-682-2462
Don Almquist, (I), Keith Batcheller, (I), Roger Bergendorff, (I), Dan Bridy, (I), Chris Butler, (I), Bob Byrd, (I), Gary Ciccarelli, (I), Jim Deigan, (I), Bob Dorsey, (I), Lane DuPont, (I), Michael Ellins, (I), Russell Farrell, (I), Jack Freas, (I), George Gaadt, (I), Rob Gage, (I), Jackie Geyer, (I), John Hamagami, (I), Pam Hamilton, (I), Karel Havileck, (I), Steve Hendricks, (I), Doug Henry, (I), John Holm, (I), Chris Hopkins, (I), Andy Hoyos, (I), Mitch Hyatt, (I), Richard Kriegler, (I), Ned Levine, (I), Maurice Lewis, (I), Ed Lindlof, (I), Jerry LoFaro, (I), Ron Mahoney, (I), Mick McGinty, (I), James Needham, (I), David Noyes, (I), Jim Owens, (I), Nan Parsons, (I), Charles Passarelli, (I), Tony Randazzo, (I), Jan Sawka, (I), Todd Schorr, (I), Michael Schumacher, (I), Victor Scocozza, (P), Joe Scrofani, (I), Mike Steirnagle, (I), Tony Ward, (P), Stan Watts, (I), Will Weston, (I), Ron Wolin, (I), Jonathan Wright, (I), Andy Zito, (I)

Anthony, Ed/133 W 19th St 3rd Fl, New York, NY — 212-924-7770
Joseph Cementi, (P)

Anton, Jerry/107 E 38th St #5A, New York, NY — 212-689-5886
Bobbye Cochran, (I), Abe Echevarria, (I), Norman Green, (I), Aaron Rezny, (P)

Aparo, Vincent/65 W 68th St, New York, NY — 212-877-5439
Edward Addeo, (P), Charles Baum, (P), Kevin CLarke, (P), Anita Giraldo, (P)

Arnold, Peter Inc/1181 Broadway 4th Fl, New York, NY — 212-481-1190
Fred Bavendam, (P), Bob Evans, (P), Jacques Jangoux, (P), Manfred Kage, (P), Stephen Krasemann, (P), Hans Pfletschinger, (P), David Scharf, (P), Erika Stone, (P), Bruno Zehnder, (P)

Art Farm, The/420 Lexington Ave, New York, NY — 212-688-4555
Dick Carroll, (I), Sururi Gumen, (I), Bob Lubbers, (I), Dick Naugler, (I), Linda Pascual, (I), Scott Pike, (I), Bob Walker, (I), Kong Wu, (I), Bill Zdinak, (I)

Artco/24 W 57th St #605, New York, NY — 212-489-8777
Ed Acuna, (I), George Angelini, (I), Dan Brown, (I), Alain Chang, (I), Jeff Cornell, (I), Bob Dacey, (I), Beau & Alan Daniels, (I), Ron DeFelice, (I), Enid Hatton, (I), Kathy Jeffers, (I), Rick McCollum, (I), Joseph Milioto, (I), Barry Phillips, (I), Rick Tulka, (I)

Artists Associates/211 E 51st St #5F, New York, NY — 212-755-1365
Norman Adams, (I), Don Braupigam, (I), Michael Deas, (I), Mark English, (I), Alex Gnidziejko, (I), Robert Heindel, (I), Steve Karchin, (I), Dick Krepel, (I), Skip Liepky, (I), Fred Otnes, (I), Daniel Schwartz, (I), Norman Walker, (I)

Arton Associates/216 E 45th St, New York, NY — 212-661-0850
Paul Giovanopoulis, (I), Jacob Knight, (I), Carveth Kramer, (I), Michelle Laporte, (I), Karen Laurence, (I)

Asciutto Art Reps/19 E 48th St 3rd Fl, New York, NY — 212-838-0050
Anthony Accardo, (I), Alex Bloch, (I), Don Bolognese, (I), Olivia Cole, (I), Daniel Delvalle, (I), Kitty Diamantis, (I), Simon Galkin, (I), Donald Gates, (I), Meryl Henderson, (I), Taylor Jones, (I), Nurit Karlin, (I), Paul Lackner, (I), Sally Marshall Larrain, (I), Goran Lindgren, (I), Morissa Lipstein, (I), Hal Lose, (I), Loreta Lustig, (I), Tod Mason, (I), Sal Murdocca, (I), Jan Pyk, (I), Donna Ward, (I), Fred Winkowski, (I)

Ash, Michael/5 W 19th St, New York, NY — 212-741-0015

Azzara, Louise/131 E 17th St, New York, NY — 212-674-8114

B

Backer, Vic/30 W 26th St, New York, NY — 212-620-0944

Badd, Linda/568 Broadway #601, New York, NY — 212-431-3377

Badin, Andy/835 Third Ave 4th Fl, New York, NY — 212-532-1222
Jeff Feinen, (I), Brian Kossoff, (P), Michael Kozmiuk, (I), Robert S Levy, (I), Harry Pincus, (I)

Bahm, Darwin/6 Jane St, New York, NY — 212-989-7074
Julian Allen, (I), Joan Landis, (I), Rick Meyerowitz, (I), Don Ivan Punchatz, (I), Arno Sternglass, (I), Sketch Pad Studio, (I), John Thompson, (I), Robert Weaver, (I)

Baker, Valerie/152 W 25th St 12th Fl, New York, NY — 212-807-9754

Barboza, Ken Assoc/853 Broadway #1603, New York, NY — 212-505-8635
Pinder Hughes, (P)

Barclay, R Francis/5 W 19th St, New York, NY — 212-255-3440

Barnes, Fran/25 Fifth Ave #9B, New York, NY — 212-505-2720

Barracca, Sal/156 Fifth Ave #1222, New York, NY — 212-645-6772
Andrea Baruffi, (I), Robert Evans, (I), Rick Fischer, (I), Yan Nascimbene, (I), Larry Noble, (I), Donna Ruff, (I), JC Suares, (I)

Bauchner, Susan/134 Beaumont St, Brooklyn, NY — 718-648-5345
Jacques Charlas, (P)

Becker, Erika/150 W 55th St, New York, NY — 212-757-8987
Richard Ely, (I), Esther Larson, (I)

Becker, Noel/150 W 55th St, New York, NY — 212-757-8987
Howard Tangye, (P), Sy Vinopoll, (P)

Beilin, Frank/405 E 56th St, New York, NY — 212-751-3074

Benedict, Brinker (Ms)/165 E 89th St, New York, NY — 212-534-1845

Berns, James/1133 Broadway #706, New York, NY — 212-627-8050

Bernstein & Andriulli/60 E 42nd St #505, New York, NY — 212-682-1490
Richard Anderson, (I), Tony Antonios, (I), Per Arnoldi, (I), Pat Bailey, (I), Garin Baker, (I), Garie Blackwell, (I), Melinda Bordelon, (I), Rick Brown, (I), Everett Davidson, (I), Cathy Deeter, (I), Ron Fleming, (I), Victor Gadino, (I), Joe Genova, (I), Marika Hahn, (I), Veronika Hart, (I), Catherine Huerta, (I), Cathy Johnson, (I), Mary Ann Lasher, (I), Bette Levine, (I), Todd Lockwood, (I), Michael Molkenthin, (P), Bill Morse, (I), Frank Moscati, (P), Craig Nelson, (I), Jake Rajs, (P), Joe Salina, (I), Marla Shega, (I), Simpson/Flint, (P), Chuck Slack, (I), Peter Stallard, (I), J C Suares, (I), Tom Szumowski, (I), Murray Tinkelman, (I), Clay Turner, (I), Pam Wall, (I), Chuck Wilkinson, (I), Paul Wollman, (I), James B. Wood, (P)

Bishop, Lynn/134 E 24th St, New York, NY — 212-254-5737
Irene Stern, (P)

Black Silver & Lord/415 Madison Ave, New York, NY — 212-725-3806
Gloria Baker, (P), Kip Brundage, (P), Norm Clasen, (P), Fred Mullane, (P), Michel Tcherevkoff, (P), Roger Tully, (P)

Black Star/450 Park Ave S, New York, NY — 212-679-3288
John W. Alexanders, (P), Nancy Rica Schiff, (P), Kim Steele, (P), Arnold Zann, (P)

Blum, Felice S/79 W 12th St, New York, NY — 212-929-2166

Boghosian, Marty/1123 Broadway #412, New York, NY — 212-242-1251
James Salzano, (P)

Booth, Tom Inc/425 W 23rd St #17A, New York, NY — 212-243-2750
Ann Field, (I), William Garrett, (P), John Goodman, (P), Joshua Greene, (P), Richard Holiman, (I), Gordon Munro, (P), Dick Nystrom, (P), Patrick Russell, (P), Geoff Spear, (P), Alexander Vethers, (I)

Boyer, Susan/39 E 12th St, New York, NY — 212-533-3113
Brett Froomer, (P)

Brackman, Henrietta/415 E 52nd St, New York, NY — 212-753-6483

Brackman, Selma/251 Park Ave S, New York, NY — 212-777-4210

Brennan, Dan/568 Broadway #1005, New York, NY — 212-925-8333
Tom Biondo, (P), Knut Bry, (P), Francois Deconnick, (P), Renato Grignaschi, (P), Bob Krieger, (P), Michel Momy, (P)

Brindle, Carolyn/203 E 89th St #3D, New York, NY — 212-534-4177

Brody, Sam/230 E 44th St #2F, New York, NY — 212-758-0640
Robert Butler, (P), Linda Clenney, (I), Fred Hilliard, (I), Gary Kufner, (P), Stanford Smilow, (P), Steen Svenson, (P), Rudi Tesa, (P)

Brown, Doug/17 E 45th St #1009, New York, NY — 212-980-4971
Abe Seltzer, (P), Andrew Unangst, (P)

Browne, Pema Ltd/185 E 85th St, New York, NY — 212-369-1925
George Angelini, (I), Robert Barrett, (I), Joe Burleson, (I), Peter Catalanotto, (I), Robert C Howe, (I), Ron Jones, (I), Kathy Krantz, (I), David Plourde, (I), Karen Pritchett, (I), John Rush, (I), John Sandford, (I), Alice deKok, (I)

Bruck, J S/157 W 57th St, New York, NY — 212-247-1130
Richard Anderson, (I), Michael Dudash, (I), Tom Freeman, (I),

Representatives

Donald Hedlin, (I), Jim Mathewuse, (I), Richard Newton, (I), Victoria Vebell, (I), Gary Watson, (I)

Bruck, Nancy/302 W 12th St, New York, NY   212-645-1547
Gary Feinstein, (P), Pamela Patrick, (I)

Bruml, Kathy/262 West End Ave, New York, NY   212-874-5659
Charles Folds, (P), Michael Skott, (P)

Bush, Nan/135 Watts St, New York, NY   212-226-0814
Bruce Weber, (P)

Byrnes, Charles/5 E 19th St #303, New York, NY   212-473-3366
Steve Steigman, (P)

C

Cafiano, Charles/140 Fifth Ave, New York, NY   212-777-7654
Kenro Izu, (P)

Cahill, Joe/135 E 50th St, New York, NY   212-751-0529
Shig Ikeda, (P), Brad Miller, (P), Howard Sochurek, (P)

Camp, Woodfin & Assoc/415 Madison Ave, New York, NY   212-750-1020
Robert Azzi, (P), Kip Brundage, (P), Jason Laure, (P)

Canter, Theresa/1483 First Ave #5G, New York, NY   212-734-1352

Caputo, Elise & Assoc/PO Box 6898, New York, NY   212-725-0503
Becker/Bishop, (P), James Kozyra, (P), Peter Papadopolous, (P), Bill Robbins, (P)

Carmel/69 Mercer St, New York, NY   212-925-6216
Guy Powers, (P)

Carp, Stan/11 E 48th St, New York, NY   212-759-8880
Nick Samardge, (P), Allen Vogel, (P)

Casey, Judy/96 Fifth Ave, New York, NY   212-255-3252
Calliope, (P), Richard Corman, (P), Torkil Gudnason, (P), Lizzie Himmel, (P), Elisabeth Novick, (P), Michael O'Brien, (P), Paolo Roversi, (P)

Casey, Marge/245 E 63rd St, New York, NY   212-486-9575
Lisa Charles, (P), Geoffrey Clifford, (P), Frank Cowan, (P), Thomas Hooper, (P), Robert Lambert, (P), Michael Lupino, (P)

Cedeno, Lucy/10 W 18th St, New York, NY   212-255-9212

Celano, Nancy/345 E 80th St, New York, NY   212-744-7258

Celnick, Manny/36 E 12th St, New York, NY   212-473-4455
Edward Selnick, (P)

Chie/15 E 11th St #2M, New York, NY   212-243-2353

Chislovsky, Carol/853 Broadway #1201, New York, NY1000   322-980-3510
Randal Birkey, (I), Alex Bostic, (I), Russell Cobane, (I), Jon Conrad, (I), Bob Cooper, (I), Jan Evans, (I), Ignacio Gomez, (I), Ken Graning, (I), John Gray, (I), Michael Haynes, (I), Tim Herman, (I), William Hosner, (I), Hubert, (I), Jim Hunt, (I), Joe Lapinski, (I), Felix Marich, (I), Joe Ovies, (I), Vincent Petragnani, (I), Chuck Schmidt, (I), Sandra Shap, (I), Danny Smythe, (I), Randy South, (I), Nighthawk Studios, (I), Bob Thomas, (I)

Cohen, Bruce/54 W 16th St, New York, NY   212-620-7839

Collignon, Daniele/1500 Broadway #2013, New York, NY   212-391-1830
Bob Aiese, (I), Dan Cosgrove, (I), Bill Frampton, (I), David Gambale, (I), Mel Greifinger, (I), Richard Hughes, (P), Mike Lester, (I), Dennis Mukai, (I), Fran Oelbaum, (I), Cindy Pardy, (I), Alex Tiani, (I), Varlet-Martinelli, (I), Vicki Yiannias, (I)

Conlon, Jean/461 Broome St, New York, NY   212-966-9897
Elizabeth Brady, (I), Kenro Izu, (P), Evan Polenghi, (I), David Riley, (P), Holly Shapiro(S), Nana Watanabe, (P)

Cornelia/448 E 37th St, New York, NY   212-947-5167
Cristof Gstalder, (P), Denis Malerbi, (P), Ron Nicolaysen, (P), Jim Varriale, (P)

Craven Design/461 Park Ave S, New York, NY   212-696-4680
Diana Magnuson, (I), Roz Schanzer, (I)

Creative Freelancers/62 W 45th St, New York, NY   212-398-9540
Harold Brooks, (I), R S Brown, (I), Rudy Cristiano, (I), Howard Darden, (I), Steve Doquette, (I), Claudia Fouse, (I), Arie Haas, (I), Blake Hampton, (I), Alice Landry, (I), Robert Pasternak, (I), Rosanne Percivalle, (I), Meryl Rosner, (I), Steve Sullivan, (I)

Creative Talent/62 LeRoy St, New York, NY   212-243-7869
Marshall Cetlin, (I), Alan Henderson, (I), Guy Smalley, (I)

Crecco, Michael/342 Madison Ave, New York, NY   212-682-5663

Cuevas, Robert/230 E 44th St, New York, NY   212-661-7149
Ray Chen, (P), Barnett Plotkin, (I), Robbie Stillerman, (I), Larry Williams, (P)

Cullom, Ellen/55 E 9th St, New York, NY   212-777-1749

D

Dagrosa, Terry/374 Eighth Ave 2nd Fl, New York, NY   212-645-4082
Rod Cook, (P)

Davies, Nora/370 E 76th St #C103, New York, NY   212-628-6657

DeBacker, Clo/29 E 19th St, New York, NY   212-420-1276
Bob Kiss, (P)

DeVito, Kitty/43 E 30th St 14th Fl, New York, NY   212-889-9670
Bart DeVito, (P)

DeVlieger, Mary/2109 Broadway, New York, NY   212-903-4321

DeWan, Michael/250 Cabrini Blvd #2E, New York, NY   212-927-9458
Nancy Bundt, (P), Don Sparks, (P)

Dedell, Jacqueline/58 W 15th St 6th Fl, New York, NY   212-741-2539
Ivan Chermayeff, (I), Teresa Fasolino, (I), David Frampton, (I), Chermayeff and Geismar, (G), Griesbach/Martucci, (I), Barry Root, (I), Kimberly B Root, (I), Isadore Seltzer, (I), Richard Williams, (I), Henry Wolf, (P)

Des Verges, Diana/73 Fifth Ave, New York, NY   212-691-8674

Deverin, Daniele/226 E 53rd St, New York, NY   212-755-4945
Greg Couch, (I), Mort Drucker, (I), David Johnson, (I), Lazlo Kubinyi, (I), Charles Shields, (I), Jeff Smith, (I), Don Weller, (I)

Dewey, Frank & Assoc/420 Lexington Ave, New York, NY   212-986-1249

DiMartino, Joseph/25 W 39th St #902, New York, NY   212-764-5591
Mark Blanton, (I), Paul DiMartino, (I), Whistl'n Dixie, (G), Mac Evans, (I), Rudy Gutierrez, (I), Mark Herron, (I), Jay, (I)

Dickinson, Alexis/175 Fifth Ave #1112, New York, NY   212-206-0410
Richard Dunkley, (P), Paul Hoffman, (P)

Dobrowolski, Nina/PO Box 1288/Mad Sq Sta, New York, NY   212-753-2310

Dorman, Paul/419 E 57th St, New York, NY   212-826-6737
Studio DGM, (P)

Drexler, Sharon/451 Westminster Rd, Brooklyn, NY   718-284-4779
Les Katz, (I)

Droske, Diane/300 E 40th St #19R, New York, NY   212-867-2383
Tom Hollyman, (P), Nancy LeVine, (P), Tobey Sanford, (P)

DuCane, Alex/135 W 70th St #9E, New York, NY   212-769-2840

Dunn, Roark/18 College Pl, Brooklyn, NY   718-875-2558

E

Eagles, Betsy/130 W 57th St, New York, NY   212-582-1501
Ron Nicolaysen, (P), Lance Steadler, (P)

Edlitz, Ann/230 E 79th St #14F, New York, NY   212-744-7945

Ellis, Mirjana/176 Westminster Rd, Brooklyn, NY   718-282-6449
Ray Ellis, (P)

Eng, Barbara/110 E 23rd St, New York, NY   212-254-8334

Engel, Mary/65 Central Pk W, New York, NY   212-580-1051

Englert, Tim/305 W 84th St #313, New York, NY   212-496-2074

Enright, Catherine/61 E 66th St, New York, NY   212-288-0249

Erika/114 E 32nd St, New York, NY   212-532-7897
Tony Mandarino, (P)

Erlacher, Bill/Artists Assoc/211 E 51st St #5F, New York, NY   212-755-1365
Norman Adams, (I), Don Braupigam, (I), Michael Deas, (I), Mark English, (I), Alex Gnidziejko, (I), Robert Heindel, (I), Steve Karchin, (I), Dick Krepel, (I), Skip Liepky, (I), Fred Otnes, (I), Daniel Schwartz, (I)

Everly, Bart/156 Fifth Ave #327, New York, NY   212-924-1510

Eyre, Susan/292 Marlboro Rd, Brooklyn, NY   718-282-5034
Robert Phillips, (P)

F

Feldman, Robert/133 W 17th St #5A, New York, NY   212-741-7254
Alen MacWeeney, (P), Terry Niefield, (P)

Fischer, Bob/135 E 54th St, New York, NY   212-755-2131
James Moore, (P)

Fishback, Lee/350 W 21st St, New York, NY   212-929-2951

Flesher, Lex/7 E 14th St #903, New York, NY   212-255-4863

Folickman, Gail/399 E 72nd St, New York, NY   212-879-1508

Foster, Peter/870 UN Plaza, New York, NY   212-593-0793
Charles Tracey, (P)

Fraser, Gaylene/211 Thompson St, New York, NY   212-475-5911
Rosemary Howard, (P), Bernard Maisner, (I)

Frazier, Victoria/40 W 27th St, New York, NY   212-689-4207

Freelance Advantage/127 E 59th St #201, New York, NY   212-593-2965

Friess, Susan/36 W 20th St, New York, NY   212-675-3021
Richard Goldman, (P)

Friscia, Salmon/20 W 10th St, New York, NY   212-228-4134

Furst, Franz/420 E 55th St, New York, NY — 212-684-0492
  Greg Pease, (P)

G

Gargagliano, Tony/216 E 45th St, New York, NY — 212-661-0850
Gaynin, Gail/241 Central Park West, New York, NY — 212-580-3141
  Terry Clough, (P)
Gebbia, Doreen/156 Fifth Ave, New York, NY — 212-807-0588
  Bruce Plotkin, (P)
Gelb, Elizabeth/856 West End Ave, New York, NY — 212-222-1215
Giraldi, Tina/54 W 39th St, New York, NY — 212-840-8225
Godfrey, Dennis/95 Horatio St #203, New York, NY — 212-807-0840
  Jeffrey Adams, (I), Daryl Cagle, (I), Joel Nakamura, (I), Wendy
  Popp, (I)
Goldman, David/41 Union Sq W #918, New York, NY — 212-807-6627
  Norm Bendell, (I), Jay Brenner, (P), Joe Marvullo, (P), Mitchell
  Rigie, (I)
Goldmann, Howard/221 W 21st St #4A, New York, NY — 212-627-2319
Goldsmith, Randi/56 W 84th St #1R, New York, NY — 212-769-4468
Goldstein, Michael L/107 W 69th St, New York, NY — 212-874-6933
  Fred Schulze, (P)
Gomberg, Susan/145 E 22nd St, New York, NY — 212-473-8747
  Colin Brown, (I), Steve Carver, (I), Julius Ciss, (I), Michael
  Conway, (I), Robert Dale, (I), Jeff Faria, (I), Richard Fried, (P),
  Allen Garns, (I), Franklin Hammond, (I), Fran Hardy, (I), Ron
  Lieberman, (I), Janeart Limited, (P), Dan McGowan, (I), Enzo
  Messi & Urs Schmidt, (I), Kathy S Schorr, (I), James Tughan, (I)
Goodman, Barbara L/50 W 34th St, New York, NY — 212-594-9209
Goodwin, Phyllis A/10 E 81st St, New York, NY — 212-570-6021
  Cosimo, (P), Carl Furuta, (P), Howard Menken, (P), Carl Zapp,
  (P)
Gordon, Barbara Assoc/165 E 32nd St, New York, NY — 212-686-3514
  Craig Bakley, (I), Ron Barry, (I), Linda Benson, (I), Judith
  Cheng, (I), Bob Clarke, (I), Keita Colton, (I), James Dietz, (I),
  Glenn Harrington, (I), Robert Hunt, (I), Nenad Jakesevic, (I),
  Jackie Jasper, (I), Sonja Lamut, (I), April Lawton, (I), Roy
  McKie, (I), Andrew Nitzberg, (I), Sharleen Pederson, (I), Jas
  Szygiel, (I), Jackie Vaux, (I)
Gordon, Fran/1654 E 13th St #5A, Brooklyn, NY — 718-339-4277
Gotham Art Agency/25 Tudor Pl, New York, NY — 212-286-9786
Green, Anita/718 Broadway, New York, NY — 212-674-4788
  Alan Dolgins, (P), Stuart Peltz, (P)
Grien, Anita/155 E 38th St, New York, NY — 212-697-6170
  Dolores Bego, (I), Fanny M Berry, (I), Julie Johnson, (I), Hal
  Just, (I), Mangal, (I), Jerry McDaniel, (I), Don Morrison, (I),
  Marina Neyman-Levikova, (I), Alan Reingold, (I), Ellen Rixford,
  (I), Bill Wilkinson, (I)
Griffith, Valerie/10 Sheridan Square, New York, NY — 212-675-2089

H

Hainy, Barry/82 Jane St, New York, NY — 212-929-4313
Hajjar, Rene/220 Park Ave S, New York, NY — 212-777-5361
  Chris Jones, (P)
Hankins + Tegenborg Ltd/60 E 42nd St #1940, New York, NY — 212-867-8092
  Peter Attard, (I), Ralph Brillhart, (I), George Bush, (I), Frederico
  Castelluccio, (I), Frederico Castelluccio, (I), Jamie Cavaliere,
  (I), Jim Cherry, (I), Mac Conner, (I), David Cook, (I), John
  Dawson, (I), Guy Deel, (I), Chris Dellorco, (I), Ron DiScensa,
  (I), John Dismukes, (I), Bill Dodge, (I), John Ennis, (I), Marc
  Ericksen, (I), George Fernandez, (I), George Fernandez, (I),
  David Gaadt, (I), Sergio Giovine, (I), James Griffin, (I), Tom
  Hall, (I), Ray Harvey, (I), Edwin Herder, (I), Michael Herring, (I),
  Kevin Hulsey, (I), Aleta Jenks, (I), Rick Johnson, (I), Uldis
  Klavins, (I), Richard Lauter, (I), John Mazzini, (I), Cliff Miller,
  (I), Wendell Minor, (I), Miro, (I), Sam Montesano, (I), Jeffery
  Oh, (I), Greg Olanoff, (I), Matt Peak, (I), Walter Rane, (I), Kirk
  Reinert, (I), Ron Runda, (I), Robert Sabin, (I), Harry Schaare,
  (I), Bill Schmidt, (I), Diane Slavec, (I), Dan Sneberger, (I), Frank
  Steiner, (I), Ludmilla Strugatsky, (I), Robert Travers, (I), Bob
  Trondsen, (I), Victor Valla, (I), Jeff Walker, (I), John Youssi, (I)
Hansen, Wendy/126 Madison Ave, New York, NY — 212-684-7139
  Minh, (P)
Hare, Fran/126 W 23rd St, New York, NY — 212-794-0043
  Peter B Kaplan, (P)

Harmon, Rod/254 W 51st St #17E, New York, NY — 212-245-8935
  Brian Hennessey, (P), Al Rubin, (P), David Spagnolo, (P)
Head, Olive/155 Riverside Dr #10C, New York, NY — 212-580-3323
Healy, Tim/251 W 30th St #16W, New York, NY — 212-279-1515
Henderson, Gayle/6 W 20th St 2nd Fl, New York, NY — 212-689-6783
  David Brown, (P), Barry Schein(p)
Henry, John/237 E 31st St, New York, NY — 212-686-6883
  Gregory Cannon, (P), Rosemary Howard, (P)
Herron, Pat/829 Park Ave, New York, NY — 212-753-0462
  Larry Dale Gordon, (P), Malcolm Kirk, (P)
Heyl, Fran/230 Park Ave #2525, New York, NY — 212-581-6470
  Phillip Harrington, (P)
Hill, James/1026 Sixth Ave #2S, New York, NY — 212-302-4646
Hoeye, Michael/120 W 70th St, New York, NY — 212-362-9546
  Lelo Raymond, (P)
Holmberg, Irmeli/280 Madison Ave #1402, New York, NY — 212-775-1810
  Vincent Amicosante, (I), Dan Bridy, (I), Georgan Damore, (I),
  Rainbow Grinder, (I), Walter Gurbo, (I), Mitchell Hyatt, (I),
  Sharmen Liao, (I), John Martinez, (I), Barbara Maslen, (I), Lu
  Matthews, (I), Marilyn Montgomery, (I), Ann Neuman, (I),
  Jacqueline Osborn, (I), Stephen Osborn, (I), Deborah Pinkney,
  (I), Bob Radigan, (I), Bill Rieser, (I), Nicholas Wilton, (I)
Holt, Rita/280 Madison Ave #1109, New York, NY — 212-683-2002
Holtzberg, Diana/166 Second Ave #11K, New York, NY — 212-829-9838
  Ori Hofmekler, (I)
Hovde, Nob/829 Park Ave, New York, NY — 212-753-0462
  Malcolm Kirk, (P), J Frederick Smith, (P)
Hurewitz, Gary/5 E 19th St #303, New York, NY — 212-473-3366
  Howard Berman, (P), Steve Bronstein, (P), Earl Culberson, (P),
  Steve Steigman(D)
Husak, John/236 W 26th St #805, New York, NY — 212-463-7025
  Frank Marchese, (G), William Sloan, (I)

IJ

Iglesias, Jose/1123 Broadway #716, New York, NY — 212-929-7962
  Stan Fellerman, (P), Sven Lindman, (I), Akio Matsuyoshi, (I),
  George Ruentiz, (I)
Jacobsen, Vi/333 Park Ave S 2nd Fl, New York, NY — 212-677-3770
Jedell, Joan/370 E 76th St, New York, NY — 212-861-7861
Johnson, Bud & Evelyne/201 E 28th St, New York, NY — 212-532-0928
  Kathy Allert, (I), Betty de Araujo, (I), Irene Astrahan, (I), Rowan
  Barnes-Murphy, (I), Cathy Beylon, (I), Lisa Bonforte, (I),
  Carolyn Bracken, (I), Jane Chambliss-Rigie, (I), Roberta
  Collier, (I), Frank Daniel, (I), Larry Daste, (I), Ted Enik, (I),
  Carolyn Ewing, (I), Bill Finewood, (I), Robert Gunn, (I), Yukio
  Kondo, (I), Tom LaPadula, (I), Turi MacCombie, (I), Dee Malan,
  (I), Brookie Maxwell, (I), Darcy May, (I), Eileen McKeating, (I),
  Mei-ku-Huang, (I), Steven Petruccio, (I), Christopher Santoro,
  (I), Stan Skardinski, (I), Barbara Steadman, (I), Pat Stewart, (I),
  Tom Tierney, (I), Tricia Zimic, (I)
Joseph Mindlin & Mulvey/156 Fifth Ave #617, New York, NY — 212-243-1333
  Ernest Albanese, (I), Joseph Dawes, (I), John Dyess, (I), Paula
  Goodman, (I), Mark Hannon, (I), Mark Kaplan, (I), Tad
  Krumeich, (I), Bruce Lemerise, (I), Anita Lovitt, (I), Mike
  McCreanor, (I), Justin Novak, (I), Frederick Porter, (I), Tom
  Powers, (I), Herb Reed, (I), John Rice, (I), Sally Scheadler, (I),
  Kyuzo Tsugami, (I), Guenther Vollath, (I)

K

Kahn, Harvey Assoc Inc/50 E 50th St, New York, NY — 212-752-8490
  Clint Clemens, (P), Alan Cober, (I), Bernard Fuchs, (I),
  Nicholas Gaetano, (I), Gerald Gersten, (I), Wilson McLean, (I),
  Bob Peak, (I), Isadore Seltzer, (I)
Kane, Barney & Friends/18 E 16th St 2nd Fl, New York, NY — 212-206-0322
  Margaret Brown, (P), Jack DeGraffenried, (I), Joe Denaro, (I),
  Michael Farina, (I), Nat Giorgio, (I), William Harrison, (I),
  Steven Keyes, (I), Harvey Kurtzman, (I), Bob Lapsley, (I), Peter
  Lloyd, (I), Ted Lodigensky, (I), Rich Mahon, (I), Robert
  Melendez, (I), Doug Rosenthal, (I), Sue Rother, (I), Gary
  Ruddell, (I), Joseph Sellars, (I), Mario Stasolla, (I), Bill
  Thompson, (I), Vahid, (I), Larry Winborg, (I), Jenny Yip, (I)
Kane, Odette/119 W 23rd St, New York, NY — 212-807-8730
  Maria Perez, (I), Charles Seesselberg, (P)
Kaplan, Holly/35 W 36th St, New York, NY Bruno, (P) — 212-563-2730

Kaufman, Hillery/206 Lincoln Pl, Brooklyn, NY   718-230-3348
Kauss, Jean-Gabriel/240 E 41st St #32H, New York, NY   212-370-4300
   Guy Fery, (I), Jesse Gerstein, (P), Francois Halard, (P),
   Jacques Malignon, (P), John Stember, (P)
Keating, Peggy/30 Horatio St, New York, NY   212-691-4654
   Bob Parker, (I), Frank Paulin, (I), Suzanne Peck, (I), Fritz
   Varady, (I), Carol Vennell, (I), Norma Welliver, (I)
Keiserman/Kandel/29 W 21st St, New York, NY   212-691-5860
   Bill Buckner, (P), Robert Epstein, (P), David Lefler, (P), Vincent
   Ricucci, (P), Steve Young, (P)
Kenney, John Assoc/251 W 30th St 16th Fl, New York, NY   212-279-1515
   Gary Hanlon, (P), Elizabeth Heyert, (P), David Stetson, (P)
Kent, Al/244 Madison Ave, New York, NY   212-687-5578
Kestner, V G/427 E 77th St #4C, New York, NY   212-535-4144
Kim/209 E 25th St, New York, NY   212-679-5628
Kimche, Tania/470 W 23rd St, New York, NY   212-242-6367
   Paul Blakey, (I), Richard Goldberg, (I), Hom & Hom, (I), Rafal
   Olbinski, (I), Donald Gordon Penny, (P), Miriam Schottland, (I),
   E T Steadman, (I)
Kirchoff-Wohlberg Inc/866 UN Plaza #4014, New York, NY   212-644-2020
   Angela Adams, (I), Bob Barner, (I), Esther Baron, (I), Brian
   Cody, (I), Gwen Connelly, (I), Floyd Cooper, (I), Betsy Day, (I),
   Lois Ehlert, (I), Al Fiorentino, (I), Frank Fretz, (I), Jon Friedman,
   (I), Jeremy Guitar, (I), Konrad Hack, (I), Ron Himler, (I),
   Rosekrans Hoffman, (I), Kathleen Howell, (I), Susan Jaekel, (I),
   Chris Kalle, (I), Mark Kelley, (I), Christa Kieffer, (I), Dora Leder,
   (I), Tom Leonard, (I), Susan Lexa, (I), Don Madden, (I), Jane
   McCreary, (I), Lyle Miller, (I), Carol Nicklaus, (I), Sharon
   O'Neil, (I), Ed Parker, (I), Jim Pearson, (I), Charles Robinson,
   (I), Bronwen Ross, (I), Arvis Stewart, (I), Pat Traub, (I), Lou
   Vaccaro, (I), Joe Veno, (I), Alexandra Wallner, (I), John
   Wallner, (I), Arieh Zeldich, (I)
Klein, Leslie D/104 E 40th St, New York, NY   212-490-1460
   Franck Levy, (I), Eric Meola, (P), Digital Productions, (P)
Klimt, Bill & Maurine/15 W 72nd St, New York, NY   212-799-2231
   Wil Cormier, (I), Jamie DeJesus, (I), Jacques Devaud, (I), Doug
   Gray, (I), Paul Henry, (I), Steven Huston, (I), Ken Joudrey, (I),
   Brain Kotzky, (I), Frank Morris, (I), Shusei Nagaoka, (I), Alan
   Neider, (I), Gary Penca, (I), Pinturov, (I), Bill Purdom, (I), Mark
   Skolsky, (I)
Knight, Harrison/1043 Lexington Ave #4, New York, NY   212-288-9777
Kontzias, Lucy/317 Washington Ave, Brooklyn, NY   718-857-1528
Kopel, Shelly & Assoc/51 E 42nd St #716, New York, NY   212-986-3282
   Bliss Brothers, (I), Penny Carter, (I), Tom Christopher, (I),
   Marcus Hamilton, (I), Jim Manos, (I)
Korman, Alison/240 E 76th St, New York, NY   212-686-0525
   David Bishop, (P), Susan Kravis, (I)
Kramer, Joan & Assoc/720 Fifth Ave, New York, NY   212-567-5545
   David Cornwell, (P), Clark Dunbar, (P), John Lawlor, (P),
   James McLoughlin, (P), Frank Moscati, (P), Jeff Perkell, (P),
   John Russell, (P), Simpson/Flint, (P), Glen Steiner, (P), Ken
   Whitmore, (P), Edward Young, (P)
Kreis, Ursula G/63 Adrian Ave, Bronx, NY   212-562-8931
   Stephen Green-Armytage, (P), John T. Hill, (P), Bruce
   Pendleton, (P), Jed Share, (P)
Krongard, Paula/210 Fifth Ave #301, New York, NY   212-683-1020
   Bill White, (P)

L   LGI/241 W 36th St 7th Fl, New York, NY   212-736-4602
Lada, Joe/330 E 19th St, New York, NY   212-254-0253
   George Hausman, (P)
Lamont, Mary/200 W 20th St, New York, NY   212-242-1087
   Jim Marchese, (P)
Lander/Osborn/333 E 30th St, New York, NY   212-679-1358
   Francois Cloteaux, (I), Mel Furukawa, (I), Helen Guetary, (I),
   Cathy Heck, (I), Frank Riley, (I)
Lane Talent Inc/104 Fifth Ave, New York, NY   212-861-7225
Larkin, Mary/308 E 59th St, New York, NY   212-308-7744
   Lynn St John, (P)
Lashua, Sonja/27 W 20th St, New York, NY   212-929-5701
   Rick Young, (P)
Lavaty, Frank & Jeff/50 E 50th St #5, New York, NY   212-355-0910

   John Berkey, (I), Jim Butcher, (I), Bernard D'Andrea, (I), Don
   Daily, (I), Michael Davis, (I), Roland DesCombes, (I), Christine
   Duke, (I), Bruce Emmett, (I), Gervasio Gallardo, (I), Tim
   Hildebrandt, (I), Martin Hoffman, (I), Stan Hunter, (I), Chet
   Jezierski, (I), David McCall Johnson, (I), Mort Kunstler, (I), Paul
   Lehr, (I), Lemuel Line, (I), Robert LoGrippo, (I), Darrel Millsap,
   (I), Carlos Ochagavia, (I)
Lee, Alan/33 E 22nd St #5D, New York, NY   212-673-2484
   Werner Kappes, (I), Peter Vaeth, (P)
Leff, Jerry/420 Lexington Ave #2738, New York, NY   212-697-8525
   Franco Accornero, (I), Ken Barr, (I), Semyon Bilmes, (I), Alex
   Boies, (I), Mike Bryan, (I), Ron DiCianni, (I), Richard Drayton,
   (I), Charles Gehm, (I), Penelope Gottlieb, (I), Richard High(GD)
   Gayle Kabaker, (I), Ron Lesser, (I), Francis Livingston, (I),
   Dennis Magdich, (I), Frank Marciuliano, (I), Mercedes
   McDonald, (I), Gary McLaughlin, (I), John Parsons, (I),
   Dazzeland Studios, (I), James Woodend, (I)
Legrand, Jean Yves & Assoc/41 W 84th St #4, New York, NY   212-724-5981
   Jim Cherry, (I), Holly Hollington, (I), Barry McKinley, (P), Peter
   Sato, (I), Jack Ward, (P)
Leone, Mindy/381 Park Ave S #710, New York, NY   212-696-5674
   Bill Kouirinis, (P)
Leonian, Edith/220 E 23rd St, New York, NY   212-989-7670
   Philip Leonian, (P)
Lerman, Gary/113 E 31st St #4D, New York, NY   212-683-5777
   Paul Barton, (P), John Bechtold, (P), Jan Cobb, (P)
Levin, Bruce/691 Third Ave #3A, New York, NY   212-410-0123
Levitt, Lee/43 W 16th St #16, New York, NY   212-206-7257
Levy, Leila/4523 Broadway #7G, New York, NY   212-942-8185
   Yoav Levy, (P)
Lewin, Betsy/152 Willoughby Ave, Brooklyn, NY   718-622-3882
   Ted Lewin, (I)
Lindgren & Smith/41 Union Sq W #1228, New York, NY   212-929-5590
   Barbara Banthien, (I), Tom Bloom(I) Bradley Clark, (I), Cam
   DeLeon, (I), Regan Dunnick, (I), Cameron Eagel, (I), Michele
   Laporte, (I), Audrey Levine, (I), Richard Mantel, (I), Kathy
   O'Brien, (I), Michael Paraskevas, (I), Charles White, (I), Darryl
   Zudeck, (I)
Lindgren & Smith/484 W 43rd St #8R, New York, NY   212-594-7756
Locke, John Studios Inc/15 E 76th St, New York, NY   212-288-8010
   John Cayea, (I), John Clift, (I), Oscar DeMejo, (I), Jean-Pierre
   Desclozeaux, (I), Blair Drawson, (I), James Endicott, (I),
   Richard Erdoes, (I), Jean Michel Folon, (I), Michael Foreman,
   (I), Andre Francois, (I), George Giusti, (I), Edward Gorey, (I),
   Peter Lippman, (I), Sam Maitin, (I), Richard Oden, (I), William
   Bryan Park, (I), Colette Portal, (I), Fernando Puigrosado, (I),
   Hans-Georg Rauch, (I), Ronald Searle, (I), Tim, (I), Roland
   Topor, (I)
Longobardi, Gerard/5 W 19th St, New York, NY   212-255-3440
Loshe, Diane/10 W 18th St, New York, NY   212-691-9920
Lott, Peter & George/60 E 42nd St #411, New York, NY   212-953-7088
   Juan Barberis, (I), Ted Chambers, (I), Tony Cove, (I), Jim
   Dickerson, (I), David Halpern, (I), Ed Kurtzman, (I), Wendell
   McClintock, (I), Tim O'Brien, (I), Marie Peppard, (I), Joun Suh,
   (I), Steen Svenson, (P)
Lynch, Alan/155 Ave of Americas 10th Fl, New York, NY   212-255-6530
   Stephen Hall, (I), Jim Warren, (I)

M   Macfie, Jennifer/18 Bank St, New York, NY   212-206-0436
Madris, Stephen/445 E 77th St, New York, NY   212-744-6668
   Gary Perweiler, (I)
Manasse, Michele/1960 Broadway #2E, New York, NY   212-873-3797
   Sheldon Greenberg, (I), Narda Lepu, (I), Wallop Manyum, (I),
   Roger Roth, (I), John Segal, (I), Terry Widener, (I)
Mandell, Ilene/61 E 86th St, New York, NY   212-860-3148
Mann, Ken/20 W 46th St, New York, NY   212-944-2853
   Rebecca Blake, (P), Hashi, (P), Dicran Studio, (P)
Mann, Ronnie/141 E 88th St, New York, NY   212-860-4046
Marchesano, Frank/35 W 36th St, New York, NY   212-563-2730
Marek & Assoc Inc/160 Fifth Ave, New York, NY   212-924-6760
Marie, Diana Rose/38 E 19th St, New York, NY   212-477-5107
Marino, Frank/35 W 36th St, New York, NY *Bruno Benvenuti, (I)*   212-563-2730

Representatives
Continued

Please send us your additions and updates.

Mariucci, Marie A/32 W 39th St, New York, NY   212-944-9590
Marshall, Mel/40 W 77th St, New York, NY   212-877-3921
Mason, Kathy/101 W 18th St 4th Fl, New York, NY   212-675-3809
   Don Mason, (P)
Mathias, Cindy/7 E 14th St, New York, NY   212-741-3191
   Vittorio Sartor, (I)
Mattelson, Judy/, ,   212-684-2974
   Karen Kluglein, (I), Marvin Mattelson, (I), Gary Viskupic, (I)
Mautner, Jane/85 Fourth Ave, New York, NY   212-777-9024
   Kozlowski, (P)
Mayo, Vicki/425 E 86th St, New York, NY   212-722-7228
McKay, Colleen/229 E 5th St #2, New York, NY   212-598-0469
Meixler, Harriet/36 W 37th St, New York, NY   212-868-0078
   Susanne Buckler, (P)
Mendelsohn, Richard/353 W 53rd St #1W, New York, NY   212-682-2462
Mendola, Joseph/420 Lexington Ave #2911, New York, NY   212-986-5680
   Paul Alexander, (I), Robert Berran, (I), Jim Campbell, (I), Carl Cassler, (I), Deborah Chabrian, (I)Karen Chandler, (I), Gary Colby, (I), Jim Deneen, (I), Kenneth Dewey, (I), John Eggert, (I), Jon Ellis, (I), Peter Fiore, (I), Antonio Gabriele, (I), Hector Garrido, (I), Ted Giavis, (I), Elaine Gigniliat, (I), Dale Gustafson, (I), Chuck Hamrick, (I), Attila Hejja, (I), Dave Henderson, (I), Mitchell Hooks, (I), Paul Jennis, (I), Bob Jones, (I), Dave Kilmer, (I), Michael Koester, (I), Richard Leech, (I), Dennis Luzak, (I), Dennis Lyall, (I), Jeff Lynch, (I), Jeffrey Mangiat, (I), Lou Marchetti, (I), Edward Martinez, (I), Goeffrey McCormack, (I), Ann Meisel, (I), Roger Metcalf, (I), Ted Michner, (I), Mike Mikos, (I), Jonathon Milne, (I), Wally Neibart, (I), Chris Notarile, (I), Mort Rosenfeld, (I), Brian Sauriel, (I), David Schleinkofer, (I), Mark Schuler, (I), Mike Smollin, (I), John Solie, (I), Kip Solowedel, (I), Cliff Spohn, (I), Jeffrey Terreson, (I), Thierry Thompson, (I), Mark Watts, (I), Alan Welkis, (I), Ben Wohlberg, (I)
Mennemeyer, RAlph/286 Fifth Ave 4th Fl, NEw York, NY   212-279-2838
   Paul Christensen, (P), Katrina DeLeon, (P), Ted Morrison, (P)
Metz, Bernard/43 E 19th St, New York, NY   212-254-4996
Michael, Pamela/36 Riverside Dr, New York, NY   212-799-8281
Michalski, Ben/118 E 28th St, New York, NY   212-683-4025
Miller, Judith/20 E 35th St, New York, NY   212-213-1772
Miller, Susan/1641 Third Ave #29A, New York, NY   212-905-8400
   David Zimmerman, (P)
Mintz, Les/111 Wooster St #PH C, New York, NY   212-925-0491
   Bernard Bonhomme, (I), Robert Burger, (I), Hovik Dilakian, (I), Mark Fisher, (I), Amy Hill, (I), George Masi, (I), Kirsten Soderlind, (I), Tommy Soloski, (I), Kurt Vargo, (I), Josie Yee, (I), Dennis Ziemienski, (I)
Moll, Jonathan/41 E 28th St #2C, New York, NY   212-679-9074
Monomakhoff, Kathleen/304 E 20th St #7B, New York, NY   212-807-7703
Moretz, Eileen P/141 Wooster St, New York, NY   212-254-3766
   Charles Moretz, (P)
Morgan, Vicki Assoc/194 Third Ave, New York, NY   212-475-0440
   John Alcorn, (I), Stephen Alcorn, (I), Willardson + Assoc, (I), Ray Cruz, (I), Patty Dryden, (I), Sabina Fascione, (I), Vivienne Flesher, (I), Kathy & Joe Heiner, (I), Ward Schumacher, (I), Nancy Stahl, (I), Dahl Taylor, (I), Bruce Wolfe, (I), Wendy Wray, (I), Brian Zick, (I)
Morse, Lauren/78 Fifth Ave, New York, NY   212-807-1551
   Alan Zenreich, (P)
Moscato, Lynn/118-14 83rd Ave #5B, Kew Gardens, NY   718-805-0069
Mosel, Sue/310 E 46th St, New York, NY   212-599-1806
   Gerard Gentil, (P), Stan Shaffer, (P)
Moses, Janice/155 E 31st St #20H, New York, NY   212-951-4229
Moskowitz, Marion/342 Madison Ave #469, New York, NY   212-719-9879
   Dianne Bennett, (I), Diane Teske Harris, (I), Arnie Levin, (I), Geoffrey Moss, (I)
Moss, Eileen/333 E 49th St #3J, New York, NY   212-980-8061
   Bill Cigliano, (I), Tom Curry, (I), Mike Davis, (I), Dennis Gottlieb, (I), Robert Pizzo, (I), Scott Pollack, (I)
Moss, Susan/29 W 38th St, New York, NY   212-354-8024
   Louis Mervar, (P)
Muth, John/37 W 26th St, New York, NY   212-532-3479
   Pat Hill, (P)

NO

Napaer, Michele/349 W Broadway, New York, NY   212-219-0325
   Michael Abramson, (P)
Neail, Pamela R Assoc/27 Bleecker St, New York, NY   212-673-1600
   Sean Daly, (I), Dennis DiVincenzo, (I), Barbara Goodrich, (I), Thea Kliros, (I), Tony Mascio, (I), Cary McKiver, (I), Manuel Nunez, (I), Ryuji Otani, (I), Brenda Pepper, (I), Janet Recchia, (I), Linda Richards, (I), Gail Severance, (I), Glenn Tunstull, (I), Gaylord Welker, (I), Pat Zadnik, (I)
Newborn, Milton/135 E 54th St, New York, NY   212-421-0050
   Braldt Bralds, (I), Carol Gillot, (I), Robert Giusti, (I), Dick Hess, (I), Mark Hess, (I), Victor Juhasz, (I), Simms Taback, (I), David Wilcox, (I)
O'Rourke-Page Assoc/219 E 69th St #11G, New York, NY   212-772-0346
   Jonathan Exley, (P), Honolulu Crtv Grp, (P), Sam Haskins, (P), Robert Kligge, (P), Rob Van Petten, (P), Lincoln Potter, (P), Jim Raycroft, (P), Eric Schweikardt, (P), Smith/Garner, (P), William Sumner, (P), John Thornton, (P), John Zimmerman, (P)
Oye, Eva/307 E 44th St, New York, NY   212-286-9103
   Carlos Eguiguren, (P)

P

Palmer-Smith, Glenn Assoc/160 Fifth Ave, New York, NY   212-807-1855
   James Moore, (P), Charles Nesbitt, (P)
Penny & Stermer Group/48 W 21st St 9th Fl, New York, NY   212-243-4412
   Bob Alcorn, (I), Manos Angelakis, (I), Ron Becker, (I), Jane Clark, (I), Julian Graddon, (I), Rich Grote, (I), Michael Hostovich, (I), Michael Kanarek, (I), Andy Lackow, (I), Julia Noonan, (I), Deborah Bazzel Pogue, (I), Steve Shub, (I), Gary Smith, (I), Terry Walsh, (I), Page Wood, (I)
Perretti, Linda/420 Lexington Ave, New York, NY   212-687-7392
   Ken Tannenbaum, (P)
Petersen, Victoria/16 W 71st St, New York, NY   212-799-7021
   Neal McPheeters, (I)
Phyllis/38 E 19th St 8th Fl, New York, NY   212-475-3798
   John Weir, (P)
Pinkstaff, Marcia/222 Central Pk S, New York, NY   212-246-2300
Pritchett, Tom/330 W 4th St, New York, NY   212-688-1080
   Steve Durke, (I), Tom Evans, (I), George Parrish Jr, (I), George Kanelous, (I), Mike Robins, (I), Terry Ryan, (I)
Puhalski, Ron Inc/1133 Broadway #221, New York, NY   212-242-2860
   Alice Brock, (I), Harry Burman, (I), Ellis Chappell, (I), Peter Cunningham, (P), Dominick Finelle, (I), Tony Meers, (I), Leonard Morgan, (I), Vince Natale, (I), Joel Spector, (I), Paul Tankersley, (I), Marc Yankus, (I)
Pushpin Assoc/215 Park Ave S, New York, NY   212-674-8080
   Istvan Banyai, (I), Lou Beach, (I), Christopher Blumrich, (I), Seymour Chwast, (I), Jose Cruz, (I), Hiro Kimura, (I), R Kenton Nelson, (I), Roy Pendleton, (I), George Stavrinos, (I), Stanislaw Zagorski, (I)

QR

Quercia, Mat/78 Irving Pl, New York, NY   212-477-4491
Rapp, Gerald & Cullen Inc/108 E 35th St #1C, New York, NY   212-889-3337
   Ray Ameijide, (I), Michael Brown, (I), Lon Busch, (I), Ken Dallison, (I), Jack Davis, (I), Bill Delvin, (I), Bob Deschamps, (I), Ray Domingo, (I), Ginnie Hoffman, (I), Lionel Kalish, (I), Sharon Knettell, (I), Lee Lorenz, (I), Allan Mardon, (I), Elwyn Mehlman, (I), Marie Michal, (I), Alex Murawski, (I), Lou Myers, (I), Gary Overacre, (I), Bob Peters, (I), Jerry Pinkney, (I), Charles Santori, (I), Bob Tanenbaum, (I), Michael Witte, (I), Barry Zaid, (I)
Ray, Marlys/350 Central Pk W, New York, NY   212-222-7680
   Bill Ray, (P)
Reese, Kay Assoc/175 Fifth Ave #1304, New York, NY   212-598-4848
   Jonathan Atkin, (P), Lee Balterman, (P), Gerry Cranham, (P), Ashvin Gatha, (P), Lowell Georgia, (P), Peter Gullers, (P), Arno Hammacher, (P), Jay Leviton, (P), George Long, (P), George Love, (P), Jon Love, (P), Lynn Pelham, (P), Richard Saunders, (P), Milkie Studio, (P), T Tanuma, (P), Peter Treiber, (P)
Reid, Pamela/66 Crosby St, New York, NY   212-925-5909
   Madeleine Cofano(H), Thierry des Fontaines, (P), Mane/Christiane(S), Laura Mercier(MU) Bob Recine(H), Bert Stern, (P), Franck Thiery, (P)

RENARD, MADELINE/501 FIFTH AVE #1407, NEW YORK, NY (P 10-19)   212-490-2450
Guy Billout, (I), Steve Bjorkman, (I), Chas Wm Bush, (P), John Collier, (I), Etienne Delessert, (I), Bart Forbes, (I), Audra Geras, (I), Tim Girvin, (I), Lamb & Hall, (P), Miles Hardiman, (I), Personality Inc, (I), John Martin, (I), Richard Newton, (I), Al Pisano, (I), Robert Rodriguez, (I), Javier Romero, (I), Michael Schwab, (I), Jozef Sumichrast, (I), Kim Whitesides, (I)

Rep Rep/211 Thompson St, New York, NY   212-475-5911
Rob Fraser, (P), Marcus Tullis, (P)

Ridgeway, Karen/330 W 42nd St #3200NE, New York, NY   212-714-0147
Scott Bricher, (I), Marilyn Jones, (I), David Rickerd, (I), Ron Ridgeway, (I), Gordon Swenarton, (I)

Riley, Edward T Inc/81 Greene St, New York, NY   212-925-3053
Elliot Banfield, (I), Quentin Blake, (I), Zevi Blum, (I), William Bramhall, (I), CESC, (I), Chris DeMarest, (I), Paul Degen, (I), David Gothard, (I), Carolyn Gowdy, (I), Paul Hogarth, (I), Edward Koren, (I), Pierre Le-Tan, (I), Joseph Mathieu, (I), Paul Meisel, (I), Sara Midda, (I), Robert A Parker, (I), Jim Parkinson(L), Cheryl Peterson, (I), J J Sempe, (I), Brenda Shahinian, (I), Philippe Weisbecker, (I)

Rindner, Barbara/216 E 45th St, New York, NY   212-661-0850

Rivelli, Cynthia/303 Park Ave S, New York, NY   212-254-0990

Roman, Helen Assoc/140 West End Ave #9H, New York, NY   212-874-7074
William Cone, (I), Andrea Mistretta, (I), Anna Rich, (I)

Rosenberg, Arlene/200 E 16th St, New York, NY   212-289-7701

Rudoff, Stan/271 Madison Ave, New York, NY   212-679-8780
David Hamilton, (P), Gideon Lewin, (P)

S

S I International/43 East 19th St, New York, NY   212-254-4996
Karen Baumann, (I), Stephen Berger, (I), Bob Blas, (I), Jack Brusca, (I), Ernie Colon, (I), Richard Corben, (I), Richard Courtney, (I), Allen Davis, (I), Robert DeMichiell, (I), Walt DeRijk, (I), Enric, (I), Fernando Fernandez, (I), Robert Fine, (I), Don Gabriel, (I), Devis Grebu, (I), Steve Haefele, (I), Susi Kilgore, (I), Gaetano Liberatore, (I), Sergio Martinez, (I), Fred Marvin, (I), Mones-Mateu, (I), Joan Palaez, (I), Vince Perez, (I), Martin Rigo, (I), Doug Rosenthal, (I), Artie Ruiz, (I), Sanjulian, (I), Paul Tatore, (I), Bodhi Wind, (I), Kathy Wyatt, (I)

Sacramone & Valentine/302 W 12th St, New York, NY   212-929-0487
Stephen Ladner, (P), Tohru Nakamura, (P), John Pilgreen, (P), Robin Saidman, (P), Gianni Spinazzola, (P)

Samuels, Rosemary/200 W 20th St, New York, NY   212-477-3567
Beth Galton, (P)

Sander, Vicki/48 Gramercy Park North #3B, New York, NY   212-674-8161
Ed Gallucci, (P), George Menda, (P)

Sandler, Cathy/PO Box 3295, New York, NY   212-242-9087
Aaron Rapoport, (P)

Santa-Donato, Paul/25 W 39th St, New York, NY   212-921-1550

Scharak, Lisa/401 E 58th St #B-4, New York, NY   212-460-8067

Schecter Group, Ron Long/212 E 49th St, New York, NY   212-752-4400

Scher, Dotty/235 E 22nd St, New York, NY   212-841-2343

Schickler, Paul/135 E 50th St, New York, NY   212-355-1044

Schochat, Kevin R/221 W 21st St #1D, New York, NY   212-243-6229
Thom DeSanto, (P), Mark Ferri, (P), Bill Kramer, (P), Frank Moscati, (P)

Schon, Herb/1240 Lexington Ave, New York, NY   212-737-2945

Schub, Peter & Robert Bear/37 Beekman Pl, New York, NY   212-246-0679
Robert Freson, (P), Alexander Lieberman, (P), Irving Penn, (P), Rico Puhlmann, (P), Snowdon, (P), Albert Watson, (P)

Seigel, Fran/515 Madison Ave 22nd Fl, New York, NY   212-486-9644
Leslie Cabarga, (I), Cheryl Cooper, (I), Kinuko Craft, (I), Peter Cross, (I), Cathy Deeter, (I), Joe English, (I), Earl Keleny, (I), Michael Vernaglia, (I)

Shamilzadeh, Sol/1155 Broadway 3rd Fl, New York, NY   212-532-1977
Ryszard Horowitz, (P), The Strobe Studio, (P)

Shapiro, Elaine/369 Lexington Ave, New York, NY   212-867-8220

Sharlowe Assoc/275 Madison Ave, New York, NY   212-683-2822
Claus Eggers, (P), Nesti Mendoza, (P)

Sheer, Doug/29 John St, New York, NY *Karen Kent, (P)*   212-732-4216

Shepherd, Judith/186 E 64th St, New York, NY   212-838-3214
Barry Seidman, (P)

Siegel, Tema/461 Park Ave S 4th Fl, New York, NY   212-696-4680

Sigman, Joan/336 E 54th St, New York, NY   212-832-7980
Robert Goldstrom, (I), John H Howard, (I), Jeff Seaver, (I), James Tennison, (I)

Simon, Debra/164 W 21st St, New York, NY   212-988-8890
Uli Rose, (P)

Simoneau, Christine/PO Box 12541, New York, NY   212-696-2085

Sims, Jennifer/1150 Fifth Ave, New York, NY   212-860-3005
Clint Clemens, (P), Robert Latorre, (P)

Sjolin, Robert Nils/117 W 13th St, New York, NY   212-242-7238
Richard Brummett, (P)

Slocum, Linda/15 W 24th St 11th Fl, New York, NY   212-243-0649

Slome, Nancy/121 Madison Ave, New York, NY   212-685-8185
Joe Berger, (P), Dennis Galante, (P)

Smith, Emily/30 E 21st St, New York, NY   212-674-8383

Smith, Rita Assoc/1407 Broadway, New York, NY   212-730-0065

Solomon, Richard/121 Madison Ave, New York, NY   212-683-1362
Rick Brown, (I), Ray-Mel Cornelius, (I), Jack E. Davis, (I), Gary Kelley, (I), Elizabeth Koda-Callan, (I), Bill Nelson, (I), David Palladini, (I), C F Payne, (I), Rodica Prato, (I), Ian Ross, (I), Douglas Smith, (I), John Svoboda, (I), Shelley Thornton, (I)

Sonneville, Dane/PO Box 20415 Greeley Sta, New York, NY   212-603-9530
Leland Bobbe, (P), Jim Kinstrey, (I), John Pemberton, (P), Jamie Phillips, (P), Bob Shein, (I), Bill Truran, (P)

Stein, Jonathan & Assoc/353 E 77th St, New York, NY   212-517-3648
Mitch Epstein, (P), Burt Glinn, (P), Ernst Haas, (P), Nathaniel Lieberman, (P), Alex McLean, (P), Gregory Murphey, (P), Joel Sternfeld, (P), Jeffrey Zaruba, (P)

Steiner, Susan/130 E 18th St, New York, NY   212-673-4704

Stevens, Norma/1075 Park Ave, New York, NY   212-427-7235
Richard Avedon, (P)

Stockland, Bill/17 E 45th St, New York, NY   212-972-4747
Joel Baldwin, (P), Walter Iooss, (P), Eric Meola, (P), Michael Pruzan, (P)

Stogo, Donald/310 E 46th St, New York, NY   212-490-1034
Tom Grill, (P), John Lawlor, (P), Tom McCarthy, (P), Peter Vaeth, (P)

Stringer, Raymond/123 W 44th St #8F, New York, NY   212-840-2891
Ajin, (I)

Susse, Ed/56 W 22nd St 5th Fl, New York, NY   212-243-1126
Karl Zapp, (P)

T

Taborda, Carlos/344 E 85th St #1E, New York, NY   212-734-1903

Tanenbaum, Dennis/286 Fifth Ave 4th Fl, New York, NY   212-279-2838

Taylor, Nancy/153 E 57th St, New York, NY   212-223-0744

Terzis, Cornelia/448 W 37th St #88, New York, NY   212-929-5174

Thomas, Brenda & Assoc/127 W 79th St, New York, NY   212-873-7236

Tise, Katherine/200 E 78th St, New York, NY   212-570-9069
Raphael Boguslav, (I), John Burgoyne, (I), Bunny Carter, (I), Roberts & Van Heusen, (I), Judy Pelikan, (I), Cathleen Toelke, (I)

Tralongo, Katrin/144 W 27th St, New York, NY   212-255-1976
Mickey Kaufman, (P)

UV

Umlas, Barbara/131 E 93rd St, New York, NY   212-534-4008
Hunter Freeman, (P), Nora Scarlett, (P)

Van Arnam, Lewis/154 W 57th St, New York, NY   212-541-4787
Paul Amato, (P), Mike Reinhardt, (P)

Van Orden, Yvonne/119 W 57th St, New York, NY   212-265-1223
Joe Schneider, (P)

Vance, Joy/515 Broadway #2B, New York, NY   212-219-0808
Al Satterwhite, (P)

VisualWorks Inc/545 W 45th St, New York, NY   212-489-1717

Vitale, Marian/151 Lexington Ave #9A, NEw York, NY   211-683-4225

Vollbracht, Michelle/225 E 11th St, New York, NY   212-475-8718
Walter Wick, (P)

Von Schreiber, Barbara/315 Central Pk West, New York, NY   212-873-6594
Hiro, (P), Jean Pagliuso, (P), Neal Slavin, (P)

WYZ

Wasserman, Ted/310 Madison Ave, New York, NY   212-867-5360

Wayne, Philip/66 Madison Ave #9C, New York, NY   212-696-5215
Roberto Brosan, (P)

Weissberg, Elyse/299 Pearl St #5E, New York, NY 212-406-2566
    Jack Reznicki, (P)
Wheeler, Paul/50 W 29th St #11W, New York, NY 212-696-9832
    John Dominis, (P), Greg Edwards, (P), Foto Shuttle Japan, (P),
    Seth Joel, (P), John McGrail, (P), Joe McNally, (P), Michael
    Melford, (P), Aaron Rapoport, (P), Steven Smith, (P), Peter
    Tenzer, (P), Leroy Woodson, (P)
Williamson, Jack/16 W 22nd St, New York, NY 212-463-8302
    DiFranza Williamson, (P)
Winfield, Sharon/455 State St, Brooklyn, NY 212-668-0340
Yellen, Bert & Assoc/575 Madison Ave, New York, NY 212-481-7744
    Bill Connors, (P), Harvey Edwards, (P), Robert Farber, (P), Joe
    Francki, (P), Olaf Wahlund, (P)
Youngs, Maralee/318 E 39th St, New York, NY 212-679-8124
Zanetti, Lucy/36 E 20th St 3rd Fl, New York, NY 212-473-4999
Zitsman, Cookie/30 Magaw Pl #3A, New York, NY 212-928-6228
    Calvin Redmond, (P), Ken Rosenberg, (P), Ricardo Salas, (P)
Zlotnick, Jenny/14 Prince St, New York, NY 212-431-7680

Northeast

AB
Ackermann, Marjorie/2112 Goodwin Lane, North Wales, 215-646-1745
    PA H Mark Weidman, (P)
Art Source, The/444 Bedford Rd, Pleasantville, NY 914-747-2220
    James Barkley, (I), Karen Baumann, (I), Larry Bernette, (I),
    Paul Birling, (I), Vince Caputo, (I), Robert Cassila, (I), Betsy
    Feeney, (I), Scott Gladden, (I), Robert Lee, (I), Robert
    Marinelli, (I), Michael McGovern, (I), John Ramon, (I), Mary
    Rankin, (I), Richard Rockwell, (I), Harry Rosenbaum, (I),
    Jonathan Rosenbaum, (I)
Artco/227 Godfrey Rd, Weston, CT 203-222-8777
Artifacts Agency/368 Grove St, Glenrock, NJ 201-445-3635
Artists International/7 Dublin Hill Dr, Greenwich, CT 203-869-8010
Bancroft, Carol & Friends/185 Goodhill Rd, Weston, CT 203-226-7674
    Bill & Judy Anderson, (I), Yvette Banek, (I), Cal & Mary
    Bausman, (I), Wendy Biggins, (I), Kristine Bollinger, (I), Denise
    Brunkus, (I), Jim Cummins, (I), Susan Dodge, (I), Andrea
    Eberbach, (I), Marla Frazee, (I), Bob Giuliani, (I), Fred Harsh,
    (I), Ann Iosa, (I)
Bassett, Lisa/173 Walnut St, Brookline, MA 617-566-6012
Beckelman, Barbara/251 Greenwood Ave, Bethel, CT 203-797-8188
Beranbaum, Cheryl/118 Newbury St, Boston, MA 617-437-9459
Birenbaum, Molly/7 Williamsburg Dr, Cheshire, CT 203-272-9253
    Alice Coxe, (I), W E Duke, (I), Sean Kernan, (P), Joanne
    Schmaltz, (P), Paul Selwyn, (I), Bill Thomson, (I)
Black Silver & Lord/66 Union St, Belfast, ME 207-338-1113
Brewster, John/601 Riverside Ave, Westport, CT 203-226-4724
    Wendy Caporale, (I), Walter Einsel, (I), Jim Herity, (P), Dolph
    LeMoult, (I), Howard Munce, (I), Alan Neider, (I)
Breza, Susan/105 Prospect Ave, Langhorne, PA 215-752-7216
    Nessa Becker, (I), Ray Dallasta, (I), Sandi Glass, (I), Polly
    Lewis, (I), Tony Mascio, (I)
Brown, Jill/911 State St, Lancaster, PA 717-393-0918
    brt Photo Illustration, (P)

CD
Camp, Woodfin Inc/925 1/2 F St NW, Washington, DC 202-638-5705
Colucci, Lou/128 Broadway #106, Patterson, NJ 201-881-7618
Crawford, Janice/123 Minortown Rd, Woodbury, CT 212-722-4964
Creative Advantage Inc/707 Union St, Schenectady, NY 518-370-0312
    Jack Graber, (I), Richard Siciliano, (I)
D'Angelo, Victoria/309 Madison Ave, Reading, PA 215-921-8430
    Andy D'Angelo, (P)
DeBren, Alan/355 Pearl St, Burlington, VT 802-864-5916
    John Goodman, (P)
Donaldson, Selina/37 Hemlock, Arlington, MA 617-646-1687
Downzzyk, Maria/113 Arch St, Philadelphia, PA 215-238-0655

EG
Ella/229 Berkeley #52, Boston, MA 617-266-3858
    Lizi Boyd, (I), Wilbur Bullock, (I), Rob Cline, (I), Richard
    Cowdrey, (I), Jack Crompton, (I), Anna Davidian, (I), Susan
    Dodge, (I), Sharon Drinkwine, (I), Anatoly Dverin, (I), Scott

Gordley, (I), Eaton & Iwen, (I), Roger Leyonmark, (I), Janet
    Mager, (I), Radiomayonnaise, (I), Bruce Sanders, (I), Ron
    Toelke, (I)
Esto Photographics/222 Valley Pl, Mamaroneck, NY 914-698-4060
    Peter Aaron, (P), Dan Cornish, (P), Wolfgang Hoyt, (P), Max
    MacKenzie, (P), Peter Mauss, (P), Jock Pottle, (P)
Geng, Maud/25 Gary St, Boston, MA 617-236-1920
    Caroline Alterio, (I), Peter Barger, (I), John Curtis, (P), Vicki
    Smith, (I), John Svoboda, (I)
Giandomenico, Terry (Ms)/13 Fern Ave, Collingswood, NJ 609-854-2222
    Bob Giandomenico, (P)
Gidley, Fenton/43 Tokeneke Rd, Darien, CT 212-772-0846
Ginsberg, Michael/200 Croton Ave, Mt Kisco, NY 212-628-2379
Goldstein, Gwen/91 Hundreds Rd, Wellesley Hills, MA 617-235-8658
    Michael Blaser, (I), Cathy Diefendorf, (I), Steve Fuller, (I), Lane
    Gregory, (I), Terry Presnall, (I), Susan Spellman, (I), Gary
    Torrisi, (I), Joe Veno, (I)
Gordon, Leslie/15 North Rd, Northport, NY 212-772-0403
Graphics Guild/1342 Berkshire Ave, Springfield, MA 413-543-6796

HK
HK Portfolio/458 Newton Trpk, Weston, CT 203-454-4687
    Randy Chewning, (I), Carolyn Croll, (I), Eldon Doty, (I), Benton
    Mahan, (I), Jan Palmer, (I), Suzanne Richardson, (I), Sandra
    Speidel, (I), Susan Swan, (I), Barbara Todd, (I), Jean & Mou-
    sien Tseng, (I), George Ulrich, (I)
Haas, Ken/PO Box 86, Oley, PA 215-987-3711
    Peter Leach, (P), Emilie Snyder, (I), Jeff Zinggeler, (I)
Heisey, Betsy/109 Somerstown Rd, Ossining, NY 914-762-5335
    Whitney Lane, (P)
Hone, Claire/2130 Arch Street, Philadelphia, PA 215-568-5434
Hopkins, Nanette/PO Box 323, Haverford, PA 215-431-3240
    Rick Davis, (P)
Hubbell, Marian/99 East Elm St, Greenwich, CT 203-629-9629
Kanefield, Andrew/14 Northgate Pk, West Newton, MA 617-965-3557
    Christopher Cunningham, (P), William Hubner, (P), Lewis
    Portnoy, (P), Lewis Portnoy, (P)
Kendy/Benser/Noble/2313 Maryland Ave, Baltimore, MD 601-235-5235
Kurlansky, Sharon/192 Southville Rd, Southborough, MA 617-872-4549
    Steve Alexander, (I), Colleen, (I), Charles Freeman, (I), Judy
    Gailen, (I), John Gamache, (I), Susan Hanson, (I), Peter Harris,
    (I), Terry Van Heusen, (I), Geoffrey Hodgkinson, (I), Mark Kelly,
    (I), Dorthea Sierra, (I)

LM
Labonty, Deborah/PO Box 7446, Lancaster, PA 717-872-8198
    Tim Schoon, (P)
Lenar, Loci/17 Central Ave, Mine Hill, NJ 201-989-0934
Lipman, Deborah/506 Windsor Dr, Framingham, MA 617-451-6528
    Mark Fisher, (I), Richard A. Goldberg, (I), James Hanlon, (I),
    Richard M. Joachim, (I), Armen Kojoyian, (I), Carol LaCourse,
    (I), Katherine Mahoney, (I), Susan Smith, (I), Karen Watson, (I)
Mattelson Assoc/37 Cary Rd, Great Neck, NY 212-684-2974
    Brian Bailey, (I), Karen Kluglein, (I), Marvin Mattelson, (I), Gary
    Viskupic, (I)
Mattie, Gary/2016 Walnut St, Philadelphia, PA 215-972-1543
McNamara, Paula B/182 Broad St, Wethersfield, CT 203-563-6159
    Jack McConnell, (P)
Metzger, Rick/186 South St, Boston, MA 617-426-2290
    Steve Grohe, (P)
Montreal Crtv Consrtm/1155 Dorchester W #1520, Montreal 514-875-5426
More, Sherry/3016 Dumbarton #11 NW, Washington, DC
Morgan, Wendy/5 Logan Hill Rd, Northport, NY 516-757-5609
    Scott Gordley, (I), Fred Labitzke, (I), Don Landwehrle, (P),
    Preston Lyon, (P), Al Margolis, (I), ParaShoot, (P), David
    Rankin, (I), Fred Schrier, (I), Art Szabo, (P), David Wilder, (P)
Murphy, Brenda/20 High Rock St, Westwood, MA 617-329-2245
    Jeanne Abboud, (I), Cheryl Cicha, (I), George Courage, (I),
    Walter Fournier, (I), Howie Green, (I), Joshua Hayes, (I), Mark
    Jenkins, (I), Loretta Krupinski, (I), Diane Kunic, (I), Stanley
    Roberts, (I), Mark Seppala, (A), Catherine Severin, (I), Rich
    Sullivan, (C)

OP
Oreman, Linda/15 Atkinson St, Rochester, NY 716-232-1585

Representatives
Continued

Please send us your additions and updates.

Nick Angello, (I), Jim & Phil Bliss, (I), Roger DeMuth, (I), Jeff Feinen, (I), Bill Finewood, (I), Doug Gray, (I), Stephen Moscowitz, (I), Vicki Wehrman, (I)

Palulian, Joanne/18 McKinley St, Rowayton, CT   203-866-3734
M John English, (I), Bonnie Hofkin, (I), David Lesh, (I), Kirk Moldoff, (I), Dickran Palulian, (I)

Publishers Graphics/251 Greenwood Ave, Bethel, CT   203-797-8188
Paul Harvey, (I)

Putscher, Tony/2303 Green St, Philadelphia, PA   215-569-8890

R
Radxevich Standke/15 Intervale Terr, Reading, MA   617-944-3166
Christian Delbert, (P)

Reese-Gibson, Jean/4 Puritan Rd, N Beverly, MA   617-927-5006

Resources/511 Broadway, Saratoga Springs, NY   518-587-4730
Russell Ley, (P), Larry Van Valkenburg, (P)

Riley, Catherine/45 Circle Dr, Hastings 0n Hudson, NY   914-478-4377
Jon Riley, (P)

Robbins, David Group/256 Arch Rd, Avon, CT   203-673-6530
Mike Eagle, (I)

Rotella, Robert/88 Beacon Hill Dr, Holland, PA   215-968-3696
Abbott, Jim, (P), Michael LaRiche, (P)

S
Satterthwaite, Victoria/115 Arch St, Philadelphia, PA   215-925-4233
Michael Furman, (P)

Sequis Ltd/PO Box 398, Stevenson, MD   301-467-7300
Jeremy Green, (P)

Shulman, Carol/6182 Chinquapin Pkwy, Baltimore, MD   301-323-8645

Smith, Russell/65 Washington St, S Norwalk, CT   203-866-8871
Gordon Smith, (P)

Smith, Wayne R/145 South St Penthouse, Boston, MA   617-426-7262
Robert Brooks, (I), John Holt, (I), Ben Luce, (I), Ed Porzio, (I)

Snitzel, Gary/1060 Durham Rd, Pineville, PA   215-598-0214

Snyder, Diane/3 Underwood Rd, Wyncote, PA   215-572-1192
Craig Bakley, (I), Gordon Kibbee, (I), Michael McNelly, (I), Verlin Miller, (I), Shelly Roseman, (P), Lee Wojnar, (P)

Spiak, Al/35 Monroe Ave, Dumont, NJ   201-387-9395

Stemrich, J David/612 N 12th St, Allentown, PA   215-776-0825
Mark Bray, (I), Kevin Bubbenmoyer, (P), Bob Hahn, (P), Montieth Studio, (P)

Stoller, Erica/222 Valley Pl, Mamaroneck, NY   914-698-4060

Sweeny, Susan/425 Fairfield Ave, Stamford, CT

TUV
Ternay, Louise/119 Birch Ave, Bala Cynwyd, PA   215-667-8626
Vince Cuccinotta, (I), Don Everhart, (I), Greg Purdon, (I), Peter Sasten, (G), Bill Ternay, (I), Victor Valla, (I)

Turner, Ward/1342 Berkshire Ave, Springfield, MA   413-543-6796
Roc Goudreau, (I), Linda Schiwall-Gallo, (I), Frederick Schneider, (I)

Unicorn/1148 Parsippany Blvd, Parsippany, NJ   201-334-0353
Greg Hildebrandt, (I)

Valen Assocs/PO Box 8, Westport, CT   203-227-7806
Chas Adams, (I), George Booth, (C), Whitney Darrow, (C), Eldon Dedini, (I), Joe Farris, (C), William Hamilton, (C), Stan Hunt, (C), Anatol Kovarsky, (I), Henry Martin, (C), Warren Miller, (I), Frank Modell, (C), Mischa Richter, (C), Charles Saxon, (C), Jim Stevenson, (C), Henry Syverson, (C), Bob Weber, (C), Gahan Wilson, (I), Rowland Wilson, (I), Bill Woodman, (I), Bill Ziegler, (I)

WZ
Wasco, Sonya/PO Box 317, Lititz, PA

Waterman, Laurie/130 South 17th St, Philadelphia, PA   215-988-0390

Watterson, Libby/PO Box 1575/Lincoln City Rd, Lakeville, CT   212-696-1461
Karen Leeds, (P)

Wayne, Lynn/99 Wilson Ave, Windsor, CT   203-522-3143

Weisbrot, Eric/145 Claudy Ln, New Hyde Pk, NY   212-254-5553

Wigon, Leslie/191 Plymouth Dr, Scarsdale, NY   914-472-9459

Wolfe, Deborah Ltd/731 North 24th St, Philadelphia, PA   215-232-6666
Skip Baker, (I), Steve Cusano, (I), Jeff FitzMaurice, (I), Robin Hotchkiss, (I), Eric Joyner, (I), Ron Lehew, (I), Bill Margerin, (I), Bob Schenker, (I), Jas Szygiel, (I), Meryl Treatner, (I), Charles Weckler, (P), Frank Williams, (I)

Worrall, Dave/2107 Chancellor St, Philadelphia, PA   215-567-2881

Weaver Lilley, (P)

Worthington, Diane/372 Marlborough St, Boston, MA   617-247-284/
Kurt Stier, (P)

Zellner, Robin/54 Applecross Cir, Chalfont, PA   215-822-8258
Charles Callahan, (P)

Southeast

ABC
Ad Artist SE/1424 N Tryon, Charlotte, NC   704-372-6007

Aldridge, Donna/755 Virginia Ave, Atlanta, GA   404-872-7980
Thomas Gonzalez, (I), Chris Lewis, (I), Marcia Wetzel, (I)

And Associates/573 Hill St, Athens, GA   404-353-8479
Dan McClure, (P), Dennis O'Kain, (P), Elaine H Rabon, (I), Drake White, (P)

Art Group, The/5856 Faringdon Pl, Raleigh, NC   919-876-6765

Beck, Susanne/2721 Cherokee Rd, Birmingham, AL   205-871-6632
Charles Beck, (P)

Burnett, Yolanda/559 Dutch Vall Rd, Atlanta, GA   404-874-0956
Jim Copland, (P), Charlie Lathem, (P)

Couch, Tom/1164 Briarcliff Rd NE #2, Atlanta, GA   404-872-5774
Granberry/Anderson Studio, (P)

FGH
Folio Five/30 S Park Sq #222, Marrietta, GA   404-424-0811

Forbes, Pat/11459 Waterview Cluster, Reston, VA   703-437-7042
Kay Chenush, (P)

Green, Cindy/280 Elizabeth St #A-105, Atlanta, GA   404-525-1333

Hathcox, Julia/5730 Arlington Blvd, Arlington, VA   703-845-5831
David Hathcox, (P)

JKL
Jett & Assoc/600 E Main St, Louisville, KY   502-561-0737
Mark Cable, (I), Cynthia Torp, (I)

Jourdan, Carolyn/520 Brickell Key Dr #1417, Miami, FL   305-372-9425

Judge, Marie/9452 SW 77th Ave, Miami, Fl33156   305-595-1700

Kohler, Chris/1105 Peachtree St, Atlanta, GA   404-876-1223

Linden, Tamara/919 Lenox Hill Ct, Atlanta, GA   404-262-1209
Tom Fleck, (I), Joe Ovies, (I), Charles Passarelli, (I), Larry Tople, (I)

MP
McGee, Linda/1816 Briarwood Ind Ct, Atlanta, GA   404-633-1286

McLean Represents/100 Colony SW #305, Atlanta, GA   404-881-6627
Joe Isom, (I), Jack Jones, (I), Martin Pate, (I), Steve Spetseris, (I), Warren Weber, (I)

Peters, Barbara/2217 Cypress Island Dr #205, Pompano Beach, FL   212-777-6384
Jacques Dirand, (P), Lizzie Himmel, (P)

Phelps, Catherine/3210 Peachtree Rd NE, Atlanta, GA   404-264-0264
Tom McCarthy, (P), Tommy Thompson, (P), Bill Weems, (P)

Pitt, Karen/503 Emory Circle, Atlanta, GA   404-378-0694

Pollard, Kiki/848 Greenwood Ave NE, Atlanta, GA   404-875-1363
Betsy Alexander, (G), John Findley, (I), Dennis Guthrie, (I), James Soukup, (I), Mark Stanton, (I)

Prentice, Nancy/315-A Pharr Rd, Atlanta, GA   404-266-9707

Propst, Sheryle/PO Box 1583, Norcross, GA   404-263-9296
Fred Gerlich, (P), Herring & Klem, (I), Reggie Stanton, (I),

ST
Silva, Naomi/2161 Peachtree St NE #502, Atlanta, GA   404-355-2160
Daryl Cagle, (C), Tom Cain, (I), Kevin Hamilton, (I), Rob Horn, (L), Cyd Moore, (I), Mike Moore, (I), Rick Paller, (I), Alan Patton, (I), Gary Penca, (I), Don Sparks, (I)

Silver Image/5128 NW 58th Ct, Gainesville, FL   904-373-5771

Sumpter, Will/1106 W Peachtree St #106, Atlanta, GA   404-874-2014
Flip Chalfant, (P)

Torres, Martha/927 Third St, New Orleans, LA   504-895-6570
Glade Bilby II, (P)

W
Wells, Susan/5134 Timber Trail, Atlanta, GA   404-255-1430
Paul Blakey, (I), Jim Caraway, (I), Don Loehle, (I), Richard Loehle, (I), Randall McKissick, (I), Monte Varah, (I), Beth White, (I)

Wexler, Marsha Brown/6108 Franklin Pk Rd, McLean, VA   703-241-1776

Williams, Phillip/1106 W Peachtree St #201, Atlanta, GA   404-873-2287

Representatives
Continued

Please send us your additions and updates.

Jamie Cook, (P), Chipp Jamison, (P), Rick Lovell, (I), Kenvin Lyman, (G), Bill Mayer, (I), David McKelvey, (I), John Robinette, (I)

Wooden/Grubbs & Bate/1151 W Peachtree St NW, Atlanta, GA   404-892-6303
  Johnna Hogenkamp, (I), Charlie Mitchell, (I), Theo Rudnak, (I)

Midwest

AB

Altman, Elizabeth/820 N Franklin St, Chicago, IL   312-266-8661
Art Staff Inc/1463 Premier, Troy, MI   313-649-8630
  John Arvan, (I), Joy Brosious, (I), Ralph Brunke, (I), Ricardo Capraro, (I), Larry Cory, (I), Caryl Cunningham, (I), Sheryl DeMorris, (I), Brian Foley, (I), Dennis Goldsworthy, (I), Jim Gutheil, (I), Vicki Hayes, (I), Jim Hodge, (I), Ben Jaroslaw, (I), Dan Kistler, (I), Baron Lesperance, (I), John Martin, (I), Dick Meissner, (I), Heidi Meissner, (I), Dick Miller, (I), Jerry Monteleon, (I), Linda Nagle, (I), Colin Payne, (I), Jeff Ridky, (I), Al Schrank, (I), Jim Slater, (I), Chris Szetela, (I), Ken Taylor, (I), Alan Wilson, (I)
Ball, John/203 N Wabash, Chicago, IL   312-332-6041
Baron, Mary/2238 N Burling, Chicago, IL   312-528-5046
Bartels, Ceci Assoc/1913 Park, St Louis, MO   314-241-4014
  Eric Dinyer, (I), Mark Fredrickson, (I), Shannon Kriegshauser, (I), Don Kueker, (I), Greg MacNair, (I), Jean Probert, (I), Terry Sirrell, (I), Terry Speer, (I), Fran Vuksanovich, (I), Tony Wade, (I)
Berk, Ida/1350 N La Salle, Chicago, IL   312-944-1339
Bernstein, Joanie/433 Thomas Ave, Minneapolis, MN   612-374-3169
Bonnen, Ed/444 Lentz Ct, Lansing, MI   517-371-3086
Bouret, Louise/208 W Kinzie St, Chicago, IL   312-467-1430
  Shanoor Photo, (P)
Bradley, Francie/7630 N Euclid, Gladstone, MO   816-436-7130
Brenna, Allen/Southgate Plaza, #515, Minneapolis   MN
  612-835-1831
Brenner, Harriet/2147 W Augusta Blvd, Chicago, IL   312-384-0008
  Dick Krueger, (P)
Brooks & Assoc/855 W Blackhawk St, Chicago, IL   312-642-3208
  Nancy Brown, (P), VanKirk Photo, (P)
Bussler, Tom/19 E Pearson #410, Chicago, IL   312-944-3837
  Sid Evans, (P)

CD

Carr, Ken/4715 N Ronald St, Harwood Heights, IL   312-867-5445
Christell, Jim & Assoc/307 N Michigan Ave #1008, Chicago, IL   312-236-2396
  Michel Ditlove, (P), Ron Harris, (P)
Clift, Susan/535 N Michigan #1808, Chicago, IL   312-670-2150
Coleman, Woody/490 Rockside Rd, Cleveland, OH   216-661-4222
  Jeffrey Bedrick, (I), Stuart Daniels, (I), Vladimir Kordic, (I), John Letostak, (I), David Moses, (I), Ernest Norcia, (I), Bob Novack, (I), Ezra Tucker, (I), Tom Utley, (I)
Commercial Images Group/15339 Center St, Harvey, IL   312-333-1047
Daguanno, Donna/211 E Ohio #621, Chicago, IL   312-644-0172
  Chris Hawker, (P)
DeWalt & Assoc/210 E Michigan St #203, Milwaukee, WI   414-276-7990
  Tom Fritz, (P), Don Glassford, (I), Mary Gordon, (G), Dennis Matz, (I), Tom Redman, (I)
Demunnik, Jack/Twin Springs Farms, Durango, IA   319-588-3019
Dodge, Tim/2412 E Stratford Ct, Milwaukee, WI   414-964-9558
  Barbara Ericksen, (I), Jeff Hangartner, (I), Ken Hanson, (G), Paul Henning, (I), Tom Kwas, (P), Dave Vander Veen, (P)
Dolby, Karen/215 W Ohio 5th Fl, Chicago, IL   312-321-1770
  Charly Palmer, (I), Paul Ristau, (I)

EF

Edsey, Steve/520 N Michigan Ave #736, Chicago, IL   312-943-1865
Emerich Studios/300 W 19th Terrace, Kansas City, MO   816-474-8888
Erdos, Kitty/210 W Chicago, Chicago, IL   312-787-4976
Fazio, Peter/617 W Fulton St, Chicago, IL   312-845-9650
Feldman, Kenneth/1821 N Dayton, Chicago, IL   312-337-0447
Fiat, Randi/612 N Michigan, Chicago, IL   312-784-2343
  Marc Hauser, (E)
Fleming, Laird Tyler/1 Memorial Dr, St Louis, MO   314-982-1700
  Willardson + Assoc, (P), John Bilecky, (P)

Fried, Monica/1546 N Orleans, Chicago, IL   312-642-8715
Frost, Brent & Laumer, Dick/4037 Queen Ave S, Minneapolis, MN   612-922-3440

GH

Graphic Access/444 N Wells St, Chicago, IL   312-222-0087
Hanson, Jim/540 N Lake Shore Dr, Chicago, IL   312-527-1114
  Bob Bender, (P), Richard Fegley, (P), Bob Gelberg, (P), Rob Johns, (P), Rick Mitchell, (P), Barry O'Rourke, (P), John Payne, (P), Al Satterwhite, (P)
Harlib, Joel/405 N Wabash #3203, Chicago, IL   312-329-1370
  Bob August, (I), Nick Backes, (I), John Casado, (I), Esky Cook, (I), Lawrence Duke, (P), Peter Elliott, (P), Marty Evans, (P), Randy Glass, (I), Scott Harris, (I), Karel Havlicek, (I), Barbara Higgins-Bond, (I), DeWitt Jones, (P), Richard Leech, (I), Tim Lewis, (I), Peter Lloyd, (I), Bret Lopez, (P), David McMacken, (I), Joe Ovies, (I), Fred Pepera, (I), Matthew Rolston, (P), Todd Shorr, (I), Jay Silverman, (P), Robert Tyrrell, (I), Bill Vann, (I), Ron Villani, (I), Allan Weitz, (P), Kim Whitesides, (I), Bruce Wolfe, (I), Bob Ziering, (I)
Harmon, Ellen/332 S Cuyler, Oak Park, IL   312-524-9743
  Harry Przekop, (P)
Hartig, Michael/3620 Pacific, Omaha, NB   402-345-2164
Heinen, Sandy/219 N 2nd St #409, Minneapolis, MN   612-332-3671
Higa, Tracy/1560 N Sandburg Terr, chicago, IL   312-440-1284
Higgens Hegner Genovese Inc/510 N Dearborn St, Chicago, IL   312-644-1882
Hogan, Myrna & Assoc/333 N Michigan, Chicago, IL   312-372-1616
  Terry Heffernan, (P)
Holcepl, Robert/2479 W 11th St, Cleveland, OH   216-621-3838
  Roman Sapecki, (P), John Watt, (P)
Horton, Nancy/939 Sanborn, Palatine, IL   312-934-8966
Hull, Scott Assoc/68 E Franklin St, Dayton, OH   513-433-8383
  Mark Braught, (I), Tracy Britt, (I), Greg Dearth, (F), David Groff, (I), Julie Hodde, (I), Greg LaFever, (I), John Maggard, (I), Larry Martin, (I), Ted Pitts, (I), Mark Riedy, (I), David Sheldon, (I), Bob Thomas, (I), Don Vanderbeek, (I), Lee Woolery, (I)

JK

J/B Assoc/1156 W Grand, Chicago, IL   312-243-5423
Jenkins, John/1147 W Ohio #403, Chicago, IL   312-243-6580
Jeske, Kurt/612 S Clinton, Chicago, IL   312-922-9200
Jordano, Charles/2623 Rhodes, Troy, MI   313-528-0593
Kamin, Vince & Assoc/111 E Chestnut, Chicago, IL   312-787-8834
  Tom Berthiaume, (P), Dave Jordano, (P), Ron Lieberman, (I), Mary Anne Shea, (I), Roy Volkman, (P)
Kapes, Jack/233 E Wacker Dr #1412, Chicago, IL   312-565-0566
  Stuart Block, (P), John Cahoon, (P), Jerry Friedman, (P), Klaus Lucka, (P), Dan Romano, (I), Nicolas Sidjakov, (G), Francine Zaslow, (P)
Kezelis, Elena/215 W Illinois, Chicago, IL   312-644-7108
Koralik, Connie/6051 N Olympia, Chicago, IL   312-944-5680
  Kazu, (P), Robert Keeling, (P)

L

Lakehomer & Assoc/405 N Wabash #1402, Chicago, IL   312-644-1766
  Tim Schultz, (P)
Lasko, Pat/452 N Halsted, Chicago, IL   312-243-6696
  Ralph King, (P)
Lawrence, Morgan/317 10th St, Toledo, OH   419-255-5117
Levey, Rebecca/211 E Ohio #518, Chicago, IL   312-661-1561
Linzer, Jeff/4001 Forest Rd, Minneapolis, MN   612-926-4390
Lonier, Terry/215 W Ohio #5W, Chicago, IL   312-527-1880
Lukmann, Geri/314 W Institute Pl, Chicago, IL   312-787-1774
  Brent Carpenter, (P), Steve Nozicka, (P)

M

McGrath, Judy/612 N Michigan Ave 4th Fl, Chicago, IL   312-944-5116
McMasters, Deborah/157 W Ontario, Chicago, IL   312-943-9007
  Richard Foster, (P)
McNamara Associates/1250 Stephenson Hwy, Troy, MI   313-583-9200
  Max Alterruse, (I), Gary Ciccarelli, (I), Garry Colby, (I), Hank Kolodziej, (I), Chuck Passarelli, (I), Tony Randazzo, (I), Gary Richardson, (I), Dick Scullin, (I), Don Wieland, (I)
McNaughton, Toni/233 E Wacker #2904, Chicago, IL   312-938-2148
  Pam Haller, (P), Rodica Prato, (I), James B. Wood, (P)

Miller Services/45 Charles St E, Toronto ON — 416-925-4323

Miller, Richard/405 N Wabash #1204, Chicago, IL — 312-527-0444
  Paul Barton, (P), Morton Beebe, (P), Rebecca Blake, (P), Chris Butler, (I), Geoffrey Clifford, (P), Richard High, (C), Bob Krogle, (I), Jim Krogle, (I), Robert Sacco, (P)

Mohlman, Jeanette/114 W Illinois, Chicago, IL — 312-321-1570

Mohlo, David/ Werremeyer Inc/12837 Flushing Meadow Dr, St Louis, MO — 314-966-3770

Moore, Connie/1540 N North Park, Chicago, IL — 312-787-4422
  Richard Shirley, (I)

Morawski & Assoc/1550 E Nine Mile Rd, Ferndale, MI — 313-543-9440
  Tim Doyle, (P)

Moshier & Maloney/535 N Michigan, Chicago, IL — 312-943-1668
  Nicolette Anastas, (I), Dave Wilson & Assoc, (I), Steve Carr, (P), Dan Clyne, (I), Ron DiCianni, (I), David Gaadt, (I), John Hamagami, (I), Rick Johnson, (I), Bill Kastan, (I), Ed Lindlof, (I), Dennis Luzak, (I), Colleen Quinn, (I), Paul Ristau, (I), Stephen Rybka, (I), Skidmore-Sahratian, (I), Al Stine, (I), Jim Trusilo, (I), John Youssi, (I)

Murphy, Sally/70 W Hubbard, Chicago, IL — 312-346-0720

NO

Nagan, Rita/1514 NE Jefferson St, Minneapolis, MN — 612-788-7923

Neis, Judy Group/336 Lakeview Ln, Plainwell, MI — 616-685-1518
  Tom Bookwater, (I), Gary Eldridge, (I), Nancy Munger, (I), Dave Schweitzer, (I)

Nelson, Sandy/315 W Walton, Chicago, IL — 312-266-8029

Newman, Richard/1866 N Burling, Chicago, IL — 312-266-2513

Nicholson, Richard B/2310 Denison Ave, Cleveland, OH — 216-398-1494
  Martin Reuben, (P), Mike Steinberg, (P), Al Teufer, (P), J David Wilder, (P)

Nicolini, Sandra/230 N Michigan #523, Chicago, IL — 312-346-1648
  Elizabeth Ernst, (P), Tom Petroff, (P)

O'Brien-Stieber/203 N wabash #1600, Chicago, IL — 312-726-9690

O'Farrel, Eileen/311 Good Ave, Des Plaines, IL — 312-297-5447

O'Grady Advertising Arts/333 North Michigan Ave #2200, Chicago, IL — 312-726-9833

O'Neill, Mary/17006 Woodbury Ave, Cleveland, OH — 216-252-6238

Ores, Kathy/17302 Hawthorne Dr, E Hazelcrest, IL — 312-410-7139

Osler, Spike/2616 Industrial Row, Troy, MI — 313-280-0640
  Mark Coppos, (P), Madison Ford, (P), Rob Gage, (P), Rick Kasmier, (P), Jim Secreto, (P)

P

Peterson, Vicki/211 E Ohio, Chicago, IL — 312-467-0780
  Charlie Gold, (P), Elyse Lewin, (P), Howard Menken, (P), Robert Stevens, (P), Charlie Westerman, (P)

Phase II/155 N Michigan Ave, Chicago, IL — 312-565-0030
  Bill Cigliano, (I), David Krainik, (I), Kathy Petrauskas, (I)

Photo Services Owens-Corning/Fiberglass Towers, Toledo, OH — 419-248-8041
  Jay Langlois, (P), Joe Sharp, (P)

Platzer, Karen & Assoc/317 Webster #1, Chicago, IL — 312-467-1981
  Larry Banner, (P), Michael Caporale, (P), Ray Cioni, (I)

Pohn, Carol/2259 N Wayne, Chicago, IL — 312-348-0751
  Ron Amis, (I), Diane O'Quinn Burke, (I), Hedwig, (I), Carl Heinz, (I), Carl Leick, (I), Roger Marchultz, (P)

Pool, Linda/7216 E 99th St, Kansas City, MO — 816-761-7314
  Michael Radencich, (P)

Potts, Carolyn/3 E Ontario #25, Chicago, IL — 312-935-1707
  Karen Bell, (I), Barbara Bersell, (P), John Craig, (I), Alan Dolgins, (P), Gregory Murphey, (P), Fred Nelson, (P), Joe Ovies, (I), Kulp Productions, (P), Leslie Wolf, (I)

Potts, Vicki/2000 N Racine #3700, Chicago, IL — 312-248-3909
  Mitchell Einhorn, (P), Mercer Engelhard, (P), David Gerhardt, (P), Kathy Sanders, (P)

Pride, Max/401 W Superior, Chicago, IL — 312-664-5392

R

Rabin, Bill & Assoc/666 N Lake Shore Dr, Chicago, IL — 312-944-6655
  John Alcorn, (I), Joel Baldwin, (P), Joe Baraban, (P), Roger Beerworth, (I), Guy Billout, (I), Howard Bjornson, (P), Thomas Blackshear, (I), R O Blechman, (I), Charles William Bush, (P), JoAnn Carney, (P), John Collier, (I), Jackie Geyer, (I), Paul Giovanopoulos, (I), Tim Girvin, (G), Robert Giusti, (I), Kunio Hagio, (I), Lamb & Hall, (P), Mark Hess, (I), Richard Hess, (I), Walter Ioss, (I), Art Kane, (P), Rudi Legname, (P), Daniel Maffia, (I), Jay Maisel, (P), Dan Malinowski, (P), Jim Matusik, (P), Eric Meola, (P), Eugene Mihaesco, (I), Richard Noble, (P), Robert Rodriguez, (I), Reynold Ruffins, (I), Michael Shwab, (I), Ed Sorel, (I), George Stavrinos, (I), Simms Taback, (I), Ezra Tucker, (I), Pete Turner, (P), David Wilcox, (I)

Ray, Rodney/455 St James Pl, Chicago, IL — 312-222-0337
  David Beck, (I), Ken Goldammer, (I)

Remien, Tami/441 E Erie #1612, Chicago, IL — 312-944-6416
  Joe DeNatale, (P)

Ritchey, Deborah/920 N Franklin #202, Chicago, IL — 312-642-5763

S

Scarff, Signe/22 W Erie, Chicago, IL — 312-266-8352
  Larry Kolze, (P)

Schofield/Trenbeth Assoc/10 E Ontario Pl #1612, Chicago, IL — 312-642-4599

Sell, Dan/233 E Wacker, Chicago, IL — 312-565-2701
  Alvin Blick, (I), Paul Bond, (I), Wayne Carey, (I), Justin Carroll, (I), Bobbye Cochran, (I), Wil Cormier, (I), Bill Ersland, (I), Rick Farrell, (I), Dick Flood, (I), Bill Harrison, (I), Jay, (I), Dave LaFleur, (I), Gregory Manchess, (I), Bill Mayer, (I), Frank Morris, (I), Tim Raglin, (I), Ian Ross, (I), Mark Schuler, (I), R J Shay, (I), Jay Songero, (I), Dale Verzaal, (I), Fran Vuksanovich, (I), Phil Wendy, (I), John Zielinski, (I)

Shulman, Salo/215 W Ohio, Chicago, IL — 312-337-3245
  Stan Stansfield, (P)

Sims, Mel/233 E Wacker Dr #4304, Chicago, IL — 312-938-8937

Sinclair, Valerie/77 Florence St #301, Toronto, ON — 416-588-1527
  John Martin, (P), James Toogan, (I)

Skillicorn, Roy/233 E Wacker #29031, Chicago, IL — 312-856-1626
  Wickart Brothers, (I), Tom Curry, (I), David Scanlon, (I)

Snowberger, Ann/3312 W Belle Plaine, Chicago, IL — 312-463-3590
  Tim Bieber, (P)

Sparka, David/2233 Kemper Ln, Cincinnati, OH — 513-861-1400

T

Timon, Clay & Assoc Inc/540 N Lake Shore Dr, Chicago, IL — 312-527-1114
  Bob Bender, (P), Michael Fletcher, (P), Larry Dale Gordon, (P), Don Klumpp, (P), Chuck Kuhn, (P), Barry O'Rourke, (P), Al Satterwhite, (P), Michael Slaughter, (P)

Trembeth, Rich/30 E Huron #4904, Chicago, IL — 312-727-1096

Trinko, Genny/126 W Kinzie St, Chicago, IL — 312-222-9242
  Cam Chapman, (P)

Trott, David/32588 Dequiendre, Warren, MI — 313-978-8932

Tuke, Joni/368 W Huron, Chicago, IL — 312-787-6826
  Jay Ahrend, (P), David Beck, (I), Dan Blanchette, (I), Chris Hopkins, (I), Susan Kindst, (P), Brian Otto, (I), John Welzenbach, (P), Ken Westphal, (I)

VWYZ

Virnig, Janet/3308 Girard Ave S, Minneapolis, MN — 612-822-6444

Wainman, Rick & Assoc/166 E Superior #212, Chicago, IL — 312-337-3960

Yunker, Kit/ Allchin, Scott/1335 N Wells St, Chicago, IL — 312-321-0655

Zann, Sheila/502 N Grove, Oak Park, IL — 312-386-2864
  Arnold Zann, (P)

Southwest

AB

Art Rep Inc/2801 W Lemmon #305, Dallas, TX — 214-521-5156
  Tom Bailey, (I), Lee Lee Brazeal, (I), Ellis Chappell, (I), Dean St Clair, (I), Tom Curry, (I), M John English, (I), Tom Evans, (I), Tim Girvin, (I), Bill Harrison, (I), Jim Jacobs, (I), Kent Kirkley, (P), Gary McCoy, (P), Genevieve Meek, (I), Frank Morris, (I), Michael Schwab, (I), Andrew Vracin, (P), Kim Whitesides, (I), Terry Widener, (I)

Assid, Carol/122 Parkhouse, Dallas, TX — 214-748-3765

Booster, Barbara/3910 Buena Vista #10, Dallas, TX — 214-559-3640

Boston, Belinda/PO Box 821095, Dallas, TX — 214-821-3042
  Kenneth Huey, (I)

Bozeman, Debbie/PO Box 147152, Dallas, TX — 214-526-3317

CD

Callahan, Joe/330 E Mitchell, Phoenix, AZ — 602-954-0224
  Tom Gerczynski, (P), Mike Gushock, (I), Jon Kleber, (I),

Representatives
Continued

Please send us your additions and updates.

Howard Post, (I), Dan Ruiz, (I), Mark Sharpls, (I), Dan Vermillion, (P), Balfour Walker, (P)

Campbell, Pamela/1821 W Alabama, Houston, TX	713-523-5328
Campbell, Patty/2610 Catherine, Dallas, TX	214-946-6597

Douglas Doering, (P)

Cobb & Friend/2811 McKinney #224, Dallas, TX	214-855-0055

Kent Barker, (P), Greg Bates, (I), Cathie Bleck, (I), Michael Johnson, (P), David Kampa, (I), Margaret Kasahara, (I), Geof Kern, (P), Mercedes McDonald, (I), Michael McGar, (I), Dennis Murphy, (P), R Kenton Nelson, (I), Steve Pietzsch, (I), Tom Ryan, (P), Jim Sims, (P), James N Smith, (I), James Tennison, (I), Michele Warner, (I), Ken Westphal, (I), Neill Whitlock, (P)

Crowder, Bob/4404 Main St, Dallas, TX	214-823-9000

Barry Kaplan, (P), Moses Olmoz, (P), Al Rubin, (P)

DiOrio, Diana/1819 Augusta Ct #148, Houston, TX	713-266-9390

John Collier, (I), Ray Mel Cornelius, (I), Regan Dunnick, (I), Larry Keith, (I), Bahid Marinfar, (I), Dennis Mukai, (I), Thom Ricks, (I)

EFH

Edwards, Nancy/2121 Regency Dr, Irving, TX	214-438-4114
Freeman, Sandra/3030 McKinney #1706, Dallas, TX	214-871-1956
Fuller, Alyson/5610 Maple Ave, Dallas, TX	214-688-1855
Hamilton, Chris/3900 Lemmon, Dallas, TX	214-526-2050

KLM

Klein, Sandy/637 Hawthorn, Houston, TX	713-522-1862
Lewis, Max/5545 Skelly Dr, Tulsa, OK	918-663-1308
Lynch, Larry/3527 Oak Lawn Ave #122, Dallas, TX	214-521-6169

Morton Beebe, (P), Robert Latorre, (P), Richard Wahlstrom, (P)

McCann, Liz/3000 Carlisle #206, Dallas, TX	214-630-7756

Bill Crumpt, (P), Michael Doret, (I), Ben James, (I), Phil Kretchmar, (P), James B. Wood, (P)

NPS

Noble, Peter/8344 East RL Thornton , Dallas, TX	214-328-6676
Photocom Inc/1707 S Ervay, Dallas, TX	214-428-8781

Robb Depenport, (P), Bart Forbes, (I), Andy Post, (P), Louis Reens, (P), Michael Steirnagle, (I), Kelly Stribling, (I), Richard Wahlstrom, (P), Gordon Willis, (P)

Production Services/1711 Hazard, Houston, TX	713-529-7916

George Craig, (P), C Bryan Jones, (P), Thaine Manske, (P)

Simpson, Elizabeth/415 N Bishop Ave, Dallas, TX	214-943-9355
Spiegal, Melanie/2412 Converse, Dallas, TX	214-428-8781

TW

Traylor, Janet/329 W Vernon Ave, Phoenix, AZ	602-254-8232

Libba Tracey, (I), Liz kenyon, (I)

Washington, Dick/914 Westmoreland, San Antonio, TX	512-342-2009

Rick Kroninger, (P), Reuben Njaa, (P)

Whalen, Judy/5551 Vanderbilt, Dallas, TX	214-630-8977
Willard, Paul Assoc/815 North First Ave #3, Phoenix, AZ	602-257-0097

Kevin Cruff, (P), Matthew Foster, (I), Rick Gayle, (P), Rick Kirkman, (I), Kevin MacPherson, (I), Curtis Parker, (I), Nancy Pendleton, (I), Bob Peters, (I), Roy & Peggy Roberts, (I), Norma Samuelson, (I), Wayne Watford, (I), Jean Wong, (I)

Rocky Mountain

FGK

Foremark Studios/PO Box 10346, Reno, NV	702-786-3150
Garrett, Ann/1100 Acoma, Denver, CO	303-893-1199
Goodman, Christine/1869 S Pearl St #201, Denver, CO	303-298-7085

Bill Koropp, (P), David X Tejada, (P), Geoffrey Wheeler, (P)

Guenzi, Carol/130 Pearl St #1602, Denver, CO	303-733-0128
Kelly, Rob/3113 E 3rd St #220, Denver, CO	303-399-3851

Pat Fujisaki, (I), Ron Sauter, (I)

MN

Marshall, Radonna/3955 E Exposition Ave , Denver, CO	303-744-8877
No Coast Graphics/2629 18th St, Denver, CO	303-458-7086

John Cuneo, (I), Cindy Enright, (I), Tom Nikosey, (I), Chris F Payne, (I), Jim Salvati, (I), Mike Steirnagle, (I)

RS

Roberts, Hallie/16 W 13th Ave, Denver, CO	303-534-7267
Sperling, Alice/1050 Corona #307, Denver, CO	303-832-4686
Synchrony/655 Broadway #800, Denver, CO	303-825-7513

West Coast

AB

Aline, France/1076 S Ogden Dr, Los Angeles, CA	213-933-2500

Guy Billout, (I), Thomas Blackshear, (I), Steve Hulen, (P), Michael Lamotte, (P), Bret Lopez, (P), Manuel Nunez, (I), Michael Schwab, (I), Veronica Sim, (P), Peggy Sirota, (P), Bob Stevens, (P), Ezra Tucker, (I), Kim Whitesides, (I), Bruce Wolfe, (I), Bob Zoell, (I)

Arnold, Wendy/4620 Coldwater Cnyn, Studio City, CA	818-762-8850
Ayerst, Deborah/828 Mission St, San Francisco, CA	415-974-1755
Baker, Kolea/2815 Alaskan Way #37-A, Seattle, WA	206-443-0326

George Abe, (I), Don Baker, (I)

Becker, Roxanne/521 State St, Glendale, CA	818-243-6400
Braun, Kathy/75 Water St, San Francisco, CA	415-543-7377

Anka, (I), Arnold & Assoc, (F), Sandra Belce, (L), Tandy Belew, (G), Michael Bull, (I), Eldon Doty, (I), Boyington Film, (F), Jim Fulp, (I), Stephen Osborn, (I), Jim Parkinson, (L), Allan Rosenberg, (P), Diane Tyler, (MU)

Brenneman, Cindy/1856 Elba Cir, Costa Mesa, CA	714-641-9700
Brooks/5290 W Washington Blvd, Los Angeles, CA	213-857-6647

Mike Chesser, (P)

Brown, Dianne/732 N Highland, Los Angeles, CA	213-464-2775

David LeBon, (P), Bill Werts, (P)

Burlingham, Tricia/10355 Ashton Ave, Los Angeles, CA	213-271-3982

Bob Stevens, (P)

Busacca, Mary/58 Corte Madera #4, Mill Valley, CA	415-381-9047

Bob August, (I), Mark Busacca, (I), Ignacio Gomez, (I), Paul Hoffman, (P), Alton Kelley, (I), Rich Mahon, (I), Joe Murray, (C), Tom Nikosey, (I)

Bybee, Gerald/1811 Folsom St, San Francisco, CA	415-863-6346

C

Caplan, Deborah/5371 Wilshire Blvd , Los Angeles, CA	213-935-8248
Church, Spencer/425 Randolph Ave, Seattle, WA	206-324-1199

John Fretz, (I), Terry Heffernan, (P), Mits Katayama, (I), Ann Marra, (G), Scott McDougall, (I), Dale Nordell, (I), Marilyn Nordell, (I), Rusty Platz, (I), Ted Rand, (I), Diane Solvang-Angell, (I), Dugald Stermer, (I), West Stock, (S), Craig Walden, (I), Dale Windham, (P)

Collier, Jan/166 South Park, San Francisco, CA	415-552-4252

Barbara Banthien, (I), Bunny Carter, (I), Chuck Eckart, (I), Cris Hammond, (I), Robert Hunt, (I), Kathy O'Brien, (I), Bernard Phillips, (P), Gretchen Schields, (I), Robert Steele, (I)

Conrad, James/2149 Lyon #5, San Francisco, CA	415-921-7140
Cook, Warren/PO Box 2159, Laguna Hills, CA	714-770-4619

Kathleen Norris Cook, (P)

Cormany, Paul/11607 Clover Ave, Los Angeles, CA	213-828-9653

Mark Busacca, (I), Bryant Eastman, (I), Dave Eichenberger, (I), Bob Gleason, (I), Lamb & Hall, (P), Jim Heimann, (I), Bob Krogle, (I), Gary Norman, (I), Ed Scarisbrick, (I), Stan Watts, (I), Dick Wilson, (I), Andy Zito, (I)

Cornell, Kathleen/1046 N Orange Dr, Los Angeles, CA	213-462-5622

Nancy Duell, (I), Miles Hardiman, (I), Masami, (I), Daniel McGowan, (I), Jan Oswald, (P), Bonnie Timmons, (I)

Courtney & Natale/8800 Venice, Los Angeles, CA	213-202-0344

Douglas Bevans, (I), Bart Doe, (I), Diane Teske Harris, (I), Matt Mahurin, (I), Paul Maxon, (P), Linda Medina, (I), Judy Reed, (I), Jeff Scales, (P), Chuck Schmidt, (I)

Crosse, Annie/10642 Vanora Dr, Sunland, CA	818-352-5173

DE

Dicker, Debbie/765 Clementina St, San Francisco, CA	415-621-0687

Keith Ovregaard, (P)

Drayton, Sheryl/5018 Dumont Pl, Woodland Hills, CA	818-347-2227
Dubow, Chuck/5550 Wilshire Blvd #202, Los Angeles, CA	213-208-8042

Terry Anderson, (I), Rick Ellescas, (I), Marc Ericksen, (I), Roger Hubbard, (I), Richard Ikkanda, (I), Paul Kratter, (I), Mike Rogers, (I)

Egbert, Lydia/190 Cervantes Blvd #7, San Francisco, CA	415-921-2415
Elliott, Christine/17806 Bailey Dr, Torrance, CA	213-542-7267
Epstein, Rhoni & Assoc/3814 Franklin Ave, Los Angeles, CA	213-663-2388
Ericson, William/1024 Mission St, South Pasadena, CA	213-461-4969

Representatives
Please send us your additions and updates.

F Feliciano, Terrianne/16782 Red Hill #B, Irvine, CA ... 714-250-3377
Finlayson & Assoc/1448 Portia St, Los Angeles, CA ... 213-481-0228
Fisher, Susan/1821 Pacific Ave #16, San Francisco, CA ... 415-928-3640
Fleming, Laird Tyler/407 1/2 Shirley Pl, Beverly Hills, CA ... 213-552-4626
Ford, Mary Ann/1800 Pacific St, San Francisco, CA ... 415-449-5209
Fox & Clark/8350 Melrose Ave #201, Los Angeles, CA ... 213-653-6484
Franco, Evelyn/29515 Bernice Dr, Rncho Palos Vrdes, CA ... 213-832-5103
 Steve McMahon, (P)

G Gardner, Jean/384 N Norton Ave, Los Angeles, CA ... 213-464-2492
George, Nancy/360 1/2 N Mansfield Ave, Los Angeles, CA ... 213-935-4696
 Brent Bear, (P), Sid Bingham, (I), Justin Carroll, (I), Bruce Dean, (I), Steve Hendricks, (I), Hank Hinton, (I), Gary Hoover, (I), Richard Kriegler, (I), Larry Lake, (I), Gary Lund, (I), Rob Sprattler, (I), Bruce Wilson, (P), Jeannie Winston, (I)
Glick, Ivy/350 Townsend St #421, San Francisco, CA ... 415-543-6056
 David Bishop, (P), Jim Blakeley, (P), Don Dudley, (I), Mike Steirnagle, (I)
Goldman, Caren/4521 Cleveland Ave, San Diego, CA ... 619-298-4043
Graham, Corey/Pier 33 North, San Francisco, CA ... 415-956-4750
 Byron Coons, (I), Joel Nakamura, (I), Gretchen Schields, (I), Mark Schroeder, (I), Debra Zinc, (I)
Gray, Pam/1912 Hermosa Ave #F, Hermosa Beach, CA ... 213-374-3606
Group West Inc/5455 Wilshire Blvd #1212, Los Angeles, CA ... 213-937-4472
 Neil Boyle, (I), Nixon Galloway, (I), Frank Germain, (I), Roger Hammond, (I), Fred Hatzer, (I), Ron McKee, (I), Norman Merritt, (I), Bill Robles, (I), Ren Wicks, (I)

H Hackett, Pat/101 Yesler #502, Seattle, WA ... 206-441-0606
 Bill Cannon, (P), Steve Coppin, (I), Larry Duke, (I), Bill Evans, (I), Norman Hathaway, (I), Ed Hauser, (I), Gary Jacobsen, (I), Larry Lubeck, (P), Bill Mayer, (I), Mike Schumacher, (I), John C Smith, (I), John Terence Turner, (P)
Hall, Marni & Assoc/620 N Citrus Ave, Los Angeles, CA ... 213-934-9420
 Kent Knudson, (P)
Harrison, Sumana/5733 La Jolla Blvd #60, La Jolla, CA ... 619-456-5868
Hart, Vikki/780 Bryant St, San Francisco, CA ... 415-495-4278
 G K Hart, (P), Kevin Hulsey, (I), Aleta Jenks, (I), Heather King, (I), Julie Tsuchiya, (I), Jonathan Wright, (I)
Hauser, Barbara/PO Box 1443, San Francisco, CA ... 415-339-1885
Hedge, Joanne/1838 El Cerrito Pl #3, Los Angeles, CA ... 213-874-1661
 Delana Bettoli, (I), Chris Dellorco, (I), Ignacio Gomez, (I), Bette Levine, (I), Kenvin Lyman, (I), Rick McCollum, (I), David McMacken, (I), Dennis Mukai, (I), Vida Pavesich, (I), William Rieser, (I), Jim Salvati, (I), Joe Saputo, (I), Julie Tsuchiya, (I)
Heimberg, Nancy/351 1/2 N Sycamore Ave, Los Angeles, CA ... 213-933-8660
Hillman, Betsy/2230 Francisco #106, San Francisco, CA ... 415-563-2243
 Chuck Bowden, (I), Tim Boxell, (I), Hiro Kimura, (I), John Marriott, (P), HKM Productions, (P), Greg Spalenka, (I), Joe Spencer, (I), Jeremy Thornton, (I), Jackson Vereen, (P)
Hjul, Diana/8696 Crescent Dr, Los Angeles, CA ... 213-654-9513
 Neal Brisker, (P), John Reed Forsman, (P), Jim Greenberg, (P)
Hodges, Jeanette/12401 Bellwood, Los Alamitos, CA ... 213-431-4343
 Ken Hodges, (I)
Hughes, April & Assoc/465 California St #809, San Francisco, CA ... 415-781-2773
 Dennis Dittrich, (I), Ernie Friedlander, (P), Mitch Heinze, (I), Kim Mak, (I), Paul Matsuda, (P), Sandra Speidel, (I)
Hyatt, Nadine/PO Box 307, Ross, CA ... 415-456-7711
 Jeanette Adams, (I), Rebecca Archey, (I), Linda Bacon, (I), Charles Bush, (P), Frank Cowan, (P), Marty Evans, (P), John Hyatt, (I), Bret Lopez, (P), K Mercedes McDonald, (I), Jan Schockner, (L), Liz Wheaton, (I)

JK Jorgensen, Donna/609 Summit Ave, Seattle, WA ... 206-284-5080
 Alice Brickner, (I), Frank Denman, (P), Fred Hilliard, (I), Richard Kehl, (I), Doug Keith, (I), David Lund, (I), Robert Peckham, (I), Tim Stevenson, (I)
Karpe, Michele/4328 Ben Ave, Studio City, CA ... 818-763-9686
Kirsch, Melanie/7316 Pryamid Dr, Los Angeles, CA ... 213-651-3706
 Bob August, (I), Kevin Hulsey, (I), Todd Smith, (P), Jeff Wack,

Knable, Ellen/PO Box 67725, Los Angeles, CA ... 213-855-8855
 Henry Bjorn, (P), Roger Chouinard, (I), Bob Commander, (I), Joe Heiner, (I), Kathy Heiner, (I), Jeff Nadler, (P), Margo Nahas, (I), Michael Ruppert, (P), Jonathan Wright, (I), Brian Zick, (I)
Koeffler, Ann/1555 Greenwich #9, San Francisco, CA ... 415-885-2714
 Randy Berrett, (I), Karl Edwards, (I), Bob Hickson, (I), Paul Kratter, (I), Kevin O'Shea, (I), Michael Pearce, (I), Stephen Peringer, (I), Ken Rosenberg, (I), Chris Shorten, (P), Sarn Suvityasiri, (I)
Kovac, Elka/1609 Greenfield Ave, Los Angeles, CA ... 213-473-6316

L Lanier, Kate/633 W 6th St, Los Angeles, CA ... 213-935-9343
Laycock, Louise/8800 Venice Blvd, Los Angeles, CA ... 213-204-6401
Lee & Lou/1548 18th St #101, Santa Monica, CA ... 213-828-2259
 Rob Gage, (P), Bob Grigg, (P), Richard Leech, (I)
Lilie, Jim/251 Kearny St #511, San Francisco, CA ... 415-441-4384
 Lou Beach, (I), Alan Dolgins, (P), David Fischer, (P), Patricia Mahoney, (I), Masami Miyamoto, (I), Larry Noble, (I), Robert Rodriguez, (I), Dugald Stermer, (I), Ezra Tucker, (I), Stan Watts, (I), Dennis Ziemienski, (I)
Linville, Betty/6546 Hollywood Blvd #220, Los Angeles, CA ... 213-467-4455
 Douglass Hyun, (P)
Lippert, Tom/1100 Glendon #732, Los Angeles, CA ... 213-279-1539
London, Valerie/9756 Charleville Blvd, Beverly Hills, CA ... 213-277-8090
Luna, Tony/45 E Walnut St, Pasadena, CA ... 213-681-3130

M MK Communications/545 Sutter St, San Francisco, CA ... 415-391-3780
 Mike Godfrey, (I), Robert Holmes, (P), Jim Sadlon, (P)
Marie, Rita & Friends/6376 W 5th St, Los Angeles, CA ... 213-934-3395
 David Beck, (I), Chris Consani, (I), Mort Drucker, (I), Brian Duggan, (I), Jim Endicott, (I), Marla Frazee, (I), Ken Goldammer, (I), Robert Gunn, (I), Haruo Ishioka, (I), Hiro Kimura, (I), Gary Pierazzi, (I), Robert Pryor, (I), Paul Rogers, (I), Gary Ruddell, (I), Dick Sakahara, (I), Danny Smyhte, (I), Greg Wray, (I)
Martha Productions/1830 S Robertson Blvd #203, Los Angeles, CA ... 213-204-1771
 Bob Brugger, (I), Brian Cronin, (I), Stan Evenson, (I), Allen Garns, (I), Bryon Gin, (I), William Harrison, (I), Jeff Hitch, (I), Dan Lavigne, (I), Catherine Leary, (I), Ron Mazellan, (I), R Kenton Nelson, (I), Rudy Obrero, (I), Cathy Pavia, (I), Steve Vance, (I), Wayne Watford, (I)
Mastrogeorge, Robin/11020 Ventura Blvd Box 294, Studio City, CA ... 818-954-8748
McBain, Morgan/650 San Juan Ave, Venice, CA ... 213-392-9341
 Joann Daley, (I), Ron Derhacopian, (P), John Taylor Dismukes, (I), Scott Ernster, (I), Bob McMahon, (I), Greg Moraes, (I)
McBride, Elizabeth/70 Broadway, San Francisco, CA ... 415-863-0655
 Keith Criss, (I), Robert Holmes, (P), Patricia Pearson, (I), Bill Sanchez, (I), Earl Thollander, (I), Tom Vano, (P)
McCargar, Lucy/652 Bair Isl Rd, Redwood City, CA ... 415-363-2130
 Tim Mitoma, (I), Mary Ross, (I)
McGuiness, Charlotte/2120 W 60th St, Seattle, WA ... 206-524-8308
McKenzie, Dianne/125 King St, San Francisco, CA ... 415-541-9051
 Victor Budnik, (P)
Melrose, Penny/1333 Lawrence Expwy #150, Santa Clara, CA ... 408-737-9494
Michaels, Martha/3279 Kifer Rd, Santa Clara, CA ... 408-735-8443
Mix, Eva/2129 Grahn Dr, Santa Rosa, CA ... 707-579-1535
Mizejewski, Max/942 Shearwater St, Ontario, CA ... 714-947-8585
Moniz, Karletta/250 Newhall Ave, San Francisco, CA ... 415-821-6358
Morgan-Friedman/PO Box 19608-329, Irvine, CA ... 714-551-6445

NO Newman & Franks/2956 Nicada Dr, Los Angeles, CA ... 213-470-0140
 Tim Huhn, (I), Jeff Peterson, (I)
Ogden, Robin/8126 Blackburn Ave, Los Angeles, CA ... 213-858-0946
 Karen Bell, (I), Joe Crabtree, (I), Jan Evans, (I), Steve Gray, (I), Gerry Hampton, (I), Jim Miller, (I), Julie Perron, (I), John Puchalski, (I), Ken Rosenberg, (I), Corey Wolfe, (I)
Ostan-Prentice/Ostan/1850 Federal Ave #1, Los Angeles, CA ... 213-305-7143

PR Padgett, Donna/13520 Terrace Pl, Whittier, CA ... 213-945-7801
Parrish, Dave/Photopia/PO Box 2309, San Francisco, CA ... 415-441-5611

Representatives
Continued

Please send us your additions and updates.

Parsons, Ralph/1232 Folsom St, San Francisco, CA	415-339-1885
Partners Reps/13480 Contour, Sherman Oaks, CA	818-995-6883
Pate, Randy/The Source/PO Box 687, N Hollywood, CA	818-985-8181
Steven Chorney, (I), Robert Florczak, (I), Mick McGinty, (I), Kazu Sano, (I)	
Peek, Pamela/1964 N Rodney Dr #201, Los Angeles, CA	213-660-1596
Phillips, Ellen/1717 Mason St #2, San Francisco, CA	415-928-6336
Piscopo, Maria/2038 Calvert Ave, Costa Mesa, CA	714-556-8133
Pohl, Jacqueline/608 Fulsom, San Francisco, CA	415-543-2907
Pribble, Laurie/911 Victoria Dr, Arcadia, CA	818-574-0288
Reece, Sandra/2565 Canyon Dr, Los Angeles, CA	213-465-7576
Ken Chernus, (P), Ralph Pleasant, (P), David Zanzinger, (P)	
Repertory/6010 Wilshire Blvd #505, Los Angeles, CA	213-931-7449
Rob Anthony, (I), Rob Anthony, (I), Steve Berman, (P), Craig Calsbeek, (I), Scott Hensey, (SC) Robert Jacobs, (R), Buena Johnson, (I), Scott Johnston, (I), Tim Jonke, (I), Karl Parry, (P), Jeff Spear, (L), Philip Velasquez, (I), Larry Vigon, (G)	
Rosenthal, Elise/3443 Wade St, Los Angeles, CA	213-390-9595
Cary Becker, (I), Saul Bernstein, (I), Chris Butler, (I), Alan Daniels, (I), Jody Eastman, (I), David English, (I), David Erramouspe, (I), Alan Hashimoto, (I), James Henry, (I), Roger Loveless, (I), Jim McKiernan, (I), Kenton Nelson, (I), Eric Vander Palen, (I), Peter Palombi, (I), Tom Pansini, (I), Kim Passey, (I), Bill Robles, (I), Larry Salk, (I), Tom Tomita, (I), Ren Wicks, (I), Larry Winborg, (I)	

S

Salisbury, Sharon/116 W Blithedale, Mill Valley, CA	415-495-4665
Keith Batcheller, (I), Craig Calsbeck, (I), Jim Endicott, (I), Bob Graham, (I), Bo Hylen, (P), Larry Keenan, (P), Bette Levine, (I), Dave McMacken, (I), Robert Mizono, (P), Vida Pavesich, (I)	
Salzman, Richard W/1352 Hornblend St, San Diego, CA	619-272-8147
Tony Baker, (I), Daniels, (I), Ruben DeAnda, (I), Kristen Funkhouser, (I), Manuel Garcia, (I), Jason Harlem, (P), Denise Hilton-Putnam, (I), Bernie Lansky, (C), Gordon Menzie, (P), Dave Mollering, (I), Imagery That Moves, (G), Dianne O'Quinn-Burke, (I), Everett Peck, (I), Nono Remos, (R), Terry Smith, (I), Debra Stine, (I), Walter Stuart, (I), Jonathan Wright, (I)	
Scott, Freda/244 Ninth St, San Francisco, CA	415-621-2992
Sherry Bringham, (I), David Campbell, (P), John Hersey, (I), Gayle Kabaker, (I), Jeff Leedy, (F), Francis Livingston, (I), Alan Mazzetti, (I), Diane Padys, (P), Susan Schelling, (P), Judy Unger, (I)	
Scroggy, David/2124 Froude St, San Diego, CA	619-222-2476
Ed Abrams, (I), Jodell D Abrams, (I), Joe Chiado, (I), Rick Geary, (I), John Pound, (I), Hal Scroggy, (I), Debbie Tilley, (I)	
Shaffer, Barry/PO Box 480888, Los Angeles, CA	213-939-2527
Shigekuni, Cindy/PO Box 2336, Beverly Hills, CA	213-838-8811
Slobodian, Barbara/745 N Alta Vista Blvd, Hollywood, CA	213-935-6668
Bob Greisen, (I), David Kaiser, (I), Tom O'Brien, (P), Forest Sigwart, (I), Scott Slobodian, (P)	
Sobol, Lynne/4302 Melrose Ave, Los Angeles, CA	213-665-5141
Frank Marquez, (I), Arthur Montes de Oca, (P)	
Stefanski, Janice/2022 Jones St, San Francisco, CA	415-928-0457
Adrian Day, (I), Michael Jay, (P), Barbara Kelley, (I), Steven Lyons, (I), George Olson, (P), Katherine Salentine, (I), Cliff Spohn, (I)	
Steinberg, John/11731 Crescenta, Los Angeles, CA	213-471-0232
Jay Ahrent, (P), John Alvin, (I), Bo Gehring & Associates, (I), Alan Daniels, (I), Beau Daniels, (I), Precision Illustration, (I), David Kimble, (I), Reid Miles, (P), Richard Moore, (P), Larry Noble, (I), Frank Page, (I), Mark Stehrenberger, (I), Ed Wexler, (I)	
Stivers, Robert/101 Scholz Plz PH 21, Newport Beach, CA	714-645-9070
Studio Artists Inc/638 S Van Ness Ave, Los Angeles, CA	213-382-6281
Chuck Coppock, (I), George Francuch, (I), Bill Franks, (I), Duane Gordon, (I)	
Sullivan, Diane/3727 Buchanan St, San Francisco, CA	415-563-8884
Lawrence Duke, (P)	
Sullivan, Martha/2395 Paradise Dr, Tiburon, CA	415-435-4181
Patricia Brabant, (P)	
Sweet, Ron/716 Montgomery St, San Francisco, CA	415-433-1222

Charles East, (D), Randy Glass, (I), John Hamagami, (I), Bob Haydock, (I), Gregg Keeling, (I), Richard Leech, (I), Tom Lochray, (I), Will Nelson, (I), Walter Swarthout, (P), Jack Unruh, (I), Don Weller, (I), Bruce Wolfe, (I), James B Wood, (P)	

TV

Taggard, Jim/PO 4064 Pioneer Square Station, Seattle, WA *Sjef's-Photographie, (P)*	206-547-0807
Thornby, Kirk/1039 S Fairfax Ave, Los Angeles, CA	213-933-9883
Tos, Debbie/7306 W 82nd St, Los Angeles, CA	213-410-0402
Carl Furuta, (P)	
Townsend, Kris/58 Polhemus Way, Larkspur, CA	212-243-2484
David W Hamilton, (P)	
Tranter, Susan/23011 Moulton Pky #E-9, Lauguna Hills, CA	714-770-1680
Trimpe, Susan/2717 Western Ave, Seattle, WA	206-728-1300
Don Baker, (I), Wendy Edelson, (I), Stephen Peringer, (I)	
Vandamme, Mary/1242 Francisco #1, San Francisco, CA	415-771-0494
Eddie Barnett() Martin Bell() Tony Cookson() Werner Hlinka()	
Vandamme, Vicki/1242 Francisco St, San Franscisco, CA	415-771-0404
Kirk Caldwell, (I), John Collier, (I), Mukai. Dennis, (I), Heiner, Kathy & Joe, (I), Alan Krosnick, (P), Jennie Oppenheimer, (I), Bill Rieser, (I), Michael Schwab, (I), Stuart Schwartz, (P), Kim Whitesides, (I), Nic Wilton, (I)	

WYZ

Wagoner, Jae/200 Westminster Ave #A, Venice, CA	213-392-4877
Tim Alt, (I), Michael Backus, (I), Roger Beerworth, (I), Stephen Durke, (I), Steve Jones, (I), Lee MacLeod, (I), Craig Nelson, (I), Robert Tanenbaum, (I), Don Weller, (I)	
Werner, Jan & Joel/2001 Freemont, S Pasadena, CA	213-255-5972
Wiegand, Chris/7106 Waring Ave, Los Angeles, CA	213-931-5942
Wiley, David/1535 Green St #207, San Francisco, CA	415-441-1623
Steve Bjorkman, (I), Dennis Carmichael, (I), Bart Forbes, (I), Merilyn Moss, (L), Woody Pirtle, (G), Studio R, (R), Dave Stephenson, (I), Raden Studio, (G), Mark Tuschman, (P), Jim Wasco, (L), Keith Witmer, (I)	
Winston, Bonnie/228 S Beverly Dr #210, Beverly Hills, CA	213-275-2858
David Andrade, (I), Garry Brod, (P), Robert Ferrone, (P), Kiko Ricotti, (P), Rob White, (P)	
Youmans, Jill/1021 1/2 N La Brea, Los Angeles, CA	213-469-8624
Dan Cooper, (I), Jeff George, (I), Brian Leng, (P), Jeff Leung, (I), Christine Nasser, (I), Joyce Patti, (I), Bill Salada, (I)	
Young, Jill/Compendium Inc/945 Front St #206, San Francisco, CA	415-392-0542
Judy Clifford, (I), Armondo Diaz, (P), Celeste Ericsson, (I), Marilee Heyer, (I), Rae Huestis, (G), Mary Jew, (G), Bonnie Matza, (I), Barbara Muhlhauser, (G), Martin Schweitzer, (G), Donna Mae Shaver, (P), Cecily Starin, (I), Sarn Suvityasiri, (I), Ed Taber, (I), Carlotta Tormey, (I)	
Zank, Elen/262 Donahue St, Sausalito, CA	415-332-3739
Chip Carroon, (P)	
Zimmerman, Delores H/9135 Hazen Dr, Beverly Hills, CA	213-273-2642

Illustrators

New York City

A

Abraham, Daniel E/Box 2528/Rockefeller Sta	718-499-4006
Abrams, Kathie/41 Union Square W #1001	212-741-1333
Accardo, Anthony/19 E 48th St 3rd Fl	212-838-0050
Accornero, Franco/620 Broadway	212-674-0068
Acuna, Ed/24 W 57th St #605	212-489-8777
Adams, Angela/866 UN Plaza #4014	212-644-2020
Adams, Jeanette/261 Broadway	212-732-3878
Adams, Jeffrey/95 Horatio St	212-807-0840
Aiese, Bob/60 Pineapple St	718-596-2240
Ajhar, Brian/321 E 12th St #30	212-254-0694
Albahae, Andrea/2364 Brigham St 1st Fl	718-934-7004
Albanese, Ernest/156 Fifth Ave #617	212-243-1333
Alcorn, John/194 Third Ave	212-475-0440
Alcorn, Stephen/194 Third Ave	212-475-0440
Allaux, Jean Francois/21 W 86th St	212-799-0399
Allen, Julian/31 Walker St	212-925-6550
Allen, Terry/164 Daniel Low Terr	718-727-0723
Allert, Kathy/201 E 28th St	212-532-0928
Aloisio, Richard/145 E 16th St	212-473-5635
Alpert, Alan/405 E 54th St	212-741-1631
Alpert, Olive/9511 Shore Rd	718-833-3092
Alter, Judy/539 Naughton Ave	718-667-5643
Amicosante, Vincent/280 Madison Ave #1402	212-775-1810
Anderson, Mark/166 Second Ave #9C	212-674-3831
Angelakis, Manos/48 W 21st St 9th Fl	212-243-4412
Angelini, George/24 W 57th St #605	212-489-8777
Angelo, Peter/328 W 46th St #1R	212-246-1243
Angerame, Diane/57-30 254th St	718-428-7794
Antonios, Tony/60 E 42nd St #505	212-682-1490
Arcelle, Joan/430 W 24th St	212-924-1865
Arisman, Marshall/314 W 100th St	212-662-2289
Aristovulos, Nick/16 E 30th St	212-725-2454
Arnold, Robert/149 W 14th St	212-989-7049
Arnoldi, Per/60 E 42nd St #505	212-682-1490
Asbaghi, Zita/104-40 Queens Blvd	718-275-1995
Assel, Steven/472 Myrtle Ave	718-789-1725
Astrahan, Irene/201 E 28th St	212-532-0928
Azzopardi, Frank/1039 Victory Blvd	718-273-4343

B

Bacall, Aaron/204 Arlene St	718-494-0711
Bailer, Brent/104 E 40th St	212-661-0257
Bailey, Pat/Airstream/60 E 42nd St #505	212-682-1490
Baker, Garin/35 W 92nd St #7A	212-865-1975
Baldus, Fred/29 Jones St	212-620-0423
Baldwin, Read/230 Fifth Ave #200	212-481-7311
Banfield, Elliot/81 Greene St	212-925-3053
Barancik, Cathy/140 Grand St	212-472-2202
Barberis, Juan C/60 E 42nd St	212-687-4185
Barner, Bob/866 UN Plaza #4014	212-644-2020
Barnes, Michele/111 Sullivan St #3B	212-219-9269
Barnes-Murphy, Rowan/201 E 28th St	212-532-0928
Baron, Esther/866 UN Plaza #4014	212-644-2020
Barr, Ken/420 Lexington Ave #2738	212-697-8525
Barrera, Alberto/463 West St #1017D	212-645-2544
Barrett, Ron/2112 Broadway #402A	212-874-1370
Barritt, Randi/240 W 15th St	212-255-5333
Barry, Ron/165 E 32nd St	212-686-3514
Bartalos, Michael/81 Second Ave #3	212-254-5858
Bartholomew, Caty/217 Dean St	718-596-8863
Bartoloni, Gary/203 W 98th St #6E	212-749-4498
Bascove/319 E 50th St	212-888-0038
Baseman, Gary/628 President St #4F	718-398-2313
Bauer, Carla Studio/156 Fifth Ave #1100	212-807-8305
Bauman, Jill/PO Box 152	718-631-3160
Baumann, Karen/43 E 19th St	212-688-1080
Beach, Lou/215 Park Ave S	212-674-8080
Becker, Ron/265 E 78th St	212-535-8052
Beecham, Tom/420 Lexington Ave #2738	212-697-8525
Bego, Dolores/155 E 38th St	212-697-6170

Bellair & Inoue Visual Comm/323 Park Ave S	212-473-8330
Ben-Ami, Doron/808 Union St	718-230-3348
Bendell, Norm/41 Union Sq W #918	212-807-6627
Benson, Linda/165 E 32nd St	212-686-3514
Berger, Stephen/43 E 19th St	212-254-4996
Berkey, John/50 E 50th St	212-355-0910
Berran, Robert/420 Lexington Ave #2911	212-986-5680
Berry, Fanny Mellet/155 E 38th St	212-697-6170
Beylon, Cathy/201 E 28th St	212-532-0928
Bianco, Geraldo/1040 82nd St	718-836-8637
BILLOUT, GUY/ 225 LAFAYETTE ST. (P 20)	**212-431-6350**
Bittman, Monika/709 Carroll St	718-622-2061
BJORKMAN, STEVE/501 FIFTH AVE #1407 (P 16)	**212-490-2450**
Blackwell, Garie/60 E 42nd St #505	212-682-1490
Blake, Marty/24 Jane St #5B	212-929-4440
Blake, Quentin/81 Greene St	212-925-3053
Blakey, Paul/470 W 23rd St	212-242-6367
Blas, Bob/43 E 19th St	212-254-4996
Blasutta, Mary Lynn/1 Union Sq W #803	212-675-0287
Bleck, Cathie/303 E 71st St #4A	212-288-3708
Blevins, Steve/475 18th St 2nd Fl	718-768-6702
Bloch, Alex/19 E 48th St 3rd Fl	212-838-0050
Bloom, Tom/235 E 84th St #17	212-628-6861
Blount, Lester/302 5th St 3rd Fl	718-768-0059
Blubaugh, Susan/191 Amity St #2	718-858-4360
Blum, Zevi/81 Greene St	212-925-3053
Blume, George/350 E 89th St	212-502-3976
Blumrich, Christoph/215 Park Ave S	212-674-8080
Bochner, Nurit/28 Tompkins Pl	718-596-3476
Boguslav, Raphael/200 E 78th St	212-570-9069
Bolognese, Don/19 E 48th St	212-838-0050
Bonforte, Lisa/201 E 28th St	212-532-0928
Bonhomme, Bernard/111 Wooster St #PH C	212-925-0491
Bono, Mary/PO Box 1502	212-475-6266
Bordelon, Melinda/60 E 42nd St #505	212-682-1490
Borea, Phyllis/245 W 104th St	212-663-4463
Bostic, Alex/853 Broadway	212-677-9100
Botas, Juan/207 E 32nd St	212-420-5984
Boyd, Harvey/24 Fifth Ave	212-475-5235
Boyd, Kris/318 E 89th St #1D	718-648-7138
Bozzo, Frank/400 E 85th St #5J	212-535-9182
Bracken, Carolyn/201 E 28th St	212-532-0928
Bralds, Braldt/135 E 54th St	212-421-0050
Bramhall, William/81 Greene St	212-925-3053
Brandt, Joan/15 Gramercy Park S	212-473-7874
Breakey, John/42-52 Layton #1H	718-507-6467
Breinberg, Aaron/1123 Broadway	212-243-4929
Bricher, Scott/330 W 42nd St #3200NE	212-714-0147
Brickner, Alice/4720 Grosvenor Ave	212-549-5909
Brillhart, Ralph/60 E 42nd St #1940	212-867-8092
Brindak, Hermine/29 W-15th St #B	212-620-0604
Broderson, Charles/873 Broadway #612	212-925-9392
Brodner, Steve/446 W 58th St	212-586-1267
Brofsky, Miriam/186 Riverside Dr	212-595-8094
Brooks, Andrea/41 Union Sq W #1228	212-645-0644
Brooks, Clare Vanacore/415 W 55th St	212-245-3632
Brooks, Hal/20 W 87th St	212-595-5980
Brooks, Lou/415 W 55th St	212-245-3632
Brothers, Barry/1922 E 18th St	718-336-7540
Brown, Bradford/4103 Lowerre Pl	212-231-8223
Brown, Colin/145 E 22nd St	212-473-8747
Brown, Dan/24 W 57th St #605	212-489-8777
Brown, Donald/129 E 29th St	212-532-1705
Brown, Judith Gwyn/522 E 85th St	212-288-1599
Brown, Kirk/1092 Blake Ave	718-342-4565
Brown, Peter D/235 E 22nd St #16R	212-684-7080
Brown, RS/62 W 45th St	212-398-9540
Brundage, Cheryl/314 Washington Ave	718-789-6392
Brusca, Jack/43 E 19th St	212-254-4996
Bryan, Diana/200 E 16th St #1D	212-475-7927
Bryan, Mike/420 Lexington Ave #2738	212-697-8525
Bryant, Rick J/18 W 37th St #301	212-594-6718

Buchanan, Yvonne/411 14th St	718-965-3021	Crews, Donald/653 Carroll St	718-636-5773
Buehler, Mark/418 Atlantic Ave	718-797-3689	Cristiano, Rudy/62 W 45th St	212-398-9540
Burger, Robert/111 Wooster St #PH C	212-925-0491	Crosthwaite, Royd/50 E 50th St #5	212-355-0910
Burgoyne, John/200 E 78th St	212-570-9069	Cruse, Howard/88-11 34th Ave #5D	718-639-4951
Buschman, Lynne/186 Franklin St	212-925-4701	Cruz, Jose/215 Park Ave S	212-674-8080
Bush, George/60 E 42nd St #1940	212-867-8092	Cruz, Ray/194 Third Ave	212-475-0440
Byskiniewicz, Maryika/75-23 113th St #4F	718-261-5883	Csatari, Joe/420 Lexington Ave #2911	212-986-5680
		Cuevas Stillerman Plotkin/230 E 44th St	212-661-7149
C Caggiano, Tom/83-25 Dongan Ave	718-651-8993	Cuevos, Stillerman, Plotkin/230 E 44th St	212-661-7149
Cain, David/200 W 20th St #607	212-633-0258	Cummings, Pat/28 Tiffany Pl	718-834-8584
Campbell, Jim/420 Lexington Ave #2911	212-986-5680	Cummings, Terrence/210 W 64th St #5B	212-586-4153
Cantarella, Virginia Hoyt/107 Sterling Pl	718-622-2061	Cusack, Margaret/124 Hoyt St	718-237-0145
Carbone, Kye/241 Union St	718-802-9143	Cushwa, Tom/303 Park Ave S #511	212-228-2615
Carr, Noell/30 E 14th St	212-675-1015		
Carter, Abby/2109 45th Ave	718-729-6822	**D** D'Andrea, Bernard/50 E 50th St #5	212-355-0910
Carter, Bunny/200 E 78th St	212-570-9069	D'Andrea, Domenick/50 E 50th St #5	212-355-0910
Carter, Penny/430 E 66th St #4	323-772-3715	D'Onofrio, Alice/866 UN Plaza #4014	212-644-2020
Carver, Steve/145 E 22nd St	212-473-8747	Dacey, Bob/24 W 57th St #605	212-489-8777
Casale, Paul/5304 11th Ave	718-871-6848	Dale, Robert/1573 York Ave #3N	212-535-2505
Cassler, Carl/420 Lexington Ave #2911	212-986-5680	Dallison, Ken/108 E 35th St #1	212-889-3337
Castelluccio, Frederico/60 E 42nd St #1940	212-867-8092	Daly, Sean/85 South St	212-668-0031
Cavaliere, Jamie/60 E 42nd St #1940	212-867-8092	Damore, Georgan/280 Madison Ave #1402	212-775-1810
Celsi, David/91 E 3rd St #2B	212-475-1325	Daniel, Frank/201 E 28th St	212-532-0928
Ceribello, Jim/11 W Cedar View Ave	718-317-5972	Daniels, Beau & Alan/24 W 57th St #605	212-489-8777
Cesc/81 Greene St	212-925-3053	Daniels, Shelley/132 Berkeley Pl	718-636-1046
Cetlin, Marshall/62 LeRoy St	212-243-7869	Daniels, Sid/12 E 22nd St #11B	212-673-6520
Chabrian, Deborah/420 Lexington Ave #2911	212-986-5680	Darden, Howard/62 W 45th St	212-398-9540
Chambless-Rigie, Jane/201 E 28th St	212-532-0928	Darrer, Tony/515 E 79th St	212-517-8544
Chang, Alain/24 W 57th St #605	212-489-8777	Daste, Larry/201 E 28th St	212-532-0928
Charmatz, Bill/25 W 68th St	212-595-3907	Davidson, Everett/60 E 42nd St #505	212-682-1490
Cheng, Judith/88-57 195th St	718-465-5598	Davis, Allen/141-10 25th Rd #3A	718-463-0966
Chermayeff, Ivan/58 W 15th St	212-741-2539	Davis, Harry/189 E 3rd St #15	212-674-5832
Chernishov, Anatoly/4 Willow Bank Ct	201-327-2377	Davis, Jack/108 E 35th St #1C	212-889-3337
Chester, Harry/501 Madison Ave	212-752-0570	Davis, Nelle/20 E 17th St 4th Fl	212-807-7737
Chironna, Ronald/135 Sturges St	718-720-6142	Davis, Paul/14 E 4th St	212-460-9644
Chow, Tad/179 Bay 35th St	718-946-8519	Day, Betsy/866 UN Plaza #4014	212-644-2020
Christopher, Tom/51 E 42nd St #716	212-986-3282	DeAraujo, Betty/201 E 28th St	212-532-0928
Chwast, Jacqueline/462 W 58th St #3C	212-246-7342	DeGraffenried, Jack/18 E 16th St	212-206-0322
Chwast, Seymour/215 Park Ave S	212-674-8080	DeJesus, Jamie/15 W 72nd St	212-799-2231
Ciardiello, Joe/2182 Clove Rd	718-727-4757	DeLattre, Georgette/100 Central Park South	212-247-6850
Ciccarelli, Gary/353 W 53rd St #1W	212-682-2462	DeMarest, Chris/81 Greene St	212-925-3053
Ciesiel, Christine G/101 MacDougal St	212-982-9461	DeMichiell, Robert/226 W 78th St #26	212-769-9192
Ciss, Julius/145 E 22nd St	212-473-8747	DeRijk, Walt/43 E 19th St	212-254-4996
Clark, Jane/48 W 21st St 9th Fl	212-243-4412	DeSeve, Peter/461 W 21st St #3	212-627-5533
Clarke, Robert/159 W 53rd St	212-581-4045	Deas, Michael/39 Sidney Pl	718-852-5630
Cloteaux, Francois/333 E 30th St	212-679-1358	Deel, Guy/60 E 42nd St #1940	212-867-8092
Cody, Brian/866 UN Plaza #4014	212-644-2020	Degen, Paul/81 Greene St	212-925-3053
Cohen, Adam/74 Charles St #213	212-924-5941	Deibler, Gordon/1 Wrld Trade Ctr #8817	212-323-8022
Cole, Olivia/19 E 48th St 3rd Fl	212-838-0050	Del Rosso, Richard/303 W 42nd St #312	212-974-1059
Collier, Roberta/201 E 28th St	212-532-0928	Delvalle, Daniel/19 E 48th St	212-838-0050
Colon, Ernie/43 E 19th St	212-254-4996	Denaro, Joseph/18 E 16th St	212-206-0322
Colton, Keita/165 E 32nd St	212-686-3514	Deneen, Jim/420 Lexington Ave #2911	212-986-5680
Cone, William/140 West End Ave #9H	212-874-7074	DesCombes, Roland/50 E 50th St #5	212-355-0910
Conner, Mona/1 Montgomery Pl #8	718-636-1527	Deschamps, Bob/108 E 35th St #1	212-889-3337
Conrad, Jon/853 Broadway #1201	212-677-9100	Design Loiminchay/210 Canal St #501	212-608-2880
Continuity Graphics Assoc'd Inc/62 W 45th St	212-869-4170	Detrich, Susan/253 Baltic St	718-237-9174
Conway, Michael/316 E 93rd St #23	212-369-0019	Devlin, Bill/108 E 35th St #1	212-889-3337
Cook, David/60 E 42nd St #1940	212-867-8092	Dewey, Kenneth F/420 Lexington Ave #2911	212-986-5680
Cook, Esky/405 N Wabash #3203	312-329-1370	DiCianni, Ron/420 Lexington Ave	212-697-8525
Cooper, Cheryl/515 Madison Ave	212-486-9644	DiComo Comp Art/120 E 34th St #12K	212-689-8670
Cooper, Floyd/866 UN Plaza #4014	212-644-2020	DiVincenzo, Dennis/27 Bleecker St	212-673-1600
Cooperstein, Sam/677 West End Ave	212-864-4064	Diamantis, Kitty/19 E 48th St 3rd Fl	212-838-0050
Corben, Richard/43 E 19th St	212-254-4996	Diamond Art Studio/11 E 36th St	212-685-6622
Cornell, Jeff/24 W 57th St #605	212-489-8777	Diamond, Ruth/95 Horatio St #521	212-243-3188
Cornell, Laura/118 E 93rd St #1A	212-534-0596	Diehl, David/222 W 20th St #16	212-242-8897
Corvi, Donna/568 Broadway #604	212-925-9622	Dietz, Jim/165 E 32nd St	212-686-3514
Couch, Greg/112 Willow St #5A	718-625-1298	Dilakian, Hovik/111 Wooster St #PH C	212-925-0491
Courtney, Richard/43 E 19th St	212-254-4996	Dinnerstein, Harvey/933 President St	718-783-6879
Cove, Tony/60 E 42nd St #411	212-953-7088	Dion, Madge/320 Palmer Terrace #1F	914-698-1027
Crawford, Margery/237 E 31st St	212-686-6883	Dircks, David/295 Park Ave S #12N	212-260-7892
Crawford, Ronald/354 22nd St #6	718-768-6194	Dittrich, Dennis/42 W 72nd St #12B	212-864-5971
Creed, Cora/651 Vanderbilt St	718-633-7753	Dodds, Glenn/392 Central Park West #9M	212-679-3630

Illustrators

Continued

Please send us your additions and updates.

Dodge, Bill/60 E 42nd St #1940	212-867-8092
Domingo, Ray/108 E 35th St #1	212-889-3337
Doniger, Nancy/361 E 10th St #45	212-475-7901
Donner, Carroll/830 Broadway 10th Fl	212-254-0069
Doret, Michael/12 E 14th St	212-929-1688
Doret/ Smith Studios/12 E 14th St	212-929-1688
Doty, Curt/4 S Portland Ave #2	718-797-5115
Downes, Nicholas/PO Box 107	718-875-0086
Drescher, Henrik/151 First Ave #55	212-777-6077
Drovetto, Richard/355 E 72nd St	212-861-0927
Dryden, Patty/194 Third Ave	212-475-0440
Duarte, Mary Young/350 First Ave #9E	212-674-4513
Dubanevich, Arlene/866 UN Plaza #4014	212-644-2020
Dudzinski, Andrzej/52 E 81st St	212-628-6959
Duerk, Chris/259 E 33rd St #3	
Dunnick, Regan/41 Union Sq W #1228	813-951-2691
Dyess, John/156 Fifth Ave	212-243-1333

E
Eagel, Cameron/41 Union Sq #1228	212-929-5590
Eastman, Norm & Bryant/420 Lexington Ave #2738	212-697-8525
Eggert, John/420 Lexington Ave #2911	212-986-5680
Egielski, Richard/463 West St	212-255-9328
Ehlert, Lois/866 UN Plaza #4014	212-644-2020
Eisner, Gil/310 W 86th St #11A	212-595-2023
Ellis, Dean/30 E 20th St	212-254-7590
Elmer, Richard/504 E 11th St #FE1A	212-522-1051
Ely, Richard/150 W 55th St	212-757-8987
Emerson, Carmela/217-11 54th Ave	718-224-4251
Emmett, Bruce/285 Park Pl	718-636-5263
Endewelt, Jack/50 Riverside Dr	212-877-0575
Enik, Ted/82 Jane St #4A	212-620-5972
Ennis, John/75 Stone Ave	914-762-9403
Enric/43 E 19th St	212-688-1080
Ensor, Barbara/90 Fulton St	212-619-6103
Erickson, Mary Anne/154 Eighth Ave #4	212-929-7964
Ettlinger, Doris/73 Leonard St	212-226-0331
Eutemy, Loring/51 Fifth Ave	212-741-0140
Evans, Jan/853 Broadway #1201	212-677-9100
Evcimen, Al/305 Lexington Ave #6D	212-889-2995
Ewing, Carolyn/201 E 28th St	212-532-0928

F
Fanelli, Carolyn/19 Stuyvesant Oval	212-533-9829
Farina, Michael/18 E 16th St 2nd Fl	212-206-0322
Farmakis, Andreas/835 Third Ave	212-758-5280
Farrell, Sean/245 E 44th St #9D	212-949-6081
Fascione, Sabina/194 Third Ave	212-475-0440
Fasolino, Teresa/58 W 15th St	212-741-2539
Faulkner, Matt/435 Clinton St #4	718-858-1724
Faust, Clifford/322 W 57th St #42P	212-581-9461
FEBLAND, DAVID/670 WEST END AVE #11B (P 26)	**212-580-9299**
Fernandes, Stanislaw/35 E 12th St	212-533-2648
Fernandez, Fernando/43 E 19th St	212-254-4996
Fernandez, George/60 E 42nd St #1940	212-867-8092
Fertig, Howard/75-15 210th St	718-468-3627
Fichera, Maryanne/120 E 34th St	212-689-8670
Filippucci, Sandra/270 Park Ave S #9B	212-477-8732
Fine, Robert/43 E 19th St	212-254-4996
Fiore, Peter/10-11 162nd St #7D	718-358-9018
Fiorentino, Al/866 UN Plaza #4014	212-644-2020
Fischer, Rick/156 Fifth Ave #1222	212-645-6772
Fitzgerald, Frank/PO Box 6113	212-722-6793
Flaherty, David/650 Ninth Ave #1R	212-262-6536
Flanagan, Dan/427 15th St #1C	718-499-5253
Fleming, Ron/Graphic Assoc/60 E 42nd St #505	212-682-1490
Flesher, Vivienne/194 Third Ave	212-475-0440
FORBES, BART/501 FIFTH AVE #1407 (P 12)	**212-490-2450**
Forest, Sandra/315 Central Park W	212-580-8510
Forrest, Sandra/315 Central Pk W #3N	212-580-8510
Foster, B Lynne/540 Ft Washington Ave #3D	212-740-7011
Foster, Pat (Ms)/6 E 36th St #1R	212-685-4580
Foster, Stephen Design/145 W 28th St 10th Fl	212-967-2533
Fox, Barbara/301 W 53rd St	212-245-7564

Francis, Judy/110 W 96th St	212-866-7204
Fraser, Betty/240 Central Park South	212-247-1937
Freas, John/353 W 53rd St #1W	212-682-2462
Freelance Solutions/369 Lexington Ave 18th Fl	212-490-3334
Freeman, Irving/145 Fourth Ave #9K	212-674-6705
Freeman, Tom/157 W 57th St	212-247-1130
Fresh, Mark/1421 First Ave	212-674-5556
Fretz, Frank/866 UN Plaza #4014	212-644-2020
Fricke, Warren/15 W 72nd St	212-799-2231
Fried, Janice/51 W 46th St #3B	212-398-0067
Friedman, Barbara/29 Bank St	212-242-4951
Friedman, Jon/866 UN Plaza #4014	212-644-2020
Friedman, Wendy/136 Grand St #5WF	212-431-8824
Froom, Georgia/62 W 39th St #803	212-944-0330
Funtastic Studios/506 W 42nd St	212-239-8245
Furukawa, Mel/116 Duane St	212-349-3225

G
Gabriel, Don/43 E 19th St	212-254-4996
Gabriele, Antonio J/420 Lexington Ave #2911	212-986-5680
Gadino, Victor/1601 Third Ave	212-534-7206
Gaetano, Nicholas/821 Broadway 6th Fl	212-674-5749
Gala, Tom/420 Lexington Ave #2911	212-986-5680
Gale, Cynthia/229 E 88th St	212-860-5429
Galkin, Simon/19 E 48th St 3rd Fl	212-838-0050
Gallardo, Gervasio/50 E 50th St	212-355-0910
Galub, Meg/405 W 57th St	212-757-3506
Gambale, David/1500 Broadway #2013	212-391-1830
Gampert, John/PO Box 219	718-441-2321
Garner, David/175 W 87th St #26H	212-874-3147
Garrick, Jacqueline/333 E 75th St	212-628-1018
Garrido, Hector/420 Lexington Ave #2911	212-986-5680
Garrison, Barbara/12 E 87th St	212-348-6382
Gates, Donald/19 E 48th St 3rd Fl	212-838-0050
Gayler, Anne/418 E 75th St 2nd Fl	212-734-7060
Gehm, Charles/420 Lexington Ave #2738	212-697-8525
Geller, Amy/11-15 45th Ave	718-786-5277
Gem Studio/420 Lexington Ave #220	212-687-3460
Genova, Joe/60 E 42nd St #505	212-682-1490
Gentile, John & Anthony/850 Seventh Ave #1006	212-757-1966
Geras, Audra/501 Fifth Ave #1407	212-490-2450
Gershinowitz, George/PO Box 204 Chelsea Sta	718-596-1492
Gersten, Gerry/1380 Riverside Dr	212-928-7957
Giavis, Ted/420 Lexington Ave #2911	212-986-5680
Giglio, Mark/143 Waverly Pl #5F	212-645-4124
Giglio, Richard/2231 Broadway #17	212-724-8118
Gillot, Carol/67 E 11th St #708	212-353-1174
Giorgio, Nate/18 E 16th St	212-206-0322
Giovanopoulos, Paul/216 E 45th St	212-661-0850
Gold, Marcy/200 E 28th St #2C	212-685-4974
Goldstrom, Robert/471 Fifth St	718-768-7367
Goodell, Jon/866 UN Plaza #4014	212-644-2020
Goodman, Paula/156 Fifth Ave	212-243-1333
Goodrich, Carter/134 W 87th St #4F	212-787-9184
Gordon, Rebecca/201 W 16th St	212-989-5762
Gore, Elissa/583 W 215th St #A3	212-567-2161
Gorton, Julia/85 South St #6N	212-825-0190
Gothard, David/81 Greene St	212-925-3053
Gottfried, Max/82-60 116th St #CC3	718-441-9868
Gottlieb, Penelope/420 Lexington Ave #2738	212-679-8525
Gourley, Robin/225 Lafayette St #407	212-219-9391
Gowdy, Carolyn/81 Greene St	212-925-3053
Grace, Alexa/70 University Pl	212-254-4424
Graddon, Julian/48 W 21st St 9th Fl	212-243-4412
Graham, Mariah/670 West End Ave	212-580-8061
Graham, Thomas/408 77th St #D4	718-680-2975
Grajek, Tim/184 E 2nd St #4F	212-995-2129
Grant, William/4114 Highland Ave	718-996-3555
Grashow, David/81 Greene St	212-925-3053
Gray, Doug/15 W 72nd St	212-799-2231
Gray, John/264 Van Duzer St	718-447-6466
Gray, Susan/42 W 12th St #5	212-675-2243
Grebu, Devis/43 E 19th St	212-688-1080

Illustrators

Continued

Please send us your additions and updates.

Greenstein, Susan/4915 Surf Ave	718-373-4475
Gregoretti, Rob/240-13 Hanford St	718-229-5647
Greif, Gene/270 Lafayette St #1505	212-966-0470
Greifinger, Mel/1500 Broadway #2013	212-391-1830
Greiner, Larry/63 E 7th St	212-982-2428
Griesbach/Martucci/35 Sterling Pl	718-622-1831
Griffel, Barbara/23-45 Bell Blvd	718-631-1753
Griffin, James/60 E 42nd St #1940	212-867-8092
Grimmett, Douglas/467 Sixth Ave	212-627-8216
Grinko, Andy/125 Cedar St	212-732-5308
Gross, Mort/2 Park Ave #1804	212-686-4788
Grossman, Dina/28 St James Pl #1A	718-789-3350
Grossman, Robert/19 Crosby St	212-925-1965
Grossman, Wendy/355 W 51st St #43	212-262-4497
Guarnaccia, Steven/430 W 14th St #508	212-645-9610
Guitar, Jeremy/866 UN Plaza #4014	212-644-2020
Gumen, Murad/33-25 90th St #6K	718-478-7267
Gunn, Robert/201 E 28th St	212-532-0928
Gurbo, Walter/55 Hudson St #3A	212-775-1810
Gurney, John Steven/523 E 16th St	718-462-5073
Gusson, Steven/105 Bergen St #2B	718-852-7791

H

Haas, Arie/62 W 45th St	212-398-9540
Hack, Konrad/866 UN Plaza #4014	212-644-2020
Hahn, Marika/11 Riverside Dr	212-580-7896
Hall, Deborah Ann/105-28 65th Ave #6B	718-896-3152
Hall, Joan/155 Bank St #H954	212-243-6059
Hallgren, Gary/231 W 29th St #805	212-947-1054
Hamann, Brad/330 Westminster Rd	718-287-6086
Hampton, Blake/62 W 45th St	212-398-9540
Hamrick, Chuck/420 Lexington Ave #2911	212-986-5680
Hannon, Mark/156 Fifth Ave	212-243-1333
Hardy, Fran/145 E 22nd St	212-473-8747
Harrington, Glenn/165 E 32nd St	212-686-3514
Harris, Diane Teske/342 Madison Ave #469	212-719-9879
Harrison, William/18 E 16th St	212-206-0322
Hart, Veronika/60 E 42nd St #505	212-682-1490
Harvey, Ray/60 E 42nd St #1940	212-867-8092
Harwood, Laurel/1239 Broadway #1350	212-689-3515
Hays, Michael/43 Cheever Pl	718-852-2731
Heapps, Bill/2441 41st St	718-726-2193
Heck, Cathy/333 E 30th St	915-686-9343
Hedin, Donald/157 W 57th St	212-247-1130
Heindel, Robert/211 E 51st St #5F	212-755-1365
Heiner, Joe & Kathy/194 Third Ave	212-475-0440
Heller, Debbie/601 West End Ave	212-580-0917
Heller, Karen/300 W 108th St	212-866-5879
Helman, Marc/425 W 46th St #4E	212-262-5039
Henderson, Alan/31 Jane St #10B	212-243-0693
Henderson, Meryl/19 E 48th St 3rd Fl	212-838-0050
Henry, Paul/15 W 72nd St	212-799-2231
Herbert, Jonathan/1205 Manhattan Ave	718-383-1251
Herbick, David/5 Montague Terrace	718-852-6450
Herder, Edwin/60 E 42nd St #1940	212-867-8092
Hering, Al/277 Washington Ave #3E	718-789-7685
Herman, Rolla/462 Greenwich St	212-226-1510
Herman, Tim/853 Broadway	212-677-9100
Hernandez, Richard/144 Chambers St	212-732-3474
Herrmann, Hal/50 E 50th St	212-752-8490
Hewitt, Margaret/31 Ocean Pkwy #2C	718-436-2039
Hill, Amy/111 Wooster St #PH C	212-925-0491
Himler, Ron/866 UN Plaza #4014	212-644-2020
Hiroko/67-12 Yellowstone Blvd #E2	718-896-2712
Hoffman, Ginnie/108 E 35th St #1	212-889-3337
Hoffman, Rosekrans/866 UN Plaza #4014	212-644-2020
Hofkin, Bonnie/204 W 80th St	212-787-6384
Hofmekler, Ori/166 Second Ave #11K	212-829-9838
Hogarth, Paul/81 Greene St	212-925-3053
Holland, Brad/96 Greene St	212-226-3675
Holland, Gary/140 W 86th St #15A	212-877-9165
Holm, John/353 W 53rd St #1W	212-682-2462
Holst, Joani/1519 81st St	718-236-6214

Hom & Hom/470 W 23rd St	212-242-6367
Hong, Min Jae/422 E 14th St #1B	212-674-4320
Hooks, Mitchell/321 E 83rd St	212-737-1853
Hortens, Walter/154 E 64th St	212-838-0014
Hosner, William/853 Broadway	212-677-9100
Hostovich, Michael/127 W 82nd St #9A	212-580-2175
Hovland, Gary/140 W 86th St #15A	212-877-9165
Howard, John/336 E 54th St	212-832-7980
Howell, Kathleen/866 UN Plaza #4014	212-644-2020
Howland, Gary/140 W 86th St #15A	212-877-9165
Huang, Mei-ku/201 E 28th St	212-532-0928
Hubert, Laurent/216 E 45th St	212-661-0850
Huerta, Catherine/60 E 42nd St #505	212-682-1490
Huffman, Tom/130 W 47th St #6A	212-819-0211
Hughes, Mary Ellen/403 E 70th St	212-288-8375
Huling, Phil/33 E 22nd St #5F	212-673-0839
Hull, Cathy/165 E 66th St	212-683-8559
Hunt, Jim/853 Broadway	212-677-9100
Hunter, Stan/50 E 50th St	212-355-0910
Huston, Steven/15 W 72nd St	212-799-2231

IJ

Idelson, Joyce/11 Riverside Dr	606-269-2190
Igarashi, Satoru/222 W 20th St #16	212-242-8897
Image Network Inc/645 West End Ave	212-877-2517
Incandescent Ink Inc/111 Wooster St #PH C	212-925-0491
Incisa, Monica/141 E 56th St	212-752-1554
Inoue, Izumi/323 Park Ave S	212-473-8330
Iskowitz, Joel/420 Lexington Ave #2911	212-986-5680
Ivens, Rosalind/483 13th St	718-499-8285
Jaben, Seth/54 W 21st St #62	212-242-3181
Jamieson, Doug/42-20 69th St	718-565-6034
Jampel, Judith/148 Columbus Ave	212-873-5234
Jasper, Jackie/165 E 32nd St	212-686-3514
Jeffers, Kathy/106 E 19th St 12th Fl	212-475-1756
Jennis, Paul/420 Lexington Ave #2911	212-986-5680
Jetter, Frances/390 West End Ave	212-580-3720
Jezierski, Chet/50 E 50th St	212-355-0910
Jinks, John/690 Greenwich St #BD	212-675-2961
Jobe, Jody/875 W 181st St	212-795-4941
Johnson, David McCall/50 E 50th St	212-355-0910
Johnson, Doug/45 E 19th St	212-260-1880
Johnson, Julie/155 E 38th St	212-697-6170
Johnson, Kristin/441 W 37th St	212-594-2343
Johnston, David McCall/50 E 50th St	212-355-0910
Jones, Bob/420 Lexington Ave #2911	212-986-5680
Jones, Randy/323 E 10th St	212-677-5387
Jones, Taylor/19 E 48th St 3rd Fl	212-838-0050
Joseph, Paula/16 W 16th St #9SN	212-242-6137
Joudrey, Ken/746 Park Ave #2R	201-659-8875
Julian, Claudia/2939 Ave Y #1E	718-891-7957
Just, Hal/155 E 38th St	212-697-6170

K

Kagansky, Eugene/515 Ave I #2H	718-253-0454
Kahn, Sandra/PO Box 20141/Dag Hammrskld Ctr	
Kalish, Lionel/30 E 10th St	212-228-6587
Kallan, Elizabeth Kada/67 Irving Place	212-674-8080
Kalle, Chris/866 UN Plaza #4014	212-644-2020
Kaloustian, Rosanne/208-19 53rd Ave	718-428-4670
Kanarek, Michael/48 W 21st St 9th Fl	212-243-4412
Kantra, Michelle/40 W 27th St	212-684-6700
Kaplan, Mark/156 Fifth Ave #617	212-243-1333
Kappes, Werner/134 W 26th St	212-673-2484
Karlin, Bernie/41 E 42nd St	212-687-7636
Karlin, Nurit/19 E 48th St	212-838-0050
Katsin, Nancy/17 E 31st St #4F	212-213-0709
KATZ, LES/451 WESTMINSTER RD (P 31)	**718-284-4779**
Kaufman, Curt/215 W 88th St	212-873-9841
KAUFTHEIL/ROTHSCHILD/220 W 19TH ST #1200 (P 32,33)	**212-633-0222**
Keleny, Earl/515 Madison Ave 22nd Fl	212-486-9644
Kelley, Barbara/555 10th St	718-788-2465
Kelley, Mark/866 UN Plaza #4014	212-644-2020
Kelly, Susannah/77 Perry St	212-206-8960

Kendrick, Dennis/99 Bank St #3G	212-924-3085
Kernan, Patrick/413 W 48th St	212-581-2069
Keyes, Steven/18 E 16th St	212-206-0322
Kibbee, Gordon/6 Jane St	212-989-7074
Kieffer, Christa/866 UN Plaza #4014	212-644-2020
Kilmer, David/420 Lexington Ave #2911	212-986-5680
Kimura, Hiro/145 Washington Ave	718-638-0372
Kingston, James/31 E 31st St #10A	212-685-2520
Kirk, Daniel/85 South St #6N	212-825-0190
Klavins, Uldis/60 E 42nd St #1940	212-867-8092
Klein, David G/257 Winsdor Pl	718-788-1818
Klein, Renee/164 Daniel Low Terr	718-727-0723
Klein/Allen Studio/164 Daniel Low Terr	718-727-0723
Kling, Culla/777 Third Ave 10th Fl	212-546-2138
Kluglein, Karen/	
Knettell, Sharon/108 E 35th St #1	212-889-3337
Knight, Jacob/216 E 45th St	212-661-0850
Kobayashi, Ann/146 Berkeley Pl	718-622-6031
Kojoyian, Armen/52 Clark St #5K	718-797-5179
Kondo, Yukio/201 E 28th St	212-532-0928
Koren, Edward/81 Greene St	212-925-3053
Kotzky, Brian/132-42 Booth Memorial Ave	718-353-5480
Kovalcik, Terry/48 W 20th St	212-620-7772
Kramer, Carveth/216 E 45th St	212-661-0850
Kretschmann, Karin/323 W 75th St #1A	212-724-5001
Kronen, Jeff/231 Thompson St #22	212-475-3166
Krumeich, Tad/156 Fifth Ave	212-243-1333
Kubinyi, Laszlo/226 E 53rd St	201-833-4428
Kuester, Bob/353 W 53rd St #1W	212-682-2462
Kukalis, Romas/420 Lexington Ave #2911	212-986-5680
Kunstler, Mort/50 E 50th St	212-355-0910
Kuper, Peter/250 W 99th St #9C	212-864-5729
Kurman, Miriam/422 Amsterdam #2A	212-580-1649
Kursar, Ray/1 Lincoln Plaza #43R	212-873-5605
Kurtzman, Edward/60 E 42nd St #411	212-953-7088
Kurtzman, Harvey/18 E 16th St	212-206-0322

L LaPadula, Tom/201 E 28th St	212-532-0928
Lacey, Lucille/77-07 Jamaica Ave	718-296-1813
Lackner, Paul/19 E 48th St	212-838-0050
Lackow, Andy/1325 Third Ave	212-472-8898
Ladas, George/157 Prince St	212-673-2208
Lakeman, Steven/115 W 85th St	212-877-8888
Lamut, Sonja & Jakesevic, Nenad/165 E 32nd St	212-686-3514
Landis, Joan/6 Jane St	212-989-7074
Landry, Alice/62 W 45th St	212-398-9540
Lang, Cecily/19 Jones St #21	212-206-1251
Lang, Gary/420 Lexington Ave #2738	212-697-8525
Langenstein, Michael/56 Thomas St 2nd Fl	212-964-9637
Lapinski, Joe/853 Broadway #1201	212-677-9100
Laporte, Michele/579 Tenth St	718-499-2178
Larrain, Sally Marshall/19 E 48th St 3rd Fl	212-838-0050
Lasher, Mary Ann/60 E 42nd St #505	212-682-1490
Laslo, Larry/179 E 71st St	212-737-2340
Laurence, Karen/216 E 45th St	212-661-0850
Lauter, Richard/60 E 42nd St #1940	212-867-8092
Law, Polly/309 W 93rd St	212-866-3754
Lazure, Catherine/593 Riverside Dr #6D	212-690-1867
Le-Tan, Pierre/81 Greene St	212-925-3053
Lebbad, James A/1133 Broadway #1229	212-645-5260
Leder, Dora/866 UN Plaza #4014	212-644-2020
Lehr, Paul/50 E 50th St #5	212-355-0910
Lemerise, Bruce/410 W 24th St	212-989-0749
Leonard, Richard/212 W 17th St #2B	212-243-6613
Leonard, Tom/866 UN Plaza #4014	212-644-2020
Lesser, Robert/412 E 11th St #3B	212-228-1371
Lesser, Ron/420 Lexington Ave #2738	212-697-8525
Levin, Arnie/342 Madison Ave #469	212-719-9879
Levine, Andy/30-85 36th St #2	718-956-8539
Levine, Bette/60 E 42nd St #505	212-682-1490
Levine, Rena/200 Bethel Loop #12G	718-642-7339
Levine, Ron/1 W 85th St #4D	212-787-7415

Lewin, Ted/152 Willoughby Ave	718-622-3882
Lewis, Howard B/246 W 22nd St	212-243-3954
Lewis, Tim/194 Third Ave	212-475-0440
Lexa, Susan/866 UN Plaza #4014	212-644-2020
Liao, Sharmen/914 Arroyo Terr	818-458-7699
Liberatore, Gaetano/43 E 19th St	212-254-4996
Lieberman, Ron/109 W 28th St	212-947-0653
Lilly, Charles/24-01 89th St	718-803-3442
Lindberg, Jeffrey/449 50th St	718-492-1114
Lindgren, Goran/19 E 48th St 3rd Fl	212-838-0050
Lindlof, Ed/353 W 53rd St #1W	212-682-2462
Line, Lemuel/50 E 50th St	212-355-0910
Lippman, Peter/410 Riverside Dr #134	212-865-1823
Lipstein, Morissa/19 E 48th St	212-838-0050
Little Apple Art/409 Sixth Ave	718-499-7045
Lloyd, Peter/18 E 16th St	212-206-0322
LoGrippo, Robert/50 E 50th St #5	212-355-0910
Lockwood, Todd/60 E 42nd St #505	212-682-1490
Lodigensky, Ted/18 E 16th St	212-206-0322
Lorenz, Lee/108 E 35th St #1C	212-889-3337
Lovitt, Anita/308 E 78th St	212-628-8171
Low, William/31 Ocean Pkwy #2C	718-436-2039
Luce, Ben/5 E 17th St 6th Fl	212-255-8193
Lulevitch, Tom/101 W 69th St #4D	212-362-3318
Lustig, Loretta/19 E 48th St 3rd Fl	212-838-0050
Lyall, Dennis/420 Lexington Ave #2911	212-986-5680
Lynch, Jeff/420 Lexington Ave #2911	212-986-5680

M MacCombie, Turi/201 E 28th St	212-532-0928
Mack, Stan/226 E 53rd St	212-755-4945
Madden, Don/866 U N Plaza #4014	212-644-2020
Magdich, Dennis/420 Lexington Ave #2738	212-697-8525
Magnuson, Diana/461 Park Ave S	212-696-4680
Mahon, Rich/18 E 16th St	212-206-0322
Mahoney, Ron/353 W 53rd St #1W	212-682-2462
Maisner, Bernard/184 Second Ave #2A	212-475-5911
Maitz, Don/50 E 50th St #5	212-355-0910
Malan, Dee/201 E 28th St	212-532-0928
Malonis, Tina/34-44 71st St	718-565-8209
Mangal/155 E 38th St	212-697-6170
Mangiat, Jeffrey/420 Lexington Ave #2911	212-986-5680
Manos, Jim/51 E 42nd St #716	212-986-3282
Mantel, Richard/41 Union Sq W #1228	212-929-5590
Manyum, Wallop/37-40 60th St	718-476-1478
Marcellino, Fred Studio/432 Park Ave S #601	212-532-0150
Marchetti, Lou/420 Lexington Ave #2911	212-986-5680
Marciuliano, Frank/420 Lexington Ave #2738	212-697-8525
Mardon, Allan/108 E 35th St #1C	212-889-3337
Margulies, Robert/561 Broadway #10B	212-219-9621
Marich, Felix/853 Broadway	212-677-9100
Marinelli, Robert/165 Bryant Ave	718-979-4018
Marridejos, Fernando/130 W 67th St #1B	212-724-7339
Martin, Bruce Rough Riders/389 Ave of Americas	212-620-0539
MARTIN, JOHN/501 FIFTH AVE #1407 (P 15)	**212-490-2450**
Martinez, Edward/420 Lexington Ave #2911	212-986-5680
Martinez, John/280 Madison Ave	212-775-1810
Martinez, Sergio/43 E 19th St	212-254-4996
Martinot, Claude/145 Second Ave #20	212-473-3137
Marvin, Fred/43 E 19th St	212-254-4996
Masi, George/111 Wooster St #PH C	212-925-0491
Maslen, Barbara/45 W 18th St	212-645-5325
Mason, Brick/349 E 14th St #3R	212-777-4297
Mason, Tod/19 E 48th St 3rd Fl	212-838-0050
Mathewuse, James/157 W 57th St	212-247-1130
Mathieu, Joseph/81 Greene St	212-925-3053
Matsuyoshi, Akio/PO Box 1150	212-683-5621
Mattelson, Marvin/	
Maxwell, Brookie/53 Irving Pl	212-475-6909
May, Darcy/201 E 28th St	212-532-0928
Mazur, Ruby (Mr)/300 E 75th St #16K	212-734-2950
McArthur, Dennis/170-44 130th Ave	212-559-0029
McClintock, Wendell/60 E 42nd St #411	212-953-7088

McCollum, Rick/24 W 57th St #605	212-489-8777
McConnell, Gerald/10 E 23rd St	212-505-0950
McCormack, Geoffrey/420 Lexington Ave #2911	212-986-5680
McCreanor, Mike/156 Fifth Ave	212-243-1333
McCreary, Jane/866 UN Plaza #4014	212-644-2020
McDaniel, Jerry/155 E 38th St	212-697-6170
McKeating, Eileen/862 Union St #6H	718-638-0760
McKenzie, Crystal/30 E 20th St #502	212-598-4567
McKie, Roy/75 Perry	212-989-5186
McLaughlin, Gary/420 Lexington Ave #2738	212-697-8525
McLean, Wilson/50 E 50th St	212-752-8490
McMullan, James/222 Park Ave S #10B	212-473-5083
McNeel, Richard/215 Park Ave S	212-674-8080
McPheeters, Neal/16 W 71st St	212-799-7021
Mead, Kimble Pendleton/125 Prospect Park West	718-768-3632
Mehlman, Elwyn/108 E 35th St #1	212-889-3337
Meisel, Ann/420 Lexington Ave #2911	212-986-5680
Meisel, Paul/90 Hudson St #5E	212-226-5463
Meisler, Meryl/553 8th St	718-499-9836
Melendez, Robert/18 E 16th St 2nd Fl	212-206-0322
Merrell, Patrick/48 W 20th St	212-620-7777
Messi, Enzo & Schmidt, Urs/145 E 22nd St	212-473-8747
Meyerowitz, Rick/68 Jane St	212-989-2446
Michaels, Bob/304 E 49 St	212-685-6225
Michal, Marie/108 E 35th St #1	212-889-3337
Michner, Ted/420 Lexington Ave #2911	212-986-5680
Midda, Sara/81 Greene St	212-925-3053
Mihaesco, Eugene/25 Tudor City Pl #1423	212-692-9271
Mikos, Mike/420 Lexington Ave #2911	212-986-5680
Milbourn, Patrick/327 W 22nd St	212-989-4594
Milicic, Michael/570 Ft Washington Ave #34B	212-927-2353
Miller, Cliff/60 E 42nd St #1940	212-867-8092
Millington, Hunter/49 W 11th St #14	212-645-8688
Milne, Jonathon/420 Lexington Ave	212-986-5680
Minor, Wendell/277 W 4th St	212-691-6925
Miro/60 E 42nd St #1940	212-867-8092
Mitchell, Celia/30-25 Steinway St #1B	718-626-4095
Mitra, Annie/237 W 15th St #4B	212-330-6444
Mitsuhashi, Yoko/43 E 29th St	212-683-7312
Miyamoto, Linda/PO Box 2310	718-596-4787
Mones-Mateu/43 E 19th St	212-254-4996
Montesano, Sam/60 E 42nd St #1940	212-867-8092
Montgomery, Marilyn/280 Madison Ave #1402	212-775-1810
Montiel, David/115 W 16th St #211	212-989-7426
Moraes, Greg/60 E 42nd St #428	212-867-8092
Morgan, Jacqui/692 Greenwich St	212-675-7208
Morgen, Barry/337 W 87th St #G	212-595-6835
Morris, Frank/15 W 72nd St	212-799-2231
Morrison, Don/155 E 38th St	212-697-6170
Morse, Bill/60 E 42nd St #505	212-682-1490
Moss, Geoffrey/315 E 68th St	212-472-9474
Mossey, Belinda/526 2nd	718-499-2588
Mukai, Dennis/1500 Broadway #2013	212-391-1830
Mulcaby, Karen/130 Jane St	212-714-2550
Murakami, Maho/34-21 61st St	718-446-3204
Murawski, Alex/108 E 35th St #1	212-889-3337
Murdocca, Sal/19 E 48th St 3rd Fl	212-838-0050
Myers, David L/228 Bleecker St #8	212-989-5260

N Nagaoka, Shusei/15 W 72nd St — 212-799-2231

Nahigan, Alan/33-08 31st Ave #2R	718-274-4042
Najaka, Marlies/241 Central Park West	212-580-0058
Nakai Sacco & Crowell/218 Madison Ave	212-213-5333
Nascimbene, Yan/156 Fifth Ave #1222	212-645-6772
Nazz, James/159 Second St #12	212-228-9713
Neff, Leland/506 Amsterdam Ave #61	212-724-1884
Nelson, Bill/121 Madison Ave	212-683-1362
Nemirov, Meredith/110 Kent St	718-389-5972
Nessim, Barbara/63 Greene St	212-677-8888
Neubecker, Robert/395 Broadway #14C	212-219-8435
Neumann, Ann/444 Broome St	212-431-7141
NEWTON, RICHARD/501 FIFTH AVE #1407 (P 13)	**212-490-2450**

Neyman-Levikova, Marina/155 E 38th St	212-697-6170
Ng, Michael/58-35 155th St	718-461-8264
Nicastre, Michael/420 Lexington Ave #2738	212-697-8525
Nicholas, Jess/18 E 16th St	212-206-0322
Nicklaus, Carol/866 UN Plaza #4014	212-644-2020
Nicotra, Rosanne/420 Lexington Ave #2738	212-697-8525
Nitzburg, Andrew/165 E 32nd St	212-686-3514
Noftsinger, Pamela/600 W 111th St #6A	212-316-4241
Noonan, Julia/873 President St	718-622-9268
North, Russ/40 W 20th St #901	212-242-6300
Nosek, Laslo/440 West End Ave	212-362-7376
Nosz Studio Inc/440 West End Ave	212-362-7376
Notarile, Chris/420 Lexington Ave #2911	212-986-5680
Novak, Justin/156 Fifth Ave	212-243-1333

O O'Brien, Tim/60 E 42nd St #411 — 212-953-7088

Oberheide, Heide/295 Washington Ave #5B	718-622-7056
Ochagavia, Carlos/50 E 50th St #5	212-355-0910
Odom, Mel/252 W 76th St #B1	212-724-9320
Oelbaum, Fran/1500 Broadway #2013	212-391-1830
Olanoff, Greg/60 E 42nd St #1940	212-867-8092
Olbinski, Rafal/470 W 23rd St	212-242-6367
Olitsky, Eve/235 W 102nd St #12K	212-678-1045
Olson, Richard A/85 Grand St	212-925-1820
Orloff, Denis/682 Carroll St #1	718-965-0385
Ortiz, Jose Luis/PO Box 6678	212-877-3081
Osaka, Rick/14-22 30th Dr	718-956-0015
Osborn, Stephen/280 Madison Ave #1402	212-775-1810

P Pace, Don/9303 Shore Rd — 718-748-7651

Palaez, Joan/43 E 19th St	212-254-4996
Pantuso, Mike/350 E 89th St	212-534-3511
Pappas, Joanne/401 20th St	718-788-7689
Paragraphics/427 3rd St	718-965-2231
Paraskevas, Michael/41 Union Sq #1228	212-929-5590
Pardy, Cindy/1500 Broadway #2013	212-391-1830
Parker, Robert Andrew/81 Greene St	212-925-3053
Parsons, John/420 Lexington Ave #2738	212-697-8525
Paslavsky, Evan/510-7 Main St N	212-759-3985
Passarelli, Charles/353 W 53rd St #1W	212-682-2462
Pasternak, Robert/114 W 27th St #55	212-675-0002
Paul, Tony/467 W 57th St	212-307-6188
Peak, Matt/60 E 42nd St #1940	212-867-8092
Peak, Robert/50 E 50th St	212-752-8490
Pearson, Jim/866 UN Plaza #4014	212-644-2020
Pechanel, Vladimir/34-43 Crescent St #4C	718-729-3973
Pedersen, Judy/96 Greene St	212-226-3675
Peele, Lynwood/344 W 88th St	212-799-3305
Pelavin, Daniel/46 Commerce St #4	212-929-2706
Pelikan, Judy/200 E 78th St	212-570-9069
Pendleton, Roy/215 Park Ave S	212-674-8080
Percivalle, Rosanne/430 W 14th St #413	212-243-6589
Perez, Maria/119 W 23rd St	212-807-8730
Perez, Vince/43 E 19th St	212-254-4996
Perini, Benny/932 President St #6	718-622-4578
Personality Inc/501 Fifth Ave #1407	212-490-2450
Peters, Bob/108 E 35th St #1C	212-889-3337
Peterson, Cheryl/81 Greene St	212-925-3053
Peterson, Robin/411 West End Ave	212-724-3479
Petragnani, Vincent/853 Broadway	212-677-9100
Petruccio, Steven/201 E 28th St	212-532-0928
Pettingill, Ondre/2 Ellwood St #3U	212-942-1993
Phillips, Barry/24 W 57th St #605	212-489-8777
Pierson, Mary Louise/310 W 56th St #11B	212-315-3516
Pietrobono, Janet/147 Sterling Pl	212-245-7300
Pincus, Harry/160 Sixth Ave @ 210 Spring St	
Pinkney, Debbie/280 Madison Ave #1402	212-775-1810
Pinturov/15 W 72nd St	212-799-2231
Pisano, Al/22 W 38th St	212-213-3204
Piscopia, Joe/114 Beadel St	718-384-2206
Podwill, Jerry/108 W 14th St	212-255-9464
Pogue, Deborah Bazzel/48 W 21st St 9th Fl	212-243-4412

Illustrators
Continued

Please send us your additions and updates.

Poladian, Girair/42 E 23rd St #6N	212-529-7878
Polenghi, Evan/159 25th St	718-499-3214
Pollack, Scott/333 E 66th St	212-517-3599
Popp, Wendy/95 Horatio St #203	212-807-0840
Porter, Frederick/156 Fifth Ave	212-243-1333
Powell, Ivan/58 W 15th St	212-741-2539
Powers, Christine/198 Berkeley Pl	203-966-1417
Powers, Tom/156 Fifth Ave	212-243-1333
Prato, Rodica/154 W 57th St #123	212-683-1362
Purdom, Bill/780 Madison Ave #7A	212-988-4566
Pyk, Jan/19 E 48th St 3rd Fl	212-838-0050

QR
Quartuccio, Dom/5 Tudor City Pl #2201	212-661-1173
Quon, Mike Design Office/568 Broadway #703	212-226-6024
Racz, Michael/18-36 26th Rd #1R	718-956-0980
Radigan, Bob/280 Madison Ave #1402	212-775-1810
Ragland, Greg/258 Broadway #4E	212-513-7218
Raglin, Tim/138 W 74th St	212-873-0538
Rainbow Grinder/55 Hudson St #3A	212-775-1810
Rane, Walter/60 E 42nd St #1940	212-867-8092
Rea, John/300 W 23rd St #26	212-546-1384
Realo, Perry A/155 E 2nd St #4B	212-254-5635
Reay, Richard/515 W 236th St	212-884-2317
Reddin, Paul/120 Windsor Pl	718-965-0647
Reed, Chris/14 E 4th St #817	212-677-7198
Reed, Herb/156 Fifth Ave	212-243-1333
Reim, Melanie/214 Riverside Dr #601	212-749-0177
Reinert, Kirk/60 E 42nd St #1940	212-867-8092
Reingold, Alan/155 E 38th St	212-697-6170
Reingold, Michael/121 Heberton Ave	718-981-1999
Renfro, Ed/250 E 83rd St #4E	212-879-3823
Reott, Paul/51-10 Van Horn St	718-426-1928
Reynolds, Scott/308 W 30th St #9B	212-239-0009
Rice, John/156 Fifth Ave	212-243-1333
Rich, Anna M/777 St Marks Ave	718-604-0121
Rich, Norman/2557 Marion Ave #3G	212-733-5140
Richards, Linda/27 Bleecker St	212-673-1600
Ridgeway, Ron/330 W 42nd St #3200 NE	212-714-0130
Rigie, Mitch/41 Union Sq W #918	212-807-6627
Rigo, Martin/43 E 19th St	212-254-4996
Risko, Robert/201 W 11th St	212-989-6987
Rixford, Ellen/308 W 97th St	212-865-5686
Roberts, Phil/420 Lexington Ave #2911	212-986-5680
Robinson, Charles/866 UN Plaza #4014	212-644-2020
Robinson, Lenor/201 E 69th St #6I	212-734-0944
RODRIGUEZ, ROBERT/501 FIFTH AVE #1407 (P 17)	**212-490-2450**
Rogers, Lilla/483 Henry St	718-624-6862
Roman, Barbara/345 W 88th St #5C	212-362-1374
Romer, Dan/125 Prospect Park W	718-768-3632
Romero, Javier/529 W 42nd St	212-206-9175
Root, Barry/58 W 15th St	212-741-2589
Roper, Bob/43-17 55th St	718-898-8591
Rosen, Terry/101 W 81st St #508	212-580-4784
Rosenblum, Richard/392 Fifth Ave	212-279-2068
Rosenfeld, Mort/420 Lexington Ave #2911	212-986-5680
Rosenthal, Doug/24 Fifth Ave	212-475-9422
Rosenthal, Marc/230 Clinton St	518-766-4191
Rosenzweiz, Myra/310 W 90th St	212-362-9871
Rosner, Meryl/21 Grammercy Park #3A	212-254-7668
ROSS CULBERT HOLLAND & LAVERY/15 W 20TH ST 9TH	
FL (P 40,41)	**212-206-0044**
Ross, Barry/211 W 102nd St #5A	212-663-7386
Ross, Bronwen/866 UN Plaza #4014	212-644-2020
Ross, Ian/106 Lexington Ave #2	212-685-4178
Ross, Richard/204 W 20th St	212-675-8800
Rothman, Mike/21 W 74th St	212-362-3302
Roy, Frederick/205 W 14th St	212-255-0775
RUBYAN, ROBERT/241 W 36TH ST #9R (P 42)	**212-563-0633**
Ruddell, Gary/18 E 16th St	212-206-0322
Rudenjack, Phyllis/245 E 72nd St	212-772-2813
Ruff, Donna/595 West End Ave	212-627-9858
Ruffins, Reynold/15 W 20th St 9th Fl	212-627-5220

Ruiz, Artie/43 E 19th St	212-254-4996
Runda, Ron/60 E 42nd St #1940	212-867-8092
Russell, Billy D/483 Columbus Ave #2B	212-873-7975
Russell, Melissa/350 E 89th St	212-502-3976
Rutherford, Stephen/69 Fifth Ave #3	718-857-5253
Ryan, Terry/330 W 4th St	212-688-1080

S
Sabanosh, Michael/433 W 34th St #18B	212-947-8161
Sabin, Robert/60 E 42nd St #1940	212-867-8092
Saffioti, Lino/61-15 218th St	718-224-3170
Saksa Art & Design/41 Union Sq W #1001	212-255-5539
Saldutti, Denise/463 West St #354H	212-255-9328
Salina, Joe/60 E 42nd St #505	212-682-1490
Samuels, Mark/25 Minetta Ln #4A	212-777-8580
Sanders, Jane/47-51 40th St #6D	718-786-3505
Sanjulian/43 E 19th St	212-688-1080
Santoro, Christopher/201 E 28th St	212-532-0928
Sargent, Claudia K/15-38 126th St	718-461-8280
Saris, Anthony/103 E 86th St	212-831-6353
Sauber, Rob/420 Lexington #2911	212-986-5680
Sauriel, Brian/420 Lexington Ave #2911	212-986-5680
Sawka, Jan/353 W 53rd St #1W	212-682-2462
Schaare, Harry/60 E 42nd St #1940	212-867-8092
Schaedler, Sally/156 Fifth Ave	212-243-1333
Schaer, Miriam/522 E 5th St	212-673-4926
Schaller, Tom/2255 Broadway #303	212-362-5524
Schanzer, Roz/461 Park Ave S	212-696-4680
Scheld, Betsy/429 E 65th St #13	212-260-0062
Scheuer, Phil/126 Fifth Ave #13B	212-620-0728
Schmidt, Bill/60 E 42nd St #1940	212-867-8092
Schmidt, Chuck/853 Broadway	212-677-9100
Schneegass, Martinu/35 Carmine St #9	212-860-6643
Schongut, Emanuel/	
Schottland, Miriam/470 W 23rd St	212-242-6367
Schreiber, Dana/89 James Pl	718-638-3505
Schreier, Joshua/466 Washington St	212-925-0472
Schumacher, Michael/353 W 53rd St #1W	212-682-2462
Schumacher, Ward/194 Third Ave	212-475-0440
Schumer, Arlen/313 E Sixth St	212-254-8242
SCHWAB, MICHAEL/501 FIFTH AVE (P 10,11)	**212-490-2450**
Schwartz, Joanie/22 E 36th St #3C	212-213-1282
Schwarz, Jill Karla/80 N Moore St	212-227-2444
Scott, Bob/106 Lexington Ave	212-684-2409
Scott, Robert/250 W 16th St St #4E	301-535-3741
Scrofani, Joe/353 W 53rd St #1W	212-682-2462
Seaver, Jeffrey/130 W 24th St #4B	212-741-2279
Segal, John/324 W 101st St	212-662-3278
Seltzer, Isadore/336 Central Park West	212-666-1561
Sempe, J J/81 Greene St	212-925-3053
Sentnor, Robert/3871 Sedgwick Ave	212-884-7048
Shafer, Ginger/113 Washington Pl	212-989-7697
Shahinian, Brenda/81 Greene St	212-925-3053
Shap, Sandra/853 Broadway #1201	212-677-9100
Shea, Mary Anne/154 Eighth Ave #4	212-929-7964
Shega, Marla/60 E 42nd St #505	212-682-1490
Shenefield, Barbara/223 Sullivan St	212-254-1946
Sherman, Mary/165 E 32nd St	212-686-3514
Sherman, Maurice/209 E 23rd St	212-679-7350
Shields, Charles/226 E 53rd St	212-755-4945
Shohet, Marti/26 W 17th St 8th Fl	212-627-1299
Shub, Steve/48 W 21st St 9th Fl	212-243-4412
Siciliano, Gerald/261 Fourth Ave	718-636-4561
Siegel, Norm/333 E 49th St	212-980-8061
Silverman, Burt/324 W 71st St	212-799-3399
Singer, Alan D/70 Prospect Park W	718-797-4083
Singer, Paul Design/494 14th St	718-499-8172
Skardinski, Stan/201 E 28th St	212-532-0928
Skolsky, Mark/15 W 72nd St	212-799-2231
Skopp, Jeniffer/1625 Emmons Ave #6H	718-789-2983
Slack, Chuck/60 E 42nd St #505	212-682-1490
Slackman, Charles B/320 E 57th St	212-758-8233
Slavin, Fran/452 Myrtle Ave	718-403-9643

Sloan, William/236 W 26th St #805	212-463-7025
Slvavec, Diane/60 E 42nd St #1940	212-867-8092
Smalley, Guy/183 Madison Ave	212-683-0339
Smith, Brett/353 W 53rd St #1W	212-682-2462
Smith, Gary/48 W 21st St 9th Fl	212-243-4412
Smith, Joseph/159 John St #6	212-825-1475
Smith, Laura/12 E 14th St #4D	212-206-9162
Smith, Mary Anne/44 E 1st St #2	212-420-0204
Smith, Trudi/866 UN Plaza #4014	212-644-2020
Smith, Vicki/504 E 5th St #6C	212-475-1671
Smollin, Mike/420 Lexington Ave #2911	212-986-5680
Smythe, Danny/853 Broadway	212-677-9100
Sneberger, Dan/60 E 42nd St #1940	212-867-8092
Sobel, Phillip Eric/80-15 41st Ave #128	718-476-3841
Soderlind, Kirsten/111 Wooster St # PH C	212-925-0491
Solie, John/420 Lexington Ave #2911	212-986-5680
Solomon, Debra/536 W 111th St #55	212-662-5619
Soloski, Tommy/49 W 85th St #1D	212-787-7142
Solowedel, Kip/420 Lexington Ave #2911	212-986-5680
Sottung, George/420 Lexington Ave #2911	212-986-5680
Spacak, Peter/611 Broadway #610	212-505-6802
Spector, Joel/130 E 16th St	212-254-3527
Spollen, Chris/362 Cromwell Ave	718-979-9695
Sposato, John/43 E 22nd St #2A	212-477-3909
Stabin, Victor/100 W 15th St #4I	212-243-7688
Stahl, Nancy/194 Third Ave	212-475-0440
Stallard, Peter/60 E 42nd St #505	212-682-1490
Staples, Matthew/141 W 36th St 14th Fl	212-279-7935
Starace, Tom/2 Stuyvesant Oval #3D	212-228-8674
Stavrinos, George/76 W 86th St #6D	212-724-1557
Steadman, Barbara/330 E 33rd St #10A	212-684-6326
Steadman, E T/470 W 23rd St	212-242-6367
Steiner, Frank/60 E 42nd St #1940	212-867-8092
Stephens, Lynn/52 W 87th St #4A	212-787-6195
Sternglass, Arno/622 Greenwich St	212-675-5667
Sterrett, Jane/160 Fifth Ave #700	212-929-2566
Stewart, Arvis/866 UN Plaza #4014	212-644-2020
Stewart, Pat/201 E 28th St	212-352-0928
Stillerman, Robbie/230 E 44th St #2F	212-661-7149
Stillman, Susan/126 W 71st St #5A	212-724-5634
Stone, Gilbert/58 W 15th St	212-741-2539
Strachan, Bruce/999 Lorimer St	718-383-1264
Streeter, Sabina/141 Wooster St	212-254-7436
Studio 23/6 W 20th St 2nd Fl	212-243-7362
Suares, J C/60 E 42nd St	212-682-1490
Suh, John/60 E 42nd St #411	212-953-7088
Sullivan, Suzanne Hughes/225 Central Pk W #1402	212-496-0162
Sweeney, Jerry/339 Blvd of Allies	412-391-4471
Sweny, Stephen/217 E 29th St #52	212-532-4072
Szabo, Gustav/440 West End Ave	212-362-7376
Szilagyi, Mary/410 Central Park West	212-666-7578
Szpura, Beata/48-02 69th St	718-424-8440
Szumowski, Tom/60 E 42nd St	212-682-1490
Szygiel, Jas/165 E 32nd St	212-686-3514

T

Taba, Eugene/1185 Sixth Ave 8th Fl	212-730-0101
Taback, Simms/15 W 20th St 9th Fl	212-627-5220
Taleporos, Plato/333 E 23rd St	212-689-3138
Tankersley, Paul/29 Bethune St	212-924-0015
Tauss, Marc/484 W 43rd St #40H	212-410-2827
Taylor, Doug/106 Lexington Ave	212-674-6346
Taylor, Katrina/216 E 45th St	212-661-0850
Tedesco, Michael/120 Boerum Pl #1E	718-596-4179
Terreson, Jeffrey/420 Lexington Ave #2911	212-986-5680
The Hub/16 E 16th St 4th Fl	212-675-8500
The Ink Tank/2 W 47th St 14th Fl	212-869-1630
The Sketch Pad Studio/6 Jane St	212-989-7074
Theakston, Greg/15 W 72nd St	212-799-2231
Thompson, Bill/18 E 16th St	212-206-0322
Thompson, Thierry/420 Lexington Ave #2911	212-986-5680
Thonnessen, Sabina/141 Wooster St #3B	212-254-7436
Thorpe, Peter/254 Park Ave S #6C	212-477-0131

Tierney, Tom/201 E 28th St	212-532-0928
Tod-Kat Studios/353 W 53rd St #1W	212-682-2462
Torpedo Studios/350 E 89th St	212-502-3976
Travers, Robert/60 E 42nd St #1940	212-867-8092
Trondsen, Bob/60 E 42nd St #1940	212-867-8092
Trossman, Michael/411 West End Ave #16D	212-799-6852
Trull, John/1573 York Ave	212-535-5383
Tsugami, Kyuzo/156 Fifth Ave #617	212-243-1333
Tunstull, Glenn/47 State St	718-834-8529
Turk, Steve/4120 Cold Stream Terrace	818-705-0660
Turner, Clay/Graphic Assoc/60 E 42nd St #505	212-682-1490

UV

Uram, Lauren/251 Washington Ave #2F	718-789-7717
Vaccaro, Lou/866 UN Plaza #4014	212-644-2020
Vahid/18 E 16th St 2nd Fl	212-206-0322
Vainisi, Jenny/225 E 10th St #1A	212-477-3086
Valla, Victor/60 E 42nd St #1940	212-867-8092
Varlet-Martinelli/1500 Broadway #2013	212-391-1830
Vaux, Jacquie Marie/165 E 32nd St	212-686-3514
Vecchio, Carmine/200 E 27th St	212-683-2679
Velasquez, Eric/226 W 113th St	212-866-2209
Ventura, Dana/134 W 32nd St #602	212-244-4270
Victor, Joan B/863 Park Ave #11E	212-988-2773
Villa, Roxanne/31 Strong Pl #3	718-797-0348
Viviano, Sam/25 W 13th St	212-242-1471
Vogt, Elaine/242 E 83rd St	212-988-6430
Vollath, Gunther/156 Fifth Ave #617	212-243-1333
Vosk, Alex/521 E 82nd St #1A	212-737-2314
Voth, Gregory/231 W 20th St	212-807-9766

W

Wajdowicz, Jurek/1123 Broadway	212-807-8144
Waldman, Michael/506 W 42nd St #G4	212-239-8245
Walker, Jeff/60 E 42nd St #1940	212-867-8092
Walker, John S/47 Jane St	212-242-3435
Wall, Pam/Airstream/60 E 42nd St #505	212-682-1490
Waller, Charles/35 Bethune St PH C	212-989-5843
Wallner, Alexandra & John/866 UN Plaza #4014	212-644-2020
Walsh, Terry/48 W 21st St	212-243-4412
Wanamaker, Jo Ann/225 W 86th St	212-724-1786
Ward, Donna/19 E 48th St 3rd Fl	212-838-0050
Warhola, James/23-11 40th Ave	718-937-6467
Waring & LaRosa/555 Madison Ave	212-755-0700
Wasserman, Randi/28 W 11th St	212-254-0468
Wasson, Cameron/4 S Portland Ave #3	718-875-8277
Weaver, Robert/42 E 12th St	212-254-4289
Weiman, Jon/147 W 85th St #3F	212-787-3184
Weinstein, Morey/35 E 20th St	212-260-6702
Weisbecker, Philippe/21 W 86th St	212-580-3143
Weisser, Carl/38 Livingston St #33	718-834-0952
Weissman, Sam/2510 Fenton Ave	212-840-3300
Welker, Gaylord/27 Bleecker St	212-673-1600
Wells, Skip/244 W 10th St	212-242-5563
Whistl'n Dixie/25 W 39th St #902	212-764-5591
White, Richard A/250 Washington Ave	718-783-3244
Whitehead, Samuel B/206 Eighth Ave	718-965-2047
Whitehouse, Debora/1457 Broadway #1001	212-840-8223
Whitesides, Kim/501 Fifth Ave #1407	212-490-2450
Wiemann, Roy/PO Box 271/Prince St Sta	212-431-3793
Wilkinson, Bill/155 E 38th St	212-697-6170
Wilkinson, Chuck/60 E 42nd St #505	212-682-1490
Willardson + Assoc/194 Third Ave	212-475-0440
Williams, Elizabeth/349 E 82nd St #8	212-517-4593
Williams, Oliver/141 Fifth Ave 12th Fl	212-674-1903
Williams, Richard/58 W 15th St	212-741-2539
Wilshire, Mary/217 E 85th St #15W	212-463-8980
Wilson, Amanda/346 E 20th St	212-260-7567
Wilson, Deborah C/339 E 33rd St #1R	212-532-5205
Wilson, Harvey/316 Clinton Ave	718-857-8525
Wind, Bodhi/43 E 19th St	212-254-4996
Winkowski, Fred/48 W 71st St	212-724-3136
Winterrowd, Turk/62 E Broadway 5th Fl	212-966-0031
Winters, Nina/20 W 77th St	212-877-3089

Illustrators

Continued

Please send us your additions and updates.

Wohlberg, Ben/43 Great Jones St	212-254-9663
Wolfe, Bruce/194 Third Ave	212-475-0440
Wolff, Punz/151 E 20th St #5G	212-254-5705
Wolfgang, Sherri/313 E 6th St	212-254-8242
Wollman, Paul/60 E 42nd St #505	212-682-1490
Womersley, David/420 Lexington Ave #2911	212-986-5680
Wood, Clare/54 Berkeley Pl	718-783-3734
Wood, Page/48 W 21st St 9th Fl	212-243-4412
Woodend, James/420 Lexington Ave #2738	212-697-8525
Woodman, Jowill/334 W 49th St #5RW	212-765-8406
Wray, Wendy/194 Third Ave	212-475-0440
Wyatt, Kathy/43 E 19th St	212-254-4996
Wynne, Patricia/446 Central Pk West	212-865-1059

Y

Yalowitz, Paul/215 E 26th St #7	212-532-0859
Yankus, Marc/179 Prince St	212-228-6539
Yee, Josie/111 Wooster St #PHC	212-925-0491
Yeldham, Ray/420 Lexington Ave #2911	212-986-5680
Yemi/77 W 15th St #3F	212-627-1269
Yiannias, Vicki/1500 Broadway #2013	212-391-1830
Yip, Jennie/6103 Twentieth Ave	718-236-0349
York, Judy/165 E 32nd St	212-686-3514
Yorke, Oliver/525-A Sixth Ave	718-965-0609
Young, Lisa/545 W 111th St	212-864-5673
Yule, Susan Hunt/176 Elizabeth St	212-226-0439

Z

Zacharow, M Christopher/109 Waverly Pl #4R	212-460-5739
Zagorski, Stanislaw/142 E 35th St	212-532-2348
Zaid, Barry/108 E 35th St #1	212-889-3337
Zamchick, Gary/137 E 25th St 1st Fl	212-213-5096
Zann, Nicky/155 W 68th St	212-724-5027
Zeldich, Arieh/866 UN Plaza #4014	212-644-2020
Zick, Brian/194 Third Ave	212-475-0440
Ziering, Bob/151 W 74th St #2B	212-873-0034
Zimic, Tricia/341 E 6th St #4A	212-598-4228
Zimmerman, Jerry/48 W 20th St 2nd Fl	212-620-7777
Zimmerman, Robert/254 Park Ave S #6C	212-477-0131
Zudeck, Michael/41 Union Sq NY	212-929-5590
Zwarenstein, Alex/15 W 72nd St	212-799-2231

Northeast

A

Abel, Ray/18 Vassar Pl, Scarsdale, NY	914-725-1899
Adam Filippo & Moran/1206 Fifth Ave, Pittsburgh, PA	412-261-3720
Adams, Norman/229 Berkeley #52, Boston, MA	617-266-3858
Addams, Charles/PO Box 8, Westport, CT	203-227-7806
Agans, Carol/3 Medford Ave, Mercerville, NJ	609-586-9071
Ahmed, Ghulan Hassan/5738 Edgepark Rd, Baltimore, MD	301-444-8246
Alcorn, Bob/434 South Main St, Heightstown, NJ	609-448-4448
Aldrich, Susan/PO Box 1164, Smithtown, NY	516-261-6220
Alexander, Paul R/37 Pine Mountain Rd, Redding, CT	203-544-9293
Allanson, Bryan/275 W Clinton St #4A, Dover, NJ	212-696-7403
Allen, Tanya/74 Washington Ave, Natick, MA	617-651-1474
Alsop, Mark/324 Auburndale Ave, Auburndale, MA	617-527-7862
Alterio, Caroline/25 Gray St, Boston, MA	617-236-1920
Ancas, Karen/7 Perkins Sq #11, Jamaica Plain, MA	617-522-2958
Anderson, Richard/490 Bleeker Ave, Mamaroneck, NY	914-381-2682
Annand, Jonathan/10 Manor Rd, Harrington Park, NJ	201-768-6072
Armstrong, Stuart/1503 Dublin Dr, Silver Spring, MD	301-681-6178
Ashmead, Hal/39 Club House Dr, Woodbury, CT	203-263-3466
Avati, Jim/345 Broad St #12, Redbank, NJ	201-842-4370

B

Bailey, Brian/461 9th St, Palisades Park, NJ	201-585-2937
Baker, Lori/33 Richdale Ave, Cambridge, MA	617-492-5689
Baker, Skip/731 N 24th St, Philadelphia, PA	215-232-6666
Bakley, Craig/68 Madison Ave, Cherry Hill, NJ	609-428-6310
Ball, Harvey/340 Main St, Wooster, MA	617-752-9154
Banek, Yvette/185 Goodhill Rd, Weston, CT	203-226-7674
Bang, Molly Garrett/43 Drumlin Rd, Falmouth, MA	617-540-5174
Bangham, Richard/2006 Cascade Rd, Silver Spring, MD	301-649-4919

Banta, Susan/17 Magazine St, Cambridge, MA	617-876-8568
Barbagallo, Ron/36 E 35th St, Bayonne, NJ	201-437-2394
Barber, David/21 Taft St, Marblehead, MA	617-631-6130
Barger, Peter/25 Gray St, Boston, MA	617-236-1920
Barkley, James/444 Bedford Rd, Pleasantville, NY	914-747-2220
Barnard, Bryn/PO Box 285, Woodbury, MA	
Barrett, Tom/151 Tremont St #14R, Boston, MA	617-426-1918
Baruffi, Andrea/341 Hudson Terrace, Piermont, NY	914-359-9542
Becker, N Neesa/241 Monroe St, Philadelphia, PA	215-925-5363
Beisel, Dan/4713 Ribble Ct, Ellicott City, MD	301-461-6377
Belser, Burkey/1818 N St NW #110, Washington, DC	202-775-0333
Bendis, Keith/275 Tanglewylde Rd, Lake Peekskill, NY	914-528-7378
Bennett, James/301 Willow Ave #1, Hoboken, NJ	201-963-1457
Benson, John D/2111-A Townhill Rd, Baltimore, MD	301-665-3395
Berg, John/305 Bryant St, Buffalo, NY	716-884-8003
Berg, Linda/34 Westwood Dr, E Rochester, NY	716-385-8513
Berlin, Frederic/220 Ferris Ave, White Plains, NY	914-946-1950
Bernette, Larry/444 Bedford Rd, Pleasantville, NY	914-747-2220
Berry, Sheila & Richard/803 E 5th St, South Boston, MA	617-269-1338
Biggins, Wendy/185 Goodhill Rd, Weston, CT	203-226-7674
Birling, Paul/444 Bedford Rd, Pleasantville, NY	914-747-2220
Birmingham, Lloyd P/Peekskill Hollow Rd, Putnam Valley, NY	914-528-3207
Blaser, Michael/91 Hundred Rd, Wellesley Hills, MA	617-235-8658
Bliss, Harry/838 Christian St, Philadelphia, PA	215-922-4169
Bollinger, Kristine/185 Goodhill Rd, Weston, CT	203-226-7674
Bonanno, Paul/142 W Golf Ave, S Plainfield, NJ	201-756-8867
Bone, Fred/28 Farm Court, New Britain, CT	203-827-8418
Bono, Peter/114 E 7th St, Clifton, NJ	201-340-1169
Booth, George/PO Box 8, Westport, CT	203-227-7806
Booth, Margot/10215 Menlo Ave, Silver Spring, MD	301-588-6839
Boston Illustration Co/371 Beacon St, Boston, MA	617-236-0350
Botsis, Peter/1239 University Ave, Rochester, NY	716-271-2140
Boyd, Lizi/229 Berkeley St #52, Boston, MA	617-266-3858
Boynton, Lee A/7 Gladden Rd, Annapolis, MD	301-263-6336
Braun, Wendy/87 Longvale Rd, Bronxville, NY	914-961-3732
Brautigan, Don/29 Cona Ct, Haledon, NJ	201-956-7710
Bray, Mark/RD 1/Box 694/Huffs Chrch Rd, Alburtis, PA	215-845-3229
Breeden, Paul M/Sullivan Harbor Farm, Sullivan Harbor, ME	207-422-3007
Bremer/Keifer Studio/21 Lake Dr, Enfield, CT	203-749-9680
Brickman, Robin/32 Fort Hoosac Pl, Williamstown, MA	413-458-9853
Bridy, Dan Visuals Inc/625 Stanwix St #2402, Pittsburgh, PA	412-288-9362
Brown, Carolyn/PO Box 33, Enosbury Falls, VT	
Brown, Michael D/932 Hungerford Dr #24, Rockville, MD	301-762-4474
Brown, Richard/3979 York Rd, Furlong, PA	212-683-1362
Brunkus, Denise/185 Goodhill Rd, Weston, CT	203-226-7674
Bucella, Martin/72 Martinique Dr, Cheektowaga, NY	716-668-0040
Bullock, Wilbur/229 Berkeley #52, Boston, MA	617-266-3858
Burroughs, Miggs/PO Box 6, Westport, CT	203-227-9667
Burrows, Bill & Assoc/103 E Read St, Baltimore, MD	301-752-4615
Buschini, Maryanne/238 W Highland Ave, Philadelphia, PA	215-242-8517
Butcher, Jim/1357 E Macphail Rd, Bel Air, MD	301-879-6380
Buterbaugh, Richard/2132 N Market St, Wilmington, DE	302-571-1124
Butterbaugh, Richard/2132 N Market St, Wilmington, DE	302-656-2365
Byrd, Robert/409 Warwick Rd, Haddonfield, NJ	609-428-9627

C

Cabib, Leila/8601 Buckhannon Dr, Potomac, MD	301-299-4158
Cable, Jerry/29 Station Rd, Madison, NJ	201-966-0124
Cagle, Daryl/17 Forest Lawn Ave, Stamford, CT	203-359-3780
Callahan, Kevin/26 France St, Norwalk, CT	203-847-2046
Callanan, Brian/5 Winston Pl, Yonkers, NY	914-779-4120
Calleja, Bob/490 Elm Ave, Bogota, NJ	201-488-3028
Calver, Dave/271 Mulberry St, Rochester, NY	716-271-6208
Cantin, Charles/809 Cartier, Quebec G1R 2R8, QC	418-524-1931
Caporale, Wende L/Studio Hill Farm Rte 116, N Salem, NY	914-669-5653
Caputo, Vince/444 Bedford Rd, Pleasantville, NY	914-747-2220
Carbone, Lou/286 Sylvan Rd, Bloomfield, NJ	201-338-8678
Cardella, Elaine/215 Clinton St, Hoboken, NJ	201-656-3244
Cardillo, James/49-D Village Green, Budd Lake, NJ	201-691-1530
Carlson, Frederick H/2335 Meadow Dr, Pittsburgh, PA	412-371-8951
Carr, Bill/1035 69th Ave, Philadelphia, PA	215-276-1819
Carson, Jim/11 Foch St, Cambridge, MA	617-661-3321
Cascio, Peter/98 Harding Rd, Glen Rock, NJ	201-445-3262

Casilla, Robert/36 Hamilton Ave, Yonkers, NY	914-963-8165
Cassila, Robert/444 Bedford Rd, Pleasantville, NY	914-747-2220
Catalano, Sal/114 Boyce Pl, Ridgewood, NJ	201-447-5318
Cayea, John/39 Lafayette St, Cornwall, NY	914-534-2942
Cellini, Eva & Joseph/415 Hillside Ave, Leonia, NJ	201-944-6519
Chadwick, Paul/RR #1 Box 90, Warren, CT	203-868-9261
Chandler, Fay/1010 Memorial Dr, Cambridge, MA	617-423-6446
Chandler, Jean/385 Oakwood Dr, Wyckoff, NJ	201-891-2381
Chandler, Karen/14 Andrew Pl, Locust Valley, NY	516-671-8562
Chen, Tony/241 Bixley Heath, Lynbrook, NY	516-596-9158
Chlumecky, Danielle/1056 Beacon St #9, Brookline, MA	617-731-6138
Chui, George/2250 Elliot St, Merrick, NY	516-223-8474
Cincotti, Gerald/371 Beacon St, Boston, MA	617-236-0456
Clark, Bradley/99 Mill St, Rhinebeck, NY	914-876-2615
Clark, Cynthia Watts/99 Mill St, Rhinebeck, NY	914-876-2615
Clark, Patricia C/6201 Benalder Dr, Bethesda, MD	301-229-2986
Clarke, Bob/55 Brook Rd, Pittsford, NY	716-248-8683
Cline, Rob/356 E Main St, Newark, DE	302-368-3757
Cober, Alan E/95 Croton Dam Rd, Ossining, NY	914-941-8696
Coddbarrett Assoc/65 Ashburton Ave, Providence, RI	401-273-9898
Cohen, Alan R/2828 N Howard St, Baltimore, MD	301-366-3855
Cohen, Dee/10407 Parkwood Dr, Kensington, MD	202-364-1118
Cohen, Sharon/7108 Horizon Terrace, Rockville, MD	301-869-0624
Cohen, Susan D/208 Park Ave #3R, Hoboken, NJ	201-659-5472
Collado, Frank/82 E 18th St, Patterson, NJ	201-289-1233
Collins, Daniel/PO Box 669, Jamaica Plains, MA	617-241-7747
Collyer, Frank/RR 1 Box 266, Stony Point, NY	914-947-3050
Concept One/Gizmo/366 Oxford St, Rochester, NY	716-461-4240
Condon, Ken/42 Jefferson St, Cambridge, MA	617-492-4301
CONGE, BOB/28 HARPER ST, ROCHESTER, NY (P 24,25)	**716-473-0291**
Console, Carmen/8 Gettysburg Dr, Voorhees, NJ	215-463-6110
Cook, Susan Anderson/675 Leone St, Woodbridge, NJ	201-750-0977
Cook, William/3804 E Northern Pkwy, Baltimore, MD	301-426-1130
Cooper, Bob/311 Fern Dr, Atco Post Office, NJ	609-767-0967
Cooper, Steven/26 Lafayette St, Wakefield, MA	617-245-7528
Cornell, Jeff/58 Noyes Rd, Fairfield, CT	203-259-7715
Cosatt, Paulette/60 South St, Cresskill, NJ	201-568-1436
Cosgrove, Mary Ann/7 Tulip Ln, Levittown, NY	516-796-5643
Costas, Laura/2707 Adams Mill Rd, Washington, DC	202-265-4499
Cowdrey, Richard/229 Berkeley St #52, Boston, MA	617-266-3858
Cox, Birck/1305 E Chocolate Ave, Hershey, PA	717-533-1878
Craft, Kinuko/RFD #1 PO Box 167, Norfolk, CT	203-542-5018
Cramer, D L/10 Beechwood Dr, Wayne, NJ	201-628-8793
Crawford, Robert/123 Minor Town Rd, Woodbury, CT	203-266-0059
Crofut, Bob/8 New St, Ridgefield, CT	203-431-4304
Croll, Carolyn/458 Newton Trnpk, Weston, CT	203-454-4687
Crompton, Jack/229 Berkeley #52, Boston, MA	617-266-3858
Cross, Peter/210 Cherry St, Katonah, NY	914-232-3975
Cunningham, Robert M/PO Box 1035/Rt 45, Warren, CT	203-868-2702
Cusano, Steve/80 Talbot Ct, Media, PA	215-565-8829

D

Daily, Don/57 Academy Rd, Bala Cynwyd, PA	215-664-5729
Dally, Lyman M/166 Beachwood Rd, Parsippany, NJ	201-887-1338
Daly, Tom/47 E Edsel Ave, Palisades Park, NJ	201-943-1837
Darrow, Whitney/PO Box 8, Westport, CT	203-227-7806
Davidian, Anna/229 Berkeley #52, Boston, MA	617-266-3858
Davis, Gary/1 Cedar Pl, Wakefield, MA	617-245-2628
Davis, Michael/516 Orange St, New Haven, CT	203-562-4334
Dawes, Joseph/20 Church St, Closter, NJ	201-767-8127
DeKiefte, Kees/185 Goodhill Rd, Weston, CT	203-226-7674
DeLapine, Jim/398 31st St, Lindenhurst, NY	516-225-1247
DeMuth, Roger Taze/4103 Chenango St, Cazenovia, NY	315-655-8599
DEAN, GLENN/RD #2 BOX 788, SUSSEX, NJ (P 18,19)	**212-490-2450**
Dedini, Eldon/PO Box 8, Westport, CT	203-227-7806
Demarest, Robert/87 Highview Terr, Hawthorne, NJ	201-427-9639
Demers, Donald/PO Box 4009, Portsmouth, NH	207-439-1463
Diefendorf, Cathy/91 Hundreds Rd, Wellesley Hills, MA	617-235-8658
Dior, Jerry/9 Old Hickory Ln, Edison, NJ	201-561-6536
Dodge, Paul/731 N 24th St, Philadelphia, PA	215-232-6666
Doney, Todd/231 Main St #2, Milburn, NJ	201-376-4157
Donnarumma, Dom/25 Stanwood Rd, New Hyde Park, NY	516-248-5113
Dorsett, Diedre/CT,	203-855-1933

Dorsey, Bob/107 H Hoopes Ave, Auburn, NY	315-255-2367
Drescher, Joan/23 Cedar, Hingham, MA	617-749-5179
Drinkwine, Sharon/229 Berkeley #52, Boston, MA	617-266-3858
Driver, Ray/5725-B Harpers Farm, Columbia, MD	301-596-6955
Drucker, Mort/42 Juneau Blvd, Woodbury, NY	516-367-4920
DuPont, Lane/6 Gorham Ave, Westport, CT	203-222-1562
Dudash, Michael/PO Box 12, Waitsfield, VT	212-247-1130
Duke, Christine/Maple Ave Box 471, Millbrook, NY	914-677-9510
Duke, W E Illustration/312 Westfield Rd, Holyoke, MA	413-536-8269
Dunne, Tom/16 Cherry St, Locust Valley, NY	516-676-3641
Dverin, Anatoly/229 Berkeley #52, Boston, MA	617-266-3858
Dwingler, Randy/124 Median Dr, Wilmington, DE	302-478-6063
Dykeman, James/14 Cherry Hill Cir, Ossining, NY	914-941-0821
Dykes, John/17 Morningside Dr S, Westport, CT	203-222-8150

E

Eagle, Mike/7 Captains Ln, Old Saybrook, CT	203-388-5654
Ebel, Alex/30 Newport Rd, Yonkers, NY	914-961-4058
Echevarria, Abe/Memory Ln Farm, Sherman, CT	203-355-1254
Eckstein, Bob/107 Cherry Lane, Medford, NY	516-654-0291
Edens, John/2464 Turk Hill Rd, Victor, NJ	716-453-3441
Eggleton, Bob/57 Eddy St #513, Providence, RI	401-831-5030
Ehrenfeld, Jane/39 Nieman Ave, Lynbrook, NY	516-599-6327
Einsel, Naiad/26 Morningside Dr S, Westport, CT	203-226-0709
Einsel, Walter/26 Morningside Dr S, Westport, CT	203-226-0709
Ellis, Jon/3204 Whitney Ct, Bensalem, PA	215-750-6180
Ellson, Randy/Arctan/8 Prince St, Rochester, NY	716-244-6327
English, M John/18 McKinley St, Rowayton, CT	203-866-3734
Enos, Randall/11 Court of Oaks, Westport, CT	203-227-4785
Epstein, Aaron/2015 Aspen Dr, Plainsboro, NJ	212-410-7169
Epstein, Len/720 Montgomery Ave, Narbeth, PA	215-664-4700
Epstein, Lorraine/Dows Ln, Irvington-on-Hudson, NY	914-591-7470
Eucalyptus Tree Studio/2220 N Charles St, Baltimore, MD	301-243-0211

F

Faria, Jeff/937 Garden St, Hoboken, NJ	201-656-3063
Farnsworth, Bill/PO Box 653, New Milford, CT	203-355-1649
Farrell, Marybeth/77 Dwight Pl, Engelwood, NJ	212-799-7486
Farris, Joe/PO Box 8, Westport, CT	203-227-7806
Feeney, Betsy/444 Bedford Rd, Pleasantville, NY	914-747-2220
Feinen, Jeff/4702 Sawmill Rd, Clarence, NY	716-759-8406
Fiedler, Joseph D/500 Sampsonia Way, Pittsburgh, PA	412-322-7245
Finewood, Bill/605 S Main St, E Rochester, NY	716-377-2126
Fisch, Paul/101-B Nipmuc Trail, N Providence, RI	401-353-2206
Fisher, Mark/111 Wooster St #PHC, New York, NY	212-925-0491
Fitz-Maurice, Jeff/720 Crown St, Morrisville, PA	215-295-3266
Flat Tulip Studio/Rt 1 Box 146, Marietta, PA	717-426-1344
Flynn, Maura/8 George St, Manhasset, NY	516-627-6608
Fondersmith, Mark/8 W Branch Ln, Baltimore, MD	301-385-3145
Ford, Pam/251 Greenwood Ave, Bethel, CT	203-797-8188
Forman, James/2 Central Pl, Lynbrook, NY	516-599-2046
Foster, Susan/3903 Rosemary St, Chevy Chase, MD	301-652-3848
Fournier, Walter/185 Forest St, S Hamilton, MA	617-468-2892
Fox, Jerry/1480 Rt 46 #63-A, Parsippany, NJ	201-299-8368
Francisco, Rid/1845 Walnut St, Philadelphia, PA	215-299-3864
Frank, Scott J/38 Prospect Pl, Croton on Hudson, NY	914-271-2992
Franke, Phil/10 Nehring Ave, Babylon Village, NY	516-661-5778
Frinta, Dagmar/150 Maple Ave, Altamont, NY	518-861-6942
Fuchs, Bernard/3 Tanglewood Ln, Westport, CT	203-227-4644
Fuller, Steve/7 Winding Brook Dr, Guilderland, NY	518-456-7496

G

Gaadt, George/888 Thorn, Sewickley, PA	412-741-5161
Gail, Roxanne/56 Worrall St, Poughkeepsie, NY	914-454-0056
Garland, Michael/78 Columbia Ave, Hartsdale, NY	914-946-4536
Gaszi, Edward/84 Evergreen Rd, New Egypt, NJ	609-758-9466
Gay-Kassel, Doreen/7 S Lanning Ave, Hopewell, NJ	609-466-9457
Gazsi, Ed/84 Evergreen, New Egypt, NJ	609-758-9466
Gebert, Warren/71 Sedgwick Ave, Yonkers, NY	914-968-5247
Geller, Andrea/45-B Hastings Ave, Rutherford, NJ	201-507-5134
Geraci, Phillip/RFD, Marlborough, NH	603-847-9009
Gerber, Mark & Stephanie/18 Oak Grove Rd, Brookfield, CT	203-775-3658
Gerlach, Cameron/2644 N Calvert St, Baltimore, MD	301-889-3093
Geyer, Jackie/107 6th St #207 Fulton Bldg, Pittsburgh, PA	412-261-1111
Giardina, Laura/12 Buckingham Ct, Pomona, NY	914-354-0871

Illustrators

Continued

Please send us your additions and updates.

Gist, Linda E/224 Madison Ave, Fort Washington, PA	215-643-3757
Giuliani, Alfred/10 Woodland Terrace, Lincroft, NJ	201-741-8756
Giusti, Robert/340 Long Mountain Rd, New Milford, CT	203-354-6539
Gladden, Scott/444 Bedford Rd, Pleasantville, NY	914-747-2220
Glanzman, Louis S/6 Zoxford Ct, Medford, NJ	609-654-6579
Glasbergen, Randy J/PO Box 611, Sherburne, NY	607-674-9492
Glazer, Ted/28 West View Rd, Spring Valley, NY	914-354-1524
Glessner, Marc/24 Evergreen Rd, Somerset, NJ	201-249-5038
Gold, Al/266 Mill St, Elmwood Park, NJ	201-794-8786
Goldberg, Richard/368 Congress St 5th Fl, Boston, MA	617-338-6369
Goldinger, Andras/215 C St SE #310, Washington, DC	202-543-9029
Goldman, Marvin/RD 3 Gypsy Trail Rd, Carmel, NY	914-225-8611
Good, Harley/30 Regina Dr, Monsey, NY	914-578-5677
Goode, Harley/30 Regina Rd, South Munsey, NY	212-687-1310
Goodreau, Roc/1342 Berkshire Ave, Springfield, MA	413-543-6796
Gordley, Scott/229 Berkeley #52, Boston, MA	617-266-3858
Gormley, Mal/RD #1/ Bonnieview, N Salem, NY	914-232-5811
Goryl, John/128 Diamond St, Swoyersville, PA	717-961-3355
GRABER, JACK/707 UNION ST, SCHENECTADY, NY (P 27)	**518-370-0312**
Grashow, James/14 Diamond Hill Rd, W Redding, CT	203-938-9195
Graves, David/74 Clifton Ave, Brockton, MA	401-726-4100
Green, Norman/11 Seventy Acres Rd, W Redding, CT	203-438-9909
Greene, Anne/34 Woodford St, Worcester, MA	617-752-2572
Gregory, Lane/91 Hundreds Rd, Wellesley Hills, MA	617-235-8658
Grewe, Nilou/4 Wakeman Pl, Larchmont, NY	914-834-6820
Grote, Rich/21 Tyndale Rd, Hamilton Square, NJ	609-586-5896
Gunning, Kevin/398 Longmeadow Rd, Orange, CT	203-795-3317
Gustafson, Dale/56 Fourbrooks Rd, Stamford, CT	203-322-5667
Gyson, Mitch/4412 Colmar Gardens Dr E, Baltimore, MD	301-243-3430

H

Haas, Gordon & Shelly/86 Prospect Ave, Montclair, NJ	201-746-0539
Haefele, Steve/2101 Crompond Rd, Peekskill, NY	914-736-0785
Haffner, Marilyn/185 Holworthy St, Cambridge, MA	617-354-0696
Hallman, Tom/38 S 17th St, Allentown, PA	215-776-1144
Hamilton, Ken/4511 Kennedy Blvd, N Bergen, NJ	201-863-8169
Hamilton, Laurie/5403 McArthur Blvd NW, Washington, DC	301-369-7171
Hamilton, William/81 Sand Rd, Ferrisburg, VT	802-877-6869
Handelsman, Bud/PO Box 8, Westport, CT	203-227-7806
Haney, William/16 River Road RD #3, Neshanic Station, NJ	201-369-3848
Harden, Laurie/RD 4/Box 31, Boonton Township, NJ	201-335-4578
Hardy, Neil O/2 Woods Grove, Westport, CT	203-226-4446
Harris, Ellen/125 Pleasant St #602, Brookline, MA	617-739-1867
Harris, Peter/37 Beech St, Wrenthem, MA	617-384-2470
Harsh, Fred/185 Goodhill Rd, Weston, CT	203-226-7674
Harvey, Paul/475-B Commanche Ln, Stratford, CT	203-381-9836
Hatton, Enid/46 Parkway, Fairfield, CT	203-259-3789
Hazelton, Betsey/106 Robbins Dr, Carlisle, MA	617-369-5309
Healy, Deborah/72 Watchung Ave, Upper Montclair, NJ	201-746-2549
Hearn, Diane Dawson/22 Spring St, Pauling, NY	914-855-1152
Hearn, Walter/22 Spring St, Pauling, NY	914-855-1152
Heath, R Mark/4338 Roland Springs Dr, Baltimore, MD	301-366-4633
Heimann, Steve/PO Box 406, Oradell, NJ	201-345-9132
Heitmann, Bob/9071 Millcreek RD #116, Levittown, PA	215-946-1394
Hejja, Attila/300 Edward St, Roslyn Heights, NY	516-621-8054
Henderson, Dave/7 Clover Ln, Verona, NJ	201-783-5791
Herrick, George W/23 Girard Ave #B4, Hartford, CT	203-232-6651
Herring, Michael/RD 1 Box 205A, Cold Spring, NY	914-265-9476
Hess, Mark/88 Quicks Lane, Katonah, NY	914-232-5870
Hess, Richard/310 Litchfield Rd, Norfolk, CT	203-354-2921
Hess, Robert/63 Littlefield Rd, E Greenwich, RI	401-885-0331
Heyck, Edith/92 Water St, Newburyport, MA	617-462-9027
Hierro, Claudia & Gregory/1099 Rosse Ave, New Milford, NJ	201-907-0423
Hildebrandt, Greg/1148 Parsippany Blvd, Parsippany, NJ	201-334-0353
Hildebrandt, Tim/10 Jackson Ave, Gladstone, NJ	201-234-2149
Hill, Michael/828 Park Ave, Baltimore, MD	301-728-8767
Hoffman, Martin/RD 2 Box 50, Worcester, MA	607-638-5472
Hoffman, Nancy/16 Ridge Dr, Berkeley Heights, NJ	201-665-2177
Hofhiemer, Steven/341 E Hudson St, Long Beach, NY	516-432-0075
Hogan, Jamie/36 Green St, Jamaica Plain, MA	617-522-5503
Hokanson, Lars/PO Box 199, Hopeland, PA	717-733-9066
Howell, Van/720 New York Ave, Huntington, NY	516-424-6499
Huehnergarth, John/196 Snowden Ln, Princeton, NJ	609-921-3211

Huelsman, Amy/24 S Calumet Ave, Hastings on Hudson, NY	914-478-0596
Huerta, Gerard/45 Corbin Dr, Darien, CT	203-656-0505
Hulsey, John/Rte 9D, Garrison, NY	914-424-3544
Hunt, Stan/PO Box 8, Westport, CT	203-227-7806
Hurd, Jane/4002 Virginia Pl, Bethesda, MD	301-229-7966
Hurd, Lauren/1715 Linden Ave, Baltimore, MD	301-523-5411
Hurwitz, Joyce/7314 Burdette Ct, Bethesda, MD	301-365-0340
Huyssen, Roger/45 Corbin Dr, Darien, CT	203-656-0200

IJ

Inouye, Carol/Gulf Schoolhouse Rd, Cornwallville, NY	518-634-7589
Iosa, Ann/185 Goodhill Rd, Weston, CT	203-226-7674
Irish, Gary/45 Newbury St, Boston, MA	617-247-4168
Irwin, Virginia/67 Spring Park Ave, Jamaica Plain, MA	617-469-3186
Jacobus, Tim/PO Box 142, Glasser, NJ	201-663-4501
Jaeger Design Studio/2025 I St NW #622, Washington, DC	202-785-8434
James, Derek/561 Main St, E Keansburg, NJ	201-787-0231
Johnson, David A/299 South Ave, New Canaan, CT	203-966-3269
Johnson, Richard/18 Rochambeau Ave, Ridgefield, CT	203-438-0348
Jones, Barry/2725 Mary St, Easton, PA	215-253-3709
Jones, Donald/15 Dehart Pl, Madison, NJ	201-765-9750
Jones, George/52 Old Highway, Wilton, CT	203-762-7242
Jones, John R/335 Town St, East Haddam, CT	203-873-9950
Jones, Marilyn/25 Sylvan Rd, Verona, NJ	201-746-7131
Jones, Robert/47 W Stewart, Lansdowne, PA	215-626-1245
Jones, Roger/15 Waldo Ave, Somerville, MA	617-628-1487
Jordan, Laurie/185 Goodhill Rd, Weston, CT	203-226-7674
Jordan, Polly/29 Warren Ave, Somerville, MA	617-776-0329
Juhasz, Victor/576 Westminster Ave, Elizabeth, NJ	201-351-4227

K

Kane, Kid/9 W Bridge St, New Hope, PA	215-862-0392
Karp, Julie/1 Ash Pl #3J, Great Neck, NY	516-466-4093
Kassel, Doreen/24-A Chestnut Ct, Princeton, NJ	609-497-0783
Keene, Donald/191 Clove Rd, New Rochelle, NY	914-636-2128
Kidd, Tom/59 Cross Brook Rd, New Milford, CT	203-355-1781
Kilroy, John/28 Fairmount Way, Nantasket, MA	617-925-0582
Kingham, Dave/42 Blue Spruce Circle, Weston, CT	203-226-3106
Kingsbery, Guy/305 High St, Milford, CT	203-878-8939
Kinstrey, Jim/1036 Broadway, W Longbranch, NJ	201-229-0312
Klim, Joseph/56 Arbor St, Hartford, CT	203-236-4061
Kline, Rob/229 Berkeley #52, Boston, MA	617-266-3858
Kluglein, Karen/37 Cary Rd, Great Neck, NY	516-487-1323
Knabel, Lonnie/34 Station St, Brookline, MA	617-566-4464
Koeppel, Gary/368 Congress, Boston, MA	617-426-8887
Kossin, Sanford/143 Cowneck Rd, Port Washington, NY	516-883-3038
Kovarsky, Anatol/PO Box 8, Westport, CT	203-227-7806
Krosnick Studio/686 Undercliff Ave, Edgewater, NJ	201-224-5495
Kulczak, Frank/412 Diller Rd, Hanover, PA	717-637-2580
Kupper, Ketti/21 Old Stone Rd, Darien, CT	203-656-0010
Kyriacos, Betty/2221 Penfield Ln, Bowie, MD	301-249-3606

L

LaCaourse, Carol/506 Windsor Dr, Framingham, MA	617-451-6528
Langdon, John/106 S Marion Ave, Wenonah, NJ	609-468-7868
Lanza, Barbara/PO Box 118, Pine Island, NY	914-258-4601
Lawton, April/31 Hampshire Dr, Farmingdale, NY	516-454-0868
Layman, Linda J/Hill Rd, South Hamilton, MA	617-468-4297
Lazarevich, Mila/185 Goodhill Rd, Weston, CT	203-226-7674
Lazarus, Robin/814 Edgewood Dr, Westbury, NY	516-334-8609
Leamon, Tom/18 Main St, Amherst, MA	413-256-8423
Lee, Bryce/120 77th St, N Bergen, NJ	201-662-9106
Lee, Robert/444 Bedford Rd, Pleasantville, NY	914-747-2220
Lefkowitz, Mark/94 Fox Meadow Ln, Dedham, MA	617-332-4353
Lehew, Ron/17 Chestnut St, Salem, NJ	609-935-1422
Leibow, Paul/369 Lantana Ave, Englewood, NJ	201-567-2561
Lemelman, Martin/1286 Country Club Rd, Allentown, PA	215-395-4536
Levine, Ned/301 Frankel Blvd, Merrick, NY	516-378-8122
Levy, Robert S/1023 Fairway Rd, Franklin Square, NY	516-872-3713
Lewczak, Scott/95 Kimberly Rd, Colonia, NJ	201-388-5262
Leyburn, Judy/41 Pine St, Arlington, MA	617-641-1727
Leyonmark, Roger/229 Berkeley #52, Boston, MA	617-266-3858
Lidbeck, Karin/185 Goodhill Rd, Weston, CT	203-226-7674
Little, Ed/8 Buttonball Dr, Newton, CT	203-226-4724
Loccisano, Karen/185 Goodhill Rd, Weston, CT	203-226-7674

Illustrators

Continued

Please send us your additions and updates.

Lofaro, Jerry/22 Bruce Lane, Farmingdale, NY	516-752-7519
Logan, Ron/PO Box 306, Brentwood, NY	516-273-4693
Longacre, Jimmy/185 Goodhill Rd, Weston, CT	203-226-7674
Lorenz, Al/185 Goodhill Rd, Weston, CT	516-354-5530
Lose, Hal/533 W Hortter St, Philadelphia, PA	215-849-7635
Lubey, Dick/726 Harvard, Rochester, NY	716-442-6075
Luzak, Dennis/88 Main St, New Canaan, CT	203-966-5681
Lyhus, Randy/4853 Cordell Ave #3, Bethesda, MD	301-986-0036
Lynn, Kathy/1741 Bainbridge, Philadelphia, PA	215-545-5039

M

MacArthur, Dave/147 E Bradford Ave #B, Cedar Grove, NJ	201-857-1046
MacFarland, Jean/Laurel Lake Rd, Lenox, MA	413-637-3647
MacNeill, Scott/74 York St, Lambertville, NJ	609-397-4631
Maddalone, John/81 Lindberg Blvd, Bloomfield, NJ	201-338-1674
Maffia, Daniel/44 N Dean St, Englewood, NJ	201-871-0435
Mager, Janet/229 Berkeley #52, Boston, MA	617-266-3858
Mahoney, John/77 W Brookline St, Boston, MA	617-267-8791
Mahoney, Katherine/60 Hurd Rd, Belmont, MA	617-489-0406
Mahoney, Ron/204 Fifth Ave, Pittsburgh, PA	412-261-3824
Mandel, Saul/163 Maytime Dr, Jericho, NY	516-681-3530
Marchesi, Steve/185 Goodhill Rd, Weston, CT	203-226-7674
Mardon, John/185 Goodhill Rd, Weston, CT	203-226-7674
Mariuzza, Pete/146 Hardscrabble Rd, Briarcliff Manor, NY	914-769-3310
Marmo, Brent/4 Davis Ct, Brookline, MA	617-566-7330
Martin, Henry/PO Box 8, Westport, CT	203-227-7806
Martin, Richard/485 Hilda St, East Meadow, NY	516-221-3630
Marton, Charles/PO Box 5151, Potsdam, NY	315-265-6372
Mascio, Tony/4 Teton Ct, Voorhees, NJ	609-424-5278
Mattelson, Marvin/37 Cary Rd, Great Neck, NY	516-487-1323
Matthews, Dale/813 Silver Spring Ave, Silver Spring, MD	301-343-1111
Mattingly, David/1112 Bloomfield St, Hoboken, NJ	201-659-7404
Mattiucci, Jim/247 N Goodman St, Rochester, NY	716-271-2280
Mayforth, Hal/121 Rockingham Rd, Londonderry, NH	603-432-2873
Mayo, Frank/265 Briar Brae, Stamford, CT	203-322-3650
Mazut, Mark/PO Box M1573, Hoboken, NJ	201-656-0657
Mazzini, John/68 Grey Ln, Levittown, NY	516-579-6518
McCollum, Rick/15 Dr Gillette Cir, Westport, CT	203-227-4455
MCCURDY, MICHAEL/66 LAKE BUEL RD, GREAT BARRINGTON, MA (P 34)	**413-528-2749**
McElfish, Susan/5725 Phillips Ave, Pittsburgh, PA	412-521-6041
McGovern, Mike/444 Bedford Rd, Pleasantville, NY	914-747-2220
McGuire, Arlene Phoebe/495 Old York Rd, Jenkintown, PA	215-576-5123
McIntosh, Jon C/17 Devon Rd, Chestnut Hill, MA	617-277-9530
McMormick, Mary Ellen/2100 Connecticut NW, Washington, DC	202-265-7661
McVicker, Charles/PO Box 183, Rocky Hill, NJ	609-924-2660
Meeker, Carlene/24 Shore Dr, Winthrop, MA	617-846-5117
MELGAR, FABIAN/14 CLOVER DR, SMITHTOWN, NY (P 35)	**516-543-7561**
Melius, John/3028 New Oak Ln, Bowie, MD	301-249-3709
Menk, France/PO Box 350, Pound Ridge, NY	914-764-8583
Merrill, David/POB 1581/1661 Big Tree Dr, Fairmont, WV	304-363-7953
Metcalf, Roger/132 Hendrie Ave, Riverside, CT	203-637-9524
Michael, Lillian/23 W Mt Pleasant Ave, Philadelphia, PA	215-247-4298
Miles, Elizabeth/185 Goodhill Rd, Weston, CT	203-226-7674
Miller, Warren/PO Box 8, Westport, CT	203-227-7806
Milnazik, Kim/73-2 Drexelbrook Dr, Drexel Hill, PA	215-259-1565
Mistretta, Andrea/5 Bohnert Pl, Waldwick, NJ	201-652-7531
Miyake, Yoshi/185 Goodhill Rd, Weston, CT	203-226-7674
Mladinich, Charles/7 Maspeth Dr, Melville, NY	516-271-8525
Modell, Frank/PO Box 8, Westport, CT	203-227-7806
Moldoff, Kirk/18 McKinley St, Rowayton, CT	203-866-3734
Mooney, Gerry/2 Main St #3S, Dobbs Ferry, NY	914-693-8076
Moore, Brian/2938 Brighton 12th St, Brooklyn, NY	718-934-1581
Moore, Jack/131 Cedar Lake West, Denville, NJ	201-627-6931
Moores, Jeff/72 S Maple Ave, Springfield, NJ	201-379-4657
Morales, Manuel/PO Box 1763, Bloomfield, NJ	201-429-0848
Moran, Mike/25 Anthony Dr, Madison, NJ	201-966-6229
Morecraft, Ron/97 Morris Ave, Denville, NJ	201-627-6728
Morrissey, Belinda/541 Hillcrest St, Teaneck, NJ	201-836-7016
Morrow, Skip/Ware Rd/Box 123, Wilmington, VT	802-464-5523
MOSCARILLO, MARK/106 BENEFIT ST, PROVIDENCE, RI (P 36)	**401-751-3919**
Moscowitz, Stephen/701 Monroe Ave, Rochester, NY	716-442-8433
Moss, Donald/232 Peaceable St, Ridgefield, CT	203-438-5633
Musy, Mark/PO Box 755, Buckingham, PA	215-764-8851
Myers, Lou/58 Lakeview Ave, Peekskill, NY	914-737-2307

N

Nachbar, Amy/57 Lorimar Ave, Providence, RI	401-274-4591
NACHT, MERLE/374 MAIN ST, WEATHERSFIELD, CT (P 37)	**203-563-7993**
Neibart, Wally/1715 Walnut St, Philadelphia, PA	215-564-5167
Neider, Alan/151 Penn Common, Milford, CT	203-878-9260
Newman, Lisa/PO Box 761, Williamsburg, MA	413-268-3040
Newman, Robert/420 Springbrook Ln, Hatboro, PA	215-672-8079
Nix, Jonathon J/Carter Rd, Becket, MA	413-684-0441
Norman, Marty/5 Radcliff Blvd, Glen Head, NY	516-671-4482
Noyes, David/20 Hemenway St #26, Boston, MA	617-262-3611
Noyse, Janet/118 Woodland Rd, Wyncote, PA	215-572-6975

O

O'Leary, John/547 N 20th St, Philadelphia, PA	215-561-7377
Oh, Jeffrey/2635 Ebony Rd, Baltimore, MD	301-661-6064
Olsen, Jimmy/50 New York Ave, Clark, NJ	201-388-0967
Olson, Victor/Fanton Meadows, West Redding, CT	203-938-2863
Otnes, Fred/Chalburn Rd, West Redding, CT	203-938-2829
Oughton, Taylor/Jamison, Bucks County, PA	215-598-3246

P

Palladini, David/PO Box 991, Water Mill, NY	212-983-1362
Palmer, Jan/458 Newton Trnpk, Weston, CT	203-454-4687
Palulian, Dickran/18 McKinley St, Rowayton, CT	203-866-3734
Parker, Earl/5 New Brooklyn Rd, Cedar Brook, NJ	609-567-2925
Parker, Ed Assoc/9 Carlisle St, Andover, MA	617-475-2659
Parry, Ivor A/4 Lorraine Dr, Eastchester, NY	914-961-7338
Passalacqua, David/325 Versa Pl, Sayville, NY	516-589-1663
Pate, Rodney/185 Goodhill Rd, Weston, CT	203-226-7674
Patrick, Pamela/398-A Burrows Run, Chadds Ford, PA	215-388-7654
Pavia, Cathy/185 Goodhill Rd, Weston, CT	203-226-7674
Payne, Thomas/11 Colonial Ave, Albany, NY	518-482-1756
Pels, Winslow Pinney/Hack Green Rd, Pound Ridge, NY	914-764-8470
Pennor, Robert/928 Summit Rd, Cheshire, CT	203-758-4008
Pentick, Joseph/RD 4 Box 231, Kingston, NY	914-331-8197
Perina, Jim/33 Regent St, N Plainfield, NJ	201-757-3010
Phillips, Alan/2 Washington Sq #41, Larchmont, NY	914-834-4528
Pidgeon, Jean/38 W 25th St, Baltimore, MD	301-235-1558
Piejko, Alex/5796 Morris Rd, Marcy, NY	315-732-4852
Pierson, Huntley S/PO Box 14430, Hartford, CT	203-549-4863
Pinkney, Jerry/41 Furnace Dock Rd, Croton-on-Hudson, NY	914-271-5238
Pizzo, Robert/26 Pondfield Rd W #4F, Bronxville, NY	914-961-5020
Platania, Nancy Anne/44 Cornell, Williston Park, NY	516-747-2417
Plotkin, Barnett/126 Wooleys Ln, Great Neck, NY	516-487-7457
Porzio, Ed/131 Bartlett Rd, Winthrop, MA	617-846-3875
Presnall, Terry/91 Hundred Rd, Wellesly Hills, MA	617-235-8658
Price, George/PO Box 8, Westport, CT	203-227-7806
Printz, Larry/1840 London Rd, Abington, PA	215-572-0331
Prokell, Jim/307 4th Ave #200, Pittsburgh, PA	412-232-3636
Provensen, Alice/Meadowbrook Ln Box 171, Staatsburg, NY	914-266-3245

R

Rabl, Lorraine/249 Queen Anne Rd, Bogota, NJ	201-342-4647
Radiomayonnaise/112-A Appleton St, Boston, MA	617-536-5440
Ramage, Alfred/5 Irwin St #7, Winthrop, MA	617-846-5955
Ramon, John/444 Bedford Rd, Pleasantville, NY	914-747-2220
Rankin, Mary/444 Bedford Rd, Pleasantville, NY	914-747-2220
Ransome, James/932 E 24th St, Patterson, NJ	201-279-3944
Ravel, Ken/2 Myrtle Ave, Stoney Creek, PA	215-779-2105
Recchia, Dennis & Janet/94 Oak St, Tenafly, NJ	201-569-6136
Reeser, Tracy P (Mr)/254 Andover Rd, Glenmoore, PA	215-942-2597
Reiner, John/107 Jackson Ave, Huntington, NY	516-360-3049
Rhodes, Nancy Muncie/146 Hathaway Rd, Dewitt, NY	315-446-8742
Richardson, Suzanne/458 Newton Trnpk, Weston, CT	203-454-4687
Richter, Mische/PO Box 8, Westport, CT	203-227-7806
Rickerd, David/22 Canvas Back Rd, Manalapan, NJ	201-446-2119
Riley, Frank/108 Bamford Ave, Hawthorne, NJ	201-423-2659
Roberts & Van Heusen/1153 Narragansett Blvd, Cranston, RI	401-785-4490
Roberts, Cheryl/1153 Narragansett Blvd, Cranston, RI	401-785-4490
Robertson, Paula Havey/65 Glenbrook Rd #7B, Stamford, CT	203-327-4199
Rockwell, Richard/444 Bedford Rd, Pleasantville, NY	914-747-2220

Rodericks, Michael/129 Lounsbury Rd, Trumbull, CT	203-268-1551
Roffo, Sergio/42 Shepard St #3, Boston, MA	617-787-5861
Rogers, Glenda/1 Fayette Pk #100, Syracuse, NY	315-478-4509
Roman, Irena & John/369 Thom Clapp Rd Box 571, Scituate, MA	617-545-6514
Romano, Al/62 Kelsey Pl, Madison, CT	203-245-3006
Roselius, Elizabeth/7309 Balt Nat'l Pike, Frederick, MD	301-473-4058
Rosenbaum, Harry/444 Bedford Rd, Pleasantville, NY	914-747-2220
Rosenbaum, Jonathan/444 Bedford Rd, Pleasantville, NY	914-747-2220
Ross, Larry/53 Fairview Ave, Madison, NJ	201-377-6859
Rosso, David/469 Palisade Ave, Jersey City, NJ	201-792-5378
Roth, Gail/185 Goodhill Rd, Weston, CT	203-226-7674
Rutherford, Jenny/185 Goodhill Rd, Weston, CT	203-226-7674
Ryan, Carol/14 Adams St, Port Washington, NY	516-944-3953
S Sahli, Barbara/8212 Flower Ave, Takoma Park, MD	301-585-5122
Saint John, Bob/320 South St, Portsmouth, NH	603-431-7345
Sanders, Bruce/229 Berkeley #52, Boston, MA	617-266-3858
Sanderson, Ruth/185 Goodhill Rd, Weston, CT	203-226-7674
Santa, Monica/185 Goodhill Rd, Weston, CT	203-226-7674
Santoliquido, Delores/60 W Broad St #6H, Mt Vernon, NY	914-667-3199
Santore, Charles/138 S 20th St, Philadelphia, PA	215-563-0430
Saunders, Rob/368 Congress St 5th Fl, Boston, MA	617-542-6114
Saxon, Charles/PO Box 8, Westport, CT	203-227-7806
Scaff, Gregory/133 Linden Dr, Fair Haven, NJ	201-758-0785
Scharf, Linda/45 Dwight St #1, Brookline, MA	617-738-9294
Schenker, Bob/31 W Circular Ave, Paoli, PA	215-640-9993
Schiwall-Gallo, Linda/1342 Berkshire Ave, Springfield, MA	413-543-6796
Schleinkofer, David/344 Crown St, Morrisville, PA	215-295-8622
Schlemme, Roy/585 Center St, Oradell, NJ	212-921-9732
Schneider, Frederick/1342 Berkshire Ave, Springfield, MA	413-543-6796
Schneider, Rick/260 Montague Rd, Leverett, MA	413-548-9304
Schofield, Glen/4 Hillside Ave, Roseland, NJ	201-941-8853
Schorr, Kathy Staico/PO Box 142, Roxbury, CT	203-266-4084
Schorr, Todd/PO Box 142, Roxbury, CT	203-266-4084
Schreck, John/371 Beacon St #2, Boston, MA	617-236-0350
Schroeder, Michael/1327 Walnut St, Reading, PA	215-375-9055
Schroeppel, Richard/12-L English Hill Rd #203, Manchester, NH	603-673-0997
Schweigert, Carol/791 Tremont St #E406, Boston, MA	617-262-8909
Sekeris, Pim/570 Milton St #10, Montreal H2X 1W4, QU	514-844-0510
Selwyn, Paul/287 Laurel St, Hartford, CT	203-278-6757
Shachat, Andrew/66 Katydid Dr, Somerville, NJ	201-722-1667
Sharpe, Jim/21 Ten O'Clock Ln, Weston, CT	203-226-9984
Shaw, Barclay/49 Elbow Hill Rd, Brookfield, CT	203-775-8477
Sherman, Gene/500 Helendale Rd, Rochester, NY	716-288-8000
Sherman, Oren/30 Ipswich #301, Boston, MA	617-437-7368
Shieldhouse, Stephanie/1321 Eutaw Pl #34, Baltimore, MD	301-383-2648
Shiff, Andrew Z/153 Clinton St, Hopkinton, MA	617-435-3607
Shigley, Neil/427 72nd St, North Bergen, NJ	201-854-3737
Sikorski, Tony/2304 Clark Bldg, Pittsburgh, PA	412-391-8366
Sims, Blanche/185 Goodhill Rd, Weston, CT	203-226-7674
Singer, Gloria/14 Disbrow Ct, E Brunswick, NJ	201-257-4728
Sisti, Jerald/34 Wiedmann Ave, Clifton, NJ	201-478-7488
Smallwood, Steve/2417 3rd St Bsmt, Fort Lee, NJ	201-585-7923
Smith, Douglas/405 Washington St #2, Brookline, MA	617-566-3816
Smith, Elwood H/2 Locust Grove Rd, Rhinebeck, NY	914-876-2358
Smith, Gail Hunter/PO Box 217, Barnegat Light, NJ	609-494-9136
Smith, Jeffrey/255 E Prospect Ave, Mt Vernon, NY	914-667-6397
Smith, Marcia/112 Linden St, Rochester, NY	716-461-9348
Smith, Raymond/222 Willow Ave, Hoboken, NJ	201-653-6638
Smith, Susan B/66 Clarendon #3, Boston, MA	617-266-4441
Snyder, Emilie/50 N Pine St #107, Marietta, PA	215-426-2906
Soileau, Hodges/350 Flax Hill Rd, Norwalk, CT	203-852-0751
Sokolowski, Ted/RD #2 Box 408, Lake Ariel, PA	717-937-4527
Somerville, Kevin/120 Sylvan Ave, Englewood Cliffs, NJ	201-944-2632
Sorensen, Robert/59 Granville Ave, Milford, CT	203-874-6381
Soyka, Ed/231 Lafayette Ave, Peekskill, NY	914-737-2230
Spanfeller, Jim/Mustato Rd, Katonah, NY	914-232-3546
Sparacio, Mark & Erin/30 Rover Ln, Hicksville, NY	516-579-6679
Sparkman, Gene/PO Box 644, Sandy Hook, CT	203-426-0061
SPARKS, RICHARD/2 W ROCKS RD, NORWALK, CT (P 43)	**203-866-2002**
Spellman, Susan/91 Hundreds Rd, Wellesley Hills, MA	617-235-8658
Spence, Jim/33 Elsie St, Patchogue, NY	516-654-4650
Spiak, Sharon/35 Monroe Ave, Dumont, NJ	201-387-9395
Springer, Sally/317 S Lawrence Ct, Philadelphia, PA	215-925-9697
Sprouls, Kevin/335 Readington Rd, Sommerville, NJ	201-722-5408
Sprovach, Craig/51 Glenwood Ave, Norwalk, CT	203-855-8885
Stahl, Benjamin F/18 Lowndes Ave, S Norwalk, CT	203-838-5308
Stasolla, Mario/37 Cedar Hill Ave, S Nyack, NY	914-353-3086
Steig, William/PO Box 8, Westport, CT	203-227-7806
Steinberg, Herb/PO Box 65, Roosevelt, NJ	609-448-4724
Steiner, Joan/Plattekill Rd, Greenville, NY	518-966-8908
Stevens, John/68 Rita Dr, East Meadow, NY	516-579-5352
Stevenson, James/PO Box 8, Westport, CT	203-227-7806
Stewart, Jonathan/113 South 20th St, Philadelphia, PA	215-546-3649
Stirweis, Shannon/31 Fawn Pl, Wilton, CT	203-762-7058
Sturrock, Walt/57 E Shawnee Trl, Wharton, NJ	201-663-0069
Sullivan, Steve/72 Revere Dr, Ridgefield, CT	203-438-4969
Swan, Susan/83 Saugatuk Ave, Westport, CT	203-226-9104
Swenarton, Gordon/40 Druid Hill Ln, Summit, NJ	201-635-2900
Syverson, Henry/PO Box 8, Westport, CT	203-227-7806
Szabo, Leslie/44 S Main St #306, S Norwalk, CT	203-838-2155
T Tandem Graphics/5313 Waneta Rd, Bethesda, MD	301-320-5008
Tarlow, Phyllis/42 Stafford Rd, New Rochelle, NY	914-235-9473
Tatore, Paul/10 Wartburg Pl, Valhalla, NY	914-769-1061
Tauss, Herb/S Mountain Pass, Garrison, NY	914-424-3765
Taylor, Dahl/508 Grand St, Troy, NY	518-274-6379
TeleVision Corp/928 Mt Carmel Rd, Parkton, MD	301-343-1111
Ten, Arnie/93 Fairview Ave, Poughkeepsie, NY	914-485-8419
Tennison, James/117 Ironworks Rd, Clinton, CT	203-669-7883
Thompson, Arthur/39 Prospect Ave, Pompton Plains, NJ	201-835-3534
Thompson, John M/708-14 Jersey Ave, Jersey City, NJ	201-653-1675
Tiani, Alex/PO Box 4530, Greenwich, CT	203-661-3891
Tinkelman, Murray/75 Lakeview Ave W, Peekskill, NY	914-737-5960
Todd, Barbara/458 Newton Trnpk, Weston, CT	203-454-4687
Toelke, Cathleen/16 Tremont St, Boston, MA	617-242-7414
Toelke, Ron/229 Berkeley #52, Boston, MA	617-266-3858
Torrisi, Gary/91 Hundreds Rd, Wellesley Hills, MA	617-235-8658
Treatner, Meryl/721 Lombard St, Philadelphia, PA	215-627-2297
Tseng, Jean & Mou-sein/458 Newton Trnpk, Weston, CT	203-454-4687
Two-H Studio/45 Corbin Dr, Darien, CT	203-656-0200
UV Ulrich, George/458 Newton Trnpk, Weston, CT	203-454-4687
Van Horn, Michael/RD 2/Box 442/Milan Hill Rd, Red Hook, NY	914-758-8407
VanHouten, Norbert/Rt 2/Box 554E, Sharon Springs, NY	518-673-5504
Vann, Bob/5306 Knox St, Philadelphia, PA	215-843-4841
Vargo, Kurt/94 New Monmouth Rd, Middletown, NJ	201-671-8679
Vebell, Victoria/1 Cedar Spring Ln, Woodbury, CT	203-266-4007
Vella, Ray/345 Main St #7D, White Plains #7D, NY	914-997-1424
Veno, Joe/20 Cutler Rd, Hamilton, MA	617-468-3165
Vernaglia, Michael/1251 Bloomfield St, Hoboken, NJ	201-659-7750
Viskupic, Gary/7 Westfield Dr, Center Port, NY	516-757-9021
Vissichelli, Joe/100 Mayfield Ln, Valley Stream, NY	516-872-3867
W Walczak, Larry/803 Park Ave, Hoboken, NJ	201-798-6176
Waldman, Neil/47 Woodlands Ave, White Plains, NY	914-693-2782
Walker, Norman/37 Stonehenge Rd, Weston, CT	203-226-5812
Wallerstein, Alan/61 Tenth St, Ronkonkoma, NY	516-736-2625
Waters, Julian/9509 Aspenwood Pl, Washington, MD	202-544-5258
Watson, Karen/100 Churchill Ave, Arlington, MA	617-641-1420
Watts, Mark/616 Iva Ln, Fairless Hills, PA	215-945-9422
Weber, Robert/PO Box 8, Westport, CT	203-227-7806
Wehrman, Richard/247 N Goodman St, Rochester, NY	716-271-2280
Weiss, Conrad/1581 Rt 23, Wayne, NJ	201-633-5198
Weissman, Bari/41 Atkins St, Brighton, MA	617-783-0230
Welkis, Alan/53 Heights Rd, Fort Salonga, NY	516-261-4160
Weller, Linda Boehm/185 Goodhill Rd, Weston, CT	203-226-7674
Westlake, Laura/7 Dublin Hill Dr, Greenwich, CT	203-869-8010
Whelan, Michael/23 Old Hayrake Rd, Danbury, CT	203-798-6063
White, Caroline/1 Langdon St #22, Cambridge, MA	617-661-1283
Whiting, Ann/2627 Woodley Place NW, Washington, DC	202-462-1519
Wilcox, David/PO Box 232, Califon, NJ	201-832-7368

Illustrators
Continued

Please send us your additions and updates.

Willert, Beth Anne/303 Brook Ave, N Plainfield, NJ	201-755-4327
Williams, Frank/731 North 24th St, Philadelphia, PA	215-232-6666
Williams, Marcia/84 Duncklee St, Newton Highlands, MA	617-332-5823
Williams, Ted/170 Elder Dr, Macedon, NY	315-986-3770
Williges, Mel/2 Hepworth Ct, W Orange, NJ	201-731-4086
Wilson, Gahan/PO Box 8, Westport, CT	203-227-7806
Wilson, Linda/PO Box 652, Lincroft, NJ	201-747-7218
Wilson, Mary Lou/247 N Goodman St, Rochester, NY	716-271-2280
Witschonke, Alan/28 Tower St #2, Somerville, MA	617-628-5601
Wolfe, Jean/27 E Central Ave #B9, Paoli, PA	215-644-2941
Woodman, Bill/PO Box 8, Westport, CT	203-227-7806
Wright, Bob Creative Group Inc/247 North Goodman St, Rochester, NY	716-271-2280
Wu, Leslie/65 Greenfield Ln, Rochester, NY	716-385-3722

YZ
Yaeger, Alice/3157 Rolling Rd, Edgewater, MD	301-261-4239
Yost, Cindy/45 Petton Rd, Norwalk, CT	203-853-8163
Young, Robert Assoc/78 North Union St, Rochester, NY	716-546-1973
Young, Wally/7 Birch Hill Rd, Weston, CT	203-227-5672
Zappler, Nina/166 Frazer Ave 2nd Fl, Collingswood, NJ	609-858-1388
Ziegler, Bill/PO Box 8, Westport, CT	203-227-7806
Ziegler, Kathy/40201 Delaire Landing, Philadelphia, PA	215-632-8238
Zinn, Ron/117 Village Dr, Jerico, NY	516-933-2767
Zuba, Bob/105 W Saylor Ave, Plains, PA	717-824-9730
Zuban, Kevin/34 Idelwild Rd, Edison, NJ	201-949-8617
Zuckerman, Craig/724 W Walnut St, Long Beach, NY	516-432-9483

Southeast

AB
Armstrong, Lynn/2510 Whisper Wind Ct, Roswell, GA	404-642-5512
Arroyo, Fian/4176 Ingraham Hwy, Coconut Grove, FL	305-663-1224
Arunski, Joe & Assoc/8600 SW 86th Ave, Miami, FL	305-271-8300
Azzinaro, Lewis/11872 St Trinians Ct, Weston, VA	703-620-5155
Bailey, R.C./255 Westward Dr, Miami Springs, FL	305-888-6309
Barbie, Michael/463 Old Post Rd, Niceville, FL	904-897-3441
Barklew, Pete/110 Alpine Way, Athens, GA	404-546-5058
Boone, Joe/ PW Inc/PO Box 99337, Louisville, KY	502-499-9220
Bowles, Aaron/1686 Sierra Woods Ct, Reston, VA	703-471-4019
Boyter, Charles/1135 Lanier Blvd NE, Atlanta, GA	404-727-5665
Burke, Gary/14418 NE Third Ct, N Miami, FL	305-893-1998
Butler, Meryl/PO Box 991, Virginia Beach, VA	804-491-2280

C
Cable, Mark/600 E Main St, Louisville, KY	502-634-4911
Carey, Mark/1209 Anne Ave, Chesapeake, VA	804-482-7646
Carey, Wayne/532 Hardendorp Ave, Atlanta, GA	404-378-0426
Carter, Kip/225 Beaverdam Dr, Winterville, GA	404-542-5384
Carter, Tony/504 Baker Dr, Birmingham, AL	205-871-8010
Carter, Zane/1008 N Randolph St #100, Arlington, VA	703-527-7338
Casciao, Gary/654 Jordan, Shreveport, LA	318-424-0635
Castellanos, Carlos/1800 W 49th St #219, Hialeah, FL	305-651-9524
Chaffee, Doug/Rt 3 Groveland Dr, Taylors, SC	803-877-9826
Coastline Studios/6959 Stapoint Ct #J, Winterpark, FL	305-657-6355
Collins, Samuel/PO Box 73004, Birmingham, AL	205-991-0557
Comport, Alan/220 Beach Pl, Tampa, FL	813-253-3435
Correnti, Sandra/Rt 1 Box 256, Leesburg, VA	703-777-9113
Covington, Neverne/2919 56th St South, Gulf Port, FL	813-347-0746
Cowan, Robert/528 Shelton Dr, Aberdeen, NC	919-944-1306
Craig, Robert/1005 Tarlton Ave, Burlington, NC	919-226-6796
Crane, Gary/523 W 24th St, Norfolk, VA	804-627-0717
Crunk, Matt/Rte 5 Box 39, Killen, AL	205-757-2029

DEF
DeBro, James/2725 Hayden Dr, Eastpoint, GA	404-344-2971
DeLahoussaye, Jeanne/816 Foucher, New Orleans, LA	504-581-2167
Dove Design Studio/2025 Rockledge Rd NE, Atlanta, GA	404-873-2209
Draper, Linda/2232 Haversham Close, Virginia Beach, VA	804-481-0052
Dunlap, Leslie/3745 Keller Ave, Alexandria, VA	703-379-9692
Eldredge, Ernie/2683 Vesclub Cir, Birmingham, AL	205-822-3879
Faure, Renee/600 Second St, Neptune Beach, FL	904-246-2781
Findley, John/213 Elizabeth St, Atlanta, GA	404-659-7103
Firestone, Bill/1506 N Ivanhoe St, Alexandria, VA	703-532-2923
Fisher, Mike/3811 General Pershing, New Orleans, LA	504-827-0382

Fleck, Tom/One Park Pl #120, Atlanta, GA	404-355-0729
Frank, Cheryll/2216 Eastgate Way, Tallahasse, FL	904-385-3717
Frank, Sheryl/2216 E Gateway, Tallahassee, FL	904-385-3717

G
Gaadt, David/2103 Tennyson Dr, Greensboro, NC	919-288-9727
Galey, Chuck/211 Lea Circle, Jackson, MS	601-372-5103
Gignilliat, Elaine/747 Bayliss Dr, Marietta, GA	404-977-5635
Glasgow, Dale/4517 Blu jay Ct, Woodbridge, VA	703-590-1702
Gonzalez, Thomas/755 Virginia Ave, Atlanta, GA	404-872-7980
Gordon, Jack/3201 S 5th St, Arlington, VA	703-979-3236
Gorman, Martha/3057 Pharr Ct Nrth NW #E6, Atlanta, GA	404-261-5632
Graphics Group/6111 PchtreeDunwdy Rd#G101, Atlanta, GA	404-391-9929
Graphics Illustrated/5720-E North Blvd, Raliegh, NC	919-878-7883
Greathead, Ian/1591 Sand Pt Dr, Roswell, GA	404-952-5067
Guthrie, Dennis/1118 Franklin Ct, Atlanta, GA	404-325-6867

HI
Hamilton, Marcus/12225 Ranburne Rd, Charlotte, NC	704-545-3121
Havaway, Jane/806 Briarcliff Rd, Atlanta, GA	404-872-7284
Henderling, Lisa/800 West Ave #345, Miami Beach, FL	305-531-1771
Herring & Klem/PO Box 48453, Atlanta, GA	404-945-8652
Hickey, John/3821 Abingdon Circle, Norfolk, VA	804-853-2956
Hicks, Richard Edward/3667 Vanet Rd, Chamblee, GA	404-365-0333
Hilfer, Susan/PO Box 50552, Columbia, SC	803-799-0689
Hinojosa, Albino/1802 Furman, Ruston, LA	318-255-2820
Hodges, Mike/10019-A Palace Ct, Richmond, VA	404-892-6303
Hogenkamp, Johnna/6928 Kessler, Shawnee Mission, KS	913-236-5133
Hunter, Katherine/819 Crater St, Charlotte, NC	
Hyatt, Mitch/4171 Buckingham Ct, Marietta, GA	404-924-1241
Hyatt, Steven/4171 Buckingham Ct, Marietta, GA	404-924-1241
Image Electronic Inc/3525 Piedmont Rd NE #110, Atlanta, GA	404-262-7610
Irvin, Trevor/330 Southerland Terrace, Atlanta, GA	404-377-4754

JK
James, Bill/15840 SW 79th Ct, Miami, FL	305-238-5709
Jarvis, David/275 Indigo Dr, Daytona Beach, FL	904-255-1296
Johnson, Pamela R/1415 N Key Blvd, Arlington, VA	703-525-5012
Jones, Jack/100 Colony SW #305, Atlanta, GA	404-881-6627
Kanelous, George/2864 Lake Valencia Blvd E, Palm Harbor, FL	813-784-8528
Kilgore, Susi/2905 Bay Villa, Tampa, FL	813-837-9759
Kissinger, Gordon/9304 Jefferson Hwy, Baton Rouge, LA	504-291-9906
Kunz, Grace/1104 W Newtown St, Dothan, AL	205-793-5723

L
Lam, John/5209 N Stanford Dr, Nashville, TN	615-297-5669
Landis, Jeff/1372 Fiftieth Ave NE, St Petersburg, FL	813-525-0757
Lee, Kelly/3511 N 22nd St, Arlington, VA	703-527-4089
Left, Stephen/1351 S Dixie Hwy #E8, Pompano Beach, FL	305-942-1851
Lester, Mike/1001 Eulalia Rd NE, Atlanta, GA	404-233-3093
Lewis, Chris/597 Coolidge Ave, Atlanta, GA	404-876-0288
Little, Pam/321 Niagara St, Orange City, FL	904-755-2919
Loehle, Don/2574 Sherbrooke Dr NE, Atlanta, CA	404-633-7145
Lovell, Rick/2860 Lakewind Ct, Alpharetta, GA	404-442-3943
Lunsford, Annie/515 N Hudson St, Arlington, VA	301-320-3912

MN
Marks, David/726 Hillpine Dr NE, Atlanta, GA	404-872-1824
Martin, Don/5110 S W 80th St, Miami, FL	305-665-2376
Matthews, Lu/547 Mount Hermon rd, Ashland, VA	804-782-9895
Mayer, Bill/240 Forkner Dr, Decatur, GA	404-378-0686
McGary, Richard/180 NE 39th St #125, Miami, FL	305-757-5720
McKelvey, David/3022 Huntshire Pl, Atlanta, GA	404-938-1949
McKinney-Levine, Deborah/95-50 Regency Sq Blvd, Jacksonville, FL	904-723-6000
McKissick, Randall/PO Box 21811, Columbia, SC	803-798-3688
McManus, Eugenia/PO Box 39, Mayhew, MS	601-328-5534
Mitchell, Charlie/1404 Regency Woods Dr, Atlanta, GA	404-634-0482
Mollica, Pat/2625 Cumberland Pkwy #290, Atlanta, GA	404-438-8352
Montgomery, Michael/PO Box 161031, Atlanta, GA	404-478-2929
Moore, Connie Illus/4242 Inverness Rd, Duluth, GA	404-449-9553
Moore, Cyd/317 W Glenwood Dr, Birmingham, AL	205-871-3906
Moore, William "Casey"/4242 Inverness Rd, Duluth, GA	404-449-9553
Moses, David/3410 Renault St, Memphis, TN	901-795-6157
Myers, Sherwood/9770 Sterling Dr, Miami, FL	305-238-0488
Nelson, Bill/1402 Wilmington Ave, Richmond, VA	804-358-9637

Illustrators

Continued

Please send us your additions and updates.

OP

Oliphant, Tim/200 MCHS Dr #2K, Lewisburg, TN	615-359-7430
Olson, Linda/1 Charter Plaza, Jacksonville, FL	904-723-6000
Overacre, Gary/3802 Vinyard Trace, Marietta, GA	404-973-8878
Ovies, Joe/3500 Piedmont St #430, Atlanta, GA	404-462-1209
Pardue, Jack/2307 Sherwood Hall Ln, Alexandria, VA	703-765-2622
Park, William B/110 Park Ave S, Winter Park, FL	305-644-1553
Parrish, George/2401 Old Concord Rd, Smyrna, GA	404-435-4189
Pate, Martin/401 W Peachtree NW, Atlanta, GA	404-881-6627
Pawelka, Rick/5720 E North Blvd, Raleigh, NC	919-878-7883
Penca, Gary/8335 NW 20th St, Coral Springs, FL	305-752-4699
Pendaro, Alton/2011 Orleans Ave, New Orleans, LA	501-822-9375

R

Rabon, Elaine Hearn/573 Hill St, Athens, GA	404-353-8479
RAINOCK, NORMAN/10226 PURCELL RD, GLEN ALLEN, VA (P 39)	**804-264-8123**
Rauchman, Bob/7021 SW 58th St, Miami, FL	305-445-5628
Rebeiz, Kathryn D/526 Druid Hill Rd, Vienna, VA	703-938-9779
Reppel, Aletha/PO Box 3914, Lafayette, LA	318-235-7282
Robinette, John/3745 Woodland, Memphis, TN	901-452-9853
Robinson, Mark/9050 Loreleigh Way, Fairfax, VA	703-280-4123
Romeo, Richard/1066 NW 96th Ave, Ft Lauderdale, FL	305-472-0072
Rudnak, Theo/1151 W Peachtree St NW, Atlanta, GA	404-892-6303

S

Saffold, Joe/719 Martina Dr NE, Atlanta, GA	404-231-2168
Salmon, Paul/5826 Jackson's Oak Ct, Burke, VA	703-250-4943
Sams, B B/PO Box A, Social Circle, GA	404-464-2956
Scheffer, Jules/240 Causeway Blvd, Dunedin, FL	813-734-1265
Schwartz, Nina/505 Fontaine St, Alexandria, VA	703-836-7366
Seif, Sue Solomon/10207 Stonemill Rd, Richmond, VA	804-747-9684
Sheets, Jeff/8350 Rose Terrace N, Largo, FL	813-536-1941
Shelly, Ron/6396 Manor Lane, S Miami, FL	305-667-0154
Shepherd, Bob/8371 W Weyburn Rd, Richmond, VA	804-320-8600
Short, Robbie/2903 Bentwood Dr, Marietta, GA	404-565-7811
Sloan, Michael/PO Box 1397, Madison, TN	615-865-7018
Smith, Donald/PO Box 391, Athens, GA	404-543-5555
Soper, Patrick/214 Stephens, Lafayette, LA	318-233-1635
Spetseris, Steve/100 Colony SW #305, Atlanta, GA	404-881-6627
Stanton, Mark/67 Jonesboro St, McDonough, GA	404-957-5966
Stanton, Reggie/411 Park Ave N #11, Winter Park, FL	305-645-1661
Stone, David K/9 Kennebec Dr, Chapel Hill, NC	914-929-0853

TUV

Taylor, Creed/206 Media Bldg/VA Tech, Blacksburg, VA	703-961-5314
The Artsmith/440 College Ave/Box 391, Athens, GA	404-543-5555
Thompson, Del/108 Sutton Dr, Taylors, SC	803-268-0883
Torp, Cynthia/600 E Main St, Louisville, KY	502-634-4911
Tull, Bobbi/317 N Howard St, Alexandria, VA	703-370-3451
Turner, Cynthia/3 Old Miller Pl, Santa Rosa Bch, FL	904-231-4112
Turner, Deannie/9721 Lakepointe Dr, Burke, VA	703-425-6523
Turner, Pete/938 Pamlico Dr, Cary, NC	919-467-8466
Ulan, Helen Cerra/4227 San Juan Dr, Fairfax, VA	703-691-0474
Vaughn, Rob/600 Curtis Pkwy/Box 660706, Miami Springs, FL	305-885-1292
Vintson, Sherry/430 Appian Way NE, St Petersburg, FL	813-822-2512
Vondracek, Woody/420 Lincoln Rd #408, Old Miami Beach, FL	305-531-7558

WXY

Wasiluck Asso/7115 University Blvd, Winter Park, FL	305-678-6964
Watts, David/9-A Glenwood Ave, Raliegh, NC	919-821-0652
Webber, Warren/100 Colony SW #305, Atlanta, GA	404-221-0700
Wetzel, Marcia/755 Virginia Ave, Atlanta, GA	404-872-7980
Whitver, Harry K/208 Reidhurst Ave, Nashville, TN	615-320-1795
Wilkinson, Joel/707 E McBee Ave, Greenville, SC	803-235-4483
Williams, Tim/520 Country Glen Rd, Alpharetta, GA	404-475-3146
Wilson, Danny/3508 Ten Oakes Cir, Powder Springs, GA	404-391-9929
Winkle, MArk/PO Box 25011, Durham, NC	919-682-5765
Xenakis, Thomas/523 W 24th St #25, Norfolk, VA	804-622-2061
Yarnell, David Andrew/PO Box 286, Occoquan, VA	202-690-2987
Young, Bruce/1262 Pasadena Ave NE, Atlanta, GA	404-892-8509

Midwest

A

AIR Studio/203 E Seventh St, Cincinnati, OH	513-721-1193
Ahearn, John D/151 S Elm, St Louis, MO	314-781-3389
Allen, David/18108 Martin Ave #2F, Homewood, IL	312-798-3283
Anastas, Nicolette/535 N Michigan Ave, Chicago, IL	312-943-1668
Andic, Mike/PO Box 500, Woodstock N4S 7Y5, ON	519-439-4661
Appleoff, Sandy/4931 Bell St, Kansas City, MO	816-753-5421
Archer, Doug/623 E Monroe, Box 307, KS	913-448-3841
Art Force Inc/21700 NW Hwy #570, Southfield, MI	313-569-1074
Artist Studios/666 Euclid Ave, Cleveland, OH	216-241-5355

B

Bachtell, Tom/185 N Wabash #1604, Chicago, IL	312-641-0190
Backes, Nick/405 N Wabash Ave #3203, Chicago, IL	312-329-1370
Baker, Strandell/505 N Lake Shore Dr #5307, Chicago, IL	312-661-1555
Bannick, Cathy/321 Springside Dr, Akron, OH	216-666-7014
Bartek-Mitchell, Shelley/608 S 55th St, Omaha, NE	402-444-1612
Beach, Jack/233 E Wacker Dr #1911, Chicago, IL	312-861-1771
Beck, Joan/2521 11th Ave S, Minneapolis, MN	612-870-7159
Bedrick, Jeffrey/490 Rockside Rd, Cleveland, OH	216-661-4222
Behum, Cliff/26384 Aaron Ave, Euclid, OH	216-261-9266
Bemus, Bart/652 W Buckingham Pl, Chicago, IL	312-975-1043
Benton, Jim/1911 Villa, Birmingham, MI	313-644-5875
Biggerstaff, Don/PO Box 3926, S Ill Univ/Med Sch, IL	217-782-2326
Birkey, Randall/635 Home, Oak park, IL	312-383-2392
Blanchette, Dan/185 N Wabash Ave, Chicago, IL	312-332-1339
Bleck, Linda/901 S First St #3, Champaign, IL	
Bobnick, Richard/4640 W 77th St #1, Edina, MN	612-831-6313
BOEHM, ROGER/529 SOUTH 7TH ST #539, MINNEAPOLIS, MN (P 21)	**612-332-0787**
Boge, Garrett/3821 Baltimore St, Kansas City, MO	816-531-2483
Boies, Alexandra/438 Portland Ave #8, St Paul, MN	612-224-6767
Bookwater, Tom/336 Lakeview Ln, Plainwell, MI	616-685-1518
Boswick, Steven/3342 Capital, Skokie, IL	312-328-2042
Bowman, Bob/163 Cedarwood Ct, Palatine, IL	312-966-2770
Boyer-Pennington, Lyn/3904 Sherwood Forest Dr, Traverse City, MI	616-938-1911
Bradley, Tracy/PO Box 10719, Chicago, IL	312-334-0541
Braught, Mark/629 Cherry St #18, Terre Haute, IN	812-234-6135
Brennan, Daniel/842 N Webster, Chicago, IL	312-822-0887
Britt, Tracy/68 E Franklin St, Dayton, OH	513-433-8383
Broderick, Ned/230 N Michigan Ave, Chicago, IL	312-368-8777
Brooks, Dick/11712 N Michigan Rd #100, Zionsville, IN	317-873-1117
Butler, Chris/743 N Dearborn, Chicago, IL	312-280-2288
BUTTRAM, ANDY/1636 HICKORY GLEN DR, MIAMISBURG, OH (P 23)	**513-859-7428**

C

Call, Ken/7611 N Sheridan #2 South, Chicago, IL	312-644-3017
Carloni, Kurt/7392 S Delaine Dr, Oak Creek, WI	414-762-5975
Carr, Ted/43 E Ohio #1001, Chicago, IL	312-467-6865
Carroll, Michael/1228 E 54th St, Chicago, IL	312-752-6262
Centaur Studios/10 Broadway, St Louis, MO	314-421-6485
Chickinelli, Mark/6348 Pierce St, Omaha, NE	402-551-6829
Cigliano, William/1525 W Glenlake, Chicago, IL	312-878-1659
Clay, Steve/245 W North Ave, Chicago, IL	312-280-7945
Clifford, Keesler/6642 West H Ave, Kalamazoo, MI	616-375-0688
Clifford, Lawrence/12 Hull St, St Louis, MO	314-771-6177
Clubb, Rick/333 N Michigan, Chicago, IL	312-853-1133
Clyne, Dan/535 N Michigan Ave #1416, Chicago, IL	312-943-1668
Cobane, Russell/8291 Allen Rd, Clarkston, MI	313-625-6132
Cochran, Bobbye/400 W Erie, #300, Chicago IL	312-943-5912
Cochran, Cynthia/6725 N Sheridan, Chicago, IL	312-743-8893
Colby, Gary/36339 Park Pl Dr, Sterling Hts, MI	313-268-9356
Cole, Grace/4342 N Clark, Chicago, IL	312-935-8605
COLLIER, JOHN/2309 WILLOW CREEK LN, LAWRENCE, KS (P 14)	**913-841-6442**
Color Forms/407 E Fort St, Detroit, MI	313-961-7100
Connelly, Gwen/233 E Wacker Dr, Chicago, IL	312-432-1830
Cook, Mark/742 N Humphrey, Oak Park, IL	312-848-6105
Cosgrove, Dan/405 N Wabash #4307, Chicago, IL	312-527-0375
Coulter, Marty/10129 Conway Rd, St Louis, MO	314-432-2721
Craig, John/RT 2 Box 81 Tower Rd, Soldiers Grove, WI	608-872-2371
Creative Source Inc/360 N Michigan Ave #805, Chicago, IL	312-649-9777
Crnkovich, Tony/5706 S Narragansett, Chicago, IL	312-586-9696
Csicsko, David/185 Wabash #1604, Chicago, IL	312-787-3256

Illustrators

Continued

Please send us your additions and updates.

Currant, Don/215 Parkland, St Louis, MO	314-965-8672

D

Dammer, Mike/323 S Franklin #600, Chicago, IL	312-663-5866
Dawson, John/116 Bedford Rd #1, Toronto M5R 2K2, ON	416-926-0730
Day, Rob/6130 Compton St #2, Indianapolis, IN	317-253-9469
Deal, Jim/2558 W Wilson Ave, Chicago, IL	312-242-3846
Dearth, Greg/4041 Beal Rd, Franklin, OH	513-746-5970
Devarj, Silva/116 W Illinois, Chicago, IL	312-266-1358
DiCianni, Ron/340 Thompson Blvd, Buffalo Grove, IL	312-634-1848
Dickens, Holly/612 N Michigan, Chicago, IL	312-280-0777
Dinyer, Eric/1913 Park, St Louis, MO	314-241-4014
Dougherty, Mike/1305-A Chesterdale Rd, Springdale, OH	413-671-6598
Doyle, Pat/333 N Michigan Ave, Chicago, IL	312-263-2065
Duggan, Lee/52 S Washington, Hinsdale, IL	312-986-9009
Dunlevy, Brad/3660 Jefferson, Kansas City, MO	816-931-8945
Dypold, Pat/26 E Huron St, Chicago, IL	312-337-6919

EF

Eastwood, Peter/3854 N Janssen, Chicago, IL	312-327-4704
Eaton & Iwen/70 E Lake St #1300, Chicago, IL	312-332-3256
Eberbach, Andrea/5301 N Delaware, Indianapolis, IN	317-253-0421
Eldridge, Gary/336 Lakeview Ln, Plainwell, MI	616-685-1518
Ellis, Christie/914 N Winchester, Chicago, IL	312-342-6343
English, Mark/Rt 3 PO Box 325, Kearney, MO	816-635-4433
Fanning, Jim/116 W 3rd St, Kansas City, MO	816-474-3922
Feldkamp-Malloy/185 N Wabash, Chicago, IL	312-263-0633
Flock, Mary/5247 S Washtenaw, Chicago, IL	312-925-0546
Flood, Dick/2210 S Lynn, Urbana, IL	217-328-3642
Foty, Tom/5420 Spring Ln, Minnetonka, MN	612-933-5570
Frampton, Bill/49 Henderson, Toronto M6J 2B9, ON	416-535-1931
Fredrickson, Mark/1913 Park, St Louis, MO	314-241-9014
Frueh, Mark/155 N Michigan Ave, Chicago, IL	312-565-0030
Fruzyna, Frank/PO Box 16545, Chicago, IL	312-666-3065

G

Gehold-Smith, William/1442 W Landt St 2nd Fl, Chicago, IL	312-262-1423
Gieseke, Thomas/7909 W 61st St, Merriam, KS	913-677-4593
Golby, Garry/36339 Park Pl Dr, Sterling Heights, MI	313-268-9356
Goldammer, Ken/405 N Wabash #3611, Chicago, IL	312-836-0143
Gonnella, Rick/230 N Michigan Ave, Chicago, IL	312-368-8777
Grace, Rob/7516 Lamar Ave #81, Prarie Village, KS	913-341-9135
Graef, Renee/403 W Washington Ave, Madison, WI	608-256-7796
Graham, Bill/116 W Illinois, Chicago, IL	312-440-0330
Graning, Ken/1975 Cragin Dr, Bloomfield Hills, MI	313-851-3665
Groff, David/2265 Avalon Ave, Kettering, OH	513-294-7700
Gsrmon, Van/1601 22nd St #201, W Des Moines, IA	515-246-6166
Gustafson, Glenn/307 N Michigan Ave #2016, Chicago, IL	312-368-4536

H

Halvert, Mike/2419 Big Ben, St Louis, MO	314-645-6480
Hamblin, George/944 Beach St, LaGrange Pk, IL	312-352-1780
Hammond, Franklin/1179-A W King St #310, Toronto M6K 3C5, ON	416-533-4434
Hannan, Peter/1341 W Melrose, Chicago, IL	312-883-9029
Harris, Scott/803 Greenleaf St, Evanston, IL	312-440-2360
Hatcher, Lois/32 W 58th St, Kansas City, MO	816-361-6230
Havlicek, Karel/405 N Wabash Ave #3203, Chicago, IL	312-329-1370
Hayes, Cliff/PO Box 1239, Chicago Hts, IL	312-755-7115
Hayes, John/224 W Huron St, Chicago, IL	312-787-1333
Haynes, Michael/3070 Hawthorn Blvd, St Louis, MO	314-772-3156
Heda, Jackie/3 Playter Blvd #3, Toronto M4K 2V6, ON	416-463-8692
Hodde, Julie/68 E Franklin St, Dayton, OH	513-433-8383
Hodge, Gerald/1241 Bending Rd, Ann Arbor, MI	313-764-6163
Holladay Prints/1510 E Rusholme, Davenport, IA	319-323-2343
Horn, Robert/405 N Wabash #2815, Chicago, IL	312-644-0058
Howard, Deborah/1800 N McCord Rd #45, Toledo, OH	419-867-0249
Hrabe, Curtis/2944 Greenwood Ave, Highland Park, IL	312-432-4632
Hranilovich, Barbara/1200 N Jenison, Lansing, MI	517-487-6474
Hunt, Harlan/900 W Jackson #7W, Chicago, IL	312-944-5680

IJ

Izold, Donald/20475 Bunker Hill Dr, Fairview Park, OH	216-333-9988
J H Illustration/1415 W 6th St, Cedar Falls, IA	319-277-2475
Jamerson, David/6367 N Guilford Ave, Indianapolis, IN	317-257-8752
Jarnes, Verzell/1521 W Sunnyside, Chicago, IL	312-784-2352
Jay/17858 Rose St, Lansing, IL	312-474-9704

Johannes, Greg/233 E Wacker Dr, Chicago, IL	312-642-5328
Johnson, BJ/151 N Michigan #2113, Chicago, IL	312-861-1342
Johnson, Diane/4609 N Claremont, Chicago, IL	312-728-5874
Johnson, Rick/1212 W Chase, Chicago, IL	312-274-4272
Johnson, WB/572 Mountain Ave, Winnepeg R2W 1K9, MB	204-582-1686
Jones, Danielle/55 W Charles St #1003, Toronto M5F 2W9, ON	416-968-6277
Jones, Jan/2332 N Halstead, Chicago, IL	312-929-1851
Jones, Mary/4511 N Campbell, Chicago, IL	312-769-1196
Jones, Michael Scott/459 W Briar Pl, Chicago, IL	312-944-2799
Juenger, Richard/1324 S 9th St, St Louis, MO	314-231-4069

K

Kahl, Konrad/26039 German Hill, Franklin, MI	313-851-7064
Kalisch, John W/4201 Levenworth, Omaha, NE	402-734-5064
Karpinski, Rick/6016 North Bay Ridge Ave, Whitefish Bay, WI	414-962-1002
KASTARIS, RIP/3301 S JEFFERSON, ST LOUIS, MO (P 30)	**314-773-9989**
Kauffman, George/, Topeka, KS	913-897-4342
Kecman, Milan/2730 Somia Dr, Cleveland, OH	216-741-8755
Kelen, Linda/1922 W Newport, Chicago, IL	312-975-9696
Kelley, Gary/301 1/2 Main St, Cedar Falls, IA	212-683-1362
Kessler Hartsock Assoc/5624 Belmont Ave, Cincinnati, OH	513-542-8775
Kessler, Clifford/6642 West H Ave, Kalamazoo, MI	616-375-0688
Kirov, Lydia/4008 N Hermitage Ave, Chicago, IL	312-248-8764
Kocar, George F/24213 Lake Rd, Bay Village, OH	216-871-8325
Kock, Carl/311 N Desplaines Ave, Chicago, IL	312-559-0440
Kordic, Vladimir/35351 Grovewood Dr, Eastlake, OH	216-951-4026
Kotik, Kenneth/9 Last Chance Ct, St Peter, MO	314-441-1091
Krainik, David/4719 Center Ave, Lisle, IL	312-963-4614
Kriegshauser, Shannon/12421 W Grafleman Rd, Hanna City, IL	309-565-7110
Kueker, Don/832 S Ballas, St Louis, MO	314-225-1566
Kunz, Anita/230 Ontario St, Toronto M5A 2V5, ON	416-364-3846

L

LaFever, Greg/68 E Franklin St, Dayton, OH	513-433-8383
Lambert, John/1911 E Robin Hood Ln, Arlington Heights, IL	312-392-6349
Langeneckert, Donald/4939 Ringer Rd, St Louis, MO	314-487-2042
Langeneckert, Mark/704 Dover Pl, St Louis, MO	314-752-0199
Lattimer, Evan/4203 Holly, Kansas City, MO	816-561-0103
Laurent, Richard/1132 W Columbia Ave, Chicago, IL	312-245-9014
Lawson, Robert/1523 Seminole St, Kalamazoo, MI	616-345-7607
Lee, Denis Charles/1120 Heatherway, Ann Arbor, MI	313-973-2795
Lee, Jared D/2942 Old Hamilton Rd, Lebanon, OH	513-932-2154
Leonard, Martha/1515 South Blvd, Evanston, IL	312-864-8638
Lesh, David/5693 N Meridan St, Indianapolis, IN	317-253-3141
Letostak, John/7801 Fernhill Ave, Parma, OH	216-885-1753
Liss, Julius/446 Lawrence Ave W, Toronto M5M 1C2, ON	416-784-1416
Lochray, Tom/3225 Oakland Ave, Minneapolis, MN	612-823-7630
Locke, Gary/1111 S John St, Springfield, MO	417-887-8207
Loos, Jean/5539 Arnsby Pl, Cincinnati, OH	513-561-8472
Loveless, Jim/4137 San Francisco, St Louis, MO	314-533-7914

M

MacDougall, Rob/72 Oakcrest Ave, Toronto M4C 1B6, ON	416-690-3033
MacNair, Greg/7515 Wayne, University City, MO	314-721-3781
Magdich, Dennis/1914 N Dayton, Chicago, IL	312-248-6492
Maggard, John/102 Marian Lane, Terrace Park, OH	513-831-8801
Mahan, Benton/PO Box 66, Chesterville, OH	419-768-2204
Manchess, Gregory/5721 Anne Lane, Dayton, OH	513-434-1138
Marlaire, Dennis/311 Kingston Dr, Frankfort, IL	312-819-4750
Mayerik, Val/20466 Drake Rd, Strongsville, OH	216-238-9492
Mayes, Kevin/1202 Tulsa St, Wichita, KS	316-522-6742
McDermott, Teri/514 S State St, Elgin, IL	312-888-2206
McInturff, Steve/1795 E Kings Creek, Urbana, OH	513-789-3590
McMahon, Mark/321 S Ridge Rd, Lake Forest, IL	312-295-2604
McMann, Brian/2108 Payne NE #907, Cleveland, OH	216-566-1605
McNicholas, Michael/7804 W College Dr, Palos Hts, IL	312-361-2850
Meade, Roy/1105 Adams St, Toledo, OH	419-244-9074
Mendheim, Mike/6619 North Shore Dr, Chicago, IL	312-338-0773
Miller, David/PO Box 474, Elkhart, IN	219-295-1492
Miller, Doug/2648 Glen Mawr Ave, Columbus, OH	614-267-6533
Miller, Jean/350 Esna Park Dr, Markham, ON	416-883-4114
Miller, William (Bill)/1355 N Sandburg Ter #2002, Chicago, IL	312-787-4093
Morgan, Leonard/1163 E Ogden Ave #705, Naperville, IL	312-759-3987
Mueller, Rob/1713 N Mohawk, Chicago, IL	312-649-9159
Munger, Nancy/PO Box 125, Richland, MI	616-623-5458

Illustrators

Continued

Please send us your additions and updates.

Musgrave, Steve/213 W Institute Pl #502, Chicago, IL	312-943-2597

N
Nagel, Mike/PO Box 610, Arlington Hts, IL	312-253-0638
Neidigh, Sherry/368 W Huron, Chicago, IL	312-787-6826
Nelson, Diane/2816 Birchwood, Wilmette, IL	312-256-6200
Nelson, Fred/3 E Ontario #25, Chicago, IL	312-935-1707
Nichols, Garry/1449 N Pennsylvania St, Indianapolis, IN	317-637-0250
Nighthawk Studio/1250 Riverbed Rd, Cleveland, OH	216-522-1809
Norcia, Ernest/3451 Houston Rd, Waynesville, OH	513-862-5761
Northerner, Will/932 W Sheridan, Chicago, IL	
Novack, Bob/6878 Fry Rd, Middlebury Hts, OH	216-234-1808
Noyes, Mary Albury/716 First St N #245, Minneapolis, MN	612-338-1270

O
O'Connell, Mitch/1427 W Farwell #35, Chicago, IL	312-743-3848
O'Malley, Kathy/4510 N Paulina #1W, Chicago, IL	312-334-7637
O'Neill, Brian/17006 Woodbury Ave, Cleveland, OH	216-252-6238
Oliveros, Edmond/5800 Monroe St, Sylvania, OH	419-882-7131
Olson, Robert A/15215 Buchanan Ct, Eden Prairie, MN	612-934-5767
Ormond, Rick/42 Portland Crscnt, Newmarket L3Y 6A5, ON	416-961-4098
Ortman, John/535 N Michigan Ave, Chicago, IL	312-266-1417
Ostresh, Michael/2034 13th St, Granite City, IL	618-876-8861
Otto, Brian/368 W Huron, Chicago, IL	312-787-6826

P
Palmer, Charly/215 W Ohio 5th Fl, Chicago, IL	312-644-8484
Pappas, Chris/323 S Franklin, Chicago, IL	312-922-2213
Pastucha, Ron/336 McNeans Ave, Winnipeg R2C 2J7, MB	204-222-3178
Patterson/Thomas/1002 E Washington St, Indianapolis, IN	317-638-1002
Pepera, Fred/405 N Wabash #3203, Chicago, IL	312-329-1370
Petrauskas, Kathy/155 N Michigan Ave, Chicago, IL	312-565-0030
Pitt Studios/1370 Ontario St #1430, Cleveland, OH	216-241-6720
Pitts, Ted/20 Lynnray Circle, Dayton, OH	513-433-8383
Pope, Giles/4222 Lindenwood, Matteson, IL	312-747-2056
Pope, Kevin/328 N Lincoln Ave, Mundelein, IL	312-566-5534
Post, Bob/2144 Lincoln Pk W, Chicago, IL	312-549-6725
Pranica, John/5702 W Henderson, Chicago, IL	312-685-1207
Prepera, Fred/405 N Wabash #3203, Chicago, IL	312-329-1370
Probert, Jean/1022 N Bompart, St Louis, MO	314-968-5076

QR
Quinn, Colleen/535 N Michigan, Chicago, IL	312-943-1668
Rasmussen, Bonnie/8828 Pendleton, St Louis, MO	314-962-1842
Rawley, Don/7520 Blaisdell Ave S, Richfield, MN	612-866-1023
Rawson, Jon/1225 S Hamilton, Lockport, IL	815-838-4462
Renaud, Phill/2830 W Leland, Chicago, IL	312-583-2681
Reynolds, Donna/2138 N clifton, Chicago, IL	312-836-0099
Riedy, Mark/68 E Franklin St, Dayton, OH	513-433-8383
Ristau, Paul/215 W Ohio 5th Fl, Chicago, IL	312-644-8484
Roberts, A Hardy/6512 Charlotte, Kansas City, MO	816-444-8210
Robinson, Brenda/718 19th Ave, Coralville, IA	319-353-6622
Rossi, Pam/39 Linden St, Winnetka, IL	312-441-5256
Roth, Hy/1300 Ashland St, Evanston, IL	312-491-1937
Rybka, Stephen/3119 W 83rd St, Chicago, IL	312-737-1981

S
Sanford, John/5038 W Berteau, Chicago, IL	312-685-0656
Schmelzer, J P/1002 S Wesley Ave, Oak Park, IL	312-386-4005
Schrag, Allan/8530 W Ninth, Wichita, KS	316-722-4585
Schrier, Fred/9058 Little Mtn Rd, Kirtland Hills, OH	216-255-7787
Schuler, Mark/5410 W 68th St, Prairie Village, KS	913-384-0646
Schweitzer, Dave/336 Lakeview Ln, Plainwell, MI	616-685-1518
Scibilia, Dom/2902 Franklin Blvd, Cleveland, OH	216-861-2561
Selfridge, MC/817 Desplaines St, Plainfield, IL	815-436-7197
Sellars, Joseph/2423 W 22nd St, Minneapolis, MN	612-377-8766
Seltzer, Meyer Design & Illustration/744 W Buckingham Pl, Chicago, IL	312-348-2885
Sereta, Bruce/3010 Parklane Dr, Cleveland, OH	216-241-5355
Shaw, Ned/2770 N Smith Pike, Bloomington, IN	812-333-2181
Shay, RJ/3301 S Jefferson Ave, St Louis, MO	314-773-9989
Sheldon, David/20 Lynnray Circle, Dayton, OH	513-433-8383
Sienkowski, Lauri/3660 Newcastle SE, Grand Rapids, MI	616-247-0127
Sinenkowski, Laurie/3660 New Castle, Grand Rapids, MI	616-247-0127
Sirrell, Terry/388 E Lambert Dr, Schaumburg, IL	312-980-7047
Sisson-Schlesser, Kathryn/707 W Wrightwood Ave, Chicago, IL	312-472-3877

Skidmore Sahratian Inc/2100 W Big Beaver Rd, Troy, MI	313-643-6000
Slack, Chuck/9 Cambridge Ln, Lincolnshire, IL	312-948-9226
Snodgrass, Steve/155 N Michigan Ave, Chicago, IL	312-565-0030
Songero, Jay/17858 Rose St, Lansing, IL	312-849-5676
Soukup, James/Route 1, Seward, NE	402-643-2339
Speer, Terry/181 Forest St, Oberlin, OH	216-774-8319
Staake, Bob/1009 S Berry Rd, St Louis, MO	314-961-2303
Stearney, Mark/405 N Wabash #2809, Chicago, IL	312-644-6669
Storyboard Studio/535 N Michigan Ave, Chicago, IL	312-266-1417
Streff, Michael/2766 Wasson Rd, Cincinnati, OH	513-731-0360
Stroster, Maria/2057 N Sheffield, Chicago, IL	312-525-2081
Sumichrast, Jozef/860 N Northwoods, Deerfield, IL	312-945-6353
Svolos, Maria/7346 N Hoyne St, Chicago, IL	312-338-4675
Swaford, Chris/PO Box 82, Republic, MO	417-744-4411
Syska, Richard/2327 N Geneva Terr, Chicago, IL	312-935-5569

T
Tate, Clark/557 N Park Blvd, Glen Ellyn, IL	312-469-0085
Tate, Don/557 N Park Blvd, Glen Ellyn, IL	312-469-0085
Taylor, David/1449 N Pennsylvania St, Indianapolis, IN	317-634-2728
Thacker, Kat/311 W Drayton Ave, Ferndale, MI	313-455-2765
Theodore, Jim/17253 Pearl Rd, Cleveland, OH	216-238-6188
Thiewes, Sam/111 N Andover Ln, Geneva, IL	312-232-0980
Thomas, Bob/68 E Franklin St, Dayton, OH	513-433-8383
Thomas, Pat/711 Carpenter, Oak Park, IL	312-383-8505
Thornton, Shelley/1600 S 22nd St, Lincoln, NE	212-683-1362
Tipton, Bill/1762 Sparrow Pt Ln, Fenton, MO	314-343-9961
Townley, Jon/61 Sunnyside Lane, Columbus, OH	614-268-9717
Trusilo, Jim/535 N Michigan Ave, Chicago, IL	312-943-1668
Tughan, James/1179-A King St W #310, Toronto M6K 3C5, ON	416-535-9149
Turgeon, James/233 E Wacker Dr #1102, Chicago, IL	312-861-1039
Tyrrell, Robert/405 N Wabash Ave #3203, Chicago, IL	312-329-1370

UV
Utley, Tom/490 Rockside Rd, Cleveland, OH	216-661-4222
Utterback, Bill/6105 Kingston Ave, Lisle, IL	312-871-8366
Vaccarello, Paul/505 N Lake Shore Dr, Chicago, IL	312-664-2233
VanZanten, Hugh/536 W Grant #10, Chicago, IL	312-871-8366
Vanderbeek, Don/235 Monterey Ave, Dayton, OH	513-293-5326
Vann, Bill Studio/1706 S 8th St, St Louis, MO	314-231-2322
Vanselow, Holly/2701 N Southport, Chicago, IL	312-975-5880
Villani, Ron/405 N Wabash Ave #3203, Chicago, IL	312-329-1370
Vokac, Lucy/24W567 Ohio St, Naperville, OH	312-357-7671
Voo, Rhonda/3 E Ontario #25, Chicago, IL	312-935-1707
Vuksanovich, Fran/3224 N Nordica, Chicago, IL	312-283-2138

W
Wade, Tony/1913 Park, St Louis, MO	314-241-4014
Wald, Carol/217 Farnsworth Ave, Detroit, MI	313-832-5805
Walker, John/4423 Wilson Ave, Chicago, IL	312-664-1882
Walker, Ken/116 W 3rd St, Kansas City, MO	816-931-7975
Walsh, Cathy/323 S Franklin, Chicago, IL	312-944-2985
Walter, Nancy Lee/PO Box 611, Elmhurst, IL	312-833-3898
Watkinson, Brent/1100 County Ln Rd/Bldg 12/#28, Kansas City, KS	913-362-9380
Westphal, Ken/7616 Fairway, Prairie Village, KS	913-381-8399
Westwood, William/211 23rd Ave SW, Rochester, MN	507-282-7140
Whitney, Bill/116 W Illinois 5th Fl, Chicago, IL	312-527-2455
Whitney, Mike/7833 Key Ridge Ln, St Louis, MO	314-968-1255
Wickart Brothers/6293 Surrey Ridge Rd, Lisle, IL	312-369-0164
Willey, Chris/3202 Windsor #2E, Kansas City, MO	816-483-1475
Williams, Gordon/1030 Glenmoor Ln, Glendale, MO	314-821-2032
Williams, Jim/1330 N Dearborn, Chicago, IL	312-469-1297
Willson Graphics/100 E Ohio #314, Chicago, IL	312-642-5328
Wilson, Donald/405 N Wabash, Chicago, IL	312-329-1370
Wimmer, Chuck/5000 Ira Ave, Cleveland, OH	216-526-2820
Wolek, Guy/323 S Franklin, Chicago, IL	312-341-1282
Wolf, Leslie/3 E Ontario #25, Chicago, IL	312-935-1707
Wolf, Paul/510 Tauromee, Kansas City, KS	913-621-4748
Woolery, Lee/7026 Corp Way #211, Dayton, OH	513-433-7912
Wozniak, Elaine & Dorothy/15520 Clifton Blvd, Cleveland, OH	216-226-3565

Y
Young & Laramore/6367 N Guilford Ave, Indianapolis, IN	317-257-8752
Young, David Jemerson/6367 N Guilford, Indianapolis, IN	317-257-8752
Youssi, John/Rt 1, 220 Powers Rd, Gilberts, IL	312-428-7398

Illustrators
Continued

Please send us your additions and updates.

Z
Zadnik, Pat/1018 Woodlane Dr, Cleveland, OH   216-521-6273
Zaresky, Don/41 Leonard Ave, Northfield Center, OH   216-467-5917
Zimnicki Design/774 Parkview Ct, Roselle, IL   312-893-2666
Zumbo, Matthew/2105 N Summit #201, Milwaukee, WI   414-277-9541

Southwest

AB
Andrew, Bill/1709 Dryden #709, Houston, TX   713-791-4924
Andrews, Chris/1515 N Beverly Ave, Tucson, AZ   602-325-5126
Archon/PO Box 200522, Austin, TX   512-447-0265
Artell, Michael/2809 LaQuinta Dr, Plano, TX   214-964-0901
Atha, Jim/1000 W Wilshire #428, Oklahoma City, OK   405-840-3201
Atwood, Marjorie/PO Box 700418, Tulsa, OK   918-747-2882
Bates, Greg/2811 McKinney #224, Dallas, TX   214-855-0055
Bleck, Cathie/1019 N Clinton, Dallas, TX   214-942-4639
Brazeal, Lee Lee/1227 Campbell Rd, Houston, TX   713-467-2820
Brown, Rod Design/2 Dals Comm Cmplx Nxs 20, Irving, TX   214-869-9393

C
CatPak Studio/3000 McKinney, Dallas, TX   214-744-4421
Chambers, Lindy/9131 Westview, Houston, TX   713-467-6819
Cheney, May/1300 N 12th St #403, Phoenix, AZ   602-239-4230
Cherry, Jim/3600 N Hayden Rd #3308, Scottsdale, AZ   602-941-2883
Chinchar, Alan/1718 Capstan, Houston, TX   713-480-3227
Cleveland, Tom/15622 Canterbury Forrest, Tomball, TX   713-370-8450
Collier, Steve/5512 Chaucer Dr, Houston, TX   713-522-0205
Connally, Connie/3333 Elm, Dallas, TX   214-340-7818
Cornelius, Ray-Mel/4512 Swiss Ave #3, Dallas, TX   214-826-8988
Criswell, Ron/2929 Wildflower, Dallas, TX   214-620-9109
Curry, Tom/302 Lakehills Dr, Austin, TX   512-263-3407

DE
Dean, Michael/2001 Sul Ross, Houston, TX   713-527-0295
Depew, Bob/2755 Rollingdale, Dallas, TX   214-241-9206
Draper, Chad/413 N Tyler, Dallas, TX   214-526-4668
Durbin, Mike/4034 Woodcraft, Houston, TX   713-667-8129
Eubank, Mary Grace/6222 Northwood, Dallas, TX   214-692-7579
Eudy, Mike/3800 Commerce, Dallas, TX   214-826-1361
Evans, Eleanor/965 Slocum, Dallas, TX   214-760-8232

FG
Falk, Rusty/707 E Alameda Dr, Tempe, AZ   602-966-1626
FORBES, BART/2706 FAIRMOUNT, DALLAS, TX (P 12)   **214-748-8436**
Garns, G Allen/3314 East El Moro, Mesa, AZ   602-830-7224
Gilliam, Charles/3903 SAn Ramon, Arlington, TX   817-861-1988
Girden, J M/2125 Cerrada Nopal E, Tucson, AZ   602-628-2740
Graves, Keith/809-A W 29th St, Austin, TX   512-478-3338
Griego, Tony/1801 W Tuckey Ln #23, Phoenix, AZ   602-242-3492
Grimes, Don/3514 Oak Grove, Dallas, TX   214-526-0040
Grimes, Rick/703 McKInney #432, Dallas, TX   214-954-0310

HJ
Hall, Bill/1235-B Colorado Ln, Arlington, TX   817-274-0817
Harr, Shane/637 Hawthorne, Houston, TX   713-523-8186
Haverfield, Mary/5531 Morningside, Dallas, TX   214-824-6889
Haynie, Jeff/225 Walnut St, Roanoke, TX   817-430-0343
High, Richard/4500 Montrose #D, Houston, TX   713-521-2772
Huey, Kenneth/4413 Sycamore St, Dallas, TX   214-821-3042
Jenkins, Bill/3000 McKinney, Dallas, TX   214-744-4421

KL
Kampa, David/309 E Live Oak, Austin, TX   512-440-1475
Karas, Brian/4518 N 12th St #108, Phoenix, AZ   602-263-9193
Kasahara, Margaret/5914 Oram, Dallas, TX   214-827-3172
Kenny, Kathleen/815 N First Ave #1, Phoenix, AZ   602-252-2332
Kenyon, Liz/329 W Vernon Ave, Phoenix, AZ   602-254-8232
Kirkman, Rick/815 N 1st Ave #3, Phoenix, AZ   602-257-0097
Kohler, Mark/701 W 7th Ave, Austin, TX   512-476-4283
Kramer, Dave/27112 Cooks Cr #4104, Dallas, TX   214-942-1944
Lapsley, Bob/3707 Nottingham, Houston, TX   713-667-4393
Lebo, Narda/4851 Cedar Springs, Dallas, TX   214-528-0375
Lewis, Maurice/3704 Harper St, Houston, TX   713-664-1807
Lindlof, Ed/603 Carolyn Ave, Austin, TX   512-472-0195
Lisieski, Peter/135 Pine St, Nacogdoches, TX   409-564-4244

MN
MacPherson, Kevin/815 N 1st Ave #3, Phoenix, AZ   602-257-0097
Martin, Larry/3040 Sundial, Dallas, TX   214-521-8700
Martini, John/8742 Welles Dale, San Antonio, TX   512-699-9318
McClain, Lynn/8730 Vinewood, Dallas, TX   214-321-9374
McCullough, Greg/1412 Summerbrook Cir #144, Arlington, TX   817-861-5813
McCullough, Lenndy/708 Canyon Rd #3, Santa Fe, NM   505-982-1964
McElhaney, Gary/5205 Airport Blvd #201, Austin, TX   512-451-3986
McGar, Michael/3330 Irwindell Blvd, Dallas, TX   214-339-0672
Miller, Lyle/3100 Carlisle St #112, Dallas, TX   214-871-1195
Moseley, Timothy/901 Cedar Hill Ave #227, Dallas, TX   214-942-8874
Nadon, Jean/7 Lincrest Dr, Galveston, TX   409-763-2162
Nelson, John/345 E Windsor, Phoenix, AZ   602-279-1131

OP
Osiecki, Lori/1001 N Pasadena #25, Mesa, AZ   602-962-5233
Payne, Chris F/6333 Goliad, Dallas, TX   214-421-3993
Pendleton, Nancy/815 N 1st Ave #3, Phoenix, AZ   602-257-0097
Phelps, Timothy/4018 Grennoch Ln, Houston, TX   413-666-7687
Phillips, Barry/, Dallas, TX   214-869-7157
Pietzsch, Steve/3057 Larry Drive, Dallas, TX   214-279-8851
Poli, Kristina/4211 Pebblegate Ct, Houston, TX   713-353-6910
Powell, Terry/8502-D Lyndon Ln, Austin, TX   512-335-0253
Punchatz, Don Ivan/2605 Westgate Dr, Arlington, TX   817-469-8151

RS
Ricks, Thom/6511 Adair Dr, San Antonio, TX   512-680-6540
Roberts, Mark/Art Direction/2127 Banks St, Houston, TX   713-623-0748
Rose, Lee/4250 TC Jester Blvd, Houston, TX   713-686-4799
Ruland, Mike/8946 Long Point Rd, Houston, TX   713-465-2413
Salem, Kay/13418 Splintered Oak, Houston, TX   713-469-0996
Senkarik, Mickey/PO Box 104, Helotes, TX   512-695-9327
Shultz, David/1047-E McLellan Blvd, Phoenix, AZ   602-230-0282
Sims, Thomas/4303 Junius St, Dallas, TX   214-828-0366
Sketch Pad/2605 Westgate Dr, Arlington, TX   817-469-8151
Skistmas, Jim/2630 N Stemmons Frwy #413, Dallas, TX   214-630-2574
Smith, James Noel/1011 North Clinton, Dallas, TX   214-946-4255
Smith, Malcolm/1309 Main #504-B, Dallas, TX   214-742-5229
Smithson, David/3760 E Presidio, Tucson, AZ   602-323-8651
Steirnagle, Michael/3576 McKinley, Sacramento, CA   916-456-8170

TVW
Taylor, Michael/9434 Viscount #180, El Paso, TX   915-594-7100
Tracy, Libba/329 W Vernon Ave, Phoenix, AZ   602-254-8232
VAS Communications/4800 N 22nd St, Phoenix, AZ   602-955-1000
Verzaal, Dale/2445 E Pebble Beach, Tempe, AZ   602-839-5536
Waltman, Lynne/PO Box 470889, Ft Worth, TX   817-738-1545
Warner, Michele/1011 North Clinton, Dallas, TX   214-946-4255
Washington, Bill/330 Glenarm, San Antonio, TX   512-340-0021
Watford, Wayne/815 N 1st Ave #3, Phoenix, AZ   602-257-0097
Weakley, Mark/105 N Alamo #618, San Antonio, TX   512-222-9543

Rocky Mountain

AB
Alexander, Hugh/3655 S Verbena St #G201, Denver, CO   303-796-9208
Anderson, Jon/1465 Ellendale Ave, Logan, UT   801-752-8936
Bhakti, LeVon/179 S 1200 E #3, Salt Lake City, UT   801-531-6951
Botero, Kirk/PO Box 3793, Logan, UT   801-753-4131

CDE
Christensen, James C/656 West 550 South, Orem, UT   801-224-6237
Cuneo, John/2629 18th St, Denver, CO   303-458-7086
Dazzeland Studios/209 Edison, Salt Lake City, UT   801-355-8555
Dolack, Monte/132 W Front St, Missoula, MT   406-549-3248
Donovan, David/437 Engel Ave, Henderson, NV   702-564-3598
Enright, Cindy/2629 18th St, Denver, CO   303-458-7086

FGHJ
Farley, Malcolm/3870 Newland, Wheatridge, CO   303-420-9135
Fujisaki, Pat/5917 S Kenton Way, Englewood, CO   303-698-0073
Fuller Bob/1055 Wazee St, Denver, CO   303-893-2260
Graphic Studio/1451 Larimer Sq #300, Denver, CO   303-830-1110
Hardiman, Miles/30 Village Dr, Littleton, CO   303-798-9143
Harris, Ralph/PO Box 1091, Sun Valley, ID   208-726-8077
Heiner, Joe & Kathy/850 N Grove Dr, Alpine, UT   801-756-6444
Ho, Quang/1553 Platte St #30, Denver, CO   303-477-4574

Illustrators
Continued

Please send us your additions and updates.

Hull, Richard/776 W 3500 South, Bountiful, UT	801-298-1632
Jensen, Patricia/6030 Belmont Way, Parker, CO	303-841-8899

KLMN
Krb, Vladimir/PO Box 2955/Drumheller Sta, Alberta T0J 0A0, AB	403-823-6385
Lane, Tammy/410 North Mill, Aspen, CO	303-925-9213
Lediard, Al/2216 Kensington Ave, Salt Lake City, UT	801-328-0573
Lyman, Kenvin/209 Edison St, Salt Lake City, UT	801-355-8555
Masami/3144 W 26th Ave, Denver, CO	303-756-8983
Maughan, William/PO Box 133, Millville, UT	801-752-9340
McGowan, Daniel/28325 Little Big Horn Dr, Evergreen, CO	303-674-0203
Meents, Len/Estes Industries, Penrose, CO	303-372-3080
Millard, Dennis/240 W 300 N, Salt Lake City, UT	801-359-8334
Morrison, Cathy/1544 Race St, Denver, CO	303-355-3443
Nelsen, Randy/2343 Dexter St, Denver, CO	303-860-7070
Nelson, Will/1517 W Hays, Boise, ID	208-345-3131

PRST
Peterson, Marty/3003 Valmont #42, Boulder, CO	303-449-8891
Price, Jeannette/1164 E 820 N, Provo, UT	801-377-3958
Regester, Sheryl/PO Box 478, Silver Plume, CO	303-569-3374
Sauter, Ron/3113 E 3rd St #220, Denver, CO	303-399-3851
Snyder, Teresa & Wayne/10155 Grant Creek Rd, Missoula, MT	406-549-6772
Strawn, Susan/1216 W olive St, Ft Collins, CO	303-493-0679
Stubbs, Diane/3890 Maulding Ave, Las Vegas, NV	702-361-3011
Twede, Brian L/430 S State St, Salt Lake City, UT	801-534-1459

UVWZ
Uhl, David/2536 Gilpin St, Denver, CO	303-860-7070
Van Schelt, Perry L/4495 Balsam Ave, Salt Lake City, UT	801-266-7097
Weller, Don/2240 Monarch Dr, Park City, UT	801-649-9859
Whitesides, Kim/PO Box 2189, Park City, UT	801-649-0490
Winborg, Larry/464 South, 275 East, Farmington, UT	801-451-5310
Zilberts, Ed/1070-A Race St, Denver, CO	303-399-6539

West Coast

A
Abe, George/2815 Alaskan Way #37-A, Seattle, WA	206-443-0326
Ace, Katherine/50 Claremont Ave, Orinda, CA	415-254-0705
Akers, Deborah/21 Lafayette Cir #201, Lafayette, CA	415-283-7793
Alleman, Annie/1183 E Main St #E, El Cajon, CA	619-495-2554
Allen, Pat/131 W Portola Ave, Los Altos, CA	416-941-3570
Allison, Gene/1808 Stanley Ave, Placentia, CA	714-524-5955
Alvin, John/15942 Londelius, Sepulveda, CA	213-471-0232
Ambler, Barbara Hoopes/2769 Nipoma St, San Diego, CA	619-222-7535
Amit, Emanuel/4322 Sunset Ave, Montrose, CA	213-249-1739
Anderson, Kevin/1267 Orkney Ln, Cardiff, CA	619-753-8410
Anderson, Sara/117 W Denny Way #214, Seattle, WA	206-285-1520
Anderson, Terry/5902 W 85th Pl, Los Angeles, CA	213-645-8469
Andreoli, Rick/467 Fair Dr #207, Costa Mesa, CA	714-556-2280
Ansley, Frank/860 Second Ave, San Francisco, CA	415-644-0585
Archey, Rebecca/PO Box 307, Ross, CA	415-456-7711
Arkle, Dave/259 W Orange Grove, Pomona, CA	714-865-2967
Arshawsky, David/9401 Alcott St, Los Angeles, CA	213-276-6058
Atkins, Bill/PO Box 1091, Laguna Beach, CA	714-499-3857

B
Backus, Michael/286 E Monecito, Sierra Madre, CA	818-449-3840
Bacon, Linda/PO Box 370, Ross, CA	415-456-7711
Baker, Don/2815 Alaskan Way #37-A, Seattle, WA	206-522-8133
Banthien, Barbara/127 Leland, Tiburon, CA	415-381-0842
Banyai, Istvan/1241 9th St #3, Santa Monica, CA	213-394-8035
Barbaria, Steve/1990 Third St #400, Sacramento, CA	916-442-3200
Barbee, Joel/209 San Pablo, San Clemente, CA	714-498-0067
Bartczak, Peter/PO Box 7709, Santa Cruz, CA	408-426-4247
Batcheller, Keith/1438 Calle Cecilia, San Dimas, CA	818-331-0439
Battles, Brian/5338 Nutmeg St, San Diego, CA	619-246-6048
Beach, Lou/5424 W Washington Blvd, Los Angeles, CA	213-934-7335
Beck, David/6376 W 5th St, Los Angeles, CA	213-934-3395
Becker, Cary/3443 Wade St, Los Angeles, CA	213-390-9595
Becker, Kerry/2054 Griffin Ave, Los Angeles, CA	213-225-9236
Beckerman, Carol/3950 Long Beach Blvd, Long Beach, CA	213-595-5896
Beerworth, Roger/1548 18th St, Santa Monica, CA	213-828-0578
Bell, Karen/1700 Decker Canyon Rd, Malibu, CA	213-457-2476

Bergendorff, Roger/17106 Sims St #A, Huntington Beach, CA	714-840-7665
Bernstein, Sol/649 Encino Vista Dr, Thousand Oaks, CA	805-497-7967
Bettoli, Delana/737 Vernon Ave, Venice, CA	213-396-0296
Biers, Nanette/29 Sixteenth Ave, San Francisco, CA	415-668-6080
Bilmes, Semyon/253 Marcy Loop, Grants Pass, OR	503-476-3509
Bingham, Sid/2550 Kemper Ave, La Crescenta, CA	818-957-0163
Biomedical Illustrations/804 Columbia St, Seattle, WA	206-682-8197
Birnbaum, Dianne/17301 Elsinore Circle, Huntington Beach, CA	714-847-7631
BJORKMAN, STEVE/1711 LANGLEY, IRVINE, CA (P 16)	**714-261-1411**
Blackshear, Tom/1428 Elm Dr, Novato, CA	415-897-9486
Blair, Barry/PO Box 7091, Laguna Niguel, CA	714-249-1577
Blank, Jerry/1048 Lincoln Ave, San Jose, CA	408-289-9095
Blonder, Ellen/PO Box 5513, Mill Valley, CA	415-388-9158
Bohn, Richard/595 W Wilson St, Costa Mesa, CA	714-548-6669
Bolourchian, Flora/12485 Rubens Ave, Los Angeles, CA	213-827-8457
Borkenhagen, Susan/3558 1/2 Fifth Ave, San Diego, CA	619-295-6891
Boyle, Neil/5455 Wilshire Blvd #1212, Los Angeles, CA	213-937-4472
Bradley, Barbara/750 Wildcat Canyon Rd, Berkeley, CA	415-673-4200
Braun, Marty/2858 Bush St, San Francisco, CA	415-929-0795
Bringham, Sherry/1440 Bush St, San Francisco, CA	415-775-6564
Broad, David/100 Golden Hinde Blvd, San Rafael, CA	415-479-5505
Brown, Bill & Assoc/1054 S Robertson Blvd #203, Los Angeles, CA	213-652-9380
Brown, Rick/1502 N Maple, Burbank, CA	818-842-0726
Brownd, Elizabeth/6955 Fernhill Dr, Malibu, CA	213-457-4816
Brugger, Bob/1132 Loma #4, Hermosa Beach, CA	213-372-0135
Buechler, Barbara/13929 Marquessa Way #108A, Marina Del Ray, CA	213-827-5106
Buerge, Bill/734 Basin Dr, Topanga, CA	213-455-3181
Bull, Michael/2350 Taylor, San Francisco, CA	415-776-7471
Burnside, John E/4204 Los Feliz Blvd, Los Angeles, CA	213-665-8913
Busacca, Mark/269 Corte Madera Ave, Mill Valley, CA	415-381-9048

C
Caldwell, Kirk/1844 Union St, San Francisco, CA	415-567-3727
Carroll, Justin/1118 Chautauqua, Pacific Palisades, CA	213-459-3104
Catom, Don/638 S Van Ness Ave, Los Angeles, CA	213-382-6281
Chan, Ron/32 Grattan St, San Francisco, CA	415-681-0646
Chase, Margo/2255 Bancroft Ave, Los Angeles, CA	213-668-1055
Chewning, Randy/410 Cherry Ave #C, Long Beach, CA	213-433-7665
Chiodo, Joe/2556 Chicago St #40, San Diego, CA	619-291-6094
Chorney, Steven/18686 Cumnock Pl, Northridge, CA	818-366-8779
Christman, Michael/104 S El Molino, Pasadena, CA	818-793-1358
Clark, Tim/8800 Venice Blvd, Los Angeles, CA	213-202-1044
Clarke, Coralie/PO Box 657, Bonsall, CA	619-941-1476
Coe, Wayne/1707 Michetorena #416, Los Angeles, CA	213-662-1259
Cole, Dick/25 Hotaling Pl, San Francisco, CA	415-986-8163
Commander, Bob/8800 Venice Blvd, Los Angeles, CA	213-202-6765
Conrad, Jon/85 N Raymond, Pasadena, CA	
Consani, Chris/2601 Walnut Ave, Manhattan Bch, CA	213-546-6622
Cook, Anne/1580 Treat Ave, San Francisco, CA	415-695-0210
Coons, Byron/Pier 33 North, San Francisco, CA	415-956-4750
Coppock, Chuck/638 S Van Ness Ave, Los Angeles, CA	213-382-6281
Cormier, Wil/1000 Concha, Altadena, CA	818-797-7999
Coviello, Ron/1682 Puterbaugh, San Diego, CA	619-265-6647
Creative Source/6671 W Sunset Blvd #1519, Los Angeles, CA	213-462-5731
Criss, Keith/1005 Camelia St, Berkeley, CA	415-525-8703
Critz, Carl/638 S Van Ness Ave, Los Angeles, CA	213-382-6281
Curtis, Todd/2032 14th St #7, Santa Monica, CA	213-452-0738

D
Dalaney, Jack/3030 Pualei Circle #317, Honolulu, HI	808-924-7450
Daniels/1352 Hornblend St, San Diego, CA	619-272-8147
Darrow, David R/9655 Derald Rd, Santee, CA	619-697-7408
Davidson, Kevin/505 S Grand St, Orange, CA	714-633-9061
Davis, Jack/3785 Mt Everest Blvd, San Diego, CA	619-565-0336
Day, Adrian/2022 Jones St, San Francisco, CA	415-928-0457
Day, Bruce/8141 Firth Green, Buena Park, CA	714-994-0338
Dayal, Antar/4521 18th St, San Francisco, CA	415-626-9676
DeAnda, Ruben/550 Oxford St #407, Chula Vista, CA	619-427-7765
DeLeon, Cam/1725 Berkeley St, Santa Monica, CA	213-453-4418
Dean, Bruce/23211 Leonora Dr, Woodland Hills, CA	818-716-5632
Dean, Donald/2560 Bancroft Way #14, Berkley, CA	415-644-1139

Illustrators

Continued

Please send us your additions and updates.

Dearstyne, John/22982 LaCadena Dr, Laguna Hills, CA	714-768-5619
Deaver, Georgia/766 Church St, San Francisco, CA	415-621-6572
Deeter, Catherine/801 Ave G #A, Coronado, CA	619-437-0238
Dellorco, Chris/18350 Hatteras #229, Tarzana, CA	818-342-7890
Dennewill, Jim/5823 Autry Ave, Lakewood, CA	213-920-3895
Devaud, Jacques/1165 Bruin Tr/Box 260, Fawnskin, CA	714-866-4563
Dietz, James/2203 13th Ave E, Seattle, WA	206-325-2857
Diffenderfer, Ed/32 Cabernet Ct, Lafayette, CA	415-254-8235
Dismukes, John Taylor/2820 Westshire Dr, Hollywood, CA	213-467-2787
Doe, Bart/3300 Temple St, Los Angeles, CA	213-383-9707
Doty, Eldon/1106 Santolina Dr, Novato, CA	415-897-7626
Dowlen, James/PO Box 475, Cotati, CA	707-579-1535
Drake, Bob/1556 N Faifax Ave, Los Angeles, CA	213-850-6808
Drayton, Richard/5018 Dumont Pl, Woodland Hills, CA	818-347-2227
Drennon, Tom/916 N Formosa #D, Hollywood, CA	213-874-1276
Duell, Nancy/1046 N Orange Dr, Los Angeles, CA	213-462-5622
Duffus, Bill/1745 Wagner, Pasadena, CA	818-792-7921
Duggan, Brian/6376 W 5th St, Los Angeles, CA	213-934-3395
Duke, Lawrence W/1258 Folsom St, San Francisco, CA	415-563-8884
Durfee, Tom/25 Hotaling Pl, San Francisco, CA	415-781-0527

E

Eastman, Jody/3443 Wade St, Los Angeles, CA	212-390-9595
Eastside Illustration/1807 SE 7th Ave, Portland, OR	503-235-6878
Eckart, Chuck/PO Box 1090, Point Reyes Sta, CA	415-663-9016
Edelson, Wendy/215 Second Ave S, Seattle, WA	206-728-1300
Eichenberger, Dave/228 Main St, Venice, CA	213-392-8781
Ellescas, Richard/321 N Martel, Hollywood, CA	213-939-7396
Ellmore, Dennis/3245 Orange Ave, Long Beach, CA	213-424-9379
Elstad, Ron/18253 Solano River Ct, Fountain Valley, CA	714-964-7753
Endicott, James R/3509 N College, Newberg, OR	503-538-5466
English, David/18410 Plummer #G, Northridge, CA	818-772-0688
Ente, Anke/50 Kings Rd, Brisbane, CA	415-467-8108
Ericksen, Marc/1045 Sansome St #306, San Francisco, CA	415-362-1214
Erickson, Kernie/Box 2175, Mission Viejo, CA	714-831-2818
Erramouspe, David/2337 Kelton Ave, Los Angeles, CA	213-473-7656
Etow, Carole/20532 Gresham St, Canoga Park, CA	213-545-0795
Evans, Bill/101 Yesler #502, Seattle, WA	206-441-0606
Evans, Jan/8126 Blackburn Ave, Los Angeles, CA	213-858-0946
Evans, Robert/1045 Sansome St #306, San Francisco, CA	415-397-5322
Evenson, Stan/1830 S Robrtsn Blvd #203, Los Angeles, CA	213-204-1995

F

Farrell, Rick/3918 N Stevens, Tacoma, WA	206-752-8814
Feigeles, Neil/1815 N Harvard Blvd, Los Angeles, CA	213-856-9849
Ferrero, Felix/215 Liedesdorff, San Francisco, CA	415-981-1162
Florczak, Robert/PO Box 687, N Hollywood, CA	818-985-8181
Forrest, William/817 12th St #2, Santa Monica, CA	213-458-9114
Foster, Matt/1555 Fifth Ave 3304, San Francisco, CA	415-759-5642
Francuch, George/638 S Van Ness Ave, Los Angeles, CA	213-382-6281
Franks, Bill/638 S Van Ness Ave, Los Angeles, CA	213-382-6281
Fraze, Jon/17081 Kenyon Dr #C, Tustin, CA	714-731-8493
Frazee, Marla/1199 N Holliston, Pasadena, CA	818-797-0612
French, Lisa/1069 Gardenia Ave, Long Beach, CA	213-599-0361
Fulp, Jim/173 Germania St, San Francisco, CA	415-621-5462
Funkhouser, Kristen/1352 Hornblend St, San Diego, CA	619-272-8147

G

Galloway, Nixon/5455 Wilshire Blvd #1212, Los Angeles, CA	213-937-4472
Garcia, Manuel/1352 Hornblend St, San Diego, CA	619-272-8147
Garner, Tracy/1830 S Robertson Blvd, Los Angeles, CA	213-204-1771
Garnett, Joe/12121 Wilshire Blvd #322, Los Angeles, CA	213-826-9378
Gay, Garry/109 Minna St #567, San Francisco, CA	415-626-6005
Geary, Rick/PO Box 99835, San Diego, CA	619-483-7429
Gellos, Nancy/20 Armour St, Seattle, WA	206-285-5838
General Graphics/746 Brannan, San Francisco, CA	415-777-3333
George, Jeff/2607 Rockefeller Ln #4, Redondo Beach, CA	213-374-8321
Gibson, Mike/6425 Woodley Ave #2, Van Nuys, CA	818-785-8928
Girvin, Tim Design/911 Western Ave #408, Seattle, WA	206-623-7918
Gisko, Max/2629 Wakefield Dr, Belmont, CA	415-595-1893
Glad, Deanna/PO Box 3261, Santa Monica, CA	213-393-7464
Glass, Randy/2706 Creston Dr, Los Angeles, CA	213-462-2706
Gleason, Bob/3700 Sepulveda Blvd, Los Angeles, CA	213-935-4696
Gleeson, Madge/Art Dept/Wstrn Wash Univ, Bellingham, WA	206-676-3000
Gleeson, Tony/2525 Hyperion Ave #4, Los Angeles, CA	213-668-2704

Gleis, Linda/6671 Sunset Blvd #1519, Los Angeles, CA	213-461-6376
Goddard, John/2774 Los Alisos Dr, Fallbrook, CA	619-728-5473
Goldstein, Howard/7031 Aldea Ave, Van Nuys, CA	818-987-2837
Gomez, Ignacio/812 Kenneth Rd, Glendale, CA	818-243-2838
Gordon, Duane/638 S Van Ness Ave, Los Angeles, CA	213-382-6281
Gray, Steve/307 Bayview Dr, Manhattan Beach, CA	213-372-7844
Green, Peter/10200 Riverside Dr, Toluca Lake, CA	818-760-1011
Gribbitt Ltd/5419 Sunset Blvd, Los Angeles, CA	213-462-7362
Griffith, Linda/13972 Hilo Ln, Santa Ana, CA	714-832-8536
Grim, Elgas/638 S Van Ness Ave, Los Angeles, CA	213-382-6281
Grossman, Myron/12 S Fair Oaks Ave, Pasadena, CA	213-559-9349
Grove, David/382 Union St, San Francisco, CA	415-433-2100
Guidice, Rick/9 Park Ave, Los Gatos, CA	408-354-7787
Gurvin, Abe/1129 Tait, Oceanside, CA	619-941-1838

H

Haasis, Michael/941 N Croft Ave, Los Angeles, CA	213-654-5412
Hale, Bruce/2916 5th Ave W, Seattle, WA	206-282-1191
Hall, Patricia/5402 Ruffin Rd #103, San Diego, CA	619-268-0176
Hamagami, John/11409 Kingsland St, Los Angeles, CA	213-390-6911
Hamilton, Pamela/4900 Overland Ave, Culver City, CA	213-837-1784
Hammond, Cris/410 Johnson St, Sausalito, CA	415-332-7556
Hammond, Roger/5455 Wilshire Blvd #1212, Los Angeles, CA	213-937-4472
Hampton, Gerry Inc/PO Box 2792, Seal Beach, CA	213-431-6979
Hannah, Halsted (Craig)/5320 College Ave #1, Oakland, CA	415-841-2273
Hasselle, Bruce/8691 Heil Rd, Westminster, CA	714-848-2924
Hatzer, Fred/5455 Wilshire Blvd #1212, Los Angeles, CA	213-937-4472
Haydock, Robert/49 Shelley Dr, Mill Valley, CA	415-383-6986
Haynes, Bryan/1733 Ellincourt Dr #F, South Pasadena, CA	818-799-7989
Hays, Jim/3809 Sunnyside Blvd, Marysville, WA	206-334-7596
Hegedus, James C/11850 Otsego, N Hollywood, CA	818-985-9966
Heimann, Jim/1548 18th St, Santa Monica, CA	213-828-1041
Heinecke, Stu/9665 Wilshire Blvd #400, Los Angeles, CA	213-837-3212
Hendricks, Steve/1050 Elsiemae Dr, Boulder Creek, CA	408-338-6639
Hernandez, Oscar/5708 Case Ave #3, N Hollywood, CA	818-506-4541
Herrero, Lowell/433 Bryant St, San Francisco, CA	415-543-6400
Hession, Kathleen/6671 Sunset Blvd #1519, Hollywood, CA	213-462-5731
Hilliard, Fred/5425 Crystal Springs Dr, Bainbridge Is, WA	206-842-6003
Hilton-Putnam, Denise/4758 Jean Dr, San Diego, CA	619-565-7568
Hinton, Hank/6118 W 6th St, Los Angeles, CA	213-938-9893
Hitch, Jeff/3001 Redhill Ave #6-210, Costa Mesa, CA	714-432-1802
Hoburg, Maryanne Regal/1695 8th Ave, San Francisco, CA	415-731-1870
Hodges, Ken/12401 Bellwood Rd, Los Alamitos, CA	213-431-4343
Holmes, Matthew/126 Mering Ct, Sacramento, CA	916-484-6080
Homad, Jewell/15209 S Prairie #34, Lawndale, CA	213-644-0598
Hoover, Anne Nelson/8457 Paseo Del Ocaso, La Jolla, CA	714-454-4294
Hopkins, Christopher/2932 Wilshire #202, Santa Monica, CA	213-828-6455
Hord, Bob/1760 Monrovia #B-9, Costa Mesa, CA	714-631-3890
Hubbard, Roger/10966 Strathmore Dr #8, Los Angeles, CA	213-208-8042
Hudson, Dave/1807 E Redwood Ave, Anaheim, CA	714-533-0533
Hudson, Ron/725 Auahi St, Honolulu, HI	808-536-2692
Huhn, Tim/4718 Kester Ave #208, Sherman Oaks, CA	818-986-2352
Hull, John/2356 Fair Park Ave, Los Angeles, CA	213-254-4647
Hulsey, Kevin/5306 Norwich Ave, Van Nuys, CA	818-501-7105
Hume, Kelly/912 S Los Robles, Pasadena, CA	818-793-8344
Humphries, Michael/11241 Martha Ann Dr, Los Alamitos, CA	213-493-3323
Hunt, Robert/4376 21st St, San Francisco, CA	415-824-1824
Hwang, Francis/999 Town & Country Rd, Orange, CA	714-538-1727

IJ

IBUSUKI, JAMES/2920 ROSANNA ST, LOS ANGELES, CA (P 28)	**818-244-1645**
Irvine, Rex John/6026 Dovetail Dr, Agoura, CA	818-991-2522
Ito, Joel/505 NW 185th St, Beaverton, OR	503-645-1141
Jacobs, Ellen Going/312 90th St, Daly City, CA	415-994-8800
Jacobsen, Gary/101 Yesler #502, Seattle, WA	206-441-0606
Jenks, Aleta/686 Mandana, Oakland, CA	415-444-4691
Jensen, David/1641 Merryton Ct, San Jose, CA	408-266-5645
Johnson, BE/297 Fairview St, Laguna Beach, CA	714-497-6717
Jost, Larry/3916 E Garfield St, Seattle, WA	206-328-1841
Joyner, Eric/660 Clipper St, San Francisco, CA	415-821-2641
Judd, Jeff/827 1/2 N McCadden Pl, Los Angeles, CA	213-469-0333

K

Kabaker, Gayle/545 Sutter St, San Francisco, CA	415-986-1946

KANNER, CATHERINE/717 HAMPDEN PL, PACIFIC PALISADES, CA (P 29)	**213-454-7675**
Kari, Morgan/22853 Mariano #226, Woodland Hills, CA	818-346-9167
Karlin, Eugene/632-A Sevilla, Laguna Hills, CA	714-472-4625
Katayama, Mits/425 Randolph Ave, Seattle, WA	206-324-1199
Keefer, Mel/415 Montana Ave #208, Santa Monica, CA	213-395-1147
Keeling, Gregg Bernard/659 Boulevard Way, Oakland, CA	415-444-8688
Kenyon, Chris/14 Wilmot, San Francisco, CA	415-923-1363
Kimble, David/711 S Flower, Burbank, CA	213-849-1576
King, Heather/1218 Cayetano Dr, Napa, CA	707-226-1232
Kitchell, Joyce/2755 Eagle St, San Diego, CA	619-291-1378
Koester, Michael/272 Gresham, Ashland, OR	503-488-0153
Koulian, Jack/442 W Harvard, Glendale, CA	818-956-5640
Kowalski, Michael/5263 Locksley Ave, Oakland, CA	415-658-2154
Kramer, Moline/854 S Sycamore, Los Angeles, CA	213-934-6280
Kratter, Paul/1904 Cortereal Ave, Oakland, CA	415-339-0219
Kriegler, Richard/2814 Third St, Santa Monica, CA	213-396-9087
Kriss, Ron/6671 W Sunset #1519, Los Angeles, CA	213-462-5731
Krogle, Bob/25112 Carolwood St, El Toro, CA	213-588-4444
Kung, Allan/250 The Village #206, Redondo Beach, CA	213-372-6691
Kung, Linda/264 Alpine St, Pasadena, CA	818-799-2301
L Labadie, Ed/1971 Glen Ave, Pasadena, CA	818-794-7705
Lagerstrom, Wendy/144 N Sierra Bonita , Pasadena, CA	818-584-6622
Lake, Larry/360 1/2 N Mansfield Ave, Los Angeles, CA	213-935-4696
Lamb, Dana/PO Box 1091, Yorba Linda, CA	714-996-3449
Larson, Ron/940 N Highland Ave, Los Angeles, CA	213-465-8451
Lauderbaugh, Lindah/2002 N Bronson, Los Angeles, CA	213-467-5444
Leary, Catherine/1125 S La Jolla Ave, Los Angeles, CA	213-937-8908
Lee, Warren/88 Meadow Valley Rd, Corte Madera, CA	415-924-0261
Leech, Richard & Associates/725 Filbert St, San Francisco, CA	415-981-4840
Leeds, Beth Whybrow/1335 Main St #103, St Helena, CA	707-963-8426
Leedy, Jeff/209 North St, Sausalito, CA	415-331-1354
Levine, Bette/601 N Hayworth Ave, Los Angeles, CA	213-658-6769
Lewis, Dennis/6671 Sunset #1519, Los Angeles, CA	213-462-5731
Liao, Jeff/1630 Calle Vaquero #505, Glendale, CA	818-244-1511
Lindsay, Martin/4469 41st St, San Diego, CA	619-281-8851
Livermore, Joanie/PO Box 828, Lake Oswego, OR	602-656-1399
Livingston, Francis/3916 Sacramento St, San Francisco, CA	415-776-1531
Lloyd, Gregory/5534 Red River Dr, San Diego, CA	619-582-3487
Losch, Diana/Pier 33 N Embarcadero, San Francisco, CA	415-956-5648
Loveless, Roger/1700 Yosemite #201D, Simi Valley, CA	805-522-0961
Lulich, Ted/7033 SW Macadamia Ave #107, Portland, OR	503-245-1951
Lund, Gary/360 1/2 N Mansfield Ave, Los Angeles, CA	213-935-4696
Lundgren-Ellis, Alvalyn/1343 Thayer Ave, Los Angeles, CA	213-202-6197
Lytle, John/PO Box 5155, Sonora, CA	209-928-4849
M MacLeod, Lee/200-A Westminster Ave, Venice, CA	213-392-4877
Machat, Mike/4426 Deseret Dr, Woodland Hills, CA	818-702-9433
Mahoney, Patricia/1414-A 20th Ave, San Francisco, CA	415-661-5915
Majlessi, Heda/1707 Boyleson #301, Seattle, WA	206-323-2694
Mann, David/186 Silas Ln, Newbury Park, CA	
Marsh, Cynthia/4434 Matilija Ave, Sherman Oaks, CA	818-789-5232
Marshall, Craig/404 Crescent Ave, San Francisco, CA	415-641-1010
Martin, Greg/731 Fourth St, Encinitas, CA	619-753-4073
Mattos, John/1546 Grant Ave, San Francisco, CA	415-397-2138
Mayeda, Kaz/243 Bickwell #A, Santa Monica, CA	213-452-0054
Mazzetti, Alan/375-A Crescent Ave, San Francisco, CA	415-541-0238
McConnell, Jim/10921 Live Oak Blvd, Live Oak, CA	916-695-1355
McDonald, Mercedes/25 Montgomery St, Los Gatos, CA	408-395-6540
McDougall, Scott/712 N 62nd St, Seattle, WA	206-783-1403
McElroy, Darlene/720-A Iris Ave, Corona de Mar, CA	714-760-9631
McGinty, Mike/PO Box 687, N Hollywood, CA	818-985-8181
McKee, Ron/5455 Wilshire Blvd #1212, Los Angeles, CA	213-937-4472
McKiernan, James E/2501 Cherry Ave #310, Signal Hill, CA	213-427-1953
McMahon, Bob/6820 Independence Ave #31, Canoga Park, CA	818-999-4127
Merritt, Norman/2116 Arlington Ave #1212, Los Angeles, CA	213-737-7685
Metz Air Art/2817 E Lincoln Ave, Anaheim, CA	714-630-3071
Meyer, Gary/227 W Channel Rd, Santa Monica, CA	213-454-2174
Mikkelson, Linda S/1624 Vista Del Mar, Hollywood, CA	213-463-3116
Millsap, Darrel/1744 6th Ave, San Diego, CA	619-543-0122
Mitchell, Kathy/828 21st St #6, Santa Monica, CA	213-828-6331
Mitoma, Tim/4865 Doyle St #9, Emeryville, CA	415-547-1343
Moats, George/PO Box 1187, Hanford, CA	209-584-9026
Moch, Paul/1414 Oakland Blvd #4, Walnut Creek, CA	415-932-5815
Mollering, David/2197 Gizot, San Diego, CA	619-222-2614
Monahan, Leo/721 S Victory Blvd, Burbank, CA	818-843-6115
Montoya, Ricardo/1025 E Lincoln Ave #D, Anaheim, CA	714-533-0507
Moreau, Alain/1461 1/2 S Beverly Dr, Los Angeles, CA	213-553-8529
Morse, Bill/173 18th Ave, San Francisco, CA	415-221-6711
Mortensen, Cristine/140 University Ave #102, Palo Alto, CA	415-321-4787
Mortensen, Gordon/140 University Ave #102, Palo Alto, CA	415-321-4787
Mouri, Gary/25002 Reflejo, Mission Viejo, CA	714-951-8136
Moyna, Nancy/1125 6th St #4, Santa Monica, CA	213-458-1291
Murphy, Michael/333 Kearny St #607, San Francisco, CA	415-391-5153
N Nagle, Candace/230 S Oakland Ave #C, Pasadena, CA	818-793-0342
Nakamura, Joel/Pier 33 North, San Francisco, CA	415-956-4750
Nasser, Christine/PO Box 3881, Manhattan Beach, CA	213-546-5106
Navarro, Arlene & Larry/1921 Comstock Ave, Los Angeles, CA	213-201-4744
Neila, Anthony/1514 11th Ave #1, Oakland, CA	415-397-2585
Nelson, Craig/11943 Nugent Dr, Granada Hills, CA	818-363-4494
Nelson, Mike/1836 Woodsdale Ct, Concord, CA	707-746-0800
Nelson, R Kenton/8800 Venice Blvd, Los Angeles, CA	213-838-1815
Nelson, Susan/2363 N Fitch Mtn Rd, Healdsburg, CA	707-431-7166
Nethery, Susan/1548 18th St, Santa Monica, CA	213-828-1343
Nicholson, Norman/21 Columbus #221, San Francisco, CA	415-421-2555
Nikosey, Tom/5550 Wilshire Blvd #307, Los Angeles, CA	213-937-2994
Noble, Larry/18603 Arminta, Reseda, CA	818-609-1605
Nordell, Dale/425 Randolph Ave, Seattle, WA	206-324-1199
Nordell, Marilyn/425 Randolph Ave, Seattle, WA	206-324-1199
Norman, Gary/11607 Clover Ave, Los Angeles, CA	213-828-9653
Nugent, Denise/PO Box 61, Burton, WA	206-463-5412
Nunez, Manuel/1073 W 9th St, San Pedro, CA	213-832-2471
Nye, Linda S/6349 Nancy Ridge Dr, San Diego, CA	619-455-5500
O O'Brien, Kathy/401 Alameda del Prado, Navato, CA	415-883-2964
O'Mary, Tom/8418 Menkar Rd, San Diego, CA	619-578-5361
O'Neil, Sharron/409 Alberto Way #6, Los Gatos, CA	408-354-3816
Oakley, Kevin/1123 N Glen Oaks, Burbank, CA	818-443-6162
Obrero, Rudy/3400 Barham, Los Angeles, CA	213-850-5700
Oden, Richard/PO Box 415, Laguna Beach, CA	714-760-7001
Oppenheimer, Jenny/163 Tunstead Ave, San Anselmo, CA	415-456-2456
ORVIDAS, KEN/832 EVELYN AVE, ALBANY, CA (P 38)	**415-525-6626**
Osborn, Jacqueline/101 Middlefield Rd, Palo Alto, CA	415-326-2276
P Pace, Julie/130 N Jackson #101, Glendale, CA	818-246-3721
Page, Frank/5315 Oakdale, Woodland Hills, CA	818-346-0816
Palay/Beaubois/724 Pine St, San Francisco, CA	415-362-0331
Pansini, Tom/16222 Howland Ln, Huntington Bch, CA	714-847-9329
Paris Productions/2207 Garnet, San Diego, CA	619-272-4992
Parkinson, Jim/6170 Broadway Terrace, Oakland, CA	415-547-3100
Parmentier, Henri/10462 Vanora Dr, Sunland, CA	818-352-5173
Passey, Kim/1319 Fremont Ave #1, S Pasadena, CA	818-441-4384
Pavesich, Vida/1152 Arch St, Berkeley, CA	415-528-8233
Peck, Everett/1352 Hornblend St, San Diego, CA	619-272-8147
Pederson, Sharleen/101 California St, Santa Montica, CA	213-306-7847
Peringer, Stephen/6046 Lakeshore Dr So, Seattle, WA	206-725-7779
Peterson, Barbara/2629 W Northwood, Santa Ana, CA	714-546-2786
Peterson, Eric/270 Termino Avenue, Long Beach, CA	213-438-2785
Peterson, Jeff/2956 Nicada Dr, Los Angeles, CA	213-470-0140
Pierazzi, Gary/1928 Cooley Ave #49, Palo Alto, CA	415-325-2677
Pina, Richard/600 Moulton #401, Los Angeles, CA	213-227-5213
Platz, Henry III/15922 118th Pl NE, Bothell, WA	206-488-9171
Podevin, J F/5812 Newlin Ave, Whittier, CA	213-739-5083
Pound, John/2124 Froude St, San Diego, CA	619-222-2476
Precision Illustration/11731 Crescenta, Los Angeles, CA	213-471-0232
Prochnow, Bill/1135 Spruce St, Berkeley, CA	415-835-8773
Pryor, Robert/2153 Charlemagne, Long Beach, CA	213-597-6161
Przewodek, Camille/4029 23rd St, San Francisco, CA	415-826-3238
Puchalski, John/1311 Centinela Ave, Santa Monica, CA	213-828-0841
Putnam, Jamie/882 S Van Ness Ave, San Francisco, CA	415-641-0513
Pyle, Chuck/146 10th Ave, San Francisco, CA	415-751-8087

Illustrators

Continued

Please send us your additions and updates.

R

Raess Design/424 N Larchmont Blvd, Los Angeles, CA	213-659-4928
Ramsay/In the Black/119 Merchant St, Honolulu, HI	808-732-5700
Rand, Ted/425 Randolph Ave, Seattle, WA	206-324-1199
Renz, Michael/1903-B E Denny Way, Seattle, WA	206-323-9257
Rhodes, Barbara/6455 La Jolla Blvd #338, La Jolla, CA	619-459-2045
Richardson, Nelva/2619 American River Dr, Sacramento, CA	916-482-7438
Rictor, Lew/3 Damon Ct, Alameda, CA	415-769-7130
Rieser, William/419 Via Linda Vista, Redondo Beach, CA	213-373-4762
Rinaldi, Linda/5717 Chicopee, Encino, CA	818-881-1578
Robles, Bill/3443 Wade St, Los Angeles, CA	213-390-9595
RODRIGUEZ, ROBERT/1548 18TH ST, SANTA MONICA, CA (P 17)	**213-828-2840**
Rogers, Art/The Old Creamery/Route 1, Point Reyes, CA	415-663-8345
Rogers, Mike/8000 Owensmouth St #9, Canoga Park, CA	818-992-8304
Rogers, Paul/1616 N Gardner St, Los Angeles, CA	213-874-0343
Rosco, Delro/6769 Yucca St #8, Los Angeles, CA	213-464-1575
Rosenberg, Kenneth/9710 E Lennon Ave, Arciada, CA	818-574-1631
Ross, Mary/652 Bair Isl Rd, Redwood City, CA	415-363-2130
Rother, Sue/19 Brookmont Circle, San Anselmo, CA	415-387-7578
Rutherford, John/55 Alvarado Ave, Mill Valley, CA	415-383-1788

S

Sakahara, Dick/28826 Cedarbluff Dr, Palos Verdes, CA	213-541-8187
Salentine, Katherine/2022 Jones St, San Francisco, CA	415-928-0457
Salk, Larry/5455 Wilshire Blvd #1212, Los Angeles, CA	213-934-1975
Salvati, Jim/983 S Euclid Ave, Pasadena, CA	818-441-2544
Sano, Kazu/105 Stadium Ave, Mill Valley, CA	415-381-6377
Saputo, Joe/4024 Jasper Rd, Springfield, OR	503-746-1737
Scanlon, Dave/1600 18th St, Manhattan Beach, CA	213-545-0773
Schields, Gretchen/4556 19th St, San Francisco, CA	415-558-8851
Schmidt, Eric/1852 Kirkby Rd, GLendale, CA	818-507-0263
Schroeder, Mark/Pier 33 North, San Francisco, CA	415-956-4750
Scribner, Jo Anne L/3314 N Lee, Spokane, WA	509-484-3208
Seckler, Judy/12 S Fair Oaks Ave, Pasadena, CA	818-508-8778
Shehorn, Gene/1672 Lynwood Dr, Concord, CA	415-687-4516
Shek, W E/1315 Ebener St #4, Redwood City, CA	415-363-0687
Shepherd, Roni/1 San Antonio Pl, San Francisco, CA	415-421-9764
Shields, Bill/14 Wilmot, San Francisco, CA	415-346-0376
Short, Kevin/PO Box 4037, Mission Vieho, CA	714-472-1035
Sigwart, Forrest/1033 S Orlando Ave, Los Angeles, CA	213-655-7734
Silberstein, Simon/1131 Alta Loma Rd #516, W Hollywood, CA	213-652-5226
Sizemore, Ted/10642 Vanora Dr, Sunland, CA	818-352-5173
Smith, J J/4239 1/2 Lexington Ave, Los Angeles, CA	213-668-2408
Smith, John C/101 Yesler #502, Seattle, WA	206-441-0606
Smith, Terry/1127 Princeton Dr, Glendale, CA	818-242-1915
Sobel, June/706 Marine St, Santa Monica, CA	213-392-2842
Solie, John/202 W Channel Rd, Santa Monica, CA	213-454-8417
Solvang-Angell, Diane/425 Randolph Ave, Seattle, WA	206-324-1199
South, Randy/1724 20th St, San Francisco, CA	415-695-9606
Spear, Jeffrey A/1228 11th St #201, Santa Monica, CA	213-395-3939
Spear, Randy/4325 W 182nd St #20, Torrance, CA	213-370-6071
Specht/Watson /1246 S La Cienega Blvd, Los Angeles, CA	213-652-2682
Speidel, Sandy/14 Wilmot, San Francisco, CA	415-923-1363
Spencer, Joe/11201 Valley Spring Ln, Studio City, CA	818-760-0216
Sprattler, Rob/360 1/2 N Mansfield Ave, Los Angeles, CA	503-692-6940
Starkweather, Teri/4633 Galendo St, Woodland Hills, CA	818-992-5938
Steele, Robert/14 Wilmot, San Francisco, CA	415-923-0741
Stehrenberger, Mark/11731 Crescenta, Los Angeles, CA	213-471-0232
Stein, Mike/4340 Arizona, San Diego, CA	619-295-2455
Steine, Debra/6561 Green Gables Ave, San Diego, CA	619-698-5854
Stepp, Don/275 Marguerita Ln, Pasadena, CA	818-799-0263
Stermer, Dugald/1844 Union St, San Francisco, CA	415-921-8281
Stewart, Barbara/1640 Tenth Ave #5, San Diego, CA	619-238-0083
Stine, Debra/1352 Hornblende St, San Diego, CA	619-272-8147
Stockman, Skipper/PO Box 60041, Los Angeles, CA	213-202-1773
Stout, William G/812 S LaBrea, Hollywood, CA	213-936-6342
Strange, Jedd/4684 Saratoga St, San Diego, CA	619-225-9733
Suma, Doug/448 Bryant St, San Francisco, CA	415-777-2120
Suvityasiri, Sarn/1811 Leavenworth St, San Francisco, CA	415-928-1602
Svoboda, John/3211-B S Shannon, Santa Ana, CA	714-979-8992
Swimm, Tom/33651 Halyard Dr, Laguna Niguel, CA	714-496-6349

T

Tachiera, Andrea/7416 Fairmount Ave, El Cerrito, CA	415-525-3484
Tanenbaum, Robert/5505 Corbin Ave, Tarzana, CA	818-345-6741
Tannenbaum, Robert/5505 Corbin Ave, Tarzana, CA	818-345-6741
Tarbox, Marla/1730 Gates Ave, Manhattan Beach, CA	213-699-0064
Tarleton, Suzanne/1740 Stanford St, Santa Monica, CA	213-478-9412
Taylor, C Winston/17008 Lisette St, Granada Hills, CA	818-363-5761
The Committee/15468-B Ventura Blvd, Sherman Oaks, CA	818-986-4420
Thompson, Brian/183 E Palm, Altadena, CA	818-798-5901
Thon, Bud/410 View Park Ct, Mill Valley, CA	415-332-5319
Thornton, Blake/48 Mozden Lane, Pleasant Hill, CA	415-676-7166
Tilley, Debbie/2821 Camino Del Mar #78, Del Mar, CA	212-473-8221
Timmons, Bonnie/1046 N Orange Dr, Los Angeles, CA	213-462-5622
Tom, Katherine/2601 Mesa School Ln, Santa Barbara, CA	805-962-2022
Tomita, Tom/3568 E Melton, Pasadena, CA	818-796-4213
Tompkins, Tish/1660 Redcliff St, Los Angeles, CA	213-662-1660
Truesdale Art & Design/5482 Complex St #112, San Diego, CA	619-268-1026
Tsuchiya, Julie/Pier 1/LOPR, San Francisco, CA	415-986-5365
Tucker, Ezra/4634 Woodman Ave #202, Sherman Oaks, CA	818-905-0758

UV

Unger, Joe/17120 NE 96th St, Redmond, WA	206-883-1419
Unger, Judy/14160 Oro Grande St, Sylmar, CA	818-362-6470
Unruh, Jack/716 Montgomery St, San Francisco, CA	415-433-1222
Van Der Palen/3443 Wade St, Los Angeles, CA	212-390-9595
Van Ryvin, Peter/558 King Rd, Petaluma, CA	707-778-1681
Vance, Jay/676 Lafayette Park Place, Los Angeles, CA	213-387-1171
Vandervoort, Gene/3201 S Ramona Dr, Santa Ana, CA	714-549-3194
Vanderwielen Designs/19000 MacArthur Blvd, Irvine, CA	714-733-0921
Vanle, Jay/638 S Van Ness Ave, Los Angeles, CA	213-382-6281
Vigon, Jay/708 S Orange Grove Ave, Los Angeles, CA	213-937-0355
Vinson, W T/4118 Vernon, Glen Avon, CA	714-685-7697
Voss, Tom/525 West B St #G, San Diego, CA	619-238-1673

W

Wack, Jeff/3614 Berry Dr, Studio City, CA	818-508-0348
Walden, Craig/425 Randolph Ave, Seattle, WA	206-324-1199
Walstead, Curt/398 Via Colinas, Westlake Village, CA	818-706-2304
Warnick, Elsa/812 SW St Clair #7, Portland, OR	503-228-2659
Waters Art Studio/1820 E Garry St #207, Santa Ana, CA	714-250-4466
Watson, Richard Jesse/PO Box 1470, Murphys, CA	209-728-2701
Watts, Stan/3896 San Marcus Ct, Newbury Park, CA	805-499-4747
Westlund Design/5410 Wilshire Blvd , Los Angeles, CA	213-938-5218
Weston, Will/135 S LaBrea, Los Angeles, CA	213-854-3666
Wexler, Ed/4701 Don Pio Dr, Woodland Hills, CA	818-888-3858
Wheaton, Liz/PO Box 307, Ross, CA	415-456-7711
Whidden Studios/6725 Mesa Ridge Rd #208, San Diego, CA	619-455-1776
White, Charles William/1725 Berkeley St, Santa Monica, CA	213-453-4418
Wicks, Ren/3443 Wade St, Los Angeles, CA	213-390-9595
Willardson + Assoc/103 W California, Glendale, CA	818-242-5688
WILLIAM & HINDS/2790 SKYPARK DR #112, TORRANCE, CA (P 45)	**213-539-3252**
Wilson, Dick/11607 Clover Ave, Los Angeles, CA	213-828-9653
Wilson, Rowland/7501 Solano St, La Costa, CA	619-944-3631
Wilton, Nicholas/163 Tunstead Ave, San Anselmo, CA	415-456-2456
Wilton/Oppenheimer/163 Tunstead Ave, San Anselmo, CA	415-456-2456
Winston, Jeannie/8800 Venice Blvd, Los Angeles, CA	213-558-0141
Winterbauer, Michael/280 S Euclid Ave, Pasadena, CA	818-578-1253
Winters, Greg/2139 Pinecrest Dr, Altadena, CA	818-798-7666
Witus, Edward/2932 Wilshire Blvd #202, Santa Monica, CA	213-828-6521
Wolfe, Bruce/206 El Cerrito Ave, Piedmont, CA	415-655-7871
Wolin, Ron/4501 Firmament, Encino, CA	818-783-0523
Woodward, Teresa/544 Paseo Miramar, Pacific Palisades, CA	213-459-2317
Wray, Greg/824 E Providencia Ave, Burbank, CA	818-845-2375
Wright, Jonathan/2110 Holly Dr, Los Angeles, CA	213-461-1091

XYZ

Xavier, Roger/23200 Los Codona Ave, Torrance, CA	213-375-1663
Yenne, Bill/111 Pine St, San Francisco, CA	415-989-2450
Yeomans, Jeff/820 Deal Ct #C, San Diego, CA	619-488-2502
Zaslavsky, Morris/228 Main St #6, Venice, CA	213-399-3666
Zebot, George/PO Box 4295, Laguna Beach, CA	714-499-5027
Zick, Brian/3251 Primera Ave, Los Angeles, CA	213-855-8855
Ziemienski, Dennis/308 Hillcrest Dr, Leucadia, CA	619-944-3751
Zinc, Debra/Pier 33 North, San Francisco, CA	415-956-4750
Zito, Andy/135 S La Brea Ave, Los Angeles, CA	213-931-1181
Zitting, Joel/2404 Ocean Park Blvd #A, Santa Monica, CA	213-452-7009

Photographers

New York City

A Abatelli, Gary/80 Charles St #3W — 212-254-2142

Abel, Jim/112 E 19th St — 212-460-5374
Abramowitz, Ellen/166 E 35th St #4H — 212-686-2409
Abramowitz, Jerry/680 Broadway — 212-420-9500
ABRAMSON, MICHAEL/214 GUERNSEY ST (P 63) — **212-737-1890**
Adamo, Jeff/50 W 93rd St #8P — 212-866-4886
Adams, Eddie/29 E 22nd St #68 — 212-477-5346
Adams, George G./15 W 38th St — 212-391-1345
Adams, Jim/15 W 38th St #1203 — 212-319-1345
Addeo, Edward/151 W 19th St — 212-206-1686
Adelman, Barbara Ellen/267 Mayfair Dr — 718-531-8054
Adelman, Bob/151 W 28th St — 212-736-0537
Adelman, Menachem Assoc/156 Fifth Ave #323 — 212-675-1202
Adler, Arnie/70 Park Terrace W — 212-304-2443
Agor, Alexander/108-28 Flatlands 7 St — 212-777-1775
Aharoni, Oudi/704 Broadway — 212-777-0847
Aich, Clara/218 E 25th St — 212-686-4220
Albert, Jade/59 W 19th St #3B — 212-242-0940
Alberts, Andrea/100 Fifth Ave 11th Fl — 212-242-5794
Alcorn, Richard/160 W 95th St #7A — 212-866-1161
Alexander, Robert/50 W 29th St — 212-684-0180
Alexanders, John W/308 E 73rd St — 212-734-9166
Allen, Jim/175 Fifth Ave #1112 — 212-473-8020
Allison, David/42 E 23rd St — 212-460-9056
Alper, Barbara/202 W 96th St — 212-316-6518
Alpern/Lukoski/250 W 88th St — 212-724-5017
Alt, Howard/314 E 41st St — 212-490-7868
Amato, Paul/881 Seventh Ave #405 — 212-541-4787
Ambrose, Ken/44 E 23rd St — 212-260-4848
Amplo, Nick/271 1/2 W 10th St — 212-741-2799
Amrine, Jamie/30 W 22nd St — 212-243-2178
Andrews, Bert/PO Box 20707 — 212-662-6732
Anik, Adam/111 Fourth Ave #1-I — 212-228-4148
Anthony, Don/79 Prall Ave — 718-317-6340
Antonio/Stephen Photo/45 E 20th St — 212-674-2350
Apple, Richard/80 Varick St #4B — 212-966-6782
Arakawa, Nobu/40 E 21st St — 212-475-0206
Aranita, Jeffrey/60 Pineapple St — 718-625-7672
Ardito, Peter/108 Reade St — 212-619-6582
Aresu, Aaul/568 Broadway — 212-334-9494
Arky, David/57 W 19th St #2A — 212-242-4760
Arlak, Victoria/40 East End Ave — 212-879-0250
Arma, Tom/38 W 26th St — 212-243-7904
Arndt, Dianne/400 Central Park West — 212-866-1902
Arslanian, Ovak/344 W 14th St — 212-255-1519
Ashe, Bill/534 W 35th St — 212-695-6473
Ashley, Pat/920 Broadway — 212-473-6180
Atkin, Jonathan/23 E 17th St — 212-242-5218
Aubry, Daniel/365 First Ave — 212-598-4191
Aurora Retouching/19 W 21st St — 212-255-0620
Auster, Evan/215 E 68th St — 212-517-9776
Auster, Walter/18 E 16th St — 212-627-8448
Avedis/381 Park Ave S — 212-685-5888
Avedon, Richard/407 E 75th St — 212-879-6325
Axon, Red/17 Park Ave — 212-532-6317
Azzato, Hank/348 W 14th St 3rd Fl — 212-929-9455
Azzi, Robert/116 E 27th St — 212-481-6900

B Baasch, Diane/41 W 72nd St #11F — 212-724-2123

Babchuck, Jacob/132 W 22nd St — 212-929-9811
Babushkin, Mark/110 W 31st St — 212-239-6630
Bacall, Robert/1059 E 99th St — 718-981-3144
Back, John/15 Sheridan Sq — 212-243-6347
Bahrt, Irv/310 E 46th St — 212-661-5260
Baillie, Allan & Gus Francisco/220 E 23rd St 11th Fl — 212-683-0418
Bak, Sunny/876 Broadway 4th Fl — 212-677-1712
Baker, Chuck/1630 York Ave — 212-517-9060
Baker, Gloria/415 Central Park W 8th Fl — 212-222-2866
Baker, Joe/35 Wooster St — 212-925-6555

Bakerman, Nelson/342 W 56th St #1D — 212-489-1647
Baldwin, Joel/29 E 19th St — 212-308-5991
Bale, J R/130 W 25th St — 212-627-1489
Baliotti, Dan/6 W 18th St — 212-627-9039
Bancroft, Monty/161 W 15th St — 212-807-8650
Barash, Howard/349 W 11th St — 212-242-6182
Baratta, Nicholas/450 W 31st St 10th Fl — 212-239-0999
Barba, Dan/201 E 16th St — 212-420-8611
Barber, James/873 Broadway — 212-598-4500
Barber, Karen/51 Warren St 5th Fl — 212-619-6790
Barboza, Tony/853 Broadway #1208 — 212-529-5027
Barcellona, Marianne/175 Fifth Ave #2422 — 212-463-9717
Barclay, Bob Studios/5 W 19th St 6th Fl — 212-255-3440
Barkentin, George/15 W 18th St — 212-243-2174
Barnell, Joe/164 Madison Ave — 212-686-8850
Barnett, Peggy/26 E 22nd St — 212-673-0500
Barns, Larry/21 W 16th St — 212-242-8833
Barr, Neal/222 Central Park South — 212-765-5760
Barrett, John/164 E 66th St — 212-517-5210
Barrett, John E/40 E 20th St 7th Fl — 212-777-7309
Barrick, Rick/12 E 18th St 4th Fl — 212-741-2304
Barrow, Scott/214 W 30th St #6 — 212-736-4567
BARROWS, WENDY/205 E 22ND ST #4H (P 64,65) — **212-685-0799**
Barton, Paul/101 W 18th St 4th Fl — 212-533-1422
Basilion, Nick/150 Fifth Ave #532 — 212-645-6568
Bates, Art/154 W 70th St #9L — 212-799-3388
Batlin, Lee/37 E 28th St 8th Fl — 212-685-9492
Baum, Charles/320 West End Ave — 212-724-8013
Baumel, Ken/175 Fifth Ave #3251 — 212-929-7550
Bava, John/51 Station Ave — 718-967-9175
Bealmear, Brad/54 Barrow St — 212-675-8060
Bean, John/5 W l9th St — 212-242-8106
Bechtold, John/117 E 31st St — 212-679-7630
Beck, Arthur/119 W 22nd St — 212-691-8331
BECKER, JONATHAN/451 WEST 24TH ST (P 66) — **212-929-3180**
Beckhard, Robert/130 E 24th St — 212-777-1411
Beebe, Rod/790 Amsterdam #4D — 212-678-7832
Begleiter, Steven/38 Greene St — 212-334-5262
Belinsky, Jon/119 E 17th St — 212-627-1246
Beller, Janet/568 Broadway — 212-334-0281
Benedict, William/5 Tudor City — 212-697-4460
Bercow, Larry/344 W 38th St — 212-629-9000
Berenholtz, Richard/600 W 111th St #6A — 212-222-1302
BERGER, JOSEPH/121 MADISON AVE #3B (P 67) — **212-685-7191**
Bergman, Beth/150 West End Ave — 212-724-1867
Bergren, John/27 W 20th St #1003 — 212-627-5292
Berkun, Phil/199 Amity St #2 — 718-237-2648
Berkwit, Lane (Ms)/262 Fifth Ave — 212-889-5911
Berman, Brad/295 Ecksford St — 718-383-8950
Berman, Howard/5 E 19th St #303 — 212-473-3366
Berman, Malcolm/60 Thomas St — 212-431-4446
Bernson, Carol/119 Fifth Ave #806 — 212-473-3884
Bernstein, Alan/365 First Ave 2nd Fl — 212-254-1355
Bernstein, Bill/59 Thompson St #9 — 212-925-6853
Bester, Roger/55 Van Dam St 11th Fl — 212-645-5810
Betz, Charles/138 W 25th St 10th Fl — 212-675-4760
Bevan, David/536 W 50th St — 212-582-5045
Bevilacqua, Joe/202 E 42nd St — 212-490-0355
Biddle, Geoffrey/5 E 3rd St — 212-505-7713
Bies, William/21-29 41st St #1A — 718-278-0236
Big City Prodctns/5 E 19th St #303 — 212-473-3366
Bijur, Hilda/190 E 72nd St — 212-737-4458
Bisbee, Terry/290 W 12th St — 212-242-4762
Bishop, David/251 W 19th St — 212-929-4355
Blachut, Dennis/145 W 28th St 8th Fl — 212-947-4270
Blackburn, Joseph M/116 W 29th St #2C — 212-699-3950
Blackman, Barry/115 E 23rd St 10th Fl — 212-473-3100
Blackman, Jeffrey/2323 E 12th St — 718-769-0986
Blackstock, Ann/400 W 43rd St #4E — 212-695-2525
Blake, Rebecca/35 W 36th St — 212-695-6438
Blechman, Jeff/591 Broadway — 212-226-0006
BLECKER, CHARLES/380 BLEECKER ST #140 (P 69) — **212-242-8390**

Photographers

Continued

Please send us your additions and updates.

Blegen, Alana/	718-769-2619
Blinkoff, Richard/147 W 15th St 3rd Fl	212-620-7883
Blitz, Irvin/114 Spring St 4th Fl	212-219-9744
Block, Helen/385 14th St	718-788-1097
Block, Ira Photography/215 W 20th St	212-242-2728
Bloom, Teri/300 Mercer St #6C	212-475-2274
Blosser, Robert/741 West End Ave #3C	212-662-0107
Bobbe, Leland/51 W 28th St	212-685-5238
Bodi Studios/340 W 39th St	212-947-7883
Bodick, Gay/11 E 80th St	212-772-8584
Bogertman, Ralph Inc/34 W 28th St	212-889-8871
Boisseau, Joseph/105 E 223rd St	212-519-8672
Bolesta, Alan/11 Riverside Dr #13SE	212-873-1932
Boljonis, Steven/555 Ft Washington Ave #4A	212-740-0003
Bonomo, Louis/118 W 27th St #2F	212-242-4630
Bordnick, Barbara/39 E 19th St	212-533-1180
Borowski, Steve/36 W 20th St 6th Fl	212-627-7642
Bosch, Peter/477 Broome St	212-925-0707
Boszko, Ron/140 W 57th St	212-541-5504
Bottomley, Jim/125 Fifth Ave	212-677-9646
Bracco, Bob/43 E 19th St	212-228-0230
BRADY, STEVE/507 E 30TH ST (P 212,213)	**212-213-6024**
Brandt, Peter/73 Fifth Ave #6B	212-242-4289
Braun, Yenachem/666 West End Ave	212-873-1985
Braune, Peter/134 W 32nd St #602	212-244-4270
Braverman, Alan/PO Box 865	212-674-1925
Bredel, Walter/21 E 10th St	212-228-8565
Breitrose, Howard/443 W 18th St	212-242-7825
Brello, Ron/400 Lafayette St	212-982-0490
Brenner, George/15 W 24th St	212-691-7436
Brenner, Jay/18 E 17th St	212-741-2244
Breskin, Michael/324 Lafayette	212-925-2858
Brett, Clifton/51 W 14th St	212-675-6236
Brewster, Don/235 West End Ave	212-874-0548
Bridges, Kiki/147 W 26th St 3rd Fl	212-807-6563
Brill Studio/270 City Island Ave	212-885-0802
Brill, James/160 W 16th St	212-645-9414
Britton, Peter/315 E 68th St	212-737-1664
Brizzi, Andrea/175 Washington Park	212-627-2341
BRODY, BOB/5 W 19TH 2ND FL (P 57)	**212-741-0013**
Bronstein, Steve/5 E 19th St #303	212-473-3366
Brooke, Randy/179 E 3rd St	212-677-2656
Brosan, Roberto/873 Broadway	212-473-1471
Brown, David/6 W 20th St 2nd Fl	212-924-3072
Brown, Nancy/5 W 19th St 10th Fl	212-924-9105
Brown, Owen Studio/134 W 29th St 2nd Fl	212-947-9470
Bruderer, Rolf/443 Park Ave S	212-684-4890
Bruno Burklin/873 Broadway	212-420-0208
Bruno Photo/43 Crosby St 1st Fl	212-925-2929
Brunswick, Cecile/127 W 96th St	212-222-2088
Bryce, Sherman E/269 W 90th St #3B	212-580-9639
Bryson, John/12 E 62nd St	212-755-1321
Buceta, Jaime/56 W 22nd St 6th Fl	212-807-8485
Buck, Bruce/39 W 14th St	212-645-1022
Buckler, Susanne/344 W 38th St	212-279-0043
Buckner, Bill/21 W 17th St	212-242-5129
Buonnano, Ray/237 W 26th St	212-675-7680
Burnette, David/280 Madison Ave #1109	212-683-2002
Burns, Tom/534 W 35th St	212-927-4678
Burquez, Felizardo/22-63 38th St #1	718-274-6139
Burrell, Fred/54 W 21st St #1207	212-691-0808
Butler, Dennis/200 E 37th St 4th Fl	212-686-5084
Byers, Bruce/11 W 20th St 5th Fl	212-242-5846

C

Cadge, Jeff/341 W 47th St #1B	212-246-6155
Cailor/Resnick/237 W 54th St 4th Fl	212-977-4300
Calicchio, Tom/30 E 21st St	212-473-8990
Callis, Chris/91 Fifth Ave	212-243-0231
Camera Communications/110 Greene St	212-925-2722
Cameron Photo/78 Fifth Ave	212-675-0089
Camp, E J (Ms)/20 E 10th St	212-475-6267
Campbell, Barbara/138 W 17th St	212-929-5620

CAMPOS, JOHN/132 W 21ST ST (P 70)	**212-675-0601**
Canady, Philip/1411 Second Ave	212-737-3855
Cannon, Gregory/876 Broadway 2nd Fl	212-228-3190
Cantor, Phil/75 Ninth Ave 8th Fl	212-243-1143
Cardacino, Michael/20 Ridge Rd	212-947-9307
Cargasacchi, Gianni/175 Fifth Ave	212-473-8020
Carlton, Chuck/36 E 23rd St 7th Fl	212-777-1099
Carrino, John/160 Fifth Ave #914	212-243-3623
Carron, Les/15 W 24th St 2nd Fl	212-255-8250
Carson, Donald/115 W 23rd St	212-807-8987
Carter, Dwight/11 W 17th St	212-627-1266
Casey/10 Park Ave #3E	212-984-1397
Cashin, Art/5 W 19th St	212-255-3440
Castellano, Peter/314 W 53rd St	212-206-6320
Castelli, Charles/41 Union Sq W #425	212-620-5536
Castillo, Luis A/60 Pineapple St	718-834-1380
Caulfield, Patricia/115 W 86th St #2E	212-362-1951
Caverly, Kat/414 W 49th St	212-757-8388
Cearley, Guy/25 W 31st St	212-714-0075
Celnick, Edward/36 E 12th St	212-420-9326
Cementi, Joseph/133 W 19th St 3rd Fl	212-924-7770
Cenicola, Tony Studio/32 Union Sq E #613	212-420-9798
Chakmakjian, Paul/35 W 36th St 8th Fl	212-563-3195
CHALK, DAVID/157 HUDSON ST (P 71)	**212-874-9042**
Chalkin, Dennis/5 E 16th St	212-929-1036
Chan, T S/174 Duane St	212-219-0574
Chaney, Scott/11 W 20th St 6th Fl	212-924-8440
Chanteau, Pierre/209 W 38th St	212-221-5860
Chao, John/51 W 81st St #6B	212-580-7912
Chapman, Mike/543 Broadway 8th Fl	212-966-9542
Charlas, Jacques/134 Beaumont	718-648-5345
Charles, Bill/265 W 37th St #PH-D	212-719-9156
Charles, Frederick/254 Park Ave S #7F	212-505-0686
Charles, Lisa/119 W 23rd St	212-807-8600
Chaulk, David/157 Hudson St	212-925-4203
Chauncy, Kim/123 W 13th St	212-242-2400
Checani, Richard/1133 Broadway	212-645-8634
Chelsea Photo/Graphics/641 Ave of Americas	212-206-1780
Chen, Paul Inc/133 Fifth Ave	212-674-4100
Chernin, Bruce/330 W 86th St	212-496-0266
Chestnut, Richard/236 W 27th St	212-255-1790
Chiba/303 Park Ave S #506	212-674-7575
Chin, Ted/118 W 27th St #3R	212-691-7612
Choi, Joon/10 E 18th St #5	212-645-1248
Christensen, Paul H/286 Fifth Ave	212-279-2838
Chrynwski, Walter/154 W 18th St	212-675-1906
Church, Diana/31 W 31st St	212-736-4116
Cipolla, Karen/103 Reade St 3rd Fl	212-619-6114
Cirone, Bettina/57 W 58th St	212-888-7649
Clarke, Kevin/900 Broadway 9th Fl	212-460-9360
Clayton, Tom/568 Broadway #601	212-431-3377
Clementi, Joseph Assoc/133 W 19th St 3rd Fl	212-924-7770
Clough, Terry/147 W 25th St	212-255-3040
Clymer, Jonathan/146 W 29th St	718-482-5493
Cobb, Jan/5 West 19th At	212-255-1400
Cobin, Martin/145 E 49th St	212-758-5742
Cochran, George/381 Park Ave S	212-689-9054
Coggin, Roy/64 W 21st St	212-929-6262
Cohen, James/36 E 20th St 4th Fl	212-533-4400
Cohen, Joel/27 E 13th St #7E	212-691-5129
Cohen, Lawrence Photo/247 W 30th St	212-967-4376
Cohen, Marc David/5 W 19th	212-741-0015
Cohen, Robert/175 Fifth Ave #1112	212-473-8020
Cohn, Ric/137 W 25th St #1	212-924-6749
COLABELLA, VINCENT/304 E 41ST ST (P 73)	**212-949-7456**
Cole, Bob/14114 249th St 2nd Fl	718-525-7471
Coleman, Bruce/381 Fifth Ave 2nd Fl	212-683-5227
Coleman, Gene/250 W 27th St	212-691-4752
Colen, Corrine/519 Broadway	212-431-7425
Colletti, Steve/200 Park Ave #303E	212-972-2218
Collins, Arlene/64 N Moore St #3E	212-431-9117
Collins, Benton/873 Broadway	212-254-7247

Photographers

Continued

Please send us your additions and updates.

Collins, Chris/381 Park Ave S	212-725-0237
Collins, Joe J/208 Garfield Pl	718-965-4836
Collins, Sheldon/27 W 24th St	212-242-0076
Colliton, Paul/310 Greenwich St	212-619-6102
Colton, Robert/1700 York Ave	212-831-3953
Connelly, Hank/6 W 37th St	212-563-9109
Connors, William/310 E 46th St	212-490-3801
Contact Press Images/135 Central Park West	212-481-6910
Cook, Irvin/534 W 43rd St	212-925-6216
Cook, Rod/29 E 19th St	212-995-0100
Cooke, Colin/380 Lafayette St	212-254-5090
Cooper, Martha/310 Riverside Dr #805	212-222-5146
Cope, Gil/135 W 26th St	212-929-1777
Corbett, Jane/303 Park Ave S #512	212-505-1177
Cornicello, John/245 W 29th St	212-564-0874
Cornish, Dan/594 Broadway #1204	212-226-3183
Corporate Photographers Inc/45 John St	212-964-6515
Corti, George/10 W 33rd St	212-239-4490
Cosimo/43 W 13th St	212-206-1818
Couzens, Larry/16 E 17th St	212-620-9790
Cowan, Frank/5 E 16th St	212-675-5960
Cox, David/25 Mercer St	212-925-0734
Crampton, Nancy/35 W 9th St	212-254-1135
Crocker, Ted/117 E 30th St	212-686-8684
Croner, Ted/15 W 28th St	212-685-3944
Cronin, Casey/115 Wooster St	212-334-9253
Crum, John R Photography/124 W 24th St	212-463-8663
Cserna, George/80 Second Ave #2	212-477-3472
Culberson, Earl/5 E 19th St	212-473-3366
Cunningham, Peter/214 Sullivan St	212-475-4866
Curatola, Tony/18 E 17th St	212-243-5478
Cutler, Craig/536 W 50th St	212-966-1652
Czaplinski, Czeslaw/90 Dupont St	718-389-9606

D

D'Addio, James/41 Union Sq W #1428	212-645-0267
D'Innocenzo, Paul/568 Broadway #604	212-925-9622
Daley, James D/568 Broadway	212-925-7192
Daly, Jack/247 W 30th St	212-695-2726
Dantuono, Paul/433 Park Ave So	212-683-5778
Dantzic, Jerry/910 President St	718-789-7478
David, Gabrielle/109-41 Ditmars Blvd	718-424-2873
Davidson, Bruce/251 Park Ave S 11th Fl	212-475-7600
Davidson, Darwin K/32 Bank Street	212-242-0095
Davis, Dick/400 E 59th St	212-751-3276
Davis, Don/61 Horatio St	212-989-2820
Davis, Hal/225 Lafayette St	212-563-3001
Davis, Richard/17 E 16th St 9th Fl	212-675-2428
Day, Bob/29 E 19th St	212-475-7387
Day, Olita/239 Park Ave South	212-673-9354
De Zanger, Arie/80 W 40th St	212-354-7327
DeFrancis, Peter/424 Broome St	212-966-1357
DeGrado, Drew/250 W 40th St 5th Fl	212-302-2760
DeLeone, Katrina/286 Fifth Ave #1206	212-714-9777
DeLessio, Len/7 E 17th St	212-206-8725
DeMarchelier, Patrick/162 W 21st St	212-924-3561
DeMelo, Antonio/126 W 22nd St	212-929-0507
DeMilt, Ronald/873 Broadway 2nd Fl	212-228-5321
DePaul, Raymond/252 W 76th St #1A	212-769-2550
DePra, Nancy/15 W 24th St	212-242-0252
DeRosa, Peter/117 W 95th St	212-864-3007
DeSanto, Thomas/116 W 29th St 2nd Fl	212-967-1390
DeToy, Ted/511 E 78th St	212-988-1869
DeVito, Bart/43 E 30th St 14th Fl	212-889-9670
DeVito, Michael Jr/48 W 25th St	212-243-5267
DeVoe, Marcus E/34 E 81st St	212-737-9073
DeWys, Leo/1170 Broadway	212-689-5580
Degrado, Drew/250 W 40th St	212-302-2760
Denker, Deborah/460 Greenwich St	212-219-9263
Denner, Manuel/249 W 29th St 4th Fl	212-947-6220
Dennis, Lisl/135 E 39th St	212-532-8226
Denson, Walt/70 W 83rd St Dplx B	212-496-7305
Dermer, Ronald/Falmouth St	718-332-2464

Derr, Stephen/420 W 45th St 4th Fl	212-246-5920
Deutsch, Jack/165 W 83rd St	212-799-7179
DiFranza Williamson Photography/16 W 22nd St	212-832-2343
DiMartini, Sally/137 Riverside Dr	516-329-1236
DiMicco/Ferris Studio/40 W 17th St	212-627-4074
DIAMOND, JOE/915 WEST END AVE (P 53)	**212-316-5295**
Dian, Russell/432 E 88th St #201	212-722-4348
Diaz, Jorge/142 W 24th St 12th Fl	212-675-4783
Dibue, Robert/40 W 20th St	212-206-0860
Dicran Studio/35 W 36th St 11th Fl	212-695-6438
Dipetto, John/245 E 54th St	212-935-4762
Dodge, Jeff/133 Eighth Ave	212-620-9652
Doerzbacher, Cliff/12 Cottage Ave	718-981-3144
Doherty, Marie/43 E 22nd St	212-674-8767
Dolgins, Alan/470 W 24th St	213-273-5794
Dominis, John/252 W 102nd St	212-841-2340
Dorf, Myron Jay/205 W 19th St 3rd Fl	212-255-2020
Dorot, Didier/48 W 21st St 9th Fl	212-206-1608
Doubilet, David/1040 Park Ave #6J	212-348-5011
Drabkin, Si Studios Inc/236 W 27th St	212-206-7040
Dresner, Harvey/302-46 46th Ave	718-225-2332
Drew, Rue Faris/177 E 77th St	212-794-8994
Drivas, Joseph/15 Beacon Ave	718-667-0696
Druskis, Laima/107 Sterling Pl	718-230-0078
Dubler, Douglas/162 E 92nd St	212-410-6300
DUCHAINE, RANDY/200 W 18TH ST #4F (P 52)	**212-243-4371**
Ducote, Kimberly/410 W 23rd St #5B	212-989-3680
Duke, Dana/620 Broadway	212-260-3334
Duke, Randy/235 E 149th St	212-292-1226
Dunand, Frank/18 W 27th St	212-686-3478
Dunkley, Richard/175 Fifth Ave #1112	212-473-8020
Dunning, Hank/50 W 22nd St	212-675-6040
Dunning, Robert & Deane/57 W 58th St	212-688-0788
Duomo Photo Inc/133 W 19th St	212-243-1150

E

Eagan, Timothy/319 E 75th St	212-517-7665
Eastep, Wayne/443 Park Ave S #1006	212-686-8404
Eberstadt, Fred/791 Park Ave	212-794-9471
Eckstein, Ed/234 Fifth Ave 5th Fl	212-685-9342
Edahl, Edward/236 W 27th St	212-929-2002
Edgeworth, Anthony/130 Madison Ave	212-679-6031
Edwards, Gregory/30 East End Ave	212-879-4339
Edwards, Harvey/575 Madison Ave	516-261-5239
Eguiguren, Carlos/139 E 57th St 3rd Fl	212-888-6732
Ehrenpreis, Dave/156 Fifth Ave	212-242-1976
Eisenberg, Steve/448 W 37th St	212-563-2061
Elbers, Johan/18 E 18th St	212-929-5783
Elgort, Arthur/300 Central Park West	212-219-8775
Elios-Zunini Studio/142 W 4th St	212-228-6827
Ellis, Ray/176 Westminster Rd	718-282-6449
Ellis, Roz/37 W 26th St 5th Fl	212-481-3770
Elmer, Jo/200 E 87th St	212-369-7077
Elmore, Steve/1640 York Ave #3B	212-472-2463
Elness, Jack/236 W 26th St	212-242-5045
Elz, Barry/13 Worth St	212-431-7910
Emberling, David/38 W 26th St	212-242-7455
Emil, Pamela/327 Central Park West	212-749-4716
Endress, John Paul/254 W 31st St	212-736-7800
Engel, Mort Studio/260 Fifth Ave	212-889-8466
Englander, Maury/43 Fifth Ave	212-242-9777
Englehardt, Duk/80 Varick St #4E	212-226-6490
Epstein, Mitch/353 E 77th St	212-517-3648
Epstein, S Karin/610 West End Ave #9C	212-472-0771
ESSEL, ROBERT/39 W 71ST ST #A (P 74,75)	**212-877-5228**
Estrada, Sigrid/902 Broadway	212-673-4300

F

Farber, Robert/232 E 58th St	212-486-9090
Faria, Rui/304 Eighth Ave #3	212-243-6343
Farrell, Bill/381 Park Ave S	212-683-1425
Farrell, John/189 Second Ave	212-460-9001
Favero, Jean P/208 Fifth Ave #3E	212-683-9188
Feibel, Theodor/102-10 66th Rd #15C	718-897-2445

Photographers
Continued

Please send us your additions and updates.

Feinstein, Gary/19 E 17th St	212-242-3373
Feintuch, Harvey/1440 E 14th St	718-339-0301
Feldman, Andy/515 10th St	718-788-6585
Feller, Nora/269 W 25th St	212-307-5923
Fellerman, Stan/152 W 25th St	212-243-0027
Fellman, Sandi/548 Broadway	212-925-5187
Ferguson, Phoebe/289 Cumberland St	718-643-1675
Ferrante, Terry/555 Third Ave	212-683-7240
FERRI, MARK/463 BROOME ST (P 60)	**212-431-1356**
Fetter, Frank/400 E 78th St	212-249-3138
Fields, Bruce/71 Greene St	212-431-8852
Filari, Katrina/286 Fifth Ave 4th Fl	212-279-2838
Finkelman, Allan/118 E 28th St #608	212-684-3487
Finlay, Alastair/38 E 21st St 9th Fl	212-260-4297
Finley, Calvin/59 Franklin St	212-219-8759
Firman, John/434 E 75th St	212-794-2794
Fischer, Carl/121 E 83rd St	212-794-0400
Fishbein, Chuck/276 Fifth Ave #1103	212-532-4452
Fisher, Jon/236 W 27th St 4th Fl	212-206-6311
Fishman, Chuck/69 1/2 Morton St	212-242-3987
Fishman, Robert/153 W 27th St #502	212-620-7976
Fiur, Lola Troy/360 E 65th St	212-861-1911
Flash Flood Enterprises/PO Box 1955/Old Chelsea Sta	212-627-7157
Flatow, Carl/20 E 30th St	212-683-8688
Floret, Evelyn/3 E 80th St	212-472-3179
Floyd, Bob/PO Box 216	212-684-0795
Flying Camera/114 Fulton St	212-619-0808
Flynn, Matt/99 W 27th St	212-927-2985
Flynn, Richard/306 W 4th St	212-243-0834
Forastieri, Marili/156 Fifth Ave #1301	212-431-1846
Forelli, Chip/316 Fifth Ave	212-564-1835
Forrest, Bob/273 Fifth Ave 3rd Fl	212-288-4458
Forschmidt, Don S/225 Park Pl #2J	212-878-7454
Foto Shuttle Japan/47 Greene St	212-966-9641
Foulke, Douglas/28 W 25th St	212-243-0822
Fox, Jeffrey/6 W 20th St	212-620-0147
Foxx, Stephanie/274 W 71st St	212-580-9158
FRAJNDLICH, ABE/30 E 20TH ST #605 (P 77)	**212-995-8648**
Francais, Isabelle/873 Broadway	212-678-7508
Francekevich, Al/73 Fifth Ave	212-691-7466
Frances, Scott/175 Fifth Ave #2401	212-749-8026
Francisco, Gus/220 E 23rd St	212-683-0418
Francki, Joe/575 Madison Ave 10th Fl	212-242-7716
Frank, Dick/11 W 25th St	212-242-4648
Frankian, Paul/59 W 19th St	212-675-1654
Fraser, Douglas/9 E 19th St	212-777-8404
Fraser, Rob/211 Thompson St #1E	212-677-4589
Frazier, David/245 W 29th St	212-279-0003
Freed, Leonard/251 Park Ave S	212-475-7600
French, Larry/273 Fifth Ave 3rd Fl	212-685-2644
Freni, Al/381 Park Ave S #809	212-679-2533
Fried, Richard/430 W 14th St Rm 204	212-929-1052
Friedman, Benno/26 W 20th St	212-255-6038
Friedman, Jerry/873 Broadway	212-505-5600
Friedman, Steve/545 W 111th St	212-864-2662
Friedman, Walter/58 W 68th St	212-874-5287
Froomer, Brett/39 E 12th St	212-533-3113
Funk, Mitchell/500 E 77th St	212-988-2886
Furones, Claude Emile/40 Waterside Plaza	212-683-0622
Fusco, Paul/251 Park Ave S	212-475-7600

G Gairy, John/11 W 17th St 2nd Fl

Gairy, John/11 W 17th St 2nd Fl	212-242-5805
Galante, Dennis/133 W 22nd St 3rd Fl	212-463-0938
Galloway, Ewing/1466 Broadway	212-719-4720
Gallucci, Ed/568 Broadway	212-226-2215
Galton, Beth/130 W 25th St	212-242-2266
GALVIN, KEVIN/OBLATTERWALLSTR 44 (P 78)	
Ganges, Halley/35 W 36th St	212-868-1810
Gans, Hank/40 Waterside Plaza	212-683-0622
Garetti, John/140 W 22nd St	212-505-0304
Garik, Alice/ Photo Comm/173 Windsor Pl	718-499-1456
Garn, Andrew/207 Eighth Ave #2R	212-353-8434

Gatehouse, Don/356 E 89th St	212-517-8979
Gatton, Beth/130 W 25th St	212-242-2266
Gee, Elizabeth/280 Madison #1109	212-683-6924
Geller, Bonnie/57 W 93rd St	212-864-5922
Gelsobello, Paul/245 W 29th St #1200	212-947-0317
Generico, Tony/130 W 25th St	212-627-9755
Gentieu, Penny/87 Barrow St	212-691-1994
Gentil, Gerard/310 E 46th St	212-599-1806
George, Michael/525 Hudson St	212-627-5868
Geradi, Marcia/38 W 21st St	212-243-8400
Germana, Michael/64 Hett Ave	718-987-2986
Gesar, Aram/417 Lafayette St	212-228-1852
Gescheidt, Alfred/175 Lexington Ave	212-889-4023
Ghergo, Christina/160 Fifth Ave	212-243-6811
Gibbons, George/292 City Islnd Ave	212-885-0769
Gidion Inc/140 W 22nd St	212-627-4769
Gigli, Ormond/327 E 58th St	212-758-2860
Gillardin, Andre/6 W 20th St	212-675-2950
Gillette, Bruce/142 W 26th St #8A	212-807-9207
Gioiello, Rick/1105 Stadium Ave	212-409-0023
Giordano, John A/60 E 9th St #538	212-477-3273
Giovanni, Raeanne/156 Fifth Ave #1230	212-206-7757
Giraldi, Frank/54 W 39th St	212-840-8225
Giraldo, Anita/83 Canal St	212-431-1193
Gladstone, Gary/237 E 20th St #2H	212-777-7772
Glancz, Jeff/38 W 21st St 12th Fl	212-741-2504
Glaser, Harold/143-30 Roosevelt Ave	718-939-1829
Glassman, Carl/80 N Moore St #37G	212-732-2458
Glaviano, Marco/222 Central Park S #41	212-307-7794
Glinn, Burt/41 Central Park W	212-877-2210
Globus Brothers/44 W 24th St	212-243-1008
Goble, Brian/365 First Ave	212-460-8329
Goff, Lee/32 E 64th St	212-223-0716
Gold, Bernie/873 Broadway #301	212-677-0311
Gold, Charles/56 W 22nd St	212-242-2600
Goldman, Richard/36 W 20th St	212-675-3021
Goldring, Barry/568 Broadway #608	212-334-9494
Goldsmith, Gary/201 E 66th St	212-288-4851
Goldstein, Art/101 Wooster St	212-966-2682
Goll, Charles R/404 E 83rd St	212-628-4881
Golob, Stanford/40 Waterside Plaza	212-532-7166
Gonzalez, Luis/85 Livingston St	718-834-0426
Gonzalez, Manuel/127 W 26th St 7th Fl	212-242-2202
Goodman, Michael/115 Central Park W #32F	212-226-4541
Gordon, Andrew/48 W 22nd St	212-807-9758
Gordon, Brad/259 W 12th St	212-206-7758
Gordon, Joel/112 Fourth Ave	212-254-1688
Gorin, Bart/1160 Broadway	212-683-3743
Gorodnitzki, Diane/160 W 71st St	212-724-6259
Gotfryd, Bernard/46 Wendover Rd	718-261-8039
Gottlieb, Dennis/5 Union Sq W	212-620-7050
Gould, Jeff/98-41 64th Rd	718-897-0610
Gould, Peter/ Images/7 E 17th St	212-675-3707
Gove, Geoffrey/117 Waverly Pl	212-260-6051
Gozo Studio/40 W 17th St	212-620-8115
Graff, Randolph/160 Bleecker St	212-254-0412
Graflin, Liz/111 Fifth Ave 12th Fl	212-529-6700
Graig, Eric/10 E 18th St	212-548-5458
Grand, Paul/1800 Ocean Pkwy	718-375-0138
Grant, Robert/62 Greene St	212-925-1121
Graphic Media/12 W 27th St 12th Fl	212-696-0880
Graves, Tom/136 E 36th St	212-683-0241
Gray, Mitchell/169 E 86th St	212-427-2287
Gray, Robert/36 W 20th St 3rd Fl	212-807-7121
Green, Allen/1601 Third Ave	212-534-1718
Green-Armytage, Stephen/171 W 57th St #7A	212-247-6314
Greenberg, David/54 King St	212-316-9196
Greenberg, Joel/265 Water St	212-285-0979
Greene, Jim/20 W 20th St	212-674-1631
Greene, Joshua/448 W 37th St #8D	212-243-2750
Greene, Richard/18 E 17th St	212-242-5282
Greenwald, Seth/195 Adams St	718-802-1531

Photographers

Continued

Please send us your additions and updates.

Gregoire, Peter/329 W 87th St #7	212-496-0584
Gregory, John/105 Fifth Ave #9C	212-691-1797
Gregory, Kevin/237 W 26th St	212-807-9859
Grehan, Farrell/5 E 22nd St #22L	212-677-3999
Greyshock, Caroline/578 Broadway #707	212-266-7563
Griffiths, Philip Jones/251 Park Ave S	212-475-7600
Grill, Tom/32 E 31st St	212-989-0500
Gross, Cy/59 W 19th St	212-243-2556
Gross, David/922 Third Ave #3R	212-688-4729
Gross, Garry/235 W 4th St	212-807-7141
Gross, Geoffrey/119 W 23rd St 10th Fl	212-645-5193
Gross, Pat/315 E 86th St #1S East	212-427-9396
Grossman, Eugene/80 N Moore St Ste 14J	212-962-6795
Grossman, Henry/37 Riverside Dr	212-580-7751
Grotell, Al/170 Park Row	212-349-3165
Gruen, John/20 W 22nd St	212-242-8415
Gscheidle, Gerhard E/381 Park Ave S	212-532-1374
Guatti, Albano/250 Mercer St #C403	212-674-2230
Gudnason, Torkil/58 W 15th St	212-929-6680
Guice, Brad Studio/132 W 21st St 7th Fl	212-206-0966
Gurovitz, Judy/207 E 74th St	212-988-8685
Guyaux, Jean-Marie/29 E 19th St	212-529-5395

H Haar, Thomas/463 West St 212-929-9054

Haas, David/330 W 86th St	212-673-8576
HAAS, KENNETH/15 SHERIDAN SQUARE (P 83)	**212-255-0707**
Haft, Emily/435 E 65th St #100	212-517-5123
Hagen, Boyd/448 W 37th St #6A	212-244-2436
Haggerty, David/17 E 67th St	212-879-4141
Hagiwara, Brian/504 La Guardia Pl	212-674-6026
Haimann, Todd/26 W 38th St	212-391-0810
Halaska, Jan/PO Box 6611 FDR Sta	718-389-8923
HALING, GEORGE/231 W 29TH ST #302 (P 84,85)	**212-736-6822**
Hall, Clayton/165 W 29th St	212-629-8659
Hamilton, Keith/749 FDR Dr	212-982-3375
Hamilton, Mark/119 W 23rd St	212-691-3504
Hammond, Maury/9 E 19th St	212-460-9990
Han, Anthony/143 Guernsey St	718-389-8973
Hanlon, Gary Inc/40 W 20th St	212-206-9144
Hansen, Barbara/1954 Bronxdale Ave	212-822-1676
Hansen, Constance/78 Fifth Ave	212-691-5162
HANSON, KENT/147 BLEECKER ST #3R (P 86)	**212-777-2399**
Hardin, Ted/119 W 23rd St #702	212-242-2958
Harrington, Grace/312 W 48th St	212-246-1749
Harris, Michael/18 W 21st St	212-255-3377
Harris, Ronald G/119 W 22nd St	212-255-2330
Harrison, Howard/20 W 20th St 8th Fl	212-989-9233
Hartman, Harry/61 W 23rd St 3rd Fl	212-675-5454
Hartmann, Erich/251 Park Ave S	212-475-7600
Harvey, Ned/129 W 22nd St	212-807-7043
Hashi Studio/49 W 23rd St 3rd Fl	212-675-6902
HASHIMOTO/153 W 27TH ST #1202 (P 88)	**212-645-1221**
Hathon, Elizabeth/8 Greene St	212-219-0685
Hausman, George/1181 Broadway 6th Fl	212-686-4810
Haviland, Brian/34 E 30th St 4th Fl	212-481-4132
Hayes, Kerry/35 Taft Ave	718-442-4804
Haynes, Richard/383 Madison Ave 2nd Fl	212-872-1927
Hayward, Bill/596 Broadway 8th Fl	212-966-6490
Hedrich, David/7 E 17th St	212-924-3324
Heery, Gary/577 Broadway 2nd Fl	212-966-6364
Hege, Laszlo/13 E 30th St	718-706-0833
Heiberg, Milton/71 W 23rd St	212-741-6405
Hein, George/13 E 16th St 8th Fl	212-741-3211
Heir, Stuart/578 Broadway	212-219-9585
Heisler, Gregory/568 Broadway #800	212-777-8100
Hellerstein, Stephen A/56 W 22nd St 6th Fl	212-645-0508
Helms, Bill/1175 York Ave	212-759-2079
Hemsay, Yvonne/4520 Henry Hudson Pkwy	212-549-0095
Henderson, Akemi/44 W 54th St	212-581-3630
Henze, Don Studio/39 W 29th St 4th Fl	212-689-7375
Heron, Michal (Ms)/28 W 71st St	212-787-1272
Herr, H Buff/56 W 82nd St	212-595-4783

Herrenbruck, David/119 Fifth Ave	212-967-5550
Hess, Brad/1201 Broadway	212-684-3131
Heuberger, William/28 W 25th St	312-242-1532
Heyert, Elizabeth/251 W 30th St	212-594-1008
Hill, Pat/37 W 26th St	212-532-3479
Hiller, Geoffrey/601 W 113th St	212-873-0555
Hine, Skip/34 W 17th St 9th Fl	212-691-5903
Hing/ Norton Photography/24 W 30th St 8th Fl	212-683-4258
Hiro/50 Central Park West	212-580-8000
Hirsch, Butch/107 W 25th St	212-807-7498
Hirst, Michael/1150 Sixth Ave	914-666-2993
Hitz, Brad/377 W 11th St #2B	212-929-1432
Hochman, Allen Studio/9-11 E 19 St	212-777-8404
Hodgson, David/550 Riverside Dr	212-864-6941
Hogan, David/352 E 91st St	212-369-4575
Holbrooke, Andrew/50 W 29th St	212-889-5995
Holland, Robin/430 Greenwich St	212-431-5351
Hollyman, Tom/300 E 40th St #19R	212-867-2383
Holtzman Photography/269 W 11th St	212-242-7985
Hooper, Thomas/126 Fifth Ave	212-691-0122
Hopkins, Douglas/636 Sixth Ave	212-243-1774
Hopkins, Stephen/57 E 11th St 6th Fl	212-460-5022
Hopson, Gareth/22 E 21st St	212-535-3800
Hori, Richard/119 W 23rd St #400	212-645-8333
Horowitz, Ross M/206 W 15th St	212-206-9216
Horowitz, Ryszard/103 Fifth Ave	212-243-6440
HOROWITZ, TED/214 WILTON RD (P 48,49)	**203-454-8766**
Horst/166 E 63rd St	212-751-4937
Horvath, Jim/95 Charles St	212-741-0300
Houze, Philippe Louis/123 Prince St	212-614-0435
Howard, Ken/50-52 Dobbin St	718-388-9610
Howard, Rosemary/902 Broadway	212-473-5552
Huang, Ming/3174 44th St	718-262-0220
Hughes, Pinder/536 W 111th St	212-662-5105
Huibregtse, Jim/14 Jay St	212-925-3351
Hume, Adam/12 E 89th St	212-758-8929
Huntzinger, Bob/514 W 37th St	212-645-9035
Hurwitz, Harrison/379 Park Ave S	212-213-4820
Huszar/156 Fifth Ave #836	212-929-2593
Hyatt, Morton/13 Laight St	212-226-6880
Hyman, Barry/319 E 78th St #3C	212-879-3294
Hyman, Paul/236 W 26th St	212-255-1532

I Ianuzzi, Tom/488 W 37th St #9D 212-563-1987

Ichi/303 Park Ave S #506	212-254-4810
Ihara/568 Broadway #507	212-219-9363
Ikeda, Shig/636 Sixth Ave #4C	212-924-4744
Illography/49 Crosby St	212-219-0244
Image Makers/310 E 23rd St #9F	212-533-4498
Ing, Francis/112 W 31st St 5th Fl	212-279-5022
Intrater, Roberta/1212 Beverly Rd	718-462-4004
Iooss, Walter/344 W 72nd St	212-769-1552
Irgens, O Christian/192-10 69th Ave #B	718-454-3157
Irish, Len/11 W 17th St	212-242-2237
Irwin, William/70 Remsen St #9B	718-237-2598
Isaacs, Norman/277 W 11th St	212-243-5547
Isgar, Scott/50 W 22nd St	212-675-1349
Ishimuro, Eisuke/130 W 25th St 10th Fl	212-255-9198
Ivany, Sandra/6 W 90th St #6	212-580-1501
Izu, Kenro/140 W 22nd St	212-254-1002

J Jackson, Martin/217 E 85th St #110 215-271-5149

Jacobs, Marty/34 E 23rd St 5th Fl	212-475-1160
Jacobs, Robert/116 Lexington Ave	212-683-3629
Jacobsen, Paul/150 Fifth Ave	212-243-4732
Jacobson, Alan/250 W 49th St #800	212-265-0170
Janeart Ltd/161 W 15th St #1C	212-691-9701
Jann, Gail/352 E 85th St	212-861-4335
Janoff, Dean/514 W 24th St	212-807-0816
Jawitz, Louis H/13 E 17th St #PH	212-929-0008
Jeffery, Richard/119 W 22nd St	212-255-2330
Jeffrey, Lance/30 E 21st St #4A	212-674-0595

Photographers
Continued

Please send us your additions and updates.

Jeffry, Alix/71 W 10th St	212-982-1835
Jem, Jason/164-52 84th Ave	718-658-2373
Jenkinson, Mark/142 Bleecker St Box 6	212-529-0488
Jensen, Peter M/22 E 31st St	212-689-5026
Jenssen, Buddy/34 E 29th St	212-686-0865
Joel, Seth Photography/440 Park Ave S	212-685-3179
JOERN, JAMES/125 FIFTH AVE (P 89)	**212-260-8025**
Johansky, Peter/27 W 20th St	212-242-7013
Jones, Chris/240 E 27th St	212-685-0679
Jones, Spencer/400 E 71st St	212-734-2798
Jones, Steve Photo/120 W 25th St #3E	212-929-3641
Joseph, Meryl/158 E 82nd St	212-861-5057
Jurado, Louis/170 Fifth Ave	212-242-7480

K

Kachaturian, Armen/330 Broome St	212-334-0986
Kahan, Eric/36 W 20th St 3rd Fl	212-243-9727
Kahn, R T/156 E 79th St	212-988-1423
Kahn, Steve/60 Thomas St	212-619-7932
Kalinsky, George/4 Pennsylvania Plaza	212-563-8095
Kamp, Eric/98-120 Queens Blvd	718-896-7780
Kamsler, Leonard/140 Seventh Ave	212-242-4678
Kan Photography/153 W 27th St #406	212-989-1083
Kana, Titus/876 Broadway	212-473-5550
Kanakis, Michael/144 W 27th St 10th Fl	212-807-8232
Kane, Art/568 Broadway	212-925-7334
Kane, Peter T/236 W 26th St #502	212-924-4968
Kane, Thomas/351 E 12th St #A	212-475-6383
Kaniklidis, James/1270 E 18th St	718-338-0931
Kaplan, Alan/7 E 20th St	212-982-9500
Kaplan, Barry/323 Park Ave S	212-254-8461
Kaplan, Peter B/7 E 20th St #4R	212-995-5000
Kaplan, Peter J/924 West End Ave	212-222-1193
Karales, James H/147 W 79th St	212-799-2483
Karia, Bhupendra/9 E 96th St #15B	212-860-5479
Kasoff, Brian/28 W 25th St	212-243-4880
Kassabian Photography/127 E 59th St	212-421-1950
Katchian, Sonia/47 Green St	212-966-9641
Katrina/286 Fifth Ave	212-279-2838
Katvan, Moshe/40 W 17th St	212-242-4895
Katz, Paul/381 Park Ave S	212-684-4395
Katzenstein, David/99 Commercial St	718-383-8528
Kaufman, Elliott/255 W 90th St	212-496-0860
Kaufman, Jeff/6353 Harring St	718-779-5753
Kaufman, Micky/144 W 27th St	212-255-1976
Kaufman, Ted/121 Madison Ave #4E	212-685-0349
Kawachi, Yutaka/33 W 17th St 2nd Fl	212-929-4825
Kaye, Nancy/77 Seventh Ave #7U	212-645-6463
Kayser, Alex/211 W Broadway	212-431-8518
Keaveny, Francis/260 Fifth Ave	212-481-9187
Keegan, Marcia/140 E 46th St	212-953-9023
Keller, Tom/440 E 78th St	212-472-3667
KELLEY, CHARLES W JR/649 SECOND AVE #6C-30 (P 90)	**212-686-3879**
Kelley, David/265 W 37th St	212-869-7896
Kellner, Jeff/16 Waverly Pl	212-475-3719
Kennedy, Donald J/521 W 23rd St 10th Fl	212-206-7740
Kent, Karen/29 John St	212-962-6793
Khornak, Lucille/425 E 58th St	212-593-0933
Kilkelly, James/30 W 73rd St #2B	212-496-2291
King, Bill/100 Fifth Ave	212-675-7575
Kingsford, Michael Studio/874 Broadway	212-475-0553
Kinmonth, Rob/85 E 10th St #5H	212-475-6370
Kirk, Barbara/447 E 65th St	212-734-3233
Kirk, Charles/333 Park Ave S	212-677-3770
Kirk, Malcolm/12 E 72nd St	212-744-3642
Kirk, Russell/31 W 21st St	212-206-1446
Kirkpatrick, Charla/348 E 92nd St	212-410-3496
Kiss, Bob/29 E 19th St	212-505-6650
Kitchen, Dennis/873 Broadway	212-674-7658
Kittle, Kit/511 E 20th St	212-673-0596
Klauss, Cheryl/463 Broome St	212-431-3569
Klein, Arthur/35-42 80th St	718-278-0457
Klein, Matthew/104 W 17th St	212-255-6400
Klein, Robert/215 W 90th St	212-580-0381
Kligge, Robert/578 Broadway	212-226-7113
Klonsky, Arthur/161 W 15th St	212-691-9701
KNOWLES, ROBERT M/2 FORDHAM HILL OVAL #9C (P 91)	**212-367-4430**
Kolansky, Palma/291 Church St	212-431-5858
Komar, Greg/30 Waterside Sq #18A	212-685-0275
Kopelow, Paul/135 Madison Ave 14th Fl	212-689-0685
Koppelman, Jozef/1717 Ave N	718-645-3548
Korsh, Ken/118 E	212-685-8864
Kosoff, Brian/28 W 25th St 6th Fl	212-243-4880
Koudis, Nick/40 E 23rd St 2nd Fl	212-475-2802
Kouirinis, Bill/381 Park Ave S #710	212-696-5674
Kozan, Dan/32 W 22nd St	212-691-2288
Kozlowski, Mark/39 W 28th St	212-684-7487
Kozyra, James/568 Broadway	212-431-1911
Kramer, Bill/33 W 17th St 4th Fl	212-242-7007
Kramer, Daniel/110 W 86th St	212-873-7777
Krasowitz, Mike/330 E 76th St #4W	212-861-4207
Krein, Jeffrey/119 W 23rd St #800	212-741-5207
Krementz, Jill/228 E 48th St	212-688-0480
Krieger, Harold/225 E 31st St	212-686-1690
Kristofik, Robert/334 E 90th St #2A	212-534-5541
Kroll, Eric/118 E 28th St #1005	212-684-2465
Kron, Dan/154 W 18th St	212-463-9333
Krongard, Steve/212-A E 26th St	212-689-5634
Krotki, Saul/170 West End Ave	212-724-4823
Krueger, Mike/300 E 95th St #6C	212-722-7638
Kuehn, Karen/49 Warren St	212-406-3005
Kugler, Dennis/43 Bond St	212-677-3826
Kuhn, Ann Spanos/1155 Broadway	212-685-1774
Kupinski, Steven/31 W 21st St	212-206-1446

L

LaMonica, Chuck/121 E 24th St	212-673-4848
Labar, Elizabeth/327 W 18th St	212-929-7463
Lachenauer, Paul/876 Broadway	212-529-7059
Langley, David/536 W 50th St	212-581-3930
Lanker, Brian/20 W 46th St	212-944-2853
Larrain, Gilles/95 Grand St	212-925-8494
Laszlo Studio/28 W 39th St	212-736-6690
Lategan, Barry/502 LaGuardia Pl	212-228-6850
Laurance, Bruce Studio/253 W 28th St	212-947-3451
Laure, Jason/8 W 13th St 11th Fl	212-691-7466
Laurence, Mary/PO Box 1763	212-903-4025
Lavine, Arthur/1361 Madison Ave	212-348-2642
Lawrence, Christopher/12 E 18th St	212-807-8028
Lax, Ken/239 Park Ave S	212-228-6191
Layman, Alex/6 W 18th St 6th Fl	212-989-5845
LeBaube, Guy/310 E 46th St	212-986-6981
LEDERMAN, ED/166 E 34TH ST #12H (P 92,93)	**212-685-8612**
Leduc, Lyle/320 E 42nd St #1014	212-697-9216
Lee, Jung (Ms)/132 W 21st St 3rd Fl	212-807-8107
Lee, Vincent/155 Wooster St #3F	212-254-7888
Lee, Wellington/305 Broadway 7th Fl	718-760-2762
LEFKOWITZ, LESTER/370 LEXINGTON AVE #2010 (P 94-97)	**212-627-8088**
Legrand, Michel/152 W 25th St 12th Fl	212-807-9754
Lehman, Amy/210 E 75th St	212-535-7457
Leibovitz, Annie/101 W 18th St	212-807-0220
Leicmon, John/200 W 15th St	212-675-3219
Leighton, Thomas/321 E 43rd St	212-370-1835
Leiter, Saul/111 E 10th St	212-475-6034
Lenore, Dan/249 W 29th St #2N	212-967-7115
Leo, Donato/170 Fifth Ave	212-989-4200
Leonian, Phillip/220 E 23rd St	212-989-7670
Lerner, Richard/807 Ave of Americas	212-481-4135
Lesinski, Martin/49 Willow St #3H	718-624-8475
Let There Be Neon/PO Box 337/Canal St	212-226-4883
LEUNG, J MING/110 E 23RD ST (P 99)	**212-254-8570**
Levin, James/1570 First Ave #3D	212-734-0315
Levine, Jonathan/11 W 9th St	212-673-4698
Levine, Nancy/60 E 9th St	212-473-0015
Levinson, Ken/35 East 10th St	212-254-6180

Photographers

Continued
Please send us your additions and updates.

LEVY, FRANCK/305 E 40TH ST #5Y (P 100)	**212-557-8256**
Levy, Peter/119 W 22nd St	212-691-6600
Levy, Richard/5 W 19th St	212-243-4220
Lewin, Gideon/25 W 39th St	212-921-5558
Lewin, Ralph/156 W 74th St	212-580-0482
Lewis, Robert/333 Park Ave S 4th Fl	212-475-6564
Lewis, Ross/460 W 24th St	212-691-6878
Lieberman, Allen/5 Union Sq 4th Fl	212-243-2240
Liebman, Phil/315 Hudson	212-269-7777
Ligeti Inc/415 W 55th St	212-246-8949
Lindner, Steven/18 W 27th St 3rd Fl	212-683-1317
Lipton, Trina/60 E 8th St	212-533-3148
Lisi-Hoeltzell Ltd/156 Fifth Ave	212-255-0303
Little, Christopher/4 W 22nd St	212-691-1024
Lloyd, Harvey/310 E 23rd St	212-533-4498
Lobell, Richard/25-12 Union St	718-445-6864
Loete, Mark/33 Gold St #405	212-571-2235
Loew, Anthony/503 Broadway	212-226-1999
Logan, Kevin/119 W 23rd St #905	212-206-0539
Lombardi, Frederick/180 Pinehurst Ave	212-568-0740
Lombroso, Dorit/67 Vestry St #B	212-219-8722
Lomeo, Angelo/336 Central Park W	212-663-2122
Londener, Hank/18 W 38th St	212-354-0293
Londoner, Hank/18 W 38th St	212-354-0293
Lonsdale, William J/35 Orange St	718-788-6652
Loppacher, Peter/56 Jane St	212-929-1322
Lorenz, Albert/49 Floral Park	516-354-5530
Lorenz, Robert/80 Fourth Ave	212-505-8483
Love, Robin/676 Broadway 4th Fl	212-777-3113
Lubianitsky, Leonid/1013 Ave of Americas	212-391-0197
Lucka, Klaus/101 Fifth Ave 2nd Fl	212-255-2424
Luftig, Allan/873 Broadway	212-533-4113
Lulow, William/302 W 86th St	212-873-5380
Luria, Dick/5 E 16th St 4th Fl	212-929-7575
Lusk, Frank/25 E 37th St	212-679-1441
Lustica, Tee/156 Fifth Ave #920	212-255-0303
Luttenberg, Gene/20 W 22nd St	212-620-8112
Lypides, Chris/119 W 23rd St	212-741-1911

M

MacLaren, Mark/430 E 20th St	212-674-8615
MacWeeney, Alen Inc/171 First Ave	212-473-2500
Macedonia, Carmine/866 Ave of Americas	212-889-8520
Mack, Donald/69 W 55th St	212-246-6086
Mackiewicz, Jim/208 E 28th St	212-689-0766
Madere, John/75 Spring St 5th Fl	212-966-4136
Maisel, Jay/190 Bowery	212-431-5013
Malignon, Jacques/34 W 28th St	212-532-7727
Maloof, Karen/110 W 94th St #4C	212-678-7737
Mandarino, Tony/114 E 32nd St	212-686-2866
Mangeim, David S/339 Hart Ave	718-442-4095
Mangia, Tony/11 E 32nd St #3B	212-889-6340
Mani, Monsor/40 E 23rd St	212-947-9116
Manna, Lou/20 E 30th St	212-683-8689
Manno, John/20 W 22nd St #802	212-243-7353
Marchese, Carole/91 Bedford St	212-627-5562
Marchese, Jim/200 W 20th St	212-242-1087
Marco, Phil/104 Fifth Ave 4th Fl	212-929-8082
Marcus, Helen/120 E 75th St	212-879-6903
Marcusson, Eric E/85 Barrow St #2R	212-924-5437
Maresca, Frank/236 W 26th St	212-620-0955
Margerin, Bill/41 W 25th St	212-645-1532
Marshall, Alec/287 Ave C #8B	212-995-0153
Marshall, Elizabeth/200 Central Pk S #31A	212-463-7884
Marshall, Jim Studio/125 VAnderbilt Ave	718-855-2802
Marshall, Lee/201 W 89th St	212-799-9717
Martin, Bard/142 W 26th St	212-929-6712
Martin, Butch/244 Madison Ave #2F	212-370-4959
Martin, Dennis/11 W 25th St	212-929-2221
Martin, Gregg/169 Columbia Hts	718-522-3237
Martinez, Oscar/303 Park Ave S #408	212-673-0932
Marvullo Photomontage/141 W 28th St #502	212-564-6501
Marx, Richard/130 W 25th St	212-929-8880

Masca/109 W 26th St	212-929-4818
MASON, DONALD/101 W 18TH ST 4TH FL (P 56)	**212-675-3809**
Mass, Rita/119 W 23rd St 10th Fl	212-645-9120
Masser, Randy/953 President	718-622-8274
Massey, Philip/475 W 186th St	212-928-8210
Masters, Charles/308 E 59th St	212-308-7744
Masullo, Ralph/33 W 17th St 2nd Fl	212-929-4825
Masunaga, Ryuzo/57 W 19th St #2D	212-807-7012
Mathews, Barbara Lynn/16 Jane St	212-691-0823
Mathews, Bruce Photo/95 E 7th St	212-529-7909
Matsumoto/PO Box 242 Cooper Station	212-228-7192
Matsuo, Toshi/105 E 29th St	212-532-1320
Matthews, Cynthia/200 E 78th St	212-288-7349
Maucher, Arnold/154 W 18th St	212-206-1535
Maynard, Chris/297 Church St	212-255-8204
Mazzurco, Phil/150 Fifth Ave #319	212-823-5621
McCabe, David/39 W 67th St #1403	212-874-7480
McCabe, Robert/117 E 24th St	212-677-1910
McCarthy, Jo Anna/535 Greenwich St	212-255-5150
McCarthy, Margaret/31 E 31st St	212-696-5971
McCartney, Susan/902 Broadway #1608	212-533-0660
McCavera, Tom/450 W 31st St 9th Fl	212-714-9122
McConnell, Chester/31 W 21st St	212-255-8141
McCurdy, John Chang/156 Fifth Ave	212-243-6949
McDermott, Brian/48 W 21st St	212-675-7273
McFarland, Nancy & Lowell/128 E 28th St	212-691-2600
McGlenn, David/18-23 Astoria Blvd	718-626-9427
McGlynn, David/18-23 Astoria Blvd	718-626-9427
McGoon, James/317 E 18th St	212-473-7680
McGrath, Norman/164 W 79th St #16	212-799-6422
McKiernan, Scott/27 W 24th St 6th Fl	212-645-3784
McLaughlin, Glenn/5 W 19th St	212-645-7028
McLaughlin-Gill, Frances/454 W 46th St #3D-S	212-664-7637
McLoughlin, James Inc/148 W 24th St 5th Fl	212-206-8207
McMullen, Mark/304 Eighth Ave #3	212-243-6343
MCNALLY, BRIAN T/234 E 81ST ST #1A (P 101)	**212-744-1263**
McNally, Joe/305 W 98th St #6D S	212-219-1014
McNamara, David/32 Union Square E	212-529-3096
McQueen, Hamilton/373 Park Ave S	212-689-7367
McSpirit, Jerry/413 E 82nd St	212-879-2332
Mead, Chris/108 Reade St	212-619-5616
Megna, Richard/210 Forsyth St	212-473-5770
Meiselas, Susan/251 Park Ave S	212-475-7600
Melford, Michael/32 E 22nd St	212-473-3095
Melillo, Nick/118 W 27th St #3R	212-691-7612
Mella, Michael/217 Thompson St	212-777-6012
Mellon/69 Perry St	212-691-4166
Meltzer, Irwin & Assoc/50 W 17th St	212-807-7464
Meltzer, Lee/2271 W 1st St	718-998-2597
Memo Studio/39 W 67th St #1402	212-787-1658
Menashe, Abraham/306 E 5th St #27	212-254-2754
Menda, George/568 Broadway #403	212-431-7440
Menken, Howard Studios/119 W 22nd St	212-924-4240
Mensch, Barbara/274 Water St	212-349-8170
Meola, Eric/535 Greenwich St	212-255-5150
Merle, Michael G/5 Union Square West	212-741-3801
Mervar, Louis/29 W 38th St 16th Fl	212-354-8024
Messin, Larry/64 Carlyle Green	718-948-7209
Meyerowitz, Joel/151 W 19th St	212-242-0740
Michals, Duane/109 E 19th St	212-473-1563
Michelson, Eric T/101 Lexington Ave #4B	212-687-6190
Milbauer, Dennis/15 W 28th St	212-532-3702
Miles, Ian/313 E 61st St	212-688-1360
Miles, Peter/20 Ave D #11l	
Milisenda, John/424 56th St	718-439-4571
Miljakovich, Helen/114 Seventh Ave #3C	212-242-0646
Miller, Bert/30 Dongan Pl	212-567-7947
Miller, Bill Photo/36 E 20th St	212-674-8026
MILLER, DONALD L/295 CENTRAL PARK WEST (P 102,103)	**212-496-2830**
Miller, Eileen/28 W 38th St	212-944-1507
Miller, Myron/23 E 17th St	212-242-3780
Miller, Sue Ann/16 W 22nd St #406	212-645-5172

Photographers

Continued

Please send us your additions and updates.

Miller, Wayne F/251 Park Ave S	212-475-7600
Millsenda, John/424 56th St	718-439-4571
Ming Photo/1200 Broadway #2E	212-213-1166
Ming Studio/110 E 23rd St	212-254-8570
Minh Studio/200 Park Ave S #1507	212-477-0649
Minks, Marlin/34-43 82nd St	718-507-9513
Mistretta, Martin/220 W 19th St 11th Fl	212-675-1547
Mitchell, Andrew/220 Berkeley Pl	718-783-6727
Mitchell, Benn/119 W 23rd St	212-255-8686
Mitchell, Diane/175 W 73rd St	212-877-7624
Mitchell, Jack/356 E 74th St	212-737-8940
Molkenthin, Michael/31 W 31st St #6E	212-594-0144
Moon, Sarah/215 Park Ave S	212-213-0941
Moore, Carla/11 W 19th St	212-633-0300
Moore, Chris/20 W 22nd St #810	212-242-0553
Moore, Jimmy/38 E 19th St	212-674-7150
Moore, Truman/873 Broadway 4th Fl	212-533-3655
Moran, Nancy/568 Broadway	212-505-9620
Morello, Joe/40 W 28th St	212-684-2340
Moretz, Charles/141 Wooster St	212-714-1357
Morgan, Jeff/27 W 20th St #604	212-924-4000
Morris, Bill/34 E 29th St 6th Fl	212-685-7354
Morris, Leonard/200 Park Ave S #1410	212-473-8485
Morrison, Ted/286 Fifth Ave	212-279-2838
Morsch, Roy J/1200 Broadway #2B	212-679-5537
Morsillo, Les/17 Laight St	212-219-8009
Morton, Keith/39 W 29th St	212-889-6643
Moscati, Frank/5 E 16th St	212-255-3434
Moskowitz, Sonia/5 W 86th St #18B	212-877-6883
Mougin, Claude/227 W 17th St	212-691-7895
Mucchi, Fabio/5 W 20th St	212-620-0167
Mucci, Tina/568 Broadway	212-206-9402
Mullane, Fred/415 Madison Ave	212-580-4045
Muller, Rick/23 W 31st St	212-967-3177
Muller, Rudy/318 E 39th St	212-679-8124
Munro, Gordon/381 Park Ave S	212-889-1610
Munson, Russell/458 Broadway 5th Fl	212-226-8875
Muresan, Jon/56 W 22nd St 5th Fl	212-242-1227
Murray, Robert/149 Franklin St	212-226-6860
Murrow, Robert/226 W 47th St	212-302-2550
Myers, Robert J/407 E 69th St	212-249-8085
Myriad Communications Inc/208 W 30th St	212-564-4340

N

Naar, Jon/230 E 50th St	212-752-4625
Nadelson, Jay/116 Mercer St	212-226-4266
Nahoum, Ken/260 W Broadway #4G	212-219-0592
Naideau, Harold/233 W 26th St	212-691-2942
Nakamura, Tohru/112 Greene St	212-334-8011
Nakano, George/8 1/2 MacDougal Alley	212-228-9370
Namuth, Hans/20 W 22nd St	212-691-3220
Nanfra, Victor/222 E 46th St	212-687-8920
Nardi, Bob/568 Broadway	212-219-8298
Nardiello, Carl/143 W 20th St	212-242-3106
Nathan, Simon/275 W 96th St	212-873-5560
Nault, Corky/251 W 19th St	212-807-7310
Needham, Steven/6 W 18th St 10th Fl	212-206-1914
Neil, Joseph/150 Fifth Ave #319	212-691-1881
Neleman, Hans/348 W 14th St	212-645-5832
Nelken, Dan/43 W 27th St	212-532-7471
Nelson, Michael/7 E 17th St 5th Fl	212-924-2892
Nemeth Studio/220 E 23rd St #700	212-686-3272
Nesbit, Charles/160 Fifth Ave	212-807-1855
Neumann, Peter/30 E 20th St 5th Fl	212-420-9538
Newler, Michael/119 W 23rd St #409	212-242-2449
Newman, Arnold/39 W 67th St	212-877-4510
Newman, Marvin E/227 Central Park West	212-219-1228
Ney, Nancy/108 E 16th St 6th Fl	212-260-4300
Ng, Norman Kaimen/36 E 20th St	212-982-3230
Niccolini, Dianora/2 W 32nd St #200	212-564-4953
Nicholas, Peter/29 Bleecker St	212-529-5560
Nicholson, Nick/121 W 72nd St #2E	212-362-8418
Nicolaysen, Ron/448 W 37th St #12A	212-947-5167

Niederman, Mark/230 W 72nd St	212-362-3902
Niefield, Terry/12 W 27th St 13th Fl	212-686-8722
Nilsen, Geoffrey/463 Broome St	212-226-3260
NISNEVICH, LEV/133 MULBERRY ST (P 54)	**212-219-0535**
Nivelle, Serge/145 Hudson St 14th Fl	212-473-2802
Niwa-Ogrudek Ltd/17 W 17th St	212-982-7120
Nobart NY Inc/33 E 18th St	212-475-5522
Nons, Leonard/5 Union Sq West	212-741-3990
Noren, Catherine/15 Barrow St	212-627-7805
Norstein, Marshall/248 6th Ave	718-768-0786

O

O'Connor, Michael/216 E 29th St	212-679-0396
O'Connor, Thom/74 Fifth Ave	212-620-0723
O'Neill, Michael/134 Tenth Ave	212-807-8777
O'Reilly, Robert/311 E 50th St	212-832-8992
O'Rourke, J Barry/578 Broadway #707	212-226-7113
Obremski, George/1200 Broadway #2A	212-684-2933
Ochi, Toru/636 Sixth Ave #5A	212-807-7711
Oelbaum, Zeva/600 W 115th St #84L	212-864-7926
Ogilvy, Stephen/876 Broadway	212-505-9005
Ohara, Ken/Pier 62/12th Ave @23rd St	212-255-0798
Ohringer, Frederick/514 Broadway	212-737-6487
Okada, Tom/45 W 18th St	212-569-0726
Olds, H F/12 W 21st St	212-691-5614
Olivo, John/545 W 45th St	212-765-8812
Olman, Bradley/15 W 24th St	212-243-0649
Oppersdorff, Mathias/1220 Park Ave	212-860-4778
Orenstein, Ronn/511 W 33rd St 3rd Fl	212-967-6075
Oringer, Hal/568 Broadway #503	212-219-1588
Ort, Samuel/3323 Kings Hwy	718-377-1218
Ortner, Jon/64 W 87th St	212-873-1950
Osonitsch, Robert/112 Fourth Ave	212-533-1920
Otfinowski, Danuta/420 E 10th St	212-254-5799
Otsuki, Toshi/241 W 36th St	212-594-1939
Oudi/704 Broadway 2nd Fl	212-777-0847
Outerbridge, Graeme/PO Box 182	809-298-0888
Owens, Sigrid/221 E 31st St	212-686-5190
Ozgen, Nebil/37 E 18th St 3rd Fl	212-505-7770

P

Paccione/73 Fifth Ave	212-691-8674
Page, Lee/310 E 46th St	212-286-9159
Paglailunga, Albert/450 Clarkson Ave Box 18	718-271-2760
Pagliuso, Jean/315 Central Pk West	212-873-6594
Pagnano, Patrick/217 Thompson St	212-475-2566
PALMISANO, GIORGIO/309 MOTT ST (P 55)	**212-431-7719**
Palubniak, Jerry/144 W 27th St	212-645-2838
Palubniak, Nancy/144 W 27th St	212-645-2838
Papadopolous, Peter/78 Fifth Ave 9th Fl	212-675-8830
Pappas, Tony/110 W 31st St 3rd Fl	212-868-2032
Paras, Michael N/28-40 34th St	718-278-6768
Parks, Claudia/210 E 73rd St #1G	212-879-9841
Passmore, Nick/150 W 80th St	212-724-1401
Pastner, Robert L/166 E 63rd St	212-838-8335
Pateman, Michael/155 E 35th St	212-685-6584
Peacock, Christian/126 W 22nd St	212-645-9837
Pearson, Lee/126 Fifth Ave	212-691-0122
Peden, John/155 W 19th St 6th Fl	212-255-2674
Pederson/Erwin/76 Ninth Ave 16th Fl	212-929-9001
PELAEZ, JOSE L/568 BROADWAY #103 (P 104)	**212-925-2283**
Peliz, Jose/172 E 7th St #4C	212-995-2283
Peltz, Stuart/33 W 21st St	212-929-4600
Pemberton, John/377 Park Ave S	212-532-9285
Pendleton, Bruce/PO Box 1060	212-921-0599
Penn, Irving/89 Fifth Ave 11th Fl	212-880-8426
Penny, Donald Gordon/505 W 23rd St #PH	212-243-6453
Peress, Gilles/251 Park Ave S	212-475-7600
Perkell, Jeff/132 W 22nd St	212-645-1506
Perweiler, Gary/873 Broadway	212-254-7247
Peterson, Grant/568 Broadway #1003	212-475-2767
Peticolas, Kip/210 Forsyth St	212-473-5770
Petoe, Denes/22 W 27th St	212-213-3311
Pettinato, Anthony/42 Greene St	212-226-9380

Photographers

Continued

Please send us your additions and updates.

Pfeffer, Barbara/40 W 86th St	212-877-9913
Pfizenmaier, Edward/42 E 23rd	212-475-0910
Phillips, James/82 Greene St	212-219-1799
Phillips, Robert/101 W 57th St	212-757-5190
Photoquest International/175 Fifth Ave	212-986-1224
Pich, Tom/2870 Dudley Ave	212-863-1837
Piel, Denis/458 Broadway 9th Fl	212-925-8929
Pierce, Richard/241 W 36th St #8F	212-947-8241
Pilgreen, John/91 Fifth Ave #300	212-243-7516
Pilossof, Judd/142 W 26th St	212-989-8971
Pioppo, Peter/50 W 17th St	212-243-0661
Pipinou, Tom/568 Broadway	212-431-4518
Piscioneri, Joe/333 Park Ave S	212-533-7982
Pite, Jonathan/244 E 21st St	212-777-5484
Pittman, Dustin/45 W 18th St	212-243-2956
Pizzolorusso, Chris/381 Park Ave S	212-686-7175
PLIMPTON, RANDY/401 W 48TH ST #2W (P 105)	**212-603-9338**
Plotkin, Bruce/3 W 18th St 7th Fl	212-691-6185
Plotkin, Burt/141 Wooster St	212-260-5900
POBERESKIN, JOSEPH/51 WARREN ST (P 61)	**212-619-3711**
Pobiner, Ted/381 Park Ave S	212-679-5911
Polsky, Herb/1024 Sixth Ave	212-730-0508
Popper, Andrew J/330 First Ave	212-982-9713
Porta, Art/29 E 32nd St	212-685-1555
Portnoy, Neal/1 Hudson St	212-619-4661
Poster, James Studio/210 Fifth Ave #402	212-206-4065
Pottle, Jock/301 W 89th St #15	212-874-0216
Powell, Dean/32 Union Sq East	212-239-9760
Powers, Guy/534 W 43rd St	212-563-3177
Pozarik, Jim/43-19 168th St	718-539-7836
Pressman, Herb/137 E 30th St	212-683-5055
Prezant, Steve Studios/1181 Broadway 9th Fl	212-684-0822
Pribula, Barry/59 First Ave	212-777-7612
Price, Clayton J/205 W 19th St	212-929-7721
Price, David/4 E 78th St	212-794-9040
Priggen, Leslie/215 E 73rd St	212-772-2230
Prochnow, Bob/43-40 161st St	212-627-3244
Prozo, Marco/122 Duane St	212-766-4490
Pruitt, David/156 Fifth Ave	212-807-0767
Pruzan, Michael/1181 Broadway 8th Fl	212-686-5505
Puhlmann, Rico/156 Fifth Ave #1218	212-620-4211
Purvis, Charles/84 Thomas St #3	212-619-8028

QR

Quat, Dan/57 Leonard St	212-431-7780
Raab, Michael/831 Broadway	212-533-0030
Rajs, Jake/36 W 20th St 11th Fl	212-675-3666
Rapoport, David/55 Perry St #2D	212-691-5528
Rattner, Robert/106-15 Jamaica Ave	718-441-0826
Ratzkin, Lawrence/392 Fifth Ave	212-279-1314
RAY, BILL/350 CENTRAL PARK WEST (P 107)	**212-222-7680**
Raymond, Lelo/212 E 14th St	212-362-9546
Rea, Jimmy/151 W 19th St 10th Fl	212-627-1473
Reed, Robert/25-09 27th St	718-278-2455
Regan, Ken/6 W 20th St	212-989-2004
Regen, David/227 E 11th St #3D	212-533-5183
Reichert, Robert/149 W 12th St	212-645-9515
Reinhardt, Mike/881 Seventh Ave #405	212-541-4787
Reinmiller, Mary Ann/163 W 17th St	212-243-4302
Rentmeester, Co/4479 Douglas Ave	212-757-4796
Reznicki, Jack/568 Broadway #704	212-925-0771
Rezny, Aaron/119 W 23rd St	212-691-1894
Rezny, Abe/28 Cadman Plz W/Eagle Wrhse	212-226-7747
Rhodes, Arthur/325 E 64th St	212-249-3974
Ricucci, Vincent/59 W 19th St	212-691-5860
Riddell, Richard/208 E 82nd St #23	212-628-9370
Riddle, Richard/208 E 82nd St #23	212-628-9370
Ries, Henry/204 E 35th St	212-689-3794
Ries, Stan/48 Great Jones St	212-533-1852
Riggs, Cole/39 W 29th St	212-481-6119
Riggs, Robert/502 Laguardia Pl	212-254-7352
Riley, David-Carin/152 W 25th St	212-741-3662
RILEY, JON/12 E 37TH ST (P 108,109)	**212-532-8326**

Rivelli, William/303 Park Ave S #508	212-254-0990
Rivera, Al/139 W 14th St	212-691-3930
Roberts, Grant/120 Eleventh Ave	212-620-7921
Roberts, John/433 W 21st St #5A	212-645-4439
Roberts, Stefan K/155 E 47th St	212-688-9798
Robins, Lawrence/50 W 17th St	212-206-0436
Robinson, CeOtis/4-6 W 101st St #49A	212-663-1231
Robinson, James/1255 Fifth Ave #3G	212-580-1793
Robison, Chuck/21 Stuyvesant Oval	212-777-4894
Rockfield, Bert/31 E 32nd St	212-689-3900
Rodin, Christine/38 Morton St	212-242-3260
Rohr, Robert/325 E 10th St #5W	212-674-1519
Rolo Photo/214 W 17th St	212-691-8355
Romanelli, Marc/244 Riverside Dr	212-865-5214
Rose, Uli/234 W 21st St #33	212-988-8890
Rosen, David/238 E 24th St	212-684-5193
Rosenberg, Ken/514 West End Ave	212-362-3149
Rosenthal, Barry/205 W 19th St	212-645-0433
Rosenthal, Marshall M/231 W 18th St	212-807-1247
Ross, Ken/80 Madison Ave 7th Fl	212-213-9205
Ross, Mark/345 E 80th St	212-744-7258
Ross, Steve/10 Montgomery Pl	718-783-6451
Rossi, Emanuel/78-29 68th Rd	718-894-6163
Rossum, Cheryl/310 E 75th St	212-628-3173
Roth, Peter/8 W 19th St	212-662-3765
Roth, Seth/137 W 25th St	212-620-7050
Rothaus, Ede/34 Morton St	212-989-8277
Roto Ad Print Studio/252 W 37th St	212-279-6590
Rozsa, Nick/325 E 64th St	212-734-5629
Rubenstein, Raeanne/8 Thomas St	212-964-8426
Rubin, Al/250 Mercer St #1501	212-674-4535
Rubin, Daniel/126 W 22nd St 6th Fl	212-989-2400
Rubinstein, Eva/145 W 27th St	212-243-4115
Rudnick, James/799 Union St	718-783-4156
Rudolph, Nancy/35 W 11th St	212-989-0392
Rugen-Kory/150 E 18th St	212-777-3889
Ruggeri, Francesco/71 St Marks Pl #9	212-505-8477
Russell, Ted/67-25 Clyde St	718-263-3725
Russell, Tom/636 Ave of Americas	212-989-9755
Ryan, Will/16 E 17th St 2nd Fl	212-242-6270
Rysinski, Edward/636 Ave of Americas	212-807-7301
Ryuzo/57 W 19th St	212-807-7012

S

Sabal, David/20 W 20th St #501	212-242-8464
Sacco, Vittorio/126 Fifth Ave #602	212-929-9225
SACHA, BOB/370 CENTRAL PARK W (P 110)	**212-749-4128**
Sahaida, Michael/5 W 19th St 5th Fl	212-924-4545
Sailors, David/123 Prince St	212-505-9654
Sakas, Peter/400 Lafayette St	212-254-6096
Salaff, Fred/322 W 57th St	212-246-3699
Salaverry, Philip/133 W 22nd St	212-807-0896
Salvati, Jerry/206 E 26th St	212-696-0454
Salzano, Jim/29 W 15th St	212-242-4820
Samardge, Nick/568 Broadway #706	212-226-6770
Sanchez, Alfredo/14-23 30th Dr	718-726-0182
Sanders, Chris/295 Park Ave S	212-529-5005
Sandone, A J/132 W 21st St 9th Fl	212-807-6472
Sanford, Tobey/888 Eighth Ave #166	212-245-2736
Sarapochiello, Jerry/47-A Beach St	212-219-8545
Sartor, Vittorio/10 Bleecker St	212-674-2994
Sasson, Bob/352 W 15th St	212-675-0973
Sato Photo/152 W 26th St	212-741-0688
Satterwhite, Al/80 Varick St	212-219-0808
Satterwhite, Steve/13 Avenue A	212-254-8844
Savides, Harris/1425 Third Ave	212-772-8745
Saylor, H Durston/219 W 16th St #4B	212-620-7122
Scarlett, Nora/37 W 20th St	212-741-2620
Scavullo, Francesco/212 E 63rd St	212-838-2450
Schecter, Lee/13-17 Laight St 3rd Fl	212-431-0088
Scheer, Stephen/261 Broadway #10E	212-233-7195
Schein, Barry/118-60 Metropolitan Ave	718-849-7808
Schenk, Fred/112 Fourth Ave	212-677-1250

Photographers
Continued

Please send us your additions and updates.

Schiavone, Carmen/271 Central Park West	212-496-6016
Schillaci, Michael/320 W 30th St #3A	212-564-2364
Schillaci/Jones Photo/400 E 71st St #14-O	212-734-2798
Schiller, Leif/244 Fifth Ave	212-532-7272
Schinz, Marina/222 Central Park S	212-246-0457
Schlachter, Trudy/160 Fifth Ave	212-741-3128
Schneider, Josef/119 W 57th St	212-265-1223
Schneider, Peter/902 Broadway	212-982-9040
Schneider, Roy/59 W 19th St	212-691-9588
Schreck, Bruno/873 Broadway #304	212-254-3078
Schulze, Fred/38 W 21st St	212-242-0930
Schupf, John/568 Broadway #106	212-226-2250
Schurink, Yonah (Ms)/666 West End Ave	212-362-2860
Schuster, Sharon/320 W 90th St	212-734-0927
Schwartz, Marvin/223 W 10th St	212-929-8916
Schwartz, Sing-Si/15 Gramercy Park S	212-228-4466
Schweitzer, Andrew/333 Park Ave S	212-473-2395
Schwerin, Ron/889 Broadway	212-228-0340
Sclight, Greg/146 W 29th St	212-736-2957
Scocozza, Victor/117 E 30th St	212-686-9440
Secunda, Sheldon/112 Fourth Ave	212-477-0241
Seesselberg, Charles/119 W 23rd St	212-807-8730
Seghers, Carroll/441 Park Ave S	212-679-4582
Seidman, Barry/85 Fifth Ave	212-255-6666
Seitz, Sepp/530 W 25th St	212-255-5959
Selby, Richard/113 Greene St	212-431-1719
Seligman, Paul/163 W 17th St	212-242-5688
Selkirk, Neil/515 W 19th St	212-243-6778
Seltzer, Abe/443 W 18th St	212-807-0660
Seltzer, Kathleen/25 E 4th St	212-475-0314
Sewell, Jim/720 W 181st St	212-923-7686
Shaffer, Stan/2211 Broadway	212-807-7700
Shaman, Harvey/109 81st Ave	718-793-0434
Shapiro, Pam/11 W 30th St 2nd Fl	212-967-2363
SHARE, JED/TOKYO/63 ADRIAN AVE (P 111)	**212-562-8931**
Sharko, Greg/103-56 103rd St	718-738-9694
Sharratt, Paul/20 W 20th St #703	212-243-3281
Shelley, George/873 Braodway 8th Fl	212-473-0519
Sherman, Guy/108 E 16th St 6th Fl	212-675-4983
Shiki/119 W 23rd St #504	212-929-8847
Shipley, Christopher/18-23 Astoria Blvd	718-626-9427
Shiraishi, Carl/137 E 25th St 11th Fl	212-679-5628
Shung, Ken/236 W 27th St	212-807-1449
Silano, Bill/138 E 27th St	212-889-0505
Silbert, Layle/505 LaGuardia Pl	212-677-0947
Silver, Larry/236 W 26th St	212-807-9560
Simko, Robert/437 Washington St	212-431-6974
Simon, Peter Angelo/568 Broadway #701	212-925-0890
Simpson, Coreen/599 West End Ave	212-877-6210
Simpson, Jerry/28 W 27th St	212-696-9738
Singer, Michelle/251 W 19th St #5C	212-969-9522
Sint, Steven/45 W 17th St 5th Fl	212-463-8844
Sirdofsky, Arthur/112 W 31st St	212-279-7557
Skalski, Ken/866 Broadway	212-777-6207
Skelley, Ariel/80 Varick St #6A	212-226-4091
Skogsbergh, Ulf/5 E 16th St	212-255-7536
SKOLNIK, LEWIS/135 W 29TH ST (P 112)	**212-239-1455**
Skott, Michael/244 Fifth Ave #PH	212-686-4807
Slade, Chuck/12 E 14th St #4B	212-807-1153
Slavin, Fred/42 E 23rd St 7th Fl	212-505-1420
Slavin, Neal/62 Greene St	212-925-8167
Sleppin, Jeff/3 W 30th St	212-947-1433
Sloan-White, Barbara/372 Fifth Ave	212-760-0057
Small, John/156 Fifth Ave #834	212-645-4720
Smilow, Stanford/333 E 30th St/Box 248	212-685-9425
Smith, David L/420 Goldway	
Smith, Jeff/30 E 21st St	212-674-8383
Smith, Kevin/446 W 55th St	212-757-4812
Smith, Michael/140 Claremont #5A	212-724-2800
Smith, Rita/666 West End Ave #10N	212-580-4842
Smith, Robert Photo/421 Seventh Ave #1112	212-563-2535
Smith, Sean/365 First Ave	212-505-5688
Smith, William E/498 West End Ave	212-877-8456
Snedeker, Katherine/16 E 30th St	212-684-0788
Snider, Lee/221 W 82nd St #9D	212-873-6141
Snyder, Norman/514 Broadway #3H	212-219-0094
So Studio/34 E 23rd St	212-475-0090
Sobel, Jane/161 W 15th St #1C	212-691-9701
Sochurek, Howard/680 Fifth Ave	212-582-1860
Solomon, Chuck/622 Greenwich St	212-243-4036
Solomon, Paul/440 W 34th St #13E	212-760-1203
Solowinski, Ray/154 W 57th St #826	212-757-7940
Soluri, Michael/95 Horatio St #633	212-645-7999
Somekh, Rick/13 Laight St	212-219-1613
Soot, Olaf/419 Park Ave S	212-686-4565
Sorce, Wayne/20 Henry St #5G	718-237-0497
Sorensen, Chris/PO Box 1760	212-684-0551
Sotres, Craig/40 W 17th St #2B	212-627-4599
Spagnolo, David/144 Reade St	212-226-4392
Spahn, David/381 Park Ave S #915	212-689-6120
Spatz, Eugene/264 Sixth Ave	212-777-6793
SPECHT, DIANE/167 W 71ST ST #10 (P 113)	**212-877-8381**
Speier, Leonard/190 Riverside Dr	212-595-5480
Spielman, Les/5 W 30th St 4th Fl	212-947-3470
Spindel, David M/18 E 17th St	212-989-4984
Spinelli, Frank/12 W 21st St 12th Fl	212-243-7718
Spinelli, Paul/1619 Third Ave #21K	212-410-3320
Spinelli, Phil/12 W 21st St	212-243-7718
Spiro, Edward/82-01 Britten	718-424-7162
Spreitzer, Andy/225 E 24th St	212-685-9669
Springston, Dan/135 Madison Ave	212-689-0685
St John, Lynn/308 E 59th St	212-308-7744
Stahman, Robert/1200 Broadway #2D	212-679-1484
Standart, Joe/5 W 19th St 5th Fl	212-924-4545
Stanton, Brian/175 Fifth Ave #3086	212-678-7574
Stanton, William/160 W 95th St #9D	212-662-3571
Stark, Philip/245 W 29th St 15th Fl	212-868-5555
Steadler, Lance/154 W 27th St	212-243-0935
Stechow, Kirsten/249 W 29th St	
Steedman, Richard C/214 E 26th St	212-684-7878
Steele, Kim/640 Broadway #7W	212-777-7753
Steigman, Steve/5 E 19th St #303	212-473-3366
Stein, Larry/568 Broadway #706	212-219-9077
Steinbrenner, Karl/135 W 29th St 4th Fl	212-629-3148
Steiner, Charles/61 Second Ave	212-777-0813
Steiner, Christian/300 Central Park West	212-724-1990
Stember, John/154 W 57th St	212-757-0067
Stephanie Studios/277 W 10th St #2D	212-929-1029
Stern, Anna/261 Broadway #3C	212-349-1134
Stern, Bert/66 Crosby St	212-925-5909
Stern, Bob/12 W 27th St	212-889-0860
Stern, John/451 W Broadway	212-477-0656
Stern, Laszlo/57 W 19th St	212-691-7696
Sternfeld, Joel/353 E 77th St	212-517-3648
Stetson, David/240 W 15th St #28	212-496-0276
Stettner, Bill/118 E 25th St	212-460-8180
Stevens, D David/175 Fifth Ave #3216	212-677-2200
Stiles, James/413 W 14th St	212-627-1766
Stock, Dennis/251 Park Ave S	212-475-7600
Stone, Erika/327 E 82nd St	212-737-6435
Stratos, Jim/150 W 36th St	212-695-5674
Strode, Mark/2026 E 29th St	718-332-1241
Stroili, Elaine/416 E 85th St #3G	212-879-8587
Strongin, Jeanne/61 Irving Pl	212-473-3718
Stuart, John/80 Varick St #4B	212-966-6783
Stucker, Hal/295 Washington Ave #5D	718-789-1180
Stucky Photo/23-38 26th St	718-278-7226
Stupakoff, Otto/80 Varick St	212-334-8032
Sugarman, Lynn/40 W 22nd St	212-691-3245
Sun Photo/19 E 21st St	212-505-9585
Sussman, Daniel/369 Seventh Ave 3rd Fl	212-947-5546
Sussman, David/115 E 23rd St	212-254-9380
Svensson, Steen/52 Grove St	212-242-7272
Swedowsky, Ben/381 Park Ave S	212-684-1454

Photographers

Continued

Please send us your additions and updates.

Swick, Danille/276 First Ave	212-777-0653
Symons, Abner/27 E 21st St 10th Fl	212-777-6660
T Takeyama, Kimio/154 W 70th St	212-873-0908
TANNENBAUM, KEN/16 W 21ST ST (P 115)	**212-675-2345**
Tanous, Dorothy/652 Hudson St	212-255-9409
Tardio, Robert/19 W 21st St	212-463-9085
Taufic, William/166 W 22nd St	212-620-8143
Taylor, Curtise/29 E 22nd St #2S	212-473-6886
Taylor, Jonathan/5 W 20th St	212-741-2805
TCHEREVKOFF, MICHEL/873 BROADWAY (P 116,117)	**212-228-0540**
Teboul, Daniel/1 Astor Pl	212-473-7757
Tedesco, Frank/Union Sq W	212-629-4353
Tegni, Ricardo/100 E Mosholu Pkwy S #6F	212-367-8972
Terk, Neil/400 E 59th St	212-838-1213
Tervenski, Steve/421 E 54th St	212-753-6990
Tessler, Stefan/115 W 23rd St	212-924-9168
Testa, Michelle/POB 1961/Old Chelsea Sta	212-627-9413
The Strobe Studio/91 Fifth Ave	212-532-1977
Thomas, Mark/141 W 26th St 4th Fl	212-741-7252
Thompson, Eleanor/147 W 25th St	212-675-6773
Thompson, Kenneth/220 E 95th St	212-348-3530
Tillinghast, Paul/20 W 20th St 7th Fl	212-924-0575
Tillman, Denny/39 E 20th St	212-674-7160
Today's Photos Inc/17 E 28th St	212-686-0071
Togashi/36 W 20th St	212-929-2290
TORNBERG-COGHLAN ASSOC/6 E 39TH ST (P 58)	**212-685-7333**
Toto, Joe/148 W 24th St	212-620-0755
Trachman, Emanuel/63 Haven Esplanade	718-447-1393
Tran, Clifford/525 E 14th St #4C	212-777-5724
Truran, Bill/54 Green St	212-406-2440
Trzeciak, Erwin/145 E 16th St	212-254-4140
Tullis, Marcus/400 Lafayette St	212-460-9096
Tully, Roger/341 W 38th St 10th Fl	212-947-3961
Tung, Matthew/5 Union Sq West	212-741-0570
Turbeville, Deborah/160 Fifth Ave #907	212-924-6760
Turner, Pete Photography/154 W 57th St	212-765-1733
Turner, Sam/321 E 21st St #3E	212-777-8715
Tweedy-Holmes, Karen/180 Claremont Ave #51	212-866-2289
Tweel, Ron/241 W 36th St	212-563-3452
Tyler, Mark/233 Broadway #822	212-962-3690
UV Uher, John/529 W 42nd St	212-594-7377
Umans, Marty/29 E 19th St	212-995-0100
Unangst, Andrew/381 Park Ave S	212-889-4888
Ursillo, Catherine/1040 Park Ave	212-722-9297
Urwuand, Dan/250 W 40th St	212-921-2730
Vaeth, Peter/295 Madison Ave	212-685-4700
Valente, Jerry/193 Meserole Ave	718-389-0469
Valentin, Augusto/202 E 29th St 6th Fl	212-888-1371
Vallini Productions/43 E 20th St 2nd Fl	212-674-6581
Van Der Heyden, Frans/60-66 Crosby St	212-226-8302
Van Otteren, Juliet/7 E 14th St	212-627-1958
Vanglintenkamp, Rik/5 E 16th St 12th Fl	212-924-9210
Varnedoe, Sam/12 W 27th St #603	212-679-1230
Varon, Malcolm/125 Fifth Ave	212-473-5957
Vartoogian, Jack/262 W 107th St #6A	212-663-1341
Vega, Julio/417 Third Ave #3B	212-889-7568
Veldenzer, Alan/160 Bleecker St	212-420-8189
Vendikos, Tasso/59 W 19th St	212-206-6451
Vest, Michael/40 W 27th St 3rd Fl	212-532-8331
Vhandy Productions/225-A E 59th St	212-759-6150
Vickers, Camille/200 W 79th St PH #A	212-580-8649
Victor, Thomas/131 Fifth Ave	212-777-6004
Vidal, Bernard/853 Seventh Ave	212-586-6074
Vidol, John/37 W 26th St	212-889-0065
Viesti, Joe/PO Box 20424	212-734-4890
Villanueva, Bill/5 E 17th St	212-924-2500
Vine, David/873 Broadway 2nd Fl	212-505-8070
Vishniac, Roman/219 W 81st St	212-787-0997
Visual Impact Productions/15 W 18th St 10th Fl	212-243-8441
Vitale, Peter/157 E 71st St	212-249-8412

Vogel, Allen/348 W 14th St	212-675-7550
Volpi, Rene/121 Madison Ave #11-I	212-532-7367
Von Hassell, Agostino/277 W 10th St PH-D	212-242-7290
Vos, Gene/440 Park Ave S	212-714-1155
W Wadler, Lois/341 E 6th St	212-777-5638
Wagner Int'l Photos/216 E 45th St 14th Fl	212-661-6100
Wagner, Daniel/50 W 29th St	212-532-8255
Wagner, David/568 Broadway	212-925-5149
Wagoner, Robert/150 Fifth Ave	212-807-6050
Wahlund, Olof/7 E 17th St	212-929-9067
Waine, Michael/873 Broadway	212-533-4200
Waldo, Maje/PO Box 1156 Cooper Sta	212-255-3155
Waldron, William/463 Broome St	212-226-0356
Wallace, Randall/43 W 13th St #3F	212-242-2930
Wallach, Louis/594 Broadway #8W	212-925-9553
Walsh, Bob/401 E 34th St	212-684-3015
Waltzer, Bill/110 Greene St #96	212-925-1242
Waltzer, Carl/873 Broadway #412	212-475-8748
Walz, Barbra/143 W 20th St	212-242-7175
Wang, John Studio Inc/30 E 20th St	212-982-2765
Wang, Tony/118 E 28th St #908	212-213-4433
Warchol, Paul/133 Mulberry St	212-431-3461
Ward, Bob Studio/151 W 25th St	212-473-7584
Warsaw Photographic Assocs/36 E 31st St	212-725-1888
Watabe, Haruo/37 W 20th St #905	212-505-8800
Watanabe, Nana/130 W 25th St 10th Fl	212-741-3248
Watson, Albert M/80-82 Greene St	212-925-8552
Watson, Michael/133 W 19th St	212-620-3125
Watt, Elizabeth/141 W 26th St	212-929-8504
Watts, Cliff/360 W 36th St	212-629-8116
Waxman, Dani/242 E 19th St	212-481-3579
Weaks, Dan/5 E 19th St	212-473-3366
Webb, Alex/251 Park Ave S	212-475-7600
Weber, Bruce/135 Watts St	212-685-5025
Weckler, Chad/210 E 63rd St	212-355-1135
Weidlein, Peter/122 W 26th St	212-989-5498
Weinberg, Carol/40 W 17th St	212-206-8200
Weinberg, Michael/5 E 16th St	212-691-1000
Weinberg, Steve/47 E 19th St 3rd Fl	212-254-9571
Weinstein, Todd/47 Irving Pl	212-254-7526
Weiss, Michael Photo/10 W 18th St 2nd Fl	212-929-4073
Werner, Perry/PO Box 3992	212-379-7434
West, Bonnie/156 Fifth Ave #1232	212-929-3338
WESTHEIMER, BILL/167 SPRING ST (P 59)	**212-431-6360**
Wettenstein, Raphael/165 Madison Ave	212-679-5555
Wexler, Mark/400 W 43rd St	212-564-7733
Wheatman, Truckin/251 W 30th St #4FW	212-239-1081
White, Bill/34 W 17th St	212-243-1780
White, Joel/36 W 20th St	212-620-3085
White, John/11 W 20th St 6th Fl	212-691-1133
White, Timothy/430 W 14th St #502	212-206-7377
Whitehurst, William/32 W 20th St	212-206-8825
Whitely Presentations/60 E 42nd St #419	212-490-3111
Whitman, Robert/1181 Broadway 7th Fl	212-213-6611
Whyte, Douglas/519 Broadway	212-431-1667
Wick, Walter/560 Broadway #404	212-966-8770
Wien, Jeffrey/160 Fifth Ave #912	212-243-7028
Wier, John Arthur/38 E 19th St 8th Fl	212-477-5107
WIER, TERRY/38 E 19TH ST 8TH FL (P 50,51)	**212-685-6021**
Wiesehahn, Charles/249 W 29th St #2E	212-563-6612
Wilcox, Shorty/DPI/19 W 21st St #901	212-246-6367
Wilkes, Stephen/48 E 13th St	212-475-4010
Wilks, Harry/234 W 21st St	212-929-4772
Williamson, Richie/514 W 24th St	212-807-0816
Wills, Bret/245 W 29th St	212-629-4878
Wilson, Mike/441 Park Ave S	212-683-3557
Wing, Peter/56-08 138th St	718-762-3617
Winstead, Jimmy/76 Charles St	212-929-2810
Wohl, Marty/40 E 21st St 6th Fl	212-460-9269
Wolf, Bernard/214 E 87th St	212-427-0220
Wolf, Bruce/123 W 28th St	212-695-8042

Photographers

Continued

Please send us your additions and updates.

Wolf, Henry/58 W 15th St 6th Fl	212-741-2539
Wolff, Brian R/131 E 23rd St #7B	212-475-7801
Wolfson Photography/156 Fifth Ave #327	212-924-1510
Wolfson, Steve and Jeff/13-17 Laight St 5th Fl	212-226-0077
Wong, Daniel Photography/652 Broadway #3	212-260-7058
Wong, Leslie/303 W 78th St	212-595-0434
Wood, Merrell/319 W 38th St/Twnhse	212-868-0262
Wood, Susan/641 Fifth Ave	212-371-0679
Woodward, Herbert/555 Third Ave	212-685-4385
Workman, Wendy/203 7th Ave	718-965-0257
Wormser, Richard L/800 Riverside Dr	212-928-0056
Wyman, Ron/36 Riverside Dr	212-799-8281
Wynn, Dan/170 E 73rd St	212-535-1551

YZ
Yalter, Memo/14-15 162nd St	718-767-3330
Yamashiro, Tad/224 E 12th St	212-473-7177
Yee, Tom/141 W 28th St	212-947-5400
YOAV/4523 BROADWAY (P 118)	**212-942-8185**
Yoshitomo Photography/119 Fifth Ave #305	212-505-8800
Young, Donald/166 E 61st St Box 148	212-593-0010
Young, James/56 W 22nd St	212-924-5444
Young, Rick/27 W 20th St #1003	212-929-5701
Young, Steve/164 W 25th St 11th Fl	212-691-5860
Youngblood, Lee/200 W 70th St #8F	212-595-7913
Zager, Howard/450 W 31st St	212-239-8082
Zakarian, Aram/25 E 20th St	212-679-6203
Zamdmer, Mona/71 E 7th St	212-982-7318
Zan/108 E 16th St 6th Fl	212-260-0271
Zander, George/141 W 28th St	212-971-0874
Zander, Peter/312 E 90th St #4A	212-348-2647
Zanetti, Gerry/36 E 20th St	212-473-4999
Zapp, Carl/873 Broadway	212-505-0510
Zappa, Tony/28 E 29th St	212-532-3476
Zegre, Francois/124 E 27th St	212-684-6517
Zehnder, Bruno/PO Box 5996	212-840-1234
Zenreich, Alan/78 Fifth Ave 3rd Fl	212-807-1551
Zeray, Peter/113 E 12th St	212-674-0332
Zimmerman, David/119 W 23rd St #909	212-243-2718
Zimmerman, Marilyn/119 W 23rd St #909	212-243-2718
Zingler, Joseph/18 Desbrosses St	212-226-3867
Zitz, Peter/6126 Firestone Rd	212-543-7896
Zoiner, John/12 W 44th St	212-972-0357
Zwiebel, Michael/42 E 23rd St	212-477-5629

Northeast

A
Aaron, Peter/222 Valley Pl, Mamaroneck, NY	914-698-4060
Abarno, Richard/11 Dean Ave, Newport, RI	401-846-5820
Abbott, Jim/303 N 3rd St, Philadelphia, PA	215-925-9706
ABDELNOUR, DOUG/RT 22 PO BOX 64, BEDFORD VILLAGE, NY (P 62)	**914-234-3123**
Abell, Ted/51 Russell Rd, Bethany, CT	203-777-1988
Abend, Jay/511 East 5th St, Boston, MA	617-268-3334
Abrams, Larry/7 River St, Milford, CT	203-878-5090
Abramson, Dean/PO Box 610, Raymond, ME	207-655-7386
Accame, Deborah/5161 River Rd Bldg 2B, Bethesda, MD	301-652-1303
Adams Studio Inc/1523 22nd St NW Courtyard, Washington, DC	202-785-2188
Adamstein, Jerome/3720 39th St NW #E167, Washington, DC	202-362-9315
Addis, Kory/144 Lincoln St #4, Boston, MA	617-451-5142
Agelopas, Mike/2510 N Charles St, Baltimore, MD	301-235-2823
Ahrens, Gene/544 Mountain Ave, Berkeley Heights, NJ	201-464-4763
Aiello, Frank/35 S Van Brunt St, Englewood, NJ	201-894-5120
Akis, Emanuel/145 Lodi St, Hackensack, NJ	201-342-8070
Alexander, Jules/9 Belmont Ave, Rye, NY	914-967-8985
Allen, C J/89 Orchard St, Boston, MA	617-524-1925
Allopp, Jean Mitchell/16 Maple St, Shirley, MA	617-425-2296
Alonso, Manuel/425 Fairfield Ave, Stamford, CT	203-359-2838
Althus, Mike/5161 River Rd Bldg 2B, Bethesda, MD	301-652-1303
Altman, Steve/79 Grand St, Jersey City, NJ	201-434-0022
Ames, Thomas Jr/Skunk Hollow Rd/Box 66, Thetford Center, VT	603-448-6168
Ancker, Clint/3 Hunter Trl, Warren, NJ	201-356-4280
Ancona, George/Crickettown Rd, Stony Point, NY	914-786-3043
Anderson, Richard Photo/2523 N Calvert St, Baltimore, MD	301-889-0585
Anderson, Theodore/235 N Madison St, Allentown, PA	215-437-6468
Anderson-Bruce, Sally/19 Old Mill Rd, New Millford, CT	203-355-1525
Andersson, Monika L/11 Ranelegh Rd, Brighton, MA	617-787-5510
Andrews Studios/RD 3/Box 277, Pine Bush, NY	914-744-5361
Andris-Hendrickson Photo/314 N 13th #404, Philadelphia, PA	215-925-2630
Angier, Roswell/65 Pleasant St, Cambridge, MA	617-354-7784
Ankers Photo/316 F St NE, Washington, DC	202-543-2111
Ansin, Mikki/2 Ellery Square, Cambridge, MA	617-661-1640
Anthony, Greg/107 South St, Boston, MA	617-423-4983
Anyon, Benjamin/206 Spring Run Ln, Downington, PA	215-363-0744
Appleton, Hal/Kingston, Doug/44 Mechanic St PO Box 421, Newton, MA	617-969-5772
Arbor Studios/56 Arbor St, Hartford, CT	203-232-6543
Arce Studios/219 Henry St, Stanford, CT	203-323-1343
Areman, Scott/5708 Warburton Ave, Yonkers, NY	914-969-5814
Aristo, Donna/80 Wheeler Ave, Pleasantville, NY 10570	
Armstrong, Christine/916 N Charles, Baltimore, MD	301-727-8800
Armstrong, James/127 Mill St, Springfield, MA	413-734-7337
Arruda, Robert/144 Lincoln St, Boston, MA	617-482-1425
Asterisk Photo/2016 Walnut St, Philadelphia, PA	215-972-1543
Auerbach, Scott/32 Country Rd, Mamaroneck, NY	914-698-9073
Augenstein, Ron/509 Jenne Dr, Pittsburgh, PA	412-653-3583
Augustine, Paula/, , PA	215-455-4311
Austin, Miles/26 Sandra Cir, Westfield, NJ	201-232-1155
Avanti Studios/46 Waltham St, Boston, MA	617-574-9424
Avatar Studio/1 Grace Dr, Cohasset, MA	617-383-1099
Aviation Photo Service/65 Riverside Ave, Concord, MA	617-371-2079
Avics Inc/116 Washington Ave, Hawthorne, NJ	201-444-8118
Avid Productions Inc/10 Terhune Place, Hackensack, NJ	201-343-1060
Avis, Paul/310 Bedford, Manchester, NH	603-627-2659

B
B & H photo/1210 Race St Box 1319, Philadelphia, PA	215-425-0888
Baehr, Sarah/708 South Ave, New Canaan, CT	203-966-6317
Baer, Rhoda/3006 Military Rd NW, Washington, DC	202-364-8480
Bain, Christopher/239 Court St, Newtown, PA	215-968-0286
Baker, Bill Photo/1045 Pebble Hill Rd RD3, Doylestown, PA	215-348-9743
Baldwin, Steve/8 Eagle St, Rochester, NY	716-325-2907
Barber, Doug/1634 E Baltimore St, Baltimore, MD	301-276-1634
Bardes, Harold/1812 Kennedy Blvd, Union City, NJ	201-867-7808
Bareish Photo/3 Briarfield Dr, Great Neck, NY	516-487-2725
Barker, Robert/1255 University Ave, Rochester, NY	716-244-6334
Barlow, Curtis/PO Box 8863, Washington, DC	202-543-5506
Barlow, Len/392 Boylston, Boston, MA	617-266-4030
Barnes, Christopher/122 Winnisimmet St, Chelsea, MA	617-884-2745
Barocas, Melanie Eve/78 Hart Rd, Guilford, CT	203-457-0898
Baron, Greg/35 E Stewart Ave, Lansdowne, PA	215-626-8677
Barone, Christopher/381 Wright Ave, Kingston, PA	717-287-4680
Barrett, Bob/323 Springtown Rd, New Paltz, NY	914-255-1591
Barrow, Pat/10 Post Office Rd, Silver Spring, MD	301-588-3131
Bartlett, Linda/3316 Runnymede Pl NW, Washington, DC	202-362-4777
Basch, Richard/2627 Connecticut Ave NW, Washington, DC	202-232-3100
Baskin, Gerry/12 Union Park St, Boston, MA	617-482-3316
Bates, Carolyn/PO Box 215, Burlington, VT	802-862-5386
Bavendam, Fred/PO Box 276, Kittery, ME	207-439-0600
Bean, Jeremiah/96 North Ave, Garwood, NJ	201-789-2200
Beards, James/409 Pine St, Providence, RI	401-273-9055
Beardsley, John/322 Summer St 5th Fl, Boston, MA	617-482-0130
Beauchesne Photo/4 Bud Way/Vantage Pt III/#2, Nashua, NH	603-880-8686
Becker, Tim/266 Burnside Ave, E Hartford, CT	203-528-7818
BEDFORD PHOTO-GRAPHIC STUDIO/PO BOX 64 RT 22, BEDFORD, NY (P 62)	**914-234-3123**
Beigel, Daniel/2024 Chesapeake Road, Annapolis, MD	301-261-2494
Bell, Mike/411 Tomlinson Rd #C3, Philadelphia, PA	215-676-7393
Belmonte, William/43 Homestead Ave, Greenfield, MA	413-773-7744
Bender, Frank/2215 South St, Philadelphia, PA	215-985-4664
Benedetto, Angelo/825 S 7th St, Philadelphia, PA	215-627-1990
Benn, Nathan/925 1/2 F St NW, Washington, DC	202-638-5705
Bennett, William/128 W Northfield Rd, Livingston, NJ	201-992-7967

Photographers

Continued

Please send us your additions and updates.

Benson, Gary/PO Box 29, Peapack, NJ	201-234-2216
Benvenuti, Judi/12 N Oak Ct, Madison, NJ	201-377-5075
Berg, Hal/67 Hilary Circle, New Rochelle, NY	914-235-9356
Bergman, LV & Assoc/East Mountain Rd S, Cold Spring, NY	914-265-3656
Berinstein, Martin/215 A St 6th Fl, Cambridge, MA	617-268-4117
Bernsau, W Marc/PO Box 1152, Sanford, ME	207-324-1741
Bernstein, Daniel/7 Fuller St, Waltham, MA	617-894-0473
Berry, Michael/838 S Broad St, Trenton, NJ	609-396-2413
Bethoney, Herb/1222 Washington St, Boston, MA	617-749-1124
BEZUSHKO, BOB/1311 IRVING ST, PHILADELPHIA, PA (P 68)	**215-735-7771**
BEZUSHKO, GEORGE/1311 IRVING ST, PHILADELPHIA, PA (P 68)	**215-735-7771**
Bibikow, Walter/76 Batterymarch St, Boston, MA	617-451-3464
Biegun, Richard/56 Cherry Ave, West Sayville, NY	516-567-2645
Bilyk, I George/314 E Mt Airy Ave, Philadelphia, PA	215-242-5431
Bindas Studio/205 A St, Boston, MA	617-268-3050
Bingham, Jack/8 Abbot St, E Rochester, NH	603-742-7718
Binzen, Bill/Indian Mountain Rd, Lakeville, CT	203-435-2485
Birn, Roger/150 Chestnut St, Providence, RI	401-421-4825
Bishop, Jennifer/2732 St Paul St, Baltimore, MD	301-366-6662
Blake, Mike/107 South Street, Boston, MA	617-451-0660
Blakeslee Lane Studios/916 N Charles St, Baltimore, MD	301-727-8800
Blank, Bruce/228 Clearfield Ave, Norristown, PA	215-539-6166
Blevins, Burgess/601 N Eutaw St #713, Baltimore, MD	301-685-0740
Bliss, Brad/42 Audubon St, Rochester, NY	716-461-9794
Bloomberg, Robert/172 Kohanza St, Danbury, CT	203-794-1764
Bloomenfeld, Richard/200-19 E 2nd St, Huntington Sta, NY	516-424-9492
Blouin, Craig/14 Main St, Rollinsford, NH	603-742-0104
Boehm, J Kenneth/96 Portland Ave, Georgetown, CT	203-544-8524
Bognovitz, Murray/4980 Wyaconda Rd, Rockville, MD	301-984-7771
Bohm, Linda/7 Park St, Montclair, NJ	201-746-3434
Boisvert, Paul/305 South Beach Rd, S Burlington, VT	802-862-7249
BOLSTER, MARK/1235 MONTEREY ST, PITTSBURGH, PA (P 124,125)	**412-231-3757**
Bolton, Bea/186 Lincoln, Boston, MA	617-423-2050
Bookbinder, Sigmund/Box 833, Southbury, CT	203-264-5137
Borg, Erik/Drew Lane, Middlebury, VT	802-388-6302
Borkoski, Matthew/1506 Noyes Dr, Silver Spring, MD	301-589-4858
Bossart, Bob/PO Box 734/Cathedral St, Boston, MA	617-423-2323
Boston Candle Power Systems/186 Lincoln St 1st Fl, Boston, MA	617-536-2277
Bowden, John/528 F Street Terrace SE, Washington, DC	202-543-5151
Bowen, Dave/RD #5 Box 176, Wellsboro, PA	717-326-1212
Bowman, Jo/1102 Manning St, Philadelphia, PA	215-625-0200
Bowman, Ron/PO Box 4071, Lancaster, PA	717-898-7716
Boxer, Jeff Photography/14 Newbury St, Boston, MA	617-266-7755
Boyer, Beverly/17 Llanfair Rd, Ardmore, PA	215-649-0657
Bradley, Dave/840 Summer St, Boston, MA	617-268-6644
Bradley, Roy/760 State St, Schenectady, NY	518-377-9457
Brady, Joseph/Rt 179 RD2 Box 198, Ringoes, NJ	201-788-5550
Braverman, Ed/337 Summer St, Boston, MA	617-423-3373
Bravo, David/1649 Main St, Bridgeport, CT	203-384-8524
Bress, Pat/7324 Arrowood Rd, Bethesda, MD	301-469-6275
Brignolo, Joseph B/Oxford Springs Rd, Chester, NY	914-496-4453
Brittany Photo/217 N Wood Ave, Linden, NJ	201-925-0055
Broock, Howard/432 Sharr Ave, Elmira, NY	607-733-1420
Brown, Dorman/POB 0700/Coach Rd #8B, Quechee, VT	802-296-6902
Brown, Jim/, Marblehead, MA	617-631-2526
Brown, Martin/Cathance Lake, Grove Post Office, ME	207-454-7708
Brown, Skip/1720 21st St NW, Washington, DC	202-234-3187
Brown, Stephen R/1882 Columbia Rd NW, Washington, DC	202-667-1965
Brownell, David/PO Box 97, Hamilton, MA	617-468-4284
Brownell, William/1411 Saxon Ave, Bay Shore, NY	516-665-0081
Brt Photographic Illustrations/911 State St, Lancaster, PA	717-393-0918
Bruemmer, Fred/5170 Cumberland Ave, Montreal H4V 2N8, QU	514-482-5098
Brundage, Kip/66 Union St, Belfast, ME	207-338-5210
Bry, Kimberly/11 S Highland #3, W Hartford, CT	203-236-8118
Bubbenmoyer, Kevin/RD #2 Box 110, Orefield, PA	215-395-9167
Buchanan, Robert/466 Lakeview Ave, Valhalla, NY	914-592-1204
Buckman, Sheldon/15 Kiley Dr, Randolph, MA	617-986-4773
Buff, Cindy/55 Marina Bay Dr, Long Beach, NJ	201-870-3222
Bulkin, Susan/Photogphy Works/548 Fairway Terrace, Philadelphia, PA	215-483-8814
Buller, Frank/2505 Village Dr, Brewster, NY	914-278-9036
Bulvony, Matt/1003 E Carson St, Pittsburgh, PA	412-431-5344
Burak, Jonathan/50 Woodward, Quincy, MA	617-770-3380
Burdick, Gary Photography/9 Parker Hill, Brookfield, CT	203-775-2894
Burger, Oded/670 South St, Waltham, MA	617-527-1024
Burke, John/31 Stanhope St, Boston, MA	617-536-4912
Burke, John & Judy/116 E Van Buren Ave, New Castle, DE	302-322-8760
Burns, George/3909 State St, Schenectady, NY	518-393-3633
Burris, Ken/PO Box 592, Shelburne, VT	802-985-3263
Buschner & Faust/450 W Metro Pk, Rochester, NY	716-475-1170
Butler, Herbert/200 Mamaroneck Ave, White Plains, NY	914-683-1767
Byron, Pete/40 King St, Morristown, NJ	201-538-7520

C

C L M Photo/272 Nassau Rd, Huntington, NY	516-423-8890
Caffee, Chris/216 Blvd of Allies, Pittsburg, PA	412-642-7734
Cafiero, James/410 Church Ln, New Brunswick, NJ	201-297-8979
Cali, Guy/Layton Rd, Clarics Summit, PA	717-587-1957
Callahan, Charles/54 Applecross Circle, Chalfont, PA	215-822-8258
Canner, Larry/413 S Ann St, Baltimore, MD	301-276-5747
Carbone, Fred/1041 Buttonwood St, Philadelphia, PA	215-236-2266
Carrier, John/601 Newbury St, Boston, MA	617-262-4440
Carrino, Nick/710 S Marshall St, Philadelphia, PA	215-925-3190
Carroll, Hanson/11 New Boston Rd, Norwich, VT	802-649-1094
Carruthers, Alan/3605 Jeanne-Mamce, Montreal H2X 2K4, QU	514-288-4333
Carstens, Don/1021 Cathedral St, Baltimore, MD	301-385-3049
Carter, J Pat/3000 Chestnut Ave #116, Baltimore, MD	301-256-2982
Carter, Philip/PO Box 479, Bedford Hills, NY	914-666-3090
Cassaday, Bruce/RD 1 Box 345 Lockwood Rd, Peekskill, NY	914-528-4343
Cataffo, Linda/PO Box 460, Palisades Park, NJ	201-694-5047
Catiero, Jeff/410 Church Ln, New Brunswick, NJ	201-297-8979
CAVANAUGH, JAMES/ON LOCATION/PO BOX 158, TONAWANDA, NY (P 123)	**716-633-1885**
Certo, Rosemarie/2519 Parrish St, Philadelphia, PA	215-789-0555
Chadman, Bob/595-603 Newbury St, Boston, MA	617-426-4926
Chalifour, Benoit/1030 St Alexandre #812, Montreal H2Z 1P3, QU	
Chandoha, Walter/RD 1 PO Box 287, Annandale, NJ	201-782-3666
Chapman, Peter/28 Randolph St, Boston, MA	617-357-5670
Chaput, Chuck/17 Stilling St, Boston, MA	617-542-8272
Chase, Thomas W/, , NH	603-875-2808
Chatwin, Jim/5459 Main St, Williamsville, NY	716-634-3436
Chauhan, Dilip/145 Ipswich St, Boston, MA	617-262-2359
Chawtsky, Ann/85 Andover Rd, Rockville Centre, NY	516-766-2417
Chiusano, Michael/39 Glidden St, Beverly, MA	617-927-7067
Choroszewski, Walter J/10 Mohave Path, Branchburg, NJ	201-526-2018
Ciaglia, Joseph/2036 Spruce St, Philadelphia, PA	215-985-1092
Ciuccoli, Stephen/575 Broad St #219, Bridgeport, CT	203-333-5228
Clark, Conley/9814 Rosensteel Ave, Silver Spring, MD	301-585-4739
Clark, Michael/PO Box 423, Stowe, VT	802-253-7927
Clayton-Hall, Gary/PO Box 38, Shelburne, VT	802-985-8380
Cleff, Bernie Studio/715 Pine St, Philadelphia, PA	215-922-4246
Clemens, Clint/346 Newbury St, Boston, MA	617-437-1309
Clemens, Peter/153 Sidney St, Oyster Bay, NY	516-922-1759
Clifford, Geoffrey C/Craggle Ridge, Reading, VT	802-484-5047
Clifford, Joan/33 Myrtle St, Quincy, MA	617-471-8310
Cohen, Daniel/744 Park Ave, Hoboken, NJ	201-659-0952
Cohen, Marc Assoc/23 Crestview Dr, Brookfield, CT	203-775-1102
Collette, Roger/PO Box 215, Woodsville, NH	603-226-1856
Collins & Collins/PO Box 10736, State College, PA	814-234-2916
Colucci, Joe/118 N 12th St, Prospect Park, NJ	201-881-7618
Comb, David/Boston, MA,	617-426-3644
Conaty, Jim/1 Winthrop Square, Boston, MA	617-482-0660
Conboy, John/1225 State St, Schenectady, NY	518-346-2346
Confer, Holt/2016 Franklin Pl, Wyomissing, PA	215-678-0131
Congalton, David/206 Washington St, Pembroke, MA	617-826-2788
Conner, Marian/456 Rockaway Rd #15, Dover, NJ	201-328-1823
Connor, Donna/PO Box 272/Fourth Ave, Sweetwater, NJ	609-965-3396
Contrino, Tom/22 Donaldson Ave, Rutherford, NJ	212-947-4450
Cooke, Doug/23 Pondview Ave #2, Jamaica Plian, MA	617-267-1754
Coolidge, Jeffrey/322 Summer St, Boston, MA	617-338-6869
Cooper, John F/One Bank Street, Summit, NJ	201-273-0368

Corcoran, John/310 Eighth St, New Cumberland, PA	717-774-0652
Cordingley, Ted/Way Rd, Gloucster, MA	617-283-2591
CORNELL, LINC/107 SOUTH ST #600, BOSTON, MA (P 126)	**617-423-1511**
Corsiglia, Betsy/32 Bolton St, Waltham, MA	617-899-8830
Cortesi, Wendy/3034 'P' St NW, Washington, DC	202-965-1204
Cosloy, Jeff/118 South St, Boston, MA	617-338-6824
Cough, George/8 Bryant Dr, Huntington, NY	516-673-9376
Coughlin, Suki/Main St, New London, NH	603-526-4645
Crabtree, Shirley Ann/1 Prospect St #2A, New Rochelle, NY	914-636-5494
Crane, Tom/113 Cumberland Pl, Bryn Mawr, PA	215-525-2444
Crawford, Carol/14 Fortune Dr Box 221, Billerica, MA	617-663-8662
Creative Image Photo/325 Valley Rd, West Orange, NJ	201-325-2352
Creative Images/122 Elmcroft Rd, Rochester, NY	716-482-8720
Croes, Larry/256 Charles St, Waltham, MA	617-625-7038
Crossley, Dorothy/Mittersill Rd, Franconia, NH	603-823-8177
Cullen, Betsy/125 Kingston St, Boston, MA	617-542-0965
Cunningham, Chris/9 East St, Boston, MA	617-542-4640
Curtis, Bruce/70 Belmont Dr, Roslyn Heights, NY	516-484-2570
Curtis, Jackie/Alewives Rd, Norwalk, CT	203-866-9198
Curtis, John/50 Melcher St, Boston, MA	617-451-9117
Cushner, Susie/354 Congress St, Boston, MA	617-542-4070
Czamanske, Marty/61 Commercial St, Rochester, NY	716-546-1434

D
D'Angelo, Andy/620 Centre Ave, Reading, PA	215-376-1100
Dai, Ping/383 Beacon St, Boston, MA	617-353-0657
Daigle, James/107 South St #403, Boston, MA	617-482-0939
Dannenberg, Mitchell/261 Averill Ave, Rochester, NY	716-473-6720
Dapkiewicz, Steve/121 Beach St, Boston, MA	617-357-6809
Davidson, Josiah Scenic Photography/PO Box 434, Jenkintown, PA	215-682-2153
Davis, Harold/299 Pavonia Ave, Jersey City, NJ	800-759-2583
Davis, Howard/19 E 21st St, Baltimore, MD	301-625-3838
Davis, Ken/Box 4447, Annapolis, MD	301-268-3870
Davis, Pat Photo/14620 Pinto Ln, Rockville, MD	301-279-8828
Davis, Rick/210 Carter Dr #9/Matlack Ind, West Chester, PA	215-436-6050
Day, Joel/PO Box 554, Lititz, PA	717-627-2778
De Lucia, Ralph/120 E Hartsdale Ave, Hartsdale, NY	914-472-2253
DeMichele, Bill/40 Broadway, Albany, NY	518-436-4927
DeVito, Mary/2528 Cedar Ave, Ronkonkoma, NY	516-981-4547
DEWAELE, JOHN/14 ALMY ST, LINCOLN, RI (P 127)	**401-726-0084**
Dean, Floyd M/2-B S Poplar St, Wilmington, DE	302-655-7193
Debren, Allen/355 Pearl St, Burlington, VT	802-864-5916
Degginger, Phil/189 Johnson Rd, Morris Plains, NJ	201-455-1733
Delano, Jon/6 Manor Ave, Cranford, NJ	201-276-4034
Delbert, Christian/19 Linell Circle, Billerica, MA	617-273-3138
Dempsey-Hart/241 A St, Boston, MA	617-338-6661
Denuto, Ellen/24 Mill St, Patterson, NJ	201-881-0614
Derenzis, Philip/PO Box 19, Wind Gap, PA	215-437-7832
Devenny, Joe/RFD 1/Box 147, Waldoboro, ME	207-549-7693
Deveraux, Joanne/123 Oxford St, Cambridge, MA	617-876-7618
DiBenedetto, Emilo/32 Touro Ave, Medford, MA	617-396-0550
DiGiacomo, Melchior/32 Norma Rd, Harrington Park, NJ	201-767-0870
DiMaggio, Joe/512 Adams St, Centerport, NY	516-271-6133
DiMarco, Salvatore C Jr/1002 Cobbs St, Drexel Hill, PA	215-789-3239
DiMarzo, Bob/109 Broad St, Boston, MA	617-720-1113
Dibble, Warren/, , VT	802-862-5386
Dickens, James/1255 University Ave, Rochester, NY	716-244-6334
Dickstein, Bob/101 Hillturn Lane, Roslyn Heights, NY	516-621-2413
Diebold, George/416 Bloomfield Ave, Montclair, NJ	201-744-5789
Dietz, Donald/PO Box 177, Dorchester, MA	617-265-3436
Dillon, George/210 South St, Boston, MA	617-482-6154
Distefano, Paul/387 Teaneck Rd, Ridgefield Pk, NJ	201-641-1784
Dittmar, Warren/217 Main St, Ossining, NY	914-762-6311
Dixon, Mel/PO Box 468, Ossining, NY	914-941-9336
Dodson, George/Schoolhouse Commons #103, Stevensville, MD	301-643-6202
Dolin, Penny Ann/190 Henry St, Stamford, CT	203-359-9932
Donovan, Bill/165 Grand Blvd, Scarsdale, NY	914-472-0938
Dorman, Terry/Coach Rd 8-B/Box 700, , VT	802-296-6902
Douglas Associates/3 Cove of Cork Ln, Annapolis, MD	301-266-5060
Douglass, James/5161 River Rd Bldg 2B, Bethesda, MD	301-652-1303
Dovi, Sal/2935 Dahlia St, Baldwin, NY	516-379-4273

Dow, Norman/52 Concord Ave, Cambridge, MA	617-492-1236
Dowling, John/521 Scott Ave, Syracuse, NY	315-446-8189
Dreyer, Peter H/916 Pleasant St, Norwood, MA	617-762-8550
Dunham, Tom/335 Gordon Rd, Robinsville, NJ	609-259-6042
Dunn, Jeffery/32 Pearl St, Cambridge, MA	617-864-2124
Dunn, Paul/29 Swallow St, S Boston, MA	617-542-9554
Dunn, Phoebe/20 Silvermine Rd, New Canaan, CT	203-966-9791
Dunoff, Rich/1313 Delmont Ave, Havertown, PA	215-627-3690
Dunwell, Steve/20 Winchester St, Boston, MA	617-423-4916
Dupont, Iris/7 Bowdoin Ave, Dorchester, MA	617-436-8474
Duran, Larry/2322 Glover Rd, Marcellus, NY	315-673-2502
Durrance, Dick/Dolphin Ledge, Rockport, ME	207-236-3990
Dwiggins, Gene/204 Westminster Mall, Providence, RI	401-421-6466
Dyekman, James E/14 Cherry Hill Circle, Ossining, NY	914-941-0821

E
Earle, John/PO Box 63, Cambridge, MA	617-628-1454
Eastern Light Photo/113 Arch St, Philadelphia, PA	215-238-0655
Edelman, Harry/2790 McCully Rd, Pittsburgh, PA	412-486-8822
Edmunds, Skip/25 E Huron, Buffalo, NY	716-842-2272
Edson, Franz Inc/26 Watch Way, Huntington, NY	516-692-4345
Edson, Steven/107 South St, Boston, MA	617-357-8032
Edwards, Robert/9302 Hilltop Ct, Laurel, MD	301-490-9659
Egan, Jim/Visualizations/220 W Exchange St, Providence, RI	401-521-7052
Ehrlich, George/PO Box 186, New Hampton, NY	914-355-1757
Eisenberg, Leonard J/85 Wallingford Rd, Brighton, MA	617-787-3366
Elder, Tommy/Chapelbrook & Ashfield Rds, Williamsburg, MA	413-628-3243
Elkins, Joel/8 Minkel Rd, Ossining, NY	914-627-4099
Ellis, Bob/15 Washington Ave, Emerson, NJ	212-874-5300
Elson, Paul/8200 Blvd East, North Bergen, NJ	201-662-2882
Emmott, Bob/700 S 10th St, Philadelphia, PA	215-925-2773
Epstein, Alan Photography/295 Silver St, Agawam, MA	413-789-3320
Epstein, Robert/3813 Ingoman NW, Washington, DC	301-320-3946
Esposito, Anthony Jr/48 Old Amity Rd, Bethany, CT	203-393-2231
Esto Photo/222 Valley Pl, Mamaroneck, NY	914-698-4060
Evans, John C/Benedum-Trees Bldg #1712, Pittsburgh, PA	412-281-3663
Evans, Michael/5520 33rd St NW, Washington, DC	202-362-4901
Everett Studios/22 Barker Ave, White Plains, NY	914-997-2200
Eyle, Nicolas Edward/304 Oak St, Syracuse, NY	315-422-6231

F
F-90 Inc/60 Sindle Ave, Little Falls, NJ	201-785-9090
Falkenstein, Roland/Strawberry St #4, Philadelphia, PA	215-592-7138
Faragan, George/1621 Wood St, Philadelphia, PA	215-928-0499
Farris, Mark/10606 Huntley Place, Silver Springs, MD	202-269-5963
Fatone, Bob/166 W Main St, Niantic, CT	203-739-2427
Fatta, C/25 Dry Dock Ave, Boston, MA	617-423-6638
FAULKNER, ROBERT I/52 COMSTOCK ST, NEW BRUNSWICK, NJ (P 76)	**201-828-6984**
Feehan, Stephen/86 Donaldson Ave, Rutherford, NJ	201-438-1514
Feil, Charles W III/7 Fox Court, Portland, ME	207-773-3754
Feiling, David/129 E Water St, Syracuse, NY	315-422-6215
Feingersh, Jon/18533 Split Rock Ln, Germantown, MD	301-428-9525
Felker, Richard/20 Melville St, Augusta, ME	207-623-2223
Fennell, Mary/57 Maple Ave, Hastings on Hudson, NY	914-478-3627
Feraulo, Richard/518 First Parish Rd, Scituate, MA	617-545-6654
Fernando Photo/2901 James St, Syracuse, NY	315-432-0065
Ferreira, Al/237 Naubuc Ave, East Hartford, CT	203-569-8812
Ferrino, Paul/PO Box 3641, Milford, CT	203-878-4785
Ficara Studios Ltd/68 Elmcroft Rd, Stamford, CT	203-327-4535
Filipe, Tony/239 A St, Boston, MA	617-542-8330
Findlay, Christine/Hwy 36 Airport Plaza, Hazlet, NJ	201-264-2211
Fine, Jerome/4594 Brookhill Dr N, Manlius, NY	315-682-7272
Fine, Ron/8600 Longacre Ct, Bethesda, MD	301-469-7960
Fink, Mark/119 W Crooked Hill Rd #104, Pearl River, NY	
Finlayson, Jim/PO Box 337, Locust Valley, NY	516-676-5816
Finnegan, Michael/PO Box 901, Plandome, NY	516-365-7942
Fischer, John/9 Shore View Rd, Port Washington, NY	516-883-3225
Fish, Dick/37 Fairfield Ave, Holyoke, MA	413-584-6500
Fisher, Al/601 Newbury St, Boston, MA	617-536-7126
Fisher, Patricia/2234 Cathedral Ave NW, Washington, DC	202-232-3781
Fiterman, Al/1415 Bayard St, Baltimore, MD	301-625-1265
Fitzgerald, Mark/87 Daly Rd, E Northport, NY	516-368-6972
Fitzhugh, Susan/3809 Beech Ave, Baltimore, MD	301-243-6112

Photographers

Continued

Please send us your additions and updates.

Five Thousand K/281 Summer St, Boston, MA	617-542-5995
Fland, Peter/20 Park St, Moravia, NY	315-497-3528
Flanigan, Jim/1325 N 5th St #F4, Philadelphia, PA	215-236-4448
Flowers, Morocco/520 Harrison Ave, Boston, MA	617-426-3692
FLYNN, BRYCE/17 CARMINE AVE, FOXBORO, MA	
(P 128,129)	**508-543-3020**
Fogliani, Tom/600 Thurnau Dr, River Vale, NJ	201-391-2245
Foley, Paul/791 Tremont, Boston, MA	617-266-9336
Folti, Arthur/8 W Mineola Ave, Valley Steam, NY	516-872-0941
Foote, James/22 Tomac Ave, Old Greenwich, CT	203-637-3228
Forbes, Fred/1 South King St, Gloucester City, NJ	609-456-1919
Forbes, Peter/916 N Charles St, Baltimore, MD	301-727-8800
Foster, Frank/323 Newbury St, Boston, MA	617-536-8267
Foster, Nicholas/143 Claremont Rd, Bernardsville, NJ	201-766-7526
Fox, Jon Gilbert/RR 1/Box 307G, Norwich, VT	802-649-2828
Fox, Peggy/701 Padonia Rd, Cockeysville, MD	301-252-0003
Fox, Seth/8 Roundtree Circle, Hockessin, DE	302-652-8644
Francois, Emmett W/208 Hillcrest Ave, Wycoff, NJ	201-652-5775
Frank, Richard/48 Woodside Ave, Westport, CT	203-227-0496
Frank-Adise, Gale/9012 Fairview Rd, Silver Spring, MD	301-585-7085
Fraser, Renee/1167 Massachusetts Ave, Arlington, MA	617-646-4296
Frederick, Leigh/3119 Lancaster Ave, Wilmington, DE	302-428-6109
Fredericks, Michael Jr/RD 2 Box 292, Ghent, NY	518-672-7616
Freer, Bonnie/265 S Mountain Rd, New City, NY	212-535-3666
Freeze Frame Studios/255 Leonia Ave, Bogota, NJ	201-343-1233
Freid, Joel Carl/812 Loxford Terr, Silver Spring, MD	301-681-7211
Freund, Bud/1425 Bedford St #9C, Stamford, CT	203-359-0147
Fries, Janet/4439 Ellicott St NW, Washington, DC	202-362-4443
Frog Hollow Studio/Box 897, Bryn Mawr, PA	215-353-9898
Furman, Michael/115 Arch St, Philadelphia, PA	215-925-4233
Furore, Don/49 Sugar Hollow Rd, Danbury, CT	203-792-9395

G

G/Q Studios/1217 Spring Garden St, Philadelphia, PA	215-236-7770
Gabrielsen, Ken/5 Hundley Ct, Stamford, CT	203-964-8254
Gale, Howard & Judy/712 Chestnut St, Philadelphia, PA	215-629-0506
Gale, John & Son/712 Chestnut St, Philadelphia, PA	215-629-0506
Galella, Ron/17 Glover Ave, Yonkers, NY	914-237-2988
Gallery, Bill/86 South St, Boston, MA	617-542-0499
Gallo, Peter/1238 Callowhill St, Philadelphia, PA	215-925-5230
Gannon, Barbara/7 Sleepy Hollow Rd, Essex Junction, VT	
Gans, Harriet/50 Church Lane, Scarsdale, NY	914-723-7017
Ganson, John/14 Lincoln Rd, Wayland, MA	617-358-2543
Garber, Ira/150 Chestnut St, Providence, RI	401-274-3723
Garcia, Richard/30 Kimberly Pl, Wayne, NJ	201-956-0885
Gardner, Charles/12 N 4th St, Reading, PA	215-376-8086
Garfield, Peter/3401 K St NW, Washington, DC	202-333-1379
Garrett-Stow, Liliane/18 Tuthill Point Rd, East Moriches, NY	516-878-8587
Gates, Ralph/364 Hartshorn Dr Box 233, Short Hills, NJ	201-379-4456
GEER, GARRY/183 ST PAUL ST, ROCHESTER, NY (P 79)	**716-232-2393**
GEORGE, FRED/737 CANAL ST/BLDG #35, STAMFORD, CT	
(P 80,81)	**203-348-7454**
George, Walter Jr/863 Mountain Ave, Berkeley Heights, NJ	201-464-2180
Geracj, Steve/125 Wilbur Place, Bohemia, NY	516-567-8777
Getgen, Linda/221 North St, Hingham, MA	617-749-7815
Giandomenico & Fiore/13 Fern Ave, Collingswood, NJ	609-854-2222
Giese, Al/RR 1/Box 302, Poundridge, NY	914-764-5512
Giglio, Harry/925 Penn Ave #305, Pittsburgh, PA	412-261-3338
Gillette, Guy/133 Mountaindale Rd, Yonkers, NY	914-779-4684
Gilligan Group/PO Box 29, Hackettstown, NJ	201-689-1343
Glasofer, David/176 Main St, Metuchen, NJ	201-549-1845
Glass, Mark/310 9th St, Hoboken, NJ	201-798-0219
Glass, Peter/15 E Oakwood St, East Hartford, CT	203-528-8559
Glazier, Brad/1811 Bryce Dr, Wilmington, DE	302-475-0495
Gluck, Mike/2 Bronxville Rd, Bronxville, NY	914-961-1677
Goell, Jonathan J/535 Albany St, Boston, MA	617-423-2057
Goembl, Ponder/617 S 10th St, Philadelphia, PA	215-928-1797
Gold, Gary D/One Madison Pl, Albany, NY	518-434-4887
Goldblatt, Steven/32 S Strawberry St, Philadelphia, PA	215-925-3825
Goldenberg, Barry/1 Baltimore Ave Box 412, Cranford, NJ	201-276-1510
Goldklang, Jay/778 New York Ave, Huntington, NY	516-421-3860
Goldman, Mel/329 Newbury St, Boston, MA	617-536-0539
Goldman, Rob/64 Division Ave, Levittown, NY	516-796-9327

Goldstein, Alan/10 Post Office Rd B-3, Silver Spring, MD	301-589-1690
Good, Richard/5226 Osage Ave, Philadelphia, PA	215-472-7659
Goodman, Howard/PO Box 433, Croton Falls, NY	914-277-3133
Goodman, John/337 Summer St, Boston, MA	617-482-8061
Goodman, John D/One Mill Street, Burlington, VT	802-864-0200
Goodman, Lou/322 Summer St, Boston, MA	617-542-8254
Gorchev & Gorchev/11 Cabot Rd, Woburn, MA	617-933-8090
Gordon, David A/1413 Hertel Ave, Buffalo, NY	716-833-2661
Gordon, Lee/354 Congress St 4th Fl, Boston, MA	617-267-3006
Gorrill, Robert B/PO Box 206, North Quincy, MA	617-328-4012
Gottheil, Philip/1278 Lednam Ct, Merrick, NY	516-378-6802
Gottlieb, Steve/3601 East-West Hwy, Chevy Chase, MD	301-951-9648
Graham, Jim/720 Chestnut St, Philadelphia, PA	215-592-7272
Grant, Gail/7006 Valley Ave, Phildelphia, PA	215-482-9857
Grant, Jarvis/1650 Harvard St NW #709, Washington, DC	202-387-8584
Graphic Accent/446 Main St PO Box 243, Wilmington, MA	617-658-7602
Gray, Sam/23 Westwood Rd, Wellesley, MA	617-237-2711
Graybeal, Sharon/PO Box 896, Hockessin, DE	302-998-4037
Grayson, Jay/9 Cockenoe Dr, Westport, CT	203-222-0072
Green, Elisabeth/54B Fore Rd, Elliot, ME	207-439-7594
Green, Jeremy/4128 Westview Rd, Baltimore, MD	301-366-0123
Greenberg, Andrew/313 N Albany Ave, Massapequa, NY	516-293-7835
Greenberg, Steven/28 Randolph St, Boston, MA	617-423-7646
Gregoire, Rogier/107 South St 2nd Fl, Boston, MA	617-574-9554
Greniers Commercial Photo/127 Mill St, Springfield, MA	413-532-9406
Griebsch, John/183 St Paul St, Rochester, NY	716-546-1303
Grohe, Stephen F/186 South St, Boston, MA	617-426-2290
Gross, Lance/PO Box 388, Manchester, CT	203-871-2641
Guarinello, Greg/252 Highwood St, Teaneck, NJ	201-836-2333
Gude, Susann/Slip 1-A/Spruce Dr, E Patchogue, NY	516-654-8093

H

Hagerman, Ron/385 Westminster St, Providence, RI	401-272-1117
Hahn, Bob/3522 Skyline Dr, Bethlehem, PA	215-868-0339
Halliwell, Harry/PO Box 1690 GMF, Boston, MA	617-623-7225
Halstead, Dirck/3332 P St NW, Washington, DC	202-338-2028
Hambourg, Serge/Box 753, Crugers, NY	212-866-0085
Hamor, Robert/2308 Columbia Cir, Merrimack, NH	603-424-6737
Handerhan, Jerome/JJH Photo/113 Edgewood Ave,	
Pittsburgh, PA	412-242-6308
Handler, Lowell/147 Main St, Coldspring, NY	914-265-4023
Hansen, Doug/402 S Patterson Park Ave, Baltimore, MD	301-522-6175
Hansen, Steve/1260 Boylston St, Boston, MA	617-236-2211
Hansen-Sturm, Robert/334 Wall St, Kingston, NY	914-338-8753
Hanstein, George/389 Belmont Ave, Haledon, NJ	201-790-0505
Haritan, Michael/1701 Eben St, Pittsburgh, PA	412-343-2112
Harkey, John/90 Larch Rd, Providence, RI	401-831-1023
Harkins, Kevin F/219 Appleton St, Lowell, MA	617-452-9704
Harrington, Blaine/374 Old Hawleyville Rd, Bethel, CT	203-798-2866
Harrington, John/455 Old Sleepy Hollow Rd, Pleasantville, NY	914-939-0702
Harrington, Phillip A/Wagner Ave/PO Box 10, Fleischmann's,	
NY	914-254-5227
HARRIS, BROWNIE/PO BOX 164, CROTON-ON-HUDSON,	
NY (P 87)	**914-271-6426**
Harrison, Jim/PO Box 266, Charleston, MA	617-242-4314
Harting, Christopher/327 Summer St, Boston, MA	617-451-6330
Harvey, Milicent/, Boston, MA	617-524-8093
Harvey, Scott/273 Speedwell, Morristown, NJ	201-538-9410
Hatos, Kathleen/3418 Keins St, Philadelphia, PA	215-425-3960
Hausner, Clifford/10 Wayne Rd, Fairlawn, NJ	201-791-7409
Hayes, Eric/Rural Route #1, Jrdn Fls B0T1J0, NS	902-875-4260
Hayman, James/100 Fourth Ave, North York, PA	717-843-8338
Haywood, Alan/39 Westmoreland Ave, White Plains, NY	914-946-1928
Heard, Gary/724 N Goodman St, Rochester, NY	716-271-6780
Heayn, Mark/17 W 24th St, Baltimore, MD	301-235-1608
Hecker, David/285 Aycrigg Ave, Passaic, NJ	201-471-2496
Heilman, Grant/PO Box 317, Lititz, PA	717-626-0296
Heinz, F Michael Photography/17 Rose Hill, Southport, CT	203-259-7456
Heist, Scott/616 Walnut St, Emmaus, PA	215-965-5479
Helmar, Dennis/134 Beach St, Boston, MA	617-451-1496
Herity, Jim/601 Riverside Ave, Westport, CT	203-454-3979
Herko, Robert/121 Hadley St, Piscataway, NJ	201-563-1613
Hermsdorf, Conrad/75 Nundlett Hill Rd, Bedford, NH	603-669-4999

Photographers
Continued

Please send us your additions and updates.

Herrera, Frank - Photoworks/318 Kentucky Ave SE, Washington, DC	301-229-7930
Herwig/36 Gloucester St, Boston, MA	617-353-1262
HEWITT, MALCOLM/179 MASSACHUSETTS AVE, BOSTON, MA (P 130)	**617-262-7227**
Higgins, James/281 Princeton St, N Chelmsford, MA	617-454-4248
Hill, Brian/PO Box 1823, Nantucket, MA	617-228-2210
Hill, John T/388 Amity Rd, New Haven, CT	203-393-0035
Hines, Harry/PO Box 10061, Newark, NJ	201-242-0214
Hirshfeld, Max/1027 33rd St NW, Washington, DC	202-333-7450
Hodges, Sue Anne/87 Gould Rd, Andover, MA	617-657-6417
Hoffman, Dave/PO Box 1299, Summit, NJ	201-277-6285
Holland, James R/104 Charles St, Boston, MA	617-321-3638
Hollander, David/11 S Springfield Ave/POB 443, Springfield, NJ	201-467-0870
Holmes, Greg/2007 Hickory Hill Ln, Silver Spring, MD	301-295-3338
Holniker, Barry/400 E 25th St, Baltimore, MD	301-889-1919
Holob, Ed/145 Comac St, Ronkohoma, NY	516-981-3100
Holoquist, Marcy/424 N Craig St, Pittsburgh, PA	412-963-8021
Holt, Chuck/535 Albany St, Boston, MA	617-338-4009
Holt, John/145 South St, Boston, MA	617-426-7262
Holt, Walter/PO Box 936, Media, PA	215-565-1977
Holz, Thomas Jay/PO Box 4, Tribes Hill, NY	518-842-7730
Hone, Stephen/859 N 28th St, Philadelphia, PA	215-765-6900
Hood, Sarah/Box #7A, Boston, MA	617-262-1355
Hopkins, Tom/15 Orchard Park, Box, Madison, CT	203-245-0824
Hornick/Rivlin/25 Dry Dock, Boston, MA	617-482-8614
Horowitz, Abby/922 Chestnut, Philadelphia, PA	215-925-3600
Hotshots/35 Congress St, Salem, MA	617-744-1557
Houck, Julie/535 Albany St, Boston, MA	617-338-4009
Houser, Robert/PO Box 299, Litchfield, CT	203-567-4241
Houser-Tartaglia Photoworks/23 Walnut Ave, Clark, NJ	201-388-8531
Howard, Jerry/12 Main St, Natick, MA	617-653-7610
Howard, Richard/144 Holworthy St, Cambridge, MA	617-628-5410
Hoyt, Russell/171 Westminister Ave, S Attleboro, MA	617-399-8611
Hoyt, Wolfgang/222 Valley Pl, Mamaroneck, NY	914-698-4060
Hubbell, William/99 East Elm St, Greenwich, CT	203-629-9629
Huber, William, Productions/481 Beacon St #14, Boston, MA	617-437-0797
Hukub, Ed/145 Comac St, Ronkonhoma, NY	516-981-3100
Hulbert, Steve/PO Box 350, Lemoyne, PA	717-731-8289
Hundertmark, Charles/6264 Oakland Mills Rd, Sykesville, MD	301-242-8150
Hungaski, Andrew/Merribrook Lane, Stamford, CT	203-327-6763
Hunsberger, Douglas/115 W Fern Rd, Wildwood Crest, NJ	609-522-6849
Hunt, Barbara/5161 River Rd Bldg 2B, Bethesda, MD	301-652-1303
Hunter, Allan/56 Main St 3rd Fl, Milburn, NJ	201-467-4920
Hurwitz, Joel/PO Box 1009, Leominster, MA	617-537-6476
Huss, W John/PO Box 399, Wethersfield, CT	203-728-0545
Hutchings, Richard/19 Jochum Ave, Larchmont, NY	914-834-9633
Hutchinson, Gardiner/280 Friend St, Boston, MA	617-523-5180
Huyler, Willard/218 South Ave E, Cranford, NJ	201-272-8874
Hyde, Dana/PO Box 1302, South Hampton, NY	516-283-1001
Hyon, Ty/65 Drumhill Rd, Wilton, CT	203-834-0870

IJ

Iacovelli, Richard/560 Harrison Ave, Boston, MA	617-451-0966
Iannazzi, Robert F/450 Smith Rd, Rochester, NY	716-624-1285
Ickow, Marvin/1824 35th St NW, Washington, DC	202-342-0250
Iglarsh, Gary/2229 N Charles St, Baltimore, MD	301-235-3385
Image Source Inc/PO Box 1929, Wilmington, DE	302-658-5897
Images Commercial Photography/360 Sylvan Ave, Englewood Cliffs, NJ	201-871-4406
Impact Multi Image Inc/117 W Washington, Pleasantville, NJ	609-484-8100
Iverson, Bruce/MA, 617-433-8429, Jackson, Cappy/914 Morris Ave, Lutherville, MD	301-252-9144
Jackson, Glenwood/3000 Chestnut Ave #10, Baltimore, MD	301-366-0049
Jackson, Martin/314 Catherine St #401, Philadelphia, PA	215-271-5149
Jackson, Reggie/135 Sheldon Terr, New Haven, CT	203-787-5191
Jagger, Warren/150 Chestnut St Box 3330, Providence, RI	401-351-7366
Jesudowich, Stanley/200 Henry St, Stamford, CT	203-359-8886
Joachim, Bruno/326 A Street, Boston, MA	617-451-6156
Joel, Yale/Woodybrook Ln, Croton-On-Hudson, NY	914-271-8172
Johnson, Paul/38 Athens St, Boston, MA	617-269-4043
Johnson, Stella/137 Langdon Ave, Watertown, MA	617-923-1263
Jones, Alexander/1243-A Maryland Ave NE, Washington, DC	202-398-8422
Jones, Lou/22 Randolph St, Boston, MA	617-426-6335
Jones, Peter/43 Charles St, Boston, MA	617-227-6400
Joseph, Nabil/445 St Pierre St #402, Montreal H2Y 2M8, QU	514-842-2444

K

Kaetzel, Gary/PO Box 3514, Wayne, NJ	201-696-6174
Kalfus, Lonny/226 Hillside Ave, Leonia, NJ	201-944-3909
Kalischer, Clemens/Main St, Stockbridge, MA	413-298-5500
Kalish, JoAnne/512 Adams St, Centerport, NY	516-271-6133
Kalisher, Simpson/North St, Roxbury, CT	203-354-8893
Kaminsky, Saul/36 Sherwood Ave, Greenwich, CT	203-531-4953
Kamper, George/62 North Union St, Rochester, NY	716-454-7006
Kan, Dennis/PO Box 248, Clarksburg, MD	301-428-9417
Kane, Alice/3380 Emeric Ave, Wantagh, NY	516-781-7049
Kane, John/POB 731, New Milford, CT	203-354-7651
Kane, Martin/, , DE	302-762-0946
Kannair, Jon/72 Cambridge St, Worcester, MA	617-757-3417
Kaplan, Carol/20 Beacon St, Boston, MA	617-720-4400
Kasper, Ken/1232 Cobbs St, Drexel Hill, PA	215-446-0108
Katz, Dan/36 Aspen Rd, W Orange, NJ	201-731-8956
Katz, Geoffrey/156 Francestown Rd, New Boston, NH	603-487-3819
KAUFFMAN, KENNETH/915 SPRING GARDEN ST, PHILADELPHIA, PA (P 131)	**215-649-4474**
Kaufman, Robert/58 Roundwood Rd, Newton Upper Falls, MA	617-964-4080
Kawalerski, Ted/7 Evergreen Way, North Tarrytown, NY	212-242-0198
Keene Studio/10510 Insley St, Silver Spring, MD	301-949-4722
Keller, Michael/15 S Grand Ave, Baldwin, NY	516-223-9604
Kelley, Edward/20 White St, Red Bank, NJ	201-747-0596
Kelly/Mooney Photography/87 Willow Ave, North Plainfield, NJ	201-757-5924
Kenik, David Photography/21 Countryside Dr, Nashua, NH	603-880-8108
Kerbs, Ken/458 Walker St, Fairview, NJ	201-945-9490
Kernan, Sean/576 Leetes Island Rd, Stony Creek, CT	203-481-4478
Kerper, David/1018 E Willow Grove Ave, Philadelphia, PA	215-836-1135
Kerson, Larry/539 Amity Rd, Woodbridge, CT	203-548-9805
Kim, Chang H/9425 Bethany Pl, Gaithersburg, MD	301-840-5741
King, Ralph/103 Broad St, Boston, MA	617-426-3565
Kinum, Drew/Glen Avenue, Scotia, NY	518-382-7566
Kirkman, Tom/58 Carley Ave, Huntington, NY	516-549-6705
Kittle, James Kent/49 Brinckerhoff Ln, New Canann, CT	203-966-2442
Klapatch, David/350 Silas Deane Hwy, Wethersfield, CT	203-563-3834
Kligman, Fred/4733 Elm St, Bethesda, MD	301-652-6333
Kline, Andrew/, Montpelier, VT	802-229-4924
Klinefelter, Eric/10963 Hickory Ridge Rd, Columbia, MD	301-964-0273
Knapp, Stephen/74 Commodore Rd, Worcester, MA	617-757-2507
Kobrin, Harold/PO Box 115, Newton, MA	617-332-8152
Korona, Joseph/178 Superior Ave, Pittsburgh, PA	412-761-4349
Kovner, Mark/14 Cindy Lane, Highland Mills, NY	914-928-6543
Kramer, Phil/122 W Church St, Philadelphia, PA	215-928-9189
Krist, Bob/228 Overlook Ave, Leonia, NJ	201-585-9464
Krubner, Ralph/4 Juniper Court, Jackson, NJ	201-364-3640
Kruper, Alexander Jr/70 Jackson Dr Box 152, Cranford, NJ	201-276-1510
Kugielsky, Joseph/Little Brook Ln, Newtown, CT	203-426-7123

L

L M Associates/20 Arlington, Newton, MA	617-232-0254
LaBua, Frank/37 N Mountain Ave, Montclair, NJ	201-783-6318
LaCourciere, Mario/1 Rue Hamel, Quebec G1R 4J6, QU	418-694-1744
LaRiche, Michael/30 S Bank St, Philadelphia, PA	215-922-0447
Labelle, Lise/4282 A Rue Delorimier, Montreal H2H 2B1, QU	514-596-0010
Labuzetta, Steve/180 St Paul St, Rochester, NY	716-546-6825
Lacko, Steve/PO Box 383, Belmar, NJ	201-280-1199
Lamar Photographics/PO Box 470, Framingham, MA	617-881-2512
Lamb, David J/78 Hollywood Ave, Rochester, NY	716-442-2243
Landsman, Gary D/12115 Parklawn Dr, Rockville, MD	301-468-2588
Landwehrle, Don/9 Hother Ln, Bayshore, NY	516-665-8221
Lane, Rhonda/8-J Darling St, Southington, CT	203-621-6334
Lane, Whitney/109 Somerstown Rd, Ossining, NY	914-762-5335
Lanman, Jonathan/41 Bristol St, Boston, MA	617-574-9420
Lapides, Susan Jane/451 Huron Ave, Cambridge, MA	617-864-7793
Larrimore/916 N Charles St, Baltimore, MD	301-727-8800
Lauber, Christopher/609 Crescent Dr, Bound Brook, NJ	201-271-4077
Laurien Photo/4 Roberta St, Farmingdale, ME	207-582-3726
Laurino, Don Studio/145 Pallisade St, Dobbs Ferry, NY	914-693-1199
Lautman, Robert C/4906 41 St NW, Washington, DC	202-966-2800

Lavine, David S/4016 The Alameda, Baltimore, MD	301-467-0523
Lawfer, Larry/107 South St, Boston, MA	617-451-0628
Lawrence, Stefan/40 Norwood Ave, Malverne, NY	516-593-2992
Lawrence, Stephanie/2422 Chetwood Circle, Timonium, MD	301-252-3704
LeBlond, Jerry/7 Court Sq, Rutland, VT	802-422-3115
Leach, Peter/116 S Seventh St, Philadelphia, PA	215-574-0230
Leaman, Chris/42 Old Lancaster Rd, Malvern, PA	215-647-8455
Ledbetter, Jack/, , VT	802-276-3730
Lee, Carol/136 Marlborough, Boston, MA	617-523-5930
Lee, Raymond/PO Box 9743, Baltimore, MD	301-323-5764
Leeds, Karen/22 Barker Ave, White Plains, NY	914-997-2200
Leeming Studios Inc/222 Richmond St, Providence, RI	401-421-1916
Lefcourt, Victoria/3207 Coquelin Terr, Chevy Chase, MD	301-652-1658
Leney, Julia/PO Box 434, Wayland, MA	617-358-7229
LENNON, JIM/358 JUNE AVE, FLANDERS, NY (P 98)	**516-369-1185**
Lent, Max/24 Wellington Ave, Rochester, NY	716-328-5126
Lent, Michael/PO Box 825, Hoboken, NJ	201-798-4866
Leomporra, Greg/2607 Barton Dr, Cinnaminson, NJ	609-829-3159
Leonard, Barney/518 Putnam Rd, Merion, PA	215-664-2525
Levart, Herb/566 Secor Rd, Hartsdale, NY	914-946-2060
Leveille, David/27-31 St Bridget's Dr, Rochester, NY	716-423-9474
Levin, Aaron M/3000 Chestnut Ave #102, Baltimore, MD	301-467-8646
Lewis, Ronald/PO Box 489, East Hampton, NY	516-267-8624
Lewitt, Peter/39 Billings Park, Newton, MA	617-244-6552
Ley, Russell/103 Ardale St, Boston, MA	617-325-2500
Lidington, John/2 "C" St, Hull, MA	617-246-0300
Lieberman, Fred/2426 Linden Ln, Silver Spring, MD	301-565-0644
Lilley, Weaver/2107 Chancellor St, Philadelphia, PA	215-567-2881
Lillibridge, David/Rt 4 Box 1172, Burlington, CT	203-673-9786
Linck, Tony/2100 Linwood Ave, Fort Lee, NJ	201-944-5454
Lincon, James/30 St John Pl, Westport, CT	203-226-3724
Lineham, Clark/74 Mt Pleasant Ave, Gloucester, MA	617-281-3903
Linehan, Clark/31 Blackburn Ctr, Gloucester, MA	617-281-3903
Litoff, Walter/2919 Union St, Rochester, NY	716-232-6140
Littlehales, Breton/9520 Seminole St, Silver Spring, MD	202-291-2422
Littlewood, John/PO Box 141, Woodville, MA	617-435-4262
Littwin, Michael/53 Smithfield Ave, Lawrence, NJ	201-886-0531
Lockwood, Lee/27 Howland Rd, West Newton, MA	617-965-6343
Lokmer, John/PO Box 2782, Pittsburgh, PA	412-765-3565
Long Shots/4421 East West Hwy, Bethesda, MD	301-654-0279
Longley, Steven/2224 North Charles St, Baltimore, MD	301-467-4185
Lowe, Shawn Michael/240 Prospect Ave #602, Hackensack, NJ	201-487-2865
Lukowicz, Jerome/122 Arch St, Philadelphia, PA	215-922-7122

M MacKay, Kenneth/127 Hillary Lane, Penfield, NY	716-385-1116
MACKENZIE, MAXWELL/2641 GARFIELD ST NW, WASHINGTON, DC (P 149)	**202-232-6686**
MacLeod, Richard/551 Boylston St, Boston, MA	617-267-6364
MacWright, Jeff/248 East Main, Chester, NJ	201-879-4545
Macchiarulo, Tony/12 Gregory Blvd, Norwalk, CT	203-866-8414
Machalaba, Robert/4 Brentwood Dr, Livingston, NJ	201-992-4674
Maciel, Chris/RD2 Box 176 Riley Rd, New Windsor, NY	914-564-6972
Macys, Mr Sandy/, , VT	802-496-2518
Maggio, Chris/180 St Paul St, Rochester, NY	716-454-3929
Maggio, Donald/Brook Hill Ln #5E, Rochester, NY	716-381-8053
Maglott, Larry/249 A St, Boston, MA	617-482-9347
Magnet, Jeff/Flight Source Intl/Box 1054, Cambridge, MA	617-547-8226
Magno, Thomas/19 Peters St, Cambridge, MA	617-492-5197
Mahoney, Bob/213 Warham St, Syracuse, NY	315-478-1858
Makris, Dave/10 Newbold Dr, Hyde Park, NY	914-462-4502
Malin, Marc/221 Crafts Rd, Brookline, MA	617-734-4916
MALITSKY, ED/337 SUMMER ST, BOSTON, MA (P 132)	**617-451-0655**
Malka, Daniel/1030 St Alexandre #203, Montreal H2Z 1P3, QU	
Maltz, Alan/182 Beach #136, Belle Harbour, NY	718-318-0110
Malyszko, Michael/90 South St, Boston, MA	617-426-9111
Mandelkorn, Richard/309 Waltham St, W Newton, MA	617-332-3246
Manheim, Michael Philip/PO Box 35, Marblehead, MA	617-631-3560
Mann, Richard J/PO Box 2712, Dix Hills, NY	516-754-8496
Manning, Ed/875 E Broadway, Stratford, CT	203-375-3384
Marchese, Frank/56 Arbor St, Hartford, CT	203-232-4417
Marcus, Joan/2311 Calvert St NW, Washington, DC	202-332-2828

Mares, Manuel/185 Chestnut Hill Ave, Brighton, MA	617-782-4208
Margolis, David/682 Howard Ave, New Haven, CT	203-777-7288
Margolis, Paul/77 S Broadway, Nyack, NY	201-569-2316
Marinelli, Jack/673 Willow St, Waterbury, CT	203-756-3273
Marinelli, Mary Leigh/48 Essex St, Salem, MA	617-745-7035
Markel, Brad/639 'E' St NE, Washington, DC	703-920-2791
Markowitz, Joel/2 Kennsington Ave, Jersey City, NJ	202-451-0413
Marshall, John/344 Boylston St, Boston, MA	617-536-2988
Martin Paul Ltd/247 Newbury St, Boston, MA	617-536-1644
Martin, Bruce/266-A Pearl St, Cambridge, MA	617-492-8009
Martin, Jeff/6 Industrial Way W, Eatontown, NJ	201-389-0888
Martin, Marilyn/130 Appleton St #2l, Boston, MA	617-262-5507
Martin-Elson, Patricia/120 Crooked Hill Rd, Huntington, NY	516-427-4799
Martines, Douglas/410 Oakwood Rd, Huntington Sta, NY	516-423-3614
Massar, Ivan/296 Bedford St, Concord, MA	617-369-4090
Mastalia, Francesco/2 Midland Ave, Hawthorne, NJ	212-772-8449
MATT, PHIL/PO BOX 10406, ROCHESTER, NY (P 133)	**716-461-5977**
Mattei, George Photography/179 Main St, Hackensack, NJ	201-342-0740
Mauro, George, Photography/211 Glenridge Ave, Montclair, NJ	201-744-7899
Mauss, Peter/222 Valley Pl, Mamaroneck, NY	914-698-4060
Mavodones, Bill/46 Waltham St #105, Boston, MA	617-423-7382
May Tell, Susan/NY,	516-433-8244
Mayernik, George/41 Wolfpit Ave #2N, Norwalk, CT	203-846-1406
Mazzone, James/1201 82nd St, N Bergen, NJ	201-861-8992
McCarron, Marc/1018 E Willow Grove Ave, Philadelphia, PA	215-836-1135
McConnell & McConnell/NY,	516-883-0058
McConnell, Jack/ 182 Broad St, Old Wethersfield, CT	203-563-6154
McConnell, Russ/8 Adler Dr, E Syracuse, NY	315-433-1005
McCormick & Nelson, Inc/34 Piave St, Stamford, CT	203-348-5062
McCoy, Dan/Main St, Housatonic, MA	413-274-6211
MCDONALD, KEVIN R/319 NEWTOWN TURNPIKE, REDDING, CT (P 134)	**203-938-9276**
McDonough Studio/3224 Kennedy Blvd, Jersey City, NJ	201-420-1056
McDowell, Bill/56 Edmonds St, Rochester, NY	716-442-8632
McGrail, John/6576 Senator Ln, Bensalem, PA	215-750-6070
McKean, Thomas R/742 Cherry Circle, Wynnewood, PA	215-642-1412
McLaren, Lynn/42 W Cedar, Boston, MA	617-227-7448
McLean, Alex/65 E India Row #10D, Boston, MA	617-523-6446
McMullin, Forest/183 St Paul St, Rochester, NY	716-262-3944
McNamara, Mr Casey/109 Broad St, Boston, MA	617-426-8641
McNeill, Brian/840 W Main St, Lansdale, PA	215-368-3326
McQueen, Ann/791 Tremont St #401, Boston, MA	617-267-6258
McWilliams, Jack/15 Progress Ave, Chelmsford, MA	617-256-9615
Meacham, Joseph/601 North 3rd St, Philadelphia, PA	215-925-8122
Meadowlands Photo Service/259 Hackensack St, East Rutherford, NJ	201-933-9121
Mecca, Jack/1508 72nd St, North Bergen, NJ	201-869-7956
Mednick, Seymour/316 S Camac, Philadelphia, PA	215-735-6100
Medvec, Emily/151 Kentucky Ave SE, Washington, DC	202-546-1220
Meech, Christopher/456 Glenbrook Rd, Stamford, CT	203-348-1158
Meehan, Joseph/RD 1/Box 39/Betwn Lakes Rd, Salisbury, CT	203-824-0866
Meek, Richard/8 Skyline Dr, Huntington, NY	516-271-0072
Mehne, Ralph/1501 Rose Terrace, Union, NJ	201-686-0668
Meiller, Henry Studios/1026 Wood St, Philadelphia, PA	215-922-1525
Melino, Gary/235 Simmonsville Ave, Johnston, RI	401-781-6320
Mellor, D W/1020 Mt Pleasant Rd, Bryn Mawr, PA	215-527-9040
Melton, Janice Munnings/692 Walkhill St, Boston, MA	617-298-1443
Mendelsohn, David/Sky Farm Rd, Northwood, NH	603-942-7622
MERCER, RALPH/239 'A' ST, BOSTON, MA (P 135)	**617-482-2942**
Merchant, Martin/22 Barker Ave, White Plains, NY	914-997-2200
Merz, Laurence/215 Georgetown Rd, Weston, CT	203-222-1936
Michael's/481 Central Ave, Cedarhurst, NY	516-374-3456
Michael, Shawn/240 Prospect Ave, Hackensack, NJ	201-487-2865
Michaels, John - MediaVisions/17 May St, Clifton, NJ	201-772-0181
Millard, Howard/220 Sixth Ave, Pelham, NY	914-738-3689
Miller, Bruce Photography/9 Tall Oaks Dr, East Brunswick, NJ	201-257-0211
Miller, David Photo/5 Lake St, Morris, NY	607-263-5060
Miller, Don/60 Sindle Ave, Little Falls, NJ	201-785-9090
Miller, Gary/PO Box 136, Bedford Hills, NY	914-666-4174
Miller, J T/12 Forest Edge Dr, Titusville, NJ	609-737-3116
Miller, Melabee/29 Beechwood Pl, Hillside, NJ	201-527-9121
Miller, R/PO Box 553, Levittown, PA	609-883-7492

Photographers
Continued

Please send us your additions and updates.

Miller, Roger/1411 Hollins St Union Sq, Baltimore, MD	301-566-1222
Millman, Lester Jay/23 Court St #23, White Plains, NY	914-946-2093
Mincey, Dale/113 Brunswick St, Jersey City, NJ	201-420-9387
Mindell, Doug/811 Boylston St, Boston, MA	617-262-3968
Mink, Mike/180 St Paul St 5th Fl, Rochester, NY	716-325-4865
Miraglia, Elizabeth/29 Drummer Ln, W Redding, CT	203-938-2261
Mirando, Gary/27 Cleveland St, Valhalla, NY	914-997-6588
Mitchell, Les/RD #4, Box 93 Pittenger Pnd Rd Freehold, NJ	201-462-2451
Mitchell, Mike/930 'F' St #800, Washington, DC	202-347-3223
Mogerley, Jean/1262 Pines Lake Dr W, Wayne, NJ	201-839-2355
Molinaro, Neil R/15 Walnut Ave, Clark, NJ	201-396-8980
Monroe, Robert/Kennel Rd, Cuddebackville, NY	914-754-8329
Moore, Marvin/1333 S Park St #1720, Halifax, NS	902-420-0389
Mopsik, Eugene/230 Monroe St, Philadelphia, PA	215-922-3489
Moran, Richard/201 S Main St, Wilkes-Barre, PA	717-287-3182
Morelli, Mark/14 Lincoln Parkway, Somerville, MA	617-625-2278
Morgan, Bruce/55 S Grand Ave, Baldwin, NY	516-546-3554
Morley, Bob/186 Lincoln St #202, Boston, MA	617-482-7279
Morris, R Kevin/5005 Baltan Rd, Bethesda, MD	301-229-6045
Morrow, Christopher W/163 Pleasant St, Arlington, MA	617-648-6770
Morse, Timothy/1133 Curve St, Carlisle, MA	617-369-8036
MOZO PHOTO DESIGN/282 SHELTON RD (RT 110),	
MONROE, CT (P 136)	**203-261-7400**
Mullen, Stephen/825 N 2nd St, Philadelphia, PA	215-574-9770
Mulligan, Bob/109 Broad St, Boston, MA	617-542-7308
Mulligan, Joseph/239 Chestnut St, Philadelphia, PA	215-592-1359
Munster, Joseph/Old Rt 28, Phoenicia, NY	914-688-5347
Murray, Ric/232 W Exchange St, Providence, RI	401-751-8806
Murry, Peggy/1913 VWaverly St, Philadelphia, PA	215-790-9239
Musto, Tom/225 S Main St, Wilkes-Barre, PA	717-822-5798
Mydans, Carl/212 Hommocks Rd, Larchmont, NY	212-841-2345
Myers Studios Inc/5775 Big Tree Rd, Orchard Park, NY	716-662-6002
Myers, Steve/Drawer 2, Almond, NY	607-276-6400
Myron/127 Dorrance St, Providence, RI	401-421-1946
N Nadel, Lee/10 Loveland Rd, Brookline, MA	617-451-6646
Nagler, Lanny/56 Arbor St, Hartford, CT	203-233-4040
Napier, Owen/2113 N Pine St, Wilmington, DE	302-656-0233
Navin, Mr Chris/, Boston, MA	617-825-3299
Nelder, Oscar/Box 661 Main St, Presque Isle, ME	207-769-5911
Nelson, Janet/Finney Farm, Croton-On-Hudson, NY	914-271-5453
Nerney, Dan/137 Rowayton Ave, Rowayton, CT	203-853-2782
Nettis, Joseph/1717 Walnut St, Philadelphia, PA	215-563-5444
Neudorfer, Brien/46 Waltham St, Boston, MA	617-451-9211
Neumann, William/96 Carmita Ave, Rutherford, NJ	201-939-0370
Neumayer, Joseph/Chateau Rive #102, Peekskill, NY	914-739-3005
Neurath, Eric/33 Richdale Ave #206, Cambridge, MA	617-935-9003
Nible, Rick/408 Vine St 4th Fl, Philadelphia, PA	215-625-0638
Nichols, Don/1241 University Ave, Rochester, NY	716-461-9666
Nighswander, Tim/315 Peck St, New Haven, CT	203-789-8529
Noble Inc/2313 Maryland Ave, Baltimore, MD	301-235-5235
Nochton, Jack/1238 W Broad St, Bethlehem, PA	215-691-2223
Noel, Peter/18 Bartlett St, Malden, MA	617-321-1264
Norris, Robert/RFD 1 Box 4480, Pittsfield, ME	207-487-5981
North Jersey Photographers/23 Vernon Terrace, Bloomfield,	
NJ	201-429-1012
Northlight Visual Comm Group Inc/21-23 Quine St, Cranford,	
NJ	201-272-1155
O O'Connell, Bill/791 Tremont St, Boston, MA	617-437-7556
O'Donnell, John/179 Westmoreland St, White Plains, NY	914-948-1786
O'Donoghue, Ken/8 Union Park St, Boston, MA	617-542-4898
O'Hare, Richard/POB 273, Clifton Heights, PA	215-626-1429
O'Neill, James/1543 Kater St, Philadelphia, PA	215-545-3223
O'Neill, Martin/1914 Mt Royal Terr 1st Fl, Baltimore, MD	301-225-0522
O'Neill, Michael Photo/162 Lakefield Rd, E Northport, NY	516-754-0459
O'Shaughnessy, Bob/50 Melcher, Boston, MA	617-542-7122
Obermeyer, Eva/PO Box 1722, Union, NJ	201-375-3322
Ogiba, Joseph/PO Box M, Somerville, NJ	201-725-4595
Olbrys, Anthony/41 Pepper Ridge Rd, Stamford, CT	203-322-9422
Oliver, Lou/8 Adler Dr, E Syracuse, NY	315-433-1005
Olivera, Bob/42 Weybossett St, Providence, RI	401-272-1170

Olmstead Studio/118 South St, Boston, MA	617-542-2024
Olsen, Peter/1415 Morris St, Philadelphia, PA	215-465-9736
Orel, Mano/PO Box E, Dove Court, Croton-On-Hudson, NY	914-271-5542
Orkin, Pete/80 Washington St, S Norwalk, CT	203-866-9978
Orlando, Fran/329 Spruce St, Philadelphia, PA	215-629-9968
Orling, Alan S/Hawley Rd, North Salem, NY	914-669-5405
Orrico, Charles/72 Barry Ln, Syosset, NY	516-364-2257
Ouzer, Louis/120 East Ave, Rochester, NY	716-454-7582
Owens, John/93 Massachusetts Ave, Boston, MA	617-423-2452
P Paez, Hugo/2301 Glenn Alan Ave #320, Silver Spring, MD	301-946-4373
Painter, Joseph/205 Fairmont Ave, Philadelphia, PA	215-592-1612
Palmer, Gabe/Fire Hill Farm, West Redding, CT	203-938-2514
Palmiere, Jorge/316 F St NE #21, Washington, DC	202-543-2111
Pamatat, Ken/165 West Ave, Rochester, NY	716-235-1222
Panioto, Mark/95 Mohawk Ln, Weathersfield, CT	203-241-3202
Pantages, Tom/7 Linden Ave, Gloucester, MA	617-525-3678
Pape, Maria/41 Magee Ave, Stamford, CT	203-348-1588
Paradigm Productions/6437 Ridge Ave, Philadelphia, PA	215-482-8404
Paredes, Cesar/Lawrence Commons, Lawrenceville, NJ	609-987-8626
Paskevich, John/1500 Locust St #3017, Philadelphia, PA	215-735-9868
Pasley, Richard/15 Bristol St, Cambridge, MA	617-864-8386
Paul, Richard/7525 Washington St, Pittsburgh, PA	412-271-6609
Pavlovich, James/MA,	617-266-9723
Paxenos, Dennis F/2125 Maryland Ave #103, Baltimore, MD	301-837-1029
PEASE, GREG/23 E 22ND ST, BALTIMORE, MD (P 150,151)	**301-332-0583**
Peckham, Lynda/65 S Broadway, Tarrytown, NY	914-631-5050
Pehlman, Barry/806 King Rd, Malvern, PA	215-296-7966
Pellegrini, Lee/381 Newtonville Ave, Newtonville, MA	617-964-7925
Pelletier, Herve/329 A Street, Boston, MA	617-423-6724
Peluso, Frank/15 Caspar Berger Rd, Whitehouse Station, NJ	201-534-9637
Pendergrast, Mark/, , VT	802-658-0337
Penneys, Robert/DE,	302-733-0444
Peoples, Joe/420 Fairview Ave #3G, Fort Lee, NJ	212-679-7575
Perez, Paul R/143 W Hoffman Ave, Lindenhurst, NY	516-226-0846
Perlman, Ilene/279 Harvard St #11, Cambridge, MA	617-497-6695
Perlmutter, Steven/246 Nicoll St, New Haven, CT	203-789-8493
Perron, Robert/119 Chestnut St, Branford, CT	203-481-2004
Peterson, Brent/73 Maple Ave, Tuckahoe, NY	212-573-7195
Petronio, Frank/74 Westchester Ave, Rochester, NY	716-288-4642
Petty, David/ The Stone Mill, Laurence, MA	617-794-0404
Pevarnik, Gervose/180 St Paul St, Rochester, NY	716-262-3579
Philiba, Allan A/3408 Bertha Dr, Baldwin, NY	516-623-7841
Philips, Jaye R/2 Crescent Hill Ave, Arlington, MA	617-646-8491
Photo Dimensions/14 S Tennessee Ave, Atlantic City, NJ	609-344-1212
Photo Synthesis/216 Blvd of Allies, Pittsburgh, PA	412-642-7734
Photo-Colortura/PO Box 1749, Boston, MA	617-522-5132
Photographers & Co/113 S Brandywine Ave, Schenectady, NY	518-377-9457
Photographic Illustration Ltd/7th & Ranstead, Philadelphia, PA	215-925-7073
Photown Studio/190 Vandervoort St, North Tonawanda, NY	716-693-2912
Photoworks/23 Walnut Ave, Clark, NJ	201-388-8531
Picarello, Carmine/12 S Main St, S Norwalk, CT	203-866-8987
Pickerell, Jim H/110-E Frederick Ave, Rockville, MD	301-251-0720
Pictorial/8081 Zionsville Rd, Indianapolis, IN	317-872-7220
Picture That Inc/880 Briarwood, Newtown Square, PA	215-353-8833
Picturehouse Assoc Inc/22 Elizabeth St, Norwalk, CT	203-852-1776
Pietersen, Alex/29 Raynor Rd, Morristown, NJ	201-267-7003
Piperno, Lauren/215 E Dean St, Freeport, NY	718-935-1550
Pivak, Kenneth/605 Pavonia Ave, Jersey City, NJ	201-656-0508
PLANK, DAVID/CHERRY & CARPENTER STS, READING, PA	
(P 137)	**215-376-3461**
Platteter, George/82 Colonnade Dr, Rochester, NY	716-334-4488
Poggenpohl, Eric/12 Walnut St, Amherst, MA	413-256-0948
Pohuski, Michael/36 S Paca St #215, Baltimore, MD	301-962-5404
Polansky, Allen/1431 Park Ave, Baltimore, MD	301-383-9021
Polumbaum, Ted/326 Harvard St, Cambridge, MA	617-491-4947
Pope-Lance, Elton/125 Stockfarm Rd, Sudbury, MD	617-443-0596
Porcella, Phil/109 Broad St, Boston, MA	617-426-3222
Portsmouth Photography/259 Miller Ave, Portsmouth, NH	603-431-3351
Potter, Anthony/509 W Fayette St, Syracuse, NY	315-428-8900
Powell, Bolling/1 Worcester Sq, Boston, MA	617-536-1199
Powers, James/15 Jerome Pl, Leominster, MA	617-534-3664

Pownall, Ron/7 Ellsworth Ave, Cambridge, MA	617-354-0846
Praus, Edgar G/176 Anderson Ave, Rochester, NY	716-442-4820
Preisler, Don/8563 Greenbelt Rd #204, Greenbelt, MD	301-552-3567
Prezio, Franco/606 Allen Ln, Media, PA	717-565-6919
Procaccini, Charles/1355 New York Ave, Huntington Sta, NY	516-549-4144
Profit, Everett R/533 Massachusetts Ave, Boston, MA	617-267-5840
Prue, Sara/, Washington, DC	202-232-2330
Putnam, Sarah/8 Newell St, Cambridge, MA	617-547-3758

QR

Quin, Clark/241 A Street, Boston, MA	617-451-2686
Quindry, Richard/200 Loney St, Philadelphia, PA	215-742-6300
Raab, Timothy/163 Delaware Ave, Delmar, NY	518-439-2298
Rabdau, Yvonne/RR2 Box 590 Kelly Ct, Stormville, NY	914-221-4643
Rabinowitz, Barry/515 Willow St, Waterbury, CT	203-574-1129
Rae, John/153 W Concord St, Boston, MA	617-266-5754
Ranck, Rosemary/323 W Mermaid Ln, Philadelphia, PA	215-242-3718
Rapp, Frank/327 A St, Boston, MA	617-542-4462
Rauch, Bonnie/Crane Rd, Somers, NY	914-277-3986
Rawle, Johnathan/7 Railroad Ave, Bedford, MA	617-275-3030
Ray, Dean/2900 Chestnut Ave, Baltimore, MD	301-243-3441
Raycroft/McCormick/326 A Street #C, Boston, MA	617-542-7229
Redding, Jim/105 Beach St, Boston, MA	617-482-2833
Reichel, Lorna/PO Box 63, E Greenbush, NY	518-477-7822
Reis, Jon Photography/141 The Commons, Ithaca, NY	607-272-1966
Renard, Jean/142 Berkeley St, Boston, MA	617-266-8673
Renckly, Joe/1200 Linden Pl, Pittsburgh, PA	412-323-2122
RESNICK, SETH/15 SLEEPER ST #507, BOSTON, MA	
(P 138,139)	**617-423-7475**
Retallack, John/207 Erie Station Rd, West Henrietta, NY	716-334-1530
Revette, David/602 W State St, Syracuse, NY	315-422-1558
Richard, George/PO Box 392, Walker Valley, NY	914-733-4300
Richards, Christopher/737 Canal St Bldg 35A, Stamford, CT	203-964-0235
Richards, Toby/1 Sherbrooke Dr., Princeton Junction, NJ	609-275-1885
Richmond, Jack/12 Farnsworth St, Boston, MA	617-482-7158
Riemer, Ken/183 St Paul St, Rochester, NY	716-232-5450
Riley, George/Sisquisic Trail PO Box 840, Yarmouth, ME	207-846-5787
Riley, Laura/Hidden Spng Fm PO Box 186, Pittstown, NJ	201-735-7707
Rimi, Jim/PO Box 2134, West New York, NJ	201-866-7463
Ritter, Frank/2414 Evergreen St, Yorktown Hts, NY	914-962-5385
Rizzi, Leonard F/5161 River Rd Bldg 2B, Bethesda, MD	301-652-1303
Rizzo, John/36 St Paul St, Rochester, NY	716-232-5140
Robb, Steve/535 Albany St, Boston, MA	617-542-6565
Roberts, Mathieu/200 Henry St, Stamford, CT	203-324-3582
Robins, Susan/124 N Third St, Philadelphia, PA	215-238-9988
Robinson, George A/4-A Stonehedge Dr, S Burlington, VT	802-862-6902
Robinson, Mike/2413 Sarah St, Pittsburgh, PA	412-431-4102
Rocheleau, Paul/Canaan Rd, Richmond, MA	413-698-2676
Rock, Dean/PO Box 392, Cape Neddick, ME	207-363-7040
Rockhill, Morgan/204 Westminster Mall, Providence, RI	401-274-3472
Rode, Robert/2670 Arleigh Rd, East Meadow, NY	516-485-6687
Romanos, Michael/30 Stanton Rd, Brookline, MA	617-277-3504
Roseman, Shelly/1238 Callowhill St, Philadelphia, PA	215-922-1430
Rosier, Gerald/PO Box 470, Framingham, MA	617-881-2512
Rosner, Eric/314 N 13th St, Philadelphia, PA	215-629-1240
Rosner, Stu/One Thompson Sq, Charlestown, MA	617-242-2112
Ross, Alex F/1622 Chestnut St, Philadelphia, PA	215-576-7799
Rossotto, Frank/184 E Main St, Westfield, NY	716-326-2792
Rossow, Lee/641 Van Doren Ct, Valley Cottage, NY	914-358-6931
Roth, Eric/337 Summer St, Boston, MA	617-338-5358
Rothstein, Jennifer/192-C Columbus Dr #1, Jersey City, NJ	201-435-5701
Rotman, Jeffrey L/14 Cottage Ave, Somerville, MA	617-666-0874
Rowan, Norm R/106 E 6th St, Clifton, NJ	201-772-5126
Rowin, Stanley/791 Tremont St, Boston, MA	617-437-0641
RUBENSTEIN, LEN/87 PINE ST, EASTON, MA (P 140)	**617-238-0744**
Ruggeri, Lawrence/10 Old Post Office Rd, Silver Spring, MD	301-588-3131
Ruggieri, Ignazio/49 Prospect St, Little Falls, NJ	201-890-0660
Ruiz, Felix/72 Smith Ave, White Plains, NY	914-949-3353
Rummel, Hal/36 S Paca St #515, Baltimore, MD	301-244-8517
Runyon, Paul/113 Arch St, Philadelphia, PA	215-238-0655
Russ, Clive/82 Barlett St, Charlestown, MA	617-242-5234
Russel, Rae/75 Byram Lake Rd, Mount Kisco, NY	914-241-0057
Russell Studios/14 Hawk St, Scotia, NY	518-370-3600

Russo, Rich/11 Clinton St, Morristown, NJ	201-538-6954

S

Sa'Adah, Jonathan/PO Box 247, Hartford, VT	802-295-5327
Sabol, George Jeremy/107 Patricia Ave, Colonia, NJ	201-574-2974
Sagala, Steve/53-A Parsippany Rd, Whippany, NJ	201-377-1418
Sakmanoff, George/179 Massachusetts Ave, Boston, MA	617-262-7227
Salamone, Anthony/1277 Commonwealth Ave, Boston, MA	617-254-5427
Salant, Robin/165 Westfield Ave, Clark, NJ	201-272-1331
Salomone, Frank/296 Brick Blvd, Bricktown, NJ	201-920-1525
Salsbery, Lee/14 Seventh St NE, Washington, DC	202-543-1222
Salstrand, Duane/503 Boylston #4, Brookline, MA	617-232-1795
Samara, Thomas/713 Erie Blvd West, Syracuse, NY	315-476-4984
Samu, Mark/39 Erlwein Ct, Massapequa, NY	516-795-1849
Samuels Studio/8 Waltham St, PO Box 201, Maynard, MA	617-897-7901
Sanderson, John/2310 Pennsylvania Ave, Pittsburgh, PA	412-391-8720
Sanford, Eric/219 Turnpike Rd, Manchester, NH	603-624-0122
Sansone, Nadine/7 River St, Milford, CT	203-878-5090
Santos, Don/175-A Boston Post Rd, Waterford, CT	203-443-5668
Sapienza, Louis A/96 West St, Colonia, NJ	201-382-5933
Saraceno, Paul/35 Kingston St, Boston, MA	617-542-2779
Sargent, William/PO Box 331, Woods Hole, MA	617-548-2673
Sasso, Ken/116 Mattabaffet Dr, Meriden, CT	203-235-1421
Sauter, Ron Photo/183 St Paul St, Rochester, NY	716-232-1361
Savage, Sally/99 Orchard Terrace, Piermont, NY	914-359-5735
Savoie, Phil/187 Lake Ave, Trumbull, CT	203-268-9917
Saydah, Gerard/PO Box 210, Demarest, NJ	201-768-2582
Sayers, Jim/325 Valley Rd, West Orange, NJ	201-325-2352
Schadt, Bob/23 Ransom Rd, Brighton, MA	617-782-3734
Schaefer, Dave/48 Grove St, Belmont, MA	617-371-2850
Schaeffer, Bruce/631 N Pottstown Pike, Exton, PA	215-363-5230
Schembri, Joseph/PO Box 4393, Metuchen, NJ	201-287-8561
Schenk, Andy/28 Mulberry Ln, Colts Neck, NJ	201-946-9459
Scherer, James/35 Kingston St, Boston, MA	617-338-5678
Scherzi, James/116 Town Line Rd, Syracuse, NY	315-455-7961
Schlanger, Irv/946 Cherokee Rd, Huntington Valley, PA	215-663-0663
Schlegel, Robert/2 Division St #10-11, Somerville, NJ	201-231-1212
SCHLEIPMAN, RUSS/298-A COLUMBUS AVE, BOSTON, MA	
(P 141)	**617-267-1677**
Schlowsky Studios/145 South St, Boston, MA	617-338-4664
Schmitt, Steve/337 Summer St, Boston, MA	617-482-5482
Schoen, Robert/241 Crescent St, Waltham, MA	617-647-5546
Schoon, Tim/PO Box 7446, Lancaster, PA	717-291-9483
Schroeder, H Robert/PO Box 7361, W Trenton, NJ	609-883-8643
Schulmeyer, LT/2019 St Paul St, Baltimore, MD	301-332-0767
Schultz, Jurgen/Rt 100 N/Box 19, Londonderry, VT	802-824-3475
Schweikardt, Eric/PO Box 56, Southport, CT	203-375-8181
Scott, Jesse/250 Washington Ave, Nutley, NJ	201-667-3829
Sculnick, Herb/611 Warren St, Hudson, NY	518-828-2178
Sedik, Joe/2419 N Broad St, Colmar, PA	215-822-3399
Seng, Walt/810 Penn Ave #400, Pittsburgh, PA	412-391-6780
Serbin, Vincent/304 Church Rd, Bricktown, NJ	201-477-5620
Serio, Steve/535 Albany st, Boston, MA	617-542-2644
Severi, Robert/813 Richmond Ave, Silver Spring, MD	301-585-1010
Shafer, Bob/3554 Quebec St N W, Washington, DC	202-362-0630
Shambroom, Eric/383 Albany St, Boston, MA	617-423-0359
Shapiro, Alan/46 University Rd, Brookline, MA	617-424-1745
Sharp, Steve/153 N 3rd St, Philadelphia, PA	215-925-2890
Shearn, Michael/214 S 12th St, Philadelphia, PA	215-232-6666
Shelton, Sybil/416 Valley View Rd, Englewood, NJ	201-568-8684
Shepherd, Francis/PO Box 204, Chadds Ford, PA	215-347-6799
Sherer, Larry/5233 Eliots Oak Rd, Columbia, MD	301-730-3178
Sherman, Steve/49 Melcher St, Boston, MA	617-542-1496
Sherriff, Bob/963 Humphrey St, Swampscott, MA	617-599-6955
Shoemake, Allan Hunter/56 Main St, Millburn, NJ	201-467-4920
Shotwell, John/241 A Street, Boston, MA	617-357-7456
Shoucais, Bill/460 Harrison Ave 3rd Fl, Boston, MA	617-423-1774
Siciliano, Richard/809 Albany St, Schenectady, NY	518-370-4417
Sickles Photo Reporting/PO Box 98, Maplewood, NJ	201-763-6355
Siegel, Hyam Photography/PO Box 356, Brattleboro, VT	802-257-0691
Silk, Georgiana B/190 Godfrey Rd E, Weston, CT	203-226-0408
Silver, David/35 N Third St, Philadelphia, PA	215-925-7277
Silverman, Paul/49 Ronald Dr, Clifton, NJ	201-472-4339

Silverstein, Abby/3315 Woodvalley Dr, Baltimore, MD	301-486-5211
Simeone, J Paul/116 W Baltimore Pike, Media, PA	215-566-7197
Simian, George/566 Commonwealth Ave, Boston, MA	617-267-3558
SIMMONS, ERIK LEIGH/241 A ST, BOSTON, MA (P 120,121)	**617-482-5325**
Simon, David/263 110th St, Jersey City, NJ	201-795-9326
Simpson/Flint/2133 Maryland Ave, Baltimore, MD	301-837-9923
Singer, Arthur/Sedgewood RD 12, Carmel, NY	914-225-6801
Singer, Jay/20 Russell Park Rd, Syosset, NY	516-935-8991
SITEMAN, FRANK/136 POND ST, WINCHESTER, MA (P 142)	**617-729-3747**
Skalkowski, Bob/310 Eighth St, New Cumberland, PA	717-774-0652
Sklute, Kenneth/210 E Nassau St, Islip Terrace, NY	516-581-7276
Skoogford, Leif/415 Church Rd #B2, Elkins Park, PA	215-635-5186
Slide Graphics/262 Summer St, Boston, MA	617-542-0700
Sloan Photo/443 Albany St, Boston, MA	617-542-3215
Smith, Brian/344 Boylston St, Boston, MA	617-262-0444
Smith, Gary & Russell/65 Washington St, S Norwalk, CT	203-866-8871
Smith, Gordon E/65 Washington St, S Norwalk, CT	203-866-8871
Smith, Hugh R/2515 Burr St, Fairfield, CT	203-255-1942
Smith, Philip W/1589 Reed Rd #2A, W Trenton, NJ	609-737-3370
Smith, Stuart/68 Raymond Lane, Wilton, CT	203-762-3158
Socolow, Carl/642 N 3rd St, Harrisburg, PA	717-236-1906
Solomon Assoc/PO Box 237, Glyndon, MD	301-833-5678
Sons, Fred/514 E St NE, Washington, dc20002	412-456-7380
Soorenko, Barry/5161 River Rd Bldg 2B, Bethesda, MD	301-652-1303
Speedy, Richard/1 Sherbrooke Dr, Princeton Junction, NJ	609-275-1885
Spelman, Steve/15 A St Mary's Ct, Brookline, MA	617-566-6578
Spencer, Michael/735 Mt Hope Ave, Rochester, NY	716-475-6817
Sperduto, Stephen/18 Willett Ave, Port Chester, NY	914-939-0296
Spiegel, Ted/RD 2 Box 353 A, South Salem, NY	914-763-3668
Spiro, Don/137 Summit Rd, Sparta, NJ	212-484-9753
St Niell Studio/209 Parker Ave, Clifton, NJ	201-340-1212
Staccioli, Marc/167 New Jersey Ave, Lake Hopatcong, NJ	201-663-5334
Stafford, Rick/26 Wadsworth, Allston, MA	617-495-2389
Stapleton, John/6854 Radbourne Rd, Upper Darby, PA	215-626-0920
Starinskas, Vyto/VT,	802-775-5511
Stearns, Stan/1814 Glade Ct, Annapolis, MD	301-268-5777
Stein, Geoffrey R/348 Newbury St, Boston, MA	617-536-8227
Stein, Howard/18 Willett Ave, Port Chester, NY	914-939-0242
Steiner, Chuck/111 Newark Ave, Union Beach, NJ	201-739-0629
Steiner, Peter/183 St Paul St 3rd Fl, Rochester, NY	716-454-1012
Stevens, Lee/2 Phillips Dr, Newburyport, MA	617-462-9385
Stier, Kurt/451 "D" St, Boston, MA	617-330-9461
Stierer, Dennis/34 Plympton St, Boston, MA	617-357-9488
STILL, JOHN/17 EDINBORO ST, BOSTON, MA (P 143)	**617-451-8178**
STILLINGS, JAMEY/87 N CLINTON AVE 5TH FL, ROCHESTER, NY (P 144,145)	**716-232-5296**
Stills/1 Winthrop Sq, Boston, MA	617-482-0660
Stites, Bill/,	203-655-7376
Stock, Jack/Newberg, Art/155 Myrtle St, Shelton, CT	203-735-3388
Stockwell, Thomas/101 Providence St, Worcester, MA	617-755-0992
Stoller, Bob/30 Old Mill Rd, Great Neck, NY	516-829-8906
Stone, Parker/6632 Temple Dr, E Syracuse, NY	315-463-0577
Stone, Steve/20 Rugg Rd, Allston, MA	617-782-1247
Storch, Otto/Box 712, 22 Pondview Ln, East Hampton, NY	516-324-5031
Stromberg, Bruce/PO Box 2052, Philadelphia, PA	215-735-3520
Stuart, Stephen Photography/10 Midland Ave, Port Chester, NY	914-939-0302
Studio 185/185 Forest St, S Hamilton, MA	617-468-2892
Studio Assoc/30-6 Plymouth St, Fairfield, NJ	201-575-2640
Studio Tech/25 Congress St, Salem, MA	617-745-5070
SUED, YAMIL/PO BOX 15558, STAMFORD, CT (P 146)	**203-353-8865**
Sullivan, Sharon/115 Columbia Ave, Jersey City, NJ	201-795-1930
Sunshine Photography/192 Newtown Rd, Plainview, NY	516-293-3399
Susoeff, Bill/3025 Wahangton Rd, McMurray, PA	412-941-8606
Sutphen, Chazz/22 Crescent Beach Dr, Burlington, VT	802-862-5912
Sutton, Humphrey/, , MA	413-245-3733
Swann/Niemann/1258 Wisconsin Ave NW 4th Fl, Washington, DC	202-342-6300
Sweeney, Dan/337 Summer St, Boston, MA	617-482-5482
Sweet, Ozzie/Mill Village Hill, Francestown, NH	603-547-6611
Swertfager, Amy/343 Manville Rd, Pleasantville, NY	914-747-1900
Swift, Dick/31 Harrison Ave, New Canaan, CT	203-966-8190
Swisher, Mark/5107 Herring Run Dr, Baltimore, MD	301-426-6665
Swoger, Arthur/18 Medway St #3, Providence, RI	401-331-0440
Szabo, Art/156-A Depot Rd, Huntington, NY	516-549-1699

T

Tadder, Morton/1010 Morton St, Baltimore, MD	301-837-7427
Taglienti, Maria/294 Whippany Rd, Whippany, NJ	201-428-4477
Tango, Rick/11 Pocconock Terrace, Ridgefield, CT	203-431-0514
Tardi, Joseph/125 Wolf Rd #108, Albany, NY	518-438-1211
Taylor, Ed/115 Patterson St, Hillsdale, NJ	201-666-8370
Tchakirides, Bill/Photography Assoc/201 Ann St, Hartford, CT	203-525-5117
Teatum, Marc/28 Goodhue St, Salem, MA	617-745-2345
Tech Photo/37 Huyler Ct, Setauket, NY	516-751-5193
Tenin, Barry/PO Box 2660 Saugatuck Sta, Westport, CT	203-226-9396
Tepper, Peter/195 Tunxis Hill Rd, Fairfield, CT	203-367-6172
Tesa, Rudi/194 Knickerbocker Rd, Demarest, NJ	201-767-4012
Tesi, Mike/12 Kulick Rd, Fairfield, NJ	201-575-7780
Thauer, Bill/542 Higgens Crowell Rd, W Yarmouth, MA	617-362-8222
Thayer, Mark/25 Dry Dock, Boston, MA	617-542-9532
The Studio Inc/818 Liberty Ave, Pittsburgh, PA	412-261-2022
Thellmann, Mark D/19 W Park Ave, Merchantville, NJ	609-488-9093
Thomas, Edward/140-50 Huyshope Ave, Hartford, CT	203-246-3293
Thompson, T Stephan/333 Pemberton Browns Mills Rd, New Lisbon, NJ	609-893-2726
Titcomb, Jeffery/PO Box 2662, Boston, MA	617-782-4939
Tkatch, James/2307 18th St NW, Washington, DC	202-462-2211
Tobey, Robert/MA, 413-586-4380, Tolbert, Brian/911 State St, Lancaster, PA	717-393-0918
Tollen, Cynthia/50 Fairmont St, Arlington, MA	617-641-4052
Tong, Darren/28 Renee Terrace, Newton, MA	617-527-3304
Tornallyay, Martin/77 Taft Ave, Stamford, CT	203-357-1777
Total Concept Photo/95-D Knickerbocker Ave, Bohemia, NY	516-567-6010
Trafidlo, James F/17 Stilling St, Boston, MA	617-338-9343
Traub, Willard/PO Box 2429, Framingham, MA	617-872-2010
Traver, Joseph/187 Hodge Ave, Buffalo, NY	716-884-8844
Treiber, Peter/917 Highland Ave, Bethlehem, PA	215-867-3303
Tretick, Stanley/4365 Embassy Park Dr NW, Washington, DC	202-537-1445
Trian, George/PO Box 2537, Hartford, CT	203-647-1372
Tribulas, Michael/1879 Old Cuthbert Rd #14, Cherry Hill, NJ	609-354-1903
Tritsch, Joseph/507 Longstone Dr, Cherry Hill, NJ	609-424-0433
Troha, John/12258 St James Rd, Potomac, MD	301-340-7220
Trola, Bob/1216 Arch St 2nd Fl, Philadelphia, PA	215-977-7078
Truslow, Bill/855 Islington St, Ponsborough, PA	603-436-4600
Trzoniec, Stanley/58 W Main St, Northboro, MA	617-393-3800
Tur, Stefan/, , NY	914-557-8857
Turin, Miranda/, Boston, MA	617-723-6087
Turner, Steve/377 Main St, Westport, CT	203-454-3999

UV

Uniphoto/1071 Wisconsin Ave, Washington, DC	202-333-0500
Urban, John/1424 Canton Ave, Milton, MA	617-333-0343
Urbina, Walt/7208 Thomas Blvd, Pittsburgh, PA	412-242-5070
Urdang, Monroe/461-A Oldham Ct, Ridge, NY	516-744-3903
Uzzle, Burk/267 S Van Pert St, Philadelphia, PA	215-629-1202
Vadnai, Peter/180 Valley Rd, Katonah, NY	914-232-5328
Valerio, Gary/278 Jay St, Rochester, NY	716-352-0163
Van Petten, Rob/109 Broad St, Boston, MA	617-426-8641
Van Schalkwyk, John/50 Melcher St, Boston, MA	617-542-4825
Van Valkenburgh, Larry/26 E High St, Ballston Spa, NY	518-885-8406
Van Zandbergen Photo/187 Riverside Dr, Binghamton, NY	607-625-3408
VanGordon, John/63 Unquowa, Fairfield, CT	203-255-6622
Vanden Brink, Brian/PO Box 419, Rockport, ME	207-236-4035
VanderWiele, John/75 Boulevard, Pequannock, NJ	201-694-2095
Vandermark, Peter/523 Medford St, Charlestown, MA	617-242-2277
Vanderwarker, Peter/56 Boyd St, Newton, MA	617-964-2728
Vandevanter, Jan/909 'C' St SE, Washington, DC	202-546-3520
Vanga, Ruhi/PO Box 344, Wayne, PA	215-293-1315
Vaughan, Ted/423 Doe Run Rd, Manheim, PA	717-665-6942
Vecchio, Dan/129 E Water St, Syracuse, NY	315-471-1064
Vecchione, Jim/4733 Elm St, Bethesda, MD	301-652-6333
Verderber, Gustav/VT,	802-644-2089
Vericker, Joe/111 Cedar St 4th Fl, New Rochelle, NY	914-632-2072
Verno, Jay/101 S 16th St, Pittsburgh, PA	412-562-9880
Vicari, Jim/PO Box 134, Berryville, NY	914-557-8506

Photographers

Continued

Please send us your additions and updates.

Vickery, Eric/4 Genetti Circle, Bedford, MA	617-275-0314
Visual Conspiracy/31 Stanhope St, Boston, MA	617-536-8909
Visual Productions/2121 Wisconsin Ave NW #470, Washington, DC	202-337-7332
Vogt, Laurie/1210 Park Ave #3, Hoboken, NJ	201-792-0485
Von Hoffmann, Bernard/2 Green Village Rd, Madison, NJ	201-377-0317
Voscar The Maine Photographer/PO Box 661, Presque Isle, ME	207-769-5911

W
Waggaman, John/2746 N 46 St, Philadelphia, PA	215-473-2827
Wagner, William/208 North Ave, Cranford, NJ	201-276-2002
Walch, Robert/310 W Main St, Kutztown, PA	215-683-5701
Waldemar/386 Brook Ave, Passaic Park, NJ	201-471-3033
Wallen, Jonathan/41 Lewis Pkwy, Yonkers, NY	914-476-8674
Walp's Photo Service/182 S 2nd St, Lehighton, PA	215-377-4370
Walsh, Dan/409 W Broadway, Boston, MA	617-268-7615
Walters, Day/PO Box 5655, Washington, DC	202-362-0022
Walther, Michael/2185 Brookside Ave, Wantagh, NY	516-783-7636
Wanamaker, Roger/PO Box 2800, Darien, CT	203-655-8383
Ward, Jack/221 Vine St, Philadelphia, PA	215-627-5311
Ward, Michael/916 N Charles St, Baltimore, MD	301-727-8800
Ward, Tony/704 South 6th St, Philadelphia, PA	215-238-1208
Warner, Lee/2300 Walnut St #421, Philadelphia, PA	215-567-0187
Warniers, Randall/35 Cleveland St, Arlington, MA	617-643-0454
Warren, Marion E/1935 Old Annapolis Blvd, Annapolis, MD	301-974-0444
Watson, H Ross/859 Lancaster Ave, Bryn Mawr, PA	215-527-2028
Watson, Linda M/38 Church St/Box 14, Hopkinton, MA	617-498-9638
Watson, Tom/2172 West Lake Rd, Skaneateles, NY	315-685-6033
Weed, John/115 Pius St, Pittsburg, PA	412-381-6826
Weems, Samuel/One Arcadia Pl, Boston, MA	617-288-8888
Weese, Carl/140-150 Huyshope Ave, Hartford, CT	203-246-6016
Weidman, H Mark/2112 Goodwin Lane, North Wales, PA	215-646-1745
Weigand, Tom/707 North 5th St, Reading, PA	215-374-4431
Weinberg, Abe/1230 Summer St, Philadelphia, PA	215-567-5454
Weinrebe, Steve/354 Congress St, Boston, MA	617-423-9130
Weisenfeld, Stanley/135 Davis St, Painted Post, NY	607-962-7314
Weisgrau, Richard/1107 Walnut St 2nd Fl, Philadelphia, PA	215-923-0348
Weiss, Michael/212 Race St, Philadelphia, PA	215-629-1685
Weitz, Allan/147 Harbinson Pl, E Windsor, NJ	609-443-5549
Welsch, Ms Ulrike/4 Dunns Lane, Marblehead, MA	617-631-1641
Wendler, Hans/RD 1 Box 191, Epsom, NH	603-736-9383
West, Judy/, Boston, MA	617-437-7645
Westwood Photo Productions/PO Box 85, Mansfield, MA	617-339-4141
Wexler, Ira/4893 MacArthur Blvd NW, Washington, DC	202-337-4886
Wheeler, Edward F/1050 King of Prussia Rd, Radnor, PA	215-964-9294
Wheeler, Nick/Turner Rd, Townsend Harbor, MA	617-597-2919
White, Frank/18 Milton Pl, Rowayton, CT	203-866-9500
White, Sharon/107 South St, Boston, MA	617-423-0577
Whitman, Edward/519 W Pratt St #105, Baltimore, MD	301-727-2220
Wiley, John Jay/147 Webster St, Boston, MA	617-567-0506
Williams, Jay/9101 W Chester Pike, Upper Darby, PA	215-789-3030
Williams, Lawrence S/9101 W Chester Pike, Upper Darby, PA	215-789-3030
Willinger, Dave/74 Pacific Blvd, Long Beach, NY	516-889-0678
Wilson, John/2416 Wynnefield Dr, Havertown, PA	215-446-4798
Wilson, Paul S/6384 Overbrook Ave, Philadelphia, PA	215-473-4455
Wilson, Robert L/PO Box 1742, Clarksburg, WV	304-623-5368
Windman, Russell/348 Congress St, Boston, MA	617-357-5140
Woloszyn, Gustav/745 McGillvray Pl, Linden, NJ	201-925-7399
Wood, Jeffrey C/808 Monroe Ave, Ardsley, PA	215-572-6848
Wood, Richard/169 Monsgnr O'Brien Hwy, Cambridge, MA	617-661-6856
Woodard, Steve/2003 Arbor Hill Ln, Bowie, MD	301-249-7705
Wrenn, Bill/200 Henry St, Stamford, CT	203-323-4409
Wright, Jeri/PO box 7, Wilmington, NY	518-946-2658
Wu, Ron/179 St Paul St, Rochester, NY	716-454-5600
Wurster, George/128 Berwick, Elizabeth, NJ	201-352-2134
Wyatt, Ronald/846 Harned St, Perth Amboy, NJ	201-442-7527
Wyman, Ira/14 Crane Ave, West Peabody, MA	617-535-2880

YZ
Yablon, Ron/834 Chestnut St #PH 105, Philadelphia, PA	215-923-1744
Yamashita, Michael/Roxticus Rd, Mendham, NJ	201-543-4473
Young, Don/PO Box 249, Exton, PA	215-363-2596
Yourman, Steve & Lisa/317 Plaza Rd N, Fairlawn, NJ	201-796-8091

Yuichi, Idaka/RR 2 Box 229D Wood Ave, Rindge, NH	603-899-6165
Z, Taran/528 F St Terrace SE, Washington, DC	202-543-5322
Zane, Steven/227 Grand St, Hoboken, NJ	201-420-8868
Zappala, John/Candlewood Echoes, Sherman, CT	203-354-6420
Zimbel, George/1538 Sherbrooke W #813, Montreal H3G1L5, QU	514-931-6387
Zimmerman, Larry/50 Grove St, Salem, MA	617-745-7117
Zmiejko, Tom/246 Center St #110, Freeland, PA	717-636-2304
Zucker, Gale/PO Box 2281/Short Beach, Branford, CT	203-488-0499
Zuckerman, Robert/100 Washington St, South Norwalk, CT	203-853-2670
Zungoli, Nick/Box 5, Sugar Loaf, NY	914-469-9382
Zurich, Robert/105 Church St, Aberdeen, NJ	201-566-7076
Zutell, Kirk/911 State St, Lancaster, PA	717-393-0918

Southeast

A
Abel, Wilton/2609 Commonwealth Ave, Charlotte, NC	704-372-6354
Adcock, James/3108 1/2 W Leigh St #8, Richmond, VA	804-358-4399
Alexander, Ric & Assoc Inc/212 S Graham St, Charlotte, NC	704-332-1254
Allard, William Albert/Marsh Run Farm Box 549, Somerset, VA	804-823-5951
Allen, Bob/710 W Lane St, Raleigh, NC	919-833-5991
Alston, Cotten/Box 7927-Station C, Atlanta, GA	404-876-7859
Alterman, Jack/285 Meeting St, Charleston, SC	803-577-0647
Alvarez, Jorge/3105 W Granada, Tampa, FL	813-831-6765
Anderson, Susanne/PO Box 6, Waterford, VA	703-882-3244
Andrea, Michael/225 South Mint St, Charlotte, NC	704-334-3992
Ashcraft, Jeff/3611 Tanglewood Dr NW, Atlanta, GA	404-438-1287
Atlantic Photo/319 N Main St, High Point, NC	919-884-1474
Avanti Photo/5750 Major Blvd #520, Orlando, FL	

B
Bachmann, Bill/PO Box 833, Lake Mary, FL	305-322-4444
Baker, I Wilson/PO Box 647, Mount Pleasant, SC	803-881-0811
Balbuza, Joseph/25 NE 210 St, Miami, FL	305-652-1728
Ball, Roger/225 West 4th St #A, Charlotte, NC	704-335-0479
Ballenberg, Bill/200 Cortland Ln, Virginia Beach, VA	804-463-3505
Baptie, Frank/1426 9th St N, St Petersburg, FL	813-823-7319
Barley, Bill/PO Box 2388, Columbia, SC	803-755-1554
Barnes, Billy E/313 Severin St, Chapel Hill, NC	919-942-6350
Barr, Ian/2640 SW 19th St, Fort Lauderdale, FL	305-584-6247
Barreras, Anthony/731-D Highland Ave, Atlanta, GA	404-681-2370
Barrs, Michael/6303 SW 69th St, Miami, FL	305-665-2047
Bartlett & Assoc/3007 Edgewater Dr, Orlando, FL	305-425-7308
Bassett, Donald/9185 Green Meadows Way, Palm Beach Gardens, FL	305-694-1109
Beck, Charles/2721 Cherokee Rd, Birmingham, AL	205-871-6632
Beck, G & Assoc/176 Ottley Dr NE, Atlanta, GA	404-872-0728
Becker, Joel/5121 Virginia Beach Blvd, Norfolk, VA	804-461-7886
Behrens, Bruce/2920 N Orange Ave, Orlando, FL	305-629-0261
Belenson, Mark/8056 NW 41st Ct, Sunrise, FL	305-749-0675
Belloise, Joe/2160 N 56th Terr, Hollywood, FL	305-966-7957
Bennett, Ken/1001 Lockwood Ave, Columbus, GA	404-324-1182
Bennett, Robert/819 Leigh Mill Rd, Great Falls, VA	703-759-4582
Bentley, Gary/240 Great Circle Rd #330, Nashville, TN	615-242-4038
Berch, Ida/POB 350335, Fort Lauderdale, FL	305-463-1912
Berg, Audrey & Fronk, Mark/7953-A Twist Ln, Springfield, VA	703-455-7343
Berger, Erica/One Herald Plaza, Miami, FL	305-376-3750
Bergeron, Joe/516 Natchez, New Orleans, LA	504-522-7503
Bertling, Norbert G Jr/2125 N Charles St, Baltimore, MD	301-727-8766
Beswick, Paul/4479 Westfield Dr, Mableton, GA	404-944-8579
Bewley, Glen/428 Armour Circle, Atlanta, GA	404-872-7277
Bilby, Glade/6901 Pritchard Pl, New Orleans, LA	504-866-0031
Blanton, Jeff/7401 Chancery Ln, Orlando, FL	305-851-7279
Blow, Jerry/PO Box 1615, Wilmington, NC	919-763-3835
Boatman, Mike/3430 Park Ave, Memphis, TN	901-324-9337
Bollman, Brooks/1183 Virginia Ave NE, Atlanta, GA	404-876-2422
Bondarenko, Marc/212 S 41st St, Birmingham, AL	205-933-2790
Borchelt, Mark/4398-D Eisenhower Ave, Alexandria, VA	703-243-7850
Borum, Michael/625 Fogg St, Nashville, TN	615-259-9750
Bose, Patti/1245 W Fairbanks #300, Winter Park, FL	305-629-5650
Bostick, Rick/6959-J Stapoint Ct, Winterpark, FL	305-677-5717
Bowie, Ed/809 W University/Box 31641, Lafayette, LA	318-234-0576

Photographers

Continued

Please send us your additions and updates.

Boyd, Richard/PO Box 5097, Roanoke, VA	703-366-3140
Boyle, Jeffrey/8725 NW 18th Terrace #215, Miami, FL	305-592-7032
Brack, Dennis/3609 Woodhill Pl, Fairfax, VA	703-280-2285
Brasher/Rucker Photography/3373 Park Ave, Memphis, TN	901-324-7447
Braun, Paulette/1500 N Orange #42, Sarasota, FL	813-366-6284
Brill, David/Route 4, Box 121-C, Fairbourn, GA	404-461-5488
Brinson, Rob/486 14th St, Atlanta, GA	404-874-2497
Brooks, Charles/800 Luttrell St, Knoxville, TN	615-525-4501
Broomell, Peter/901 N Columbus St, Alexandria, VA	703-548-5767
Brown, Billy/2700 Seventh Ave S, Birmingham, AL	205-251-8327
Brown, Richard Photo/PO Box 1249, Asheville, NC	704-253-1634
Browne, Turner/1634 Washington Ave, New Orleans, LA	504-899-8883
Bryant, Doug/PO Box 80155, Baton Rouge, LA	504-387-1620
Bumpus, Ken/1770 W Chapel Dr, Deltona, FL	305-695-0668
Burgess, Ralph/PO Box 36, Chrstnsted/St Croix, VI	809-773-6541
Burns, Jerry/331-B Elizabeth St, Atlanta, GA	404-522-9377
Busch, Scherley/4186 Pamona Ave, Coconut Grove, FL	305-661-6605
Byrd, Syndey/7932 S Clairborne #6, New Orleans, LA	504-865-7218

C
Calamia, Ron & Assoc/8140 Forshey St, New Orleans, LA	504-482-8062
Call, Douglas/8279-A Severn Dr, Boca Raton, FL	305-977-5591
Callendrillo, Frank/2485 E Sunrise Rd #205, Fort Lauderdale, FL	305-566-8236
Camera Graphics/1230 Gateway Rd, Lake Park, FL	305-844-3399
Cameron, Larry/1314 Lincoln St #301, Columbia, SC	803-799-7558
Carnes, John/3730 Central Ave, Nashville, TN	615-321-5506
Carpenter, Michael/5127 Hartford Ln, Burke, VA	703-978-2196
Carriker, Ronald/565 Alpine Rd, Winston Salem, NC	919-765-3852
Case, Sam/PO Box 1139, Purcellville, VA	703-338-2725
Caswell, Sylvia/807 9th Court S, Birmingham, AL	205-252-2252
Caudle, Dennis/909 Felle St, Baltimore, MD	301-563-0906
Caudle, Rod Studio/1708 Defoor Pl, Atlanta, GA	404-351-6385
Cavedo, Brent/9 W Main St, Richmond, VA	804-344-5374
Centner, Ed Productions/12950 SW 122nd Ave, Miami, FL	305-238-3338
Chalfant, Flip/283 Hope St, Marietta, GA	404-422-1796
Chambers, Terrell/6843 Tilton Lane, Doraville, GA	404-396-4648
Chamowitz, Mel/3931 N Glebe Rd, Arlington, VA	703-536-8356
Chapple, Ron/501 N College, Charlotte, NC	704-377-4217
Chernush, Kay/3855 N 30th St, Arlington, VA	703-528-1195
Chesler, Donna & Ken/6941 NW 12th St, Plantation, FL	305-581-6489
Choiniere, Gerin/1424 N Tryon St, Charlotte, NC	704-372-0220
Clark, Marty/1105 Peachtree St NE, Atlanta, GA	404-873-4618
Clayton, Al/141 The Prado NE, Atlanta, GA	404-577-4141
Cochrane, Craig/PO Box 2316, Virginia Beach, VA	804-468-1065
Cody, Dennie/5820 SW 51st Terrace, Miami, FL	305-666-0247
Colbroth, Ron/4421 Airlie Way, Annandale, VA	703-354-2729
Collins, Michael/PO Box 608522, Orlando, FL	305-889-9242
Compton, Grant/7004 Sand Nettles Dr, Savannah, GA	912-897-3771
Contorakes, George/PO Box 430901, South Miami, FL	305-661-0731
Cook, Jamie/653 Ethel St, Atlanta, GA	404-892-1393
Cooke, Bill/7761 SW 88th St, Miami, FL	305-596-2454
Copeland, Jim/2135-F Defoor Hills Rd, Atlanta, GA	404-352-2025
Corn, Jack/27 Dahlia Dr, Brentwood, TN	615-373-3301
Cornelia, William/PO Box 5304, Hilton Head Island, SC	803-671-2576
Cornelius, John/915 W Main St, Abington, MA	703-628-1699
COSBY-BOWYER INC./209 N FOUSHEE ST, RICHMOND, VA (P 160)	**804-643-1100**
Coste, Kurt/929 Julia, New Orleans, LA	504-523-6060
Cox, Whitney/2042 W Grace St #3, Richmond, VA	804-358-3061
Cromer, Peggo/1206 Andora Ave, Coral Gables, FL	305-667-3722
Crum, Lee/1536 Terpsichore St, New Orleans, LA	504-529-2156
Culpepper, Mike/1227 Sixth Ave, Columbus, GA	404-323-5703

D
Dakota, Irene/Miami, FL,	305-325-8727
Dale, John/576 Armour Circle NE, Atlanta, GA	404-872-3203
Daniel, Ralph/915 Argonne Ave #2, Atlanta, GA	404-872-3946
David, Alan/1186-D N Highland Ave, Atlanta, GA	404-872-2142
Davidson, Cameron/5316 Admiralty Ct, Alexandria, VA	703-922-3922
Dawson, Bill/1853 Madison Ave, Memphis, TN	901-726-6043
DeKalb, Jed/PO Box 22884, Nashville, TN	615-331-8527
DeVault, Jim/2400 Sunset Pl, Nashville, TN	615-269-4538
Deal Bowie & Assoc/809 W University, Lafayette, LA	318-234-0576

Degast, Robert/Rt 1 Box 323, Onancock, VA	804-787-8060
Demolina, Raul/3903 Ponce De Leon, Coral Gables, FL	305-448-8727
Design & Visual Effects/1228 Zonolite Rd, Atlanta, GA	404-872-3283
DiModica, James/139 Sevilla Ave, Coral Gables, FL	305-666-7710
Diaz, Rick/7395 SW 42nd St, Miami, FL	305-264-9761
Dickerson, John/1895 Annwicks Dr, Marietta, GA	404-977-4138
Dickinson, Dick/1854 University Pkwy, Sarasota, FL	813-351-2036
Dix, Paul/106 W Bonito Dr, Ocean Springs, MS	601-875-7691
Dixon, Tom/3404-D W Windover Ave, Greensboro, NC	919-294-6076
Dobbs, David/1536 Monroe Dr NE #110, Atlanta, GA	404-885-1460
Donica, John/4204 Wallace Ln, Nashville, TN	615-269-5024
Dorin, Jay/800 West Ave #345, Miami Beach, FL	305-866-3888
Doty, Gary/PO Box 23697, Ft Lauderdale, FL	305-928-0645
Douglas, Keith/405 NE 8th Ave, Ft Lauderdale, FL	305-763-5883
Draper, Fred/259 S Willow Ave, Cookeville, TN	615-526-1315
Dressler, Brian/300-A Huger, Columbia, SC	803-254-7171
Dugas, Henri/PO Box 250, Amelia, LA	501-631-0687
Duvall, Joe/1601 Philadelphia Ave, Orlando, FL	305-894-5052
Duvall, Thurman III/1021 Northside Dr NW, Atlanta, GA	404-875-0161

E
Eastmond, Peter/PO Box 856 E, Barbados,W Indies,	809-429-7757
Edwards, Jack/6250 Edgewater Dr #2600, Orlando, FL	305-581-6220
Edwards, Jim/416 Armour Circle NE, Atlanta, GA	404-875-1005
Eighme, Bob/1520 E Sunrise Blvd, Ft Lauderdale, FL	305-527-8445
Elliot, Tom/19756 Bel Aire Dr, Miami, FL	305-251-4315
Ellis, Bill/3410E W Andover Ave, Greensboro, NC	919-299-5074
Ellis, Gin/1203 Techwood Dr, Atlanta, GA	404-892-3204
Elmore, James/4807 5th St W, Bradenton, FL	813-755-0546
Engelman, Suzanne/1621 Woodbridge Lk Cir, W Palm Beach, FL	305-969-6666
English, Melissa Hayes/1195 Woods Circle NE, Atlanta, GA	404-261-7650
Epley, Paul/PO Box 9092, Charlotte, NC	704-332-5466
Erickson, Jim/302 Jefferson St #300, Raleigh, NC	919-833-9955

F
Felipe, Giovanni/3465 SW 73rd Ave, Miami, FL	305-266-5308
FERNANDEZ, JOSE/1011 VALENCIA AVE, CORAL GABLES, FL (P 161)	**305-443-6501**
Fineman, Michael/7521 SW 57th Terrace, Miami, FL	305-666-1250
Fisher, Kurt/679-A Durrant Pl, Atlanta, GA	404-874-5572
Fisher, Ray/10700 SW 72nd Ct, Miami, FL	305-665-7659
Fitzgerald, Barry/808 Charlotte St, Fredericksburg, VA	703-371-3253
Foley, Roger/519 N Monroe St, Arlington, VA	703-524-6274
Forer, Dan/1970 NE 149th St, North Miami, FL	305-949-3131
Fortenberry, Mark/128 Wonderwood Dr, Charlotte, NC	704-365-4774
Fowley, Douglas/103 N Hite Ave, Louisville, KY	502-897-7222
Frazier, Jeff/1025 8th Ave S, Nashville, TN	615-242-5642
Frazier, Steve/1425 US 19 S Bldg 26 #102, Clearwater, FL	813-531-3631
Freeman, Tina/2113 Decatur Sr, New Orleans, LA	504-523-3000
Frink, Stephen/PO Box 2720, Key Largo, FL	305-451-3737
Fulton, George/1237-F Gadsden St, Columbia, SC	803-779-8249

G
Gandy, Skip/302 East Davis Blvd, Tampa, FL	813-253-0340
Gardella Photography & Design/781 Miami Cr NE, Atlanta, GA	404-231-1316
Garrett, Kenneth/PO Box 208, Broad Run, VA	703-347-5848
Garrison, Gary/1052 Constance St, New Orleans, LA	504-588-9422
Gefter, Judith/1725 Clemson Rd, Jacksonville, FL	904-733-5498
Gelabert, Bill/PO Box 3231, Old San Juan, PR	809-725-4696
GELBERG, BOB/7035-E SW 47TH ST, MIAMI, FL (P 159)	**305-665-3200**
Gemignani, Joe/13833 NW 19th Ave, Miami, FL	305-685-7636
Geniac, Ruth/13353 Sorrento Dr, Largo, FL	813-595-2275
Genser, Howard/1859 Seventh Ave, Jacksonville, FL	904-734-9688
Gentile, Arthur Sr/7335 Connan Lane, Charlotte, NC	704-541-0227
GERLICH, FRED/1220 SPRING ST NW, ATLANTA, GA (P 158)	**404-872-3487**
Glaser, Ken & Assoc/5270 Annunciation St, New Orleans, LA	504-895-7170
Gleasner, Bill/132 Holly Ct, Denver, NC	704-483-9301
Godfrey, Mark/3526 N Third St, Arlington, VA	703-527-8293
Good, Jay/20901 NE 26th Ave, N Miami Beach, FL	305-935-4884
Gornto, Bill/590 Ponce De Leon Ave, Atlanta, GA	404-876-1331
Graham, Curtis/648 First Ave S, St Petersburg, FL	813-821-0444
Granberry/Anderson Studios/1211 Spring St NW, Atlanta, GA	404-874-2426
Green, Jack/1 N Pack Sq, Asheville, NC	704-274-4153
Greenberg, Bob/5277 NW 161st St, Miami, FL	305-621-8500

Photographers

Continued

Please send us your additions and updates.

Grigg, Roger Allen/PO Box 52851, Atlanta, GA	404-876-4748
Groendyke, Bill/6344 NW 201st Ln, Miami, FL	305-625-8293
Guider, John/517 Fairground Ct, Nashville, TN	615-255-4495
Guillermety, Edna/3133 Lakestone Dr, Tampa, Fl33618	813-962-1748
Gupton, Charles/Route 2 Box 206, Wake Forest, NC	919-556-6511
Guravich, Dan/PO Box 891, Greenville, MS	601-335-2444

H
Haggerty, Richard/656 Ward St, High Point, NC	919-889-7744
Hall, Don/2922 Hyde Park st, Sarasota, FL	813-365-6161
Hall, Ed/7010 Citrus Point, Winter Park, FL	305-657-8182
Hamilton, Tom/2362 Strathmore Dr, Atlanta, GA	404-266-0177
Hannau, Michael/3800 NW 32nd Ave, Miami, FL	305-633-1100
Hansen, Eric/3005 7th Ave S/Box 55492, Birmingham, AL	205-251-5587
Harbison, Steve/1516 Crestwood Dr, Greeneville, TN	615-638-2535
Hardy, Frank/1003 N 12th Ave, Pensacola, FL	904-438-2712
Harkins, Lynn S/1900 Byrd Ave #101, Richmond, VA	804-285-2900
Harrelson, Keith/4505 131st Ave N, Clearwater, FL	813-577-9812
Harris, Christopher/PO Box 2926, Covington, LA	504-893-4898
Hathcox, David/5730 Arlington Blvd, Arlington, VA	703-845-5831
Haviland, Patrick/323 E Kingston Ave, Charlotte, NC	701-332-7273
Hayden, Kenneth/1318 Morton Ave, Louisville, KY	502-583-5596
HENDERSON/MUIR PHOTO/6005 CHAPEL HILL RD,	
RALEIGH, NC (P 162)	**919-851-0458**
Hendley, Arington/454 Irwin St, Atlanta, GA	404-577-2300
Henley & Savage/113 S Jefferson St, Richmond, VA	804-780-1120
Heston, Ty/4505 131st Ave N #18, Clearwater, FL	813-573-4878
Higgins, Neal/1540 Monroe Dr, Atlanta, GA	404-876-3186
Hill, Dan/9132 O'Shea Ln, W Springfield, VA	703-451-4705
Hill, Jackson/2032 Adams St, New Orleans, LA	504-861-3000
Hill, Tom/207 E Parkwood Rd, Decatur, GA	404-377-3833
Hillyer, Jonathan/450-A Bishop St, Atlanta, GA	404-351-0477
Hirsch, Alan/1259 Ponce de Leon #6C, San Juan, PR	809-723-2224
Hoflich, Richard/544 N Angier Ave NE, Atlanta, GA	404-584-9159
HOGBEN, STEVE/468 ARMOUR DR, ATLANTA, GA (P 163)	**404-266-2894**
Holland, Ralph/3706 Alliance Dr, Greensboro, NC	919-855-6422
Holland, Robert/PO Box 162099, Miami, FL	305-255-6758
Holt Group/403 Westcliff Rd/Box 35488, Greensboro, NC	919-668-2770
HOOD, ROBIN/1101 W MAIN ST, FRANKLIN, TN (P 156,157)	**615-794-2041**
Horan, Eric/PO Box 6373, Hilton Head Island, SC	803-842-3233
Hosack, Loren/2301-F Sabal Ridge Ct, Palm Beach Gardens, FL	305-627-8313
Houghtaling, Jim/403 Westcliff/Box 3548, Greensboro, NC	919-668-2770
Humphries, Gordon/Boozer Shopping Ctr, Columbia, SC	803-772-3535
Humphries, Vi/Boozer Shopping Ctr, Columbia, SC	803-772-3535
Hunter, Bud/1917 1/2 Oxmoor Rd, Birmingham, AL	205-879-3153
Huntley, Robert/1210 Spring St NW, Atlanta, GA	404-892-6450

IJ
International Defense Images/2419 Mt Vernon Ave, Alexandria, VA	703-548-7217
Isaacs, Lee/2321 First Ave N #105, Birmingham, AL	205-252-2698
Jamison, Chipp/2131 Liddell Dr NE, Atlanta, GA	404-873-3636
Jeffcoat, Russell/1201 Hagood St, Columbia, SC	803-799-8578
Jeffcoat, Wilber L/1864 Palomino Cir, Sumter, SC	803-773-3690
Jenkins, Dave Prdctns/1084 Duncan Ave, Chattanooga, TN	615-629-5380
Jimison, Tom/5929 Annunciation, New Orleans, LA	504-891-8587
Joens, Samuel A/131 Pineview Rd, W Columbia, SC	803-791-4896
Johns, Douglas/2535 25th Ave N, St Petersburg, FL	813-321-7235
Johnson, Forest/7755 SW 86th St #406, Miami, FL	305-279-6074
Johnson, George L/16603 Round Oak Dr, Tampa, FL	813-963-3222
Johnson, Silvia/6110 Brook Dr, Falls Church, VA	703-532-8653
Jones, Samuel A/131 Pineview Rd, West Columbia, SC	803-791-4896
Jordan/Rudolph Studios/1446 Mayson St NE #5L, Atlanta, GA	404-874-1829
Jureit, Robert A/916 Aguero Ave, Coral Gables, FL	305-667-1346

K
Kaplan Studio/PO Box 7206, McLean, VA	703-893-1660
Kaplan, Al/PO Box 611373, North Miami, FL	305-891-7595
Kaplan, Martin & Laura/PO Box 7206, McLean, VA	703-893-1660
Kappiris, Stan/PO Box 14331, Tampa, FL	813-254-4866
Katz, Arni/PO Box 724507, Atlanta, GA	404-953-1168
Kaufman, Len/5119 Arthur St, Hollywood, FL	305-920-7822
Kearney, Mitchell/301 E 7th St, Charlotte, NC	704-377-7662
Kennedy, Chuck/2745-B Hidden Lake Blvd, Sarasota, FL	813-365-5564

Kennedy, M Lewis/2700 7th Ave S, Birmingham, AL	205-252-2700
Kenner, Jack/PO Box 3269, Memphis, TN	901-527-3686
Kent, David/7515 SW 153rd Ct #201, Miami, FL	305-382-1587
Kern Photography/1243 N 17th Ave, Lake Worth, FL	305-582-2487
Kersh, Viron/PO Box 51201, New Orleans, LA	504-524-4515
King, J Brian/1267 Coral Way, Miami, FL	305-856-6534
King, Tom/2806 Edgewater Dr, Orlando, FL	305-841-4421
Kinney, Greg/912 Burford Pl, Nashville, TN	615-297-8084
Kinsella, Barry/1010 Andrews Rd, West Palm Beach, FL	305-832-8736
Klass, Rubin & Erika/5200 N Federal Hwy #2, Fort Lauderdale, FL	305-565-1612
Klemens, Susan/7423 Foxleigh Way, Alexandria, VA	703-971-1226
Kling, David Photography/502 Armour Circle, Atlanta, GA	404-881-1215
KNIBBS, TOM/5907 NE 27TH AVE, FT LAUDERDALE, FL (P 164)	**305-491-6263**
Knight, Steve/1212 E 10th St, Charlotte, NC	704-334-5115
Kogler, Earl/PO Box 3578, Longwood, FL	305-331-4035
Kohanim, Parish/1130 W Peachtree NW, Atlanta, GA	404-892-0099
Kollar, Robert E/1431 Cherokee Trail #52, Knoxville, TN	615-573-8191
Koplitz, William/729 N Lime St, Sarasota, FL	813-366-5905
Kralik, Scott/210 N Fillmore, Arlington, VA	703-522-8261
Kufner, Gary/2032 Harrison St, N Hollywood, FL	305-944-7740

L
Lackey, Larry/2400 Poplar Ave #514, Memphis, TN	901-323-0811
Lafayette, James/148 Windward Hill, Hilton Head, SC	803-785-3201
Lai, Bill/2500-A Morosgo Pl, Atlanta, GA	404-237-0003
Lair, John/1122 Roger St, Louisville, KY	502-589-7779
Langone, Peter/516 NE 13th St, Ft Lauderdale, FL	305-467-0654
Lanpher, Keith/865 Monticello Ave, Norfolk, VA	804-627-3051
Lanzone, John/10 E Madison St #1D, Baltimore, MD	301-385-0230
Latham, Charles/559 Dutch Valley Rd NE, Atlanta, GA	404-873-5858
Lathem, Charles & Assoc/559 Dutch Valley Rd NE, Atlanta, GA	404-873-5858
Lavenstein, Lance/4605 Pembroke Lake Cir, Virginia Beach, VA	804-499-9959
Lawrence, David/PO Box 835, Largo, FL	813-586-2112
Lawrence, John R/Box 330570, Coconut Grove, FL	305-447-8621
Lawrence, Mark/PO Box 23950, Ft Lauderdale, FL	305-565-8866
Lawson, Slick/3801 Whitland Ave, Nashville, TN	615-383-0147
Lazzo, Dino/655 SW 20th Rd, Miami, FL	305-856-1148
Lee, Chung P/7820 Antiopi St, Annandale, VA	703-560-3394
Lee, George/423 S Main St, Greenville, SC	803-232-4119
Lee, Joe/PO Box 22941, Jackson, MS	601-948-5255
Leggett, Albert/1415 Story Ave, Louisville, KY	502-584-0255
Leo, Victor/121 W Main St, Louisville, KY	502-589-2423
Lipson, Stephen/15455 SW Terrace, Miami, FL	305-382-3502
Little, Chris/PO Box 467221, Atlanta, GA	404-641-9688
Llewellyn, Robert/PO Drawer L, Charlottesville, VA	804-973-8000
Long, Lewis/3130 SW 26th St, Miami, FL	305-448-7667
Loumakis, Constantinos/826 SW 13th St, Ft Lauderdale, FL	305-525-7367
Lubin, Jeff/8472 Rainbow Bridge Ln, Springfield, VA	703-569-5086
Lucas, Steve/7925 SW 104th St #E-202, Miami, FL	305-238-6024
Luttrell, David/1500 Highland Dr, Knoxville, TN	615-588-5775
Lynch, Warren/306 Production Ct, Louisville, KY	502-491-8233

M
Magee, Ken/3519 Live Oak, New Orleans, LA	504-889-3928
Magruder, Mary and Richard/2156 Snap Finger Rd, Decatur, GA	404-289-8985
Mahen, Rich/4301 SW 10th St, Ft Lauderdale, FL	305-792-5429
Malles, Ed/1013 S Semoran Blvd, Winter Park, FL	305-679-4155
Mann, James/1007-B Norwalk, Greensboro, NC	919-292-1190
Mann, Rod/5082 Woodleigh Rd, Knotts Island, NC	919-429-3009
Maratea, Ronn/4338 Virginia Beach Blvd, Virginia Beach, VA	804-340-6464
Marden, Bruce F Productions/611 Honeybear Ln, Marietta, GA	404-351-8152
Markatos, Jerry/Rt 2 Box 419/Rock Rest Rd, Pittsboro, NC	919-542-2139
Marquez, Toby/1709 Wainwright Dr, Reston, VA	703-471-4666
Mason, Chuck/8755 SW 96th St, Miami, FL	305-270-2070
May, Clyde/1037 Monroe Dr NE, Atlanta, GA	404-873-4329
Mayo, Michael/710 Tenth St, Atlanta, GA	404-873-2410
Mayor, Randy/2007 15th Ave S, Birmingham, AL	212-645-8737
Mazey, Jon/2724 NW 30th Ave, Ft Lauderdale, FL	305-731-3300
McCannon, Tricia/1536 Monroe Dr, Atlanta, GA	404-873-3070
McCarthy, Tom/8960 SW 114th St, Miami, FL	305-233-1703

Photographers

Continued

Please send us your additions and updates.

McClure, Dan/320 N Milledge, Athens, GA	404-354-1234
McCord, Fred/2720 Piedmont Rd NE, Atlanta, GA	404-262-1538
McCoy, Frank T/131 Donmond Dr, Hendersonville, TN	615-822-4437
McGee, E Alan/1816-E Briarwd Ind Ct, Atlanta, GA	404-633-1286
McIntyre, William/3746 Yadkinville Rd, Winston-Salem, NC	919-922-3142
McKee, Lee/1004 Ruth Jordano Ct, Ocoee, FL	305-656-9289
McKenzie & Dickerson/133 W Vermont Ave/Box 152, Southern Pines, NC	919-692-6131
McLaughlin, Ken/623 7th Ave S, Nashville, TN	615-256-8162
McNabb, Tommy/4015 Brownsboro Rd, Winston-Salem, NC	919-723-4640
McNeely, Burton/PO Box 338, Land O'Lakes, FL	813-996-3025
McVicker, Sam/PO Box 880, Dunedin, FL	813-734-9660
Meacham, Ralph/Rt 1/Box 215, Spring Hill, TN	615-486-2973
Melyana Assoc/2740 Alton Rd, Miami Beach, FL	305-673-0094
Meredith, David/2900 NE 30th St #2H, Ft Lauderdale, FL	305-564-4579
Michot, Walter/1520 E Sunrise Blvd, Ft Lauderdale, FL	305-527-8445
Mikeo, Rich/5399 N E 14th Ave, Ft Lauderdale, FL	305-491-5399
Miller, Brad/3645 Stewart, Coconut Grove, FL	305-666-1617
Miller, Bruce/9401 61st Court SW, Miami, FL	305-666-4333
Miller, Randy/6666 SW 96th St, Miami, FL	305-667-5765
Millington, Rod/526 N Washington Dr, Sarasota, FL	813-388-1420
Mills, Henry/5514 Starkwood Dr, Charlotte, NC	704-535-1861
Mims, Allen/107 Madison Ave, Memphis, TN	901-527-4040
Minardi, Mike/PO Box 14247, Tampa, FL	813-684-7138
Mitchell, Michael/2803 Foster Ave, Nashville, TN	615-333-1008
Molony, Bernard/PO Box 15081, Atlanta, GA	404-457-6934
Montage Studio/429-A Armour Cir, Atlanta, GA	404-892-3650
Moore, George Photography/1301 Admiral St, Richmond, VA	804-355-1862
Moore, Leslie/8551 NW 47th Ct, Fort Lauderdale, FL	305-742-4074
Moore, Mark/3803 W Gray, Tampa, FL	813-874-0410
Morgan, Frank/789 Seahawk Circle #112, Virginia Beach, VA	804-422-9328
Morgan, Red/970 Hickory Trail, W Palm Beach, FL	305-793-6085
Morrah, Linda/201 E Coffee St, Greenville, SC	803-242-9108
Morris, Paul/PO Box 530894, Miami, FL	305-758-8150
Muldez, Richard/404 Investors Pl #108, Virginia Beach, VA	804-490-6640
Murphy, Lionel Jr/2311 Waldemere, Sarasota, FL	813-365-0595
Murray, Kevin/Box 212, Winston-Salem, NC	919-722-5107
Murray, Steve/1330 Mordecai, Raleigh, NC	919-828-0653
Myers, Fred/114 Regent Ln, Florence, AL	205-386-2207
Myhre, Gordon/PO Box 1226, Ind Rocks Beach, FL	813-584-3717
Mykietyn, Walt/10110 SW 133 St, Miami, FL	305-235-2342

NO

Nelson, Jon/PO Box 8772, Richmond, VA	804-359-0642
Nemeth, Judy/930 N Poplar St, Charlotte, NC	704-375-9292
Neubauer, John/1525 S Arlington Ridge Rd, Arlington, VA	703-920-5994
Norling Studios Inc/221 Swathmore Ave/Box 7167, High Point, NC	919-434-3151
Norris, Robert Photo/224 Lorna Square, Birmingham, AL	205-979-7005
North Light Studio/1803 Hendricks Ave, Jacksonville, FL	904-398-2501
Norton, Mike/4917 W Nassau, Tampa, FL	813-876-3390
Novak, Jack/PO Box 971, Alexandria, VA	703-836-4439
Novicki, Norb/6800 North West 2nd St, Margate, FL	305-971-8954
Nurnberg, Paul/810 E Sixth St, Washington, NC	617-327-3920
O'Boyle, Erin/7001 N Atlantic Ave #122, Cape Canaveral, FL	305-783-1923
O'Brian, Brian/102 W Clinton Ave #404, Huntsville, AL	205-539-0407
O'KAIN, DENNIS/102 W MAIN, LEXINGTON, GA (P 165)	**404-743-3140**
O'Sullivan, Brian/1401 SE 8th St, Deerfield Beach, FL	305-429-0712
Oesch, James/3706 Ridge Rd, Annadale, VA	703-941-3600
Olive, Tim/754 Piedmont Ave NE, Atlanta, GA	404-872-0500
Olson, Carl/3325 Laura Way, Winston, GA	404-949-1532
Osborne, Mitchel L/920 Frenchman St, New Orleans, LA	504-949-1366

P

Parker, Phillip M/192 Williford, Memphis, TN	901-529-9200
Patterson, M N/1615 Brown Ave #2, Cookeville, TN	615-528-8025
Patterson, Pat/1635 Old Louisburg Rd, Raleigh, NC	919-834-2223
Payne, Steve/1524 Virginia St E, Charleston, WV	304-343-7254
Pelosi & Chambers/684 Greenwood Ave NE, Atlanta, GA	404-872-8117
Peters, J Dirk/PO Box 15492, Tampa, FL	813-884-6272
Petrey, John/670 Clay St/Box 2401, Winter Park, FL	305-645-1718
Phillips, David/20 Topsail Tr, New Port Richey, FL	813-849-9458
Photo-Synthesis/1239 Kensington Rd, McLean, VA	703-734-8770
Photographic Group/7407 Chancery Ln, Orlando, FL	305-855-4306

Photographic Ideas/701 E Bay St/Box 1216, Charleston, SC	803-577-7020
Photography Unlimited/3662 S West Shore Blvd, Tampa, FL	813-839-7710
Pierce, Nancy J/1715 Merry Oaks Rd, Charlotte, NC	704-535-7409
Pierson, Art/1107 Lincoln Ave, Falls Church, VA	703-237-5937
Pocklington, Mike/9 W Main St, Richmond, VA	804-783-2731
PORTRAIT ALLIANCE/6083 ARLINGTON BLVD, FALLS CHURCH, VA (P 152)	**703-533-9453**
Posey, Mike/3524 Canal St, New Orleans, LA	504-488-8000
Prism Studios/1027 Elm Hill Pike, Nashville, TN	615-255-1919
Purin, Thomas/14190 Harbor Lane, Lake Park, FL	305-622-4131

R

Ramirez, George/303 Canals St, Santurce, PR	809-724-5727
Ramos, Victor/8390 SW 132 St, Miami, FL	305-255-3111
Randolph, Bruce/132 Alan Dr, Newport News, VA	804-877-0992
Rank, Don/1980 Will Ross Ct, Atlanta, GA	404-452-1658
Rathe, Robert A/8451-A Hilltop Rd, Fairfax, VA	703-560-7222
Raymond, Tom/Rt 6 Box 424-C, Jonesborough, TN	615-753-9061
Reus-Breuer, Sandra/Cal Josefa Cabrera Final #3, Rio Piedras, PR	809-767-1568
Rickles, Tom/5401 Alton Rd, Miami, FL	305-866-5762
Riggall, Michael/403 8th St NE, Atlanta, GA	404-872-8242
Riley, Richard/34 N Ft Harrison, Clearwater, FL	813-446-2626
Rippey, Ray/PO Box 50093, Nashville, TN	615-646-1291
Rob/Harris Productions/PO Box 15721, Tampa, FL	813-258-4061
Rodgers, Ted/544 Plasters Ave, Atlanta, GA	404-892-0967
Rogers, Brian/689 Antone St NW, Atlanta, GA	404-355-8069
Rogers, Chuck/1226-28 Spring St NW, Atlanta, GA	404-872-0062
Rosen, Olive/3415 Arnold Ln, Falls Church, VA	703-560-5557
Rossmeissl, Kirk/1921 Woodford Rd, Vienna, VA	301-899-4866
Rubio, Manny/1203 Techwood Dr, Atlanta, GA	404-892-0783
Runion, Britt/7409 Chancery Ln, Orlando, FL	305-857-0491
Russell, John Photo/PO Box 2141, High Point, NC	919-887-1163
Rutherford, Michael W/623 Sixth Ave S, Nashville, TN	615-242-5953
Rutledge, Don/13000 Edgetree Ct, Midlothian, VA	804-353-0151

S

Saenz, C M/PO Box 117, Alachua, FL	904-462-5670
Salmon, George/10325 Del Mar Circle, Tampa, FL	813-961-8687
Sambrook, Don/13 W 25th St, Baltimore, MD	301-235-0900
Sanacore, Steve/1829 Abbey Rd, West Palm Beach, FL	305-439-7883
Sander, Neil/PO Box 819, Maggie Valley, NC	704-456-9912
Saylor, Ted/2312 Farwell Dr, Tampa, FL	813-879-5636
Schaedler, Tim/PO Box 1081, Safety Harbor, FL	813-796-0366
Schatz, Bob/112 Second Ave N, Nashville, TN	615-254-7197
Schenck, Gordon H/PO Box 35203, Charlotte, NC	704-332-4078
Schenker, Richard/6304 Benjamin Rd #504, Tampa, FL	813-885-5413
Schermerhorn, Tim/325 Model Farm Rd, High Point, NC	919-889-6121
Schiavone, George/355 NE 59th Terr, Miami, FL	305-662-6057
Schiff, Ken/4406 SW 74th Ave, Miami, FL	305-262-2022
Schneider, John/3702-B Alliance Dr, Greensboro, NC	919-855-0261
Schulke, Debra/6770 SW 101st St, Miami, FL	305-667-0961
Schulke, Flip/14730 SW 158th St, Miami, FL	305-251-7717
Schumacher, Karl/6254 Park Rd, McLean, VA	703-241-7424
Schwartz, Alan/8400 SW 133rd Ave Rd #409, Miami, FL	305-596-6720
Seifried, Charles/Rt 3 Box 162, Decatur, AL	205-355-5558
Seitelman, M D/PO Box 2477, Alexandria, VA	703-548-7217
Seitz, Arthur/1905 N Atlantic Blvd, Ft Lauderdale, FL	305-563-0060
Sharpe, David/816 N St Asaph St, Alexandria, VA	703-683-3773
Shea, David/#12 Miracle Strip Pkwy SE, Ft Walton Beach, FL	904-244-3602
Sheffield, Scott/2707 W Broad St, Richmond, VA	804-358-3266
Sheldon, Mike/Rt 2 Box 61A, Canton, NC	704-235-8345
Sherbow, Robert/1607 Colonial Terr, Arlington, VA	202-522-3644
Sherman, Pam/103 Bonnie Brae Way, Hollywood, FL	305-652-0566
SHERMAN, RON/PO BOX 28656, ATLANTA, GA (P 166)	**404-993-7197**
Shooters Photographic/1001-C W Tremont Ave, Charlotte, NC	704-334-7267
Shrout, Bill/Route 1 Box 317, Theodore, AL	205-973-1379
Silla, Jon/229 S Brevard St, Charlotte, NC	704-377-8694
Sink, Richard/1225 Cedar Dr, Winston Salem, NC	919-784-8759
Sisson, Barry/6813 Bland St, Springfield, VA	703-569-6051
Smeltzer, Robert/29 Stone Plaza Dr, Greenville, SC	803-235-2186
Smith, Clark/618 Glenwood Pl, Dalton, GA	404-226-2508
Smith, Richard & Assoc/1007 Norwalk St #B, Greensboro, NC	919-292-1190
Smith, Richard Photo/1625 NE 3rd Ct, Ft Lauderdale, FL	305-523-8861

Photographers

Continued

Please send us your additions and updates.

Smith/Garner Studios/1114 W Peachtree St, Atlanta, GA	404-875-0086
Snow, Chuck/2700 7th Ave S, Birmingham, AL	205-251-7482
Snyder, Lee/4150-D 112th Terr N, Clearwater, FL	813-578-2332
Sparkman, Clif/161 Mangum St SW #301, Atlanta, GA	404-588-9687
Sparks, Don/670 11th St NW, Atlanta, GA	404-876-7354
Spartana, Stephen/1802 E Lombard St, Baltimore, MD	301-327-1918
Speidell, Bill/1030 McConville Rd, Lynchburg, VA	804-846-2133
St John, Chuck/2724 NW 30th Ave, Ft Lauderdale, FL	305-731-3300
St John, Michael/PO Box 1202, Oldsmar, FL	813-725-4817
STANSFIELD, ROSS/4938-D EISENHOWER AVE, ALEXANDRIA, VA (P 153)	**703-370-5142**
Staples, Neil/5092 NE 12th Ave, Ft Lauderdale, FL	305-792-2448
Stein Photo/20240 SW 92nd Ave, Miami, FL	305-251-2868
Stein, Art/2419 Mt Vernon Ave, Alexandria, VA	703-684-0675
Stein, Marc/402 Rustic Trail, Birmingham, AL	205-987-1359
Stewart, Harvey & Co Inc/836 Dorse Rd, Lewisville, NC	919-945-2101
Stoppee Photographics Group/13 W Main St, Richmond, VA	804-644-0266
Strode, William A/1008 Kent Rd, Prospect, KY	502-228-4446
Suraci, Carl/216 Hillsdale Dr, Sterling, VA	703-620-6645
Swann, David/776 Juniper St, Atlanta, GA	404-873-3003
Sweetman, Gary Photography/2904 Manatee Ave W, Bradenton, FL	813-748-4004
Symmes Jr, Edwin C/PO Box 8101, Atlanta, GA	404-876-7620

T

Tast, Jerry/8880 Old King's Rd S #34, Jacksonville, FL	904-731-5887
Taylor, Randy/555 NE 34th St #701, Miami, FL	305-573-5200
Telesca, Chris/PO Box 51449, Raliegh, NC	919-846-0101
Tesh, John/904-A Norwalk St, Greensboro, NC	919-299-1400
Thomas, J Clark/2305 Elliston Place, Nashville, TN	615-327-1757
Thomas, Larry/1212 Spring St, Atlanta, GA	404-881-8850
Thomas/Bruce Studio/79-25 4th St N, St Petersburg, FL	813-577-5626
Thompson & Thompson Photo/5180 NE 12th Ave, Ft Lauderdale, FL	305-772-4411
Thompson, Darrell/124 Rhodes Dr, Marietta, GA	404-641-2020
Thompson, Ed C/2381 Drew Valley Rd, Atlanta, GA	404-636-7258
Thompson, Michael Photography/1579-F Monroe Dr #240, Atlanta, GA	404-874-4054
Thompson, Rose/4338 NE 11th Ave, Oakland Park, FL	305-563-7937
Thompson, Thomas L/3210 Peachtree Rd NW #14, Atlanta, GA	404-524-6929
Tilley, Arthur/1925 College Ave NE, Atlanta, GA	404-371-8086
Tobias, Jerry/2117 Opa-Locka Blvd, Miami, FL	305-685-3003
TOUCHTON, KEN/3011 NORTHEAST 40TH ST, FT LAUDERDALE, FL (P 167)	**305-566-9756**
Traves, Stephen/360 Elden Dr, Atlanta, GA	404-255-5711
Trufant, David/1902 Highland Rd, Baton Rouge, LA	504-344-9690
Truman, Gary/PO Box 7144, Charleston, WV	304-755-3078
Tucker, Mark Studio/117 Second Ave N, Nashville, TN	615-254-5555
Turnau, Jeffrey/7210 Red Rd #216, Miami, FL	305-666-5454

UV

Ustinick, Richard/12 North 18th St, Richmond, VA	804-649-1477
Uzzell, Steve/2505 N Custis Rd, Arlington, VA	703-522-2320
Uzzle, Warren/5201 William & Mary Dr, Raleigh, NC	919-266-6203
Valada, M C/204 Park Terr Ct SE, Vienna, VA	703-938-0324
Van Calsem, Bill/824 Royal St, New Orleans, LA	504-522-7346
Van Camp, Louis/713 San Juan Rd, New Bern, NC	919-633-6081
Van de Zande, Doug/515 Hillsborough St, Raliegh, NC	919-832-2499
Vance, David/13760 NW 19th Ave #14, Miami, FL	305-685-2433
Vaughn, Marc/11140 Griffing Blvd, Biscayne Park, FL	305-895-5790
Victor, Ira/2026 Prairie Ave, Miami Beach, FL	305-532-4444
Vullo, Phillip Photography/565 Dutch Valley Rd NE, Atlanta, GA	404-874-0822

W

Wagoner, Mark/12-H Wendy Ct Box 18974, Greensboro, NC	919-854-0406
Walker, Reuel Jr/PO Box 5421, Greenville, SC	803-834-9836
Walker, Wes/201 E Coffee St, Greenville, SC	803-242-9108
Walpole, Gary/284 N Cleveland, Memphis, TN	901-726-1155
Walters, Tom/804 Atando Ave, Charlotte, NC	704-333-6294
Wark, Mark/Rte 5 Box 239-A, Charlottesville, VA	804-973-3370
Warren, Bob/1511 Gilford Ave, Baltimore, MD	301-539-2807
Watt, John/3480 Matilda, Miami, FL	216-621-3838
Wax, Bill/6880 Abbott Ave #201, Miami Beach, FL	305-864-8650
Webb, Jon/2023 Kenilworth Ave, Louisville, KY	502-459-7081

Webster & Co/2401 Euclid Ave, Charlotte, NC	704-522-0647
Weinlaub, Ralph/81 SW 6th St, Pompano Beach, FL	305-941-1368
Weithorn, Mark/13740 NW 19th Ave #6, Miami, FL	305-688-7070
Westerman, Charlie/Central Amer Bldg/Bowman Fld, Louisville, KY	502-458-1532
Wheless, Rob/2239 Faulkner Rd NE, Atlanta, GA	404-321-3557
White, Drake/PO Box 40090, Augusta, GA	404-733-4142
Whitman, Alan/724 Lakeside Dr, Mobile, AL	205-661-0400
Whitman, John/604 N Jackson St, Arlington, VA	703-524-5569
Wiener, Ray/4300 NE 5th Terrace, Oakland Park, FL	305-565-4415
Wiley Jr, Robert/1145 Washington Ave, Winter Park, FL	305-629-5823
Williams, Jimmy/3801 Beryl Rd, Raleigh, NC	919-832-5971
Williams, Ron/105 Space Park Dr #A, Nashville, TN	615-331-2500
Williams, Sonny/741 Monroe Dr, Atlanta, GA	404-892-5551
Willis, Joe/105 Lake Emerald Dr #314, Ft Lauderdale, FL	305-485-7185
Wilson, Andrew/1720 Cumberland Point Dr #20, Marietta, GA	404-980-1289
Wilson, Vickie/21 W Country Cove, Kifsimmee, FL	305-348-4906
Wilt, Greg/PO Box 212, Clearwater, FL	813-442-4360
Winner, Alan/20151 NE 15th Court, Miami, FL	305-653-6778
Wolf, David/1770 Quail Ridge Rd, Raleigh, NC	919-876-1387
Woodbury, Mark/6801 NW 9th Ave #102, Ft Lauderdale, FL	305-977-9000
Woodson, Richard/PO Box 12224, Raliegh, NC	919-833-2882
Wray, Michael/3501 Royal Palm Ave, Ft Lauderdale, FL	305-564-3433
Wright, Chris (Ms)/4131 Walnut Grove, Memphis, TN	901-761-5215
Wright, Christopher/2001-A Dekle Ave, Tampa, FL	813-251-5206
Wright, Timothy/PO Box 5425, Virginia Bch, VA	804-464-6710
Wrisley, Bard/55 Bennett St NW, Atlanta, GA	404-524-6929

YZ

Yankus, Dennis/223 S Howard Ave, Tampa, FL	813-254-4156
Young, Chuck/1199-R Howell Mill Rd, Atlanta, GA	404-351-1199
Zeck, Gerry/1939 S Orange Ave, Sarasota, FL	813-953-4888
Zimmerman, Mike/7821 Shalimar, Mira Mar, FL	305-987-8482
Zinn, Arthur/2661 S Course Dr, Pompano Beach, FL	305-973-3851
Zonner, Anthony/850 Montrose St, Shreveport, LA	318-865-0307

Midwest

A

AGS & R Studios/425 N Michigan Ave, Chicago, IL	312-836-4500
Abel Photographics/7035 Ashland Dr, Cleveland, OH	216-526-5732
Abramson, Michael Photo/3312 W Belle Plaine, Chicago, IL	312-267-9189
Accola, Harlan J/207 E 29th St, Marshfield, WI	715-387-8682
Adamo, Sam/490 Parkview Dr, Seven Hills, OH	216-447-9249
Adams, Steve Studio/3101 S Hanley, Brentwood, MO	314-781-6676
Alan, Andrew/20727 Scio Church Rd, Chelsea, MI	313-475-2310
Albiez, Scott/4144 N Clarendon, Chicago, IL	312-327-8999
Albright, Dave/200 S Main, Northville, MI	313-348-2248
Alexander, Gordon/1848 Porter St SW, Wyoming, MI	616-531-1204
Alexander, Mark/412 Central Ave, Cincinnati, OH	413-651-5020
Allan-Knox Studios/450 S 92nd St, Milwaukee, WI	414-774-7900
Allen, Carter/8081 Zionsville Rd/POB 68520, Indianapolis, IN	317-872-7720
Altman, Ben/820 N Franklin, Chicago, IL	312-944-1434
Amenta/555 W Madison #3802, Chicago, IL	312-248-2488
Anderson Studios Inc/546 S Meridian #300, Indianapolis, IN	317-632-9405
Anderson, Craig/105 7th St, W Des Moines, IA	515-279-7766
Anderson, Curt/Box 3213, Minneapolis, MN	612-332-2008
Anderson, Rob/900 W Jackson, Chicago, IL	312-666-0417
Anderson, Whit/219 W Chicago, Chicago, IL	312-973-5683
Andre, Bruce/436 N Clark, Chicago, IL	312-661-1060
Andrew, Larry/1632 Broadway, Kansas City, MO	816-471-5565
Ann Arbor Photo/670 Airport Blvd, Ann Arbor, MI	313-995-5778
Apolinski, John/735 N Oriole Ave, Park Ridge, IL	312-696-3156
Arciero, Anthony/70 E Long Lake Rd, Bloomfield Hills, MI	313-645-2222
Ardisson Photography/2719 N Wayne, Chicago, IL	312-836-0464
Armour, Tony/1726 N Clybourn Ave, Chicago, IL	312-664-2256
Arndt, David M/4620 N Winchester, Chicago, IL	312-334-2841
Arndt, Jim/400 First Ave N #510, Minneapolis, MN	612-332-5050
Arsenault, Bill/1244 W Chicago Ave, Chicago, IL	312-421-2525
Ascherman, Herbert Jr/1846 Coventry Vill-4, Cleveland Heights, OH	216-321-0055
Askenas, Ulf/409 W Huron, Chicago, IL	312-944-4630
Atevich, Alex/325 N Hoyne Ave, Chicago, IL	312-942-1453

PHOTOGRAPHERS

341

Photographers

Continued

Please send us your additions and updates.

Atkinson, David/3923 W Pine Blvd, St Louis, MO	314-535-6484
Audio Visual Impact Group/233 E Erie, Chicago, IL	312-664-6247
Ayala/320 E 21 St, Chicago, IL	312-326-0728
Azuma, Don/1335 N Wells, Chicago, IL	312-337-2101

B

Baer Studio/5807 Capri Ln, Morton Grove, IL	312-966-4759
Baer, Gordon/PO Box 2467, Cincinnati, OH	513-281-2339
Bagnoli, Susan/74-24 Washington Ave, Eden Prairie, MN	612-944-5750
Bahm, Dave/711 Commercial, Belton, MO	816-331-0257
Baker, Jim/1632 Broadway, Kansas City, MO	816-471-5565
Balterman, Lee/910 N Lake Shore Dr, Chicago, IL	312-642-9040
Banna, Kevin/617 W Fulton St, Chicago, IL	312-845-9650
Banner & Burns Inc/153 W Ohio, Chicago, IL	312-644-4770
Bannister, Will/2312 N Lincoln, Chicago, IL	312-327-2143
Barge, Mike/7618 W Myrtle, Chicago, IL	312-762-1749
Barkan Keeling Photo/905 Vine St, Cincinnati, OH	513-721-0700
Barlow Photography Inc/1125 S Brentwood Blvd, Richmond Hts, MO	314-721-2385
Barnett, Jim/1502 S Keystone Ave, Indianapolis, IN	317-783-6797
BARRETT, BOB PHOTO/3733 PENNSYLVANIA, KANSAS CITY, MO (P 175)	**816-753-3208**
Bart, Casimir/205 Ridgemont W #703, Toronto M5V 1V5,	
Bartholomew, Gary/263 Columbia Ave, Des Plaines, IL	312-824-8473
Barton, Mike/5019 Nokomis Ave S, Minneapolis, MN	612-721-1349
Bartone, Tom/436 N Clark St, Chicago, IL	312-836-0464
Bartz, Carl Studio Inc/321 N 22nd St, St Louis, MO	314-231-8690
Basdeka, Pete/1254 N Wells, Chicago, IL	312-944-3333
Bass, Alan/126 W Kinzie, Chicago, IL	312-280-9140
Battrell, Mark/1611 N Sheffield, Chicago, IL	312-642-6650
Baver, Perry L/2923 W Touhy, Chicago, IL	312-674-1695
Bayles, Dal/4431 N 64th St, Milwaukee, WI	414-464-8917
Beasley, Michael/1210 W Webster, Chicago, IL	312-248-5769
Beaugureau Studio/7843 W Berwyn Ave, Chicago, IL	312-696-1299
Beaulieu, Allen/127 N 7th St #208, Minneapolis, MN	612-338-2327
Beckett Photography/510 N Water St, Milwaukee, WI	414-271-2061
Beckett Studios/340 W Huron St, Chicago, IL	312-943-2648
Bednersti, Paul/5735 Bishop Rd, Detroit, MI	313-882-0427
Bellville, Cheryl Walsh/2823 8th St S, Minneapolis, MN	612-333-5788
Belter, Mark/640 N LaSalle St #555, Chicago, IL	312-337-7676
Benda, Tom/20555 LaGrange, Frankfurt, IL	815-469-3600
Bender/Bender/281 Klingel Rd, Waldo, OH	614-726-2470
Benkert, Christine/27 N 4th St #501, Minneapolis, MN	612-340-9503
Bennarski, Paul/5735 Bishop Rd, Detroit, MI	313-882-0427
Benoit, Bill/1708 1/2 Washington, Wilmette, IL	312-251-7634
Bentley, David/208 West Erie, Chicago, IL	312-836-0242
Benyas-Kaufman Photo/8775 W 9 Mile Rd, Oak Park, MI	313-548-4400
Berglund, Peter/126 N 3rd St #402, Minneapolis, MN	612-371-9318
Bergos, Jim Studio/122 W Kinzie St, Chicago, IL	312-527-1769
Berkman, Elie/125 Hawthorn Ave, Glencoe, IL	312-835-4158
Berlin Chic Photo/1708 W School Rd 3rd Fl, Chicago, IL	312-327-2266
Berliner, Sheri/2815 N Pine Grove #1A, Chicago, IL	312-477-6692
Berlow, Marc Photography/325 W Huron St #406, Chicago, IL	312-787-6528
Berr, Keith/1220 W 6th St #608, Cleveland, OH	216-566-7950
BERTHIAUME, TOM/1008 NICOLLET MALL, MINNEAPOLIS, MN (P 176)	**612-338-1999**
Bevacqua, Alberto/720 N Wabash, Chicago, IL	312-266-2575
Bidak, Lorne/827 Milwaukee Ave, Chicago, IL	312-733-3997
Bieber, Tim/3312 W Belle Plaine, Chicago, IL	312-463-3590
Biel Photographic Studios/2289-91 N Moraine Blvd, Dayton, OH	513-298-6621
Bilsley, Bill/126 W Kinzie, Chicago, IL	312-661-1379
Bishop, Robert/5622 Delmar #103, St Louis, MO	314-367-8787
Bjornson, Howard/300 N Ashland, Chicago, IL	312-243-8200
Block, Ernie/1138 Cambridge Cir Dr, Kansas City, KS	913-321-3080
Block, Stuart/1242 W Washington Blvd, Chicago, IL	312-733-3600
Bochsler, Tom/3514 Mainway, Burlington L7M 1A8, ON	
Bock, Edward/400 N First Ave #207, Minneapolis, MN	612-332-8504
Bodenhansen, Gary/201 Main St, Kansas City, MO	816-221-2456
Bolber Studio/6706 Northwest Hwy, Chicago, IL	312-763-5860
Borde, Richard & Dawn/5328 29th Ave S, Minneapolis, MN	612-729-1913
Bornefeld, William/586 Hollywood Pl, St Louis, MO	314-962-5596
Boschke, Les/4200 N Hermitage, Chicago, IL	312-929-1119

Bosek, George/1301 S Wabash 2nd Fl, Chicago, IL	312-828-0988
Bosy, Peter/564 W Randolph, Chicago, IL	312-559-0042
Boucher, Joe/5765 S Melinda St, Milwaukee, WI	414-281-7653
Bowen, Paul/Box 3375, Wichita, KS	316-263-5537
Boyer, Dick/45W Erie #201, Chicago, IL	312-337-7211
Brackenbury, Vern/1516 N 12th St, Blue Springs, MO	816-229-6703
Braddy, Jim/PO Box 11420, Chicago, IL	312-337-5664
Bradley, Rodney/329 10th Ave SE, Cedar Rapids, IA	319-365-5071
Brandenburg, Jim/708 N 1st St, Minneapolis, MN	612-341-0166
Brandt & Assoc/Route 5 Box 148, Barrington Hills, IL	312-428-6363
Braun Photography/3966 W Bath Rd, Akron, OH	216-666-4540
Brayne, TW/326 W Kalamazoo Ave, Kalamazoo, MI	616-344-0283
Brettell, Jim/2152 Morrison Ave, Lakewood, OH	216-228-0890
Brimacombe, Gerald/7212 Mark Terrace, Minneapolis, MN	612-941-5860
Broderson, Fred/215 W Huron, Chicago, IL	312-787-1241
Brody, David & Assoc/6001 N Clark, Chicago, IL	312-761-2735
Brody, Jerry/70 W Hubbard, Chicago, IL	312-329-0660
Brookins, Carl/PO Box 80096, St Paul, MN	612-636-1733
Brooks, John/5663 Carrollton Ave, Indianapolis, IN	317-253-5663
Brosilow, Michael/208 W Kinzie 4th Fl, Chicago, IL	312-645-0628
Brown, Alan J/815 MAin St, Cincinnati, OH	513-421-5588
Brown, James F/1349 E McMillan St, Cincinnati, OH	513-221-1144
Brown, Ron/1324 N Street, Lincoln, NE	402-476-1760
Brown, Steve/107 W Hubbard, Chicago, IL	312-467-4666
Bruno, Sam/1630 N 23rd, Melrose Park, IL	312-345-0411
Bruton, Jon/3838 W Pine Blvd, St Louis, MO	314-533-6665
Brystrom, Roy/6127 N Ravenswood, Chicago, IL	312-973-2922
Bukva, Walt/118 Anchor Rd, Michigan City, IN	219-872-9469
Bundt, Nancy/1908 Kenwood Parkway, Minneapolis, MN	612-377-7700
Burjoski, David/3524 Washington Ave 4th Fl, St Louis, MO	314-534-4060
Burns Copeland Photography/6651 N Artesian, Chicago, IL	312-465-3240
Burress, Cliff/5420 N Sheridan, Chicago, IL	312-334-5332
Burris, Zack/445 W Erie, Chicago, IL	312-951-0131
BUSCHAUER, AL/11416 S HARLEM AVE, WORTH, IL (P 177)	**312-448-2222**
Bush, Tim/617 W Fulton St, Chicago, IL	312-993-0666

C

C-H Studios/517 S Jefferson 7th Fl, Chicago, IL	312-922-8880
CR Studio/1859 W 25th St, Cleveland, OH	216-861-5360
Cabanban, Orlando/410 S Michigan Ave, Chicago, IL	312-922-1836
Cable, Wayne/2212 N Racine, Chicago, IL	312-525-2240
Cain, C C/420 N Clark, Chicago, IL	312-644-2371
Cairns, Robert/2035 W Charleston #4-SE, Chicago, IL	312-384-3114
Camacho, Mike/124 W Main St, West Dundee, IL	312-428-3135
Camera Works Inc/1260 Carnegie Ave, Cleveland, OH	216-687-1788
Camerawork, Ltd/400 S Greens St #203, Chicago, IL	312-666-8802
Campbell, Bob/722 Prestige, Joliet, IL	815-725-1862
Candee & Assoc/1212 W Jackson, Chicago, IL	312-829-1212
Caporale, Michael/6710 Madison Rd, Cincinnati, OH	513-561-4011
Carell, Lynn/3 E Ontario #25, Chicago, IL	312-935-1707
Carney, Joann/368 W Huron, Chicago, IL	312-266-7620
Carosella, Tony/4138-A Wyoming, St Louis, MO	314-664-3462
Carr, Steve/311 N Desplaines #608, Chicago, IL	312-454-0984
Carter, David/510 W Wellington, Chicago, IL	312-929-0306
Carter, Garry/179 Waverly, Ottawa K2P 0V5, ON	613-233-3306
Carter, Mary Ann/5954 Crestview, Indianapolis, IN	317-255-1351
Casalini, Tom/10 1/2 N Main St, Zionsville, IN	317-873-5229
Cascarano, John/657 W Ohio, Chicago, IL	312-733-1212
Caswell, George/700 Washington Ave N #308, Minneapolis, MN	612-332-2729
Cates, Gwendolen/1942 N Dayton, Chicago, IL	312-880-5571
Caulfield, James/430 W Erie, Chicago, IL	312-951-7260
Ceolla, George/5700 Ingersoll Ave, Des Moines, IA	515-279-3508
Cermak Photo/96 Pine Ave, Riverside, IL	312-447-6446
Chadwick Taber Inc/617 W Fulton, Chicago, IL	312-454-0855
Chambers, Tom/153 W Ohio, Chicago, IL	312-828-9488
Chapman, Cam/126 W Kinzie, Chicago, IL	312-222-9242
Chapman, John/311 N Des Plaines, Chicago, IL	312-930-9127
Chare, Dave/1045 N Northwest Hwy, Park Ridge, IL	312-696-3188
Charlie Company/2000 Superior Ave #2, Cleveland, OH	216-566-7464
Chauncey, Paul C/1029 N Wichita #13, Wichita, KS	316-262-6733
Cherup, Thomas/PO Box 84, Dearborn Hts, MI	313-561-9376
Chicago Photographers/60 W Superior, Chicago, IL	312-944-4828

Chin, Ruth/108 E Jackson, Muncie, IN	317-284-4582
Chobot, Dennis/2857 E Grand Blvd, Detroit, MI	313-875-6617
Christian Studios Inc/5408 N Main St, Dayton, OH	513-275-3775
Christman, Gerald/985 Ridgewood Dr, Highland Park, IL	312-433-2279
Clark, Harold/9 Lloyd Manor, Islington M9B 5H5, ON	416-236-2958
Clark, Junebug/30419 W Twelve Mile Rd, Farmington Hills, MI	313-478-3666
Clarke, Jim/3721 Grandel Sq, St Louis, MO	314-652-6262
Clawson, David/6800 Normal Blvd, Lincoln, NE	402-489-1302
Clawson, Kent/740 18th St, Des Moines, IA	515-244-8975
Clayton, Curt/23263 Woodward Ave, Ferndale, MI	313-548-0039
Clemens, Jim/1147 W Ohio, Chicago, IL	312-280-2289
CLICK/ CHICAGO/213 W INSTITUTE PL #503, CHICAGO, IL	
(P 178)	**312-787-7880**
Cloudshooters/Aerial Photo/4620 N Winchester, Chicago, IL	312-334-2841
Clough, Jean/4440 N California, Chicago, IL	312-583-8681
Coats & Greenfield Inc/2928 Fifth Ave S, Minneapolis, MN	612-827-4676
Cocase, Ellen/18 W Hubbard St, Chicago, IL	312-384-0718
Cochrane, Jim/25 1/2 York St #1, Ottawa K1N 5S7, ON	613-234-3099
Cocose, Ellen/445 E Ohio #222, Chicago, IL	312-527-9444
Coha, Dan/9 W Hubbard, Chicago, IL	312-664-2270
Coil, Ron Studio/15 W Hubbard St, Chicago, IL	312-321-0155
Compton, Ted/112 N Washington, Hinsdale, IL	312-654-8781
Condie, Thomas M/527 N 27th St, Milwaukee, WI	414-342-6363
Copeland, Burns/6651 N Artesian, Chicago, IL	312-465-3240
Corey, Carl/222 S Morgan, Chicago, IL	312-421-3232
Corson, Mark/1709 Washington Ave, St Louis, MO	314-241-0054
Coster-Mullen, John E/PO Box 1637, Appleton, WI	414-733-9001
Cowan, Ralph/452 N Halsted St, Chicago, IL	312-243-6696
Cox, Dennis/14555 Champaign #212, Allen Park, MI	313-386-4802
Cralle, Gary/83 Elm Ave #205, Toronto M4W 1P1, ON	416-923-2920
Crandall, Greg/1742 McKinley St, Mishawaka, IN	219-259-1913
Crane, Arnold/666 N Lake Shore Dr, Chicago, IL	312-337-5544
Crane, Michael/1717 Wyandotte St, Kansas City, MO	816-221-9382
Creightney, Dorrell/1729 W Melrose, Chicago, IL	312-528-0816
Crofoot, Ron/6140 Wayzata Blvd, Minneapolis, MN	612-546-0643
Crofton, Bill/326R Linden Ave, Wilmette, IL	312-256-7862
Cromwell, Patrick/1739 Coolidge, Berkley, MI	313-543-5610
Crosby, Paul/1701 E 79th St #17B, Minneapolis, MN	612-854-3060
Cross, Emil/1886 Thunderbird, Troy, MI	313-362-3111
Crowther Photography/2210 Superior Viaduct W, Cleveland, OH	216-566-8066
Culbert-Aguilar, Kathleen/1338 W Carmen, Chicago, IL	312-561-1266
Curtis, Lucky/1540 N Park Ave, Chicago, IL	312-787-4422

D

D'Orio, Tony/1147 W Ohio, Chicago, IL	312-421-5532
Dacuisto, Todd/4455 W Bradley Rd #204, Milwaukee, WI	414-352-7527
Dale, LB/7015 Wing Lake Rd, Birmingham, MI	313-851-3296
Dali, Michael/1737 McGee, Kansas City, MO	816-931-0570
Dapkus, Jim/Westfield Photo/Rte 1 Box 247, Westfield, WI	608-296-2623
Davito, Dennis/638 Huntley Heights, Manchester, MO	314-394-0660
Day, Michael/264 Seaton St, Toronto M5A 2T4, ON	416-920-9135
DeBolt, Dale/120 West Kinzie St, Chicago, IL	312-644-6264
DeLaittre, Bill/1307 5th St South, Minneapolis, MN	612-936-9840
DeMarco Photographers/7145 W Addison, Chicago, IL	312-282-1422
DENATALE, JOE/215 W OHIO, CHICAGO, IL (P 179)	**312-329-0234**
Deahl, David/70 W Hubbard, Chicago, IL	312-644-3187
Debacker, Michael/231 Ohio, Wichita, KS	316-265-2776
Debold, Bill/1801 N Halsted, Chicago, IL	312-337-1177
Delich, Mark/304 W 10th St #200, Kansas City, MO	816-474-6699
Denning, Warren/27 Laurel, Wichita, KS	316-262-4163
Desala, Enrique/3752 N Fremont, Chicago, IL	
Design Photography/1324 Hamilton Ave, Cleveland, OH	216-687-0099
Deutsch, Owen/1759 N Sedgwick, Chicago, IL	312-943-7155
DIERINGER, RICK/19 WEST COURT ST, CINCINNATI, OH	
(P 180)	**513-621-2544**
Dierkes, Barry/1600 Thoroughbred Ln, Florissant, MO	314-831-3600
Dinerstein, Matt/606 W 18th St, Chicago, IL	312-243-4766
Dinn, Peter/54B Fore Rd, Elliot, ME	207-439-7594
Ditlove, Michel/18 W Hubbard, Chicago, IL	312-644-5233
Ditz, Michael/8138 W 9 Mile Rd, Oak Park, MI	313-546-1759
Donner, Michael/5534 S Dorchester, Chicago, IL	312-241-7896
Donofrio, Randy/6459 S Albany, Chicago, IL	312-737-0990

Dovey, Dean/1917 N Milwaukee, Chicago, IL	312-292-1737
Doyle, Tim/1550 E 9 Mile Rd, Ferndale, MI	313-543-9440
Drake, Brian Photo/1355 E Canton Ct, Deerfield, IL	312-446-5248
Drew, Terry-David/219 W Chicago, Chicago, IL	312-943-0301
Drickey, Pat/406 S 12th St, Omaha, NE	402-344-3786
Drier, David/804 Washington St #3, Evanston, IL	312-475-1992
DuBroff, Don/2031 W Cortez, Chicago, IL	312-252-7390
Dublin, Rick/414 Third Ave W, Minneapolis, MN	612-332-8924
Dzielak, Dennis/350 W Ontario #600, Chicago, IL	312-786-9364

E

ETM Studios/130 S Morgan, Chicago, IL	312-666-0660
Eagle, Joe/415 W Superior, Chicago, IL	312-280-1919
Eagle, Lin/1308 W Wrightwood, Chicago, IL	312-525-2170
Ebel, Bob Photography/1376 W Carroll, Chicago, IL	312-222-1123
Ebenoh, Tom/8439 Lake Dr, Cedar Hill, MO	314-285-2467
Eckhard, Kurt/1306 S 18th St, St Louis, MO	314-241-1116
Eggebenn, Mark/1217 Center Ave, Dostburg, WI	414-564-2344
Eiler, Lynthia & Terry/330-B Barker Rd Rt 2, Athens, OH	614-592-1280
Einhorn, Mitchell/311 N Des Plaines #603, Chicago, IL	312-944-7028
Eisner, Scott Photography/314 W Superior, Chicago, IL	312-670-2217
Eldridge, Dave/916 Olive St #300, St Louis, MO	314-231-6800
Elinchev, Chris/1324 1/2 N Milwaukee, Chicago, IL	
Elledge, Paul/1808 W Grand Ave, Chicago, IL	312-733-8021
Ellingsen/1411 Peterson, Park Ridge, IL	312-823-0192
Elliott, Peter/405 N Wabash Ave, Chicago, IL	312-329-1370
Elmore, Bob and Assoc/315 S Green St, Chicago, IL	312-641-2731
Englehard, J Versar/1723 N Honore #2F, Chicago, IL	312-787-2024
Ernst, Elizabeth/1020 Elm St, Winnetka, IL	312-441-8993
Evans, Patricia/1153 E 56th St, Chicago, IL	312-288-2291
Ewert, Steve/17 N Elizabeth, Chicago, IL	312-733-5762

F

Faitage, Nick Photography/1910 W North Ave, Chicago, IL	312-276-9321
Farber, Gerald/445 W Erie, Chicago, IL	312-337-3324
Farmer, Jerry/620 E Adams, Springfield, IL	217-785-6102
Faverty, Richard/340 W Huron, Chicago, IL	312-943-2648
Fay, Mark/5200 W 73rd, Edina, MN	612-835-5447
Feferman, Steve/462 Fern Dr, Wheeling, IL	312-459-3695
Fegley, Richard/6083 N Kirkwood, Chicago, IL	312-527-1114
Feher, Paul/3138 Flame Dr, Oregon, OH	419-698-4254
Feldman, Stephen L/2705 W Agatite, Chicago, IL	312-539-0300
Ferguson, Ken/920 N Franklin St, Chicago, IL	312-642-6255
Ferguson, Scott/7110 Oakland Ave, St Louis, MO	314-647-7466
Ficht, Bill/244 Blue Spruce La, Aurora, IL	312-851-2185
Fichter, Russ/1500 N Halstead, Chicago, IL	312-787-9768
Finlay & Finlay Photo/141 E Main St, Ashland, OH	419-289-3163
Firak Photography/11 E Hubbard, Chicago, IL	312-467-0208
First Light Assoc/78 Rusholme Rd, Toronto M6J 3H6, ON	416-532-6108
Fish Studios/4318 W Irving Park, Chicago, IL	312-282-4001
Fitzsimmons, J Kevin/2380 Wimbledon Rd, Columbus, OH	614-457-2010
Fleming, Larry/1029 N Wichita #3, Wichita, KS	316-267-0780
Fletcher, Mike/7467 Kingsbury, St Louis, MO	314-721-2279
Flood, Kevin/1329 Macklind St, St Louis, MO	314-647-2485
Floyd, Bill/215 W Ohio, Chicago, IL	312-321-1770
Fong, John/13 N Huron St, Toledo, OH	419-243-7378
Fontayne Studios Ltd/4528 W Oakton, Skokie, IL	312-676-9872
Foran, Bob/3930 Varsity Dr, Ann Arbor, MI	313-973-0960
Ford, Madison/2616 Industrial Row, Troy, MI	313-280-0640
Forrest, Michael/2150 Plainfield Ave NE, Grand Rapids, MI	616-361-2556
Forsyte, Alex/1180 Oak Ridge Dr, Glencoe, IL	312-835-0307
Forth, Ron/316 W 4th St, Cincinnati, OH	513-621-0841
Foss, Kurt/4147 Pleasant Ave S, Minneapolis, MN	612-822-4694
Foster, Richard/157 W Ontario St, Chicago, IL	312-943-9005
Foto-Graphics/2402 N Shadeland Ave, Indianapolis, IN	317-353-6259
Foto/Ed Sacks/Box 7237, Chicago, IL	312-871-4700
Fox Commercial Photo/119 W Hubbard, Chicago, IL	312-664-0162
Fox, Fred & Sons/2746 W Fullerton, Chicago, IL	312-342-3233
Francis, Dan/4515 Delaware St N, Indianapolis, IN	317-283-8244
Frantz, Ken/706 N Dearborn, Chicago, IL	312-951-1077
Franz, Bill/820 E Wisconsin, Delavan, WI	414-728-3733
Freeman, George/1061 W Balmoral, Chicago, IL	312-275-1122
French, Graham/387 Richmond St E, Toronto M5A 1P6, ON	416-860-0300
Frerck, Robert/4158 N Greenview 2nd Fl, Chicago, IL	312-883-1965

Frey, Jeff/405 E Superior St, Duluth, MN	218-722-6630
Frick, Ken/66 Northmore Pl, Colombus, OH	614-263-9955
Friedman, Susan J/215 W Ohio, Chicago, IL	312-527-1880
Fritz, Tom/2930 W Clybourn, Milwaukee, WI	414-344-8300
Futran, Eric/3454 N Bell, Chicago, IL	312-525-5020

G

GSP/156 N Jefferson, Chicago, IL	312-944-3000
Gabriel Photo/160 E Illinois, Chicago, IL	312-743-2220
Gale, Bill/3041 Aldrich Ave S, Minneapolis, MN	612-827-5858
Galloway, Scott/177 Benson Rd, Akron, OH	216-666-4477
Gardner, Al/7120 Eugene, St Louis, MO	314-752-5278
Garmon, Van/1601 22nd St #201, W Des Moines, IA	515-225-0001
Gates, Bruce/356 1/2 S Main St, Akron, OH	216-375-5282
Gaymont, Gregory/1812 N Hubbard St, Chicago, IL	312-421-3146
Gerding, Gary/8025 W Dodge Rd, Omaha, NE	402-390-2677
Gerlach, Monte/705 S Scoville, Oak Park, IL	312-848-1193
GETSUG, DON/610 N FAIRBANKS CT, CHICAGO, IL	
(P 170,171)	**312-440-1311**
Giannetti, Joseph/127 N 7th St #402, Minneapolis, MN	612-339-3172
Gillette, Bill/2917 Eisenhower, Ames, IA	515-294-4340
Gilo, Dave/121 N Broadway, Milwaukee, WI	414-273-1022
GILROY, JOHN/2407 WEST MAIN ST, KALAMAZOO, MI	
(P 181)	**616-349-6805**
Girard, Connie/609 Renolda Woods Ct, Dayton, OH	513-294-2095
Girard, Jennifer/1455 W Roscoe, Chicago, IL	312-929-3730
Glenn, Eileen/300 W Superior, Chicago, IL	312-944-1756
Gluth, Bill/5207 N Wayne, Chicago, IL	312-334-1150
Goddard, Will/1496 N Albert St, St Paul, MN	612-645-9516
Goez, Bill/9657 S Winchester, Chicago, IL	312-881-1964
Goff, D R/66 W Wittier St, Columbus, OH	614-443-6530
Goldberg, Lenore/210 Park Ave, Glencoe, IL	312-835-4226
Goldstein, Steven/14982 Country Ridge, St Louis, MO	314-532-0660
Goodwin, Andy/400 E Randolf St #1926, Chicago, IL	312-748-5426
Gorecki Studio/5011 W Fullerton, Chicago, IL	312-622-8146
Goss, James M/1737 McGee St, Kansas City, MO	816-471-8069
Goss, Michael/117 S Morgan, Chicago, IL	312-421-3808
Gould, Christopher/224 W Huron, Chicago, IL	312-944-5545
Gould, Rick Studios/217 N 10th St, St Louis, MO	314-241-4862
Graenicher, Kurt/112 Seventh Ave, Monroe, WI	608-328-8400
Graham, Stephen/1120 W Stadium #2, Ann Arbor, MI	313-761-6888
Graham-Henry, Diane/613 W Belden, Chicago, IL	312-327-4493
Grajczyk, Chris/126 North 3rd St #405, Minneapolis, MN	612-333-6265
Gray, Walter/1035 W Lake, Chicago, IL	312-733-3800
Grayson, Dan/831 W Cornelia, Chicago, IL	312-477-8659
Greenblatt, William/20 Nantucket Ln, St Louis, MO	314-726-6151
Gregg, Rene/4965 McPherson, St Louis, MO	314-361-1963
Gregg, Robb T/4715 N Ronald St, Harwood Heights, IL	312-777-4756
Gremmler, Paul/221 W Walton, Chicago, IL	312-787-1877
Griffin, Maria/PO Box 14397, Chicago, IL	312-248-5372
Griffith, Sam/345 N Canal, Chicago, IL	312-648-1900
Grignon Studios/1300 W Altgeld Dr, Chicago, IL	312-975-7200
Grippentrag, Dennis/70 E Long Lake Rd, Bloomfield Hills, MI	313-645-2222
Groen, John/676 N LaSalle, Chicago, IL	312-266-2331
Grondin, Timothy/815 Main St, Cincinnati, OH	513-421-5588
Gross, Werner/465 S College, Valparaiso, IN	219-462-3453
Grubman, Steve/219 W Chicago, Chicago, IL	312-787-2272
Grunewald, Jeff/161 W Harrison St, Chicago, IL	312-663-5799
Gubin, Mark/2893 S Delaware Ave, Milwaukee, WI	414-482-0640
Guerry, Tim/711 S Dearborn #304, Chicago, IL	312-294-0070
Gyssler, Glen/411 S Sangamon #5D, Chicago, IL	312-243-8482

H

Haberman, Mike/529 S 7th St #427, Minneapolis, MN	612-338-4696
Haefner, Jim/1407 N Allen, Troy, MI	313-583-4747
Haines, W C (Bill)/3101 Mercier Ste 484, Kansas City, MO	816-531-0561
Halbe, Harrison/710 N Tucker Blvd #218, St Louis, MO	314-993-1145
Hall, Brian/1015 N LaSalle St, Chicago, IL	312-642-6764
Haller, Pam/215 W Huron, Chicago, IL	312-649-0920
Halsey, Daniel/1017 E 145th St, Minneapolis, MN	612-431-1679
Hamill, Larry/77 Deshler, Columbus, OH	614-444-2798
Hammarlund, Vern/135 Park St, Troy, MI	313-588-5533
Hampton, Chris/3522 N Marshfield, Chicago, IL	312-467-0135
Handley, Robert E/1920 E Croxton, Bloomington, IL	309-828-4661

Hanselman, Linda/PO Box 8072, Cincinnati, OH	513-321-8669
Harbron, Patrick/366 Adelaide St E #331, Toronto, ON	416-863-9412
Harding Studio/727 Hudson, Chicago, IL	312-943-4010
Harlan, Bruce/52922 Camellia Dr, South Bend, IN	219-239-7350
Harquail, John/67 Mowat Ave #40, Toronto M6K 3E3,	416-535-1620
Harrig, Rick/3316 South 66th Ave, Omaha, NE	402-397-5529
Harris, Bart/70 W Hubbard St, Chicago, IL	312-751-2977
Hart, Bob/116 W Illinois, Chicago, IL	312-644-3636
Harvey, Jeff/PO Box 262, Palos Hts, IL	312-535-4900
Hauser, Marc/1810 W Cortland, Chicago, IL	312-486-4381
Hawker, Chris/119 N Peoria, Chicago, IL	312-829-4766
Hedrich, Sandi/10-A W Hubbard, Chicago, IL	312-321-1151
Hedrich-Blessing/11 W Illinois St, Chicago, IL	312-321-1151
Heil, Peter/225 S Morgan, Chicago, IL	312-544-9130
Helmick, William/129 Geneva, Elmhurst, IL	312-834-4798
Henebry, Jeanine/1154 Locust Rd, Wilmette, IL	312-251-8747
Henning, Paul/PO Box 92218, Milwaukee, WI	414-765-9441
Hermann, Dell/676 N LaSalle, Chicago, IL	312-664-1461
Hertzberg, Richard/436 N Clark, Chicago, IL	312-836-0464
Hetisimer, Larry/3439 Magnolia AVe, St Louis, MO	309-797-1010
Hill, John/4234 Howard, Western Springs, IL	312-246-3566
Hill, Roger/4040 W River Dr, Comstock Park, MI	616-784-9620
Hillery, John/PO Box 2916, Detroit, MI	313-345-9511
Hirneisen, Richard/306 S Washington St #218, Royal Oak, MI	313-399-2410
Hirschfeld, Corson/316 W Fourth St, Cincinnati, OH	513-241-0550
Hodes, Charles S/233 E Erie, Chicago, IL	312-951-1186
Hodge, Adele/465 N Wabash Ave #1211, Chicago, IL	312-828-0611
Hodges, Charles/539 W North Ave, Chicago, IL	312-664-8179
Hoffman-Wilber Inc/618 W Jackson, Chicago, IL	312-454-0303
Hogan, Thomas/187 Johnstown Rd, Columbus, OH	614-471-1727
Holographics Design System/1134 W Washington, Chicago, IL	312-226-1007
Holzemer, Buck/3448 Chicago Ave, Minneapolis, MN	612-824-3874
Honor, David/415 W Superior, Chicago, IL	312-751-1644
Hooke Photography/1147 W Ohio, Chicago, IL	312-829-4568
Hoppe, Ed Photography/3057 N Kimball Ave, Chicago, IL	312-787-2136
Hoskins, Sarah/1206 Isabella, Wilmette, IL	312-256-5724
Houghton, Michael/Studiohio/55 E Spring St, Columbus, OH	614-224-4885
Howrani, Armeen/2820 E Grand Blvd, Detroit, MI	313-875-3123
Hrdlicka, Mitch/4201 Levinworth, Omaha, NE	402-551-0887
Hsi, Kai/160 E Illinois, Chicago, IL	312-642-9853
Huet, John/107 South St, Boston, MA	617-423-6317
Hurling, Robert/325 W Huron, Chicago, IL	312-944-2022
Hutson, David/8120 Juniper, Prairie Village, KS	913-383-1123
Hyman, Randy/7709 Carnell Ave, St Louis, MO	314-721-7489

I

Iacono, Michael/412 Central Ave, Cleveland, OH	513-621-9108
Iann-Hutchins/2044 Euclid Ave, Cleveland, OH	216-579-1570
Image Productions/115 W Church, Libertyville, IL	312-680-7100
Image Studiio/1100 S Lynndale, Appleton, WI	414-739-7824
Imagematrix/2 Garfield Pl, Cincinnati, OH	513-381-1380
Imagination Unlimited/PO Box 268709, Chicago, IL	312-764-1880
Imbrogno, James/411 N LaSalle St, Chicago, IL	312-644-7333
Ingram, Russell/1000-02 W Monroe St, Chicago, IL	312-829-4652
Ingve, Jan & Assoc/128 Wedgewood Dr, Barrington, IL	312-381-3456
International Photo Corp/1035 Wesley, Evanston, IL	312-475-6400
Irving, Gary/PO Box 38, Wheaton, IL	312-653-0641
Isenberger, Brent/1710-J Gutherie Ave, Des Moines, IA	515-262-5466
Itahara, Tets/676 N LaSalle, Chicago, IL	312-649-0606
Iwata, John/336 W 15th Ave, Oshkosh, WI	414-424-0317
Izquierdo, Abe/213 W Institute #208, Chicago, IL	312-787-9784
Izui, Richard/315 W Walton, Chicago, IL	312-266-8029

J

Jackson, David/1021 Hall St, Grand Rapids, MI	616-243-3325
Jackson, Jack/117-A W Walker St 4th Fl, Milwaukee, WI	414-672-7444
Jacobs, Todd/3336 N Sheffield, Chicago, IL	312-472-4401
Jacobson, Scott/3435 N County Rd #18, Plymouth, MN	612-546-9191
Jacquin Enterprise/1219 Holly Hills, St Louis, MO	314-832-4221
James Studio/730 Lee St, Des Plaines, IL	312-824-0007
James, E Michael/9135 S LaSalle, Chicago, IL	312-468-9746
JAMES, PHILLIP MACMILLAN/2300 HAZELWOOD AVE, ST	
PAUL, MN (P 182)	**612-777-2303**
Jedd, Joseph/1624 S Courtland, Park Ridge, IL	312-696-1745

Photographers

Continued

Please send us your additions and updates.

Jenkins, David/1416 S Michigan Ave, Chicago, IL	312-922-2299
Jennings, Bill/1322 S Wabash, Chicago, IL	312-987-0124
Jensen, Michael/1101 Stinson Blvd NE, Minneapolis, MN	612-379-1944
Jilling, Helmut/1759 State Rd, Cuyahoga Falls, OH	216-928-1330
Jochim, Gary/1324 1/2 N Milwaukee, Chicago, IL	312-252-5250
JOEL, DAVID/1342 W HOOD AVE, CHICAGO, IL (P 183)	**312-262-0794**
Johnson, Dave/679 E Mandoline, Madison Hts, MI	313-589-0066
Johnson, Donald/2807 Brindle, Northbrook, IL	312-480-9336
Johnson, Jim/802 W Evergreen, Chicago, IL	312-943-8864
Jolly, Keith/32049 Milton Ave, Madison Hts, MI	313-588-6544
Jones, Arvell/8232 W McNichols, Detroit, MI	313-533-6313
Jones, Brent/9121 S Merrill Ave, Chicago, IL	312-933-1174
JONES, DAWSON/44 E FRANKLIN ST, DAYTON, OH (P 184)	**513-435-1121**
Jones, Dick/325 W Huron St, Chicago, IL	312-642-0242
Jones, Duane/5605 Chicago Ave S, Minneapolis, MN	612-823-8173
Jones, Harrison/445 W Erie #209, Chicago, IL	312-337-4997
Jones, Mark/718 Washington Ave N, Minneapolis, MN	612-338-5712
Jons Studio/35 E Wacker, Chicago, IL	312-236-0243
Jordan, Jack/840 John St, Evansville, IN	812-423-7676
Jordano, Dave/1335 N Wells, Chicago, IL	312-280-8212
Joseph, Mark/1007 N La Salle, Chicago, IL	312-951-5333
Julian, Percy/2613 Waunona Way, Madison, WI	608-225-6400
Justice Patterson Studio/7609 Production Dr, Cincinnati, OH	513-761-4023
K Kalyniuk, Jerry/4243 N Winchester, Chicago, IL	312-666-5588
Kapal Photo Studio/1314 W Lincoln Hwy, Schereville, IN	219-322-8305
Kaplan, Brian/1643 N Milwaukee Ave, Chicago, IL	312-489-0676
Kaplan, Dick/708 Waukegan, Deerfield, IL	312-945-3425
Kaplan, Matthew/5452 N Glenwood, Chicago, IL	312-769-5903
Karant & Assoc/215 W Ohio St, Chicago, IL	312-527-1880
Kaspar, Tom/650 S Clark, Chicago, IL	312-968-2442
Kauck, Jeff/205 W 4th St #460, Cincinnati, OH	513-241-5435
Kauffman, Kim/444 Lentz Court, Lansing, MI	517-371-3036
Kavula, Ken/19 E Pearson, Chicago, IL	312-280-9060
Kazu Studio/6051 N Olympia, Chicago, IL	312-348-5393
Kean, Christopher/624 West Adams St, Chicago, IL	312-559-0880
Keeling, Robert/6051 N Olympia, Chicago, IL	312-944-5680
Keisman & Keisman/518 W 37th St, Chicago, IL	312-268-7955
Kelly, Tony/828 Colfax, Evanston, IL	312-864-0488
Ketchum, Art/1 E Oak, Chicago, IL	312-544-1222
Kezar, Mitch/2207 Oakview Ln N, Minneapolis, MN	612-559-1733
Kimbal, Mark/23860 Miles Rd, Cleveland, OH	216-587-3555
Kinast, Susan/1035 West Lake St, Chicago, IL	312-738-0068
King, Jay Studios/1024 W Armitage, Chicago, IL	312-327-0011
Kingsbury, Andrew/700 N Washington #306, Minneapolis, MN	612-340-1919
Kitahara, Joe/304 W 10th St, Kansas City, MO	816-474-6699
Kleber, Gordon/525 Dearborn, Chicago, IL	312-341-9764
Klein Photography/952 W Lake, Chicago, IL	312-226-1878
Klein, Daniel/1301 E 12th St, Kansas City, MO	816-474-6491
Klutho, Dave/4617 Brookroyal Ct, St Louis, MO	314-487-3626
Knize, Karl/1034 W Washington, Chicago, IL	312-243-5503
Kodama, Kiyoshi/424 N Benton, St Charles, MO	314-946-9247
KOGAN, DAVID/1242 W WASHINGTON, CHICAGO, IL (P 185)	**312-243-1929**
Kolesar, Jerry Photographics/679 E Mandoline, Madison Hts, MI	313-589-0066
Kolze, Larry/22 W Erie, Chicago, IL	312-266-8352
Kompa, Jeff/25303 Lorain Rd, N Olmstead, OH	216-777-1611
Kondas, Thom Assoc/P O Box 1162, Indianapolis, IN	317-637-1414
Kondor, Linda/430 N Clark St, Chicago, IL	312-642-7365
Korab, Balthazar/PO Box 895, Troy, MI	313-641-8881
Kransberger, Jim/2247 Boston SE, Grand Rapids, MI	616-245-0390
Krantz, Jim/5017 S 24th St, Omaha, NE	402-734-4848
Krantz, John/2907 Bridge Ave, Cleveland, OH	216-241-3411
Krantzen Studios/100 S Ashland, Chicago, IL	312-942-1900
Krejci, Donald/1825 E 18th St, Cleveland, OH	216-831-4730
Krueger, Dick/2147 W Augusta Blvd, Chicago, IL	312-384-0008
Kufrin, George/535 N Michigan #1407, Chicago, IL	312-787-2854
Kulp, Curtis/1255 S Michigan, Chicago, IL	312-786-1943
L LaRoche, Andre/32588 Dequindre, Warren, MI	313-978-7373
LaTona, Tony/1317 E 5th, Kansas City, MO	816-474-3119
LaVoies Photo/01423 US 127, BRyan, OH	419-636-4602
Lacey, Ted/4733 S Woodlawn, Chicago, IL	312-624-2419
Lachman, Gary/1927 Grant St, Evanston, IL	
Lacroix, Pat/25 Brant St, Toronto, ON	416-864-1858
Landau, Allan/1147 West Ohio, Chicago, IL	312-942-1382
Landis, Mike/1030 N Crooks Rd #O, Clawson, MI	313-435-5420
Lane, Jack Studio/5 W Grand Ave, Chicago, IL	312-337-2326
Lanza, Scott/3200 S 3rd St, Milwaukee, WI	414-482-4114
Larsen, Kim/ Soren Studio/325 N Hoyne, Chicago, IL	312-577-0344
Lause, Lew/127 Prospect St, Marion, OH	614-383-1155
Lauth, Lyal/833 N Orleans, Chicago, IL	312-787-5615
LeGrand, Peter/413 Sandburg, Park Forest, IL	312-747-4923
Leavenworth Photo Inc/929 West St, Lansing, MI	517-482-4658
Leavitt, Debbie/2756 N Pine Grove Ave #212, Chicago, IL	312-348-2833
Leavitt, Fred/916 Carmen, Chicago, IL	312-784-2344
Lecat, Paul/820 N Franklin, Chicago, IL	312-664-7122
Lee, Robert Photo/1512 Northlin Dr, St Louis, MO	314-965-5832
Lee, Terry/4420 N Paulina, Chicago, IL	312-561-1153
LEHN, JOHN/2601 E FRANKLIN AVE, MINNEAPOLIS, MN (P 186)	**612-338-0257**
Leick, Jim/1709 Washington Ave, St Louis, MO	314-241-2354
Leinwohl, Stef/439 W Oakdale #3, Chicago, IL	312-975-0457
Lempke, Jack/1324 Hamilton Ave, Cleveland, OH	216-687-0099
Leonard, Steve/825 W Gunnison, Chicago, IL	312-275-8833
Leslie, William F/53 Tealwood Dr, Creve Coeur, MO	314-993-8349
Levey, Don/15 W Delaware Pl, Chicago, IL	312-329-9040
Levin, Jonathan/1035 W Lake St, Chicago, IL	312-226-3898
Lewandowski, Leon/210 N Racine, Chicago, IL	312-467-9577
Lightfoot, Robert/311 Good Ave, Des Plaines, IL	312-297-5447
Linc Studio/1163 Tower, Schaumberg, IL	312-882-1311
Lindblade, George R/PO Box 1342, Sioux City, IA	712-255-4346
Lindwall, Martin/1269 Briarwood Ln, Libertyville, IL	312-680-1578
Lipschis, Helmut Photography/2053 N Sheffield, Chicago, IL	312-935-7886
Liss, Leroy/6243 N Ridgeway Ave, Chicago, IL	312-539-4540
Little, Scott/1515 Linden, Des Moines, IA	515-243-4428
Lohbeck, Stephen/1226 Ambassador Blvd, St Louis, MO	314-991-4657
Lord, David/8140 Castle Lake Rd, Indianapolis, IN	317-841-7813
Love, Ken/6911 N Mcalpin Ave, Chicago, IL	312-775-5779
Lowenthal, Jeff/PO Box 1031, Oak Park, IL	312-386-9137
Lowry, Miles/222 S Morgan #3B, Chicago, IL	312-666-0882
Loynd, Mel/208 Queen St S, Streetsville L5M1L5, ON	416-821-0477
Lubeck, Larry/405 N Wabash Ave, Chicago, IL	312-726-5580
Lucas, John V/4100 W 40th St, Chicago, IL	312-927-4500
Lucas, Joseph/20 N Wacker Dr #1425, Chicago, IL	312-782-6905
Ludwigs, David/3600 Troost St, Kansas City, MO	816-531-1363
Lutynski, Dennis/5517 Odana Rd, Madison, WI	608-274-9838
Lyles, David/401 W Superior 5th Fl, Chicago, IL	312-642-1223
M Magin, Betty/412 Spring Valley Ct, Chesterfield, MO	314-878-5388
MAAS, CURT/5860 MERLE HAY RD/BOX 127, JOHNSTON, IA (P 192)	**515-270-3732**
MacDonald, Al/32 Martin Lane, Elk Grove, IL	312-437-8850
MACK, RICHARD/2119 LINCOLN, EVANSTON, IL (P 187)	**312-869-7794**
Mactavish, Arndt/4620 N Winchester, Chicago, IL	312-334-2841
Maguire, Jim/144 Lownsdale, Akron, OH	216-630-9050
Maki & Smith Photo/6156 Olson Mem Hwy, Golden Valley, MN	612-541-4722
Malinowski, Stan/1150 N State #312, Chicago, IL	312-951-6715
Mally Assoc/20 W Hubbard #3E, Chicago, IL	312-644-4367
Maloney, Michael/517 W Third St, Cincinnati, OH	513-721-2384
Manarchy, Dennis/229 W Illinois, Chicago, IL	312-828-9117
Mandel, Avis/40 E Cedar, Chicago, IL	312-642-4776
Mankus, Gary/1520 N LaSalle, Chicago, IL	312-787-5438
Mann, Milton & Joan/PO Box 413, Evanston, IL	312-777-5656
Mar, Jan/111 Westgate, Oak Park, IL	312-524-1898
Marden Photo/4515 N Delaware, Indianapolis, IN	317-283-8244
Marienthal, Michael/1832 S Halsted, Chicago, IL	312-226-5505
Marovitz, Bob/3450 N Lake Shore Dr, Chicago, IL	312-975-1265
Marsalle/PO Box 300063, Minneapolis, MN	612-872-8717
Marshall, Don Photography/361 W Superior, Chicago, IL	312-944-0720
Marshall, Paul/117 N Jefferson St #304, Chicago, IL	312-559-1270
Marshall, Simeon/1043 W Randolph, Chicago, IL	312-243-9500
Martin, Barbara E/46 Washington Terrace, St Louis, MO	314-361-0838
Marvy, Jim/41 Twelfth Ave N, Minneapolis, MN	612-935-0307

Masheris, R Assoc Inc/1338 Hazel Ave, Deerfield, IL	312-945-2055
Mathews, Bruce/16520 Ellison Way, Independence, MO	816-373-2920
Matlow, Linda/300 N State St #3926, Chicago, IL	312-321-9071
Matusik, Jim/3714 N Racine, Chicago, IL	312-327-5615
Mauney, Michael/1405 Judson Ave, Evanston, IL	312-869-7720
May, Ron/PO Box 8359, Ft Wayne, IN	219-483-7872
May, Sandy/18 N 4th St #506, Minneapolis, MN	612-332-0272
Mayse, Steve/666 N Lake Shore Dr, Chicago, IL	312-944-6655
McCabe, Mark/1301 E 12th St, Kansas City, MO	816-474-6491
McCall Photo/320 W Ohio, Chicago, IL	312-280-2580
McCann, Larry/666 W Hubbard, Chicago, IL	312-942-1924
McCann, Michael/27 N 4th St, Minneapolis, MN	612-333-2115
McCay, Larry Inc/3926 N Fir Rd #12, Mishawaka, IN	219-259-1414
McClelan, Thompson/206 S First St, Champaign, IL	217-356-2767
McDonald, Neal/1515 W Cornelia, Chicago, IL	312-525-5401
McDunn, James/PO Box 8053, Rolling Meadows, IL	312-934-4288
McGleam, Patrick/, Chicago, IL	312-691-2847
McHale Studios Inc/2827 Gilbert Ave, Cincinnati, OH	513-961-1454
McKay, Doug/7830 Cornell, St Louis, MO	314-863-7167
McKellar, William/1200 W Webster, Chicago, IL	312-935-5511
McKinley, William/113 N May, Chicago, IL	312-666-5400
McLean & Friends/25800 Northwestern Hwy, Southfield, MI	313-358-2660
McLuckie Graphic Photo/121 S Wheeling, Wheeling, IL	312-639-8909
McMahon, David/304 Washington Ave #202, Minneapolis, MN	612-339-9709
McMahon, Franklin/1319 Chestnut, Wilmette, IL	312-256-5528
McNamara, Norris/646 N Michigan Ave #325, Chicago, IL	312-266-8455
McNichol, Greg/1638 W Greenleaf Ave, Chicago, IL	312-973-1032
MEAD, ROBERT/711 HILLGROVE AVE, LA GRANGE, IL	
(P 188)	**312-354-8300**
Meier, Lori/9100 Guthrie, St Louis, MO	314-428-0120
Melkus, Larry/679-E Mandoline, Madison Hts, MI	313-589-0066
Meoli, Rick/710 N Tucker #306, St Louis, MO	314-231-6038
Meredith, Paul/737 W Randolph, Chicago, IL	312-559-9209
Merrithew, Jim/PO Box 1510, Almonte K0A 1A0, ON	613-729-3862
Meyer, Aaron/1302 W Randolph, Chicago, IL	312-243-1458
Meyer, Fred/415 N Dearborn, Chicago, IL	312-527-4873
Meyer, Gordon/216 W Ohio, Chicago, IL	312-642-9303
Meyer, Jim/7727 Frontier Trail, Chanhassen, MN	612-934-2908
Meyer, Robert/208 W Kinzie St, Chicago, IL	312-467-1430
Michael, William/225 W Hubbard, Chicago, IL	312-644-6137
Micus Photo/PO Box 38, Lombard, IL	312-941-8945
Mignard Associates/1950-R South Glenstone, Springfield, MO	417-881-7422
Mihalevich, Mike/9235 Somerset Dr, Overland Park, KS	913-642-6466
Miller Photo/7237 W Devon, Chicago, IL	312-631-1255
Miller, Buck/PO Box 33, Milwaukee, WI	414-273-0985
Miller, Daniel D/1551 North Orleans, Chicago, IL	312-944-7192
Miller, Frank/6016 Blue Circle Dr, Minnetonka, MN	612-935-8888
Miller, Jon/11 W Illinois, Chicago, IL	312-738-1816
Miller, Pat/1101 Stinson Blvd NE, Minneapolis, MN	612-378-9043
Miller, Spider/833 North Orleans, Chicago, IL	312-944-2880
Mills, Gary/PO Box 260, Granger, IN	219-232-4221
Milne, Brian/78 Rusholme Rd, Toronto M6J 3H6, ON	416-532-6108
Mitchell, John Sr/2617 Greenleaf, Elk Grove, IL	312-956-8230
Mitchell, Rick/652 W Grand, Chicago, IL	312-829-1700
Mitzit, Bruce/331 S Peoria/Box 6638, Chicago, IL	312-508-1937
Mooney, Kevin/511 N Noble, Chicago, IL	312-738-1816
Moore, Bob c/o Mofoto Graphics/1615 S 9th St, St Louis, MO	314-231-1430
Moore, Dan/1029 N Wichita #9, Wichita, KS	316-264-4168
Morrill, Dan/1811 N Sedgewick, Chicago, IL	312-787-5095
Morton & White/6665-H Huntley Rd, Columbus, OH	614-885-8687
Moshman Photo/401 W Superior, Chicago, IL	312-869-6770
Moss, Jean/1255 S Michigan Ave, Chicago, IL	312-786-9110
Mottel, Ray/760 Burr Oak Dr, Westmont, IL	312-323-3616
Moustakas, Daniel/1255 Rankin, Troy, MI	313-589-0100
Moy, Clinton Photography/4815 W Winnemar, Chicago, IL	312-666-5577
Moy, Willie/364 W Erie, Chicago, IL	312-943-1863
Mueller, Linda/1900 Delmar, St Louis, MO	314-621-2400
Murphey, Gregory/2232 N Seminary, Chicago, IL	312-327-4856
Musich, Jack/325 W Huron, Chicago, IL	312-644-5000
Mutrux, John L/5217 England, Shawnee Missn, KS	913-722-4343

N Nagler, Monte/38881 Lancaster Dr, Farmington Hills, MI — 313-661-0826

Najdychor, Elvira/441 E Erie #2213, Chicago, IL	312-943-7670
Nathanson, Neal/7531 Cromwell, St Louis, MO	314-727-7244
Nawrocki, William S/332 S Michigan Ave, Chicago, IL	312-427-8625
Neal, Les/319 N Albany, Chicago, IL	312-508-5299
Negative Approach/23309 Commerce Park Rd, Cleveland, OH	216-831-0688
Nelson, Tom/400 First Ave N, Minneapolis, MN	612-339-3579
Nelson-Curry, Loring/1012 W Randolph St, Chicago, IL	312-226-0779
Neumann, Robert/101 S Mason St, Saginaw, MI	517-790-9000
New View Photo/5275 Michigan Ave, Rosemont, IL	312-671-0300
Nexus Productions/10-A Ashdale Ave, Toronto M4L 2Y7, ON	416-463-5078
NIEDORF, STEVE/700 WASHINGTON AVE N #304,	
MINNEAPOLIS, MN (P 189)	**612-332-7124**
Nobart Inc/1133 S Wabash Ave, Chicago, IL	312-427-9800
Nolan, Tim/2548 Shirley, St Louis, MO	314-388-4125
Norris, James/2301 N Lowell, Chicago, IL	312-342-1050
Northlight Studio/1539 E 22nd St, Cleveland, OH	216-621-3111
Norton, Ron/2609 Vine St, Cincinnati, OH	513-281-5002
Novak, Ken/2483 N Bartlett Ave, Milwaukee, WI	414-962-6953
Novak, Sam/230 W Huron, Chicago, IL	312-664-6733
Nozicka, Steve/314 W Institute Pl, Chicago, IL	312-787-8925
Nugent Wenckus Inc/110 Northwest Hwy, Des Plaines, IL	312-694-4151

O | | |
|---|---|
| **O'BARSKI, DON/17239 PARKSIDE AVE, S HOLLAND, IL** | |
| **(P 190)** | **312-596-0606** |
| O'Rourke, John/PO Box 52, Wilmington, OH | 513-382-3782 |
| Oakes, Kenneth Ltd/902 Yale Ln, Highland Park, IL | 312-432-4809 |
| Oberle, Frank/6633 Delmar, St Louis, MO | 314-721-5838 |
| Oberreich, S/1930 N Alabama St, Indianapolis, IN | 317-923-1980 |
| Officer, Hollis/905 E 5th St, Kansas City, MO | 816-474-5501 |
| **OLAUSEN, JUDY/213 1/2 N WASHINGTON AVE,** | |
| **MINNEAPOLIS, MN (P 172)** | **612-332-5009** |
| Ollis, Karen/1231 Superior Ave E, Cleveland, OH | 216-781-8646 |
| Olsson, Russ/215 W Illinois, Chicago, IL | 312-329-9358 |
| Ontiveros, Don/1378 N Wolcott 2nd Fl, Chicago, IL | 312-342-0900 |
| Oscar & Assoc/63 E Adams, Chicago, IL | 312-922-0056 |
| Oxendorf, Eric/1442 N Franklin Pl Box 92337, Milwaukee, WI | 414-273-0654 |

P | | |
|---|---|
| Pacific Studio/632 Krenz Ave, Cary, IL | 312-639-5654 |
| Palmisano, Vito/1147 W Ohio St, Chicago, IL | 312-565-0524 |
| Panama, David/1100 N Dearborn, Chicago, IL | 312-642-7095 |
| Parker, Norman/710 N 2nd St #300N, St Louis, MO | 314-621-8100 |
| Parks, Jim/210 W Chicago, Chicago, IL | 312-321-1193 |
| Passman, Roger/719 W Willow, Chicago, IL | 312-664-4085 |
| Paszkowski, Rick/7529 N Claremont #1, Chicago, IL | 312-761-3018 |
| Paternite, David/1245 S Clevelnd-Massilon Rd #3, Akron, OH | 216-666-7720 |
| Paulson, Bill/5358 Golla Rd, Stevens Point, WI | 715-341-6100 |
| Payne, John/2250 W Grand, Chicago, IL | 312-997-2288 |
| Payne-Garrett Photo/5301 Michigan Ave, Chicago, IL | 312-671-0300 |
| Pazovski, Kazik/2340 Laredo Ave, Cincinnati, OH | 513-281-0030 |
| Perkins, Ray/222 S Morgan St, Chicago, IL | 312-421-3438 |
| Perman, Craig/1645 Hennepin #311, Minneapolis, MN | 612-338-7727 |
| Perno, Jack/1147 W Ohio, Chicago, IL | 312-829-5292 |
| Perraud, Gene/Box 2025, Northbrook, IL | 312-564-5278 |
| **PERRY, ERIC/600 AJAX DR, MADISON HTS, MI (P 191)** | **313-589-0111** |
| Perspective Inc/2322 Pennsylvania St, Fort Wayne, IN | 219-424-8136 |
| Peterson, Garrick/216 W Ohio St, Chicago, IL | 312-266-8986 |
| Peterson, Jan/325 16th St, Bettendorf, IA | 319-355-5032 |
| Peterson, Richard Photo/529 S 7th St #315, Minneapolis, MN | 612-341-0480 |
| Petroff, Tom/19 W Hubbard, Chicago, IL | 312-836-0411 |
| Petrovich, Steve/679-E Mandoline, Madison Hts, MI | 313-589-0066 |
| Phelps Photo/1057 W Dakin, Chicago, IL | 312-248-2536 |
| Phillips, David R/1230 W Washington Blvd, Chicago, IL | 312-733-3277 |
| Photo Concepts Inc/23042 Commerce Dr #2001, Farmington | |
| Hills, MI | 313-477-4301 |
| Photo Group/1945 Techny Rd, Northbrook, IL | 312-564-9220 |
| Photo Ideas Inc/804 W Washington Blvd, Chicago, IL | 312-666-3100 |
| Photo Images/1945 Techny #9, Northbrook, IL | 312-272-3500 |
| Photo Reserve/2924 N Racine St, Chicago, IL | 312-871-7371 |
| Photographic Arts/624 W Adams, Chicago, IL | 312-876-0818 |
| Photographic Illustrators/405 1/2 E Main, Muncie, IN | 317-288-1454 |
| Pierce, Rod/236 Portland Ave, Minneapolis, MN | 612-332-2670 |

Photographers

Continued

Please send us your additions and updates.

Pieroni, Frank/2432 Oak Industrial Dr NE, Grand Rapids, MI	616-459-8325
Pintozzi, Peter/42 E Chicago, Chicago, IL	312-266-7775
PIONEER HI-BRED INTERNATIONAL/5860 MERLE HAY RD/	
BOX 127, JOHNSTON, IA (P 192,193)	**515-270-3732**
Pitt, Tom/1201 W Webster, Chicago, IL	312-281-5662
Pohlman Studios Inc/535 N 27th St, Milwaukee, WI	414-342-6363
Pokempner, Marc/1453 W Addison, Chicago, IL	312-525-4567
Polaski, James/9 W Hubbard, Chicago, IL	312-644-3686
Poli, Frank/158 W Huron, Chicago, IL	312-944-3924
Polin, Jack Photography/7306 Crawford, Lincolnwood, IL	312-676-4312
Pomerantz, Ron/325 W Huron #406, Chicago, IL	312-787-6407
Poon On Wong, Peter/516 First Ave #305, Minneapolis, MN	612-340-0798
Pope, Kerig/414 N Orleans, Chicago, IL	312-222-8999
Poplis, Paul/3599 Refugee Rd Bldg B, Columbus, OH	614-231-2942
Portney, Michael/4975 Gateshead, Detroit, MI	313-881-0378
Portnoy, Lewis/5 Carole Lane, St Louis, MO	314-567-5700
Powell, Jim/326 W Kalamazoo, Kalamazoo, MI	616-381-2302
Price, Paul/8138 W Nine Mile Rd, Oak Park, MI	313-546-1759
Proctor & Proctor Photo/360 N Michigan #2105, Chicago, IL	312-798-6849
Przekop, Harry J/950 W Lake St, Chicago, IL	312-829-8201
Puffer, David/213 W Institute, Chicago, IL	312-266-7540
Puza, Greg/PO Box 1986, Milwaukee, WI	414-444-9882
Pyrzynski, Larry/2241 S Michigan, Chicago, IL	312-472-6550

QR

Quinn, James/518 S Euclid, Oak Park, IL	312-383-0654
Quist, Bruce/1370 N Milwaukee, Chicago, IL	312-252-3921
Rack, Ron/215 E Ninth St, Cincinnati, OH	513-421-6267
Radencich, Michael/1007 McGee, Kansas City, MO	816-421-5076
Radlund & Associates/4704 Pflaum Rd, Madison, WI	608-222-8177
Randall, Bob/2340 W Huron, Chicago, IL	312-235-4613
Randolph, Jon/1434 W Addison, Chicago, IL	312-248-9406
Rawls, Ray/, , MN	612-895-9717
Reames-Hanusin Studio/3306 Commercial Ave, Northbrook, IL	312-564-2706
REED, DICK/1330 COOLIDGE, TROY, MI (P 173)	**313-280-0090**
Reeve, Catherine/822 Madison St, Evanston, IL	312-327-3734
Reffner, Wayne/4178 Dayton-Xenia Rd, Dayton, OH	513-429-2760
Reid, Ken/800 W Huron #3S, Chicago, IL	312-733-2121
Reiss, Ray/2144 N Leavitt, Chicago, IL	312-384-3245
Remington, George/1455 W 29th St, Cleveland, OH	216-241-1440
Renerts, Peter Studio/633 Huron Rd, Cleveland, OH	216-781-2440
RENKEN, ROGER/PO BOX 11010, ST LOUIS, MO (P 194)	**314-394-5055**
Reuben, Martin/1231 Superior Ave, Cleveland, OH	216-781-8644
Ricco, Ron/207 E Buffalo #619, Milwaukee, WI	414-645-6450
Rice, Ted/2599 N 4th St, Columbus, OH	614-263-8656
Rich, Larry/29731 Everett, Southfield, MI	313-557-7676
Richland, Kathy/839 W Wrightwood, Chicago, IL	312-935-9634
Ritter, Gene/2440 W 14th St, Cleveland, OH	216-521-5494
River, Melissa/2500 Lakeview, Chicago, IL	312-929-5031
Robert, Francois/740 N Wells, Chicago, IL	312-787-0777
Robinson, David/1147 W Ohio, Chicago, IL	312-942-1650
Roessler, Ryan/401 W Superior, Chicago, IL	312-951-8702
Rogowski, Tom/214 E 8th St, Cincinnati, OH	513-621-3826
Rohman, Jim/2254 Marengo, Toledo, OH	419-865-0234
Rosmis, Bruce/118 W Ohio, Chicago, IL	312-787-9046
Ross, Allan/430 W Erie St #3W, Chicago, IL	312-642-2288
Rostron, Philip/489 Wellington St W, Toronto, ON	416-596-6587
Rothrock, Douglas/215 W Ohio, Chicago, IL	312-951-9045
Rottinger, Ed/5409 N Avers, Chicago, IL	312-583-2917
Rowley, Joe/368 W Huron, Chicago, IL	312-266-7620
Rubin, Laurie/1111 W Armitage, Chicago, IL	312-348-6644
Rush, Michael/415 Delaware, Kansas City, MO	816-471-1200
Russetti, Andy/1260 Carnegie St, Cleveland, OH	216-687-1788
Rustin, Barry/934 Glenwood Rd, Glenview, IL	312-724-7600
Rutt, Don/324 Munson St, Traverse City, MI	616-946-2727
Rutten, Bonnie/414 Sherburne Ave, St Paul, MN	612-224-5777
Ryan, Gary/23245 Woodward, Ferndale, MI	313-861-8199

S

S T Studio/362 W Erie, Chicago, IL	312-943-2565
Sacco Photography Ltd/833 North Orleans St, Chicago, IL	312-943-5757
SACKS, ANDREW/20727 SCIO CHURCH RD, CHELSEA, MI	
(P 195)	**313-475-2310**
Sacks, Ed/Box 7237, Chicago, IL	312-871-4700
Sadin Photo Group/820 N Franklin, Chicago, IL	312-944-1434
Sala, Don/950 W Willow, Chicago, IL	312-751-2858
Salisbury, Mark/161 W Harrison 12th Fl, Chicago, IL	312-922-7599
Salter, Tom/685 Pallister, Detroit, MI	313-874-1155
Saltzman, Ben/700 N Washington, Minneapolis, MN	612-332-5112
Sanders, Kathy/368 W Huron, Chicago, IL	312-943-2627
Sanderson, Glenn/2936 Gross St, Green Bay, WI	414-336-6500
Sandoz Studios/118 W Kinzie, Chicago, IL	312-440-0004
Santow, Loren/3057 N racine, Chicago, IL	312-929-1993
Sapecki, Roman/56 E Oakland Ave, Columbus, OH	614-262-7497
Sarnacki, Michael/18101 Oakwood Blvd, Dearborn, MI	313-548-1149
Sauer, Neil W/1554 S 7th St, St Louis, MO	314-241-9300
SCHABES, CHARLES/1220 W GRACE ST, CHICAGO, IL	
(P 196)	**312-787-2629**
Schaefer, Ginzy/4336 Genesse, Kansas City, MO	816-753-4068
Schanuel, Anthony/10901 Oasis Dr, St Louis, MO	314-849-3495
Schaugnessy, Abe/32 Martin Ln, Elk Grove Village, IL	312-437-8850
Schewe, Jeff/624 West Willow, Chicago, IL	312-951-6334
Schnepf, James/4518 W Dean Rd, Milwaukee, WI	414-354-1331
Schoenbach, Glenn/329 Enterprise Ct, Bloomfield Hills, MI	313-335-5100
Scholtes, Marc/726 Central Ave NE, Minneapolis, MN	612-378-1888
Schrempp, Erich/723 W Randolph, Chicago, IL	312-454-3237
Schridde, Charles/600 Ajax Dr, Madison Hts, MI	313-589-0111
Schroeder, Loranelle/400 First Ave N #626, Minneapolis, MN	612-339-3191
Schube-Soucek/1735 Carmen Dr, Elk Grove Village, IL	312-439-0640
Schuemann, Bill/1591 S Belvoir Blvd, South Euclid, OH	216-382-4409
Schuessler, Dave/40 E Delaware, Chicago, IL	312-787-6868
Schuette, Bob/207 E Buffalo #645, Milwaukee, WI	414-347-1113
Schulman, Bruce/1102 W Columbia, Chicago, IL	312-917-6420
SCHULMAN, LEE/669 COLLEGE AVE/BOX 09506,	
COLUMBUS, OH (P 197)	**614-235-5307**
Schultz, Karl/740 W Washington, Chicago, IL	312-454-0303
Schultz, Tim/215 W Huron, Chicago, IL	312-943-3318
Schwartz, Linda/2033 N Orleans, Chicago, IL	312-327-7755
Scott, Denis/216 W Ohio St, Chicago, IL	312-467-5663
Secreto, Jim/2626 Industrial Row, Troy, MI	313-280-0640
Seed, Brian/213 W Institute Pl #503, Chicago, IL	312-787-7880
Segal Panorama Photo/230 N Michigan Ave, Chicago, IL	312-236-8545
Segal, Mark/230 N Michigan Ave, Chicago, IL	312-236-8545
Segielski, Tony/1886 Thunderbird, Troy, MI	313-362-3111
Semeniuk, Robert/78 Rusholme Rd, Toronto M6J 3H6, ON	416-532-6108
Sereta, Greg/2108 Payne Ave #400, Cleveland, OH	216-861-7227
Severson, Kent/529 S 7th St #637, Minneapolis, MN	612-375-1870
Sexton, Ken/221 W Walton, Chicago, IL	312-854-0180
Seymour, Ronald/314 W Superior, Chicago, IL	312-642-4030
Shafer, Ronald/4428 N Malden, Chicago, IL	312-878-1346
Shaffer, Mac/526 E Dunedin Rd, Columbus, OH	614-268-2249
Shafman, Frank/466 Bathurst St #4, Toronto M5T 2S6, ON	
Shambroom, Paul/1607 Dupont Ave N, Minneapolis, MN	612-521-5835
Shanoor Photo/116 W Illinois, Chicago, IL	312-266-0465
Shapiro, Terry/1147 W Ohio St, Chicago, IL	312-226-3384
Sharp, Joe/PO Box 1494, Toledo, OH	419-243-1450
Shaughnessy & MacDonald/32 Martin Ln, Elk Grove Village, IL	312-437-8850
Shay, Arthur/618 Indian Hill Rd, Deerfield, IL	312-945-4636
Shelli, Bob/PO Box 2062, St Louis, MO	314-772-8540
Sheppard, Richard/421 N Main St, Mt Prospect, IL	312-259-4375
Shigeta-Wright Assoc/1546 N Orleans St, Chicago, IL	312-642-8715
Shirmer, Bob/11 W Illinois St, Chicago, IL	312-321-1151
Shotwell, Chuck/2111 N Clifton, Chicago, IL	312-929-0168
Shoulders, Terry/676 N LaSalle, Chicago, IL	312-642-6622
Siede/Preis Photo/1526 N Halsted, Chicago, IL	312-787-2725
Sieracki, John/676 N LaSalle, Chicago, IL	312-664-7824
Sigman, Gary/2229 W Melrose St, Chicago, IL	312-871-8756
SILBER, GARY CRAIG/300 MAIN ST, RACINE, WI (P 198)	**414-637-5097**
Silker, Glenn/5249 W 73rd St #A, Edina, MN	612-835-1811
Sills, Anne Margaret/411 N LaSalle St, Chicago, IL	312-670-3660
Sills, Casey/411 N Lasalle, Chicago, IL	312-670-3660
Silver, Jared N/660 La Salle Pl, Chicago, IL	312-433-3866
Simeon, Marshall/1043 W Randolph St, Chicago, IL	312-243-9500
Simmons Photography Inc/326 Chicago Ave, Chicago, IL	312-944-0326
Sindelar, Dan/2517 Grove Springs Ct, St Louis, MO	314-846-4775

Photographers

Continued

Please send us your additions and updates.

Singer, Beth/25741 River Dr, Franklin, MI	313-626-4860
Sinkler, Paul/510 N First Ave #307, Minneapolis, MN	612-343-0325
SINKLIER, SCOTT/5860 MERLE HAY RD/BOX 127,	
JOHNSTON, IA (P 193)	**515-270-3732**
Skalak, Carl/47-46 Grayton Rd, Cleveland, OH	216-676-6508
Skrebneski, Victor/1350 N LaSalle St, Chicago, IL	312-944-1339
Skutas, Joe/17 N Elizabeth, Chicago, IL	312-733-1266
Sladcik, William/215 W Illinois, Chicago, IL	312-644-7108
Smetzer, Donald/2534 N Burling St, Chicago, IL	312-327-1716
Smith, Bill/600 N McClurgh Ct #802, Chicago, IL	312-787-4686
Smith, Doug Photo/2911 Sutton, St Louis, MO	314-645-1359
Smith, Mike/521 Cottonwood Circle, Bolingbrook, IL	312-759-0262
Smith, R Hamilton/1021 W Montana Ave, St Paul, MN	612-488-9068
Smith, Richard/PO Box 455, Round Lake, IL	312-546-0977
Smith, Robert/496 W Wrightwood Ave, Elmhurst, IL	312-941-7755
Snook, Allen/1433 W Fullerton, Addison, IL	312-495-3939
Snook, J J/118 W Ohio, Chicago, IL	312-495-3939
Snow, Andy/346 Shadywood Dr, Dayton, OH	513-836-8566
Snyder, Don/1452 Davenport, Cleveland, OH	216-771-6811
Snyder, John/368 W Huron, Chicago, IL	312-440-1053
Soluri, Tony/1147 W Ohio, Chicago, IL	312-243-6580
Sorokowski, Rick/1051 N Halsted, Chicago, IL	312-280-1256
Spahr, Dick/1133 E 61st St, Indianapolis, IN	317-255-2400
Spectra Studios/213 W Institute #512, Chicago, IL	312-787-0667
Spencer, Gary/3546 Dakota Ave S, Minneapolis, MN	612-929-7803
Spingola, Laurel/1233 W Eddy, Chicago, IL	312-883-0020
Spitz, Robert/317 Howard, Evanston, IL	312-869-4992
Stansfield, Stan/215 W Ohio, Chicago, IL	312-337-3245
Starkey, John/2250 Rome Dr, Indianapolis, IN	317-299-5758
Starmark Photo/706 N Dearborn, Chicago, IL	312-944-6700
Stealey, Jonathan/PO Box 611, Findlay, OH	419-423-1149
Steele, Charles/531 S Plymouth Ct #22, Chicago, IL	312-922-0201
Stegbauer, Jim/421 Transit, Roseville, MN	612-333-1982
Stein, Frederic/409 W Huron St, Chicago, IL	312-642-7171
Steinbacher, Ed/5745 Overture Way, Clinton, OH	216-825-9138
STEINBERG, MIKE/633 HURON RD, CLEVELAND, OH	
(P 199)	**216-589-9953**
Steinhart Photography/325 W Huron, Chicago, IL	312-944-0226
Stemo Photo/1880 Holste Rd, Northbrook, IL	312-498-4844
Stenberg, Pete Photography/225 W Hubbard, Chicago, IL	312-644-6137
Stenbroten, Scott/107 W Van Buren #211, Chicago, IL	312-929-4677
Sterling, Joseph/2216 N Cleveland, Chicago, IL	312-348-4333
Stewart, Ron/314 E Downer Pl, Aurora, IL	312-897-4317
Stornello, Joe/4319 Campbell St, Kansas City, MO	816-756-0419
Straus, Jerry/247 E Ontario, Chicago, IL	312-787-2628
Strouss, Sarah/134 Upland Ave, Youngstown, OH	216-744-2774
Struse, Perry L Jr/232 Sixth St, West Des Moines, IA	515-279-9761
Stump Studio/1920 N Dayton, Chicago, IL	312-477-5569
Styrkowicz, Tom/4426 Shields Pl, Columbus, OH	614-261-6952
Summers Studio/153 W Ohio, Chicago, IL	312-527-0908
SUNDLOF, JOHN/1324 ISABELLA, WILMETTE, IL (P 201)	**312-256-8877**
Sutter, Greg/6621-B Century Ave, Middleton, WI	608-836-5744
Swan, Tom/2417 N Burling, Chicago, IL	312-871-8370
Swanson, Michael/215 W Ohio, Chicago, IL	312-337-3245

T

TPS Studio/4016 S California, Chicago, IL	312-847-1221
Taback, Sidney/415 Eastern Ave, Toronto M4M1B7, ON	416-463-5718
Taber, Gary/305 S Green St, Chicago, IL	312-726-0374
Tappin, Mike/4410 N Hermitage, Chicago, IL	312-275-7735
Tarleton, Gary/755 Cole Creek Dr, Omaha, NE	402-399-8616
Taxel, Barney/4614 Prospect Ave, Cleveland, OH	216-431-2400
Taylor, Dale E/8505 Midcounty Ind Ctr, St Louis, MO	314-426-2655
Technigraph Studio/1212 Jarvis, Elk Grove Village, IL	312-437-3334
Teeter, Brian/5607 Green Circle Dr #217, Minnetonka, MN	612-935-5666
Teschl, Josef/31 Brock Ave #203, Toronto, ON	416-743-5146
Teufen, Al/600 E Smith Rd, Medina, OH	216-723-3237
The Photo Place/4739 Butterfield, Hillside, IL	312-544-1222
The Picture Place/3721 Grandel Sq, St Louis, MO	314-652-6262
The Studio, Inc/4239 N Lincoln, Chicago, IL	312-348-3556
Thien, Alex/2754 N Prospect Ave, Milwaukee, WI	414-964-4349
Thill, Nancy/70 W Huron St, Chicago, IL	312-944-7164
Thoen, Greg/14940 Minnetonka Rd, Minnetonka, MN	612-938-2433

Thoman, Fred/6710 Madison Rd, Cincinnati, OH	513-561-4011
Thomas, Bill/Rt 4 Box 387, Nashville, IN	812-988-7865
Thomas, Tony/676 N Lasalle St 6th Fl, Chicago, IL	312-337-2274
Thompson, Ken/215 W Ohio, Chicago, IL	312-951-6356
Tillis, Harvey/1050 W Kinzie, Chicago, IL	312-733-7336
Tirotta, John/420 W Sample St, South Bend, IN	219-234-4244
Tolchin, Robert/1057 Kenton Rd, Deerfield, IL	312-729-2522
Torno, Laurent/1709 Washington #9000, St Louis, MO	314-231-4883
Toro, Mark/778 S Wall St, Columbus, OH	614-460-4635
Tower Photo/4327 N Elston, Chicago, IL	312-478-8494
Townsend, Wesley/, Lombard, IL	312-620-7118
Tracy, Janis/213 W Institute Pl, Chicago, IL	312-787-7166
Trantafil, Gary/222 S Morgan, Chicago, IL	312-666-1029
Trotter, Jim/12342 Conway Rd, St Louis, MO	314-878-0777
Trujillo, Edward/345 N Canal St #1604, Chicago, IL	312-454-9798
Tucker, Bill/114 W Illinois, Chicago, IL	312-321-1570
Tunison, Richard/5511 E Lake Dr, Lisle, IL	312-944-1188
Tushas, Leo/111 N Fifth Ave #309, Minneapolis, MN	612-333-5774
Tweton, Roch/700 Manvel Ave, Grafton, ND	701-352-1513
Tyson, Joye/PO Box 778, Normal, IL	309-454-2922

UV

Uhlmann, Gina/1611 N Sheffield, Chicago, IL	312-642-6650
Umland, Steve/600 Washington Ave N, Minneapolis, MN	612-332-1590
Upitis, Alvis/620 Morgan Ave S, Minneapolis, MN	612-374-9375
Urba, Alexis/148 W Illinois, Chicago, IL	312-644-4466
Van Allen, John/U of Iowa Fndtn/Alumni Ctr, Iowa City, IA	319-354-9512
Van Marter, Robert/1209 Alstott Dr S, Howell, MI	517-546-1923
VANKIRK, DEBORAH/855 W BLACKHAWK ST, CHICAGO, IL	
(P 202,203)	**312-642-7766**
Vandenberg, Greg/161 W Harrison 12th Fl, Chicago, IL	312-939-2969
Vander Lende, Craig/129 S Division St, Grand Rapids, MI	616-235-3233
Vander Veen, David/5151 N 35th St, Milwaukee, WI	414-527-0450
Vanmarter, Robert/1209 Alstott Dr S, Howell, MI	517-546-1923
Variakojis, Danguole/5743 S Campbell, Chicago, IL	312-776-4668
Vaughan, Jim/321 S Jefferson, Chicago, IL	312-663-0369
Vedros, Nick/215 W 19th St, Kansas City, MO	816-471-5488
Ventola, Giorgio/230 W Huron, Chicago, IL	312-951-0880
Verdos, Nick/215 W 19th St, Kansas City, MO	816-471-5488
Vergos Studio/122 W Kinzie 3rd Fl, Chicago, IL	312-527-1769
Viernum, Bill/1629 Mandel Ave, Westchester, IL	312-562-4143
Villa, Armando/1872 N Clybourne, Chicago, IL	312-472-7003
Visser, James/4274 Shenandoah Ave, St Louis, MO	314-771-6857
Visual Data Systems Inc/5617 63rd Pl, Chicago, IL	312-585-3060
Vizanko Advertising Photo/11511 K-Tel Drive, Minnetonka, MN	612-933-1314
Voiggs, Tim/3546 Dakota St, Minneapolis, MN	612-929-7803
Vollan, Michael/175 S Morgan, Chicago, IL	312-644-1792
Von Baich, Paul/78 Rusholme Rd, Toronto M6J 3H6, ON	416-532-6108
Von Photography/685 W Ohio, Chicago, IL	312-243-8578
Voyles, Dick & Assoc/2822 Breckenridge Ind Ctr, St Louis, MO	314-968-3851
Vuksanovich/401 W Superior, Chicago, IL	312-664-7523

W

Wagenaar, David/1035 W Lake St, Chicago, IL	312-942-0943
Waite, Tim/717 S Sixth St, Milwaukee, WI	414-643-1500
Walker, Jessie Assoc/241 Fairview, Glencoe, IL	312-835-0522
Wans, Glen/325 W 40th, Kansas City, MO	816-931-8905
Ward, Les/21477 Bridge St #C & D, Southfield, MI	313-350-8666
Warkenthien, Dan/117 South Morgan, Chicago, IL	312-666-6056
Warren, Lennie/401 W Superior, Chicago, IL	312-664-5392
Watts, Dan/245 Plymouth, Grand Rapids, MI	616-451-4693
Watts, Ron/78 Rusholme Rd, Toronto M6J 3H6, ON	416-532-6108
Weber, J Andrew/303 S Donald Ave, Arlington Hts, IL	312-255-2738
Wedlake, James/750 Jossman Rd, Ortonville, MI	313-627-2711
Weidemann, Skot/6621-B Century Ave, Middleton, WI	608-836-5744
Weiland, Jim/1100 S Lynndale Dr, Appleton, WI	414-739-7824
Weiner, Jim/540 N Lakeshore Dr, Chicago, IL	312-644-0040
Weinstein, John/3119 N Seminary Ave, Chicago, IL	312-327-8184
Weinstein, Phillip/343 S Dearborn, Chicago, IL	312-922-1945
Weispfenning, Donna/815 W 53rd St, Minneapolis, MN	612-823-8405
Welzenbach, John/368 W Huron St, Chicago, IL	312-337-3611
Wengroff, Sam/2052 N Dayton, Chicago, IL	312-248-6623
West, Mike/300 Howard Ave, Des Plaines, IL	312-699-7886
West, Stu/430 First Ave #210, Minneapolis, MN	612-375-0404

Photographers

Continued

Please send us your additions and updates.

Westerman, Charlie/630 W Oakdale, Chicago, IL	312-248-5709
Whitford, T R/1900 Delmar #2, St Louis, MO	314-621-2400
Whitmer, Jim/125 Wakeman, Wheaton, IL	312-653-1344
Wicks, L Photography/1235 W Winnemac Ave, Chicago, IL	312-878-4925
Wiegand, Eric/2339 Ferndale, Sylvan Lake, MI	313-682-8746
Wilcox, Anthony/PO Box 148191, Chicago, IL	312-935-4050
Wilder, J David/411 W St Clair Ave, Cleveland, OH	216-771-7687
Wilker, Clarence/2021 Washington Ave, Lorain, OH	216-244-5497
Willette, Brady T/2720 W 43rd St, Minneapolis, MN	612-926-4261
Williams, Alfred G/Box 10288, Chicago, IL	312-947-0991
Williams, Barry/2361 N High St, Columbus, OH	614-291-9774
Williams, Basil/4068 Tanglefoot Terrace, Bettendorf, IA	319-355-7142
WILLIAMS, BOB/32049 MILTON AVE, MADISON HEIGHTS,	
MI (P 174)	**313-588-6544**
Williamson, John/224 Palmerston Ave, Toronto M6J 2J4, ON	416-530-4511
Wilson, Jack/2133 Bellvue, St Louis, MO	314-645-2211
Wilson, Tim/1643 N Milwaukee, Chicago, IL	312-486-0500
Wirthlin, Walter/PO Box 660, Osage Beach, MO	314-348-3058
Witte, Scott J/3025 W Highland Blvd, Milwaukee, WI	414-933-3223
Woburn/4715 N Ronald St, Harwood Heights, IL	312-867-5445
Woehrle, Mark/1709 Washington Ave, St Louis, MO	314-231-9949
Wojcik, Richard R/151 Victor Ave, Highland Park, MI	313-868-2200
Wolf, Bobbe/1011 W Armitage, Chicago, IL	312-472-9503
Wolf, Don/3117 Merriam L:ane, Kansas City, MO	913-384-9653
Wolff, Ed/11357 S Second St, Schoolcraft, MI	616-679-4702
Wolford, Rick/2300 E Douglas, Wichita, KS	316-264-3013
Wooden, John/219 N 2nd St J#306, Minneapolis, MN	612-339-3032
Woodward, Greg/401 W Superior, Chicago, IL	312-337-5838
Worzala, Lyle/8164 W Forest Preserve #1, Chicago, IL	312-434-7156
Wright, James/5740 S Kenwood #1, Chicago, IL	312-856-1838

YZ

Yamashiro, Paul Studio/1500 N Halstead, Chicago, IL	312-321-1009
Yapp, Charles/723 Randolph, Chicago, IL	312-558-9338
Yates, Peter/515 Spring St, Ann Arbor, MI	313-995-0839
Yaworski, Don/600 White Oak Ln, Kansas City, MO	816-455-4814
Zaitz, Dan/1643 N Milwaukee Ave, Chicago, IL	312-276-3565
ZAKE, BRUCE/633 HURON RD 3RD FL, CLEVELAND, OH	
(P 204)	**216-694-3686**
Zamiar, Thomas/210 W Chicago, Chicago, IL	312-787-4976
Zann, Arnold/502 N Grove Ave, Oak Park, IL	312-386-2864
Zarlengo, Joseph/419 Melrose Ave, Boardman, OH	216-782-7797
Zena Photography/633 Huron Rd SE 5th Fl, Cleveland, OH	216-621-6366
Zimion/Marshall Studio/1043 W Randolph, Chicago, IL	312-243-9500
Zoom Photo/427 Queen St West, Toronto M5V 2A5, ON	416-593-0690
Zukas, R/311 N Desplaines #500, Chicago, IL	312-648-0100

Southwest

A

Abraham, Joe/11944 Hempstead Rd #C, Houston, TX	713-460-4948
AKER/BURNETTE STUDIO/4710 LILLIAN, HOUSTON, TX	
(P 208,209)	**713-862-6343**
Alford, Jess/1800 Lear St #3, Dallas, TX	214-421-3107
Allen, Jim Photo/4410 Lovers Lane, Dallas, TX	214-368-0563
Anderson, Derek Studio/3959 Speedway Blvd E, Tucson, AZ	602-881-1205
Anderson, Randy/1606 Lewis Trail, Grand Prairie, TX	214-660-1071
Angle, Lee/1900 Montgomery, Fort Worth, TX	817-737-6469
Annerino, John/PO Box 1545, Prescott, AZ	602-445-4094
Ashe, Gil/Box 686, Bellaire, TX	713-668-8766
Ashley, Constance/2024 Farrington St, Dallas, TX	214-747-2501
Associated Photo/2344 Irving Blvd, Dallas, TX	214-630-8730
Austin, David/2412 Fifth Ave, Fort Worth, TX	817-335-1881

B

Badger, Bobby/1355 Chemical, Dallas, TX	214-634-0222
Bagshaw, Cradoc/603 High St NE, Albuquerque, NM	505-243-1096
Baker, Bobbe C/1119 Ashburn, College Station, TX	409-696-7185
BAKER, JEFF/2401 S ERVAY #302, DALLAS, TX (P 210)	**214-720-0178**
Baker, Lane/1429 W Elna Rae #103, Tempe, AZ	602-829-7455
Baldwin/Watriss Assoc/1405 Branard St, Houston, TX	713-524-9199
Baraban, Joe/2426 Bartlett #2, Houston, TX	713-526-0317
Barker, Kent/2039 Farrington, Dallas, TX	214-760-7470
BAXTER, SCOTT/PO BOX 25041, PHOENIX, AZ (P 211)	**602-254-5879**

Bayanduryan, Rubik/PO Box 1791, Austin, TX	512-451-8960
Beebower Brothers/9995 Monroe #209, Dallas, TX	214-358-1219
Bender, Robert/1345 Chemical, Dallas, TX	214-631-4538
Bennett, Sue/PO Box 1574, Flagstaff, AZ	602-774-2544
Bennett, Tony R/122 Parkhouse, Dallas, TX	214-747-0107
Benoist, John/PO Box 20825, Dallas, TX	214-692-8813
Berman, Bruce/140 N Stevens #301, El Paso, TX	915-544-0352
Berrett, Patrick L/2425-C NE Monroe, Albuquerque, NM	505-881-0935
Berry, George S Photography/Rt 2 Box 325B, San Marcos, TX	512-396-4805
Bishop, Gary/PO Box 12394, Dallas, TX	214-368-0889
Bissell, Gary/120 Paragon #217, El Paso, TX	915-833-1942
Blackwell, J Michael/2032 Farrington, Dallas, TX	214-760-8742
Bland, Ron/2424 S Carver Pkwy #107, Grand Prairie, TX	214-660-6600
Blue, Janice/1708 Rosewood, Houston, TX	713-522-6899
Bondy, Roger/309 NW 23rd St, Oklahoma City, OK	405-521-1616
Booth, Greg/1322 Round Table, Dallas, TX	214-688-1855
Bouche, Len/PO Box 5188, Sante Fe, NM	505-471-7434
Bowman, Matt/8602 Santa Clara, Dallas, TX	214-320-8202
Bradley, Matt/15 Butterfield Ln, Little Rock, AR	501-224-0692
Bradshaw, Reagan/PO Box 12457, Austin, TX	512-458-6101
BRADY, STEVE/5250 GULFTON #2G, HOUSTON, TX	
(P 212,213)	**713-660-6663**
Britt, Ben/2401 S Ervay #205, Dallas, TX	214-428-2822
Brousseau, J/2408 Farrington, Dallas, TX	214-638-1248
Brown, David Photo/280 Edgewood Ct, Prescott, AZ	602-445-2485
Buffington, David/2401 S Ervay #105, Dallas, TX	214-428-8221
Bumpass, R O/1222 N Winnetka, Dallas, TX	214-742-3414
Burger, Steven/544 E Dunlap Ave, Phoenix, AZ	602-997-4625
Burkey, J W/2739 Irving Blvd, Dallas, TX	214-630-1369

C

Cabluck, Jerry/Box 9601, Fort Worth, TX	817-336-1431
CALDWELL, JIM/2422 QUENBY, HOUSTON, TX (P 214)	**713-527-9121**
Campbell, Doug/5617 Matalee, Dallas, TX	214-823-9151
Cannedy, Carl/2408 Farrington, Dallas, TX	214-638-1247
Captured Image Photography/5131 E Lancaster, Fort Worth,	
TX	817-457-2302
Cardellino, Robert/315 Ninth St #2, San Antonio, TX	512-224-9606
Carr, Fred/3346 Walnut Bend, Houston, TX	713-266-2872
Case, Bob/126 E Texas St, Grapevine, TX	817-481-4854
Chavanell, Joe/PO Box 32383, San Antonio, TX	512-377-1552
Chenn, Steve/6301 Ashcroft, Houston, TX	713-271-0631
Chisholm, Rich & Assoc/3233 Marquart, Houston, TX	713-623-8790
Clair, Andre/11415 Chatten Way, Houston, TX	713-465-5507
Clark, H Dean/18405 FM 149, Houston, TX	713-469-7021
Claussen, Peter/6901-C Mullins, Houston, TX	713-661-7498
Clintsman, Dick/3001 Quebec #102, Dallas, TX	214-630-1531
Cobb, Lynn/3505 Turtle Creek #109, Dallas, TX	214-528-6694
Cohen, Stewart Charles/2401 S Ervay #206, Dallas, TX	214-421-2186
Cole, Alan Michael/Route A Box 197, Flippin, AR	501-425-9107
Colombo, Michel/3311 Oaklawn #200, Dallas, TX	214-522-1238
Connolly, Danny F/PO Box 1290, Houston, TX	713-862-8146
Cook, Robert Ames/2525 Tingley Dr SW #314, Albuquerque,	
NM	505-275-3934
Cooke, Richard & Mary/209 E Ben White Blvd #110, Austin, TX	512-444-6100
Cotter, Austin/1350 Manufacturing #211, Dallas, TX	214-742-3633
Countryman, Mike/1609 Grantland Circle, Fort Worth, TX	817-481-7051
Cowlin, James/PO Box 34205, Phoenix, AZ	602-264-9689
Craig, George/314 E 13th St, Houston, TX	713-862-6008
Crane, Christopher/5455 Dashwood #300, Bellaire, TX	713-661-1098
Crittendon, James/5914 Lake Crest, Garland, TX	214-226-2196
Cruff, Kevin/2318 E Roosevelt, Phoenix, AZ	602-267-8845
Crump, Bill/1357 Chemical, Dallas, TX	214-630-7745

D

Davey, Robert/PO Box 2421, Prescott, CA	602-445-1160
David, Jerry/3314 Silver Maple Court, Garland, TX	214-495-9600
Davidson, Josiah/, Cloudcroft, NM	800-JDSP-810
Davis, Mark/8718 Boundbrook Ave, Dallas, TX	214-348-7679
Dawson, Greg/2211 Beall St, Houston, TX	713-862-8301
Debenport, Robb/2412 Converse, Dallas, TX	214-631-7606
Drews, Buzzy/1555 W Mockingbird #202, Dallas, TX	214-351-9968
DuBose, Bill/5627 Richard Ave, Dallas, TX	214-630-0086
Duncan, Nena/306 Shady Wood, Houston, TX	713-782-3130

Photographers
Continued

Please send us your additions and updates.

Duran, Mark/66 East Vernon, Phoenix, AZ	602-279-1141
Durham, Thomas/PO Box 4665, Witchita Falls, TX	817-691-2202
Dyer, John/107 Blue Star, San Antonio, TX	512-223-1891
Dykinga, Jack/3808 Calle Barcelona, Tucson, AZ	602-326-6094

EF
Eclipse/2727 E 21st St #600, Tulsa, OK	918-747-1991
Edens, Swain/110 N Leona, San Antonio, TX	512-226-2210
Edwards, Bill/3820 Brown, Dallas, TX	214-521-8630
Eglin, Tom/3950 W Mais St, Tucson, AZ	602-748-1299
Eilers, Rick/4030 Swiss, Dallas, TX	214-823-2103
Ewasko, Tommy/5645 Hillcroft #202, Houston, TX	713-784-1777
Fantich, Barry/PO Box 70103, Houston, TX	713-520-5434
Findysz, Mary/3550 E Grant, Tucson, AZ	602-325-0260
Fontenot, Dallas/6002 Burning Tree Dr, Houston, TX	713-988-2183
Ford, Bill/202 S Center Valley, Irving, TX	214-986-7887
Foxall, Steve/3417 Main St, Dallas, TX	214-939-9120
Frady, Connie/2808 Fifth Ave, Fort Worth, TX	817-927-7589
Freeman, Charlie/3333-A Elm St, Dallas, TX	214-742-1446
Fry, John/5416 Wateka, Dallas, TX	214-350-9565
FULLER, TIMOTHY WOODBRIDGE/135 1/2 S SIXTH AVE, TUCSON, AZ (P 215)	**602-622-3900**

G
Gaber, Brad/4946 Glen Meadow, Houston, TX	713-723-0030
Galloway, Jim/2201 N Lamar, Dallas, TX	214-954-0355
Gary & Clark Photographic Studio/2702 Main, Dallas, TX	214-939-9070
Gatz, Larry/5250 Gulfton #3B, Houston, TX	713-666-5203
Gaudet, Joe/2524 Farington St, Dallas, TX	214-630-5452
Gayle, Rick/2318 E Roosevelt, Phoenix, AZ	602-267-8845
Geffs, Dale/15715 Amapola, Houston, TX	713-933-3876
Gerczynski, Tom/2211 N 7th Ave, Phoenix, AZ	602-252-9229
Germany, Robert/3102 Commerce St, Dallas, TX	214-747-4548
Gilbert, Bruce/12335 Braesridge, Houston, TX	713-723-1486
Giles-Cardellino Inc/315 9th St #2, San Antonio, TX	512-224-9606
Gilmore, Dwight/2437 Hillview, Fort Worth, TX	817-536-4825
Gilstrap, L C/132 Booth Calloway, Hurst, TX	817-284-7701
Glentzer, Don Photography/3814 S Shepherd Dr, Houston, TX	713-529-9686
Gomel, Bob/10831 Valley Hills, Houston, TX	713-988-6390
Gonzalez, Peter/PO Box 2775, Austin, TX	512-444-9737
Goodman, Robert/2025 Levee, Dallas, TX	214-653-1120
Graham, Boyce/2809 Canton St, Dallas, TX	214-748-2809
Grass, Jon/1345 Chemical St, Dallas, TX	214-634-1455
GREEN, MARK/2406 TAFT ST, HOUSTON, TX (P 216,217)	**713-523-6146**
Grider, James/732 Schilder, Fort Worth, TX	817-732-7472
Guerrero, Charles/2207 Comal St, Austin, TX	512-477-6642

H
Hagler, Skeeter/PO Box 628, Red Oak, TX	214-576-5620
Hale, Butch Photography/1319 Conant, Dallas, TX	214-637-3987
Halpern, David/7420 E 70th St, Tulsa, OK	918-252-4973
Ham, Dan/965-B Slocum, Dallas, TX	214-742-8700
Hamburger, Jay/1817 State St, Houston, TX	713-869-0869
Hamilton, Jeffrey/6719 Quartzite Canyon Pl, Tucson, AZ	602-299-3624
Handel, Doug/1001 3rd St, Carrollton, TX	214-446-2236
Harness, BRian/1402 S Montreal Ave, Dallas, TX	214-330-4419
Hart, Len/2100 Wilcrest #102, Houston, TX	713-974-3265
Hart, Michael/7320 Ashcroft #105, Houston, TX	713-271-8250
Hartman, Gary/911 South St Marys St, San Antonio, TX	512-225-2404
Hatcok, Tom/113 W 12th St, Deer Park, TX	713-479-2603
Haverfield, Patrick/2831 Irving Blvd #101, Dallas, TX	214-630-5881
Hawks, Bob/1345 E 15th St, Tulsa, OK	918-584-3351
Hawn, Gray Photography/PO Box 16425, Austin, TX	512-451-7561
Haynes, Mike/4906 Don Dr, Dallas, TX	214-688-1841
Heiner, Gary/2039 Farrington, Dallas, TX	214-760-7471
Heinsohn, Bill/5455 Dashwood #200, Bellaire, TX	713-666-6515
Heit, Don/8502 Eustis Ave, Dallas, TX	214-324-0305
Henry, Steve/7403 Pierrepont Dr, Houston, TX	713-937-4514
Hix, Steve/209 E Ben White Blvd #109, Austin, TX	512-441-2600
Hollenbeck, Phil/4044 Hawthorne Ave, Dallas, TX	214-331-8328
Hollingsworth, Jack/3141 Irving Blvd #209, Dallas, TX	214-634-2632
Hood, Bob/2312 Grand, Dallas, TX	214-428-6080
Hubbard, Tim/Box 44971/Los Olivos Sta, Phoenix, AZ	602-274-6985
Huber, Phil/13562 Braemar Dr, Dallas, TX	214-243-4011
Hulsey, Jim Photography/8117 NW 80th St, Oklahoma City, OK	405-720-2767

IJ
Ives, Tom/2250 El Moraga, Tucson, AZ	602-743-0750
Jacoby, Doris/1317 Conant, Dallas, TX	214-526-5026
Jennings, Steve/PO Box 33203, Tulsa, OK	918-745-0836
Jew, Kim/1518 Girard NE, Albuquerque, NM	505-255-6424
Johnson, Michael/830 Exposition #215, Dallas, TX	214-828-9550
Jones, C Bryan/2900 N Loop W #1130, Houston, TX	713-956-4166
Jones, Jerry/6207 Edloe, Houston, TX	713-668-4328

K
Kaluzny, Zigy/4700 Strass Dr, Austin, TX	512-452-4463
Kasie Photos/2123 Avignon, Carrollton, TX	214-492-7837
Katz, John/5222 Red Field, Dallas, TX	214-637-0844
Kearn, Judy/4105 Prescott #201, Dallas, TX	214-630-0101
Kendrick, Robb/2700 Albany #303, Houston, TX	713-528-4334
Kennedy, David Michael/PO Box 254, Cerrillos, NM	505-473-2745
Kenny, Gill/3515 N Camino De Vista, Tucson, AZ	602-743-0963
Kern, Geof/1337 Crampton, Dallas, TX	214-630-0856
Kirkley, Kent/4906 Don St, Dallas, TX	214-688-1841
Klumpp, Don/804 Colquitt, Houston, TX	713-521-2090
Knowles, Jim/6102 E Mockingbird Ln #499, Dallas, TX	214-699-5335
Knudson, Kent/PO Box 10397, Phoenix, AZ	602-277-7701
Koppes, Neil/1611 N 36th St, Phoenix, AZ	602-231-0918
Korab, Jeanette/2264 Vantage, Dallas, TX	214-337-0114
Kretchmar, Phil Photography/3333 Elm, Dallas, TX	214-744-2039
Kroninger, Rick/PO Box 15913, San Antonio, TX	512-733-9931
Kuehnel, Jaime/901 Cedar Hill #223, Dallas, TX	214-946-3382
KUPER, HOLLY/5522 ANITA ST, DALLAS, TX (P 218)	**214-827-4494**

LM
Larsen, Peter/1350 Manufacturing #206, Dallas, TX	214-742-1014
Latorre, Robert/2336 Farrington St, Dallas, TX	214-630-8977
Lawrence, David/2720 Stemmons #1206, Dallas, TX	214-637-4686
Lawrie, Bill/3030 Sundail Dr, Dallas, TX	214-243-4188
Lettner, Hans/830 North 4th Ave, Phoenix, AZ	602-258-3506
Loven, Paul/1405 E Marshall, Phoenix, AZ	602-253-0335
Luker, Tom/PO Box 6112, Coweta, OK	918-486-5264
Mader, Bob/2570 Promenade Center N, Richardson, TX	214-690-5511
Magee, Mike/1325 Conant St, Dallas, TX	214-638-6868
Mageors & Rice Photo Service Inc/240 Turnpike Ave, Dallas, TX	214-941-3777
Major, Bert/11056 Shady Trail #119, Dallas, TX	214-956-9338
Maloney, John W/170 Leslie, Dallas, TX	214-741-6320
Manley, Dan/1350 Manufacturing Suite 215, Dallas, TX	214-748-8377
Manske, Thaine/7313 Ashcroft #216, Houston, TX	713-771-2220
Manstein, Ralph/5353 Institute Ln, Houston, TX	713-523-2500
Maples, Carl/1811 Cohn, Houston, TX	713-868-1289
Mark, Richard/3102 W Lewis St #8, Phoenix, AZ	602-272-6610
Markham, Jim/2739 S E Loop 410, San Antonio, TX	512-648-0403
Markow, Paul/2222 E McDowell Rd, Phoenix, AZ	602-273-7985
Marks, Stephen/4704-C Prospect NE, Albuquerque, NM	505-884-6100
Marshall, Jim/7451 Long Rifle Rd/Box 2421, Carefree, AZ	602-488-3373
Matthews, Michael/2727 Cancun, Dallas, TX	214-306-8000
Maxham, Robert/223 Howard St, San Antonio, TX	512-223-6000
Maxim, Robert/223 Howard St, San Antonio, TX	512-223-6000
Mayer, George H/933 Stonetrail, Plano (Dallas), TX	214-424-4409
McClain, Edward/756 N Palo Verde, Tucson, AZ	602-326-1873
McCormick, Mike/5950 Westward Ave, Houston, TX	713-988-0775
McCoy, Gary/2700 Commerce St, Dallas, TX	214-320-0002
McIntosh, W S/12201 Merit Dr #222, Richardson, TX	214-783-1711
McMichael, Garry D/RT 1 Box 312, Paris, AR	501-963-6429
McNee, Jim/PO Box 741008, Houston, TX	713-796-2633
Messina, John/4440 Lawnview, Dallas, TX	214-388-8525
Meyerson, Arthur/4215 Bellaire Blvd, Houston, TX	713-660-0405
MEYLER, DENNIS/1903 PORTSMOUTH #25, HOUSTON, TX (P 219)	**713-778-1700**
Mills, Jack R/PO Box 32583, Oklahoma City, OK	405-787-7271
Moberley, Connie/215 Asbury, Houston, TX	713-864-3638
Molen, Roy/3302 N 47 Pl, Phoenix, AZ	602-840-5439
Monteaux, Michele/223 Ojo De La Vaca, Santa Fe, NM	505-982-5598
Montoya, Andy/1800 Lear #5, Dallas, TX	214-421-3993
Moore, Terrence/PO Box 41536, Tucson, AZ	602-623-9381
Moot, Kelly/6606 Demoss #508, Houston, TX	713-683-6400
Morgan, Roger/828 Birdsong, Bedford, TX	817-282-2170

Photographers

Continued

Please send us your additions and updates.

Morris, Garry/9281 E 27th St, Tucson, AZ	602-795-2334
Morris, Mike/4003 Gilbert #6, Dallas, TX	214-528-3600
Morrison, Chet Photography/2917 Canton, Dallas, TX	214-939-0903
Muir, Robert/Box 42809 Dept 404, Houston, TX	713-784-7420
Murdoch, Lane/1350 Manufacturing #205, Dallas, TX	214-651-0200
Murphy, Dennis/101 Howell St, Dallas, TX	214-651-7516
Myers, Jim/165 Cole, Dallas, TX	214-698-0500

N
Neely, David/11163 Shady Trail #103, Dallas, TX	214-241-1950
Netzer, Don/8585 Stemmons #M29, Dallas, TX	214-869-0826
Newby, Steve/4501 Swiss, Dallas, TX	214-821-0231
Njaa, Reuben/104 Heiman, San Antonio, TX	512-227-8208
Noland, Lloyd (Weaver)/PO Box 9456, Santa Fe, NM	505-982-2488
Norrell, J B/7320 Ashcroft #106, Houston, TX	713-981-6409
NORTON, MICHAEL/PO BOX 20807, PHOENIX, AZ (P 221)	**602-840-9463**

OP
Olvera, James/235 Yorktown St, Dallas, TX	214-760-0025
Palmetto, Chuck/2707 Stemmons #160, Dallas, TX	214-638-1885
PANTIN, TOMAS/1601 E 7TH ST #100, AUSTIN, TX	
(P 222,223)	**512-474-9968**
Parsons, Bill/518 W 9th St, Little Rock, AR	501-372-5892
Patrick, Richard/215 W 4th St #B, Austin, TX	512-472-9092
Payne, A F/830 North 4th Ave, Phoenix, AZ	602-258-3506
Payne, C Ray/2643 Manana, Dallas, TX	214-350-1055
Payne, Richard/2029 Haddon St, Houston, TX	713-524-7525
Payne, Tom/2425 Bartlett, Houston, TX	713-527-8670
Perlstein, Mark/1844 Place One Ln, Garland, TX	214-690-0168
Peterson, Bruce/1222 E Edgemont, Phoenix, AZ	602-252-6088
Pettit, Steve/206 Weeks, Arlington, TX	817-265-8776
PFUHL, CHRIS/PO BOX 542, PHOENIX, AZ (P 224)	**602-253-0525**
Phelps, Greg/2360 Central Blvd, Brownsville, TX	512-541-4909
Photo Media, Inc/2805 Crockett, Fort Worth, TX	817-332-4172
Poulides, Peter/PO Box 202505, Dallas, TX	214-350-5395
Probst, Kenneth/3527 Oak Lawn Blvd #375, Dallas, TX	214-522-2031

QR
Quilia, Jim/3125 Ross, Dallas, TX	214-276-9956
Raphaele Inc/616 Hawthorne, Houston, TX	713-524-2211
Raymond, Rick/1244 E Utopia, Phoenix, AZ	602-581-8160
Records, Bill/505 W 38, Austin, TX	512-458-1017
Redd, True/2328 Farrington, Dallas, TX	214-638-0602
Reens, Louis/4814 Sycamore, Dallas, TX	214-827-3388
REESE, DONOVAN/3007 CANTON, DALLAS, TX (P 225)	**214-357-6615**
Reisch, Jim/235 Yorktown St, Dallas, TX	214-748-0456
Rich, Wilburn/3233 Marquart, Houston, TX	713-623-8790
Robbins Jr, Joe D/7320 Ashcroft Ste 213, Houston, TX	713-271-1111
Robson, Howard/3807 E 64th Pl, Tulsa, OK	918-492-3079
Roe, Cliff/47 Woodelves Pl, The Woodlands, TX	713-363-5661
Rogers, John/PO Box 35753, Dallas, TX	214-351-1751
Rubin, Janice/705 E 16th St, Houston, TX	713-868-6060
Running, John/PO Box 1237, Flagstaff, AZ	602-774-2923
Rusing, Rick/22 E 15th St, Tempe, AZ	602-967-1864
Russell, Gail/PO Box 241, Taos, NM	505-776-8474
Russell, Nicholas/849-F Harvard, Houston, TX	713-864-7664
Ryan, Tom/1821 Levee, Dallas, TX	214-651-7085

S
Sall, Narinder/2024 Karbach #3, Houston, TX	713-680-3717
Savant, Joseph/4756 Algiers St, Dallas, TX	214-951-0111
Sawada, Spencer/2810 S 24th St #109, Phoenix, AZ	602-275-5078
Saxon, John/1337 Crampton, Dallas, TX	214-630-5160
Scheer, Tim/1521 Centerville Rd, Dallas, TX	214-328-1016
Scheyer, Mark/3317 Montrose #A1003, Houston, TX	713-861-0847
Schlesinger, Terrence/PO Box 32877, Phoenix, AZ	602-957-7474
Schmidt, Dave/837 E Peoria #1, Phoenix, AZ	602-870-3090
Schneps, Michael/21 Pinedale #6, Houston, TX	713-520-8224
Schultz, Dave/1047-E McLellan Blvd, Phoenix, AZ	602-230-0282
Schuster, Ellen/3719 Gilbert, Dallas, TX	214-526-6712
SCOTT, RON/1000 JACKSON BLVD, HOUSTON, TX (P 226)	**713-529-5868**
Segrest, Jerry Photography/1707 S Arvay, Dallas, TX	214-426-6360
Segroves, Jim/170 Leslie, Dallas, TX	214-827-5482
Self, James/15oo Dragon St, Dallas, TX	214-742-3611
Sellers, Dan/1317 Conant, Dallas, TX	214-631-4705
Shands, Nathan/1107 Bryan, Mesquite, TX	214-285-5382

Shaw, Robert/1723 Kelly SE, Dallas, TX	214-428-1757
Siegel, Dave/224 N 5th Ave, Phoenix, AZ	602-257-9509
Sieve, Jerry/PO Box 1777, Cave Creek, AZ	602-488-9561
Simon, Frank/3102 W Louis #8, Phoenix, AZ	602-272-0715
SIMPSON, MICHEAL/415 N BISHOP AVE, DALLAS, TX	
(P 227)	**214-943-9347**
Sims, Jim/2811 McKinney #224, Dallas, TX	214-855-0055
Sims, John/336 Melrose #14A, Richardson, TX	214-231-6065
Smith, Ralph/2211 Beall, Houston, TX	713-862-8301
Smith/Garza Photography/PO Box 10046, Dallas, TX	214-941-4611
Smothers, Brian/834 W 43rd St, Houston, TX	713-695-0873
Smusz, Ben/2511 W Holcombe Blvd, Houston, TX	713-666-1511
Sperry, Bill/3300 E Stanford, Paradise Valley, AZ	602-955-5626
St Angelo, Ron/350 Turtle Creek #109, Dallas, TX	817-481-1833
St Gil & Associates/PO Box 820568, Houston, TX	713-870-9458
Staarjes, Hans/20 Lana Lane, Houston, TX	713-621-8503
Starnes, Mac/2703 Fondren #136, Dallas, TX	214-279-3055
Stewart, Craig/1900 W Alabama, Houston, TX	713-529-5959
Stibbens, Steve/104 Cole St, Dallas, TX	817-461-3518
Stiller, Rick/1311 E 35th St, Tulsa, OK	918-749-0297
Stroud, Dan/1350 Manufacturing #211, Dallas, TX	214-783-7133
Studio 3 Photography/2804 Lubbock, Fort Worth, TX	817-923-9931
Suddarth, Robert/3402 73rd St, Lubbock, TX	806-795-4553
Sumner, Bill/122 Parkhouse, Dallas, TX	214-748-3766
Svacina, Joe/2209 Summer, Dallas, TX	214-748-3260
Swindler, Mark/206 Santa Rita, Odessa, TX	915-332-3515

TV
TALLEY, PAUL/4756 ALGIERS ST (P 229)	**214-951-0039**
Tenney, Bob/PO Box 17236, Dallas, TX	214-288-9291
Terry, Phillip/1222 Manufacturing St, Dallas, TX	214-749-0515
Thatcher, Charles/4220 Main St, Dallas, TX	214-823-4356
The Quest Group/3007 Paseo, Oklahoma City, OK	405-525-6591
Thompson, Dennis/4153 S 87th Ave, Tulsa, OK	918-582-8850
Thompson, Wesley/800 W Airport Frwy #301, Irving, TX	214-438-7762
Timmerman, Bill/1725 W University/Bldg 844, Tempe, AZ	602-968-9474
Tomlinson, Doug/5651 East Side Ave, Dallas, TX	214-821-1192
Trent, Rusty/7205 Cecil, Houston, TX	713-526-3651
Turner, Danny/2030 Farrington, Dallas, TX	214-760-7472
Van Warner, Steven/1637 W Wilshire, Phoenix, AZ	602-254-2618
Vantage Point Studio/1109 Arizona Ave, El Paso, TX	915-533-9688
Vener, Ellis/3601 Allen Pkwy #123, Houston, TX	713-523-0456
Viewpoint Photographers/217 McKinley, Phoenix, AZ	602-245-0013
VINE, TERRY/5455 DASHWOOD #200, HOUSTON, TX	
(P 230,231)	**713-664-2920**
Vracin, Andrew/4609 Don, Dallas, TX	214-688-1841

WYZ
Walker, Balfour/1838 E 6th St, Tucson, AZ	602-624-1121
Weeks, Christopher/1260 E 31st Pl, Tulsa, OK	918-749-0297
Wells, Craig/537 W Granada, Phoenix, AZ	602-252-8166
Welsch, Diana/PO Box 1791, Austin, TX	512-451-8960
WERRE, BOB/2437 BARTLETT ST, HOUSTON, TX (P 232)	**713-529-4841**
Wheeler, Don/220 N Main, Tulsa, OK	918-592-5099
White, Frank Photo/2702 Sackett, Houston, TX	713-524-9250
Whitlock, Neill/122 E 5th St, Dallas, TX	214-948-3117
Wilke, Darrell/2608 Irving Blvd, Dallas, TX	214-631-6459
Willecke, Brian/PO Box 16603, Ft Worth, TX	817-346-6121
Williams, Oscar/8535 Fairhaven, San Antonio, TX	512-690-8807
Williamson, Thomas A/10830 N Central Expy #201, Dallas, TX	214-373-4999
Willis, Gordon/3910 Buena Vista #11, Dallas, TX	214-520-7035
WOLENSKI, STAN/2201 N LAMAR, DALLAS, TX (P 207)	**214-720-0044**
Wolfhagen, Vilhelm/4916 Kelvin, Houston, TX	713-522-2787
WOLLAM, LES/5215 GOODWIN AVE, DALLAS, TX (P 233)	**214-760-7721**
WOOD, KEITH/1308 CONANT ST, DALLAS, TX (P 234,235)	**214-634-7344**
Workman, Walter/4101 Commerce St #8, Dallas, TX	214-826-9770
Wristen, Don/2025 Levee St, Dallas, TX	214-748-5317
Yeung, Ka Chuen/4901 W Lovers Lane, Dallas, TX	214-350-8716
Zerschling, Jim/19521 Preston Rd, Dallas, TX	214-558-7226

Rocky Mountain

A
Adams, Butch/1414 S 700 W, Salt Lake City, UT	801-973-0939

Photographers

Continued

Please send us your additions and updates.

AIUPPY, LARRY/522 W CHINOOK/BOX 26, LIVINGSTON, MT
(P 239)   **406-222-7308**
Alaxandar/820 Humboldt St #6, Denver, CO   303-863-8844
Allen, Lincoln/1705 Woodbridge Dr, Salt Lake City, UT   801-277-1848
Alston, Bruce/PO Box 2480, Steamboat Springs, CO   303-879-1675
Anderson, Borge/234 South 200 East, Salt Lake City, UT   801-359-7703
Appleton, Roger/3106 Pennslyvania, Colorado Springs, CO   303-635-0393
Archer, Mark/228 S Madison St, Denver, CO   303-399-5272
Auben, Steven/590 Dover, Lakewood, CO   303-232-0243

B
Bailey, Brent P/PO Box 70681, Reno, NV   702-826-4104
Bako, Andrew/3047 4th St SW, Calgary T2S 1X9, AB   403-243-9789
Barry, Dave/6669 S Kit CArson St, Littleton, CO   303-798-9995
Bartay Studio/721 Santa Fe Dr, Denver, CO   303-628-0700
Bartek, Patrick/PO Box 26994, Las Vegas, NV   702-368-2901
Batchlor, Paul/655 Wolff St #42, Denver, CO   303-623-4465
Bator, Joe/2011 Washington Ave, Golden, CO   303-279-4163
Bauer, Erwin A/Box 543, Teton Village, WY   307-733-4023
BEEBE, KEVIN/2460 ELIOT ST, DENVER, CO (P 240)   **303-455-3627**
Beery, Gale/150 W Byers, Denver, CO   303-777-0458
BERCHERT, JAMES H/2886 W 119TH AVE, DENVER, CO
(P 241)   **303-466-7414**
Berge, Melinda/1280 Ute Ave, Aspen, CO   303-925-2317
Birnbach, Allen/3600 Tejon St, Denver, CO   303-455-7800
Blake, John/4132 20th St, Greeley, CO   303-330-0980
Bluebaugh, David Studio/1594 S Acoma St, Denver, CO   303-778-7214
Bonmarito, Jim/PO Box 599, Durango, CO   303-247-1166
Bosworth/Graves Photo Inc/1055 S 700 W, Salt Lake City, UT   801-972-6128
Burggraf, Chuck/2941 W 23rd Ave, Denver, CO   303-480-9053
Busath, Drake/701 East South Temple St, Salt Lake City, UT   801-364-6645
Bush, Michael/2555 Walnut St, Denver, CO   303-292-2874

C
Cambon, Jim/216 Racquette Dr, Fort Collins, CO   303-571-4555
Chesley, Paul/Box 94, Aspen, CO   303-925-1148
Christensen, Barry/4505 South 2300 West, Roy, UT   801-731-3521
Clasen, Norm/PO Box 4230, Aspen, CO   303-925-4418
Coca, Joe/213 1/2 Jefferson St, Ft Collins, CO   303-482-0858
Collector, Stephen/1836 Mapleton Ave, Boulder, CO   303-442-1386
Cook, James/PO Box 11608, Denver, CO   303-433-4874
Coppock, Ron/1764 Platte St, Denver, CO   303-893-2299
Cronin, Bill/2543 Xavier, Denver, CO   303-458-0883
Crowe, Steven/1150 S Cherry #1-202, Denver, CO   303-782-0346
Cruickshank/505 C Street, Lewiston, ID   208-743-9411
Cupp, David/2520 Albion St, Denver, CO   303-321-3581

D
Dahlquist, Ron/PO Box 1606, Steamboat Springs, CO   808-879-4169
Dannen, Kent & Donna/851 Peak View/Moraine Rte, Estes Park, CO   303-586-5794
DeHoff, RD/632 N Sheridan, Colorado Springs, CO   303-635-0263
DELESPINASSE, HANK/2300 E PATRICK LN #21, LAS VEGAS, NV (P 256)   **702-798-6693**
DeMancznk, Phillip/1625 Wilber Pl, Reno, NV   702-329-0339
DeSciose, Nick/2700 Arapahoe St #2, Denver, CO   303-296-6386
DeVore, Nicholas III/1280 Ute, Aspen, CO   303-925-2317
Dean, Bill/621 West 1000 North, West Bountiful, UT   801-295-9746
Dickey, Marc/2500 Curtis #115, Denver, CO   303-298-7691
Dimond, Craig/831 S Richards St, Salt Lake City, UT   801-363-7158
Dolan, J Ross/6094 S Ironton Ct, Englewood, CO   303-770-8454
DOUGLASS, DIRK/2755 S 300 W #D, SALT LAKE CITY, UT
(P 242)   **801-485-5691**
Dowbenko, Uri/PO Box 207, Emigrant, MT   406-333-4322
Downs, Jerry/1315 Oak Ct, Boulder, CO   303-444-8910

EF
Elder, Jim/PO Box 1600, Jackson Hole, WY   307-733-3555
Fader, Bob/14 Pearl St, Denver, CO   303-744-0711
Farace, Joe Photo/14 Inverness #B100, Englewood, CO   303-799-6606
Feld, Stephen/1572 E 9350 S, Sandy, UT   801-571-1752
Firth, Peter/54 E 1440 S, Salt Lake City, UT   801-486-2454
Ford, David/954 S Emerson, Denver, CO   303-778-7044
FRAZIER, VAN/2770 S MARYLAND PKWY, LAS VEGAS, NV
(P 258)   **702-735-1165**
Freeman, Hunter/852 Santa Fe Dr, Denver, CO   303-893-5730

GH
Gallian, Dirk/2301 Kuhio Ave, Honolulu, HI   808-924-0401
Gamba, Mark/705 19th St, Glenwood Springs, CO   303-945-5903
Goetze, David/3215 Zuni, Denver, CO   303-458-5026
Gorfkle, Gregory D/6901 E Baker Pl, Denver, CO   303-759-2737
Graf, Gary/1870 S Ogden St, Denver, CO   303-722-0547
H B R Studios/3310 South Knox Court, Denver, CO   303-789-4307
Harris, Richard/935 South High, Denver, CO   303-778-6433
Haun, Lora/8428 Fenton St, Arvada, CO   303-428-8834
Havey, James/1836 Blake St #203, Denver, CO   303-296-7448
Held, Patti/PO Box 44441, Denver, CO   303-341-7248
Henderson, Gordon/182 Gariepy Crescent, Edmonton T6M 1A2, AB   403-483-8049
Herridge, Brent/736 South 3rd West, Salt Lake City, UT   801-363-0337
Hiser, David C/1280 Ute Ave, Aspen, CO   303-925-2317
Holdman, Floyd/1908 Main St, Orem, UT   801-224-9966
Hooper, Robert Scott/4330 W Desert Inn Rd, Las Vegas, NV   702-873-5823
HUNT, STEVEN/1139 W SHEPARD LN, FARMINGTON, UT
(P 238)   **801-451-6552**
Huntress, Diane/3337 W 23rd Ave, Denver, CO   303-480-0219

JK
J T Photographics/10490-C West Fair Ave, Littleton, CO   303-972-8847
Jacobs, V Joseph/3961 Fuller Ct, Boulder, CO   303-499-9771
Jensen, Curt/PO Box 2092, Rock Spring, WY   307-382-7794
Johns, Rob/1075 Piedmont, Boulder, CO   303-449-9192
Johnson, Jim Photo/16231 E Princeton Circle, Denver, CO   303-680-0522
Johnson, Ron/2460 Eliot St, Denver, CO   303-458-0288
Kay, James W/4463 Wander Ln, Salt Lake City, UT   801-277-4489
King, Jennifer/9810 E Colorado #107, Denver, CO   303-337-3137
Kitzman, John/3060 22nd St, Boulder, CO   303-440-7623
Koropp, Robert/901 E 17th Ave, Denver, CO   303-830-6000
Kramer, Andrew/PO Box 6023, Boulder, CO   303-449-2280
Krause, Ann/1039 Maxwell Ave, Boulder, CO   303-444-6798

L
Laidman, Allan/PO Box 4739, Aspen, CO   303-920-1431
Laszlo, Larry/110ʋ Acoma St, Denver, CO   303-832-2299
LeGoy, James M/PO Box 21004, Reno, NV   702-322-0116
Lee, Jess/6799 N Derek Ln, Idaho Falls, ID   208-529-4535
LEVY, PATRICIA BARRY/4467 UTICA, DENVER, CO (P 243)   **303-458-6692**
Lichter, Michael/3300 14th St, Boulder, CO   303-443-9198
Lissy, David/14472 Applewood Ridge Rd, Golden, CO   303-277-0232
Lokey, David/PO Box 7, Vail, CO   303-949-5750
LONCZYNA, LONGIN/257-R S RIO GRANDE ST, SALT LAKE CITY, UT (P 244)   **801-355-7513**
Lotz, Fred/4220 W 82nd Ave, Westminster, CO   303-427-2875

M
MANGELSEN, TOM/PO BOX 2935, JACKSON, WY (P 275)   **307-733-6179**
Marlow, David/111-R Atlantic Ave, Aspen, CO   303-925-8882
Mathews, T R/9206 W 100th St, Broomfield, CO   303-469-1436
McDonald, Kirk/350 Bannock, Denver, CO   303-733-2958
McDowell, Pat/PO Box 283, Park City, UT   801-649-3403
McManemin, Jack/662 S State St, Salt Lake City, UT   801-533-0435
Meleski, Mike/505 24th St, Denver, CO   303-297-0632
Melick, Jordan/1250 W Cedar St, Denver, CO   303-744-1414
Messineo, John/PO Box 1636, Fort Collins, CO   303-482-9349
MILES, KENT/465 E NINTH AVE, SALT LAKE CITY, UT (P 245)   **801-364-5755**
Milmoe, James O/14900 Cactus Cr, Golden, CO   303-279-4364
Milne, Lee/3615 W 49th Ave, Denver, CO   303-458-1520
Mitchell, Paul/1517 S Grant, Denver, CO   303-722-8852
Mock, Wanda/Po Box 85, Roberts, MT   406-445-2356
Moore, Janet/4350 S Bannock St, Englewood, CO   303-781-0035
Mosbisch, Dick/5480 E Gill Pl, Denver, CO   303-333-9651
Munro, Harry/2355 W 27th Ave, Denver, CO   303-355-5612

OP
Ordway, Robert/105 N Edison #17, Reno, NV   702-322-4889
Oswald, Jan/921 Santa Fe, Denver, CO   303-893-8038
Outlaw, Rob/519 E Lamme/Box 1275, Bozeman, MT   406-586-2254
Patryas, David/26 Birch Ct #4, Long Mont, CO   303-678-0959
Paul, Howard/2460 Eliot St, Denver, CO   303-458-0288
Payne, Brian/2685 Forest, Denver, CO   303-355-5373
Peregrine Studio/1541 Platte St, Denver, CO   303-455-6944
Perkin, Jan/428 L St, Salt Lake City, UT   801-355-0112

Photographers

Continued

Please send us your additions and updates.

Phillips, Ron/12201 E Arapahoe #B2, Englewood, CO	303-790-8114
Proctor, Keith/, Park City, UT	

QR
QUINNEY, DAVID/423 E BROADWAY, SALT LAKE	
CITY, UT (P 246)	**801-363-0434**
Rafkind, Andrew/1702 Fairview Ave, Boise, ID	208-344-9918
Ramsey, Steve/4800 N Washington St, Denver, CO	303-295-2135
Ranson Photographers Ltd/26 Airport Rd, Edmonton	
T5G 0W7, AB	403-454-9674
Redding, Ken/PO Box 717, Vail, CO	303-949-6123
Rehn, Gary/860 Toedtli Dr, Boulder, CO	303-499-9550
Reynolds, Roger/3310 S Knox Ct, Englewood, CO	303-789-4307
Rosen Barry/1 Middle Rd, Englewood, CO	303-758-0648
Rosenberg, David/1545 Julian SE, Denver, CO	303-893-0893
Rosenberger, Edward/2248 Emerson Ave, Salt Lake City, UT	801-355-9007
Russell, John/PO Box 4739, Aspen, CO	303-920-1431

S
Saehlenou, Kevin/3478 W 32nd Ave, Denver, CO	303-455-1611
Sahula, Peter/CO, 303-927-3475, Sallaz, William/PO Box	
6050, Helena, MT	406-442-0522
Saviers, Trent/2606 Rayma Ct, Reno, NV	702-747-2591
Scherer, William D/PO Box 274, Greeley, CO	303-353-6674
Schlack, Greg/1510 Lehigh St, Boulder, CO	303-499-3860
Schmiett, Skip/740 W 1700 S #10, Salt Lake City, UT	801-973-0642
Schneider, Beth/1666 Race St, Denver, CO	303-733-3388
Schoenfeld, Michael/PO Box 876, Salt Lake City, UT	801-532-2006
Shupe, John R/4090 Edgehill Dr, Ogden, UT	801-392-2523
Simons, Randy/3320 S Knox Ct, Englewood, CO	303-761-1458
Smith, David Scott/1437 Ave E, Billings, MT	406-259-5656
Smith, Derek/925 SW Temple, Salt Lake City, UT	801-363-1061
Smith, Dorn/1201-A Santa Fe, Denver, CO	303-571-4331
Sokol, Howard/3006 Zuni St, Denver, CO	303-433-3353
St John, Charles/1760 Lafayette St, Denver, CO	303-860-7300
Staver, Barry/5122 S Iris Way, Littleton, CO	303-973-4414
STEARNS, DOUG/1738 WYNKOOP ST #102, DENVER, CO	
(P 247)	**303-296-1133**
Stewert, Sandy/18230 W 4th Ave, Golden, CO	303-278-8039
Stoecklein, DAvid/PO Box, Ketchum, ID	208-726-5191
Stott, Barry/2427 Chamonix Rd, Vail, CO	303-476-5774
Stouder, Carol/5421 W Geddes Pl, Littleton, CO	303-979-5402
Sunlit Ltd/1523 E Montane Dr, Genesse, CO	303-526-1162
Swartz, Bill/5992 S Eudora Ct, Littleton, CO	303-773-2776
Sweitzer, David/4800 Washington, Denver, CO	303-295-0703

T
Tanner, Scott/2755 South 300 West #D, Salt Lake City, UT	801-466-6884
TEJADA, DAVID X/1553 PLATTE ST #205, DENVER, CO	
(P 248)	**303-458-1220**
Tharp, Brenda/901 E Seventeenth Ave, Denver, CO	303-980-0639
Till, Tom/P O Box 337, Moab, UT	801-259-5327
Tobias, Philip/3614 Morrison Rd, Denver, CO	303-936-1267
Tradelius, Bob/738 Santa Fe Dr, Denver, CO	303-825-4847
Travis, Tom/1219 S Pearl St, Denver, CO	303-377-7422
Tregeagle, Steve/2994 S Richards St #C, Salt Lake City, UT	801-484-1673
Trice, Gordon/2046 Arapahoe St, Denver, CO	303-298-1986

VWY
Van Hemert, Martin/5481 Cyclamen Ct,	
Salt Lake City, UT	801-969-3569
Viggio Studio/2400 Central Ave, Boulder, CO	303-444-3342
Walker, Rod/PO Box 2418, Vail, CO	303-926-3210
Wapinski, David/10 Valdez Circle, Dugway, UT	801-831-5481
Warren, Cameron A/PO Box 10588, Reno, NV	702-746-2121
Wayda, Steve/5725 Immigration Canyon, Salt Lake City, UT	801-582-1787
Weeks, Michael/PO Box 6965, Colorado Springs, CO	303-632-2996
Wellisch, Bill/2325 Clay St, Denver, CO	303-455-8766
Welsh, Steve/518 Americana Blvd, Boise, ID	208-336-5541
Wheeler, Geoffrey/721 Pearl St, Boulder, CO	303-449-2137
White, Stuart/4229 Clark Ave, Great Falls, MT	406-761-6666
Wordal, Eric/3640 Keir Lane, Helena, MT	406-475-3304
Worden, Kirk/3215 Zuni Ave, Denver, CO	303-477-5621
Yarborough, Carl/PO Box 4739, Aspen, CO	303-920-1431

West Coast

A
Abecassis, Andree L/756 Neilson St, Berkeley, CA	415-526-5099
ABRAHAM, RUSSELL/17 BROSNAN ST, SAN FRANCISCO,	
CA (P 253)	**415-558-9100**
Abramowitz, Alan/PO Box 45121, Seattle, WA	206-621-0710
Ackroyd, Hugh S/Box 10101, Portland, OR	503-227-5694
Addor, Jean-Michel/1456 63rd St, Emeryville, CA	415-653-1745
Adler, Allan S/PO Box 2251, Van Nuys, CA	818-901-6555
Adler, Bob/33 Ellert St, San Francisco, CA	415-695-2867
Agee, Bill & Assoc/715 Larkspur Box 612, Corona Del Mar, CA	714-760-6700
Ahrend, Jay/1046 N Orange Dr, Hollywood, CA	213-462-5256
All Sport Photo/10234 Nevada Ave, Chatsworth, CA	818-704-5118
Allan, Larry/3503 Argonne St, San Diego, CA	619-270-1850
Allen, Charles/537 S Raymond Ave, Pasadena, CA	818-795-1053
Allen, Judson Photo/654 Gilman St, Palo Alto, CA	415-324-8177
Allison, Glen/PO Box 1833, Santa Monica, CA	213-392-1388
Alt, Tim/3699 Wilshire Blvd #870, Los Angeles, CA	213-387-8384
Ambrose, Paul Studios/1931-J Old Middlefield Wy, Mountain	
View, CA	415-965-3555
Amdal, Philip/916 W Raye, Seattle, WA	206-448-9679
Amer, Tommy/1858 Westerly Terrace, Los Angeles, CA	213-664-7624
Andersen, Kurt/250 Newhall, San Francisco, CA	415-641-4276
Anderson, Karen/1170 N Western Ave, Los Angeles, CA	213-461-9100
Anderson, Rick/8871-B Balboa Ave, San Diego, CA	619-268-1957
Angelo, Michael/PO Box 2069, Mill Valley, CA	415-381-4224
Ansa, Brian/2605 N Lake Ave, Altadena, CA	818-797-2233
Aperture PhotoBank/1530 Westlake Ave N, Seattle, WA	206-282-8116
Apton, Bill/577 Howard St, San Francisco, CA	415-543-6313
Arend, Christopher/5401 Cordova St Ste 204, Anchorage, AK	907-562-3173
Armas, Richard/6913 Melrose Ave, Los Angeles, CA	213-931-7889
Arnesen, Erik/605 25th St, Manhattan Beach, CA	213-546-2363
Arnold, Robert Photo/1379 Natoma, San Francisco, CA	415-621-6161
Arnone, Ken/3886 Ampudia St, San Diego, CA	619-298-3141
Aron, Jeffrey/17801 Sky Park Cir #H, Irvine, CA	714-250-1555
Aronovsky, James/3356-C Hancock St, San Diego, CA	619-296-4858
Atiee, James/922 N Formosa Ave, Hollywood, CA	213-850-6112
Atkinson Photo/505 S Flower B Level, Los Angeles, CA	213-624-5970
Aurness, Craig/1526 Pontius Ave #A, Los Angeles, CA	213-477-0421
Avery, Franklin/800 Duboce #201, San Francisco, CA	415-986-3701
Avery, Ron/820 N La Brea, Los Angeles, CA	213-465-7193
Avery, Sid/820 N La Brea, Los Angeles, CA	213-465-7193
Ayres, Robert Bruce/5635 Melrose Ave, Los Angeles, CA	213-461-3816

B
Bacon, Garth/18576 Bucknall Rd, Saratoga, CA	408-866-5858
Bagley, John/730 Clemintina, San Francisco, CA	415-861-1062
Baker, Bill/265 29th St, Oakland, CA	415-832-7685
BAKER, FRANK/15031-B PARKWAY LOOP, TUSTIN, CA	
(P 254)	**714-259-1462**
Balderas, Michael/5837-B Mission Gorge Rd, San Diego, CA	619-563-7077
Baldwin, Doug/10518-2 Sunland Blvd, Sunland, CA	818-353-7270
Banko, Phil/1249 First Ave S, Seattle, WA	206-621-7008
Banks, Ken/135 N Harper Ave, Los Angeles, CA	213-930-2831
Bardin, James/111 Villa View Dr, Pacific Palisades, CA	213-459-4775
Bare, John/3001 Red Hill Ave #4-102, Costa Mesa, CA	714-979-8712
Barkentin, Pamela/1218 N LaCienga, Los Angeles, CA	213-854-1941
Barnes, John/301 Parnassus #209, San Francisco, CA	415-431-5264
Barnhurst, Noel/34 Mountain Spring Ave, San Francisco, CA	415-731-9979
Barros, Bob/1813 E Sprague, Spokane, WA	509-535-6455
Barros, Robert/1813 E Sprague, Spokane, WA	509-535-6455
Bartholick, Robin/89 Yesler Way 4th Fl, Seattle, WA	206-467-1001
Barton, Hugh G/33464 Bloomberg Rd, Eugene, OR	503-747-8184
Bartone, Laurence/335 Fifth St, San Francisco, CA	415-974-6010
Bartruff, Dave/PO Box 800, San Anselmo, CA	415-457-1482
Bates, Frank/5158 Highland View Ave, Los Angeles, CA	213-258-5272
Batista-Moon Studio/444 Pearl #B-1, Monterey, CA	408-373-1947
Bayer, Dennis/1261 Howard St, San Francisco, CA	415-552-6575
Beaman, Quee/2325 3rd St #408, San Francisco, CA	415-621-1109
Bear, Brent/8659 Hayden Pl, Culver City, CA	213-558-4471
Becker Bishop Studios/1830 17th St, San Francisco, CA	415-552-4254
Beebe, Morton/150 Lombard St #207, San Francisco, CA	415-362-3530

Photographers

Continued

Please send us your additions and updates.

Beer, Rafael/14535 Arminta #F, Van Nuys, CA	213-384-9532
Behrman, C H/8036 Kentwood, Los Angeles, CA	213-216-6611
Belcher, Richard/2565 Third St #206, San Francisco, CA	415-641-8912
Benchmark Photo/1442 N Hundley, Anaheim, CA	714-630-7965
Bencze, Louis/2442 NW Market St #86, Seattle, WA	206-783-8033
Benet, Ben/333 Fifth St #A, San Francisco, CA	415-974-5433
Bennett, James Photo/280 Cajon St, Laguna Beach, CA	714-497-4309
Bennion, Chris/5234 36th Ave NE, Seattle, WA	206-526-9981
Benson, Gary Photo/11110 34th Pl SW, Seattle, WA	206-242-3232
Benson, Hank/653 Bryant St, San Francisco, CA	415-543-8153
Benson, John/1261 Howard St 2nd Fl, San Francisco, CA	415-621-5247
Benton, Richard/4773 Brighton Ave, San Diego, CA	619-224-0278
Bergman, Alan/8241 W 4th St, Los Angeles, CA	213-852-1408
Berman, Ellen/5425 Senford Ave, Los Angeles, CA	213-641-2783
Berman, Steve/7955 W 3rd, Los Angeles, CA	213-933-9185
Bernstein, Andrew/1415 N Chester, Pasadena, CA	818-797-3430
Bernstein, Gary/8735 Washington Blvd, Culver City, CA	213-550-6891
Bertholomey, John/17962 Sky Park Cir #J, Irvine, CA	714-261-0575
Betz, Ted R/527 Howard 2nd Fl, San Francisco, CA	415-777-1260
Bez, Frank/1880 Santa Barbara Ave, San Luis Obispo, CA	805-541-2878
Bielenberg, Paul/2447 Lanterman Terr, Los Angeles, CA	213-669-1085
Biggs, Ken/1147 N Hudson Ave, Los Angeles, CA	213-462-7739
Bilecky, John/5047 W Pico Blvd, Los Angeles, CA	213-931-1610
Bilyell, Martin/600 NE Couch St, Portland, OR	503-238-0349
Bjoin, Henry/146 N La Brea Ave, Los Angeles, CA	213-937-4097
Black, Laurie/540 Seventh Ave, San Francisco, CA	415-668-5144
Blakeley, Jim/1061 Folsom St, San Francisco, CA	415-558-9300
Blakeman, Bob/710 S Santa Fe, Los Angeles, CA	213-624-6662
Blattel, David/740 S Mariposa St, Burbank, CA	213-937-0366
Blaustein, Alan/885 Autumn Ln, Mill Valley, CA	415-383-1511
Blaustein, John/911 Euclid Ave, Berkeley, CA	415-525-8133
Bleyer, Pete/807 N Sierra Bonita Ave, Los Angeles, CA	213-653-6567
Blumensaadt, Mike/306 Edna, San Francisco, CA	415-333-6178
Boonisar, Peter/PO Box 2274, Atascadero, CA	805-466-5577
Boudreau, Bernard/1015 N Cahuenga Blvd, Hollywood, CA	213-467-2602
Boulger & Kanuit/503 S Catalina, Redondo Beach, CA	213-540-6300
Bowen, John E/PO Box 1115, Hilo, HI	808-959-9460
Boyd, Bill/614 Santa Barbara St, Santa Barbara, CA	805-962-9193
Boyd, Jack/2038 Calvert Ave, Costa Mesa, CA	714-556-8133
Boyer, Dale/PO Box 391535, Mountainview, CA	415-968-9656
Boyer, Neil/1416 Aviation Blvd, Redondo Beach, CA	213-374-0443
Brabant, Patricia/245 S Van Ness 3rd Fl, San Francisco, CA	415-864-0591
Bracke, Vic/560 S Main St #4N, Los Angeles, CA	213-623-6522
Bradley, Leverett/Box 1793, Santa Monica, CA	213-394-0908
Bragstad, Jeremiah O/1041 Folsom St, San Francisco, CA	415-776-2740
Brandon, Randy/PO Box 1010, Girdwood, AK	907-783-2773
Brenneis, Jon/2576 Shattuck, Berkeley, CA	415-845-3377
Brewer, Art/27324 Camino Capistrano #161, Laguna Nigel, CA	714-582-9085
Brewer, James/102 S St Andrews Pl, Los Angeles, CA	213-461-6241
Brian, Rick/555 S Alexandria Ave, Los Angeles, CA	213-387-3017
Britt, Jim/140 N LaBrea, Los Angeles, CA	213-936-3131
Brod, Garry/6502 Santa Monica Blvd, Hollywood, CA	213-463-7887
Brookhause, Win/2316 Porter St #11, Los Angeles, CA	213-448-9255
Brown, George/1417 15th St, San Francisco, CA	415-621-3543
Brown, Matt/420 Commercial Ave, Anacortes, WA	206-293-3540
Brown, Michael/PO Box 45969, Los Angeles, CA	213-379-7254
Browne, Rick/145 Shake Tree Ln, Scotts Valley, CA	408-438-3919
Brun, Kim/5555-L Santa Fe St, San Diego, CA	619-483-2124
Bubar, Julie/12559 Palero Rd, San Diego, CA	619-234-4020
Buchanan, Bruce/PO Box 48892, Los Angeles, CA	213-462-7086
Buchanan, Craig/1026 Folsom St #207, San Francisco, CA	415-861-5566
Budnik, Victor/125 King St, San Francisco, CA	415-541-9050
Buelteman, Robert/237 Clara St, San Francisco, CA	415-974-5470
Burke, Kevin/1015 N Cahuenga Blvd, Los Angeles, CA	213-467-0266
Burke, Leslie/947 La Cienega, Los Angeles, CA	213-652-7011
Burke/Triolo Photo/940 E 2nd St #2, Los Angeles, CA	213-687-4730
Burkhart, Howard Photography/8513 1/2 Horner St, Los Angeles, CA	213-671-2283
Burkholder, Jeff/3984 Park Circ Ln, Carmichael, CA	916-944-2128
Burman & Steinheimer/2648 Fifth Ave, Sacramento, CA	916-457-1908
Burr, Bruce/2867 1/2 W 7th St, Los Angeles, CA	213-388-3361
Burr, Lawrence/76 Manzanita Rd, Fairfax, CA	415-456-9158
Burroughs, Robert/6713 Bardonia St, San Diego, CA	619-469-6922
Burry, D L/PO Box 1611, Los Gatos, CA	408-354-1922
Burt, Pat/1412 SE Stark, Portland, OR	503-284-9989
Bush, Chan/PO Box 819, Montrose, CA	818-957-6558
Bush, Charles/940 N Highland Ave, Los Angeles, CA	213-937-8246
Bush, Dave/2 St George Alley, San Francisco, CA	415-981-2874
Busher, Dick/7042 20th Place NE, Seattle, WA	206-523-1426
Butchofsky, Jan/325 S Sierra #3, Solano Beach, CA	619-259-2418
Butler, Erik/655 Bryant St, San Francisco, CA	415-777-1656

C

C & I Photography/3523 Ryder St, Santa Clara, CA	408-733-5855
Cable, Ron/17835 Skypark Cir #N, Irvine, CA	714-261-8910
Caccavo, James/10002 Crescent Hts Blvd, Los Angeles, CA	213-939-9594
Cacitti, Stanley R/589 Howard, San Francisco, CA	415-974-5668
Cahoon, John/613 S LaBrea Ave, Los Angeles, CA	213-930-1144
Campbell Comm Photo/8586 Miramar Pl, San Diego, CA	619-587-0336
Campbell, David/244 Ninth St, San Francisco, CA	415-864-2556
Campbell, Kathleen Taylor/4751 Wilshire Blvd, Los Angeles, CA	213-931-6202
Campbell, Tom + Assoc/PO Box 1409, Topanga Canyon, CA	213-473-6054
Campos, Michael/705 13th St, San Diego, CA	619-233-9914
Cannon, Bill/516 Yale Ave North, Seattle, WA	206-682-7031
Caplan, Stan/7014 Santa Monica Blvd, Los Angeles, CA	213-462-1271
Capps, Alan/137 S La Peer Dr, Los Angeles, CA	213-276-3724
Capra, Robert/1256 Lindell Dr, Walnut Creek, CA	415-947-0323
Caputo, Tony/6636 Santa Monica Blvd, Hollywood, CA	213-464-6636
Carey, Ed/60 Federal St, San Francisco, CA	415-543-4883
Carlson, Craig/266 J Street, Chula Vista, CA	619-422-4937
Carlson, Joe/901 El Centro, S Pasadena, CA	213-682-1020
Carofano, Ray/1011 1/4 W 190th St, Gardena, CA	213-515-0310
Carpenter, Mert/2020 Granada Wy, Los Gatos, CA	408-370-1663
Carroll, Bruce/517 Dexter Ave N, Seattle, WA	206-623-2119
Carroll, Tom/26712 Calle Los Alamos, Capistrano Beach, CA	714-493-2665
Carroon, Chip/PO Box 590451, San Francisco, CA	415-864-1082
Carruth, Kerry/7153 Helmsdale Circle, Canoga Park, CA	818-704-6570
Carry, Mark/3375 Forest Ave, Santa Clara, CA	408-248-7872
Casilli, Mario/2366 N Lake Ave, Altadena, CA	213-681-4476
Casler, Christopher/1600 Viewmont Dr, Los Angeles, CA	213-854-7733
Cato, Eric/7224 Hillside Ave #38, Los Angeles, CA	213-851-5606
Caulfield, Andy/PO Box 41131, Los Angeles, CA	213-258-3070
Chamberlain, Paul/319 1/2 S Robertson Blvd, Beverly Hills, CA	213-659-4647
Chaney, Brad/1750 Army St #H, San Francisco, CA	415-826-2030
Charles, Cindy/1040 Noe St, San Francisco, CA	415-821-4457
Chen, James/1917 Anacapa St, Santa Barbara, CA	805-569-1849
Cherin, Alan/220 S Rose St, Los Angeles, CA	213-680-9893
Chernus, Ken/9531 Washington Blvd, Culver City, CA	213-838-3116
Chesser, Mike/5290 W Washington Blvd, Los Angeles, CA	213-934-5211
Chester, Mark/PO Box 99501, San Francisco, CA	415-922-7512
Chiarot, Roy/846 S Robertson Blvd, Los Angeles, CA	213-659-9173
Chin, Albert/1150 Homer St, Vancouver V6B2X6, BC	604-685-2000
Chin, K P/PO Box 421737, San Francisco, CA	415-282-3041
Chmielewski, David/230-C Polaris, Mountain View, CA	415-969-6639
Chubb, Ralph/850 2nd St, Santa Rosa, CA	707-579-9995
Chun, Mike/35 Russia St #H, San Francisco, CA	415-469-7220
Chung, Ken-Lei/5200 Venice Blvd, Los Angeles, CA	213-938-9117
Ciskowski, Jim/2444 Wilshire Blvd #B100, Santa Monica, CA	213-829-7375
Clark, Richard/334 S LaBrea, Los Angeles, CA	213-933-7407
Clark, Tom/2042 1/2 N Highland, Hollywood, CA	213-851-1650
Clayton, John/160 South Park, San Francisco, CA	415-495-4562
Clement, Michele/221 11th St, San Francisco, CA	415-558-9540
Cobb, Bruce/1537-A 4th St #102, San Rafael, CA	415-454-0619
Cobb, Rick/10 Liberty Ship Way, Sausalito, CA	415-332-8739
Coccia, Jim/PO Box 81313, Fairbanks, AK	907-479-4707
Cogen, Melinda/1112 N Beachwood Dr, Hollywood, CA	213-467-9414
Coit, Jim/5555-L Santa Fe St, San Diego, CA	619-272-2255
Coleman, Arthur Photography/303 N Indian Ave, Palm Springs, CA	619-325-7015
Colladay, Charles/711 12th Ave, San Diego, CA	619-231-2920
Collison, James/6950 Havenurst, Van Nuys, CA	818-902-0770
Coluzzi, Tony Photography/897 Independence Ave #2B, Mountain View, CA	415-969-2955
Connell, John/1218 Parnell Place, Costa Mesa, CA	714-540-1199
Conrad, Chris/719 East Pike, Seattle, WA	206-324-2208

Photographers

Continued

Please send us your additions and updates.

Cook, Kathleen Norris/PO Box 2159, Laguna Hills, CA	714-770-4619
Corell, Volker/3797 Lavell Dr, Los Angeles, CA	213-255-3336
Cormier, Glenn/828 K St #202, San Diego, CA	619-237-5006
Cornfield, Jim/454 S La Brea Ave, Los Angeles, CA	213-938-3553
Cornwell, David/1311 Kalakaua Ave, Honolulu, HI	808-949-7000
Corwin, Jeff/CPC Assoc/1910 Weepah Way, Los Angeles, CA	213-656-7449
Courbet, Yves/6516 W 6th St, Los Angeles, CA	213-655-2181
Courtney, William/4524 Rutgers Way, Sacramento, CA	916-487-8501
Cowin, Morgin/5 Windsor Ave, San Rafael, CA	415-459-7722
Crane, Wally/PO Box 81, Los Altos, CA	415-960-1990
Crowley, Eliot/3221 Benda Pl, Los Angeles, CA	213-851-5100
Cummings, Ian/2400 Kettner Blvd, San Diego, CA	619-231-1270
Cummins, Jim/1527 13th Ave, Seattle, WA	206-322-4944

D Dahlstrom Photography Inc/2312 NW Savier St, Portland, OR   503-222-4910

Dajani, Haas/405 Eldridge Ave, Mill Valley, CA	415-383-3291
Dancs, Andras/518 Beatty St #603, Vancouver V6B 2L3, BC	604-684-6760
Dang, Tai/426 Jefferson St, Oakland, CA	415-832-8642
DANIEL, JAY/517 JACOBY ST #11, SAN RAFAEL, CA	
(P 255)	**415-459-1495**
Dannehl, Dennis/3303 Beverly Blvd, Los Angeles, CA	213-388-3888
David/Gayle Photo/911 Western Ave #510, Seattle, WA	206-624-5207
Davidson, Dave/25003 S Beeson Rd, Beavercreek, OR	503-632-7650
Davidson, Jerry/3923 W Jefferson Blvd, Los Angeles, CA	213-735-1552
Davis, Tim/PO Box 1278, Palo Alto, CA	415-327-4192
Dayton, Ted/1112 N Beachwood, Los Angeles, CA	213-462-0712
DeCastro, Mike/2415 De La Cruz, Santa Clara, CA	408-988-8696
DeCruyenaere, Howard/1825 E Albion Ave, Santa Ana, CA	714-997-4446
DeGennaro, George Assoc/902 South Norton Ave, Los Angeles, CA	213-935-5179
DePaola, Mark/1560 Benedict Cnyn Dr, Beverly Hills, CA	213-550-5910
DeSilva, Dennis/190 Hubbell St, San Francisco, CA	415-861-7707
DeWilde, Roc/1200 Clover Ct, Lafayette, CA	415-934-1119
DeYoung, Skip/1112 N Beachwood, Los Angeles, CA	213-462-0712
Degler, Curtis/1050 Carolan Ave #311, Burlingame, CA	415-342-7381
Del Re, Sal/211-E East Columbine Ave, Santa Ana, CA	714-432-1333
Delancie, Steve/790 Church St #202, San Francisco, CA	415-864-2640
Demerdjian, Jacob/3331 W Beverly Blvd, Montebello, CA	213-724-9630
Denman, Frank B/1201 First Ave S, Seattle, WA	206-325-9260
Denny, Michael/2631 Ariane Dr, San Diego, CA	619-272-9104
Der Cruyenaere, Howard/1825 E Albion Ave, Santa Ana, CA	714-997-4446
Der, Rick Photography/50 Mandell St #10, San Francisco, CA	415-824-8580
Derhacopian, Ronald/3109 Beverly Blvd, Los Angeles, CA	213-388-6724
Devine, W L Studios/PO Box 67, Maple Falls, WA	206-599-2927
Diaz, Armando/19 S Park, San Francisco, CA	415-495-3552
Digital Art/3699 Wilshire Blvd #870, Los Angeles, CA	213-387-8384
Dominick/833 N LaBrea Ave, Los Angeles, CA	213-934-3033
Donaldson, Peter/118 King St, San Francisco, CA	415-957-1102
Dorr, Ken/1 Grand View Ave, San Francisco, CA	415-647-1087
Dow, Larry/1537 W 8th St, Los Angeles, CA	213-483-7970
Drake, Brian/407 Southwest 11th Ave, Portland, OR	503-241-4532
Dreiwitz, Herb/145 N Edgemont St, Los Angeles, CA	213-383-1746
Dressler, Rick/1322 Bell Ave #M, Tustin, CA	714-730-9113
Driver, Wallace/2540 Clairemont Dr #305, San Diego, CA	619-275-3159
Duff, Rodney/4901 Morena Blvd #323, San Diego, CA	619-270-4082
Duffey, Robert/9691 Campus Dr, Anaheim, CA	714-956-4731
Duka, Lonnie/919 Oriole Dr, Laguna Beach, CA	714-494-7057
Dull, Ed/1745 NW Marshall, Portland, OR	503-224-3754
Dumentz, Barbara/39 E Walnut St, Pasadena, CA	213-467-6397
Dunbar, Clark/1260-B Pear Ave, Mountain View, CA	415-964-4225
Dunmire, Larry/PO Box 338, Balboa Island, CA	714-673-4058
Dunn, Roger/544 Weddell Dr #3, Sunnyvale, CA	408-730-1630
Dyer, Larry/1659 Waller St, San Francisco, CA	415-668-8049

E Ealy, Dwayne/2 McLaren #B, Irvine, Ca92718   714-951-5089

Eastabrook, William R/3281 Oakshire Dr, Los Angeles, CA	213-851-3281
EDMUNDS, DANA/188 N KING ST, HONOLULU, HI (P 257)	**808-521-7711**
Edwards, Grant P/6837 Nancy Ridge Dr #G, San Diego, CA	619-458-1999
Ehrlich, Seth/1046 N Orange Dr, Hollywood, CA	213-462-5256
Elias, Robert Studio/959 N Cole, Los Angeles, CA	213-460-2988
Elk, John III/583 Weldon, Oakland, CA	415-834-3024
Emanuel, Manny/2257 Hollyridge Dr, Hollywood, CA	213-465-0259

Emberly, Gordon/1479 Folsom, San Francisco, CA	415-621-9714
Enkelis, Liane/764 Sutter Ave, Palo Alto, CA	415-326-3253
Esgro, Dan/PO Box 38536, Los Angeles, CA	213-932-1919
Estel, Suzanne/2325 3rd St, San Francisco, CA	415-864-3661
Evans, Marty/11112 Ventura Blvd, Studio City, CA	818-762-5400

F Falconer, Michael/2339 Third St #46, San Francisco, CA   415-626-7774

Falk, Randolph/123 16th Ave, San Francisco, CA	415-751-8800
Fallon, Bernard/524 N Juanita Ave #3, Redondo Beach, CA	213-318-6006
Faries, Tom/16431 Sandalwood, Fountain Valley, CA	714-775-5767
Farruggio, Matthew J/3239 Kempton, Oakland, CA	415-444-0665
Faubel, Warren/627 S Highland Ave, Los Angeles, CA	213-939-8822
Feldman, Marc/6442 Santa Monica Blvd, Hollywood, CA	213-463-4829
Felt, Jim/1316 SE 12th Ave, Portland, OR	503-238-1748
Felzman, Joe/421 NW Fourth Ave, Portland, OR	503-224-7983
Ferro, Daniel/559 Matadero Ave #6, Palo Alto, CA	415-424-9681
Finnegan, Kristin/3045 NW Thurman St, Portland, OR	503-241-2701
Firebaugh, Steve/6750 55th Ave S, Seattle, WA	206-721-5151
Fischer, Curt/51 Stillman, San Francisco, CA	415-974-5568
Fisher, Arthur Vining/271 Missouri St, San Francisco, CA	415-626-5483
Fitch, Wanelle/17845-D Sky Pk Cir, Irvine, CA	714-261-1566
Flavin, Frank/901 W 54th St, Anchorage, AK	907-561-1606
Flinn, Jim/8617 Sandpoint Way NE, Seattle, WA	206-524-1409
Flood, Alan/206 14th Ave, San Mateo, CA	415-572-0439
Fogg, Don/259 Clara St, San Francisco, CA	415-974-5244
Foothorap, Robert/426 Bryant St, San Francisco, CA	415-957-1447
Forsman, John/8696 Crescent Dr, Los Angeles, CA	213-933-9339
Forster, Bruce/431 NW Flanders, Portland, OR	503-222-5222
Fort, Daniel/PO Box 11324, Costa Mesa, CA	714-546-5709
Fowler, Bradford/1946 N Serrano Ave, Los Angeles, CA	213-464-5708
Fox, Arthur/2194 Cable St, San Diego, CA	619-223-4784
Frankel, Tracy/7250 Hillside Ave #308, Los Angeles, CA	213-851-9668
Franklin, Charly/3352 20th St, San Francisco, CA	415-543-5400
Franz-Moore, Paul/855 Folsom St #204, San Francisco, CA	415-495-6183
Franzen, David/746 Ilaniwai St #200, Honolulu, HI	808-537-9921
Frazier, Kim Andrew/PO Box 6132, Hayward, CA	415-889-7050
Freed, Jack/749 N La Brea, Los Angeles, CA	213-931-1015
Freis, Jay/416 Richardson St, Sausalito, CA	415-332-6709
French, Peter/PO Box 100, Kamuela, HI	808-889-6488
Friedlander, Ernie/82 Ringold Alley, San Francisco, CA	415-626-6111
Friedman, Todd/PO Box 3737, Beverly Hills, CA	213-550-0831
Friend, David/3886 Ampudia St, San Diego, CA	619-260-1603
Frigge, Eric/, ,	714-854-2985
Frisch, Stephen/ICB - Gate 5 Rd, Sausalito, CA	415-332-4545
Frisella, Josef/340 S Clark Dr, Beverly Hills, CA	213-462-2593
Fritz, Michael/PO Box 4386, San Diego, CA	419-281-3297
Fritz, Steve/1023 S Santa Fe Ave, Los Angeles, CA	213-629-8052
Fritze, Jack/2106 S Grand, Santa Ana, CA	714-545-6466
Fronk, Peter/203 Indian Way, Novato, CA	415-883-5253
Fruchtman, Jerry/8735 Washington Blvd, Culver City, CA	213-839-7891
Fry, George B III/PO Box 2465, Menlo Park, CA	415-323-7663
Fujioka, Robert/715 Stierlin Rd, Mt View, CA	415-960-3010
Fukuda, Curtis/2239-F Old Middlefield Way, Mountain View, CA	415-962-9131
Fukuda, Steve/454 Natoma, San Francisco, CA	415-543-9339
Fukuhara, Richard Yutaka/1032-2 Taft Ave, Orange, CA	714-998-8790
Furuta, Carl/7360 Melrose Ave, Los Angeles, CA	213-655-1911
Fusco, Paul/7 Melody Ln, Mill Valley, CA	415-388-8940

G Gage, Rob/789 Pearl St, Laguna Beach, CA   714-494-7265

Galante, Nick/1002 Kihei Rd #301, Kihei, HI	808-879-5476
Gallagher, John/PO Box 4070, Seattle, WA	206-937-2422
Galvan, Gary/4626 1/2 Hollywood Blvd, Los Angeles, CA	213-667-1457
Gardner, Robert/800 S Citrus Ave, Los Angeles, CA	213-931-1108
Garrabrandts, Doug/431 Winchester Ave, Glendale, CA	818-502-0271
Garretson, Jim/333 Fifth St, San Francisco, CA	415-974-6464
Gasperini, Robert/PO Box 954, Folsom, CA	916-985-3383
Geissler, Rick/1095 Cosmo Ave, El Cajon, CA	619-440-5594
Gelineau, Val/1041 N McCadden Pl, Los Angeles, CA	213-465-6149
GENDREAU, RAYMOND/303 BELMONT AVE E,	
SEATTLE, WA (P 259)	**206-329-9902**
Gerretsen, Charles/1714 N Wilton Pl, Los Angeles, CA	213-462-6342

Gersten, Paul/1021 1/2 N La Brea, Los Angeles, CA	213-850-6045
Gervais, Lois/754 Battery St, San Pedro, CA	213-547-1796
Gervase, Mark/PO Box 38573, Los Angeles, CA	213-877-0928
Ghelerter, Michael/1020 41st St, Emeryville, CA	415-547-8456
Giannetti Photography/730 Clementina St, San Francisco, CA	415-864-0270
Gibbs, Christopher/4640 Business Pk Blvd, Anchorage, AK	907-563-6112
Gibson, Mark/PO Box 14542, San Francisco, CA	415-524-8118
Giefer, Sebastian/3132 Hollyridge Dr, Hollywood, CA	213-461-1122
Gilbert, Elliot/311 N Curson Ave, Los Angeles, CA	213-939-1846
Gillman, Mitchell/610 22nd St #307, San Francisco, CA	415-621-5334
Gilmore, Ed/9000 Broadway Terrace, Oakland, CA	415-547-2194
Giraud, Steve/2960 Airway Ave #B-103, Costa Mesa, CA	714-751-8191
Gleis, Nick/4040 Del Rey #7, Marina Del Rey, CA	213-823-4229
Glendinning, Edward/1001 East 1st St, Los Angeles, CA	213-617-1630
Glenn, Joel/439 Bryant St, San Francisco, CA	415-957-1273
Gnass, Jeff/PO Box 2196, Oroville, CA	916-533-6788
Goavec, Pierre/1464 La Playa #303, San Francisco, CA	415-564-2252
Goble, James/620 Moulton Ave #205, Los Angeles, CA	213-222-7661
Goble, Jeff/300 Second Ave W, Seattle, WA	206-285-8765
Godwin, Bob/1427 E 4th St #1, Los Angeles, CA	213-269-8001
Going, Michael/1117 N Wilcox Pl, Los Angeles, CA	213-465-6853
Goldman, Larry/5310 Circle Dr #206, Van Nuys, CA	818-347-6865
Goldner, David/833 Traction Ave, Los Angeles, CA	212-617-0761
Goldstein, Larry/21 E 5th St, Vancouver V6H 1NF, BC	604-877-1117
Gondolf, Carl/PO Box 1395, Davis, CA	916-756-6150
Goodman, Jamison/120 S Vignes, Los Angeles, CA	213-617-1900
Goodman, Todd/1417 26th #E, Santa Monica, CA	213-453-3621
GORDON, JON/2052 LOS FELIZ DR, THOUSAND OAKS, CA	
(P 252)	**805-496-1485**
Gordon, Larry Dale/25 Eighteenth Ave, Venice, CA	213-392-6719
Gorman, Greg/1351 Miller Dr, Los Angeles, CA	213-650-5540
Gottlieb, Mark/1915 University Ave, Palo Alto, CA	415-321-8761
Gowans, Edward/10316 NW Thompson Rd, Portland, OR	503-223-4573
Grady, Noel/277 Rodney Ave, Encinitas, CA	619-753-8630
Graham, Don/1545 Marlay Dr, Los Angeles, CA	213-656-7117
Graham, Ellen/614 N Hillcrest Rd, Beverly Hills, CA	213-275-6195
Graves, Robert/30 NW 1st Ave #202, Portland, OR	503-226-0099
Gray, Dennis/250 Newhall St, San Francisco, CA	415-641-4009
Gray, Keehn/625 Locust Rd, Sausalito, CA	415-332-8831
Gray, Marion/42 Orben Pl, San Francisco, CA	415-931-5689
Gray, Todd/1962 N Wilcox, Los Angeles, CA	213-466-6088
Greenleigh, John/756 Natoma, San Francisco, CA	415-864-4147
Grigg, Robert/1050 N Wilcox Ave, Hollywood, CA	213-469-6316
Grimm, Tom & Michelle/PO Box 83, Laguna Beach, CA	714-494-1336
Groenekamp, Greg/2922 Oakhurst Ave, Los Angeles, CA	213-838-2466
Gross, Richard/1810 Harrison St, San Francisco, CA	415-558-8075
Groutoge, Monty/2214 S Fairview Rd, Santa Ana, CA	714-751-8734
H Hagopian, Jim/915 N Mansfield Ave, Hollywood, CA	213-856-0018
Hagyard, Dave/1205 E Pike, Seattle, WA	206-322-8419
Haislip, Kevin/PO Box 1862, Portland, OR	503-254-8859
Hall, Alice/1033 N Myra Ave, Los Angeles, CA	213-666-0535
Hall, George/82 Macondray Ln, San Francisco, CA	415-775-7373
Hall, Steven/645 N Eckhoff St #P, Orange, CA	714-634-1132
Hall, William/19881 Bushard St, Huntington Bch, CA	714-968-2473
Halle, Kevin/11125-D Flintkote Ave, San Diego, CA	619-452-7759
Hamilton, David W/725 S Eliseo Dr #4, Greenbrea, CA	415-461-5901
Hammid, Tino/PO Box 69-A109, Los Angeles, CA	213-652-6626
Hammond, Paul/34 Hill St, San Francisco, CA	415-824-7656
Hampton, Wally/4190 Rockaway Beach, Bainbridge Isl, WA	206-842-9900
Hanauer, Mark/1717 N Vine St #12, Los Angeles, CA	213-462-2421
Hands, Bruce/PO Box 16186, Seattle, WA	206-938-8620
Hansen, Jim/2800 S Main St #1, Santa Ana, CA	714-545-1343
Hara/265 Prado Rd #4, San Luis Obispo, CA	805-543-6907
Harding, C B/660 N Thompson St, Portland, OR	503-281-9907
Harmel, Mark/714 N Westbourne, West Hollywood, CA	213-659-1633
Harrington, Marshall/2775 Kurtz St #2, San Diego, CA	619-291-2775
Harris, Paul/4601 Larkwood Ave, Woodland Hills, CA	818-347-8294
Hart, G K/780 Bryant St, San Francisco, CA	415-495-4278
Hartman, Raiko/6916 Melrose, Los Angeles, CA	213-278-4700
Harvey, Stephen/7801 W Beverly Blvd, Los Angeles, CA	213-934-5817
Hathaway, Steve/173 Bluxome 4th Fl, San Francisco, CA	415-495-3473

Hawkes, William/5757 Venice Blvd, Los Angeles, CA	213-931-7777
Hawley, Larry/6502 Santa Monica Blvd, Hollywood, CA	213-466-5864
Heffernan, Terry/352 6th St, San Francisco, CA	415-626-1999
Henderson, Tom/11722 Sorrento Vly Rd #A, San Diego, CA	619-481-7743
Hendrick, Howard/839 Bridge Rd, San Leandro, CA	415-483-1483
Herrmann, Karl/3165 S Barrington Ave #F, Los Angeles, CA	213-397-5917
Herron, Matt/PO Box 1860, Sausalito, CA	415-479-6994
Hess, Geri/134 S Roxbury Dr, Beverly Hills, CA	213-276-3638
Hewett, Richard/5725 Buena Vista Terr, Los Angeles, CA	213-254-4577
Hicks, Alan/333 N W Park, Portland, OR	503-226-6741
Higgins, Donald/201 San Vincente Blvd #14, Santa Monica, CA	213-393-8858
Hildreth, James/2374 25th Ave, San Francisco, CA	415-821-7398
Hill, Dennis/20 N Raymond Ave #14, Pasadena, CA	818-795-2589
Hines, Richard/734 E 3rd St, Los Angeles, CA	213-625-2333
Hirshew, Lloyd/750 Natoma, San Francisco, CA	415-861-3902
Hishi, James/612 S Victory Blvd, Burbank, CA	213-849-4871
Hixson, Richard/1261 Howard St, San Francisco, CA	415-621-0246
Hodges, Rose/2325 3rd St #401, San Francisco, CA	415-550-7612
Hodges, Walter/1605 Twelfth Ave #25, Seattle, WA	206-325-9550
Hoffman, Davy/1923 Colorado Ave, Santa Monica, CA	213-453-4661
Hoffman, Paul/4500 19th St, San Francisco, CA	415-863-3575
Hofmann, Mark/827 N Fairfax Ave, Los Angeles, CA	213-658-7376
Hogg, Peter/1221 S La Brea, Los Angeles, CA	213-937-0642
Holcomb, Mark/610 22nd St #302, San Francisco, CA	415-431-9959
Hollenbeck, Cliff/Box 4247 Pioneer Sq, Seattle, WA	206-682-6300
Holmes, Mark/PO Box 556, Mill Valley, CA	415-383-6783
Holmes, Robert/PO Box 556, Mill Valley, CA	415-383-6783
Holt, David/1624 Cotner Ave #B, Los Angeles, CA	213-478-1188
Holz, William/7630 W Norton Ave, Los Angeles, CA	213-656-4061
Honolulu Creative Group/424 Nahua St, Honolulu, HI	808-926-6188
Honowitz, Ed/39 E Walnut St, Pasadena, CA	818-584-4050
Hooper, H Lee/30708 Monte Lado Dr, Malibu, CA	213-457-2897
Hopkins, Stew/414 Rose Ave, Venice, CA	213-396-8649
Horikawa, Michael/508 Kamakee St, Honolulu, HI	808-538-7378
Housel, James F/84 University Pl #409, Seattle, WA	206-682-6182
Hudetz, Larry/11135 SE Yamhill, Portland, OR	503-245-6001
Hunt, Phillip/3435 Army St #206, San Francisco, CA	415-821-9879
Hunter, Jeff/4626 1/2 Hollywood Blvd, Los Angeles, CA	213-669-0468
Hussey, Ron/1164 Katella St, Laguna Beach, CA	714-494-6988
Hylen, Bo/1640 S LaCienega, Los Angeles, CA	213-271-6543
Hyun, Douglass/459 1/2 N Fairfax Ave, Los Angeles, CA	213-655-0571
IJ Illusion Factory/4657 Abargo St, Woodland Hills, CA	818-883-4501
Imstepf, Charles/620 Moulton Ave #216, Los Angeles, CA	213-222-8773
Iri, Carl/5745 Scrivener, Long Beach, CA	213-658-5822
Irwin, Dennis/164 Park Ave, Palo Alto, CA	415-321-7959
Isaacs, Robert/1646 Mary Ave, Sunnyvale, CA	408-245-1690
Iverson, Michele/1527 Princeton #2, Santa Monica, CA	213-829-5717
Jacobs, Michael/646 N Cahuenga Blvd, Los Angeles, CA	213-461-0240
James, Patrick/1412 Santa Cruz, San Pedro, CA	213-519-1357
Jarrett, Michael/16812 Red Hill, Irvine, CA	714-250-3377
Jay, Michael/1 Zeno Pl #345 Folsom Cmplx, San Francisco, CA	415-543-7101
Jenkin, Bruce/11577-A Slater Ave, Fountain Valley, CA	714-546-2949
Jenner, Steve/5950 Grizzly Peak Blvd, Oakland, CA	415-547-3300
Jennings, William/PO Box 2030, Beaverton, OR	503-646-4752
Jensen, John/449 Bryant St, San Francisco, CA	415-957-9449
Johnson, Conrad/PO Box 3881, Laguna Hills, CA	714-643-5089
Johnson, Payne B/4650 Harvey Rd, San Diego, CA	619-299-4567
JOHNSON, RON PHOTO/2104 VALLEY GLEN, ORANGE, CA	
(P 261)	**714-637-1145**
Jones, Aaron/608 Folsom St, San Francisco, CA	415-495-6333
Jones, William B/2171 India St #B, San Diego, CA	619-235-8892
K Kaestner, Reed/2120 J Durante Blvd #4, Del Mar, CA	619-755-1200
Kaldor, Kurt/1011 Grandview Dr, S San Francisco, CA	415-583-8704
Kamens, Les/333-A 7th St, San Francisco, CA	415-431-9040
KARAGEORGE, JIM/610 22ND ST #309, SAN FRANCISCO, CA (P 262,263)	**415-648-3444**
Karjalas' Photo Vision/231 E Imperial Hwy #260, Fullerton, CA	714-992-1210
Kasmier, Richard/441 E Columbine #I, Santa Ana, CA	714-545-4022
Kasparowitz, Josef/PO Box 14408, San Luis Obispo, CA	805-544-8209

Photographers

Continued

Please send us your additions and updates.

Katano, Nicole/2969 Jackson #104, San Francisco, CA	415-563-2646
Katzenberger, George/211-D E Columbine St, Santa Ana, CA	714-545-3055
Kauffman, Helen/9017 Rangeley Ave, Los Angeles, CA	213-275-3569
Kaufman, Robert/259 Ridge Rd, San Carlos, CA	415-369-5908
Kauschke, Hans-Gerhard/16 Una Way #D, Mill Valley, CA	415-383-4230
Kearney, Ken/8048 Soquel Dr, Aptos, CA	408-688-4546
Keenan, Elaine Faris/90 Natoma St, San Francisco, CA	415-546-9246
KEENAN, LARRY/421 BRYANT ST, SAN FRANCISCO, CA	
(P 264)	**415-495-6474**
Kehl, Robert/769 22nd St, Oakland, CA	415-452-0501
Keller, Greg/769 22nd St, Oakland, CA	415-452-0501
Kelley, Tom/8525 Santa Monica Blvd, Los Angeles, CA	213-657-1780
Kermani, Shahn/109 Minna St #210, San Francisco, CA	415-567-6073
Kerns, Ben/1201 First Ave S, Seattle, WA	206-621-7636
Kessler/McKinnon Photo/2101 Las Palmas, Carlsbad, CA	619-931-9299
Kiesow, Paul/7247 Camellia Ave, N Hollywood, CA	213-655-1897
Kilberg, James/3371 Cahuenga Blvd W, Los Angeles, CA	213-874-9514
Killian, Glen/1270 Rio Vista, Los Angeles, CA	213-263-6567
Kimball, Ron/2582 Sun-Mor Ave, Mt View, CA	415-948-2939
Kimball-Nanessence/3421 Tripp Ct #4, San Diego, CA	619-453-1922
King, Kathleen/1932 1st Ave, Seattle, WA	206-443-2800
King, Nicholas/3102 Moore St, San Diego, CA	619-296-8200
Kious, Gary/9800 Sepulvada Blvd #304, Los Angeles, CA	213-536-4880
Kirkendall/ Spring/18819 Olympic View Dr, Edmonds, WA	206-776-4685
Kirkland, Douglas/9060 Wonderland Park Ave, Los Angeles, CA	
CA	213-656-8511
Kirkpatrick, Mike/1115 Forest Way, Brookdale, CA	408-395-1447
Kleinman, Kathryn/542 Natoma St, San Francisco, CA	415-864-2406
Kobayashi, Ken/1750-H Army St, San Francisco, CA	415-826-4382
Koch, Jim/1360 Logan Ave #106, Costa Mesa, CA	714-957-5719
Kodama & Moriarty Photo/4081 Glencoe Ave, Marina Del Rey,	
CA	213-306-7574
Koehler, Rick/1622 Edinger #A, Tustin, CA	714-259-8787
Kohler, Heinz/163 W Colorado Blvd, Pasadena, CA	213-681-9195
Kopp, Pierre/PO Box 8337, Long Beach, CA	213-430-8534
Kosta, Jeffrey/2565 Third St #306, San Francisco, CA	415-285-7001
Kramer, David/5121 Santa Fe St #A, San Diego, CA	619-270-5501
Krasner, Carin/3239 Helms Ave, Los Angeles, CA	213-280-0082
Kredenser, Peter/2551 Angelo Dr, Los Angeles, CA	213-278-6356
Krisel, Ron/1925 Pontius Ave, Los Angeles, CA	213-477-5519
Krosnick, Alan/2800 20th St, San Francisco, CA	415-285-1819
Krueger, Gary/PO Box 543, Montrose, CA	818-249-1051
Krupp, Carl/PO Box 910, Merlin, OR	503-479-6699
Kubly, Jon/604 Moulton, Los Angeles, CA	213-747-7259
Kuhn, Chuck/206 Third Ave S, Seattle, WA	206-624-4706
Kuhn, Robert/3022 Valevista Tr, Los Angeles, CA	213-461-3656
Kupersmith, Dan/PO Box 7401, Studio City, CA	213-935-6232
Kurihara, Ted/601 22nd St, San Francisco, CA	415-285-3200
Kurisu/819 1/2 N Fairfax, Los Angeles, CA	213-655-7287
Kuslich, Lawrence J/3386 SE 20th Ave, Portland, OR	503-236-3454

L

LaRocca, Jerry/3734 SE 21st Ave, Portland, OR	503-232-5005
LaTona, Kevin/159 Western Ave W #454, Seattle, WA	206-285-5779
Lachata, Carol/411 E las Flores Dr, Altadena, CA	818-794-6860
Lamb & Hall/7318 Melrose, Los Angeles, CA	213-931-1775
Lammers, Bud/211-A East Columbine, Santa Ana, CA	714-546-4441
Lamont, Dan/117 W Denny Way #213, Seattle, WA	206-285-8252
Lamotte, Michael/828 Mission St, San Francisco, CA	415-777-1443
Lan, Graham/PO Box 211, San Anselmo, CA	415-492-0308
Landau, Robert/7275 Sunset Blvd #4, Los Angeles, CA	213-851-2995
Landecker, Tom/288 7th St, San Francisco, CA	415-864-8888
Landreth, Doug/1940 124th Ave NE #A-108, Bellevue, WA	206-453-0466
Lane, Bobbi/7213 Santa Monica Blvd, Los Angeles, CA	213-874-0557
Langdon, Harry/8275 Beverly Blvd, Los Angeles, CA	213-651-3212
Larson, Dean/7668 Hollywood Blvd, Los Angeles, CA	213-876-1033
Lauderborn, Lawrence/301 8th St #213, San Francisco, CA	415-863-1132
Lauterborn, Lawrence/301-8th St #213, San Francisco, CA	415-863-1132
Law, Graham/PO Box 211, San Anselmo, CA	415-492-0308
Lawder, John/2672 S Grand, Santa Ana, CA	714-557-3657
Lawlor, John/6101 Melrose, Hollywood, CA	213-468-9050
LeBon, David/732 N Highland Ave, Los Angeles, CA	213-464-2775
LeCoq, John Land/2527 Fillmore St, San Francisco, CA	415-563-4724

Lea, Thomas/181 Alpine, San Francisco, CA	415-864-5941
Leach, David/7408 Beverly Blvd, Los Angeles, CA	213-932-1234
Leatart, Brian/520 N Western, Los Angeles, CA	213-856-0121
Lee, Larry/PO Box 4688, North Hollywood, CA	818-766-2677
Lee, Roger Allyn/1628 Folsom St, San Francisco, CA	415-861-1147
Lee, Sherwood/632 Alta Vista Crst, Pasadena, CA	213-255-1338
Legname, Rudi/389 Clementina St, San Francisco, CA	415-777-9569
Lehman, Danny/6643 W 6th St, Los Angeles, CA	213-652-1930
Leighton, Ron/1360 Logan #105, Costa Mesa, CA	714-641-5122
Leng, Brian/1021 1/2 N La Brea, Los Angeles, CA	213-469-8624
Levasheff, Michael/1112 N Beachwood, Los Angeles, CA	213-946-2511
Levy, Paul/2830 S Robertson Blvd, Los Angeles, CA	213-838-2252
Levy, Richard J/1015 N Kings Rd #115, Los Angeles, CA	213-654-0335
Levy, Ronald/PO Box 3416, Soldotna, AK	907-262-1383
Lewin, Elyse/820 N Fairfax, Los Angeles, CA	213-655-4214
LEWINE, ROB/8929 HOLLY PL, LOS ANGELES, CA (P 265)	**213-654-0830**
Lewis, Cindy/2554 Lincoln Blvd #1090, Marina Del Rey, CA	213-301-1977
Lewis, Don/2350 Stanley Hills Dr, Los Angeles, CA	213-656-2138
Li, Jeff/8954 Ellis Ave, Culver City, CA	213-837-5377
Lidz, Jane/33 Nordhoff St, San Francisco, CA	415-587-3377
Liles, Harry/1060 N Lillian Way, Hollywood, CA	213-466-1612
Lindsey, Gordon/2311 Kettner Blvd, San Diego, CA	619-234-4432
Lindstrom, Eric/111 S Lander #104, Seattle, WA	206-583-0601
Lindstrom, Mel/2510-H Old Middlefld Way, Mountain View, CA	415-962-1313
Linn, Alan/5121 Santa Fe St #B, San Diego, CA	619-483-2122
Littell, Dorothy/PO Box 5199, Chatsworth, CA	818-402-1181
Livzey, John/1510 N Las Palmas, Hollywood, CA	213-469-2992
London, Matthew/10391 Camino Ruiz #95, San Diego, CA	619-457-3251
Longwood, Marc/67 Nutwood Cir, Sacramento, CA	916-924-0551
Lopez, Bret/533 Moreno Ave, Los Angeles, CA	213-393-8841
Lorenzo/4654 El Cajon Blvd, San Diego, CA	619-280-6010
Louie, Ming/14 Otis St, San Francisco, CA	415-558-8663
Lovell, Craig/Rt 1 Box 53A, Carmel, CA	408-624-5241
Luhn, Jeff/ Visioneering/2565 3rd St #339, San Francisco, CA	415-282-6630
Lund, John M/860 Second St, San Francisco, CA	415-957-1775
Lund, John William/741 Natoma St, San Francisco, CA	415-552-7764
Lyon, Fred/237 Clara St, San Francisco, CA	415-974-5645
Lyons, Marv/2865 W 7th St, Los Angeles, CA	213-384-0732

M

Madden, Daniel J/PO Box 965, Los Alamitos, CA	213-429-3621
Madison, David/2330 Old Middlefield Rd, Mountain View, CA	415-961-6297
Maharat, Chester/15622 California St, Tustin, CA	714-832-6203
Maher, John/1425 SE Main #3, Portland, OR	503-297-7451
Mahieu, Ted/PO Box 42578, San Francisco, CA	415-641-4747
Maloney, Jeff/2646 Taffy Dr, San Jose, CA	408-274-6027
Malphettes, Benoit/816 S Grand St, Los Angeles, CA	213-629-9054
Manchee, Doug/2343 3rd St #297, San Francisco, CA	415-552-2422
Mangold, Steve/PO Box 1001, Palo Alto, CA	415-969-9897
Mar, Tim/PO Box 3488, Seattle, WA	206-583-0093
Marcus, Ken/6916 Melrose Ave, Los Angeles, CA	213-937-7214
Mareschal, Tom/5816 182nd Pl SW, Lynnwood, WA	206-771-6932
Margolies, Paul/480 Potrero, San Francisco, CA	415-621-3306
Marks, Michael/, Los Angeles, CA	
Marley, Stephen/1160 Industrial Way, San Carlos, CA	415-966-8301
Marriott, John/1830 McAllister, San Francisco, CA	415-922-2920
Marsden, Dominic/3783 W Cahuenga Blvd, Studio City, CA	818-508-5222
Marshall, Jim/3622 16th St, San Francisco, CA	415-864-3622
Marshall, Kent/899 Pine St #1912, San Francisco, CA	415-641-0932
Marshutz, Roger/1649 S La Cienega Blvd, Los Angeles, CA	213-273-1610
Martin, John F/118 King St, San Francisco, CA	415-957-1355
Martinelli, Bill/608 S Railroad Ave, San Mateo, CA	415-347-3589
Martinez, David/2325 Third St #433, San Francisco, CA	415-558-8088
Mason, Pablo/3026 North Park Way, San Diego, CA	619-298-2200
Mastandrea, Michael/PO Box 68944, Seattle, WA	206-244-6756
Masterson, Ed/11211-S Sorrento Val Rd, San Diego, CA	619-457-3251
Mauskopf, Norman/615 W California Blvd, Pasadena, CA	818-578-1878
May, P Warwick/PO Box 19308, Oakland, CA	415-530-7319
McCall, Stuart/518 Beatty St #603, Vancouver V6B 2L3, BC	604-684-6760
McClain, Stan/39 E Walnut St, Pasadena, CA	818-795-8828
McCrary, Jim/211 S LaBrea Ave, Los Angeles, CA	213-936-5115
McCumsey, Robert/2600 E Coast Hwy, Corona Del Mar, CA	714-720-1624
McDermott, John/31 Genoa Place, San Francisco, CA	415-982-2010

Photographers

Continued

Please send us your additions and updates.

McGraw, Chelsea/1722 Mackinnon, Cardiff by the Sea, CA	619-436-0602
McGuire, Gary/1248 S Fairfax Ave, Los Angeles, CA	213-938-2481
McKinney, Andrew/1628 Folsom St, San Francisco, CA	415-621-8415
McMahon, Steve/1164 S LaBrea, Los Angeles, CA	213-937-3345
MCNALLY, BRIAN/9937 DURANT DR, BEVERLY HILLS, CA	
(P 101)	**213-462-6565**
McVay, Matt/PO Box 1103, Mercer Island, WA	206-236-1343
Mears, Jim/1471 Elliot Ave W, Seattle, WA	206-284-0929
Meisels, Penina/917 20th St, Sacramento, CA	916-443-3330
Melgar Photographers Inc/2971 Corvin Dr, Santa Clara, CA	408-733-4500
Mendenhall, Jim/PO Box 3695, Newport Beach, CA	714-834-9240
Menzel, Peter J/136 N Deer Run Lane, Napa, CA	707-255-3528
Menzie, W Gordon/2311 Kettner Blvd, San Diego, CA	619-234-4431
Merfeld, Ken/3951 Higuera St, Culver City, CA	213-837-5300
Merkel, Dan/PO Box 1025, Haleiwa, HI	808-373-2710
Merken, Stefan/900 N Citrus Ave, Los Angeles, CA	213-466-4533
Mihulka, Chris/PO Box 1515, Springfield, OR	503-741-2289
Miles, Reid/1136 N Las Palmas, Hollywood, CA	213-462-6106
Milholland, Richard/8271 W Norton, Los Angeles, CA	213-650-5458
Milkie Studio Inc/127 Boylston Ave E, Seattle, WA	206-324-3000
Miller, Bill/7611 Melrose Ave, Los Angeles, CA	213-651-5630
MILLER, DENNIS/1467-C 12TH ST, MANHATTAN BEACH, CA	
(P 266)	**213-546-3205**
Miller, Donald/447 S Hewitt, Los Angeles, CA	213-680-1896
Miller, Earl/3212 Bonnie Hill Dr, Los Angeles, CA	213-851-4947
Miller, Ed/705 32nd Ave, San Francisco, CA	415-221-5687
Miller, Jim/1122 N Citrus Ave, Los Angeles, CA	213-466-9515
Miller, Jordan/506 S San Vicente Blvd, Los Angeles, CA	213-655-0408
Miller, Peter Read/3413 Pine Ave, Manhattan Beach, CA	213-545-7511
Miller, Ray/PO Box 450, Balboa, CA	714-646-5748
Miller, Wynn/4083 Glencoe Ave, Marina Del Rey, CA	213-821-4948
Milliken, Brad/3341 Bryant St, Palo Alto, CA	415-424-8211
Milne, Robbie/2717 Western, Seattle, WA	206-682-6828
MILROY/ MCALEER/3857 BIRCH ST #170, NEWPORT	
BEACH, CA (P 267)	**714-957-0219**
Mineau, Joe/8921 National Blvd, Los Angeles, CA	213-558-3878
Mishler, Clark/1238 G St, Anchorage, AK	907-279-0892
Mitchell, David Paul/564 Deodar Ln, Bradbury, CA	818-358-3328
Mitchell, Josh/1984 N Main St #501, Los Angeles, CA	213-225-5674
Mitchell, Margaretta K/280 Hillcrest Rd, Berkeley, CA	415-655-4920
Mizono, Robert/14 Otis St 3rd Fl, San Francisco, CA	415-558-8663
Mock, Dennis/10983 Cool Lake Terrace, San Diego, CA	619-693-3201
Molenhouse, Craig/PO Box 7678, VAn Nuys, CA	818-901-9306
Montague, Chuck/18005 Skypark Cir #E, Irvine, CA	714-250-0254
Montes de Oca, Arthur/4302 Melrose Ave, Los Angeles, CA	213-665-5141
Moore, Gary/1125 E Orange Ave, Monrovia, CA	818-359-9414
Moran, Edward/5264 Mount Alifan Dr, San Diego, CA	619-693-1041
Moratti, Brian/27411 Lindvog Rd NE, Kingston, WA	206-297-3158
Morduchowicz, Daniel/2020 N Main St #223, Los Angeles, CA	213-223-1867
Morfit, Mason/897 Independence Ave #D, Mountain View, CA	415-969-2209
Morgan, Jay P/618-D Moulton Ave, Los Angeles, CA	213-224-8288
Morgan, Mike/16252 E Construction, Irvine, CA	714-551-3391
Morgan, Scott/2210 Wilshire #433, Santa Monica, CA	213-829-5318
Morrell, Paul/300 Brannan St #207, San Francisco, CA	415-543-5887
Mosgrove, Will/250 Newhall, San Francisco, CA	415-282-7080
Motil, Guy/253 W Canada, San Clemente, CA	714-492-1350
Muckley, Mike Photography/8057 Raytheon Rd #3, San Diego, CA	619-565-6033
Mudford, Grant/5619 W 4th St #2, Los Angeles, CA	213-936-9145
Mullen, Kevin/71 Sunhurst Crescent SE, Calgary T2X 1W5, AB	403-256-5749
Mullenski, Steven/P O Box 2199, La Jolla, CA	619-454-4331
Muna, R J/63 Encina Ave, Palo Alto, CA	415-328-1131
Murphy, Suzanne/2442 Third St, Santa Monica, CA	213-399-6652
Murray, Derik/1128 Homer St, Vancouver V6B 2X6, BC	604-669-7468
Murray, Michael/15431 Redhill Ave #E, Tustin, CA	714-259-9222
Murray, Tom/592 N Rossmore Ave, Los Angeles, CA	213-937-3821
Murray, William III/15454 NE 182nd Pl, Woodinville, WA	206-485-4011
Musilek, Stan/610 22nd St #307, San Francisco, CA	415-621-5336
Myers, Jeffry W Photography/1218 3rd Ave #510, Seattle, WA	206-527-1853
N NTA Photo/600 Moulton Ave #101-A, Los Angeles, CA	213-226-0506
Nadler, Jeff/520 N Western Ave, Los Angeles, CA	213-467-2135

Nakamura, Michael/5429 Russell NW, Seattle, WA	206-784-4323
Nance, Ancil/915-A SE 33rd St, Portland, OR	503-233-7778
Nation, Bill/1514 S Stanley, Los Angeles, CA	213-937-4888
Nease, Robert/441 E Columbine #E, Santa Ana, CA	714-545-6557
Nebeux, Michael/13450 S Western Ave, Gardena, CA	213-532-0949
Nels/811 Traction Ave, Los Angeles, CA	213-680-2414
Newman, Greg/1356 Brampton Rd, Pasadena, CA	213-257-6247
Niedopytalski, Dave/1415 E Union, Seattle, WA	206-329-7612
Nishihira, Robert/6150 Yarrow Dr #G, Carlsbad, CA	619-438-0366
Noble, Richard/7618 Melrose Ave, Los Angeles, CA	213-655-4711
Nolton, Gary/107 NW Fifth Ave, Portland, OR	503-228-0844
Normark, Don/1622 Taylor Ave N, Seattle, WA	206-284-9393
Norwood, David/4040 Del Rey Ave #7, Marina Del Rey, CA	213-827-2020
Noyle, Ric/733 Auahi St, Honolulu, HI	808-524-8269
Nuding, Peter/3181 Melendy Dr, San Carlos, CA	415-967-4854
Nyerges, Suzanne/413 S Fairfax, Los Angeles, CA	213-938-0151
O O'Brien, Tom/450 S La Brea, Los Angeles, CA	213-938-2008
O'Hara, Yoshi/6341 Yucca St, Hollywood, CA	213-466-8031
O'Rear, Chuck/PO Box 361, St Helena, CA	707-963-2663
Odgers, Jayme/703 S Union, Los Angeles, CA	213-461-8173
Ogilvie, Peter/90 Natoma, San Francisco, CA	415-391-1646
Oldenkamp, John/3331 Adams Ave, San Diego, CA	619-283-0711
Olson, George/451 Vermont, San Francisco, CA	415-864-8686
Olson, Jon/4045 32nd Ave SW, Seattle, WA	206-932-7074
Omni Color/4320 Viewridge Ave #C, San Diego, CA	619-565-0672
Orazem, Scott/1150 1/2 Elm Dr, Los Angeles, CA	213-277-7447
Osbourne, Jan/460 NE 70th St, Seattle, WA	206-524-5220
Oshiro, Jeff/2534 W 7th St, Los Angeles, CA	213-383-2774
Otto, Glenn/10625 Magnolia Blvd, North Hollywood, CA	818-762-5724
Ounjian, Michael/612 N Myers St, Burbank, CA	818-842-0880
Ovregaard, Keith/765 Clementina St, San Francisco, CA	415-621-0687
Owen & Owen Photo/1108 Anahist, Honolulu, HI	808-943-6936
P Pacheco, Robert/11152 3/4 Morrison, N Hollywood, CA	818-761-1320
Pacific Image/930 Alabama, San Francisco, CA	415-282-2525
Pacura, Tim/756 Natoma St, San Francisco, CA	415-552-3512
Padys, Diane/650 Alabama, San Francisco, CA	415-285-6443
Pagos, Terry/3622 Albion Pl N, Seattle, WA	206-633-4616
Pan, Richard/722 N Hoover St, Los Angeles, CA	213-661-6638
Panography/1514 Fruitvale, Oakland, CA	415-261-3327
Parks, Ayako/PO Box 6552, Laguna Nigel, CA	714-240-8347
Parks, Jeff/12936 133rd Pl NE, Kirkland, WA	206-821-5450
Parrish, Al/3501 Buena Vista Ave, Glendale, CA	818-957-3726
Parry, Karl/8800 Venice Blvd, Los Angeles, CA	213-558-4446
Pasquali, Art/1061 Sunset Blvd, Los Angeles, CA	213-250-0134
Patterson, Robert/915 N Mansfield Ave, Hollywood, CA	213-462-4401
Pavloff, Nick/PO Box 2339, San Francisco, CA	415-452-2468
Pearlman, Andy/1920 Main St #2, Santa Monica, CA	213-550-4505
Pedrick, Frank/2690 Union st, Oakland, CA	415-465-5080
Percey, Roland/626 N Hoover, Los Angeles, CA	213-660-7305
Perry, David/Box 4165 Pioneer Sq Sta, Seattle, WA	206-932-6614
Perry, David/837 Traction Ave, Los Angeles, CA	213-625-3567
Peterman, Joan & Herbert/3185 Rossini Pl, Topanga, CA	818-883-1229
Peterson, Bryan/PO Box 892, Hillsboro, OR	503-985-3276
Peterson, Darrell/84 University #306, Seattle, WA	206-624-1762
Peterson, Richard/733 Auahi St, Honolulu, HI	808-536-8222
Peterson, Richard Studio/711 8th Ave #A, San Diego, CA	619-236-0284
Peterson, Scott/735 Harrison St, San Francisco, CA	415-442-0189
Pett, Laurence J/5907 Cahill Ave, Tarzana, CA	818-344-9453
Pfleger, Mickey/PO Box 280727, San Francisco, CA	415-355-1772
Phase Infinity/Ron Jones/10225 Barns Canyon Rd #A110, San Diego, CA	619-546-0551
Phillips, Bernard/1810 Harrison St, San Francisco, CA	415-621-7982
Phillips, Lee/4964 Norwich Place, Newark, CA	415-794-7447
Photo File/110 Pacific Ave #102, San Francisco, CA	415-397-3040
Photography Northwest/1415 Elliot Ave W, Seattle, WA	206-285-5249
Pildas, Ave/1568 Murray Circle, Los Angeles, CA	213-664-1313
Pinckney, Jim/PO Box 1149, Carmel Valley, CA	408-375-3534
Piper, Jim/922 SE Ankeny, Portland, OR	503-231-9622
Piscitello, Chuck/6502 Santa Monica Blvd, Los Angeles, CA	213-460-6397
Pizur, Joe/194 Ohukai Rd, Kihie, Maui, HI	808-879-6633

Photographers

Continued

Please send us your additions and updates.

Place, Chuck/2940 Lomita Rd, Santa Barbara, CA	805-682-6089
Pleasant, Ralph B/8755 W Washington Blvd, Culver City, CA	213-202-8997
Plummer, Bill/963 Yorkshire Ct, Lafayette, CA	415-284-1535
Poppleton, Eric/1341 Ocean Ave #259, Santa Monica, CA	213-209-3765
Porter, James/3955 Birch St #F, Newport Beach, CA	714-852-8756
Poulsen, Chriss/104-A Industrial Center, Sausalito, CA	415-331-3495
Powers, David/17 Brosnan St, San Francisco, CA	415-864-7974
Powers, Lisa/2073 Outpost Dr, Los Angeles, CA	213-874-5877
Prater, Yvonne/Box 940 Rt 1, Ellensburg, WA	509-925-1774
Preuss, Karen/369 Eleventh Ave, San Francisco, CA	415-752-7545
Pribble, Paul/911 Victoria Dr, Arcadia, CA	213-262-8305
Price, Tony/PO Box 5216, Portland, OR	503-239-4228
Pritchett, Bill/1771 Yale St, Chula Vista, CA	619-421-6005
Proehl, Steve/916 Rodney Dr, San Leandro, CA	415-483-3683
Professional Photo Services/1011 Buenos Ave #A-B, San Diego, CA	619-299-4410
Pruitt, Brett/2343-B Rose St, Honolulu, HI	808-845-3811

QR

Quinn, Allen/4781 Pel #5, Sacramento, CA	916-920-8090
Raabe, Dan/256 S Robertson Blvd #4504, Beverly Hills, CA	213-461-7060
Radstone, Richard/3480 Spring Mt Ave, Las Vegas, NV	702-364-2004
Rahn, Stephen/259 Clara St, San Francisco, CA	415-495-3556
Ramey, Michael/612 Broadway, Seattle, WA	206-329-6936
Rampy, Tom/PO Box 3980, Laguna Hills, CA	714-850-4048
Ramsey, Gary/1412 Ritchey #A, Santa Ana, CA	714-547-0782
Rand, Marvin/13432 Beach, Marina Del Rey, CA	213-306-9779
Randall, Bob/1118 Mission St, S Pasadena, CA	818-441-1003
Randlett, Mary/Box 10536, Bainbridge Island, WA	206-842-3935
Rapoport, Aaron/3119 Beverly Blvd, Los Angeles, CA	213-738-7277
Rausin, Chuck/1020 Woodcrest Ave, La Habra, CA	213-697-0408
Rawcliffe, David/7609 Beverly Blvd, Los Angeles, CA	213-938-6287
Rayniak, J Bart/3510 N Arden Rd, Otis Orchards, WA	509-924-0004
Reed, Bob/1816 N Vermont Ave, Los Angeles, CA	213-662-9703
Reiff, Robert/1920 Main St #2, Santa Monica, CA	213-938-3064
Ressmeyer, Roger/2269 Chestnut #400, San Francisco, CA	415-921-1675
Rhoney, Ann/2264 Green St, San Francisco, CA	415-922-4775
Rice, Mark/2337 El Camino Real, San Mateo, CA	415-345-8377
Rich, Bill/109 Minna #459, San Francisco, CA	415-775-8214
Ricketts, Mark/2809 NE 55th St, Seattle, WA	206-526-1911
Riggs, Robin/3785 Cahuenga W, N Hollywood, CA	818-506-7753
Ripley, John/281 Green St, San Francisco, CA	415-781-4940
Ritts, Herb/7927 Hillside Ave, Los Angeles, CA	213-876-6366
Robbins, Bill/7016 Santa Monica Blvd, Los Angeles, CA	213-930-1382
Roberge, Earl/764 Bryant, Walla Walla, WA	509-525-7385
Rodal, Arney A/395 Winslow Way E, Bainbridge Island, WA	206-842-4989
Rogers, Kenneth/PO Box 3187, Beverly Hills, CA	213-553-5532
Rogers, Peter/15621 Obsidian Ct, Chino Hills, CA	714-597-4394
Rojas, Art/1588 N Batavia Unit 2, Orange, CA	714-921-1710
Rokeach, Barrie/32 Windsor, Kensington, CA	415-527-5376
Rolston, Matthew/8259 Melrose Ave, Los Angeles, CA	213-658-1151
Rorke, Lorraine/146 Shrader St, San Francisco, CA	415-386-2121
Rose, Peter/651 N Russell, Portland, OR	503-249-5864
Rosenberg, Allan/410 E Mission, San Jose, CA	408-986-8484
Ross, Alan C/202 Culper Ct, Hermosa Beach, CA	213-379-2015
Ross, Bill/1526 Pontius Ave #A, Los Angeles, CA	818-703-7605
Ross, Dave/130 McCormick #106, Costa Mesa, CA	714-432-1355
Ross, James Studio/2565 3rd St #220, San Francisco, CA	415-821-5710
Rothman, Michael/1816 N Vermont Ave, Los Angeles, CA	213-662-9703
Rowan, Bob/209 Los Banos Ave, Walnut Creek, CA	415-930-8687
Rowe, Wayne/567 North Beverly Glen, Los Angeles, CA	213-475-7810
Rowell, Galen/1483-A Solano Ave, Albany, CA	415-524-9343
Rubins, Richard/3757 Wilshire Blvd #204A, Los Angeles, CA	213-387-9989
Ruppert, Michael/5086 W Pico, Los Angeles, CA	213-938-3779
Ruscha, Paul/940 N Highland Ave, Los Angeles, CA	213-465-3516
Ruthsatz, Richard/8735 Washington Blvd, Culver City, CA	213-838-6312
Ryder Photo/136 14th St Apt B, Seal Beach, CA	315-622-3499

S

Sabransky, Cynthia/3331 Adams Ave, San Diego, CA	619-283-0711
Sacks, Ron/PO Box 5532, Portland, OR	503-641-4051
Sadlon, Jim/2 Clinton Park, San Francisco, CA	415-626-1900
SAFRON, MARSHAL/506 S SAN VICENTE BLVD, LOS ANGELES, CA (P 269)	**213-653-1234**
Sagara, Peter/1847 Nichols Canyn Rd, Los Angeles, CA	213-933-7531
Sakai, Steve/1111 N Tamarind Ave, Los Angeles, CA	213-460-4811
Salazar, Tim/4057 Brant St #6, San Diego, CA	619-574-1176
Saloutos, Pete/11225 Huntley Pl, Culver City, CA	213-397-5509
Samerjan, Peter/743 N Fairfax, Los Angeles, CA	213-653-2940
Sanders, Paul/7378 Beverly Blvd, Los Angeles, CA	213-933-5791
Sandison, Teri/1545 N Wilcox #102, Hollywood, CA	213-461-3529
Santullo, Nancy/7213 Santa Monica Blvd, Los Angeles, CA	213-874-1940
Sarpa, Jeff/555 Rose Ave #G, Venice, CA	213-392-7400
Sassy, Gene/1285 Laurel Ave, Pomona, CA	714-623-7424
Saunders, Paul/9272 Geronimo #111, Irvine, CA	714-768-4624
Scharf, David/2100 Loma Vista Pl, Los Angeles, CA	213-666-8657
Schelling, Susan/1440 Bush St, San Francisco, CA	415-441-3662
Schenker, Larry/2830 S Robertson Blvd, Los Angeles, CA	213-837-2020
Scherl, Ron/1301 Guerrero, San Francisco, CA	415-285-8865
Schermeister, Phil/472 22nd Ave, San Francisco, CA	415-386-0218
Schiff, Darryll/8153 W Blackburn Ave, Los Angeles, CA	213-658-6179
Schiff, Nancy Rica/, Los Angeles, CA	
Schmidt, Brad/1417 26th St, Santa Monica, CA	213-828-0754
Schubert, John/5959 W Third, Los Angeles, CA	213-935-6044
Schwartz, George J/PO Box 413, Bend, OR	503-389-4062
Schwartz, Stuart/301 8th St #204, San Francisco, CA	415-863-8393
Schwob, Bill/1033 Heinz St, Berkeley, CA	415-848-3579
Scoffone, Craig/1169 Husted Ave, San Jose, CA	408-723-7011
Scott, Mark/1208 S Genesee, Hollywood, CA	213-931-9319
Sebastian Studios/5161-A Santa Fe St, San Diego, CA	619-581-9111
Sedam, Mike/16907 80th Ave NE, Bothell, WA	206-488-9375
Segal, Susan/11738 Moor Pk #B, Studio City, CA	818-763-7612
Seidemann, Bob/14130 LeMay, Van Nuys, CA	818-997-3289
Selig, Jonathan/29206 Heathercliff Rd, Malibu, CA	213-457-5856
Selland Photography/461 Bryant St, San Francisco, CA	415-495-3633
Selman, George/3609 E Olympic Blvd, Los Angeles, CA	213-855-0938
Sessions, David/2210 Wilshire Blvd #205, Santa Monica, CA	213-394-8379
Sexton, Richard/128 Laidley St, San Francisco, CA	415-550-8345
Shaffer, Bob/PO Box 2538, San Francisco, CA	415-552-4884
Shaneff, Carl/1100 Alakea St #224, Honolulu, HI	808-533-3010
Sharpe, Dick/2475 Park Oak Dr, Los Angeles, CA	213-462-4597
Sheret, Rene/2532 W 7th St, Los Angeles, CA	213-385-8587
Shipps, Raymond/1325 Morena Blvd #A, San Diego, CA	619-276-1690
Shirley, Ron/5757 Venice Blvd, Los Angeles, CA	213-937-0919
Sholik, Stan/15455 Red Hill Ave #E, Tustin, CA	714-259-7826
Short, Glenn/14641 La Maida, Sherman Oaks, CA	818-990-5599
Shorten, Chris/60 Federal St, San Francisco, CA	415-543-4883
Shrum, Steve/PO Box 6360, Ketchikan, AK	907-225-5453
Shuman, Ronald/1 Menlo Pl, Berkeley, CA	415-527-7241
Shvartzman, Eddie/224 Barbara Dr, Los Gatos, CA	408-988-6040
Sibley, Scott/764 Bay, San Francisco, CA	415-673-7468
Silk, Gary Photography/6546 Hollywood Blvd #215, Hollywood, CA	213-466-1785
Silva, Keith/771 Clementina Alley, San Francisco, CA	415-863-5655
Silverman, Jay Inc/920 N Citrus Ave, Hollywood, CA	213-466-6030
Sim, Veronica/4961 W Sunset Blvd, Los Angeles, CA	213-661-7356
Simon, Wolfgang/PO Box 807, La Canada, CA	818-790-1605
Simpson, Stephen/701 Kettner Blvd #124, San Diego, CA	619-239-6638
Sinick, Gary/3246 Ettie St, Oakland, CA	415-655-4538
Sirota, Peggy/451 N Harper Ave, Los Angeles, CA	213-653-1903
Sjef's Fotographie/2311 NW Johnson St, Portland, OR	503-223-1089
Skarsten & Dunn Studios/1062 N Rengstorff #E, Mountain View, CA	415-969-5759
Slabeck, Bernard/2565 Third St #316, San Francisco, CA	415-282-8202
Slatery, Chad/11627 Ayres Ave, Los Angeles, CA	213-477-0734
Slaughter, Paul D/771 El Medio Ave, Pacific Palisades, CA	213-454-3694
Slenzak, Ron/7106 Waring Ave, Los Angeles, CA	213-934-9088
Slobin, Marvin/1065 15th St, San Diego, CA	619-239-2828
Slobodian, Scott/6519 Fountain Ave, Los Angeles, CA	213-464-2341
Smith, Charles J/7163 Construction Crt, San Diego, CA	619-271-6525
Smith, Don/1527 Belmont #1, Seattle, WA	206-324-5748
Smith, Elliott Varner/PO Box 5268, Berkeley, CA	415-654-9235
Smith, Gil/2865 W 7th St, Los Angeles, CA	213-384-1016
Smith, Steve/228 Main St #E, Venice, CA	213-392-4982
Smith, Todd/2643 S Fairfax, Culver City, CA	213-559-0059
Snook, Randy/4220 Frida Maria Ct, Carmichael, CA	916-944-8419

Photographers
Continued

Please send us your additions and updates.

PHOTOGRAPHERS

Snyder, Mark/2415 Third St #265, San Francisco, CA	415-861-7514
Sokol, Mark/6518 Wilkinson Ave, North Hollywood, CA	818-506-4910
Sollecito, Tony/1120-B W Evelyn Ave, Sunnyvale, CA	408-773-8118
SOLOMON, MARC/PO BOX 480574, LOS ANGELES, CA (P 270,271)	**213-935-1771**
Speier, Brooks/6022 Haviland Ave, Whittier, CA	213-695-3552
Spitz, Harry Photography/7723 Varna Ave, North Hollywood, CA	818-761-9828
Spradling, David/2515 Patricia Ave, Los Angeles, CA	213-559-9870
Spring, Bob & Ira/18819 Olympic View Dr, Edmonds, WA	206-776-4685
Springmann, Christopher/PO Box 745, Point Reyes, CA	415-663-8428
St Jivago Desanges/PO Box 24AA2, Los Angeles, CA	213-931-1984
Staley, Bill/1160 21st St, W Vancouver V7V 4B1, BC	604-922-6695
Stampfli, Eric/50 Mendell #10, San Francisco, CA	415-824-2305
Starkman, Rick/544 N Rios Ave, Solana Beach, CA	619-481-8259
Steele, Melissa/PO Box 280727, San Francisco, CA	415-355-1772
Stees, M S/PO Box 2775, Costa Mesa, CA	714-545-7993
Stein, Robert/319 1/2 S Robertson Blvd, Beverly Hills, CA	213-652-2030
Steinberg, Bruce/2128 18th St, San Francisco, CA	415-864-0739
Steinberg, Mike Photo/PO Box 4525, Laguna Beach, CA	714-240-2997
STEINER, GLENN RAKOWSKY/301 EIGHTH ST #212, SAN FRANCISCO, CA (P 272)	**415-863-1214**
Stevens, Bob/9048 Santa Monica Blvd, Los Angeles, CA	213-271-8123
Stinson, John/376 W 14th St, San Pedro, CA	213-831-8495
Stoaks, Charles/PO Box 6417, Portland, OR	503-243-2635
Stock, Richard Photography/1767 N Orchid Ave #312, Los Angeles, CA	213-559-3344
Stockton, Michael/567 Prescott St, Pasadena, CA	818-794-6087
Stone, Pete/1410 NW Johnson, Portland, OR	503-224-7125
Strauss, Andrew/6442 Santa Monica Blvd, Los Angeles, CA	213-464-5394
Streano, Vince/PO Box 662, Laguna Beach, CA	714-497-1908
Street-Porter, Tim/6938 Camrose Dr, Los Angeles, CA	213-874-4278
Streshinsky, Ted/PO Box 674, Berkeley, CA	415-526-1976
Strickland, Steve/Box 3486, San Bernardino, CA	714-883-4792
Stryker, Ray/12029 76th Ave S, Seattle, WA	206-772-5680
Stuart, James Peter/PO Box 84744, Seattle, WA	206-463-5888
Studio AV/1227 First Ave S, Seattle, WA	206-292-9931
Studio B/5121-B Santa Fe St, San Diego, CA	619-483-2122
Su, Andrew/5733 Benner St, Los Angeles, CA	213-256-0598
Sugar, James/45 Midway Ave, Mill Valley, CA	415-388-3344
Sullivan, Jeremiah S/PO Box 7870, San Diego, CA	619-224-0070
Sund, Harald/PO Box 16466, Seattle, WA	206-938-1080
Sutton, John/333 Fifth St, San Francisco, CA	415-974-5452
Swarthout, Walter & Assoc/370 Fourth St, San Francisco, CA	415-543-2525
Swartz, Fred/135 S LaBrea, Los Angeles, CA	213-939-2789
Swenson, John/4353 W 5th St #D, Los Angeles, CA	213-384-1782

T

Tachibana, Kenji/1067 26th Ave East, Seattle, WA	206-325-2121
Taggart, Fritz/1117 N Wilcox Pl, Los Angeles, CA	213-469-8227
Tankersley, Todd/390 Carmelita Dr, Mountain View, CA	415-964-5346
Tapp, Carlan/114 Alaskan Way S, Seattle, WA	206-621-8344
Taub, Doug/5800 Fox View Dr, Malibu, CA	213-457-8600
Tauber, Richard/4221 24th St, San Francisco, CA	415-824-6837
Teeter, Jeff/2205 Dixon St, Chico, CA	916-895-3255
Teke/4338 Shady Glade Ave, Studio City, CA	818-985-9066
Theis, Rocky/2955 4th Ave, San Diego, CA	619-295-1923
Thimmes, Timothy/2805 S La Cienega Ave, Los Angeles, CA	213-204-6851
Thomas, Neil/7622 Jayseel St, Sunland, CA	213-202-0051
Thompson, Michael/7811 Alabama Ave #14, Canoga Park, CA	818-883-7870
Thompson, William/PO Box 4460, Seattle, WA	206-621-9069
Thomson, Sydney (Ms)/PO Box 1032, Keaau, HI	808-966-8587
Thornton, Tyler/4706 Oakwood Ave, Los Angeles, CA	213-465-0425
Tidwell, Dan/PO Box 384, Folsom, CA	916-985-2923
Tilger, Stewart/71 Columbia #206, Seattle, WA	206-682-7818
Tise, David/975 Folsom St, San Francisco, CA	415-777-0669
Tracy, Tom/115 Samsone #812, San Francisco, CA	415-340-9811
Trafficanda, Gerald/1111 N Beachwood Dr, Los Angeles, CA	213-466-1111
Trailer, Martin/11125-D Flintkote Ave, San Diego, CA	619-452-7759
Trindl, Gene/3950 Vantage Ave, Studio City, CA	213-877-4848
Tucker, Kim/2428 Canyon Dr, Los Angeles, CA	213-465-9233
Turner & DeVries/1200 College Walk #212, Honolulu, HI	808-537-3115
Turner, John Terence/173 37th Ave E, Seattle, WA	206-325-9073

Turner, Richard P/Box 64205 Rancho Pk Sta, Los Angeles, CA	213-279-2127
Tuschman, Mark/300 Santa Monica, Menlo Park, CA	415-322-4157
Tyler, Laura/6494 Gloria St #23, Sacramento, CA	916-424-3998

UV

Ueda, Richard/618 Moulton Ave St E, Los Angeles, CA	213-224-8709
Underwood, Ron/918 Hilldroft Rd, Glendale, CA	818-246-3628
Undheim, Timothy/1039 Seventh Ave, San Diego, CA	619-232-3366
Uniack/8933 National Blvd, Los Angeles, CA	213-938-0287
Upton, Tom/1879 Woodland Ave, Palo Alto, CA	415-325-8120
Urie, Walter Photography/1810 E Carnegie, Santa Ana, CA	714-261-6302
Vallely, Dwight/2027 Charleen Circle, Carlsbad, CA	619-434-3828
Vanderpoel, Fred/1118 Harrison, San Francisco, CA	415-621-4405
Varie, Bill/2210 Wilshire Blvd, Santa Monica, CA	213-395-9337
Vaughn, Ray/7167 Woodmore Oaks Dr, Citrus Heights, CA	916-726-3468
Vega, Raul/3511 W 6th Tower Suite, Los Angeles, CA	213-387-2058
Veitch, Julie/5757 Venice Blvd, Los Angeles, CA	213-936-4231
Venezia, Jay/1373 Edgecliffe Dr, Los Angeles, CA	213-665-7382
Vereen, Jackson/570 Bryant St, San Francisco, CA	415-777-5272
Viarnes, Alex/Studio 33/Clementina, San Francisco, CA	415-543-1195
Vignes, Michelle/654 28th St, San Francisco, CA	415-550-8039
Villaflor, Francisco/PO Box 883274, San Francisco, CA	415-921-4238
Visually Speaking/3609 E Olympic Blvd, Los Angeles, CA	213-269-9141
Vogt, Jurgen/936 E 28th Ave, Vancouver V5V 2P2, BC	604-876-5817
Vollenweider, Thom/3430 El Cajon Blvd, San Diego, CA	619-280-3070
Vollick, Tom/5245 Melrose, Los Angeles, CA	213-464-4415

W

Wade, Bill/5608 E 2nd St, Long Beach, CA	213-439-6826
Wahlstrom, Richard/650 Alabama St 3rd Fl, San Francsico, CA	415-550-1400
Walker, Douglas/416 Duncan St, San Francisco, CA	415-821-4379
Wallace, Marlene/1624 S Cotner, Los Angeles, CA	213-826-1027
Warden, John/9201 Shorecrest Dr, Anchorage, AK	907-243-1667
Warren Aerial Photography/1585 E Locust, Pasadena, CA	213-681-1006
Warren, William James/509 S Gramercy Pl, Los Angeles, CA	213-383-0500
Wasserman, David/252 Caselli, San Francisco, CA	415-552-4428
Watanabe, David/14355 132nd Ave NE, Kirkland, WA	206-823-0692
Waterfall, William/1160-A Nuuanu, Honolulu, HI	808-521-6863
Watson, Alan/710 13th St #300, San Diego, CA	619-239-5555
Watson, Stuart/620 Moulton Ave, Los Angeles, CA	213-221-3886
Waz, Tony/1115 S Trotwood Ave, San Pedro, CA	213-548-3758
Webber, Phil/2466 Westlake Ave N, Seattle, WA	206-282-2423
Werner, Jeffery R/14002 Palawan Way, Marina Del Rey, CA	213-821-2384
Werts Studios/732 N Highland, Los Angeles, CA	213-464-2775
Werts, Bill/732 N Highland, Los Angeles, CA	213-464-2775
West, Andrew/342 Sycamore Rd, Santa Monica, CA	213-459-7774
West, Charles/3951 Duncan Pl, Palo Alto, CA	415-856-4003
Wexler, Glen/736 N Highland, Los Angeles, CA	213-465-0268
Wheeler, Richard/PO Box 3739, San Rafael, CA	415-457-6914
Whetstone, Wayne/149 W Seventh Ave, Vancouver V5Y1L8, BC	604-873-8471
White, Randall/1514 Fruitvale, Oakland, CA	415-261-3327
Whitmore, Ken/PO Box 49373, Los Angeles, CA	213-472-4337
Whittaker, Steve/111 Glen Way #8, Belmont, CA	415-595-4242
Wiener, Leigh/2600 Carman Crest Dr, Los Angeles, CA	213-876-0990
Wietstock, Wilfried/877 Valencia St, San Francisco, CA	415-285-4221
Wilcox, Jed/PO Box 4091, Palm Springs, CA	714-659-3945
Wildschut, Sjef/2311 NW Johnson, Portland, OR	503-223-1089
WILHELM, DAVE/2565 THIRD ST #303, SAN FRANCISCO, CA (P 250,251)	**415-826-9399**
Wilkings, Steve/Box 22810, Honolulu, HI	808-732-6288
Williams, David Jordan/6122 W Colgate, Los Angeles, CA	213-936-3170
Williams, Harold/705 Bayswater Ave, Burlingame, CA	415-340-7017
Williams, Sandra/PO Box 16130, San Diego, CA	619-283-3100
Williams, Steven Burr/8260 Grandview, Los Angeles, CA	213-469-5749
Williams, Wayne/7623 Beverly Blvd, Los Angeles, CA	213-937-2882
Williamson, Scott/1901 E Carnegie #1G, Santa Ana, CA	714-261-2550
Wilson, Don/10754 2nd Ave NW, Seattle, WA	206-367-4075
Wilson, Douglas M/10133 NE 113th Pl, Kirkland, WA	206-822-8604
Wimpey, Christopher/627 Eighth Ave, San Diego, CA	619-232-3222
Windus, Scott/928 N Formosa Ave, Los Angeles, CA	213-874-3160
Wing, Frank/2325 Third, San Francisco, CA	415-626-8066
Winholt, Bryan/PO Box 331, Sacramento, CA	916-725-0592
Winter-Green Photo/3823 Mt Albertine Ave, San Diego, CA	619-278-3535

Photographers

Please send us your additions and updates.

Witbeck, Sandra/581 Seaver Dr, Mill Valley, CA	415-383-6834
Wittner, Dale/507 Third Ave #209, Seattle, WA	206-623-4545
Wolfe, Dan E/45 E Walnut, Pasadena, CA	213-681-3130
Wolman, Baron/PO Box 1000, Mill Valley, CA	415-388-0181
Wong, Ken/3431 Wesley St, Culver City, CA	213-836-3118
Wood, Darrell/517 Aloha St, Seattle, WA	206-283-7900
Wood, James/1746 N Ivar, Los Angeles, CA	213-461-3861
Woodward, Jonathan/5121 Santa Fe St #A, San Diego, CA	619-270-5501
Woolslair, James/17229 Newhope St #H, Fountain Valley, CA	714-957-0349
Wortham, Robert/521 State St, Glendale, CA	818-243-6400
Wright, Armand/4026 Blairmore Ct, San Jose, CA	408-629-0559
Wyatt, Tom Photography/585 Mission St, San Francisco, CA	415-543-2813

YZ

Young, Bill/PO Box 27344, Honolulu, HI	808-595-7324
Young, Edward/860 2nd St, San Francisco, CA	415-543-6633
Yudelson, Jim/33 Clementina, San Francisco, CA	415-543-3325
Zaboroskie, K Gypsy/5584 Mission, San Francisco, CA	415-239-4230
Zajack, Greg/1517 W Alton Ave, Santa Ana, CA	714-432-8400
Zak, Ed/80 Tehama St, San Francisco, CA	415-781-1611
Zanzinger, David/2411 Main St, Santa Monica, CA	213-399-8802
Zaruba, Jeff/906 Venezia, Venice, CA	213-653-3341
Zens, Michael/84 University St, Seattle, WA	206-623-5249
Zenuk, Alan/POB 3531, Vancouver, BC, Canada V6B 3Y6	604-733-8271
Zimberoff, Tom/31 Wolfback Ridge Rd, Sausalito, CA	415-331-3100
Zimmerman, Dick/8743 W Washington Blvd, Los Angeles, CA	213-204-2911
Zimmerman, John/9135 Hazen Dr, Beverly Hills, CA	213-273-2642
Zippel, Arthur/2110 E McFadden #D, Santa Ana, CA	714-835-8400
Zurek, Nikolay/276 Shipley St, San Francisco, CA	415-777-9210
Zwart, Jeffrey R/1900-E East Warner, Santa Ana, CA	714-261-5844
Zyber, Tom/11577-A Slater Ave, Fountain Valley, CA	714-546-2949

Stock

New York City

American Heritage Picture Library/10 Rockefeller Plaza	212-399-8930
American Library Color Slide Co/222 W 23rd St	212-255-5356
Archive Pictures/111 Wooster St	212-431-1610
Argent and Aurum/470 W 24th St	212-807-1186
Art Resource Inc/65 Bleecker St 9th Fl	212-505-8700
Beck's Studio/37-44 82nd St	718-424-8751
Bettmann Archive/136 E 57th St	212-758-0362
Camera 5 Inc/6 W 20th St	212-989-2004
Camera Five Inc/6 W 20th St	212-989-2004
Camera Prees Ltd/529 E 88th St #2A	212-737-1225
Camerique Stock Photography/1181 Broadway 2nd Fl	212-685-3870
Camp, Woodfin Assoc/415 Madison Ave	212-750-1020
Coleman, Bruce Inc/381 Fifth Ave 2nd Fl	212-683-5227
Comstock/30 Irving Pl	212-889-9700
Consolidated Poster Service/341 W 44th St	212-581-3105
Contact Stock Images/415 Madison Ave	212-750-1020
Cooke, Jerry/161 E 82nd St	212-288-2045
Culver Pictures Inc/150 W 22nd St 3rd Fl	212-684-5054
DMI Inc/341 First Ave	212-777-8135
DPI Inc/19 W 21st St #901	212-627-4060
DeWys, Leo Inc/1170 Broadway	212-986-3190
Design Conceptions/Elaine Abrams/112 Fourth Ave	212-254-1688
Dot Picture Agency/50 W 29th St	212-684-3441
FPG International/251 Park Ave S	212-777-4210
Flex Inc/342 Madison Ave	212-722-5816
Flying Camera Inc/114 Fulton St	212-619-0808
Focus on Sports/222 E 46th St	212-661-6860
Four by Five Inc/485 Madison Ave	212-355-2323
Fundamental Photographs/210 Forsythe St	212-473-5770
Gabriel Graphic News Service/38 Madison Sq Sta	212-254-8863
Galloway, Ewing/1466 Broadway	212-719-4720
Gamma-Liaison Photo Agency/150 E 58th St 15th Fl	212-888-7272
Globe Photos Inc/275 Seventh Ave 21st Fl	212-689-1340
Gottscho-Schleisner Inc/150-35 86th Ave	718-526-2795
Gross, Lee Assoc/366 Madison Ave	212-682-5240
Heyman, Ken/3 E 76th St	212-226-3725
THE IMAGE BANK/111 FIFTH AVE (P BACK COVER)	**212-529-6700**
Image Resources/134 W 29th St	212-736-2523
Index Stock International Inc/126 Fifth Ave	212-929-4644
International Stock Photos/113 E 31st St #1A	212-696-4666
Keystone Press Agency Inc/202 E 42nd St	212-924-8123
Kramer, Joan & Assoc Inc/720 Fifth Ave	212-567-5545
Lewis, Frederick Inc/134 W 29th St #1003	212-594-8816
Life Picture Service/Rm 28-58 Time-Life Bldg	212-841-4800
London Features Int'l USA Ltd/215 W 84th St #406	212-724-8780
Magnum Photos Inc/251 Park Ave S	212-475-7600
Maisel, Jay/190 Bowery	212-431-5013
Manhattan Views/41 Union Sq W #1027	212-255-1477
MediChrome/271 Madison Ave	212-679-8480
Memory Shop Inc/109 E 12th St	212-473-2404
Monkmeyer Press Photo Agency/118 E 28th St #615	212-689-2242
Omni Photo Communication/521 Madison Ave	212-751-6530
Photo Assoc News Service/PO Box 306 Station A	718-961-0909
Photo Files/1235 E 40th St	718-338-2245
Photo Library Inc/325 W 45th St	212-246-1349
Photo Researchers Inc/60 E 56th St	212-758-3420
Photo World/251 Park Ave S	212-777-4214
PhotoNet/250 W 57th St	212-757-0320
Photography for Industry/230 W 54th St	212-757-9255
Photoreporters/875 Ave of Americas #1003	212-736-7602
Phototake/4523 Broadway #76	212-942-8185
Phototeque/156 Fifth Ave #415	212-242-6406
Pictorial Parade/130 W 42nd St	212-840-2026
RDR Productions/351 W 54th St	212-586-4432
Rangefinder Corp/275 Seventh Ave	212-689-1340
Reese, Kay/175 Fifth Ave #1304	212-598-4848
Reference Pictures/119 Fifth Ave	212-254-0008
Retna Ltd/36 W 56th St	212-489-1230
Roberts, H Armstrong/1181 Broadway	212-685-3870
SO Studio Inc/34 E 23rd St	212-475-0090
Science Photo Library Int'l/118 E 28th St	212-683-4025
Shashinka Photo/501 Fifth Ave #2102	212-490-2180
Shostal Assoc/145 E 32nd St	212-686-8850
Sochurek, Howard Inc/680 Fifth Ave	212-582-1860
Sovfoto-Eastphoto Agency/25 W 43rd St	212-921-1922
Spano/Roccanova/16 W 46th St	212-840-7450
Sports Illustrated Pictures/Time-Life Bldg 19th Fl	212-841-3663
Steinhauser, Art Ent/305 E 40th St	212-953-1722
Stockphotos Inc/373 Park Ave S 6th Fl	212-686-1196
Sygma Photo News/225 W 57th St 7th Fl	212-765-1820
Tamin Stock Photos/440 West End Ave #4E	212-807-6691
Taurus Photos/118 E 28th St	212-683-4025
Telephoto/8 Thomas St	212-406-2440
The Bethel Agency/513 W 54th St #1	212-664-0455
The Granger Collection/1841 Broadway	212-586-0971
The Stock Market/1181 Broadway 3rd Fl	212-684-7878
The Stock Shop/232 Madison Ave	212-679-8480
The Strobe Studio Inc/91 Fifth Ave	212-691-5270
UPI Photo Library/48 E 21st St	212-777-6200
Uncommon Stock/1181 Broadway 4th Fl	212-481-1190
Vierheller, Shirley/11 W 19th St 6th Fl	212-633-0300
Wheeler Pictures/50 W 29th St #11W	212-696-9832
Wide World Photos Inc/50 Rockefeller Plaza	212-621-1930
Winiker, Barry M/173 W 78th St	212-572-7364

Northeast

Authenticated News Int'l/29 Katonah Ave, Katonah, NY	914-232-7726
Bergman, LV & Assoc/East Mountain Rd S, Cold Spring, NY	914-265-3656
Blizzard, William C/PO Box 1696, Beckley, WV	304-755-0094
Camerique Stock Photo/1701 Skippack Pike, Blue Bell, PA	215-272-4000
Camerique Stock Photography/45 Newbury St, Boston, MA	617-267-6450
Cape Scapes/542 Higgins Crowell Rd, West Yarmouth, MA	617-362-8222
Chandoha, Walter/RD 1 PO Box 287, Annandale, NJ	201-782-3666
Chimera Productions/PO Box 1742, Clarksburg, WV	304-623-5368
Consolidated News Pictures/209 Pennsylvania Ave SE, Washington, DC	202-543-3203
Cyr Color Photo/PO Box 2148, Norwalk, CT	203-838-8230
DCS Enterprises/12806 Gaffney Rd, Silver Spring, MD	301-622-2323
Devaney Stock Photos/7 High St #308, Huntington, NY	516-673-4477
Dunn, Phoebe/20 Silvermine Rd, New Canaan, CT	203-966-9791
Earth Scenes/Animals Animals/17 Railroad Ave, Chatham, NY	518-392-5500
Educational Dimension Stock/PO Box 126, Stamford, CT	203-327-4612
F/Stop Pictures Inc/PO Box 359, Springfield, VT	802-885-5261
Folio/2651 Conn Ave NW 3rd Fl, Washington, DC	202-965-2410
Heilman, Grant/506 W Lincoln Ave, Lititz, PA	717-626-0296
Illustrators Stock Photos/PO Box 1470, Rockville, MD	301-279-0045
Image Photos/Main St, Stockbridge, MA	413-298-5500
Jones, G P - Stock/45 Newbury St, Boston, MA	617-267-6450
Lambert, Harold M Studio/2801 W Cheltenham Ave, Philadelphia, PA	215-224-1400
Light, Paul/1430 Massachusetts Ave, Cambridge, MA	617-628-1052
Lumiere/512 Adams St, Centerport, NY	516-271-6133
Mercier, Louis/15 Long Lots Rd, Westport, CT	203-227-1620
Myers Studios/PO Box 122, Orchard Park, NY	716-662-6002
Natural Selection/177 St Paul St, Rochester, NY	716-232-1502
Newsphoto Worldwide/902 National Press Bldg, Washington, DC	202-737-0450
North Wind Picture Archives/RR 1 Box 172, Alfred, ME	207-490-1940
Philba, Allan/3408 Bertha Dr, Baldwin, NY	212-286-0948
Photo Media Ltd/3 Forest Glen Rd, New Paltz, NY	914-255-8661
Photo Resources Stock/511 Broadway, Saratoga Springs, NY	518-587-4730
Photo Stock Unlimited/7208 Thomas Blvd, Pittsburgh, PA	412-242-5070
Picture Group/5 Steeple St, Providence, RI	401-273-5473
Positive Images/12 Main St, Natick, MA	617-653-7610
Rainbow/PO Box 573, Housatonic, MA	413-274-6211
Roberts, H Armstrong/4203 Locust St, Philadelphia, PA	215-386-6300
Sandak Inc/180 Harvard Ave, Stamford, CT	203-348-4721
Sequis Stock Photo/PO Box 215, Stevenson, MD	301-467-7300
Sportschrome/10 Brynkerhoff Ave 2nd Fl, Palisades Park, NJ	201-568-1412
Starwood/PO Box 40503, Washington, DC	202-362-7404
Stock Boston Inc/36 Gloucester St, Boston, MA	617-266-2300

Stock

Continued

Please send us your additions and updates.

The Image Works Inc/PO Box 443, Woodstock, NY	914-679-7172
The Picture Cube/89 State St, Boston, MA	617-367-1532
Transtock/15 S Grand Ave, Baldwin, NY	516-223-9649
Undersea Systems/PO Box 29M, Bay Shore, NY	516-666-3127
Uniphoto Picture Agency/1071 Wisconsin Ave NW, Washington, DC	202-333-0500
View Finder Stock Photo/2310 Penn Ave, Pittsburgh, PA	412-391-8720
Weidman, H Mark/2112 Goodwin Lane, North Wales, PA	215-646-1745

Southeast

Cactus Clyde/3623 Perkins Rd Box 14876, Baton Rouge, LA	504-887-3704
Camera MD Studios/8290 NW 26 Pl, Ft Lauderdale, FL	305-741-5560
Florida Image File/222 2nd St N, St Petersburg, FL	813-894-8433
THE IMAGE BANK/3490 PIEDMONT RD NE #1106, ATLANTA, GA (P BACK COVER)	**404-233-9920**
In Stock/516 NE 13th St, Ft Lauderdale, FL	305-527-4111
National Stock Network/8960 SW 114th St, Miami, FL	305-233-1703
Phelps Agency/3210 Peachtree St NW, Atlanta, GA	404-264-0264
Photo Options/1432 Linda Vista Dr, Birmingham, AL	205-979-8412
Photri(Photo Research Int'l)/505 W Windsor/ Alexandria, VA	703-836-4439
Picturesque/1520 Brookside Dr #3, Raleigh, NC	919-828-0023
Reynolds, Charles/1715 Kirby Pkwy, Memphis, TN	901-754-2411
Sharp Shooters/7210 Red Rd #216, Miami, FL	305-666-1266
Sherman, Ron/PO Box 28656, Atlanta, GA	404-993-7197
Southern Stock /3601 W Commercial Blvd Ft Lauderdale, FL	305-486-7117
Stills Inc/3210 Peachtree Rd NE, Atlanta, GA	404-233-0022
Stockfile/2107 Park Ave, Richmond, VA	804-358-6364
The Waterhouse/PO Box 2487, Key Largo, FL	305-451-3737

Midwest

A-Stock Photo Finder /1030 N State St, Chicago, IL	312-645-0611
Artstreet/111 E Chestnut St, Chicago, IL	312-664-3049
Blasdel, John/2815 W 89th St, Leawood, KS	913-648-5973
Brooks & VanKirk/855 W Blackhawk St, Chicago, IL	312-642-7766
Bundt, Nancy/1908 Kenwood Pkw, Minneapolis, MN	612-377-7700
Cameramann International/PO Box 413, Evanston, IL	312-777-5657
Camerique Stock Photography/180 Bloor St W, Toronto	416-925-4323
Camerique Stock Photography/233 E Wacker Dr Chicago, IL	312-938-4466
Campbell Stock /28000 Middlebelt Rd Farmington Hills, MI	313-626-5233
Charlton Photos/11518 N Pt Washington Rd, Mequon, WI	414-241-8634
Click/ Chicago Ltd/213 W Institute Pl #503, Chicago, IL	312-787-7880
Collectors Series/161 W Harrison, Chicago, IL	312-427-5311
Custom Medical Stock /3819 N Southport Ave, Chicago, IL	312-248-3200
Gartman, Marilyn/510 N Dearborn, Chicago, IL	312-661-1656
Gibler, Mike/2716 Pestalozzi, St Louis, MO	314-776-5885
Hedrich-Blessing/11 W Illinois St, Chicago, IL	312-321-1151
Historical Picture Service/921 W Van Buren #201, Chicago, IL	312-346-0599
Ibid Inc/727 N Hudson, Chicago, IL	312-944-0020
THE IMAGE BANK/510 N DEARBORN #930, CHICAGO, IL (P BACK COVER)	**312-329-1817**
THE IMAGE BANK/822 MARQUETTE AVE, MINNEAPOLIS, MN (P BACK COVER)	**612-332-8935**
THE IMAGE BANK/550 QUEEN ST E #300, TORONTO ON (P BACK COVER)	**416-362-6931**
Journalism Services Stock/118 E 2nd St, Lockport, IL	312-951-0269
Masterfile/2 Carlton St #617, Toronto M5B 1J3, ON	
Miller Services/45 East Charles St, Toronto M4Y 1S6, ON	416-925-43
Panoramic Stock Images/230 N Michigan Ave, Chicago, IL	312-236-8545
Pix International/300 N State #3926, Chicago, IL	312-321-9071
Studio B Stock/107 W Van Buren #211, Chicago, IL	312-939-4677
The Photoletter/Pine Lake Farm, Osceola, WI	715-248-3800
Thill, Nancy/70 W Huron St, Chicago, IL	312-944-7164
Third Coast Stock/PO Box 92397, Milwaukee, WI	414-765-9442
Weathers, Ginny/708 Gage, Topeka, KS	913-272-1190
Zehrt, Jack/PO Box 122A Rt5, Pacific, MO	314-458-3600

Southwest

Far West Photo/1104 Hermosa Dr SE, Albuquerque, NM	505-255-0646
Image Venders/1222 N Winnetka, Dallas, TX	214-742-3414

THE IMAGE BANK/1336 CONANT ST, DALLAS, TX (P BACK COVER)	**214-631-3808**
McLaughlin, Herb & Dorothy/2344 W Holly, Phoenix, AZ	602-258-6551
Photobank/PO Box 1086, Scottsdale, AZ	602-265-5591
Photoworks/Uniphoto International/215 Asbury, Houston, TX	713-864-3638
Raphaele/Digital Transparencies /616 Hawthorne, Houston, TX	713-524-2211
Running Productions/PO Box 1237, Flagstaff, AZ	602-774-2923
Southern Images/Rt 1 Box 312, Paris, AR	501-963-6429
The Stock House Inc/9261 Kirvy, Houston, TX	713-796-8400
Visual Images West/600 E Baseline Rd #B-6, Tempe, AZ	602-820-5403

Rocky Mountain

Aspen Stock Photo/PO Box 4063, Aspen, CO	303-925-8280
Bair, Royce & Assoc/6640 South 2200 West, Salt Lake City, UT	801-569-1155
GTA Limited/2046 Arapahoe Sr, Denver, CO	303-298-1986
IMAGES OF NATURE/PO BOX 2935, JACKSON HOLE, WY (P 275)	**307-733-6179**
International Photo File/PO Box 343, Magna, UT	801-250-3447
Stack, Tom /1322 N Academy Blvd, Colorado Springs, CO	303-570-1000
Stock Imagery/711 Kalamath St, Denver, CO	303-592-1091
The Photo Bank/271 Second Ave N Box 3069, Ketchum, ID	208-726-5731
The Stock Broker/450 Lincoln St #110, Denver, CO	303-698-1734
The Stock Solution/6640 South, 2200 West, Salt Lake City, UT	801-569-1155

West Coast

Adventure Photo/3750 W Pacific Coast Hwy, Ventura, CA	805-643-7751
After Image Inc/3807 Wilshire Blvd #250, Los Angeles, CA	213-480-1105
Alaska Pictorial Service/Drawer 6144, Anchorage, AK	907-344-1370
Beebe, Morton & Assoc/150 Lombard St #207, San Francisco, CA	415-362-3530
Burr, Lawrence/76 Manzanita Rd, Fairfax, CA	415-456-9158
Camerique Stock Photography/6640 Sunset Blvd #100, Hollywood, CA	213-469-3900
Catalyst/PO Box 689, Haines, AK	907-766-2670
Dae Flights/PO Box 1086, Newport Beach, CA	714-676-3902
Dritsas, George/207 Miller Ave, Mill Valley, CA	415-381-5485
ERGENBRIGHT, RIC/PO BOX 1067, BEND, OR (P 274)	**503-389-7662**
Focus West/4112 Adams Ave, San Diego, CA	619-280-3595
French, Peter/PO Box 100, Kamuela, HI	808-889-6488
Great American Stock/3955 Pacific Hwy, San Diego, CA	619-297-2205
Grubb, T D/11102 Blix St, N Hollywood, CA	818-760-1236
Havens, Carol/POB 662, Laguna Beach, CA	714-497-1908
THE IMAGE BANK/8228 SUNSET BLVD #310, LOS ANGELES, CA (P BACK COVER)	**213-656-9003**
Jeton/483 Index Pl NE, Kenton, WA	206-226-1408
Long Photo Inc/57865 Rickenbacher Rd, Los Angeles, CA	213-933-7219
MUENCH, DAVID/PO BOX 30500, SANTA BARBARA, CA (P 276)	**805-967-4488**
Madison, David/2330 Old Middlefield Rd, Mt View, CA	415-961-6297
Pacific Ocean Stock/, Koloa, HI	808-742-7274
Peebles, Douglas Photography/1100 Alekea St #221, Honolulu, HI	808-533-6686
Photo Network/1541 Parkway Loop #J, Tustin, CA	714-259-1244
Photo Vault/1045 17th St, San Francisco, CA	415-552-9682
Photographsanstuff/730 Clementina, San Francisco, CA	415-861-1062
Photophile/2311 Kettner Blvd, San Diego, CA	619-234-4431
Simpson, Ed/PO Box 397, S Pasadena, CA	213-682-3131
Spectrum/115 Sansome St #812, San Francisco, CA	415-340-9811
Stock Orange/2511 W Sunflower #D9, Santa Ana, CA	714-546-0485
TRW/9841 Airport Blvd #1414, Los Angeles, CA	213-536-4880
Terraphotographics/BPS/PO Box 490, Moss Beach, CA	415-726-6244
The New Image Inc/38 Quail Ct 200, Walnut Creek, CA	415-934-2405
Visual Impact/733 Auahi St, Honolulu, HI	808-524-8269
West Light/1526 Pontius Ave #A, Los Angeles, CA	213-477-0421
WEST STOCK/83 S KING ST #520, SEATTLE, WA (P 277)	**206-621-1611**
Zephyr Pictures/2120 Jimmy Durante Blvd, Del Mar, CA	619-755-1200

Graphic Designers

New York City

A
AKM Associates/41 E 42nd St	212-687-7636
Abramson, Michael R Studio/21 E 40th St	212-683-1271
Adams, Gaylord Design/236 E 36th St	212-684-4625
Adlemann, Morton/30 W 32nd St	212-564-8258
Adler, Stan Assoc/1140 Ave of Americas	212-719-1944
Adzema, Diane/17 Bleecker St	212-982-5657
Album Graphics Inc/115 W 55th St	212-489-0793
Alexander, Martha/106 E 85th St	212-772-7382
Aliman, Elie/134 Spring St	212-925-9621
Allied Graphic Arts/1515 Broadway	212-730-1414
American Express Publishing Co/1120 Ave of Americas	212-382-5600
Amorello, Frank Assoc/17 E 45th St	212-972-1775
Anagraphics Inc/104 W 29th St 2nd Fl	212-279-2370
Ancona Design Atelier/524 W 43rd St	212-947-8287
And Co/49 W 27th St #900	212-213-8888
Andersen, Bill/27 Minkel Rd	914-762-4867
Anspach Grossman Portugal/711 Third Ave, 12th flr	212-692-9000
Antler & Baldwin Graphics/7 E 47th St	212-751-2031
Antupit and Others Inc/16 E 40th St	212-686-2552
Appelbaum Company/333 E 49th St #5D	212-593-0003
Aron, Michael & Co/20 W 20th St	212-627-4054
Art Department/2 W 46th St	212-391-1826
Athey, Diane/425 W 23rd St	212-787-7415

B
BN Associates/299 Madison Ave	914-964-8102
Balasas, Cora/651 Vanderbilt St	718-633-7753
Bantam Books Inc/666 Fifth Ave	212-765-6500
Barmache, Leon Design Assoc Inc/225 E 57th St	212-752-6780
Barnett Design Group/149 Fifth Ave	212-677-8830
Barry, Jim/69 W 68th St	212-873-6787
Becker Hockfield Design Assoc/35 E 21st St	212-505-7050
Beckerman, Ann Design/50 W 29th St	212-684-0496
Bell, James Graphic Design Inc/119 W 23rd St	212-929-8855
Benvenutti, Chris/12 W 27th St 12t Fl	212-696-0880
Bernhardt/Fudyma/133 E 36th St	212-889-9337
Besalel, Ely/235 E 49th St	212-759-7820
Bessen & Tully, Inc/880 Third Ave #1010	212-838-6406
Binns, Betty Graphic Design/31 E 28th St	212-679-9200
Biondo, Charles Design Assoc/389 W 12th St	212-645-5300
Birch, Colin Assoc Inc/147 E 61st St	212-223-0499
Bloch, Graulich & Whelan, Inc/333 Park Ave S	212-473-7033
Boker Group/37 W 26th St	212-686-1132
Bonnell Design Associates Inc/1457 Broadway	212-921-5390
Bordnick, Jack & Assoc/224 W 35th St	212-563-1544
Botero, Samuel Assoc/150 E 58th St	212-935-5155
Bradford, Peter/11 E 22nd St	212-982-2090
Brainchild Designs/108 E 16th St	212-420-1222
Branin, Max/135 Fifth Ave #801	212-254-9608
Braswell, Lynn/320 Riverside Dr	212-222-8761
Bree/Taub Design/648 Broadway #703	212-254-8383
Breth, Jill Marie/870 W 181st St	212-781-8370
Brochure People/14 E 38th St #1466	212-696-9185
Brodsky Graphics/270 Madison Ave #605	212-684-2600
Brown, Alastair Assoc/500 Fifth Avenue	212-221-3166
Brown, Kim/20 Bogardus Pl	212-567-5671
Brown, Kirk Q/1092 Blake Ave	718-346-8281
Buckley Designs Inc/310 E 75th St	212-861-0626
Burns, Tom Assoc Inc/330 E 42nd St	212-594-9883
By Design/14 E 38th St	212-684-0388

C
Cain, David/200 W 20th St #607	212-633-0258
Cannan, Bill & Co Inc/529 W 42nd St #2Q	212-563-1004
Caravello Studios/165 W 18th St	212-620-0620
Carnase, Inc/30 E 21st St	212-679-9880
Carson, Carol/138 W 88th St	212-580-0514
Cetta, Al/111 Bank St	212-989-9696
Chajet Design Group Inc/148 E 40th St	212-684-3669
Chang, Ivan/30 E 10th St	212-777-6102
Chapman, Sandra S/122 Ashland Pl #7E	718-855-7396

Charles, Irene Assoc/104 E 40th St #206	212-765-8000
Chermayeff & Geismar/15 E 26th St 12th Fl	212-532-4499
Chin, E T Assoc/1160 Third Ave	212-645-6800
Chu, H L & Co Ltd/39 W 29th St	212-889-4818
Church, Wallace Assoc/305 E 46th St	212-755-2903
Cliffer, Jill/9 E 16th St	212-691-7013
Cohen, Hayes/17-22 215th St	718-225-3355
Cohen, Norman Design/201 E 28th St #8K	212-679-3906
Comart Assoc/360 W 31st St	212-714-2550
Condon, J & M/126 Fifth Ave	212-242-7811
Corchia Woliner Assoc/130 W 56th St	212-977-9778
Corey & Company/155 Sixth Ave 15th Fl	212-924-4311
Corpographics, Inc./47 West St	212-483-9065
Corporate Annual Reports Inc./112 E 31st St	212-889-2450
Corporate Graphics Inc/655 Third Ave	212-599-1820
Cosgrove Assoc Inc/223 E 31st St	212-889-7202
Cotler, Sheldon Inc/80 W 40th St	212-719-9590
Cousins, Morison S & Assoc/599 Broadway 8th Fl	212-751-3390
Crane, Susan Inc/120 E 23rd St	212-260-0580
Cranner, Brian Inc/454 W 46th St #2D South	212-582-2030
Creamer Dickson Basford/1633 Broadway	212-887-8670
Crow, John/34 W 37th St	212-594-2636
Csoka/Benato/Fleurant Inc/134 W 26th St	212-242-6777
Curtis Design Inc./29 E 32nd St	212-685-0670

D
Daniels Design/150 E 35th St	212-889-0071
Davis, Jed/303 Lexington Ave	212-481-8481
Davis-Delaney-Arrow Inc/141 E 25th St	212-686-2500
DeHarak, Rudolph/150 Fifth Avenue	212-929-5445
DeMartin-Marona-Cranstoun-Downes/630 Third Ave 14th Fl	212-682-9044
DeMartino/Schultz/233 Broadway	212-513-0300
Deibler, Gordon/1 Wrld Trade Ctr #8817	212-565-8022
Delgado, Lisa/22 W 21st St	212-645-0097
Delphan Company/515 Madison Ave #3300	212-371-6700
Design Loiminchay/210 Canal St #501	212-608-2880
Designed to Print/130 W 25th St	212-924-2090
Designers Three/25 W 43rd St	212-221-5900
Designframe/1 Union Square	212-924-2426
Deutsch Design/166 Lexington	212-684-4478
DiComo, Charles & Assoc/12 W 27th St	212-689-8670
DiFranza Williamson Inc/16 W 22nd St	212-463-8302
Diamond Art Studio/11 E 36th St	212-685-6622
Dickens, Holly/60 E 42nd St #505	212-682-1490
Displaycraft/41-21 28th St	718-784-8186
Donovan & Green Inc/1 Madison Ave	212-725-2233
Doret, Michael/12 E 14th St #4D	212-929-1688
Douglas, Barry Design/300 E 71st St #4H	212-734-4137
Downey Weeks + Toomey/519 Eighth Ave 22nd Fl	212-564-8260
Drate, Spencer/160 Fifth Ave #613	212-620-4672
Dreyfuss, Henry Assoc/423 W 55th St	212-957-8600
Dubins, Milt Designer Inc/353 W 22nd St	212-691-0232
Dubourcq, Hilaire/110 Christopher St	212-924-1564
Dubrow, Oscar Assoc/18 E 48th St	212-688-0698
Duffy, William R/201 E 36th St	212-682-6755
Dvorak Goodspeed & Assoc/165 Lexington Ave	212-475-4580
Dwyer, Tom/420 Lexington Ave	212-986-7108

E
Edgar, Lauren/26 E 20th St 8th Fl	212-673-6060
Edge, Dennis Design/36 E 38th St	212-679-0927
Eichinger, Inc/595 Madison Ave	212-421-0544
Eisenman and Enock/25 Hudson St	212-431-1000
Emerson, Matt/1123 Broadway	212-807-8144
Environetics Inc/145 E 32nd St 8th Fl	212-481-9700
Environment Planning Inc/342 Madison Ave	212-661-3744
Erikson Assoc./345 Park Ave	212-688-0048
Etheridge, Palombo, Sedewitz/1500 Broadway	212-944-2530
Eucalyptus Tree Studio/73 Leonard St	212-226-0331

F
FDC Planning & Design Corp/434 E 57th St	212-355-7200
Failing, Kendrick G Design/80 Fourth Ave	212-677-5764
Falkins, Richard Design/15 W 44th St	212-840-3045
Farmlett Barsanti Inc/1123 Broadway	212-691-9398

Graphic Design

Continued

Please send us your additions and updates.

Feucht, Fred Design Group Inc/300 Madison Ave	212-682-0040
Fineberg Associates/333 E 68th St	212-734-1220
Flaherty, David/650 Ninth Ave #1R	212-262-6536
Florville, Patrick Design Research/94-50 39 Ave	718-475-2278
Flying Eye Graphics/208 Fifth Ave/Unit 2	212-725-0658
Forman, Yale Designs Inc/11 Riverside Dr	212-799-1665
Foster, Stephen Design/145 W 28th St 10th Fl	212-967-2533
Freeman, Irving/145 Fourth Ave #9K	212-674-6705
Freyss, Christina/267 Broadway 2nd Fl	212-571-1130
Friday Saturday Sunday Inc/210 E 15th St	212-260-8479
Friedlander, Ira/502 E 84th St	212-580-9800
Fulgoni, Louis/233 W 21st St #4D	212-243-2959
Fulton & Partners/330 W 42nd St, 11th Fl	212-695-1625

G
Gale, Cynthia/229 E 88th St	212-860-5429
Gale, Robert A Inc/970 Park Ave	212-535-4791
Gamarello, Paul/21 E 22nd St #4G	212-485-4774
Gardner, Beau Assoc Inc/541 Lexington Ave 18th Fl	212-832-2426
Gaster, Joanne/201 E 30th St #43	212-686-0860
Gentile Studio/333 E 46th St	212-986-7743
George, Hershell/30 W 15th St	212-929-4321
Gerstman & Meyers Inc./60 W 55th St	212-586-2535
Gianninoto Assoc, Inc./133 E 54th St #2D	212-759-5757
Giber, Lauren/152 E 22nd St	212-473-2062
Giovanni Design Assoc./137 E 36th St	212-725-8536
Gips & Balkind & Assoc/244 E 58th St	212-421-5940
Girth, Marcy/213 E 34th St #3A	212-685-0734
Gladstein, Renee/628 West End Ave	212-877-2966
Gladych, Marianne/25 Prince St	212-925-9712
Glaser, Milton/207 E 32nd St	212-889-3161
Glazer & Kalayjian/301 E 45th St	212-687-3099
Glusker Group/154 W 57th St	212-757-4438
Goetz Graphics/60 Madison Ave	212-679-4250
Gold, Susan/136 W 22nd St	212-645-6977
Goldman, Neal Assoc/230 Park Ave #1507	212-687-5058
Gorbaty, Norman Design/14 E 38th St	212-684-1665
Gordon, Sam & Assoc/226 W 4th St	212-741-9294
Gorman, Chris Assoc/12 E 41st St	212-696-9377
Grant, Bill/4114 Highland Ave	718-996-3555
Graphic Art Resource Assoc/257 W 10th St	212-929-0017
Graphic Chart & Map Co/236 W 26th St #8SE	212-463-0190
Graphic Expression/330 E 59th St	212-759-7788
Graphics 60 Inc./155 E 55th St	212-687-1292
Graphics Institute/1633 Broadway	212-887-8670
Graphics by Nostradamus/250 W 57th St #1128A	212-581-1362
Graphics for Industry/8 W 30th St	212-889-6202
Graphics to Go/133 E 36th St	212-889-9337
Gray, George/385 West End Ave	212-873-3607
Green, Douglas/251 E 51st St	212-752-6284
Griffler Designs/17 E 67th St	212-794-2625
Grossberg, Manuel/88 University Pl 9th Fl	212-620-0444
Grunfeld Graphics Ltd/80 Varick St	212-431-8700
Gucciardo & Shapokas/244 Madison Ave	212-683-9378

H
HBO Studio Productions Inc/120 E 23rd St	212-477-8600
Halle, Doris/355 South End Ave #4C	212-321-2671
Halversen, Everett/874 58th St	718-438-4200
Handler Group Inc/55 W 45th St	212-391-0951
Haydee Design Studio/27 W 20th St	212-242-3110
Hecker, Mark Studio/321 W 11th St	212-620-9050
Heimall, Bob Inc/250 W 57th St #1206	212-245-4525
Herbick, David/5 Montague Terrace	718-852-6450
Holden, Cynthia/858 West End Ave #2B	212-222-4214
Holland, DK/27 W 20th St	718-789-3112
Holzsager, Mel Assoc Inc/275 Seventh Ave	212-741-7373
Hooper, Ray Design/1123 Broadway 8th Fl	212-924-5480
Hopkins, Will/80 Fifth Ave	212-580-9800
Horvath & Assoc Studios Ltd/93-95 Charles St	212-741-0300
Hub Graphics/18 E 16th St 4th Fl	212-675-8500
Human Factors/Industrial Design Inc/575 8th Ave	212-730-8010
Huttner & Hillman/137 E 25th St	212-532-6062

I J
Image Communications Inc/85 Fifth Ave	212-807-9677
Infield & D'Astolfo/49 W 24th St	212-924-9206
Inkwell Inc/5 W 30th St	212-279-2066
Inner Thoughts/118 E 25th St	212-674-1277
Intersight Design Inc/419 Park Ave S	212-696-0700
Jaffe Communications, Inc/122 E 42nd St	212-697-4310
Johnson, Dwight/162 E 36th St	718-834-8529
Johnston, Shaun & Susan/890 West End Ave #11E	212-663-4686
Jonson Pedersen Hinrichs & Shakery/141 Lexington Ave	212-889-9611

K
KLN Publishing Services Inc/36 E 30th St	212-686-8200
Kacik Design/201 E 56th St	212-753-0031
Kaeser & Wilson Design/330 Seventh Ave	212-563-2455
Kahn, Al Group/221 W 82nd St	212-580-3517
Kahn, Donald/39 W 29th St 12th Fl	212-889-8898
Kallir Phillips Ross Inc./605 Third Ave	212-878-3700
Karlin, Bernie/41 E 42nd St	212-687-7636
Kass Communications/505 Eighth Ave 19th Fl	212-868-3133
KAUFTHEIL/ROTHSCHILD/220 W 19TH ST #1200 (P 32,33)	**212-633-0222**
Kaye Graphics/151 Lexington Ave	212-924-7800
Keithley & Assoc/32 W 22nd St 6th Fl	212-807-8388
Kleb Associates/25 W 45th St	212-246-2847
Kneapler, John/99 Lexington Ave 2nd Fl	212-696-1150
Ko Noda and Assoc International/950 Third Ave	212-759-4044
Kollberg-Johnson Assoc Inc/254 Fifth Ave	212-686-3648
Koons, Irv Assoc/635 Madison Ave	212-752-4130
Koppel & Scher Inc/22 W 27th St 8th Fl	212-683-0870
Kosarin, Linda/185 Madison Ave 10th Fl	212-684-1100

L
LCL Design Assoc Inc/120 E 56th St #320	212-758-2604
Lacy, N Lee/121 E 30th St	212-532-6200
Lake, John/38 E 57th St 7th Fl	212-644-3850
Lamlee, Stuart/55 W 86th St	212-844-8991
Leach, Richard/62 W 39th St #803	212-869-0972
Lebbad, James A/1133 Broadway #1229	212-645-5260
Lee & Young Communications/One Park Ave	212-689-4000
Lesley-Hille Inc/32 E 21st St	212-677-7570
Lester & Butler/437 Fifth Ave	212-889-0578
Levine, Gerald/9 E 46th St #1102	212-986-1068
Levine, Ron/1 W 85th St #4D	212-787-7415
Levine, William V & Assoc/31 E 28th St	212-683-7177
Levirne, Joel/151 W 46th St	212-869-8370
Lichtenberg, Al Graphic Art/10 E 40th St	212-865-4312
Lieber, Anna/324 W 87th St	212-874-2874
Lieberman, Ron/109 W 28th St	212-947-0653
Liebert Studios Inc/6 E 39th St #1200	212-686-4520
Lika Association/160 E 38th St	212-490-3660
Lind Brothers Inc/111 Eighth Ave 7th Fl	212-924-9280
Lippincott & Margulies Inc/499 Park Ave	212-832-3000
Little Apple Art/409 Sixth Ave	718-499-7045
Loiacono Adv/353 Lexington Ave	212-683-5811
Lubliner/Saltz/183 Madison Ave	212-679-9810
Luckett Slover & Partners/18 W 23rd St	212-620-9770
Lukasiewicz Design Inc/119 W 57th St	212-581-3344
Lundgren, Ray Graphics/122 E 42nd St #216	212-370-1686
Luth & Katz Inc/40 E 49th St 9th Fl	212-644-5777

M
M & Co Design Group/50 W 17th St 12th Fl	212-243-0082
Maggio, Ben Assoc Inc/420 Lexington Ave	212-697-8600
Maggio, J P Design Assoc Inc/561 Broadway	212-725-9660
Maleter, Mari/25-34 Crescent St	718-726-7124
Marchese, Frank/444 E 82nd St	212-988-6267
Marckrey Design Group Inc/7 W 18th St 7th Fl	212-620-7077
Marcus, Eric/386 Waverly Ave	718-789-1799
Mauro, C L & Assoc Inc/12 W 31st St	212-868-3940
Mauro, Frank Assoc Inc/18 W 45th St	212-719-5570
Mayo-Infurna Design/635 Madison Ave	212-888-7883
McDonald, B & Assoc/1140 Ave of the Americas	212-869-9717
McGovern & Pivoda/39 W 38th St	212-840-2912
McNicholas, Florence/1419 8th Ave	718-965-0203
Meier Adv/37 W 57th St	212-355-6460

Graphic Design
Continued

Please send us your additions and updates.

Mendola Design/420 Lexington Ave	212-986-5680
Mentkin, Robert/51 E 97th St	212-534-5101
Merrill, Abby Studio Inc/153 E 57th St	212-753-7565
Millenium Design/240 Madison Ave	212-683-3400
Miller, Irving D Inc/641 Lexington Ave	212-755-4040
Mirenburg, Barry/413 City Island Ave	718-885-0835
Mitchell, E M Inc/820 Second Ave	212-986-5595
Mizerek Design/48 E 43rd St 2nd Fl	212-986-5702
Modular Marketing Inc/1841 Broadway	212-581-4690
Mont, Howard Assoc Inc/132 E 35th St	212-683-4360
Morris, Dean/307 E 6th St #4B	212-420-0673
Moshier, Harry & Assoc/18 E 53rd St	212-873-6130
Moskof & Assoc/154 W 57th St #133	212-333-2015
Mossberg, Stuart Design Assoc/11 W 73rd St	212-873-6130
Muir, Cornelius, Moore/750 Third Ave 18th Fl	212-687-4055
Murtha Desola Finsilver Fiore/800 Third Ave	212-832-4770

N N B Assoc Inc/435 Fifth Ave — 212-684-8074
Nelson, George & Assoc Inc/PO Box 243 Madison Sq Sta	212-777-4300
Nemser, Robert/635 Madison Ave	212-832-9595
New American Graphics/240 Madison Ave 8th Fl	212-532-3551
Newman, Harvey Assoc/1466 Broadway #802	212-391-8060
Nicholson Design/148 W 24th St 12th Fl	212-206-1530
Nitzburg, Andrew/165 E 32nd St	212-686-3514
Nobart NY Inc/33 E 18th St	212-475-5522
Noneman & Noneman Design/230 E 18th St	212-473-4090
North, Charles W Studio/40 W 20th St	212-242-6300
Notovitz & Perrault Design Inc/47 E 19th St 4th Fl	212-677-9700
Novus Visual Communications Inc/18 W 27th St	212-689-2424

OP Oak Tree Graphics Inc/570 Seventh Ave — 212-398-9355
Offenhartz, Harvey Inc/1414 Ave of Americas	212-751-3241
Ohlsson, Eskil Assoc Inc/625 Madison Ave 2nd Fl	212-758-4412
Ong & Assoc/11 W 19th St 6th Fl	212-633-6702
Orlov, Christian/42 W 69th St	212-873-2381
Ortiz, Jose Luis/PO Box 6678	212-877-3081
Oz Communications Inc/36 E 30th St	212-686-8200
Page Arbitrio Resen Ltd/305 E 46th St	212-421-8190
Pahmer, Hal/8 W 30th St 7th Fl	212-889-6202
Palladino, Tony/400 E 56th St	212-751-0068
Paragraphics/427 3rd St	718-965-2231
Parsons School of Design/66 Fifth Ave	212-741-8900
Patel, Harish Design Assoc/218 Madison Ave	212-686-7425
Peckolick & Prtnrs/108 E 31st St	212-532-6166
Pellegrini & Assoc/16 E 40th St	212-686-4481
Pencils Portfolio Inc/333 E 49th St	212-355-2468
Penpoint Studio Inc/444 Park Ave S	212-243-5435
Penraat Jaap Assoc/315 Central Park West	212-873-4541
Performing Dogs/45 E 19th St	212-260-1880
Perlman, Richard Design/305 E 46th St	212-935-2552
Perlow, Paul/123 E 54th St #6E	212-758-4358
Peslak, Vickie/123 E 54th St #3C	212-720-5070
Peters, Stan Assoc Inc/236 E 36th St	212-684-0315
Peterson Blythe & Cato/216 E 45th St	212-557-5566
Pettis, Valerie/88 Lexington Ave #17G	212-683-7382
Plumb Design Group Inc/57 E 11th St 7th Fl	212-673-3490
Podob, Al/9 E 46th St	212-697-6643
Pop Shots Corporate Design/545 W 45th St	212-489-1717
Pouget, Evelyn/23 E 7th St	212-228-7935
Prendergast, J W & Assoc Inc/605 Third Ave	212-687-8805
Primary Design Group/138 Spring St	212-219-1000
Projection Systems International/219 E 44th St	212-682-0995
Puiying/433 Park Ave S	212-689-5148
Pushpin Group/215 Park Ave S	212-674-8080

QR Quon, Mike Design Office/568 Broadway #703 — 212-226-6024
RC Graphics/157 E 57th St	212-755-1383
RD Graphics/151 Lexington Ave #5F	212-889-5612
Rafkin Rubin Inc/1466 Broadway #1507	212-869-2540
Ratzkin, Lawrence/392 Fifth Ave	212-279-1314
Regn-Califano Inc/330 W 42nd St #1300	212-239-0380
Robinson, Mark/904 President St	718-638-9067

Rogers, Ana/20 W 20th St 7th Fl	212-741-4687
Rogers, Richard Inc/300 E 33rd St	212-685-3666
Romero, Javier/529 W 42nd St	212-206-9175
Rosenthal, Herb & Assoc Inc/207 E 32nd St	212-685-1814
ROSS CULBERT HOLLAND & LAVERY/15 W 20TH ST 9TH FL (P 40,41)	**212-206-0044**
Ross/Pento Inc/301 W 53rd St	212-757-5604
Rothschild, Joyce/305 E 46th St 15th Fl	212-888-8680
Rouya, E S/45-19 42nd St	718-392-5887
Russell, Anthony Inc/170 Fifth Ave 11th Fl	212-255-0650
Russo, Rocco Anthony/184 Lexington Ave	212-213-4710

S SCR Design Organization/1114 First Ave — 212-752-8496
Sabanosh, Michael/433 W 34th St #18B	212-947-8161
Saiki & Assoc/154 W 18th St #2D	212-255-0466
Sakin, Sy/17 E 48th St	212-688-3141
Saks, Arnold/16 E 79th St	212-861-4300
Saksa Art & Design/41 Union Sq W #1001	212-255-5539
Salavetz, Judith/160 Fifth Ave #613	212-620-4672
Salisbury & Salisbury Inc/15 W 44th St	212-575-0770
Salpeter, Paganucci, Inc/142 E 37th St	212-683-3310
Saltzman, Mike Group/27 W 20th St	212-929-4655
Sandgren Associates Inc/60 E 42nd St	212-679-4650
Sarda, Thomas/875 Third Ave 4th Fl	212-303-8326
Sawyer, Arnie Studio/15 W 28th St 4th Fl	212-685-4927
Saxton Communications Group/605 Third Ave #1600	212-953-1300
Say It In Neon/434 Hudson St	212-691-7977
Schaefer-Cassety Inc/42 W 39th St	212-840-0175
Schaeffer/Boehm Ltd/315 W 35th St	212-947-4345
Schechter Group Inc/212 E 49th St	212-752-4400
Schecterson, Jack Assoc Inc/274 Madison Ave	212-889-3950
Schumach, Michael P/159-10 Sanford Ave	718-539-5328
Scott, Louis Assoc/22 E 21st St	212-674-0215
Shapiro, Ellen Graphic Design/55 W 45th St	212-221-2625
Shareholder Graphics/6 E 46th St 2nd Fl	212-661-1070
Shareholders Reports/600 Third Ave 14th Fl	212-686-9099
Sherin & Matejka Inc/404 Park Ave S	212-686-8410
Sherowitz, Phyllis/310 E 46th St	212-532-8933
Shreeve, Draper Design/28 Perry St	212-675-7534
Siegel & Gale Inc/1185 Ave of Americas 8th Fl	212-730-0101
Siegel, Marion/87 E 2nd St #4A	212-460-9817
Silberlicht, Ira/210 W 70th St	212-595-6252
Silverman, Bob Design/304 E 49th St	212-371-6472
Singer, Paul Design/494 14th St	718-449-8172
Sloan, William/236 W 26th St #805	212-463-7025
Smith, Edward Design/1133 Broadway #1211	212-255-1717
Smith, Laura/12 E 14th St #4D	212-206-9162
Sobel, Phillip Eric/80-15 41st Ave	718-476-3841
Sochynsky, Ilona/200 E 36th St	212-686-1275
Solay/Hunt/28 W 44th St 21st Fl	212-840-3313
Sorvino, Skip/51 W 76th St #2B	212-580-9638
St Vincent Milone & McConnells/1156 Sixth Ave	212-921-1414
Stillman, Linda/1556 Third Ave	212-410-3225
Stuart, Gunn & Furuta/95 Madison Ave	212-689-0077
Studio 42/1466 Broadway	212-354-7298
Swatek and Romanoff Design Inc/156 Fifth Ave #1100	212-807-0236
Systems Collaborative Inc/52 Duane St	212-608-0584

T Tapa Graphics/174 Fifth Ave — 212-243-0176
Taurins Design Assoc/280 Madison Ave	212-679-5955
Tauss, Jack George/484 W 43rd St #40H	212-279-1658
Taylor & Ives/989 Sixth Ave	212-244-0750
Taylor, Stan Inc/6 E 39th St	212-685-4741
Teague, Walter Dorwin Assoc/711 Third Ave	212-557-0920
Tercovich, Douglas Assoc Inc/575 Madison Ave	212-838-4800
The Byrne Group/250 Fifth Ave	212-889-0502
The Design Office/38 E 23rd St	212-420-1722
The Lamplight Group/342 Madison Ave	212-682-6270
The Sukon Group, Inc/355 Lexington Ave 8th Fl	212-986-2290
The Whole Works/28 W 44th St	212-575-0765
Thompson Communications/1 Madison Ave 28th Fl	212-685-4400
Three/444 East 82nd St #12C	212-988-6267

Tobias, William/101 Fifth Ave 6th Fl	212-741-1712
Todd, Ann/317 W 87th St #PH	212-799-1016
Tower Graphics Arts Corp/575 Lexington Ave	212-421-0850
Tribich/Glasman Design/150 E 35th St	212-679-6016
Tscherny, George Design/238 E 72nd St	212-734-3277
Tunstull Studio/47 State St	718-834-8529

UV
Ultra Arts Inc/150 E 35th St	212-679-7493
Un, David/130 W 25th St	212-924-2090
Vecchio, Carmine/200 E 27th St #11K	212-683-2679
Viewpoint Graphics/10 Park Ave	212-685-0560
Visible Studio Inc/99 Lexington Ave	212-683-8530
Visual Accents Corp/30 Irving Pl	212-777-7766

W
Wajdowicz, Jurek/1123 Broadway	212-807-8144
Waldman, Veronica/115 E 9th St	212-260-3552
Waters, John Assoc Inc/3 W 18th St 8th Fl	212-807-0717
Waters, Pamela Studio Inc/320 W 13th St	212-620-8100
Webster, Robert Inc/331 Park Ave S	212-677-2966
Weed, Eunice Assoc Inc/370 Lexington Ave	212-725-4933
Whelan Design Office/144 W 27th St	212-691-4404
Wijtvliet, Ine/440 E 56th St	212-319-4444
Wilke, Jerry/18 W 27th St	212-689-2424
Wilson, Rex Co/330 Seventh Ave	212-594-3646
Withers, Bruce Graphic Design/236 E 46th St	212-599-2388
Wizard Graphics Inc/36 E 30th St	212-686-8200
Wolf, Henry Production Inc/167 E 73rd St	212-472-2500
Wolff, Rudi Inc/135 Central Park West	212-873-5800
Wood, Alan/274 Madison Ave #1202	212-889-5195
Word-Wise/325 W 45th St	212-246-0430
Works/45 W 27th St	212-696-1666

YZ
Yoshimura-Fisher Graphic Design/284 Lafayette St	212-431-4776
Young Goldman Young Inc/320 E 46th St	212-697-7820
Zahor & Bender/200 E 33rd St	212-686-1121
Zamchick, Gary/137 E 25th St Grnd Fl	212-608-3232
Zazula, Hy Inc/2 W 46th St	212-581-2747
Zeitsoff, Elaine/241 Central Park West	212-580-1282
Zimmerman & Foyster/22 E 21st St	212-674-0259
Zuzzolo Graphics/98-51 64th Ave #6C	718-896-7872

Northeast

A
Action Incentive/2 Townlake Cir, Rochester, NY	716-427-2410
Adam Filippo & Moran/1206 Fifth Ave, Pittsburgh, PA	412-261-3720
Adler-Schwartz Graphics/6 N Park Dr #107 Park Ctr, Hunt Valley, MD	301-628-0600
Advertising Design Assoc Inc/1220 Ridgley St, Baltimore, MD	301-752-2181
Anderson, Bill/27 Minkel Rd, Ossining, NY	914-762-4867
Another Color Inc/1439 Rhode Island Ave NW, Washington, DC	202-328-1414
Aries Graphics/Massabesic, Manchester, NH	603-668-0811
Arts and Words/1025 Conn Ave NW #300, Washington, DC	202-463-4880
Artwork Unlimited Inc/1411 K St NW, Washington, DC	202-638-6996
Autograph/616 Third St, Annapolis, MD	301-268-3300

B
Bachman Design Assoc/979 Summer St, Stamford, CT	203-325-9104
Baese, Gary/2229 N Charles St, Baltimore, MD	301-235-2226
Bain, S Milo/3 Shaw Lane, Hartsdale, NY	914-946-0144
Baker, Arthur/PO Box 29, Germantown, NY	518-537-4438
Baldwin, Jim/47 Warren St, Salem, MA	617-745-6462
Bally Design Inc/219 Park Rd, Carnegie, PA	412-621-9009
Banks & Co/607 Boylston St, Boston, MA	617-262-0020
Barancik, Bob/1919 Panama Ave, Philadelphia, PA	215-893-9149
Barton-Gillet/10 S Gay St, Baltimore, MD	301-685-6800
Bedford Photo-Graphic Studio/PO Box 64 Rt 22, Bedford, NY	914-234-3123
Belser, Burkey/1818 N St NW #110, Washington, DC	202-775-0333
Bennardo, Churik Design Inc/1311 Old Freeport Rd, Pittsburgh, PA	412-963-0133
Berns & Kay Ltd/1611 Connecticut Ave, Washington, DC	202-387-7032
Blum, William Assoc/210 Lincoln St, Boston, MA	617-232-1166
Bodzioch, Leon/59 Smith St, Chelmsford, MA	617-250-0265

Bogus, Sidney A & Assoc/22 Corey St, Melrose, MA	617-662-6660
Bomzer Design Inc/66 Canal St, Boston, MA	617-227-5151
Bookmakers/305 N Main St, Westport, CT	203-226-4293
Bowers, John/PO Box 101, RADnor, PA	215-688-5541
Bradbury, Robert & Assoc/26 Halsey Ln, Closter, NJ	201-768-6395
Brady, John Design Consultants/130 7th St, Century Bldg, Pittsburgh, PA	412-288-9300
Breckenridge Designs/2025 I St NW #300, Washington, DC	202-833-5700
Breiner, Joanne/11 Webster St, Medford, MA	617-354-8378
Bressler, Peter Design Assoc/301 Cherry St, Philadelphia, PA	215-925-7100
Bridy, Dan/119 First Ave, Pittsburgh, PA	412-288-9362
Brier, David/51 Prospect Terrace, E Rutherford, NJ	201-896-8476
Brown and Craig Inc/407 N Charles St, Baltimore, MD	301-837-2727
Bruno, Peggy/51 Grove St, Marshfield, MA	617-837-6896
Buckett, Bill Assoc/137 Gibbs St, Rochester, NY	716-546-6580
Byrne, Ford/100 N 20th St, Philadelphia, PA	215-564-0500

C
Cable, Jerry Design/29 Station Rd, Madison, NJ	201-966-0124
Calingo, Diane/3711 Lawrence Ave, Kensington, MD	301-949-3557
Cameron Inc/9 Appleton St, Boston, MA	617-338-4408
Campbell Harrington & Brear/352 W Market St, York, PA	717-846-2947
Carlson, Tim/4 Davis Ct, Brookline, MA	617-566-7330
Carmel, Abraham/7 Peter Beet Dr, Peekskill, NY	914-737-1439
Cascio, Chris/456 Glenbrook Rd, Stamford, CT	203-358-0519
Case/11 Dupont Circle NW #400, Washington, DC	202-328-5900
Casey Mease Inc/917 N Washington St, Wilmington, DE	302-655-2100
Chaparos Productions Limited/1112 6th St NW, Washington, DC	202-289-4838
Charysyn & Charysyn/Route 42, Westkill, NY	518-989-6720
Chase, David O Design Inc/E Genesee St, Skaneateles, NY	315-685-5715
Chronicle Type & Design/1333 New Hampshire Ave NW, Washington, DC	202-828-3519
Clark, Dave/112 Main St #303, Annapolis, MD	301-269-1856
Cleary Design/118-A N Division St, Salisbury, MD	301-546-1040
Cliggett, Jack/703 Redwood Ave, Yeadon, PA	215-623-1606
Colangelo, Ted Assoc/340 Pemberwick Rd (The Mill), Greenwich, CT	203-531-3600
Colopy Dale Inc/850 Ridge Ave, Pittsburgh, PA	412-332-6706
Communications Graphics Group/3717 Columbia Pike #211, Arlington, VA	703-979-8500
Concept Packaging Inc/5 Horizon Rd, Ft Lee, NJ	201-224-5762
Consolidated Visual Center Inc/2529 Kenilworth Ave, Tuxedo, MD	301-772-7300
Cook & Shanosky Assoc/103 Carnegie Ctr #203, Princeton, NJ	609-452-1666
Corcetto, Tony/RD 1 Box 300, Reinholds, PA	215-678-0866
Corey & Company/, Boston, MA	617-266-1850
Creative Presentations Inc/1221 Massachusetts Ave NW, Washington, DC	202-737-7152
Crozier, Bob & Assoc/1201 Pennsylvania Ave NW, Washington, DC	202-638-7134
Curran & Connors Inc/333 Jericho Tpke, Jericho, NY	516-433-6600

D
D'Art Studio Inc/176 Federal #518, Boston, MA	617-482-4442
Dakota Design/Rte 363, Leighton Bldg, King of Prussia, PA	215-265-1255
Dale, Terry/2824 Hurst Terrace NW, Washington, DC	202-244-3866
Dawson Designers Associates/21 Dean St, Assonet, MA	617-644-2940
DeCesare, John/1091 Post Rd, Darien, CT	203-655-6057
DeMartin-Marona-Cranstoun-Downes/911 Washington St, Wilmington, DE	302-654-5277
Dean, Jane/13 N Duke St, Lancaster, PA	717-295-4638
Design Associates/1601 Kent St #1010, Arlington, VA	703-243-7717
Design Center Inc/210 Lincoln St #408, Boston, MA	617-542-1254
Design Communication Collaboration/1346 Connecticut Ave NW, Washington, DC	202-833-9087
Design Group of Boston/437 Boylston St, Boston, MA	617-437-1084
Design Technology Corp/5 Suburban Park Dr, Billerica, MA	617-272-8890
Design Trends/4 Broadway PO Box 119, Valhalla, NY	914-948-0902
Design for Medicine Inc/301 Cherry St, Philadelphia, PA	215-925-7100
Designworks Inc/5 Bridge St, Watertown, MA	617-926-6286
DiFiore Associates/625 Stanwix St #2507, Pittsburgh, PA	412-471-0608
Dimmick, Gary/47 Riverview Ave, Pittsburgh, PA	412-321-7225

Graphic Design
Continued

Please send us your additions and updates.

Dohanos, Steven/271 Sturges Highway, Westport, CT	203-227-3541
Downing, Allan/50 Francis St, Needham, MA	617-449-4784
Duffy, Bill & Assoc/3286 M Street NW, Washington, DC	202-965-2216

EF
Edigraph Inc/45 Cantitoe St, RFD 1, Katonah, NY	914-232-3725
Educational Media/Graphics Division/GU Med Ctr 3900 Reservoir Rd, Washington, DC	202-625-2211
Egress Concepts/20 Woods Bridge Rd, Katonah, NY	914-232-8433
Erickson, Peter/147 Main St, Maynard, MA	617-369-8060
Eucalyptus Tree Studio/2220 N Charles St, Baltimore, MD	301-243-0211
Evans Garber & Paige/2631 Genesee St, Utica, NY	315-733-2313
Fader Jones & Zarkades/797 Boylston St, Boston, MA	617-267-7779
Falcone & Assoc/13 Watchung Ave Box 637, Chatham, NJ	201-635-2900
Fannell Studio/8 Newbury St, Boston, MA	617-267-0895
Fink Graphics/11 W 25th St, Baltimore, MD	301-366-1540
Finnin, Teresa/655 Washington Blvd #602, Stamford, CT	203-348-4104
Forum Inc/1226 Post Rd, Fairfield, CT	203-259-5686
Fossella, Gregory Assoc/479 Commonwealth Ave, Boston, MA	617-267-4940
Fraser, Robert & Assoc Inc/1101 N Calvert St, Baltimore, MD	301-685-3700
Fresh Produce/1307 Warwick Dr, Lutherville, MD	301-821-1815
Froelich Advertising Service/8 Wanamaker Ave, Mahwah, NJ	201-529-1737
Frohman, Al/2277 4th St, East Meadow, NY	516-735-2771

G
GK+D Communications/2311 Calvert St NW #300, Washington, DC	202-328-0414
Gasser, Gene/300 Main St, Chatham, NJ	201-635-6020
Gateway Studios/225 Ross St, Pittsburgh, PA	412-471-7224
Gatter Inc/68 Purchase St, Rye, NY	914-967-5600
Genesis Design/360 Pleasnt St, Ashland, MA	617-881-2471
Glass, Al/3312 M St NW, Washington, DC	202-333-3993
Glenn, Raymond/39 Edgerton Rd, Wallinford, CT	203-269-5643
Glickman, Frank Inc/180 Mosshill Rd, Boston, MA	617-524-2200
Goldner, Linda/709 Rittenhouse Savoy, Philadelphia, PA	215-735-8370
Good, Peter Graphic Design/Pequot Press Bldg, Chester, CT	203-526-9597
Gorelick, Alan & Assoc/1 High St #3B, Morristown, NJ	201-898-1991
Graham Associates Inc/1899 L St NW, Washington, DC	202-833-9657
Grant Marketing Assoc./1100 E Hector St, Conshohocken, PA	215-834-0550
Graphic Workshop/466 Old Hook Rd, Emerson, NJ	201-967-8500
Graphicenter/1101 2nd St NE, Washington, DC	202-544-0333
Graphics By Gallo/1800-B Swann St NW, Washington, DC	202-234-7700
Graphics Plus Corp/198 Ferry St, St Malden, MA	617-321-7500
Graphicus Corp/2025 Maryland Ave, Baltimore, MD	301-727-5553
Graves Fowler & Assoc/14532 Carona Dr, Silver Spring, MD	301-236-9808
Grear, Malcolm Designers Inc/391 Eddy St, Providence, RI	401-331-5656
Green, Mel/31 Thorpe Rd, Needham Hts, MA	617-449-6777
Greenebaum Design/86 Walnut St, Natick, MA	617-655-8146
Greenfield, Peggy/2 Lewis Rd, Foxboro, MA	617-543-6644
Gregory & Clyburne/59 Grove St, New Canaan, CT	203-966-8343
Groff, Jay Michael/515 Silver Spring Ave, Silver Spring, MD	301-565-0431
Group Four Design/PO Box 717, Avon, CT	203-678-1570
Gunn Associates/275 Newbury St, Boston, MA	617-267-0618

H
Hain, Robert Assoc/346 Park Ave, Scotch Plains, NJ	201-322-1717
Hammond Design Assoc/35 Amherst St, Milford, NH	603-673-5253
Harrington-Jackson/10 Newbury St, Boston, MA	617-536-6164
Harvey, Ed/PO Box 23755, Washington, DC	703-671-0880
Hegemann Associates/One S Franklin St, Nyack, NY	914-358-7348
Herbick & Held/1117 Wolfendale St, Pittsburgh, PA	412-321-7400
Herbst Lazar Rogers & Bell Inc/10 N Market St #406, Lancaster, PA	717-291-9042
Herman & Lees/930 Massachusetts Ave, Cambridge, MA	617-876-6463
Hill, Michael/828 Park Ave, Baltimore, MD	301-728-8767
Hillmuth, James/3613 Norton Pl, Washington, DC	202-244-0465
Holl, RJ/ Art Directions/McBride Rd, Wales, MA	413-267-5024
Holloway, Martin/56 Mt Horeb Rd, Plainfield, NJ	201-563-0169
Hough, Jack Inc/25 Seirhill Rd, Norwalk, CT	203-846-2666
Hrivnak, James/10822 Childs Ct, Silver Spring, MD	301-681-9090
Huerta, Gerard/45 Corbin Dr, Darien, CT	203-656-0505
Huyysen, Roger/45 Corbin Dr, Darien, CT	203-656-0200

IJ
Image Consultants/3 Overlook Dr, Amherst, NH	603-673-5512
Innovations & Development Inc/115 River Rd, Edgewater, NJ	201-941-5500

Irish, Gary Graphics/45 Newbury St, Boston, MA	617-247-4168
Itin, Marcel/Visual Concepts/100 Cutler Rd, Greenwich, CT	203-869-1928
Jaeger Design Studio/2025 I St NW, Washington, DC	202-785-8434
Jarrin Design Inc/PO Box 421, Pound Ridge, NY	914-764-4625
Jensen, R S/819 N Charles St, Baltimore, MD	301-727-3411
Jezierny, John Michael/20 Kenter Pl, Westville, CT	203-689-8170
Johnson & Simpson Graphic Design/49 Bleeker St, Newark, NJ	201-624-7788
Johnson Design Assoc/403 Massachusetts Ave, Acton, MA	617-263-5345
Jones, Tom & Jane Kearns/2803 18th ST NW, Washington, DC	202-232-1921

K
KBH Graphics/1023 St Paul Street, Baltimore, MD	301-539-7916
Kahana Associates/419 Benjamin #A Fox Pavilion, Jenkintown, PA	215-887-0422
Karp, Rudi/28 Dudley Ave, Landsowne, PA	215-284-5949
Katz-Wheeler Design/37 S 20th St, Philadelphia, PA	215-567-5668
Kaufman, Henry J & Assoc Inc/2233 Wisconsin Ave NW, Washington, DC	202-333-0700
Kell & Co/110 Fidler Ln #1400, Silver Spring, MD	202-585-4000
Ketchum International/4 Gateway Ctr, Pittsburgh, PA	412-456-3693
King-Casey Inc/199 Elm St, New Canaan, CT	203-966-3581
Klim, Matt & Assoc/PO Box Y, Avon Park N, Avon, CT	203-678-1222
Klotz, Don/296 Millstone Rd, Wilton, CT	203-762-9111
Knabel, Lonnie/34 Station St, Brookline, MA	617-566-4464
Knox, Harry & Assoc/1312 18th St NW, Washington, DC	202-833-2305
Konoda Assoc/PO Box 837, New Bradford, CT	
Kostanecki, Andrew Inc/47 Elm St, New Canaan, CT	203-966-1681
Kovanen, Erik/102 Twin Oak Lane, Wilton, CT	203-762-8961
Kramer/Miller/Lomden/Glossman/1528 Waverly, Philadelphia, PA	215-545-7077
Krohne, David/2727 29th St NW, Washington, DC	202-265-2371
Krone Graphic Design/426 S 3rd St, Lemoyne, PA	717-774-7431
Krueger Wright Design/106 Bromfield Rd, Somerville, MA	617-666-4880

L
LAM Design Inc/661 N Broadway, White Plains, NY	914-948-4777
Landersman, Myra/PO Box 346, Malaga, NJ	609-694-1011
Langdon, John/106 S Marion Ave, Wenonah, NJ	609-468-7868
Lapham/Miller Assoc/34 Essex St, Andora, MA	617-367-0110
Latham Brefka Associates/833 Boylston St, Boston, MA	617-536-8787
Lausch, David Graphics/2613 Maryland Ave, Baltimore, MD	301-235-7453
Lebowitz, Mo/2599 Phyllis Dr, N Bellemore, NY	516-826-3397
Leeds, Judith K Studio/14 Rosemont Ct, N Caldwell, NJ	201-226-3552
Lenney, Ann/2737 Devonshire Pl NW, Washington, DC	202-667-1786
Leotta Designers Inc/303 Harry St, Conshohocken, PA	215-828-8820
Lester Associates Inc/100 Snake Hill Rd Box D, West Nyack, NY	914-358-6100
Levinson Zaprauskis Assoc/15 W Highland Ave, Philadelphia, PA	215-248-5242
Lewis, Hal Design/104 S 20th St, Philadelphia, PA	215-563-4461
Lion Hill Studio/1233 W Mt Royal Ave, Baltimore, MD	301-837-6218
Livingston Studio/29 Robbins Ave, Elmsford, NY	914-592-4220
Lizak, Matt/Blackplain Rd RD #1, N Smithfield, RI	401-766-8885
Logan, Denise/203 Rugby Ave, Rochester, NY	716-235-0893
Lose, Hal/533 W Hortter St, Philadelphia, PA	215-849-7635
Loukin, Serge Inc/PO Box 425, Solomons, MD	212-645-2788
Luebbers Inc/2300 Walnut St #732, Philadelphia, PA	215-567-2360
Luma/702 N Eutaw St, Baltimore, MD	301-523-5903
Lussier, Mark/21 First St, E Norwalk, CT	203-852-0363

M
MDB Communications Inc/932 Hungerford Dr #23, Rockville, MD	301-279-9093
MacIntosh, Rob Communication/93 Massachusetts, Boston, MA	617-267-4912
Maglio, Mark/PO Box 872, Plainville, CT	203-793-0771
Major Assoc/1101 N Calvert #1703, Baltimore, MD	301-752-6174
Mandala/520 S Third St, Philadelphia, PA	215-923-6020
Mandle, James/300 Forest Ave, Paramus, NJ	201-967-7900
Mansfield, Malcom/20 Aberdeen St, Boston, MA	617-437-1922
Marcus, Sarna/4720 Montgomery Ln #903, Bethesda, MD	301-951-7044
Mariuzza, Pete/146 Hardscrabble Rd, Briarcliff Manor, NY	914-769-3310
Mark Color Studios/7677 Canton Center Dr, Baltimore, MD	301-282-5980
Martucci Studio/116 Newbury St, Boston, MA	617-266-6960

Graphic Design

Continued

Please send us your additions and updates.

Mason, Kim/1301 Delaware Ave SW, Washington, DC	202-646-0118
Media Concepts/14 Newbury St, Boston, MA	617-437-1382
Media Loft/7200 France Ave, Minneapolis, MN	612-831-0226
Melanson, Donya Assoc/437 Main St, Charlestown, MA	617-241-7300
Melone, Michael/RD 3 Box 123, Canonsburg, PA	412-746-5165
Micolucci, Nicholas Assoc/515 Schumaker Rd, King of Prussia, PA	215-265-3320
Miho, J Inc/46 Chalburn Rd, Redding, CT	203-938-3214
Millbergs, Aida/2901 18th St NW #615, Washington, DC	202-387-4172
Mitchell & Company/1029 33rd St NW, Washington, DC	202-342-6025
Monti, Ron/106 W University, Baltimore, MD	301-366-8952
Morlock Graphics/7400 York Rd, Towson, MD	301-825-5080
Moss, John C/4805 Bayard Blvd, Chevy Chase, MD	301-320-3912
Mossman Art Studio/2514 N Charles St, Baltimore, MD	301-243-1963
Mueller & Wister/1211 Chestnut St #607, Philadelphia, PA	215-568-7260
Muller-Munk, Peter Assoc/2100 Smallman St, Pittsburgh, PA	412-261-5161
Murphy, Martha/8 August Ave, Baltimore, MD	301-747-4555
Myers, Gene Assoc/5575 Hampton, Pittsburgh, PA	412-661-6314

N

Nason Design Assoc/329 Newbury, Boston, MA	617-266-7286
Navratil Art Studio/905 Century Bldg, Pittsburgh, PA	412-471-4322
Nimeck, Fran/RD #4, 358 Riva Ave #A, South Brunswick, NJ	201-821-8741
Noi-Viva Design/220 Ferris Ave, White Plains, NY	914-946-1950
Nolan & Assoc/4100 Cathedral Ave NW, Washington, DC	202-363-6553
North Charles St Design/222 W Saratoga St, Baltimore, MD	301-539-4040

OP

Odyssey Design Group/918 F St NW, Washington, DC	202-783-6240
Ollio Studio/Fulton Bldg, Pittsburgh, PA	412-281-4483
Omnigraphics/19 Mt Auburn St, Cambridge, MA	617-354-7444
On Target/1185 E Putnam Ave, Riverside, CT	203-637-8300
Paganucci, Bob/17 Terry Ct, Montvale, NJ	201-391-1752
Paine/ Bluett/ Paine Inc/4617 Edgefield Rd, Bethesda, MD	301-493-8445
Papazian Design/224 Clarendon St, Boston, MA	617-262-7848
Parks, Franz & Cox, Inc/2425 18th St NW, Washington, DC	202-797-7568
Parry, Ivor A/4 Lorraine Dr, Eastchester, NY	914-961-7338
Parshall, C A Inc/200 Henry St, Stamford, CT	212-947-5971
Pasinski, Irene Assoc/4951 Centre Ave, Pittsburgh, PA	412-683-0585
Patazian Design Inc/224 Clarendon St, Boston, MA	617-262-7848
Peck, Gail M/1637 Harvard St NW, Washington, DC	202-667-7448
Pentick, Joseph/RD 4 Box 231, Kingston, NY	914-331-8197
Perry, Ivor/Eastchester, NY,	914-961-7338
Perspectives In Communications/1637 Harvard St NW, Washington, DC	202-667-7448
Pesanelli, David Assoc/4301 Connecticut Ave NW, Washington, DC	202-363-4760
Petty, Daphne/1460 Belmont St NW, Washington, DC	202-667-8222
Phase One Graphics/315 Market St, Sudbury, PA	717-286-1111
Phillips Design Assoc/25 Dry Dock Ave, Boston, MA	617-423-7676
Picture That Inc/880 Briarwood Rd, Newtown Square, PA	215-353-8833
Pinkston, Steve/24 N New St 2nd Fl, West Chester, PA	215-692-2939
Planert, Paul Design Assoc/4650 Baum Blvd, Pittsburgh, PA	412-621-1275
Plataz, George/516 Martin Bldg, Pittsburgh, PA	412-322-3177
Porter, Al/Graphics Inc/5431 Connecticut Ave NW, Washington, DC	202-244-0403
Porter, Eric/37 S 20th St, Philadelphia, PA	215-563-1904
Porter, John/7056 Carroll Ave, Takoma Park, MD	301-270-8990
Presentation Associates/1346 Connecticut Ave NW, Washington, DC	202-333-0080
Production Studio/382 Channel Dr, Port Washington, NY	516-944-6688
Profile Press Inc/40 Greenwood Ave, E Islip, NY	516-277-6319
Prokell, Jim/307 4th Ave #200, Pittsburgh, PA	412-232-3636
Publication Services Inc/990 Hope St, PO Box 4625, Stamford, CT	203-348-7351

R

RKM Inc/5307 29th St NW, Washington, DC	202-364-0148
RSV/437 Boylston St, Boston, MA	617-262-9450
RZA Inc/122 Mill Pond Rd, Park Ridge, NJ	201-391-8500
Rajcula, Vincent/176 Long MEadow Hill, Brookfield, CT	203-775-2420
Ralcon Inc/431 W Market St, West Chester, PA	215-692-2840
Rand, Paul Inc/87 Goodhill Rd, Weston, CT	203-227-5375
Redtree Associates/1740 N St NW, Washington, DC	202-628-2900
Renaissance Communications/7835 Eastern Ave, Silver	

Spring, MD	301-587-1505
Research Planning Assoc/1831 Chestnut St, Philadelphia, PA	215-561-9700
Richardson/Smith/139 Lewis Wharf, Boston, MA	617-367-1491
Richman, Mel/15 N Presidential Blvd, Bala Cynwyd, PA	215-667-8900
Rieb, Robert/10 Reichert Circle, Westport, CT	203-227-0061
Ringel, Leonard Design/18 Wheeler Rd, Kendall Park, NJ	201-297-9084
Ritter, Richard Design Inc/31 Waterloo Ave, Berwyn, PA	215-296-0400
Ritzau van Dijk Design/7 Hart Ave, Hopewell, NJ	609-466-2797
Rogalski Assoc/186 Lincoln St, Boston, MA	617-451-2111
Romax Studio/32 Club Circle, Stamford, CT	203-324-4260
Rosborg Inc/15 Commerce Rd, Newton, CT	203-426-3171
Roth, J H Inc/13 Inwood Ln E, Peekskill, NY	914-737-6784
Roth, Judee/103 Cornelia St, Boonton, NJ	201-316-5411
Rubin, Marc Design Assoc/PO Box 440, Breesport, NY	607-739-0871

S

Sanchez/138 S 20th St, Philadelphia, PA	215-564-2223
Schneider Design/2633 N Charles St, Baltimore, MD	301-467-2611
Schoenfeld, Cal/6 Colony Ct #B, Parsippany, NJ	201-263-1635
Schrecongost, Paul/284 Liberty St, Salem, WV	304-782-3499
Selame Design Associates/2330 Washington St, Newton Lower Falls, MA	617-969-6690
Shapiro, Deborah/150 Bentley Ave, Jersey City, NJ	201-432-5198
Silvia, Ken/15 Story St, Cambridge, MA	617-451-1995
Simpson Booth Designers/14 Arrow St, Cambridge, MA	617-661-2630
Smarilli Graphics Inc/602 N front St, Warmleysburg, PA	717-737-8141
Smith, Agnew Moyer/850 Ridge Ave, Pittsburgh, PA	412-322-6333
Smith, Doug/17 Althea Lane, Larchmont, NY	914-834-3997
Smith, Gail Hunter/PO Box 217, Barnegat Light, NJ	609-494-9136
Smith, Tyler Art Direction/127 Dorrance St, Providence, RI	401-751-1220
Smizer Design/59 Wareham St, Boston, MA	617-423-3350
Snowden Associates Inc/5217 Wisconsin Ave NW, Washington, DC	202-362-8944
Soree, Sal/97 Forest Hill Rd, W Orange, NJ	201-325-3591
Sparkman & Bartholomew/1144 18th St NW, Washington, DC	202-785-2414
Spectrum Boston/79-A Chestnut St, Boston, MA	617-367-1008
Stansbury Ronsaville Wood Inc/17 Pinewood St, Annapolis, MD	301-261-8662
Star Design Inc/PO Box 30, Moorestown, NJ	609-235-8150
Steel Art Co Inc/75 Brainerd Rd, Allston, MA	617-566-4079
Stettler, Wayne Design/2311 Fairmount Ave, Philadelphia, PA	215-235-1230
Stockman & Andrews Inc/684 Warren Ave, E Providence, RI	401-438-0694
Stolt, Jill Design/1239 University Ave, Rochester, NY	716-461-2594
Stuart, Neil/RD 1 Box 64, Mahopac, NY	914-618-1662
Studio Six Design/6 Lynn Dr, Springfield, NJ	201-379-5820
Studio Three/1617 J F Kennedy Blvd, Philadelphia, PA	215-925-4700

T

Takajian, Asdur/17 Merlin Ave, N Tarrytown, NY	914-631-5553
Taylor, Pat/3540 'S' St NW, Washington, DC	202-338-0962
Telesis/107 E 25th, Baltimore, MD	301-235-2000
Tetrad Inc/309 Third St, Annapolis, MD	301-268-8680
The Artery/12 W Biddle St, Baltimore, MD	301-752-2979
The Avit Corp/799 Abbott Blvd, Fort Lee, NJ	201-886-1100
The Creative Dept/130 S 17th, Philadelphia, PA	215-988-0390
The Graphic Suite/235 Shady Ave, Pittsburgh, PA	412-661-6699
The Peregrine Group/375 Sylvan Ave, Englewood Cliffs, NJ	201-567-8585
The Studio Group/1713 Lanier Pl NW, Washington, DC	202-332-3003
The Visualizers/1100 E Carson St, Pittsburgh, PA	412-488-0944
Theoharides Inc/303 South Broadway, Tarrytown, NY	914-631-5363
Thompson, Bradbury/Jones Park, Riverside, CT	203-637-3614
Thompson, George L/603 Main St, Reading, MA	617-944-6256
Toelke, Cathleen/16 Tremont St, Boston, MA	617-242-7414
Torode, Barbara/2311 Lombard St, Philadelphia, PA	215-732-6792
Total Collateral Grp/992 Old Eagles School Rd, Wayne, PA	215-687-8016
Town Studios Inc/212 9th St Victory Bldg, Pittsburgh, PA	412-471-5353
Troller, Fred Assoc Inc/12 Harbor Ln, Rye, NY	914-698-1405

V

Van Der Sluys Graphics /3303 18th St NW, Washington, DC	202-265-3443
VanDine, Horton, McNamara, Manges Inc/100 Ross St, Pittsburgh, PA	412-261-4280
Vance Wright Adams & Assoc/930 N Lincoln Ave, Pittsburgh, PA	412-322-1800
Vann, Bob/5306 Knox St, Philadelphia, PA	215-843-4841

Vinick, Bernard Assoc Inc/211 Wethersfield Ave, Hartford, CT	203-525-4293
Viscom Inc/PO Box 10498, Baltimore, MD	301-764-0005
Visual Research & Design Corp/360 Commonwealth Ave, Boston, MA	617-536-2111

WYZ

Warkulwiz Design/1704 Locust St, Philadelphia, PA	215-546-0880
Wasserman's, Myron Graphic Design Group/113 Arch St, Philadelphia, PA	215-922-4545
Weadock, Rutka/1627 E Baltimore St, Baltimore, MD	301-563-2100
Webb & Co/839 Beacon St, Boston, MA	617-262-6980
Weymouth Design/234 Congress St, Boston, MA	617-542-2647
White, E James Co/5750 B General Washington Dr, Alexandria, VA	703-750-3680
Wickham & Assoc Inc/1133 15 St, NW, Washington, DC	202-296-4860
Willard, Janet Design Assoc/4284 Route 8, Allison Park, PA	412-486-8100
Williams Associates/200 Broadway #206, Lynnfield, MA	617-599-1818
Wilsonwork Graphic Design/1811 18th St NW, Washington, DC	202-332-9016
Winick, Sherwin/115 Willow Ave #2R, Hoboken, NJ	201-659-9116
Wood, William/68 Windsor Pl, Glen Ridge, NJ	201-743-5543
Wright, Kent M Assoc Inc/22 Union Ave, Sudbury, MA	617-443-9909
Yeo, Robert/746 Park Ave, Hoboken, NJ	201-659-3277
Yurdin, Carl Industrial Design Inc/2 Harborview Rd, Port Washington, NY	516-944-7811
Zeb Graphics/1312 18th St NW, Washington, DC	202-293-1687
Zmiejko & Assoc Design Agcy/PO Box 126, Freeland, PA	717-636-2304

Southeast

A

Ace Art/171 Walnut St, New Orleans, LA	504-861-2222
Alphabet Group/1441 Peachtree NE, Atlanta, GA	404-892-6500
Alphacom Inc/14955 NE Sixth Ave, N Miami, FL	305-949-5588
Art Services/1135 Spring St, Atlanta, GA	404-892-2105
Arts & Graphics/4010 Justine Dr, Annandale, VA	703-941-2560
Arunski, Joe & Assoc/8600 SW 86th Ave, Miami, FL	305-271-8300
Aurelio & Friends Inc/11110 SW 128th Ave, Miami, FL	305-385-0723

B

Baskin & Assoc/1021 Prince St, Alexandria, VA	703-836-3316
Bender, Diane/2729 S Cleveland St, Arlington, VA	703-521-1006
Beveridge and Associates, Inc/2020 N 14th St #444, Arlington, VA	202-243-2888
Blair Incorporated/5819 Seminary Rd, Bailey's Crossroads, VA	703-820-9011
Bodenhamer, William S Inc/7380 SW 121st St, Miami, FL	305-253-9284
Bonner Advertising Art/1315 Washington Ave, New Orleans, LA	504-895-7938
Bono Mitchell Graphics/2118 N Oakland St, Arlington, VA	703-276-0612
Bowles, Aaron/1686 Sierra Woods Ct, Reston, VA	703-471-4019
Brimm, Edward & Assoc/140 S Ocean Blvd, Palm Beach, FL	305-655-1059
Brothers Bogusky/11950 W Dixie Hwy, Miami, FL	305-891-3642
Bugdal Group/7227 NW 7th St, Miami, FL	305-264-1860
Burch, Dan Associates/2338 Frankfort, Louisville, KY	502-895-4881

C

Carlson Design/1218 NW 6th St, Gainesville, FL	904-373-3153
Chartmasters Inc/3525 Piedmont,7 Pdmt Ctr, Atlanta, GA	404-262-7610
Clavena, Barbara/6000 Stone Lake, Birgmingham, AL	205-991-8909
Cooper-Copeland Inc/1151 W Peachtree St NW, Atlanta, GA	404-892-3472
Corporate Design/Plaza Level-Colony Sq, Atlanta, GA	404-876-6062
Creative Design Assoc/9330 Silver Thorn Rd, Lake Park, FL	305-627-2467
Creative Services Inc/2317 Esplanade St, New Orleans, LA	504-943-0842
Creative Services Unlimited/3080 N Tamiami Tr #3, Naples, FL	813-262-0201
Creative Technologies Inc/7630 Little River Tnpk, Annandale, VA	703-256-7444
Critt Graham & Assoc/1190 W Orvid Hills Dr #T45, Atlanta, GA	404-320-1737

D

Design Alliance/2914 Lenox Rd #2, Atlanta, GA	
Design Consultants Inc/301 Park Ave, Falls Church, VA	703-241-2323
Design Inc/9304 St Marks Pl, Fairfax, VA	703-273-5053
Design Workshop Inc/9791 NW 91st Ct, Miami, FL	305-884-6300
Designcomp/202 Dominion Rd NE, Vienna, VA	703-938-1822
Dodane, Eric/8525 Richland Colony Rd, Knoxville, TN	615-693-6857

EF

Emig, Paul E/3900 N 5th St, Arlington, VA	703-522-5926
Ferris, Dianne/10732 NW 40th St, Sunrise, FL	
First Impressions/4411 W Tampa Bay Blvd, Tampa, FL	813-875-0555
Foster, Kim A/1801 SW 11th St, Miami, FL	305-642-1801
From Us Advertising & Design/273 Connecticut Ave NE, Atlanta, GA	404-373-0373

G

Gerbino Advertising Inc/2000 W Commercial Blvd, Ft Lauderdale, FL	305-776-5050
Gestalt Associates, Inc/1509 King St, Alexandria, VA	703-683-1126
Get Graphic Inc/160 Maple Ave E #201, Vienna, VA	202-938-1822
Graphic Arts Inc/1433 Powhatan St, Alexandria, VA	703-683-4303
Graphic Consultants Inc/5133 Lee Hwy, Arlington, VA	703-536-8377
Graphics Group/6111 PchtreeDunwdy Rd#G101, Atlanta, GA	404-391-9929
Graphicstudio/12305 NE 12th Ct, N Miami, FL	305-893-1015
Graphix Inc/2675 Paces Ferry Rd, Atlanta, GA	
Great Incorporated/601 Madison St, Alexandria, VA	703-836-6020
Gregg, Bill Advertising Design/2465 SW 18th Ave A-3309, Miami, FL	305-854-7657
Group 2 Atlanta/3500 Piedmont Rd, Atlanta, GA	404-262-3239

H

Haikalis, Stephanie/3310 Coryell Ln, Alexandria, VA	703-998-8695
Hall Graphics/2600 Douglas Rd #608, Coral Gables, FL	305-443-8346
Hall, Stephen Design Office/535 Louisville Galleria, Louisville, KY	502-458-2200
Hannau, Michael Ent. Inc/950 SE 8th St, Hialeah, FL	305-887-1536
Hauser, Sydney/9 Fillmore Dr, Sarasota, FL	813-388-3021
Helms, John Graphic Design/4191 Cottonwood, Memphis, TN	901-363-6589

IJ

Identitia Incorporated/1000 N Ashley Dr #515, Tampa, FL	813-221-3326
Jensen, Rupert & Assoc Inc/1800 Peachtree Rd #525, Atlanta, GA	404-352-1010
Johnson Design Group Inc/3426 N Washington Blvd #102, Arlington, VA	703-525-0808
Johnson, Charlotte/1614 N Cleveland St, Arlington, VA	202-544-7936
Jordan Barrett & Assoc/6701 Sunset Dr, Miami, FL	305-667-7051

KL

Kelly & Co Graphic Design Inc/4639 Lown St N, St Petersburg, FL	813-526-1009
Ketchum, Barbara/3948 Browning Pl #200, Raleigh, NC	919-782-4599
Kjeldsen, Howard Assoc Inc/PO Box 420508, Atlanta, GA	404-266-1897
Klickovich Graphics/1638 Eastern Parkway, Louisville, KY	502-459-0295
Lowell, Shelley Design/1449 Bates Ct NE, Atlanta, GA	404-636-9149

M

Marks, David/726 Hillpine Dr NE, Atlanta, GA	404-872-1824
Maxine, J & Martin Advertising/1497 Chain Bridge Rd #204, McLean, VA	703-356-5222
McGurren Weber Ink/705 King St 3rd Fl, Alexandria, VA	703-548-0003
MediaFour Inc/7638 Trail Run Rd, Falls Church, VA	703-573-6117
Michael, Richard S/4722 Old Kingston Pike, Knoxville, TN	615-584-3319
Miller, Hugh K/2473 John Young Pkwy, Orlando, FL	305-293-8220
Moore, William "Casey"/4242 Inverness Rd, Duluth, GA	404-449-9553
Morgan-Burchette Assoc/1020 N Fairfax St, Alexandria, VA	703-549-2393
Morris, Robert Assoc Inc/6015 B NW 31 Ave, Ft Lauderdale, FL	305-973-4380
Muhlhausen, John Design Inc/1146 Green St, Roswell, GA	404-642-1146

P

PL&P Advertising Studio/1500 NW 62nd St #202, Ft Lauderdale, FL	305-776-6505
PRB Design Studio/1900 Howell Brnch Rd #3, Winter Park, FL	305-671-7992
Parallel Group Inc/3091 Maple Dr, Atlanta, GA	404-261-0988
Pertuit, Jim & Assoc Inc/302 Magazine St #400, New Orleans, LA	504-568-0808
Platt, Don Advertising Art/1399 SE 9th Ave, Hialeah, FL	305-888-3296
Point 6/770 40th Court NE, Ft Lauderdale, FL	305-563-6939
Polizos, Arthur Assoc/220 W Freemason St, Norfolk, VA	804-622-7033
Positively Main St Graphics/290 Coconut Ave, Sarasota, FL	813-366-4959
Pre-Press Studio Design/1105N Royal St, Alexandria, VA	703-548-9194
Prep Inc/2615-B Shirlington Rd, Arlington, VA	703-979-6575
Price Weber Market Comm Inc/2101 Production Dr, Louisville, KY	502-499-9220
Promotion Graphics Inc/12787 W Dixie Hwy, N Miami, FL	305-891-3941

QR

Quantum Communications/1730 N Lynn St, Arlington, VA	703-841-1400

Rasor & Rasor/1145-D Executive Cir, Cary, NC	919-467-3353
Rebeiz, Kathryn Dereki/526 Druid Hill Rd, Vienna, VA	703-938-9779
Reinsch, Michael/32 Palmetto Bay Rd, Hilton Head Island, SC	803-842-3298
Revelations Studios/3100 Clay Ave #287, Orlando, Fl32804	305-896-4240
Richardson, Hank/2675 Paces Ferry Rd #225, Atlanta, GA	404-433-0973
Rodriguez, Emilio Jr/8270 SW 116 Terrace, Miami, FL	305-235-4700

S

Sager Assoc Inc/739 S Orange Ave, Sarasota, FL	813-366-4192
Salmon, Paul/5826 Jackson's Oak Ct, Burke, VA	703-250-4943
Santa & Assoc/3960 N Andrews Ave, Ft Lauderdale, FL	305-561-0551
Schulwolf, Frank/524 Hardee Rd, Coral Gables, FL	305-665-2129
Showcraft Designworks/603 Pinellas, Clearwater, FL	813-586-0061
Sirrine, J E/PO Box 5456, Greenville, SC	803-298-6000
Studio + Co/13353 Sorento Valley Dr, Largo, FL	813-595-2275

TUV

Tash, Ken/6320 Castle Pl, Falls Church, VA	703-237-1712
Thayer Dana Industrial Design/Route 1, Monroe, VA	804-929-6359
The Associates Inc/5319 Lee Hwy, Arlington, VA	703-534-3940
Thomas, Steve Design/1121 Kenilworth Ave, Charlotte, NC	704-332-4624
Turpin Design Assoc/1762 Century Blvd #B, Atlanta, GA	404-320-6963
Unique Communications/1034 Saber Ln, Herndon, VA	703-471-1406
Varisco, Tom Graphic Design Inc/1925 Esplanade, New Orleans, LA	504-949-2888
Visualgraphics Design/1211 NW Shore Blvd, Tampa, FL	813-877-3804

W

Walton & Hoke/7247 Lee Hwy, Falls Church, VA	703-538-5727
Whitford, Kim/242 Mead Rd, Decatur, GA	404-371-0860
Whitver, Harry K Graphic Design/208 Reidhurst Ave, Nashville, TN	615-320-1795
Winner, Stewart Inc/550 W Kentucky St, Louisville, KY	502-583-5502
Wood, Tom/3925 Peachtree Rd NE, Atlanta, GA	404-262-7424

Midwest

A

AKA Design/7380 Marietta St, St Louis, MO	314-781-3389
Aarons, Allan Design/666 Dundee Rd #1701, Northbrook, IL	312-291-9800
Ades, Leonards Graphic Design/666 Dundee Rd #1103, Northbrook, IL	312-564-8863
Album Graphics/1950 N Ruby St, Melrose Park, IL	312-344-9100
Allied Design Group/1701 W Chase, Chicago, IL	312-743-3330
Ampersand Assoc/2454 W 38th St, Chicago, IL	312-523-2282
Anderson Studios/209 W Jackson Blvd, Chicago, IL	312-922-3039
Anderson, I K Studios/215 W Huron, Chicago, IL	312-664-4536
Art Forms Inc/5150 Prospect Ave, Cleveland, OH	216-361-3855
Arvind Khatkate Design/200 E Ontario St, Chicago, IL	312-337-1478

B

Babcock & Schmid Assoc/3689 Ira Rd, Bath, OH	216-666-8826
Bagby Design/225 N Michigan, Chicago, IL	312-861-1288
Bal Graphics Inc/314 W Superior, Chicago, IL	312-337-0325
Banka Mango Design Inc/274 Merchandise Mart, Chicago, IL	312-467-0059
Barnes, Jeff/666 N Lake Shore Dr #1408, Chicago, IL	312-951-0996
Bartels & Cartsens/3284 Ivanhoe, St Louis, MO	314-781-4350
Bay Graphics/341 W Superior, Chicago, IL	312-337-0325
Beda Ross Design/310 W Chicago Ave, Chicago, IL	312-944-2332
Benjamin, Burton E Assoc/3391 Summit, Highland Park, IL	312-432-8089
Berg, Don/207 E Michigan, Milwaukee, WI	414-276-7828
Bieger, Walter Assoc/1689 W County Rd F, Arden Hills, MN	612-636-8500
Blake, Hayward & Co/834 Custer Ave, Evanston, IL	312-864-9800
Blau-Bishop & Assoc/401 N Michigan Ave, Chicago, IL	312-321-1420
Boelter Industries Inc/5198 W 76th St, Minneapolis, MN	612-831-5338
Boller-Coates-Spadero/742 N Wells, Chicago, IL	312-787-2798
Bowlby, Joseph A/53 W Jackson #711, Chicago, IL	312-922-0890
Bradford-Cout Graphic Design/9933 Lawler, Skokie, IL	312-539-5557
Brooks Stevens Assoc Inc/1415 W Donges Bay Rd, Mequon, WI	414-241-3800
Busch, Lonnie/11 Meadow Dr, Fenton, MO	314-343-1330

C

CMO Graphics/160 E Illinois, Chicago, IL	312-527-0900
Campbell Art Studio/2145 Luray Ave, Cincinnati, OH	513-221-3600
Campbell Creative Group Inc/8705 N Port Washington, Milwaukee, WI	414-351-4150

Carter, Don W/ Industrial Design/8809 E 59th St, Kansas City, MO	816-356-1874
Centaur Studios Inc/10 S Broadway, St Louis, MO	314-421-6485
Chartmasters Inc/150 E Huron St, Chicago, IL	312-787-9040
Chestnut House/200 E Ohio, Chicago, IL	312-822-9090
Claudia Janah Designs Inc/222 N Dearborn, Chicago, IL	312-726-4560
Clifford, Keesler/6642 West H Ave, Kalamazoo, MI	616-375-0688
Combined Services Inc/1414 Laurel Ave, Minneapolis, MN	612-339-7770
Container Corp of America/1 First National Plaza, Chicago, IL	312-580-5500
Contours Consulting Design Group/864 Stearns Rd, Bartlett, IL	312-837-4100
Coons/Beirise Design Assoc/2344 Ashland Ave, Cincinnati, OH	513-751-7459
Crosby, Bart/676 St Clair St, Chicago, IL	312-951-2800

D

Day, David Design & Assoc/700 Walnut St, Cincinnati, OH	513-621-4060
DeBrey Design/6014 Blue Circle #D, Minneapolis, MN	612-935-2292
DeGoede & Others/435 N Michigan Ave, Chicago, IL	312-951-6066
Dektas Eger Inc/1077 Celestial St, Cincinnati, OH	513-621-7070
Design Alliance Inc/114 E 8th St, Cincinnati, OH	513-621-9373
Design Consultants/505 N Lakeshore Dr #4907, Chicago, IL	312-642-4670
Design Factory/7543 Floyd, Overland Park, KS	913-383-3085
Design Group Three/1114 W Armitage Ave, Chicago, IL	312-337-1775
Design Innovations Inc/75 Berkeley St, Toronto M5A 2W5, ON	416-362-8470
Design Mark Inc/5455 W 86th St, Indianapolis, IN	317-872-3000
Design Marketing/900 N Franklin #610, Chicago, IL	312-787-9409
Design Marks Corp/1462 W Irving Park, Chicago, IL	312-327-3669
Design North Inc/8007 Douglas Ave, Racine, WI	414-639-2080
Design One/437 Marshman St, Highland Park, IL	312-433-4140
Design Planning Group/223 W Erie, Chicago, IL	312-943-8400
Design Train/434 Hidden Valley Ln, Cincinnati, OH	513-761-7099
Design Two Ltd/600 N McClurg Ct #330, Chicago, IL	312-642-9888
Deur, Paul/109 Ottawa NW, Grand Rapids, MI	616-458-5661
Dezign House III/1701 E 12th #8FW, Cleveland, OH	216-621-7777
Di Cristo & Slagle Design/741 N Milwaukee, Milwaukee, WI	414-273-0980
Dickens Design Group/13 W Grand, Chicago, IL	312-222-1850
Dimensional Designs Inc/1101 Southeastern Ave, Indianapolis, IN	317-637-1353
Distinction Design/8337 Capton Ln, Darien, IL	
Doty, David Design/661 W Roscoe, Chicago, IL	312-348-1200
Douglas Design/2165 Lakeside Ave, Cleveland, OH	216-621-2558
Dresser, John Design/180 Crescent Knoll E, Libertyville, IL	312-362-4222
Dynamic Graphics Inc/6000 N Forrest Park Dr, Peoria, IL	309-688-9800

E

Eaton and Associates/2116 2nd Ave S, Minneapolis, MN	612-871-1028
Egger/Assoc Inc/812 Busse Hwy, Park Ridge, IL	312-296-9100
Ellies, Dave Indstrl Design/2015 W 5th Ave, Columbus, OH	614-488-7995
Elyria Graphics/147 Winckles St, Elyria, OH	216-365-9384
Emphasis 7 Communications/43 E Ohio #1000, Chicago, IL	312-951-8887
Engelhardt Design/1738 Irving Ave S, Minneapolis, MN	612-377-3389
Environmental Graphics Inc/1101 Southeastern Ave, Indianapolis, IN	317-634-1458
Epstein & Assoc/11427 Bellflower, Cleveland, OH	216-421-1600
Eurographics/727 N Hudson, Chicago, IL	312-951-5110

F

Falk, Robert Design Group/4425 W Pine, St Louis, MO	314-531-1410
Feldkamp-Malloy/185 N Wabash, Chicago, IL	312-263-0633
Ficho & Corley Inc/875 N Michigan Ave, Chicago, IL	312-787-1011
Fleishman-Hillard, Inc/1 Memorial Dr, St Louis, MO	314-982-1700
Fleming Design Office/7101 York Ave S, Minneapolis, MN	612-830-0099
Flexo Design/57 W Grand, Chicago, IL	312-321-1368
Ford & Earl Assoc Inc/28820 Mound Rd, Warren, MI	313-536-1999
Forsythe-French Inc/4115 Broadway, Kansas City, MO	816-561-6678
Frederiksen Design/609 S Riverside Dr, Villa Park, IL	312-343-5882
Frink, Chin, Casey Inc/505 E Grant, Minneapolis, MN	612-333-6539

G

Gellman, Stan Graphic Design Studio/4509 Laclede, St Louis, MO	314-361-7676
Gerhardt and Clements/162 W Hubbard St, Chicago, IL	312-337-3443
Glenbard Graphics Inc/333 Kimberly Dr, Carol Stream, IL	312-653-4550
Goldsholl Assoc/420 Frontage Rd, Northfield, IL	312-446-8300
Goldsmith Yamasaki Specht Inc/840 N Michigan Ave,	

Graphic Design

Continued

Please send us your additions and updates.

Chicago, IL	312-266-8404
Golon, Mary/1112 Hull Terr, Evanston, IL	312-328-3935
Goodwin, Arnold/730 N Franklin, Chicago, IL	312-787-0466
Goose Graphics/716 First St N, Minneapolis, MN	612-333-3502
Gournoe, M Inc/60 E Elm, Chicago, IL	312-787-5157
Graphic Corp/727 E 2nd St PO Box 4806, Des Moines, IA	515-247-8500
Graphic House Inc/672 Woodbridge, Detroit, MI	313-259-7790
Graphic Productions/162 N Clinton, Chicago, IL	312-236-2833
Graphic Specialties Inc/2426 East 26th St, Minneapolis, MN	612-722-6601
Graphica Corp/3184 Alpine, Troy, MI	313-649-5050
Graphics Group/8 S Michigan Ave, Chicago, IL	312-782-7421
Graphics-Cor Associates/549 W Randolph St, Chicago, IL	312-332-3379
Greenberg, Jon Assoc Inc/2338 Coolidge, Berkley, MI	313-548-8080
Greenlee-Hess Ind Design/750 Beta Dr, Mayfield Village, OH	216-461-2112
Greiner, John & Assoc/8 W Hubbard, Chicago, IL	312-644-2973
Grusin, Gerald Design/232 E Ohio St, Chicago, IL	312-944-4945

H

Handelan-Pedersen/333 N Michigan #1005, Chicago, IL	312-782-6833
Hans Design/663 Greenwood Rd, Northbrook, IL	312-272-7980
Harley, Don E Associates/1740 Livingston Ave, West St Paul, MN	612-455-1631
Harris, Judy/550 Willow Creek Ct, Clarendon Hill, IL	312-789-3821
Herbst Lazar Rogers & Bell Inc/345 N Canal, Chicago, IL	312-454-1116
Higgins Hegner Genovese Inc/510 N Dearborn St, Chicago, IL	312-644-1882
Hirsch, David Design Group Inc/205 W Wacker Dr, Chicago, IL	312-329-1500
Hirsh Co/8051 N Central Park Ave, Skokie, IL	312-267-6777
Hoekstra, Grant Graphics/333 N Michigan Ave, Chicago, IL	312-641-6940
Hoffar, Barron & Co/53 W Jackson #711, Chicago, IL	312-922-0890
Hoffman York & Compton/2300 N Mayfair Rd, Milwaukee, WI	414-259-2000
Horvath, Steve Design/301 N Water St, Milwaukee, WI	414-271-3992

IJ

IGS Design Div of Smith Hinchman & Grylls/455 W Fort St, Detroit, MI	313-964-3000
Identity Center/955 N Plumgrove Rd, Schaumburg, IL	312-843-2378
Indiana Design Consortium/102 N 3rd St 300 Rvr Cty Bldg, Lafayette, IN	317-423-5469
Industrial Technological Assoc/30675 Solon Rd, Cleveland, OH	216-349-2900
Ing, Victor Design/5810 Lincoln, Morton Grove, IL	312-965-3459
Inteplex/12215 Dorsett Rd, Maryland Hts, MO	314-739-9996
J M H Corp/1200 Waterway Blvd, Indianapolis, IN	317-639-2535
James, Frank Direct Marketing/120 S Central #500 Chrmal Plz, Clayton, MO	314-726-4600
Jansen, Ute/410 S Michigan Ave #919, Chicago, IL	312-922-5048
Jnah Design/400 W Erie #304, Chicago, IL	312-944-2799
Johnson, Stan Design Inc/21185 W Gumina Rd, Brookfield, WI	414-783-6510
Johnson, Stewart Design Studio/218 W Walnut, Milwaukee, WI	414-265-3377
Jones, Richmond Designer/1921 N Hudson St, Chicago, IL	312-935-6500
Joss Design Group/232 E Ohio, Chicago, IL	312-828-0055

KL

KDA Industrial Design Consultants Inc/ Cortland Ct, Addison, IL	312-495-9466
Kaulfuss Design/200 E Ontario St, Chicago, IL	312-943-2161
Kearns, Marilyn/442 North Wells, Chicago, IL	312-645-1888
Keller Lane & Waln/8 S Michigan #814, Chicago, IL	312-782-7421
Kerr, Joe/405 N Wabash #2013, Chicago, IL	312-661-0097
Kornick & Lindsay/161 E Erie #107, Chicago, IL	312-280-8664
Kovach, Ronald Design/719 S Dearborn, Chicago, IL	312-461-9888
LVK Associates Inc/4235 Cinell, St Louis, MO	314-534-2104
Laney, Ron/15 Fern St/Box 423, St Jacob, IL	618-644-5883
Lange, Jim Design/213 W Institute, Chicago, IL	312-943-2589
Larsen Design/7101 York Ave S, Minneapolis, MN	612-835-2271
Larson Design/7101 York Ave South, Minneapolis, MN	612-835-2271
Lehrfeld, Gerald/43 E Ohio, Chicago, IL	312-944-0651
Lenard, Catherine/509 W Wrightwood Ave, Chicago, IL	312-248-6937
Lerdon, Wes Assoc/3070 Riverside Dr, Columbus, OH	614-486-8188
Lesniewicz/Navarre/222 N Erie St, Toledo, OH	419-243-7131
Lipson Associates Inc/666 Dundee Rd #103, Northbrook, IL	312-291-0500
Lipson Associates Inc/2349 Victory Pkwy, Cincinnati, OH	513-961-6225
Liska & Assoc/213 W Institute Pl #605, Chicago, IL	312-943-5910
Loew, Dick & Assoc/1308 N Astor St, Chicago, IL	312-787-9032

Lubell, Robert/2946 E Lincolnshire, Toledo, OH	419-531-2267

M

Maddox, Eva Assoc Inc/440 North Wells, Chicago, IL	312-670-0092
Madsan/Kuester/1 Main @ River Pl #500, Minneapolis, MN	612-378-1895
Manning Studios Inc/613 Main St, Cincinnati, OH	513-621-6959
Market Design/1010 Euclid Ave, Cleveland, OH	216-771-0300
Marsh, Richard Assoc Inc/203 N Wabash #1400, Chicago, IL	312-236-1331
McCoy, Steven/5414 1/2 NW Radio Hwy, Omaha, NE	402-554-1416
McDermott, Bill Graphic Design/1410 Hanley Industrial Ct, St Louis, MO	314-962-6286
McGuire, Robert L Design/7943 Campbell, Kansas City, MO	816-523-9164
McMurray Design Inc/405 N Wabash Ave, Chicago, IL	312-527-1555
Media Corporation/3070 Riverside Dr, Columbus, OH	614-488-7767
Minnick, James Design/535 N Michigan Ave, Chicago, IL	312-527-1864
Miska, John/192 E Wallings Rd, Cleveland, OH	216-526-0464
Moonink Inc/233 N Michigan Ave, Chicago, IL	312-565-0040
Murrie White Drummond Leinhart/58 W Huron, Chicago, IL	312-943-5995

NO

Naughton, Carol & Assoc/345 N Canal #901, Chicago, IL	312-454-1888
Nemetz, Jeff/900 N Franklin #600, Chicago, IL	312-664-8112
Nottingham-Spirk Design Inc/11310 Juniper Rd, Cleveland, OH	216-231-7830
Oak Brook Graphics, Inc/287 W Butterfield Rd, Elmhurst, IL	312-832-3200
Obata Design/1610 Menard, St Louis, MO	314-241-1710
Oberg, Richard/327 15th Ave, Moline, IL	319-359-3831
Osborne-Tuttle/233 E Wacker Dr #2409, Chicago, IL	312-565-1910
Oskar Designs/616 Sheridan Rd, Evanston, IL	312-328-1734
Our Gang Studios/3120 St Marys Ave, Omaha, NE	402-341-4965
Overlock Howe Consulting Group/4484 W Pine, St Louis, MO	314-533-4484

P

Pace Studios/3730 W Morse Ave, Lincolnwood, IL	312-676-9770
Painter/Cesaroni Design, Inc/1865 Grove St, Glenview, IL	312-724-8840
Palmer Design Assoc/3330 Old Glenview Rd, Wilmette, IL	312-256-7448
Paragraphs Design/10 E Huron St 4th Fl, Chicago, IL	312-943-4866
Paramount Technical Service Inc/31811 Vine St, Cleveland, OH	216-585-2550
Perlstein, Warren/560 Zenith Dr, Glenview, IL	312-827-7884
Perman, Norman/233 E Erie #2304, Chicago, IL	312-642-1348
Peterson, Ted/23 N Lincoln St, Hinsdale, IL	312-920-1091
Phares Associates Inc/Hills Tech Dr, Farmington Hills, MI	313-553-2232
Pinzke, Herbert/1935 N Kenmore, Chicago, IL	312-528-2277
Pitlock Design/300 N Michigan #200, South Bend, IN	219-233-8606
Pitt Studios/1370 Ontario St #1430, Cleveland, OH	216-241-6720
Polivka-Logan Design/5100 Thimsen Ave, Minnetonka, MN	612-474-1124
Porter-Matjasich/154 W Hubbard #404, Chicago, IL	312-670-4355
Powell/Kleinschmidt Inc/115 S LaSalle St, Chicago, IL	312-726-2208
Pride and Perfomance/970 Raymond Ave, St Paul, MN	612-646-4800
Prodesign Inc/2500 Niagara Ln, Plymouth, MI	612-476-1200
Purviance, George Marketing Comm/7404 Bland Dr, Clayton, MO	314-721-2765
Pycha and Associates/16 E Pearson, Chicago, IL	312-944-3679

QR

Qually & Co Inc/30 E Huron #2502, Chicago, IL	312-944-0237
RHi Inc/213 W Institute Pl, Chicago, IL	312-943-2585
Ramba Graphics/1575 Merwin Ave, Cleveland, OH	216-621-1776
Red Wing Enterprises/666 N Lake Shore Dr #211, Chicago, IL	312-951-0441
Redmond, Patrick Design/420 Summit Ave/Univ Club, St Paul, MN	612-224-7155
Reed, Stan/1900 University Ave, Madison, WI	608-238-1900
Richardson/Smith Inc/10350 Olentangy River Rd, Worthington, OH	614-885-3453
Roberts Webb & Co/111 E Wacker Dr, Chicago, IL	312-861-0060
Robinson, Thompson & Wise/8717 W 110th St, Overland Park, KS	913-451-9473
Ross & Harvey/500 N Dearborn, Chicago, IL	312-467-1290
Roth, Randall/535 N Michigan #2312, Chicago, IL	312-467-0140
Rotheiser, Jordan I/1725 McGovern St, Highland Park, IL	312-433-4288

S

Samata Assoc/213 W Main Street, West Dundee, IL	312-428-8600
Sargent, Ann Design/432 Ridgewood Ave, Minneapolis, MN	612-870-9995
Savlin/ Williams Assoc/1335 Dodge, Evanston, IL	312-328-3366
Schlatter Group Inc/40 E Michigan Mall, Battle Creek, MI	616-964-0898
Schmidt, Wm M Assoc/20296 Harper Ave, Harper Woods, MI	313-881-8075
Schultz, Ron Design/838 W Webster, Chicago, IL	312-528-1853

Graphic Design

Continued

Please send us your additions and updates.

Scott, Jack/600 S Dearborn #1308, Chicago, IL	312-922-1467
Selfridge, Mary/817 Desplaines St, Plainfield, IL	815-436-7197
Seltzer, Meyer Design & Illustration/744 W Buckingham Pl, Chicago, IL	312-348-2885
Sherman, Roger Assoc Inc/13530 Michigan Ave, Dearborn, MI	313-582-8844
Shilt, Jennifer/1010 Jorie Blvd, Oak Brook, IL	312-325-8657
Sigalos, Alex/520 N Michigan Ave #606, Chicago, IL	312-321-0349
Simanis, Vito/4 N 013 Randall Rd, St Charles, IL	312-584-1683
Simons, I W Industrial Design/975 Amberly Pl, Columbus, OH	614-451-3796
Skidmore Sahratian/2100 W Big Beaver Rd, Troy, MI	313-643-6000
Skolnick, Jerome/200 E Ontario, Chicago, IL	312-944-4568
Slavin Assoc Inc/229 W Illinois, Chicago, IL	312-822-0559
Smith, Glen Co/337 Oak Grove, Carriage House, Minneapolis, MN	612-871-1616
Sosin, Bill/415 W Superior St, Chicago, IL	312-751-0974
Source Inc/180 N Michigan Ave, Chicago, IL	312-236-7620
Space Design International Inc/309 Vine St, Cincinnati, OH	513-241-3000
Spatial Graphics Inc/7131 W Lakefield Dr, Milwaukee, WI	414-545-4444
Speare, Ray/730 N Franklin #501, Chicago, IL	312-943-5808
Stepan Design/317 S Prairie, Mt Prospect, IL	312-364-4121
Strandell Design Inc/233 E Wacker Dr #3609, Chicago, IL	312-861-1654
Strizek, Jan/213 W Institute Pl, Chicago, IL	312-664-4772
Stromberg, Gordon H Visual Design/5423 Artesian, Chicago, IL	312-275-9449
Studio 7/2770 State St NE, Middlebranch, OH	216-454-1622
Studio One Graphics/16329 Middlebelt, Livonia, MI	313-522-7505
Studio One Inc/4640 W 77th St, Minneapolis, MN	612-831-6313
Svolos, Maria/7246 N Hoyne St, Chicago, IL	312-338-4675
Swoger Grafik/12 E Scott St, Chicago, IL	312-943-2491
Synthesis Concepts/612 N Michigan Ave #501, Chicago, IL	312-787-1201

T

T & Company/3553 W Peterson Ave, Chicago, IL	312-463-1336
Tassian, George Org/702 Gwynne Bldg, Cincinnati, OH	513-721-5566
Taylor & Assoc/8601 Urbandale Rd, Des Moines, IA	515-276-0992
Tepe Hensler & Westerkamp/632 Vine St #1100, Cincinnati, OH	513-241-0100
Teubner, Peter & Assoc/2341 N Cambridge St, Chicago, IL	312-248-6797
The Design Group/2976 Triverton Pike, Madison, WI	608-274-5393
The Design Partnership/124 N 1st St, Minneapolis, MN	612-338-8889
Thorbeck & Lambert Inc/1409 Willow, Minneapolis, MN	612-871-7979
Toth, Joe/20000 Eldra Rd, Rocky River, OH	216-356-0745
Turgeon, James/233 E Wacker Dr #1102, Chicago, IL	312-861-1039

UV

UVG & N/4415 W Harrison St, Hillside, IL	312-449-1500
Underwood, Muriel/173 W Madison Ave, #1011, Chicago, IL	312-236-8472
Unicom/4100 W River Ln, Milwaukee, WI	414-354-5440
Vallarta, Frederick Assoc Inc/875 N Michigan #1545, Chicago, IL	312-944-7300
Vanides-Mlodock/323 S Franklin St, Chicago, IL	312-663-0595
Vann, Bill Studio/1706 S 8th St, St Louis, MO	314-231-2322
Vista Three Design/4820 Excelsior Blvd, Minneapolis, MN	612-920-5311
Visual Image Studio/1599 Selby Ave #22, St Paul, MN	612-644-7314

WXZ

Wallner Harbauer Bruce & Assoc/500 N Michigan Ave, Chicago, IL	312-787-6787
Weber Conn & Riley/444 N Michigan #2440, Chicago, IL	312-527-4260
Weiss, Jack Assoc/820 Davis St, Evanston, IL	312-866-7480
Widmer, Stanley Assoc Inc/Staples Airport Ind Park, RR2, Staples, MN	218-894-3466
Willson, William/100 E Ohio St #314, Chicago, IL	312-642-5328
Winbush Design/444 N Lake Shore Dr 4th Fl, Chicago, IL	312-527-4478
Wooster + Assoc/314 Walnut, Winnetka, IL	312-726-7944
Worrel, W Robert Design/716 N First St, Minneapolis, MN	612-623-3391
Xeno/PO Box 10030, Chicago, IL	312-327-1989
Zender and Associates/3914 Miami Rd, Cincinnati, OH	513-561-8496
Ziegler, Nancy/874 Greenbay Rd, Wilmet, IL	312-446-3707

Southwest

A

A Worthwhile Place Comm/2505 Wedglea #279, Dallas, TX	214-946-1348
A&M Associates Inc/2727 N Central Ave, Phoenix, AZ	602-263-6504

Ackerman & McQueen/5708 Mosteller Dr, Oklahoma City, OK	405-843-9451
Ad-Art Studios/813 6th Ave, Ft Worth, TX	817-335-9603
Advertising Inc/2202 E 49th St, Tulsa, OK	918-747-8871
Anderson Pearlstone & Assoc/PO Box 6528, San Antonio, TX	512-826-1897
Apple Graphics/5440 Harvest Hill Rd #235, Dallas, TX	214-522-6261
Ark, Chuck/3825 Bowser Ave, Dallas, TX	214-522-5356
Arnold Harwell McClain & Assoc/4131 N Central Expwy #510, Dallas, TX	214-521-6400
Art Associates/1300 Walnut Hill Ln #103, Irving, TX	214-258-6001

BC

Baugh, Larry/1417 N Irving Hts, Irving, TX	214-438-5696
Beals Advertising Agency/5005 N Pennsylvania, Oklahoma City, OK	405-848-8513
Bleu Design Assoc/345 E Windsor, Phoenix, AZ	602-279-1131
Boughton, Cindy/1617 Fannin #2801, Houston, TX	713-951-9113
Brooks & Pollard Co/1650 Union Nat'L Plaza, Little Rock, AR	501-375-5561
Central Advertising Agency/1 Tandy Circle #300, Fort Worth, TX	817-390-3011
Chandler, Jeff/PO Box 224427, Dallas, TX	214-946-1348
Chesterfield Interiors Inc/2213 Cedar Springs, Dallas, TX	214-747-2211
Coffee Design Inc/5810 Star Ln, Houston, TX	713-780-0571
Condroy, Scott/5038 E McDowell, Phoenix, AZ	602-231-0020
Connaster & Co/3111 Cole #1, Dallas, TX	214-744-3555
Cranford/ Johnson & Assoc/1st Commercial Bldg #2200, Little Rock, AR	501-376-6251
Creative Directions/3302 Shore Crest, Dallas, TX	214-358-3433

DE

Design Bank/PO Box 33459, Austin, TX	512-445-7584
Design Enterprises, Inc/9434 Viscount Blvd #180, El Paso, TX	915-594-7100
Designmark/1800 W Loop South #1390, Houston, TX	713-626-0953
Drebelbis, Marsha/1341 W Mockingbird Ln #1039 W, Dallas, TX	214-951-0266
Eisenberg Inc/4924 Cole, Dallas, TX	214-528-5990
Executive Image/16479 Dallas Pkwy #20, Dallas, TX	214-733-0496

FG

Fischer, Don/3636 Lemmon #204, Dallas, TX	214-522-2995
Ford, Deborah/202 Senter Valley, Irving, TX	214-579-9472
Friesenhahn, Michelle/717 W Ashby, San Antonio, TX	512-342-1997
Funk, Barbara/3174 Catamore Ln, Dallas, TX	214-350-8534
GKD/PO Box 12860, Oklahoma City, OK	405-943-2333
Galen, D/5335 Bent Tree Forest #192, Dallas, TX	214-385-7855
Gluth & Weaver/3911 Stony Brook, Houston, TX	713-784-4141
Graphics Hardware Co/3532 W Northern #2, Phoenix, AZ	602-242-4687
Gregory Dsgn Group/3636 Lemmon #302, Dallas, TX	214-522-9360
Grimes, Don/3514 Oak Grove, Dallas, TX	214-526-0040

H

Hanagriff King Design/4151 SW Freeway, Houston, TX	714-622-4260
Harman, Gary/1025 S Jennings #403, Ft Worth, TX	817-332-7687
Harrison Allen Design/6633 Hillcroft #252B, Houston, TX	713-729-3938
Herman, Ben/701 Pennsylvania, Fort Worth, TX	817-731-9941
Hermsen Design Assoc/5626 Preston Oaks #34-D, Dallas, TX	214-233-5090
Herring, Jerry/1216 Hawthorne, Houston, TX	713-526-1250
High, Richard/4500 Montrose #D, Houston, TX	713-521-2772
Hill, Chris/3512 Lake, Houston, TX	713-523-7363
Hixo/2204 Rio Grande St, Austin, TX	512-477-0050
Hood Hope & Assoc/8023 E 63rd Box 35408, Tulsa, OK	918-250-9511
Hubler-Rosenburg Assoc/1405-A Turtle Creek, Dallas, TX	214-742-2491

IJ

Image Excellence/3312 Shore Crest, Dallas, TX	214-352-9958
Image Group Studio/2808 Cole St, Dallas, TX	214-745-1411
Jacob, Jim/3333 Elm #102, Dallas, TX	214-939-0033
Jettun, Carol/4212 Cumberland Rd, Ft Worth, TX	817-737-4708
Johnson, Carla/9010 Windy Crest, Dallas, TX	214-522-1449
Jones, Don/10529 Sinclair, Dallas, TX	214-327-0819

KL

Kilmer/Geer/5650 Kirby Dr #205, Houston, TX	713-668-1708
Konig Design Group/4001 Broadway, San Antonio, TX	512-824-7387
Ledbetter, James/10818 Ridge Spring, Dallas, TX	214-341-4858
Lindgren Design/5350 Interfirst Two, Dallas, TX	214-742-3573
Loucks Atelier/2900 Weslyan #530, Houston, TX	713-877-8551
Lowe Runkle Co/6801 Broadway Extension, Oklahoma City, OK	405-848-6800

M

Mantz & Associates/3707 Rawlins, Dallas, TX	214-521-7432
Martin, Hardy/7701 Stemmons #860, Dallas, TX	214-630-2977
Martin, Randy/701 E Plano Pkwy, Dallas, TX	214-881-1647
McCulley, Mike/412 Knollwood Ct, Euless, TX	214-528-4889
McEuen, Roby/600 Eighth Ave, Ft Worth, TX	817-335-5153
McFarlin, Steven/208 W Keaney #103, Mesquite, TX	214-289-1893
McGrath, Michael Design/1201 Richardson Dr, Richardson, TX	214-644-4358
Moore Co/5427 Redfield, Dallas, TX	214-631-9443
Morales, Frank Design/12770 Coit Rd #905, Dallas, TX	214-233-0667
Morris, Carroll/14970 Trafalgar Ct, Dallas, TX	214-233-6616
Morrison & Assoc/3900 Lemmon #2, Dallas, TX	214-528-7410
Muse. Pete/5501 LBJ Freeway #1200, Dallas, TX	214-770-1473

NOP

Neumann, Steve & Friends/3000 Richmond, Houston, TX	713-629-7501
Overton, Janet/2927 Bay Oaks Dr, Dallas, TX	214-357-1272
Owens & Assoc Advertising Inc/2600 N Central Ave #1700, Phoenix, AZ	602-264-5691
Pencil Point/14330 Midway #210, Dallas, TX	214-233-0776
Pirtle Design/4528 McKinney Ave #104, Dallas, TX	214-522-7520

QRS

Quad Type & Graphics/14004 Goldmark, Dallas, TX	214-238-0733
Richards Brock Miller Mitchell & Assoc/12700 Hillcrest #242, Dallas, TX	214-386-9077
Sawyer, Sandra/1319 Ballinger, Ft Worth, TX	817-332-1611
Serigraphics Etc/4907 W Lovers Ln, Dallas, TX	214-352-6440
Slaton, Richard/3514 Oak Grove #9, Dallas, TX	214-231-3000
Squires, James/2913 N Canton, Dallas, TX	214-939-9194
Stoler, Scott/5015-A N Central Expwy, Dallas, TX	214-521-4024
Strickland, Michael & Co/3000 Post Oak Blvd, Houston, TX	713-961-1323
Struthers, Yvonne/2110 Mossy Oak, Arlington, TX	214-469-1377
Studio Renaissance/3200 Main St, Dallas, TX	214-939-0401
Studiographix/411 Northgate Plaza, Dallas, TX	214-258-8446
Sullivan, Jack Design Group/1320 N 7th Ave, Phoenix, AZ	602-271-0117
Suntar Designs/PO Box 1901, Prescott, AZ	602-778-2714
Sweeney, Jim/250 Decker, Irving, TX	214-258-1705

TUVW

Tarasoff, Neal/3019 Caribbean, Mesquite, TX	214-681-0480
Tellagraphics/401-D N Interurban, Richardson, TX	214-238-9297
Texas Art & Media/500 W 13th St #220, Ft Worth, TX	817-334-0443
The Ad Department/1412 Texas St, Ft Worth, TX	817-335-4012
The Art Works/4409 Maple St, Dallas, TX	214-521-2121
The Belcher Group Inc/8300 Bissonnet #240, Houston, TX	713-271-2727
The Goodwin Co/7598 N Mesa #200, El Paso, TX	915-584-1176
3D/International/1900 W Loop South #200, Houston, TX	713-871-7000
Total Designers/3511 Pinemont #3, Houston, TX	713-688-7766
Turnipseed, Allan/2719-C Laclede, Dallas, TX	214-871-2828
Unigraphics/2700 Oak Lawn, Dallas, TX	214-526-0930
Vanmar Assoc/1440 Empire Central #458, Dallas, TX	214-630-7603
WW3 Papagalos/313 E Thomas #208, Phoenix, AZ	602-279-2933
Walker Fuld & Assoc/8800 N Central Expwy #458, Dallas, TX	214-692-7775
Warden, Bill/1349 Empire Central #802, Dallas, TX	214-634-8434

Rocky Mountain

ABC

Allison & Schiedt/219 E 7th Ave, Denver, CO	303-830-1110
Ampersand Studios/315 St Paul, Denver, CO	303-388-1211
Arnold Design Inc/1635 Ogden, Denver, CO	303-832-7156
Barnstorm Studios/2502 1/2 Colorado Ave, Colorado Springs, CO	303-630-7200
Brogren/Kelly & Assoc/3113 E Third Ave #220, Denver, CO	303-399-3851
Chen, Shih-chien/2839 35th St, Edmonton T6L5K2, AB	403-462-8617
CommuniCreations/2130 S Bellaire, Denver, CO	303-759-1155
Consortium West/Concept Design/2290 E 4500 St #120, Salt Lake City, UT	801-278-4441
Cuerden Advertising Design/1730 Gaylord St, Denver, CO	303-321-4163

DEF

Danford, Chuck/1556 Williams St, Denver, CO	303-320-1116
Design Center/734 W 800 S, Salt Lake City, UT	801-532-6122
Duo Graphics/3907 Manhattan Ave, Ft Collins, CO	303-463-2788

Entercom/425 S Cherry St #200, Denver, CO	303-393-0405
Fleming, Ron/724 6th St NW, Great Falls, MT	406-761-7887

GM

Gelotte, Mark/3485 S Arrow #82, Denver, CO	303-750-5941
Gibby, John Design/1140 E 1250 N, Layton, UT	801-544-0736
Graphic Concepts Inc/145 Pierpont Ave, Salt Lake City, UT	801-359-2191
Graphien Design/6950 E Belleview #250, Englewood, CO	303-779-5858
Gritz Visual Graphics/5595 Arapahoe Rd, Boulder, CO	303-449-3840
Markowitz & Long/900 28th St #203, Boulder, CO	303-449-7394
Martin, Janet/1112 Pearl, Boulder, CO	303-442-8202
Matrix International Inc/3773 Cherry Creek Dr N #690, Denver, CO	303-388-9353
Monigle, Glenn/150 Adams, Denver, CO	303-388-9358
Multimedia/450 Lincoln #100, Denver, CO	303-777-5480

ORT

Okland Design Assoc/1970 SW Temple, Salt Lake City, UT	801-484-7861
Radetsky Design Associates/2342 Broadway, Denver, CO	303-629-7375
Tandem Design Group Inc/217 E 7th Ave, Denver, CO	303-831-9251
Taylor, Robert W Design Inc/2260 Baseline Rd, Boulder, CO	303-443-1975
Three B Studio & Assoc/1475 S Pearl St, Denver, CO	303-777-6359

VW

Visual Comm/4475 E Hinsdale Pl, Littleton, CO	303-773-0128
Visual Images Inc/1626 Franklin, Denver, CO	303-388-5366
Walker Design Associates/1873 S Bellaire St #715, Denver, CO	303-773-0426
Weller Institute for Design/2240 Monarch Dr, Park City, UT	801-649-9859
Woodard Racing Graphics Ltd/3116 Longhorn Rd, Boulder, CO	303-443-1986
Worthington, Carl A Partnership/1309 Spruce St, Boulder, CO	303-449-8900

West Coast

A

A & H Graphic Design/11844 Rncho Brndo, Rancho Bernardo, CA	619-486-0777
ADI/1100 W Colorado Blvd, Los Angeles, CA	213-254-7131
AGI/424 N Larchmont Blvd, Los Angeles, CA	213-462-0821
Ace Design/310 Industrial Ctr Bldg, Sausalito, CA	415-332-9390
Adfiliation Design/323 W 13th Ave, Eugene, OR	503-687-8262
Advertising Design & Production Service/1929 Emerald St #3, San Diego, CA	619-483-1393
Advertising/Design Assoc/1906 Second Ave, Walnut Creek, CA	415-421-7000
Alatorre, Sean/1341 Ocean Ave #259, Santa Monica, CA	213-209-3765
Alvarez Group/1516 N Vista Street, Los Angeles, CA	213-876-3491
Andrysiak, Michele/13534 Cordary Ave #14, Hawthorne, CA	213-973-8480
Antisdel Image Group/3252 De La Cruz, Santa Clara, CA	408-988-1010
Art Zone/404 Piikoi St PH, Honolulu, HI	808-537-6647
Artists In Print/Bldg 314, Fort Mason Center, San Francisco, CA	415-673-6941
Artmaster Studios/547 Library St, San Fernando, CA	818-365-7188
Artworks/115 N Sycamore St, Los Angeles, CA	213-933-5763
Asbury & Assoc/3450 E Spring St, Long Beach, CA	213-595-6481

B

Bailey, Robert Design Group/0121 SW Bancroft St, Portland, OR	503-228-1381
Ballard, Laurie/2400-D Main St, Santa Monica, CA	213-392-9749
Banuelos Design/111 S Orange St, Orange, CA	714-771-4335
Baptiste, Bob/20360 Orchard Rd, Saratoga, CA	408-867-6569
Barile, Michael & Assoc/7062 Saroni Dr, Oakland, CA	415-339-8360
Barnes, Herb Graphics/1844 Monterey Rd, S Pasadena, CA	213-682-2420
Basic Designs Inc/Box 479 Star Rt, Sausalito, CA	415-388-5141
Bass, Yager and Assoc/7039 Sunset Blvd, Hollywood, CA	213-466-9701
Bee, Paula/17952-B Sky Park Cir, Irvine, CA	
Beggs Langley Design/156 University Ave #201, Palo Alto, CA	415-323-6160
Bennett, Douglas Design/1966 Harvard Ave E, Seattle, WA	206-324-9966
Bennett, Ralph Assoc/6700 Densmore Ave, Van Nuys, CA	818-782-3224
Beuret, Janis/404 Piikoi St PH, Honolulu, HI	808-537-6647
Bhang, Samuel Design Assoc/824 S Burnside, Los Angeles, CA	213-382-1126
Blazej, Rosalie Graphics/127 Mateo St, San Francisco, CA	415-586-3325
Blik, Ty/715 J' St #102, San Diego, CA	619-232-5707
Bloch & Associates/2800 28th St #105, Santa Monica, CA	213-450-8863

Graphic Design
Continued

Please send us your additions and updates.

Boelter, Herbert A/1544 El Miradero, Glendale, CA	818-242-4206
Bohn, Richard/595 W Wilson St, Costa Mesa, CA	714-548-6669
Boyd, Douglas Design/8271 Melrose Ave, Los Angeles, CA	213-655-9642
Bramson + Assoc/7400 Beverly Blvd, Los Angeles, CA	213-938-3595
Bright & Associates, Inc/8322 Beverly Blvd, Los Angeles, CA	213-658-8844
Briteday Inc/970 Terra Bella #7, Mountain View, CA	415-968-5668
Brookins, Ed/4333 Farmdale Ave, Studio City, CA	213-766-7336
Brosio Design/3539 Jennings St, San Diego, CA	619-226-4322
Brown, Bill/1054 S Robertson Blvd #203, Los Angeles, CA	213-652-9380
Burns & Associates Inc/2700 Sutter St, San Francisco, CA	415-567-4404
Burridge, Robert/4681 Tajo, Santa Barbara, CA	805-964-2087
Business Graphics/1717 N Highland, Los Angeles, CA	213-467-0292

C

Camozzi, Teresa/770 California St, San Francisco, CA	415-392-1202
Carlson, Keith Advertising Art/251 Kearny St, San Francisco, CA	415-397-5130
Carre Design/1424 4th St #500 Ctr Tower, Santa Monica, CA	213-395-1033
Catalog Design & Production Inc/1485 Bay Shore Blvd, San Francisco, CA	415-468-5500
Chan Design/1334 Lincoln Blvd #150, Santa Monica, CA	213-393-3735
Chartmasters Inc/639 Howard St, San Francisco, CA	415-421-6591
Chase, Margo/2255 Bancroft Ave, Los Angeles, CA	213-668-1055
Chris Von-Veh/143 Finch Pl, Winslow, WA	206-842-1140
Churchill, Steven/4757 Cardin St, San Diego, CA	619-560-1225
Clark, Tim/8800 Venice Blvd, Los Angeles, CA	213-202-1044
Coak, Steve/2870 N Haven Lane, Altadena, CA	818-797-5477
Coates Advertising/115 SW Ash St #323, Portland, OR	503-241-1124
Cognata Associates Inc/2247 Webster, San Francisco, CA	415-931-3800
Cojean, Lonnie/1454 W 8th St, Upland, CA	714-985-9335
Conber Creations/3326 NE 60th, Portland, OR	503-288-2938
Corporate Comms Group/310 Washington St, Marina Del Rey, CA	213-821-9086
Corporate Graphics/2800 Van Ness, San Francisco, CA	415-474-2888
Cowart, Jerry/1144-C S Robertson Blvd, Los Angeles, CA	213-278-5605
Crawshaw, Todd Design/345-D Folsom, San Francisco, CA	145-777-3939
Creative Source/6671 W Sunset Blvd #1519, Los Angeles, CA	213-462-5731
Cronan, Michael Patrick/1 Zoe St, San Francisco, CA	415-543-6745
Cross Assoc/113 Stewart St, San Francisco, CA	415-777-2731
Cross, James/10513 W Pico Blvd, Los Angeles, CA	213-474-1484
Crouch + Fuller Inc/853 Camino Del Mar, Del Mar, CA	619-450-9200
Curtis, Todd/2032 14th St #7, Santa Monica, CA	213-452-0738

D

Dahm & Assoc Inc/26735 Dhorewood Rd, Rncho Palos Verdes, CA	213-373-4408
Dancer Fitzgerald & Sample/1010 Battery St, San Francisco, CA	415-981-6250
Danziger, Louis/7001 Melrose Ave, Los Angeles, CA	213-935-1251
Davis, Pat/818 19th St, Sacramento, CA	916-442-9025
Dawson, Chris/7250 Beverly Blvd #101, Los Angeles, CA	213-937-5867
Dayne, Jeff The Studio/731 NE Everett, Portland, OR	503-232-8777
Daystar Design/4641 Date Ave #1, La Mesa, CA	619-463-5014
DeMaio Graphics & Advertising/7101 Baird St #3, Reseda, CA	818-342-1800
Dellaporta Adv & Graphic/2020 14th St, Santa Monica, CA	213-452-3832
Design & Direction/2275 Torrance Blvd #201, Torrance, CA	213-320-0822
Design Bank Graphic Design/9605 Sepulveda #5, Sepulveda, CA	818-894-9123
Design Corps/501 N Alfred St, Los Angeles, CA	213-651-1422
Design Direction Group/595 S Pasadena Ave, Pasadena, CA	818-792-4765
Design Element/8624 Wonderland Ave, Los Angeles, CA	213-656-3293
Design Graphics/2647 S Magnolia, Los Angeles, CA	213-749-7347
Design Graphics/30 NE 23rd Pl, Portland, OR	503-223-0678
Design Group West/853 Camino Del Mar, Del Mar, CA	619-450-9200
Design Office/55 Stevenson, San Francisco, CA	415-543-4760
Design Projects Inc/16200 Ventura Blvd #418, Encino, CA	818-995-0303
Design Vectors/408 Columbus Ave #2, San Francisco, CA	415-391-0399
Detanna & Assoc/8200 Wilshire Blvd #400, Beverly Hills, CA	213-852-0808
Diniz, Carlos/676 S Lafayette Park Pl, Los Angeles, CA	213-387-1171
Doane, Dave Studio/215 Riverside Dr, Orange, CA	714-548-7285
Doerfler Design/8742 Villa La Jolla Dr #29, La Jolla, CA	619-455-0506
Dupre Design/415 2nd St, Coronado, CA	619-435-8369
Dyer-Cahn/5550 Wilshire Blvd #301, Los Angeles, CA	213-937-4100
Dyna Pac/7926 Convoy St, San Diego, CA	619-560-0280

EF

Earnett McFall & Assoc/2409 NE 133 St, Seattle, WA	206-364-4956
Ehrig & Assoc/4th & Vine Bldg 8th Fl, Seattle, WA	206-623-6666
Engle, Ray & Assoc/626 S Kenmore, Los Angeles, CA	213-381-5001
Exhibit Design Inc/101 S Claremont, San Mateo, CA	415-342-3060
Farber, Melvyn Design Group/406 Bonhill Rd, Los Angeles, CA	213-829-2668
Finger, Julie Design Inc/8467 Melrose Pl, Los Angeles, CA	213-653-0541
Five Penguins Design/269 W Alameda, Burbank, CA	818-841-5576
Floyd Design & Assoc/3451 Golden Gate Way, Lafayette, CA	415-283-1735
Flying Colors/2806 Laguna, San Francisco, CA	415-563-0500
Follis, Dean/2124 Venice Blvd, Los Angeles, CA	213-735-1283
Fox, BD & Friends Advertising Inc/6671 Sunset Blvd, Los Angeles, CA	213-464-0131
Frazier, Craig/173 7th St, San Francisco, CA	415-863-9613
Furniss, Stephanie Design/1327 Via Sessi, San Rafael, CA	415-459-4730
Fusfield, Robert/8306 Wilshire Blvd #2550, Beverly Hills, CA	213-933-2818

G

Garner, Glenn Graphic Design/2366 Eastlake Ave E, Seattle, WA	206-323-7788
Garnett, Joe/12121 Wilshire Blvd #322, Los Angeles, CA	213-826-9378
Georgopoulos/Imada Design/5410 Wilshire Blvd #405, Los Angeles, CA	213-933-6425
Gerber Advertising Agency/1305 SW 12th Ave, Portland, OR	503-221-0100
Gillian/Craig Assoc/165 Eighth St #301, San Francisco, CA	415-558-8988
Girvin, Tim Design/911 Western Ave #408, Seattle, WA	206-623-7918
Glickman, Abe Design/14547 Titus, #201, Van Nuys, CA	818-989-3223
Global West Studio/201 N Occidental Blvd, Los Angeles, CA	213-384-3331
Gold, Judi/8738 Rosewood Ave, West Hollywoood, CA	213-659-4690
Gordon, Roger/10799 N Gate St, Culver City, CA	213-559-8287
Gotschalk's Graphics/3157 Third Ave #3, San Diego, CA	619-298-0085
Gould & Assoc/10549 Jefferson, Culver City, CA	213-879-1900
Graformation/5233 Bakman Ave, N Hollywood, CA	818-985-1224
Graphic Data/804 Tourmaline POB 99991, San Diego, CA	619-274-4511
Graphic Designers Inc/2975 Wilshire Blvd, Los Angeles, CA	213-381-3977
Graphic Ideas/3108 Fifth Ave, San Diego, CA	619-299-3433
Graphic Studio/811 N Highland Ave, Los Angeles, CA	213-466-2666

H

Hale, Dan Ad Design Co/21241 Ventura Blvd #279, Woodland Hills, CA	818-347-4021
Harper and Assoc/2285 116th Ave NE, Bellevue, WA	206-462-0405
Harrington and Associates/11480 Burbank Blvd, N Hollywood, CA	818-508-7322
Harte-Yamashita & Forest/5735 Melrose Ave, Los Angeles, CA	213-462-6486
Hauser, S G Assoc Inc/24009 Ventura Blvd #200, Calabasas, CA	818-884-1727
Helgesson, Ulf Ind Dsgn/4285 Canoga Ave, Woodland Hills, CA	818-883-3772
Hernandez, Daniel/13443 Mulberry Dr #31, Whittier, CA	213-696-0607
Hornall Anderson Design Works/411 First Ave S, Seattle, WA	206-467-5800
Hosick, Frank Design/PO Box H, Vashon Island, WA	206-463-5454
Hubert, Laurent/850 Arbor Rd, Menlo Park, CA	415-321-5182
Humangraphic/4015 Ibis St, San Diego, CA	619-299-0431
Hyde, Bill/751 Matsonia, Foster City, CA	415-345-6955

IJ

Ikkanda, Richard/2800 28th St #105, Santa Monica, CA	213-450-4881
Imag'Inez/41 Grant Ave, San Francisco, CA	415-254-2444
Image Stream/5450 W Washington Blvd, Los Angeles, CA	213-933-9196
Imagination Creative Services/2415 De La Cruz, Santa Clara, CA	408-988-8696
Imagination Graphics/2760 S Harbor Blvd #A, Santa Ana, CA	714-662-3114
J J & A/405 S Flower, Burbank, CA	213-849-1444
Jaciow Design Inc/201 Castro St, Mountain View, CA	415-962-8860
Jerde Partnership/2798 Sunset Blvd, Los Angeles, CA	213-413-0130
Johnson Rodger Design/704 Silver Spur Rd, Rolling Hills, CA	213-377-8860
Johnson, Paige Graphic Design/535 Ramona St, Palo Alto, CA	415-327-0488
Joly Major Product Design Group/2180 Bryant St, San Francisco, CA	415-641-1933
Jones, Steve/1081 Nowita Pl, Venice, CA	213-396-9111
Jonson Pedersen Hinrichs & Shakery/620 Davis St, San Francisco, CA	415-981-6612
Juett, Dennis & Assoc/672 S Lafayette Pk Pl #48, Los Angeles, CA	213-385-4373

KL

K S Wilshire Inc/10494 Santa Monica Blvd, Los Angeles, CA 213-879-9595
Kageyama, David Designer/2119 Smith Tower, Seattle, WA 206-622-7281
Kamins, Deborah/16255 Ventura Blvd #304, Encino, CA 818-905-8536
Keating, Kate Assoc/249 Front St, San Francisco, CA 415-398-6611
Kessler, David & Assoc/1300 N Wilton Pl, Hollywood, CA 213-462-6043
Klein/1111 S Robertson Blvd, Los Angeles, CA 213-278-5600
Kleiner, John A Graphic Design/2627 10th Ct #4, Santa Monica, CA 216-472-7442
Kuey, Patty/20341 Ivy Hill Ln, Yorba Linda, CA 714-970-5286
Lacy, N Lee Assoc Ltd/8446 Melrose Pl, Los Angeles, CA 213-852-1414
Lancaster Design/1810 14th St, Santa Monica, CA 213-450-2999
Landes & Assoc/20313 Mason Court, Torrance, CA 213-540-0907
Landor Associates/Ferryboat Klamath Pier 5, San Francisco, CA 415-955-1200
Larson, Ron/940 N Highland Ave, Los Angeles, CA 213-465-8451
Laurence-Deutsch Design/751 N Highland, Los Angeles, CA 213-937-3521
Leong, Russell Design/535 Ramona #33, Palo Alto, CA 415-321-2443
Leonhardt Group/411 First Ave S #400, Seattle, WA 206-624-0551
Lesser, Joan/Etcetera/3565 Greenwood Ave, Los Angeles, CA 213-397-4575
Levine, Steve & Co/228 Main St, #5, Venice, CA 213-399-9336
Logan Carey & Rehag/353 Folsom St, San Francisco, CA 415-543-7080
Loveless, J R Design/3617 MacArthur Blvd, Santa Ana, CA 714-754-0886
Lumel-Whiteman Assoc/4721 Laurel Canyon #203, North Hollywood, CA 818-769-5332

M

Mabry, Michael/212 Sutter St, San Francisco, CA 415-982-7336
Maddu, Patrick & Co/1842 Third Ave, San Diego, CA 619-238-1340
Manwaring, Michael Office/1005 Sansome St, San Francisco, CA 415-421-3595
Marketing Comm Grp/124 S Arrowhead Ave, San Bernadino, CA 714-885-4976
Marketing Tools/384 Trailview Rd, Encinitas, CA 619-942-6042
Markofski, Don/525 S Myrtle #212, Monrovia, CA 818-446-1222
Marra & Assoc/2800 NW Thurman, Portland, OR 503-227-5207
Matrix Design Consultants/2525 W 7th St, Los Angeles, CA 213-487-6300
Matthews, Robert/1101 Boise Dr, Campbell, CA 408-378-0878
McCargar Design/652 Bair Island Rd #306, Redwood City, CA 415-363-2130
McKee, Dennis/350 Townsend St, San Francisco, CA 415-543-7107
Media Services Corp/10 Aladdin Ter, San Francisco, CA 415-928-3033
Meek, Kenneth/90 N Berkeley, Pasadena, CA 818-449-9722
Mikkelson, Linda S/1624 Vista Del Mar, Hollywood, CA 213-463-3116
Miller, Marcia/425 E Hyde Park, Ingelwood, CA 213-677-4171
Miura Design/1326 Crenshaw #A, Torrance, CA 213-320-1957
Mize, Charles Advertising Art/300 Broadway #29, San Francisco, CA 415-421-1548
Mizrahi, Robert/6256 San Harco Circle, Buena Park, CA 714-527-6182
Mobius Design Assoc/7250 Beverly Blvd #101, Los Angeles, CA 213-937-0331
Molly Designs Inc/15 Chrysler, Irvine, CA 714-768-7155
Murphy, Harry & Friends/225 Miller Ave, Mill Valley, CA 415-383-8586
Murray/Bradley Inc/1904 Third Ave #432, Seattle, WA 206-622-7082

N

N Graphic/480 2nd St #101, San Francisco, CA 415-896-5806
Naganuma, Tony K Design/1100 Montgomery St, San Francisco, CA 415-433-4484
Nagel, William Design Group/167 Hamilton Ave, Palo Alto, CA 415-328-0251
Neill, Richard/9724 Olive St, Bloomington, CA 714-877-5824
New Concepts Industrial Design Corp/1902 N 34th, Seattle, WA 206-633-3111
Nicholson Design/662 Ninth Ave, San Diego, CA 619-235-9000
Nicolini Associates/4046 Maybelle Ave, Oakland, CA 415-531-5569
Niehaus, Don/2380 Malcolm Ave, Los Angeles, CA 213-279-1559
Nine West/9 West State St, Pasadena, CA 818-799-2727
Nordenhook Design/901 Dove St #115, Newport Beach, CA 714-752-8631

OP

Olson Design Inc/853 Camino Del Mar, Del Mar, CA 619-450-9200
Orr, R & Associates Inc/22282 Pewter Ln, El Toro, CA 714-770-1277
Osborn, Michael Design/105 South Park, San Francisco, CA 415-495-4292
Oshima, Carol/1659 E Sachs Place, Covina, CA 818-966-0796
Pacific Rim Design/720 E 27th Ave, Vancouver V5V2K9, BC 604-879-6689
Package Deal/18211 Beneta Way, Tustin, CA 714-541-2440

Pease, Robert & Co/11 Orchard St, Alamo, CA 415-820-0404
Peddicord & Assoc/2290 Walsh, Santa Clara, CA 408-727-7800
Pentagram/620 Davis St, San Francisco, CA 415-981-6612
Persechini & Co/357 S Robertson Blvd, Beverly Hills, CA 213-657-6175
Petzold & Assoc/11830 SW Kerr Pkwy #350, Lake Oswego, OR 503-246-8320
Pihas Schmidt Westerdahl Co/517 SW Fourth Ave, Portland, OR 503-228-4000
Pittard, Billy/6335 Homewood Ave, Hollywood, CA 213-462-2300
Popovich, Mike/15428 E Valley Blvd, City of Industry, CA 818-336-6958
Powers Design International/822 Production Pl, Newport Beach, CA 714-645-2265
Primo Angeli Graphics/508 4th St, San Francisco, CA 415-974-6100

R

RJL Design Graphics/44110 Old Warm Springs Blvd, Fremont, CA 415-657-2038
Rand, Vicki/4087 Glencoe Ave, Marina Del Rey, CA 213-306-9779
Rankin, Bob Assoc/13804 NE 20th St #C, Bellevue, WA 206-641-4020
Reid, Scott/432 State St, Santa Barbara, CA 805-963-8926
Reineck & Reineck/1425 Cole St, San Francisco, CA 415-566-3614
Reineman, Richard Industrial Design/601 Clubhouse Ave, Newport Beach, CA 714-673-2485
Reis, Gerald & Co/560 Sutter St #301, San Francisco, CA 415-421-1232
Rickabaugh Design/213 SW Ash #209, Portland, OR 503-223-2191
Ritola, Roy Inc/714 Sansome St, San Francisco, CA 415-788-7010
Roberts, Eileen/PO Box 1261, Carlsbad, CA 619-439-7800
Robinson, David/3607 Fifth Ave #6, San Diego, CA 619-298-2021
Rogow & Bernstein Dsgn/5971 W 3rd St, Los Angeles, CA 213-936-9916
Rohde, Gretchen/411 First Ave S #550, Seattle, WA 206-623-9459
Rolandesign/21833 De La Luz Ave, Woodland Hills, CA 818-346-9752
Runyan, Richard Design/12016 Wilshire Blvd, West Los Angeles, CA 213-477-8878
Runyan, Robert Miles & Assoc/200 E Culver Blvd, Playa Del Rey, CA 213-823-0975
Rupert, Paul Designer/728 Montgomery St, San Francisco, CA 415-391-2966

S

Sackheim, Morton Enterprises/170 N Robertson Blvd, Beverly Hills, CA 213-652-0220
San Diego Art Prdctns/2752 Imperial Ave, San Diego, CA 619-239-6666
Sanchez/Kamps Assoc/60 W Green St, Pasadena, CA 213-793-4017
Sant'Andrea, Jim West Inc/855 W Victoria St #1A, Compton, CA 213-979-5449
Schaefer, Robert Television Art/738 N Cahuenga, Hollywood, CA 213-462-7877
Schockner, Jan/PO Box 306, Ross, CA 415-456-7711
Schorer, R Thomas/27580 Silver Spur Rd #201, Palos Verdes, CA 213-377-0207
Schwab, Michael Design/118 King St, San Francisco, CA 415-546-7559
Schwartz, Bonnie/Clem/2941 4th Ave, San Diego, CA 619-291-8878
Seiniger & Assoc/8201 W 3rd, Los Angeles, CA 213-653-8665
Shaw, Michael Design/819 17th St, Manhattan Beach, CA 213-545-0516
Shenon, Mike/576 Cambridge Ave, Palo Alto, CA 415-493-6878
Shimokochi/Reeves Design/6043 Hollywood Blvd #203, Los Angeles, CA 213-460-4916
Shoji Graphics/4121 Wilshire Blvd #315, Los Angeles, CA 213-384-3091
Sidjakov, Nicholas/3727 Buchanan, San Francisco, CA 415-931-7500
Signworks/7710 Aurora Ave N, Seattle, WA 206-525-2718
Slavin, David/1901 Ave Of Stars #450, Los Angeles, CA 213-557-1331
Smidt, Sam/666 High St, Palo Alto, CA 415-327-0707
Sorensen, Hugh Industrial Design/841 Westridge Way, Brea, CA 714-529-8493
Soyster & Ohrenschall Inc/575 Sutter St, San Francisco, CA 415-956-7575
Spear, Jeffrey A/1228 11th St #201, Santa Monica, CA 213-395-3939
Specht/Watson Studio/1246 S La Cienega BLvd, Los Angeles, CA 213-652-2682
Sperling, Lauren/128 S Bowling Green Way, Los Angeles, CA 213-472-9957
Spivey, William Design Inc/21911 Winnebago, Lake Forrest, CA 714-770-7931
Starr Seigle McCombs Inc/1001 Bishop Sq #19 Pcfc Twr, Honolulu, HI 808-524-5080
Stephenz, The Group/145 Dillon Ave Bldg D, Campbell, CA 408-379-4883
Strong, David Design Group/2030 First Ave #201, Seattle, WA 206-447-9160
Studio A/5801-A S Eastern Ave, Los Angeles, CA 213-721-1802

GRAPHIC DESIGNERS

Graphic Design
Continued

Please send us your additions and updates.

Sugi, Richard Design & Assoc/844 Colorado Blvd #202, Los Angeles, CA	213-385-4169
Superior Graphic Systems/1700 W Anaheim St, Long Beach, CA	213-433-7421
Sussman & Prejza/1651 18th St, Santa Monica, CA	213-829-3337

T

Tackett/Barbaria/1990 3rd St #400, Sacramento, CA	916-442-3200
The Blank Co/1048 Lincoln Ave, San Jose, CA	408-289-9095
The Coakley Heagerty Co/122 Saratoga Ave # 28, Santa Clara, CA	408-249-6242
The Design Works/2205 Stoner Ave, Los Angeles, CA	213-477-3577
The Designory Inc/351 E 6th St, Long Beach, CA	213-432-5707
The Gnu Group/2200 Bridgeway Blvd, Sausalito, CA	415-332-8010
The Quorum/305 NE Mapleleaf Pl, Seattle, WA	206-522-6872
The Smith Group/520 NW Davis St #325, Portland, OR	503-224-1905
The Stansbury Company/9304 Santa Monica Blvd, Beverly Hills, CA	213-273-1138
The Studio/45 Houston, San Francisco, CA	415-928-4400
Thomas & Assoc/532 Colorado Ave, Santa Monica, CA	213-451-8502
Thomas, Greg/2238 1/2 Purdue Ave, Los Angeles, CA	213-479-8477
Thomas, Keith M Inc/3211 Shannon, Santa Ana, CA	714-261-1161
Torme, Dave/55 Francisco St, San Francisco, CA	415-391-2694
Trade Marx/1100 Pike St, Seattle, WA	206-623-7676
Tribotti Design/15234 Morrison St, Sherman Oaks, CA	818-784-6101
Trygg Stefanic Advertising/127 Second St #1, Los Altos, CA	415-948-3493
Tycer Fultz Bellack/1731 Embarcadero Rd, Palo Alto, CA	415-856-1600

V

VanNoy & Co Inc/19750 S Vermont, Torrance, CA	213-329-0800
Vanderbyl Design/One Zoe St, San Francisco, CA	415-543-8447
Vantage Advertising & Marketing Assoc/433 Callan Ave POB 3095, San Leandro, CA	415-352-3640
Vigon, Larry/101 S Sycamore Ave #1, Los Angeles, CA	213-394-6502
Visual Resources Inc/1556 N Fairfax, Los Angeles, CA	213-851-6688
Voltec Associates/560 N Larchmont, Los Angeles, CA	213-467-2106

W

Walton, Brenda/PO Box 161976, Sacramento, CA	916-456-5833
Webster, Ken/67 Brookwood Rd #6, Orinda, CA	415-954-2516
Weideman and Associates/4747 Vineland Ave, North Hollywood, CA	818-769-8488
Wells, John/407 Jackson St, San Francisco, CA	415-956-3952
Wertman, Chuck/559 Pacific Ave, San Francisco, CA	415-433-4452
West End Studios/40 Gold St, San Francisco, CA	415-434-0380
West, Suzanne Design/535 Ramona St, Palo Alto, CA	415-324-8068
White + Assoc/137 N Virgil Ave #204, Los Angeles, CA	213-380-6319
Whitely, Mitchell Assoc/716 Montgomery St, San Francisco, CA	415-398-2920
Wilkins & Peterson Graphic Design/206 Third Ave S #300, Seattle, WA	206-624-1695
Willardson + Assoc/103 W California, Glendale, CA	818-242-5688
WILLIAM & HINDS/2790 SKYPARK DR #112, TORRANCE, CA (P 45)	**213-539-3252**
Williams & Ziller Design/330 Fell St, San Francisco, CA	415-621-0330
Williams, John/330 Fell St, San Francisco, CA	415-621-0330
Williamson & Assoc Inc/8800 Venice Blvd, Los Angeles, CA	213-836-0143
Winters, Clyde Design/2200 Mason St, San Francisco, CA	415-391-5643
Woo, Calvin Assoc/4015 Ibis St, San Diego, CA	619-299-0431
Workshop West/9720 Wilshire Blvd #700, Beverly Hills, CA	213-278-1370

YZ

Yamaguma & Assoc/12 S First St #500, San Jose, CA	408-279-0500
Yanez, Maurice & Assoc/770 S Arroyo Pky, Pasadena, CA	818-792-0778
Yee, Ray/424 Larchmont Blvd, Los Angeles, CA	213-465-2514
Young & Roehr Adv/6415 SW Canyon Ct, Portland, OR	503-297-4501
Yuguchi Krogstad/3378 W 1st St, Los Angeles, CA	213-383-6915
Zamparelli & Assoc/1450 Lomita Dr, Pasadena, CA	818-799-4370

Labs & Retouchers

New York City

ACS Studios/2 West 46th St	212-575-9250
ASAP Photolab/40 E 49th St	212-832-1223
AT & S Retouching/230 E 44th St	212-986-0977
AZO Color Labs/149 Madison Ave	212-982-6610
Accu-Color Group Inc/103 Fifth Ave	212-989-8235
Adams Photoprint Co Inc/60 E 42nd St	212-697-4980
Alchemy Color Ltd/125 W 45th St	212-997-1944
American Blue Print Co Inc/7 E 47th St	212-751-2240
American Photo Print Co/350 Fifth Ave	212-736-2885
American Photo Print Co/285 Madison Ave	212-532-2424
Andy's Place/17 E 48th St	212-371-1362
Apco-Apeda Photo Co/250 W 54th St	212-586-5755
Appel, Albert/119 W 23rd St	212-989-6585
Arkin-Medo/30 E 33rd St	212-685-1969
Atlantic Blue Print Co/575 Madison Ave	212-755-3388
Authenticolor Labs Inc/227 E 45th St	212-867-7905
Avekta Productions Inc/164 Madison Ave	212-686-4550
Bebell Color Labs/416 W 45th St	212-245-8900
Bell-Tait, Carolyn/10 W 33rd St	212-947-9449
Bellis, Dave/15 E 55th St	212-753-3740
Bellis, Dave Studios/155 E 55th St	212-753-3740
Benjamin, Bernard/1763 Second Ave	212-722-7773
Berger, Jack/41 W 53rd St	212-245-5705
Berkey K & L/222 E 44th St	212-661-5600
Bishop Retouching/236 E 36th St	212-889-3525
Blae, Ken Studios/1501 Broadway	212-869-3488
Bluestone Photoprint Co Inc/19 W 34th St	212-564-1516
Bonaventura Studio/307 E 44th St #1612	212-687-9208
Broderson, Charles Backdrops/873 Broadway #612	212-925-9392
Brunel, Jean Inc/11 Jay St	212-226-3009
C & C Productions/445 E 80th St	212-472-3700
Cacchione & Sheehan/1 West 37th St	212-869-2233
Carlson & Forino Studios/230 E 44th St	212-697-7044
Cavalluzzo, Dan/49 W 45th St	212-921-5954
Certified Color Service/2812 41st Ave	212-392-6065
Chapman, Edwin W/20 E 46th St	212-697-0872
Chroma Copy/423 West 55th St	212-399-2420
Chrome Print/104 E 25th St	212-228-0840
CitiChrome Lab/158 W 29th St	212-695-0935
Clayman, Andrew/334 Bowery #6F	212-674-4906
Colmer, Brian-The Final touch/310 E 46th St	212-682-3012
Coln, Stewart/563 Eleventh Ave	212-868-1440
Color Design Studio/19 W 21st St	212-255-8103
Color Masters Inc/143 E 27th St	212-889-7464
Color Perfect Inc/200 Park Ave S	212-777-1210
Color Pro Labs/40 W 37th St	212-563-5599
Color Unlimited Inc/443 Park Ave S	212-889-2440
Color Vision Photo Finishers/642 9th Avenue	212-757-2787
Color Wheel Inc/227 E 45th St	212-697-2434
Colorama Labs/40 W 37th St	212-279-1950
Colorite Film Processing/115 E 31st St	212-532-2116
Colotone Litho Seperator/555 Fifth Ave	212-557-5564
Columbia Blue & Photoprint Co/14 E 39th St	212-532-9424
Commerce Photo Print Co/415 Lexington Ave	212-986-2068
Compo Photocolor/18 E 48th St	212-758-1690
Copy-Line Corp/40 W 37th St	212-563-3535
Copycolor/8 W 30th St	212-725-8252
Copytone Inc/8 W 45th St	212-575-0235
Cordero, Felix/159 E 104th St	212-289-2861
Corona Color Studios Inc/10 W 33rd St	212-239-4990
Cortese, Phyllis/306 E 52nd St	212-421-4664
Crandall, Robert Assoc/306 E 45th St	212-661-4710
Creative Color Inc/25 W 45th St	212-582-3841
Crowell, Joyce/333 E 30th St	212-683-3055
Crown Photo/370 W 35th St	212-279-1950

Dai Nippon Printing/1633 Broadway	212-397-1880
Davis-Ganes/15 E 40th St	212-687-6537
DiPierro-Turiel/210 E 47th St	212-752-2260
Diamond Art Studio/11 E 36th St	212-685-6622
Diamond, Richard/50 E 42nd St	212-697-4720
Diana Studio/301 W 53rd St	212-757-0445
Dimension Color Labs Inc/1040 Ave of Amer	212-354-5918
Drop Everything/20 W 20th St	212-242-2735
Duggal Color Projects Inc/9 W 20th St	212-924-6363
Dzurella, Paul Studio/15 W 38th St	212-840-8623
Ecay, Thom/49 W 45th St	212-840-6277
Edstan Productions/240 Madison Ave	212-686-3666
Egelston Retouching Services/333 Fifth Ave 3rd Fl	212-213-9095
Evans-Avedisian DiStefano Inc/29 W 38th St	212-697-4240
Filmstat/520 Fifth Ave	212-840-1676
Fine-Art Color Lab Inc/221 Park Ave S	212-674-7640
Finley Photographics Inc/488 Madison Ave	212-688-3025
Flax, Sam Inc/111 Eighth Ave	212-620-3000
Flushing Photo Center/36-33 Main St	718-658-6033
Fodale Studio/247 E 50th St	212-755-0150
Forway Studios Inc/441 Lexington Ave	212-661-0260
Four Colors Photo Lab Inc/10 E 39th St	212-889-3399
Foursome Color Litho/30 Irving Pl	212-475-9219
Frenchys Color Lab/10 E 38th St	212-889-7787
Frey, Louis Co Inc/90 West St	212-791-0500
Friedlob, Herbert/1810 Ave N #3C	718-375-4857
Friedman, Estelle Retouchers/160 E 38th St	212-532-0084
Fromia, John A/799 Broadway	212-473-7930
FUJI FILM/350 FIFTH AVE	
GW Color Lab/36 E 23rd St	212-677-3800
Gads Color/135 W 41st St	212-221-0923
Gayde, Richard Assoc Inc/515 Madison Ave	212-421-4088
Gilbert Studio/210 E 36th St	212-683-3472
Giraldi, Bob Prodctns/581 Sixth Ave	212-691-9200
Goodman, Irwin Inc/1156 Avenue of the Americas	212-944-6337
Graphic Images Ltd/151 W 46th St	212-869-8370
Gray, George Studios/230 E 44th St	212-661-0276
Greller, Fred/325 E 64th St	212-535-6240
Grubb, Louis D/155 Riverside Dr	212-873-2561
H-Y Photo Service/16 E 52nd St	212-371-3018
Hadar, Eric Studio/10 E 39th St	212-889-2092
Hudson Reproductions Inc/76 Ninth Ave	212-989-3400
J & R Color Lab/29 W 38th St	212-869-9870
J M W Studio Inc/230 E 44th St	212-986-9155
JFC Color Labs Inc/443 Park Ave S	212-889-0727
Jaeger, Elliot/49 W 45th St	212-840-6278
Jellybean Photographics Inc/99 Madison Ave 14th Fl	212-679-4888
KG Studios Inc/56 W 45th St	212-840-7930
Katz, David Studio/6 E 39th St	212-889-5038
Kaye Graphics Inc/151 Lexington Ave	212-889-8240
Kurahara, Joan/611 Broadway	212-505-8589
LaFerla, Sandro/108 W 25th St	212-620-0693
Langen & Wind Color Lab/265 Madison Ave	212-686-1818
Larson Color Lab/123 Fifth Ave	212-674-0610
Laumont Color Labs/333 W 52nd St	212-245-2113
Lieberman, Ken Laboratories/118 W 22nd St 4th Fl	212-633-0500
Loy-Taubman Inc/34 E 30th St	212-685-6871
Lucas, Bob/10 E 38th St	212-725-2090
Lukon Art Service Ltd/56 W 45th St 3rd Fl	212-575-0474
Mann & Greene Color Inc/320 E 39th St	212-481-6868
Manna Color Labs Inc/42 W 15th St	212-691-8860
Marshall, Henry/6 E 39th St	212-686-1060
Martin, Tulio G Studio/140 W 57th St	212-245-6489
Martin/Arnold Color Systems/150 Fifth Ave #429	212-675-7270
Mayer, Kurt Color Labs Inc/1170 Broadway	212-532-3738
McCurdy & Cardinale Color Lab/65 W 36th St	212-695-5140
McWilliams, Clyde/151 West 46th St	212-221-3644
Media Universal Inc/116 W 32nd St	212-695-7454
Medina Studios Inc/141 E 44th St	212-867-3113
Miller, Norm & Steve/17 E 48th St	212-752-4830
Modernage Photo Services/312 E 46th St	212-661-9190
Moser, Klaus T Ltd/127 E 15th St	212-475-0038

Production/Support Services

Continued

Please send us your additions and updates.

Motal Custom Darkrooms/25 W 45th St 3rd Fl	212-757-7874
Murray Hill Photo Print Inc/32 W 39th St	212-921-4175
My Lab Inc/117 E 30th St	212-686-8684
My Own Color Lab/45 W 45th St	212-391-8638
National Reprographics Co/110 W 32nd St	212-736-5674
New York Camera/131 W 35th St	212-564-4398
New York Film Works Inc/928 Broadway	212-475-5700
New York Flash Rental/156 Fifth Ave	212-741-1165
Olden Camera/1265 Broadway	212-725-1234
Ornaal Color Photos/24 W 25th St	212-675-3850
PIC Color Corp/25 W 45th St	212-575-5600
Paccione, E S Inc/150 E 56th St	212-755-0965
Palevitz, Bob/333 E 30th St	212-684-6026
Pastore dePamphilis Rampone/145 E 32nd St	212-889-2221
Pergament Color/305 E 47th St	212-751-5367
Photo Retouch Inc/160 E 38th St	212-532-0084
Photographic Color Specialists Inc./10-36 47th Rd	718-786-4770
Photographics Unlimited/43 W 22nd St	212-255-9678
Photorama/239 W 39th St	212-354-5280
Portogallo Photo Services/72 W 45th St	212-840-2636
Positive Color Inc/405 Lexington	212-687-9600
Precision Chromes Inc/310 Madison Ave	212-687-5990
Preferred Photographic Co/165 W 46th St	212-757-0237
Procil Adstat Co Inc/7 W 45th St	212-819-0155
Prussack, Phil/155 E 55th St	212-755-2470
Quality Color Lab/305 E 46th St	212-753-2200
R & V Studio/32 W 39th St	212-944-9590
Rahum Supply Co/1165 Broadway	212-685-4784
Rainbow Graphics & Chrome Services/49 W 45th St	212-869-3232
Ram Retouching/380 Madison Ave	212-599-0985
Ramer, Joe Assoc/509 Madison Ave	212-751-0894
Rasulo Graphics Service/36 E 31st St	212-686-2861
Regal Velox/25 W 43rd St	212-840-0330
Reiter Dulberg/157 W 54th St	212-582-6871
Renaissance Retouching/136 W 46th St	212-575-5618
Reproduction Color Specialists/9 E 38th St	212-683-0833
Retouchers Gallery/211 E 53rd St	212-751-9203
Retouching Inc/9 E 38th St	212-683-4188
Retouching Plus/125 W 45th St	212-764-5959
Rio Enterprises/240 E 58th St	212-758-9300
Rivera and Schiff Assoc Inc/21 W 38th St	212-354-2977
Robotti, Thomas/5 W 46th St	212-840-0215
Rogers Color Lab Corp/165 Madison Ave	212-683-6400
Russo Photo Service/432 W 45th St	212-247-3817
Sa-Kura Retouching/123 W 44th St	212-764-5944
San Photo-Art Service/165 W 29th St	212-594-0850
Sang Color Inc/19 W 34th St	212-594-4205
Scala Fine Arts Publishers Inc/65 Bleecker St	212-673-4988
Schiavone, Joe/301 W 53rd St #4E	212-757-0660
Scope Assoc/11 E 22nd St	212-674-4190
Scott Screen Prints/228 E 45th St	212-697-8923
Scott, Diane Assoc/339 E 58th St	212-355-4616
Sharkey, Dick The Studio/301 W 53rd St	212-265-1036
Sharron Photographic Labs/260 W 36th St	212-239-4980
Simmons-Beal Inc/3 E 40th St	212-532-6261
Skeehan Black & White/61 W 23rd St	212-675-5454
Slide Shop Inc/220 E 23rd St	212-725-5200
Slide by Slide/445 E 80th St	212-879-5091
Spano/Roccanova Retouching Inc/16 W 46th St	212-840-7450
Spector, Hy Studios/56 W 45th St	212-221-3656
Spectrum Creative Retouchers Inc/230 E 44th St	212-687-3359
Stanley, Joseph/211 W 58th St	212-246-1258
Steinhauser, Art Retouching/305 E 40th St	212-953-1722
Stewart Color Labs Inc/563 Eleventh Ave	212-868-1440
Studio 55/39 W 38th St	212-840-0920
Studio Chrome Lab Inc/36 W 25th St	212-989-6767
Studio Macbeth Inc/130 W 42nd St	212-921-8922
Studio X/20 W 20th St	212-989-9233
Sunlight Graphics/401 5th Ave	212-683-4452
Super Photo Color Services/165 Madison Ave	212-686-9510
Sutton Studio/112 E 17th St	212-777-0301
T R P Slavin Colour Services/920 Broadway	212-674-5700
Tanksley, John Studios Inc/210 E 47th St	212-752-1150
Tartaro Color Lab/29 W 38th St	212-840-1640
The Creative Color Print Lab Inc/25 W 45th St	212-582-6237
The Darkroom Inc/222 E 46th St	212-687-8920
Todd Photoprint Inc/1600 Broadway	212-245-2440
Trio Studio/18 E 48th St	212-752-4875
Truglio, Frank & Assoc/835 Third Ave	212-371-7635
Twenty/Twenty Photographers Place/20 W 20th St	212-675-2020
Ultimate Image/443 Park Ave S 7th Fl	212-683-4838
Van Chromes Corp/311 W 43rd St	212-582-0505
Venezia, Don Retouching/488 Madison Ave	212-688-7649
Verilen Reproductions/3 E 40th St	212-686-7774
Vidachrome Inc/25 W 39th St 6th Fl	212-391-8124
Vogue Wright Studios/423 West 55th St	212-977-3400
Wagner Photoprint Co/121 W 50th St	212-245-4796
Ward, Jack Color Service/220 E 23rd St	212-725-5200
Way Color Inc/420 Lexington Ave	212-687-5610
Weber, Martin J Studio/171 Madison Ave	212-532-2695
Weiman & Lester Inc/21 E 40th St	212-679-1180
Welbeck Studios Inc/39 W 38th St	212-869-1660
Wind, Gerry & Assoc/265 Madison Ave	212-686-1818
Winter, Jerry Studio/333 E 45th St	212-490-0876
Wolf, Bill/212 E 47th St	212-697-6215
Wolsk, Bernard/509 Madison Ave	212-751-7727
Zazula, Hy Assoc/2 W 46th St	212-819-0444

Northeast

Able Art Service/8 Winter St, Boston, MA	617-482-4558
Adams & Abbott Inc/46 Summer St, Boston, MA	617-542-1621
Alfie Custom Color/155 N Dean St, Englewood, NJ	201-569-2028
Alves Photo Service/14 Storrs Ave, Braintree, MA	617-843-5555
Artography Labs/2419 St Paul St, Baltimore, MD	301-467-5575
Asman Custom Photo Service Inc/926 Pennsylvania Ave SE, Washington, DC	202-547-7713
Assoc Photo Labs/1820 Gilford, Montreal, QU	514-523-1139
Blakeslee Lane Studio/916 N Charles St, Baltimore, MD	301-727-8800
Blow-Up/2441 Maryland Ave, Baltimore, MD	301-467-3636
Bonaventure Color Labs/425 Guy St, Montreal, QU	514-989-1919
Boris Color Lab/35 Landsdowne St, Boston, MA	617-437-1152
Boston Photo Service/112 State St, Boston, MA	617-523-0508
Calverts Inc/938 Highland Ave, Needham Hts, MA	617-444-8000
Campbell Photo & Printing/1328 'I' St NW, Washington, DC	202-347-9800
Central Color/1 Prospect Ave, White Plains, NY	914-681-0218
Chester Photo/398 Centrl Pk Ave/Grnvl Plz, Scarsdale, NY	914-472-8088
Color Film Corp/440 Summer St, Boston, MA	617-426-5655
Colorama/420 Valley Brook Ave, Lyndhurst, NJ	201-933-5660
Colorlab/5708 Arundel Ave, Rockville, MD	301-770-2128
Colortek/111 Beach St, Boston, MA	617-451-0894
Colotone Litho Seperator/260 Branford Rd/Box 97, North Branford, CT	203-481-6190
Complete Photo Service/703 Mt Auburn St, Cambridge, MA	617-864-5954
Delbert, Christian/19 Linell Circle, Billerica, MA	617-273-3138
Dimension Systems/680 Rhd Islnd Ave NE/Upper Lvl, Washington, DC	202-832-5401
Dunigan, John V/62 Minnehaha Blvd, PO Box 70, Oakland, NJ	201-337-6656
Dunlop Custom Photolab Service/2321 4th St NE, Washington, DC	202-526-5000
Durkin, Joseph/25 Huntington, Boston, MA	617-267-0437
EPD Photo Service/67 Fulton Ave, Hempstead, NY	516-486-5300
Eastman Kodak/343 State St, Rochester, NY	716-724-4688
Five-Thousand K/281 Summer St, Boston, MA	617-542-5995
Foto Fidelity Inc/35 Leon St, Boston, MA	617-267-6487
G F I Printing & Photo Co/2 Highland St, Port Chester, NY	914-937-2823
Gould, David/76 Coronado St, Atlantic Beach, NY	516-371-2413
Gourdon, Claude Photo Lab/60 Sir Louis VI, St Lambert, QU	514-671-4604
Graphic Accent/446 Main St PO Box 243, Wilmington, MA	617-658-7602
Iderstine, Van/148 State Hwy 10, E Hanover, NJ	201-887-7879
Image Inc/1919 Pennsylvania Ave, Washington, DC	202-833-1550
Industrial Color Lab/P O Box 563, Framingham, MA	617-872-3280
JTM Photo Labs Inc/125 Rt 110, Huntington Station, NY	516-549-0010
K E W Color Labs/112 Main St, Norwalk, CT	203-853-7888

Leonardo Printing Corp/529 E 3rd St, Mount Vernon, NY	914-664-7890
Light-Works Inc/77 College St, Burlington, VT	802-658-6815
Meyers, Tony/W 70 Century Rd, Paramus, NJ	201-265-6000
Modern Mass Media/Box 950, Chatham, NJ	201-635-6000
Moore's Photo Laboratory/1107 Main St, Charleston, WV	304-357-4541
Muggeo, Sam/63 Hedgebrook Lane, Stamford, CT	212-972-0398
Musy, Mark/PO Box 755, Buckingham, PA	215-794-8851
National Color Labs Inc/306 W 1st Ave, Roselle, NJ	201-241-1010
National Photo Service/1475 Bergen Blvd, Fort Lee, NJ	212-860-2324
Noll, Chris/Photo Hand-Tinting, , NJ	201-775-6825
Northeast Color Research/40 Cameron Ave, Somerville, MA	617-666-1161
Ogunquit Photo School/PO Box 568, Ogunquit, ME	207-646-7055
Photo Dynamics/PO Box 731, 70 Jackson Dr, Cranford, NJ	201-272-8880
Photo Publishers/1899 'L' St NW, Washington, DC	202-833-1234
Photo-Colortura/PO Box 1749, Boston, MA	617-522-5132
Regester Photo Service/50 Kane St, Baltimore, MD	301-633-7600
Retouching Graphics Inc/205 Roosevelt Ave, Massapequa Park, NY	516-541-2960
Riter, Warren/2291 Penfield, Pittsford, NY	716-381-4368
Rothman, Henry/6927 N 19th St, Philadelphia, PA	215-424-6927
STI Group/606 W Houstatonic St, Pittsfield, MA	413-443-7900
Select Photo Service/881 Montee de Liesse, Montreal, QU	514-735-2509
Snyder, Jeffrey/915 E Street NW, Washington, DC	202-347-5777
Spaulding Co Inc/301 Columbus, Boston, MA	617-262-1935
Starlab Photo/4727 Miller Ave, Washington, DC	301-986-5300
Sterling Photo Processing/345 Main St, Norwalk, CT	203-847-9145
Stone Reprographics/44 Brattle St, Cambridge, MA	617-495-0200
Subtractive Technology/338-B Newbury St, Boston, MA	617-437-1887
Superior Photo Retouching Service/1955 Mass Ave, Cambridge, MA	617-661-9094
Technical Photography Inc/1275 Bloomfield Ave, Fairfield, NJ	201-227-4646
The Darkroom/443 Broadway, Saratoga Springs, NY	518-587-6465
The Darkroom Inc/232 First Ave, Pittsburgh, PA	412-261-6056
Trama, Gene/571 South Ave, Rochester, NY	716-232-6122
Universal Color Lab/810 Salaberry, Chomeday, QU	514-384-2251
Van Vort, Donald D/71 Capital Hts Rd, Oyster Bay, NY	516-922-5234
Visual Horizons/180 Metropark, Rochester, NY	716-424-5300
Von Eiff, Damon/7649 Old Georgeton Std 9, Bethesda, MD	301-951-8887
Weinstock, Bernie/162 Boylston, Boston, MA	617-423-4481
Wilson, Paul/25 Huntington Ave, Boston, MA	617-437-1236
Zoom Photo Lab/45 St Jacques, Montreal, QU	514-288-5444

Southeast

A Printers Film Service/904-D Norwalk, Greensboro, NC	919-852-1275
AAA Blue Print Co/3649 Piedmont Rd, Atlanta, GA	404-261-1580
Advance Color Processing Inc/1807 Ponce de Leon Blvd, Miami, FL	305-443-7323
Allen Photo/3808 Wilson Blvd, Arlington, VA	703-524-7121
Associated Photographers/19 SW 6th St, Miami, FL	305-373-4774
Atlanta Blue Print/1052 W Peachtree St N E, Atlanta, GA	404-873-5911
B & W Processing/6808 Hanging Moss, Orlando, FL	305-677-8078
Barral, Yolanda/100 Florida Blvd, Miami, FL	305-261-4767
Berkey Film Processing/1200 N Dixie Hwy, Hollywood, FL	305-927-8411
Bristow Photo Service/2018 Wilson St, Hollywood, FL	305-920-1377
Chromatics/625 Fogg St, Nashville, TN	615-254-0063
Clark Studio/6700 Sharon Rd, Charlotte, NC	704-552-1021
Color Copy Center/5745 Columbia Cir, W Palm Beach, FL	305-842-9500
Color Copy Inc/925 Gervais St, Columbia, SC	803-256-0225
Color Image-Atlanta/478 Armour Circle, Atlanta, GA	404-876-0209
Colorcraft of Columbia/331 Sunset Shopping Center, Columbia, SC	803-252-0600
Customlab/508 Armour Cr, Atlanta, GA	404-875-0289
Dixie Color Lab/520 Highland S, Memphis, TN	901-458-1818
E-Six Lab/53 14th St NE, Atlanta, GA	404-885-1293
Eagle Photographics/3612 Swann Ave, Tampa, FL	813-870-2495
Florida Color Lab/PO Box 10907, Tampa, FL	813-877-8658
Florida Photo Inc/781 NE 125th St, N Miami, FL	305-891-6616
Fordyce, R B Photography/4873 NW 36th St, Miami, FL	305-885-3406
Gables Blueprint Co/4075 Ponce De Leone Blvd, Coral Gables, FL	305-443-7146
General Color Corporation/604 Brevard Ave, Cocoa Beach, FL	305-631-1602

Infinite Color/2 East Glebe Rd, Alexandria, VA	703-549-2242
Inter-American Photo/8157 NW 60th St, Miami, FL	305-592-3833
Janousek & Kuehl/3300 NE Expressway #1-I, Atlanta, GA	404-458-8989
Klickovich, Robert Retouching/1638 Eastern Pkwy, Louisville, KY	502-459-0295
Laser Color Labs/Fairfield Dr, W Palm Beach, FL	305-848-2000
Litho Color Plate/7887 N W 55th St, Miami, FL	305-592-1605
Mid-South Color Laboratories/496 Emmet, Jackson, TN	901-422-6691
Northside Blueprint Co/5141 New Peachtree Rd, Atlanta, GA	404-458-8411
Par Excellence/2900 Youree Dr, Shreveport, LA	318-869-2533
Photo-Pros/635 A Pressley Rd, Charlotte, NC	704-525-0551
Plunkett Graphics/1052 W Peachtree St, Atlanta, GA	404-873-5976
Remington Models & Talent/2480 E Commercial Blvd PH, Ft Lauderdale, FL	305-566-5420
Reynolds, Charles/1715 Kirby Pkwy, Memphis, TN	901-754-2411
Rich, Bob Photo/12495 NE 6th Ave, Miami, FL	305-893-6137
Rothor Color Labs/1251 King St, Jacksonville, FL	904-388-7717
S & S Pro Color Inc/2801 S MacDill Ave, Tampa, FL	813-831-1811
Sheffield & Board/18 E Main St, Richmond, VA	804-649-8870
Smith's Studio/2420 Wake Forest Rd, Raleigh, NC	919-834-6491
Spectrum Custom Color Lab/302 E Davis Blvd, Tampa, FL	813-251-0338
Studio Masters Inc/1398 NE 125th St, N Miami, FL	305-893-3500
Supreme Color Inc/71 NW 29th St, Miami, FL	305-573-2934
Taffae, Syd/3550 N Bayhomes Dr, Miami, FL	305-667-5252
The Color Lab/111 NE 21st St, Miami, FL	305-576-3207
Thomson Photo Lab Inc/4210 Ponce De Leon Blvd, Coral Gables, FL	305-443-0669
Viva-Color Labs/121 Linden Ave NE, Atlanta, GA	404-881-1313
World Color Inc/1281 US #1 North, Ormond Beach, FL	904-677-1332

Midwest

A-1 Photo Service/105 W Madison St #907, Chicago, IL	312-346-2248
AC Color Lab Inc/2160 Payne Ave, Cleveland, OH	216-621-4575
Absolute Color Slides/197 Dundas E, Toronto 15A 124, ON	416-868-0413
Ad Photo/2056 E 4th St, Cleveland, OH	216-621-9360
Advantage Printers/1307 S Wabash, Chicago, IL	312-663-0933
Airbrush Arts/1235 Glenview Rd, Glenview, IL	312-998-8345
Amato Photo Color/818 S 75th St, Omaha, NE	402-393-8380
Anderson Graphics/521 N 8th St, Milwaukee, WI	414-276-4445
Anro Color/1819 9th St, Rockford, IL	815-962-0884
Arrow Photo Copy/523 S Plymouth St, Chicago, IL	312-427-9515
Artstreet/111 E Chestnut St, Chicago, IL	312-664-3049
Astra Photo Service/6 E Lake, Chicago, IL	312-372-4366
Astro Color Labs/61 W Erie St, Chicago, IL	312-280-5500
BGM Color Labs/497 King St E, Toronto, ON	416-947-1325
Benjamin Film Labs/287 Richmond St, Toronto, ON	416-863-1166
Boulevard Photo/333 N Michigan Ave, Chicago, IL	312-263-3508
Brookfield Photo Service/9146 Broadway, Brookfield, IL	312-485-1718
Buffalo Photo Co/60 W Superior, Chicago, IL	312-787-6476
Carriage Barn Studio/2360 Riverside Dr, Beloit, WI	608-365-2405
Chroma Studios/2300 Maryland Ln, Columbus, OH	614-471-1191
Chromatics Ltd/4507 N Kedzie Ave, Chicago, IL	312-478-3850
Cockrell, Ray/1737 McGee, Kansas City, MO	816-471-5959
Color Central/612 N Michigan Ave, Chicago, IL	312-321-1696
Color Corp of Canada/1198 Eglinton W, Toronto, ON	416-783-0320
Color Darkroom Corp/3320 W Vliet St, Milwaukee, WI	414-344-3377
Color Detroit Inc/310 Livernois, Ferndale, MI	313-546-1800
Color Graphics Inc/5809 W Divison St, Chicago, IL	312-261-4143
Color International Labs/593 N York St, Elmhurst, IL	312-279-6632
Color Perfect Inc/24 Custer St, Detroit, MI	313-872-5115
Color Service Inc/325 W Huron St, Chicago, IL	312-664-5225
Color Studio Labs/1553 Dupont, Toronto, ON	416-531-1177
Color Systems/5719 N Milwaukee Ave, Chicago, IL	312-763-6664
Color Technique Inc/57 W Grand Ave, Chicago, IL	312-337-5051
Color West Ltd/1901 W Cermak Rd, Broadview, IL	312-345-1110
Coloron Corp/360 E Grand Ave, Chicago, IL	312-265-6766
Colorprints Inc/410 N Michigan Ave, Chicago, IL	312-467-6930
Commercial Colorlab Service/41 So Stolp, Aurora, IL	312-892-9330
Copy-Matics, Div Lith-O-Lux/6324 W Fond du Lac Ave, Milwaukee, WI	414-462-2250
Corley D & S Ltd/3610 Nashua Dr #7, Mississaugua, ON	416-675-3511

Production/Support Services

Continued

Please send us your additions and updates.

Custom Color Processing Lab/1300 Rand Rd, Des Plaines, IL	312-297-6333
Cutler-Graves/535 N Michigan Ave, Chicago, IL	312-828-9310
D-Max Colorgraphics/1662 Headlands Dr, Fenton, MO	314-343-3570
Diamond Graphics/6324 W Fond du Lac Ave, Milwaukee, WI	414-462-2250
Drake, Brady Copy Center/413 N 10th St, St Louis, MO	314-421-1311
Draper St Photolab/1300 W Draper St, Chicago, IL	312-975-7200
Duncan, Virgil Studios/4725 E State Blvd, Ft Wayne, IN	219-483-6011
Dzuroff Studios/1020 Huron Rd E, Cleveland, OH	216-696-0120
Eastman Kodak Co/1712 S Prairie Ave, Chicago, IL	312-922-9691
Emulsion Stripping Ltd/4 N Eighth Ave, Maywood, IL	312-344-8100
Fotis Photo/25 E Hubbard St, Chicago, IL	312-337-7300
Foto-Comm Corporation/215 W Superior, Chicago, IL	312-943-0450
Fromex/188 W Washington, Chicago, IL	312-853-0067
Gallery Color Lab/620 W Richmond St, Toronto, ON	416-367-9770
Gamma Photo Lab Inc/314 W Superior St, Chicago, IL	312-337-0022
Graphic Lab Inc/124 E Third St, Dayton, OH	513-461-3774
Graphic Spectrum/523 S Plymouth Ct, Chicago, IL	312-427-9515
Greenhow, Ralph/333 N Michigan Ave, Chicago, IL	312-782-6833
Grignon Studios/1300 W Altgeld, Chicago, IL	312-975-7200
Grossman Knowling Co/7350 John C Lodge, Detroit, MI	313-832-2360
Harlem Photo Service/6706 Northwest Hwy, Chicago, IL	312-763-5860
Hill, Vince Studio/119 W Hubbard, Chicago, IL	312-644-6690
Imperial Color Inc/618 W Jackson Blvd, Chicago, IL	312-454-1570
J D H Inc/1729 Superior Ave, Cleveland, OH	216-771-0346
Jahn & Ollier Engraving/817 W Washington Blvd, Chicago, IL	312-666-7080
Janusz, Robert E Studios/1020 Huron Rd, Cleveland, OH	216-621-9845
John, Harvey Studio/823 N 2nd St, Milwaukee, WI	414-271-7170
Jones & Morris Ltd/24 Carlaw Ave, Toronto, ON	416-465-5466
K & S Photographics/180 N Wabash Ave, Chicago, IL	312-207-1212
K & S Photographics/1155 Handley Industrial Ct, St Louis, MO	314-962-7050
Kai-Hsi Studio/160 E Illinois St, Chicago, IL	312-642-9853
Kier Photo Service/1627 E 40th St, Cleveland, OH	216-431-4670
Kitzerow Studios/203 N Wabash, Chicago, IL	312-332-1224
Kluegel, Art/630 Fieldston Ter, St Louis, MO	314-961-2023
Kolorstat Studios/415 N Dearborn St, Chicago, IL	312-644-3729
Kremer Photo Print/228 S Wabash, Chicago, IL	312-922-3297
LaDriere Studios/1565 W Woodward Ave, Bloomfield Hills, MI	313-644-3932
Lagasca, Dick & Others/203 N Wabash Ave, Chicago, IL	312-263-1389
Langen & Wind Color Service Inc/2871 E Grand Blvd, Detroit, MI	313-871-5722
Lim, Luis Retouching/405 N Wabash, Chicago, IL	312-645-0746
Lubeck, Larry & Assoc/405 N Wabash Ave, Chicago, IL	312-726-5580
Merrill-David Inc/3420 Prospect Ave, Cleveland, OH	216-391-0988
Meteor Photo Company/1099 Chicago Rd, Troy, MI	313-583-3090
Midwest Litho Arts/5300 B McDermott Dr, Berkeley, IL	312-449-2442
Multiprint Co Inc/153 W Ohio St, Chicago, IL	312-644-7910
Munder Color/2771 Galilee Ave, Zion, IL	312-764-4435
NCL Graphics/575 Bennett Rd, Elk Grove Village, IL	312-593-2610
NVK Image Systems/110 W Beaver Cr #24, Richmond Hill L4B1J9, ON	416-764-8196
National Photo Service/114 W Illinois St, Chicago, IL	312-644-5211
Noral Color Corp/5560 N Northwest Hwy, Chicago, IL	312-775-0991
Norman Sigele Studios/270 Merchandise Mart, Chicago, IL	312-642-1757
O'Brien, Tom & Assoc/924 Terminal Rd, Lansing, MI	517-321-0188
O'Connor-Roe Inc/111 E Wacker, Chicago, IL	312-856-1668
O'Donnell Studio Inc/333 W Lake St, Chicago, IL	312-346-2470
P-A Photocenter Inc/310 W Washington St, Chicago, IL	312-641-6343
Pallas Photo Labs/319 W Erie St, Chicago, IL	312-787-4600
Pallas Photo Labs/207 E Buffalo, Milwaukee, WI	414-272-2525
Parkway Photo Lab/57 W Grand Ave, Chicago, IL	312-467-1711
Photocopy Inc/104 E Mason St, Milwaukee, WI	414-272-1255
Photographic Specialties Inc/225 Border Ave N, Minneapolis, MN	612-332-6303
Photomatic Corp/59 E Illinois St, Chicago, IL	312-527-2929
Precision Photo Lab/5787 N Webster St, Dayton, OH	513-898-7450
Procolor/909 Hennepin Ave, Minneapolis, MN	612-332-7721
Proctor, Jack/2050 Dain Tower, Minneapolis, MN	612-338-7777
Professional Photo Colour Service/126 W Kinzie, Chicago, IL	312-644-0888
Quantity Photo Co/119 W Hubbard St, Chicago, IL	312-644-8288
Race Frog Stats/207 E Michigan Ave, Milwaukee, WI	414-276-7828
Rahe, Bob/220 Findlay St, Cincinnati, OH	513-241-9060
Rees, John/640 N LaSalle, Chicago, IL	312-337-5785

Reichart, Jim Studio/2301 W Mill Rd, Milwaukee, WI	414-228-9089
Reliable Photo Service/415 N Dearborn, Chicago, IL	312-644-3723
Repro Inc/912 W Washington Blvd, Chicago, IL	312-666-3800
Rhoden Photo & Press Service/7833 S Cottage Grove, Chicago, IL	312-488-4815
Robb Ltd/362 W Erie, Chicago, IL	312-943-2664
Robin Color Lab/2106 Central Parkway, Cincinnati, OH	513-381-5116
Ross-Ehlert/225 W Illinois, Chicago, IL	312-644-0244
SE Graphics Ltd/795 E Kings St, Hamilton, ON	416-545-8484
Schellhorn Photo Techniques/3916 N Elston Ave, Chicago, IL	312-267-5141
Scott Studio & Labs/26 N Hillside Ave, Hillsdale, IL	312-449-3800
Sladek, Dean/8748 Hollyspring Trail, Chagrin Falls, OH	216-543-5420
Speedy Stat Service/566 W Adams, Chicago, IL	312-939-3397
Standard Studios Inc/3270 Merchandise Mart, Chicago, IL	312-944-5300
Superior Bulk Film/442 N Wells St, Chicago, IL	312-644-4448
The Color Market/3177 MacArthur Blvd, Northbrook, IL	312-564-3770
The Foto Lab Inc/160 E Illinois St, Chicago, IL	312-321-0900
The Retouching Co/360 N Michigan Ave, Chicago, IL	312-263-7445
The Stat Center/666 Euclid Ave #817, Clevland, OH	216-861-5467
Thorstad, Gordy Retouching Inc/119 No 4th St #311, Minneapolis, MN	612-338-2597
Transparency Duplicating Service/847 W Jackson Blvd, Chicago, IL	312-733-4464
Transparency Processing Service/324 W Richmond St, Toronto, ON	416-593-0434
UC Color Lab/3936 N Pulaski Rd, Chicago, IL	312-545-9641
Uhlir, Louis J/2509 Kingston Rd, Cleveland Hts, OH	216-932-4837
Wichita Color Lab/231 Ohio, Wichita, KS	316-265-2598
Williams, Warren E & Assoc/233 E Wacker Dr, Chicago, IL	312-565-2689
Winnipeg Photo Ltd/1468 Victoria Park Ave, Toronto, ON	416-755-7779
Witkowski Art Studio/52098 N Central Ave, South Bend, IN	219-272-9771
Wood, Bruce/185 N Wabash, Chicago, IL	312-782-4287
Yancy, Helen/421 Valentine St, Dearborn Heights, MI	312-278-9345

Southwest

Alamo Photolabs/3814 Broadway, San Antonio, TX	512-828-9079
Alied & WBS/6305 N O'Connor #111, Irving, TX	214-869-0100
Baster, Ray Enterprises/246 E Watkins, Phoenix, AZ	602-258-6850
Casey Color Inc/2115 S Harvard Ave, Tulsa, OK	918-744-5004
Century Copi-Technics Inc/710 N St Paul St, Dallas, TX	214-741-3191
Collins Color Lab/2714 McKinney Ave, Dallas, TX	214-824-5333
Color Mark Laboratories/2202 E McDowell Rd, Phoenix, AZ	602-273-1253
Commercial Color Corporation/1621 Oaklawn St, Dallas, TX	214-744-2610
Custom Photographic Labs/601 W ML King Blvd, Austin, TX	512-474-1177
Dallas Printing Co/3103 Greenwood St, Dallas, TX	214-826-3331
Five-P Photographic Processing/2122 E Governor's Circle, Houston, TX	713-688-4488
Floyd & Lloyd Burns Industrial Artist/3223 Alabama Courts, Houston, TX	713-622-8255
H & H Blueprint & Supply Co/5042 N 8th St, Phoenix, AZ	602-279-5701
Hall Photo/6 Greenway Plaza, Houston, TX	713-961-3454
Hot Flash Photographics/5933 Bellaire Blvd #114, Houston, TX	713-666-9510
Hunter, Marilyn Art Svc/8415 Gladwood, Dallas, TX	214-341-4664
Kolor Print Inc/PO Box 747, Little Rock, AR	501-375-5581
Magna Professional Color Lab/2601 N 32nd St, Phoenix, AZ	602-955-0700
Master Printing Co Inc/220 Creath St, Jonesboro, AR	501-932-4491
Meisel Photochrome Corp/9645 Wedge Chapel, Dallas, TX	214-350-6666
NPL/1926 W Gray, Houston, TX	713-527-9300
Optifab Inc/1550 W Van Buren St, Phoenix, AZ	602-254-7171
PSI Film Lab Inc/3011 Diamond Park Dr, Dallas, TX	214-631-5670
PhotoGraphics/1700 S Congress, Austin, TX	512-447-0963
Photographic Works Lab/3550 E Grant Rd, Tucson, AZ	602-327-7291
Pounds/909 Congress, Austin, TX	512-472-6926
Pounds Photo Lab Inc/2507 Manor Way, Dallas, TX	214-350-5671
Pro Photo Lab Inc/2700 N Portland, Oklahoma City, OK	405-942-3743
Raphaele/Digital Transparencies Inc/616 Hawthorne, Houston, TX	713-524-2211
River City Silver/906 Basse Rd, San Antonio, TX	512-734-2020
Spectro Photo Labs Inc/4519 Maple, Dallas, TX	214-522-1981
Steffan Studio/1905 Skillman, Dallas, TX	214-827-6128

Texas World Entrtnmnt/8133 Chadbourne Rd, Dallas, TX	214-351-6103
The Black & White Lab/4930 Maple Ave, Dallas, TX	214-528-4200
The Color Place/1330 Conant St, Dallas, TX	214-631-7174
The Color Place/2927 Morton St, Fort Worth, TX	817-335-3515
The Color Place/4201 San Felipe, Houston, TX	713-629-7080
The Photo Company/124 W McDowell Rd, Phoenix, AZ	602-254-5138
Total Color Inc/1324 Inwood Rd, Dallas, TX	214-634-1484
True Color Photo Inc/710 W Sheridan Ave, Oklahoma City, OK	405-232-6441

Rocky Mountain

Cies/Sexton Photo Lab/275 S Hazel Ct, Denver, CO	303-935-3535
Pallas Photo Labs/700 Kalamath, Denver, CO	303-893-0101
Rezac, R Retouching/7832 Sundance Trail, Parker, CO	303-841-0222

West Coast

A & I Color Lab/933 N Highland, Los Angeles, CA	213-464-8361
ABC Color Corp/3020 Glendale Blvd, Los Angeles, CA	213-662-2125
Action Photo Service/251 Keany, San Francisco, CA	415-543-1777
Alan's Custom Lab/1545 Wilcox, Hollywood, CA	213-461-1975
Aristo Art Studio/636 N La Brea, Los Angeles, CA	213-939-0101
Art Craft Custom Lab/1900 Westwood Blvd, Los Angeles, CA	213-475-2986
Atkinson-Stedco Color Film Svc/7610 Melrose Ave, Los Angeles, CA	213-655-1255
Bakes, Bill Inc/265 29th St, Oakland, CA	415-832-7685
Black & White Color Reproductions/38 Mason, San Francisco, CA	415-989-3070
Bogle Graphic Photo/1117 S Olive, Los Angeles, CA	213-749-7461
Boston Media Productions/330 Townsend St #112, San Francisco, CA	415-495-6662
CPS Lab/1759 Las Palmas, Los Angeles, CA	213-464-0215
Chrome Graphics/449 N Huntley Dr, Los Angeles, CA	213-657-5055
Chromeworks Color Processing/425 Bryant St, San Francisco, CA	415-957-9481
Coletti, John/333 Kearny #703, San Francisco, CA	415-421-3848
Color Lab Inc/742 Cahuenga Blvd, Los Angeles, CA	213-466-3551
Colorscope/250 Glendale Blvd, Los Angeles, CA	213-250-5555
Colortek/10425 Venice Blvd, Los angeles, CA	213-870-5579
Complete Negative Service/6007 Waring Ave, Hollywood, CA	213-463-7753
Cre-Art Photo Labs Inc/6920 Melrose Ave, Hollywood, CA	213-937-3390
Croxton, Stewart Inc/8736 Melrose, Los Angeles, CA	213-652-9720
Custom Graphics/15162 Goldenwest Circle, Westminster, CA	714-893-7517
Custom Photo Lab/123 Powell St, San Francisco, CA	415-956-2374
Faulkner Color Lab/1200 Folsom St, San Francisco, CA	415-861-2800
Focus Foto Finishers/138 S La Brea Ave, Los Angeles, CA	213-934-0013
Frosh, R L & Sons Scenic Studio/4114 Sunset Blvd, Los Angeles, CA	213-662-1134
G P Color Lab/215 S Oxford Ave, Los Angeles, CA	213-386-7901
Gamma Photographic Labs/555 Howard St, San Francisco, CA	415-495-8833
Gibbons Color Lab/606 N Almont Dr, Los Angeles, CA	213-275-6806
Giese, Axel Assoc/544 Starlight Crest Dr, La Canada, CA	213-790-8768
Glusha, Laura/1053 Colorado Blvd #F, Los Angeles, CA	213-255-1997
Good Stats Inc/1616 N Cahuenga Blvd, Hollywood, CA	213-469-3501
Gornick Film Production/4200 Camino Real, Los Angeles, CA	213-223-8914
Graphic Center/7386 Beverly, Los Angeles, CA	213-938-3773
Graphic Process Co/979 N LaBrea, Los Angeles, CA	213-850-6222
Graphicolor/8134 W Third, Los Angeles, CA	213-653-1768
Hecht Custom Photo/Graphics/1711 N Orange Dr, Hollywood, CA	213-466-7106
Hollywood Photo Reproduction/6413 Willoughby Ave, Hollywood, CA	213-469-5421
Imperial Color Lab/365 Howard St, San Francisco, CA	415-777-4020
Ivey-Seright/424 8th Ave North, Seattle, WA	206-623-8113
Jacobs, Ed/937 S Spaulding, Los Angeles, CA	213-935-1064
Jacobs, Robert Retouching/6010 Wilshire Blvd #505, Los Angeles, CA	213-931-3751
Johnston, Chuck/1111 Wilshire, Los Angeles, CA	213-482-3362
Kawahara, George/250 Columbus, San Francisco, CA	415-543-1637
Kimbo Color Laboratory Inc/179 Stewart, San Francisco, CA	415-288-4100
Kinney, Paul Productions/818 19th St, Sacramento, CA	916-447-8868

Landry, Carol/8148-L Ronson Rd, San Diego, CA	619-560-1778
Laursen Color Lab/1641 Reynolds, Irvine, CA	714-261-1500
Lee Film Processing/8584 Venice Blvd, Los Angeles, CA	213-559-0296
M P S Photo Services/17406 Mt Cliffwood Cir, Fountain Valley, CA	714-540-9515
M S Color Labs/740 Cahuenga Blvd, Los Angeles, CA	213-461-4591
MC Photographics/PO Box 1515, Springfield, OR	503-741-2289
Maddocks, J H/4766 Melrose Ave, Los Angeles, CA	213-660-1321
Marin Color Lab/41 Belvedere St, San Rafael, CA	415-456-8093
Mark III Colorprints/7401 Melrose Ave, Los Angeles, CA	213-653-0433
Metz Air Art/2817 E Lincoln Ave, Anaheim, CA	714-630-3071
Modern Photo Studio/5625 N Figueroa, Los Angeles, CA	213-255-1527
Modernage/470 E Third St, Los Angeles, CA	213-628-8194
Newell Color Lab/630 Third St, San Francisco, CA	415-974-6870
Olson, Bob Photo Blow-Up Lab/7775 Beverly Blvd, Los Angeles, CA	213-931-6643
Ostoin, Larry/22943 B Nadine Cr, Torrance, CA	213-530-1121
Pacific Production & Location/424 Nahua St, Honolulu, HI	808-924-2513
Paragon Photo/7301 Melrose Ave, Los Angeles, CA	213-933-5865
Personal Color Lab/1552 Gower, Los Angeles, CA	213-467-0721
Petron Corp/5443 Fountain Ave, Los Angeles, CA	213-461-4626
Pevehouse, Jerry Studio/3409 Tweedy Blvd, South Gate, CA	213-564-1336
Photoking Lab/6612 W Sunset Blvd, Los Angeles, CA	213-466-2977
Prisma Color Inc/5619 Washington Blvd, Los Angeles, CA	213-728-7151
Professional Color Labs/96 Jessie, San Francisco, CA	415-397-5057
Quantity Photos Inc/5432 Hollywood Blvd, Los Angeles, CA	213-467-6178
RGB Lab Inc/816 N Highland, Los Angeles, CA	213-469-1959
Rapid Color Inc/1236 S Central Ave, Glendale, CA	213-245-9211
Remos, Nona/4053 Eighth Ave, San Diego, CA	619-692-4044
Repro Color Inc/3100 Riverside Dr, Los Angeles, CA	213-664-1951
Retouching Chemicals/5478 Wilshire Blvd, Los Angeles, CA	213-935-9452
Revilo Color/4650 W Washington Blvd, Los Angeles, CA	213-936-8681
Reynolds, Carol Retouching/1428 N Fuller Ave, Hollywood, CA	213-874-7083
Ro-Ed Color Lab/707 N Stanley Ave, Los Angeles, CA	213-651-5050
Roller, S J/6881 Alta Loma Terrace, Los Angeles, CA	213-876-5654
Ross, Deborah Design/10806 Ventura Blvd #3, Studio City, CA	818-985-5205
Rudy Jo Color Lab Inc/130 N La Brea, Los Angeles, CA	213-937-3804
Schaeffer Photo Rapid Lab/6677 Sunset Blvd, Hollywood, CA	213-466-3343
Snyder, Len/238 Hall Dr, Orinda, CA	415-254-8687
Staidle, Ted & Assocs/544 N Larchmont Blvd, Los Angeles, CA	213-462-7433
Stat House/8126 Beverly Blvd, Los Angeles, CA	213-653-8200
Still Photo Lab/1216 N LaBrea, Los Angeles, CA	213-465-6106
Studio Photo Service/733 N LaBrea Ave, Hollywood, CA	213-935-1223
Technicolor Inc/1738 No Neville, Orange, CA	714-998-3424
The Darkroom Custom B&W Lab/897-2B Independence Ave, Mountain View, CA	415-969-2955
Thomas Reproductions/1147 Mission St, San Francisco, CA	415-431-8900
Timars/918 N Formosa, Los Angeles, CA	213-876-0175
Tom's Chroma Lab/514 No LaBrea, Los Angeles, CA	213-933-5637
Trans Tesseract/715 N San Antonio Rd, Los Altos, CA	415-949-2185
Tri Color Camera/1761 N Vermont Ave, Los Angeles, CA	213-664-2952
Universal Color Labs/1076 S La Cienega Blvd, Los Angeles, CA	213-652-2863
Vloeberghs, Jerome/333 Kearny St, San Francisco, CA	415-982-1287
Waters Art Studio/1820 E Garry St #207, Santa Ana, CA	
Wild Studio/1311 N Wilcox Ave, Hollywood, CA	213-463-8369
Williams, Alan & Assoc Inc/8032 W Third St, Los Angeles, CA	213-653-2243
Wolf Color Lab/6416 Selma, Los Angeles, CA	213-463-0766
Zammit, Paul/5478 Wilshire Blvd #300, Los Angeles, CA	213-933-8563
Ziba Photographics/591 Howard St, San Francisco, CA	415-543-6221

Lighting

New York City

Altman Stage Lighting Co Inc/57 Alexander	212-569-7777
Artistic Neon by Gasper/75-49 61st St	718-821-1550
Balcar Lighting Systems/15 E 30th St	212-889-5080
Barbizon Electric Co Inc/426 W 55th St	212-586-1620

Production/Support Services

Continued

Please send us your additions and updates.

Bernhard Link Theatrical Inc/104 W 17th St	212-929-6786
Big Apple Cine Service/49-01 25th Ave	718-626-5210
Big Apple Lights Corp/533 Canal St	212-226-0925
Camera Mart/456 W 55th St	212-757-6977
Electra Displays/122 W 27th St	212-924-1022
F&B/Ceco Lighting & Grip Rental/315 W 43rd St	212-974-4640
Feature Systems Inc/512 W 36th St	212-736-0447
Ferco/707 11th Ave	212-245-4800
Filmtrucks, Inc/450 W 37th St	212-868-7065
Fiorentino, Imero Assoc Inc/44 West 63rd St	212-246-0600
Four Star Stage Lighting Inc/585 Gerard Ave	212-993-0471
Kliegl Bros Universal/32-32 48th Ave	718-786-7474
Lee Lighting America Ltd/534 W 25th St	212-924-5476
Litelab Theatrical & Disco Equip/76 Ninth Ave	212-675-4357
Lowel Light Mfg Inc/475 10th St	212-949-0950
Luminere/160 W 86th St	212-724-0583
Metro-Lites Inc/750 Tenth Ave	212-757-1220
Movie Light Ltd/460 W 24th St	212-989-2318
New York Flash/156 Fifth Ave	212-741-1165
Paris Film Productions Ltd/213-23 99th Ave	718-740-2020
Photo-Tekniques/119 Fifth Ave	212-254-2545
Production Arts Lighting/636 Eleventh Ave	212-489-0312
Ross, Charles Inc/333 W 52nd St	212-246-5470
Stage Lighting Discount Corp/346 W 44th St	212-489-1370
Stroblite Co Inc/10 E 23rd St	212-677-9220
Tekno Inc/15 E 30th St	212-887-5080
Times Square Stage Lighting Co/318 W 47th St	212-541-5045
Vadar Ltd/150 Fifth Ave	212-989-9120

Northeast

Barbizon Light of New England/3 Draper St, Woburn, MA	617-935-3920
Blake, Ben Films/104 W Concord St, Boston, MA	617-266-8181
Bogen/PO Box 448, Engelwood, NJ	201-568-7771
Capron Lighting & Sound/278 West St, Needham, MA	617-444-8850
Cestare, Thomas Inc/188 Herricks Rd, Mineola, NY	516-742-5550
Cody, Stuart Inc/300 Putnam Ave, Cambridge, MA	617-661-4540
Dyna-Lite Inc/140 Market St, Kenilworth, NJ	201-245-7222
Film Associates/419 Boylston St ((n))209, Boston, MA	617-266-0892
Filmarts/38 Newbury St, Boston, MA	617-266-7468
Heller, Brian/200 Olney St, Providence, RI	401-751-1381
Lighting Products, GTE Sylvania/Lighting Center, Danvers, MA	617-777-1900
Limelight Productions/Yale Hill, Stockbridge, MA	413-298-3771
Lycian Stage Lighting/P O Box 68, Sugar Loaf, NY	914-469-2285
Martorano, Salvatore Inc/9 West First St, Freeport, NY	516-379-8097
McManus Enterprises/111 Union Ave, Bala Cynwyd, PA	215-664-8600
Norton Assoc/53 Henry St, Cambridge, MA	617-876-3771
Packaged Lighting Systems/29-41 Grant, PO Box 285, Walden, NY	914-778-3515
Penrose Productions/4 Sandalwood Dr, Livingston, NJ	201-992-4264
R & R Lighting Co/813 Silver Spring Ave, Silver Spring, MD	301-589-4997
Reinhard, Charles Lighting Consultant/39 Ocean Ave, Massapequa, NY	516-799-1615

Southeast

Kupersmith, Tony/320 N Highland Ave NE, Atlanta, GA	404-577-5319

Midwest

Duncan, Victor Inc/32380 Howard St, Madison Heights, MI	313-589-1900
Film Corps/3101 Hennepin Ave, Minneapolis, MN	612-338-2522
Frost, Jack/234 Piquette, Detroit, MI	313-873-8030
Grand Stage Lighting Co/630 W Lake, Chicago, IL	312-332-5611
Midwest Cine Service/304 W 79th Terr, Kansas City, MO	816-333-0022
Midwest Stage Lighting/2104 Central, Evanston, IL	312-328-3966
Studio Lighting/1345 W Argyle St, Chicago, IL	312-989-8808

Southwest

ABC Theatrical Rental & Sales/825 N 7th St, Phoenix, AZ	602-258-5265
Astro Audio-Visual/1336 W Clay, Houston, TX	713-528-7119

Chase Lights/1942 Beech St, Amarillo, TX	806-381-0575
Dallas Stage Lighting & Equipment Co/2813 Florence, Dallas, TX	214-827-9380
Duncan, Victor Inc/2659 Fondren Dr, Dallas, TX	214-369-1165
FPS Inc/11250 Pagemill Rd, Dallas, TX	214-340-8545
Gable, Pee Wee Inc/PO Box 11264, Phoenix, AZ	602-242-7660
MFC-The Texas Outfit/5915 Star Ln, Houston, TX	713-781-7703
Southwest Film & TV Lighting/904 Koerner Ln, Austin, TX	512-385-3483

Rocky Mountain

Rocky Mountain Cine Support/1332 S Cherokee, Denver, CO	303-795-9713

West Coast

Aguilar Lighting Works/3230 Laurel Canyon Blvd, Studio City, CA	213-766-6564
American Mobile Power Co/3218 W Burbank Blvd, Burbank, CA	213-845-5474
Astro Generator Rentals/2835 Bedford St, Los Angeles, CA	213-838-3958
B S Rental Co/18857 Addison St, North Hollywood, CA	213-761-1733
B S Rental Co/1082 La Cresta Dr, Thousand Oaks, CA	805-495-8606
Backstage Studio Equipment/5554 Fairview Pl, Agoura, CA	213-889-9816
Casper's Camera Cars/8415 Lankershim Blvd, Sun Valley, CA	213-767-5207
Castex Rentals/591 N Bronson Ave, Los Angeles, CA	213-462-1468
Ceco, F&B of CA Inc/7051 Santa Monica Blvd, Hollywood, CA	213-466-9361
Cine Turkey/2624 Reppert Ct, Los Angeles, CA	213-654-6495
Cine-Dyne Inc/9401 Wilshire Blvd #830, Beverly Hills, CA	213-622-7016
Cine-Pro/1037 N Sycamore Ave, Hollywood, CA	213-461-4794
Cinemobile Systems Inc/11166 Gault St, North Hollywood, CA	213-764-9900
Cineworks-Cinerents/5724 Santa Monica Blvd, Hollywood, CA	213-464-0296
Cool Light Co Inc/5723 Auckland Ave, North Hollywood, CA	213-761-6116
Denker, Foster Co/1605 Las Flores Ave, San Marino, CA	213-799-8656
Fiorentino, Imero Assoc Inc/6430 Sunset Blvd, Hollywood, CA	213-467-4020
Great American Market/PO Box 178, Woodlands Hill, CA	213-883-8182
Grosso & Grosso/7502 Wheatland Ave, Sun Valley, CA	213-875-1160
Hollywood Mobile Systems/7021 Hayvenhurst St, Van Nuys, CA	213-782-6558
Independent Studio Services/11907 Wicks St, Sun Valley, CA	213-764-0840
Kalani Studio Lighting/129-49 Killion St, Van Nuys, CA	213-762-5991
Key Lite/333 S Front St, Burbank, CA	213-848-5483
Leoinetti Cine Rentals/5609 Sunset Blvd, Hollywood, CA	213-469-2987
Mobile Power House/3820 Rhodes Ave, Studio City, CA	213-766-2163
Mole Richardson/937 N Sycamore Ave, Hollywood, CA	213-851-0111
Pattim Service/10625 Chandler, Hollywood, CA	213-766-5266
Picture Package Inc/22236 Cass Ave, Woodland Hills, CA	213-703-7168
Producer's Studio/650 N Bronson St, Los Angeles, CA	213-466-3111
Production Systems Inc/5759 Santa Monica Blvd, Hollywood, CA	213-469-2704
RNI Equipment Co/7272 Bellaire Ave, North Hollywood, CA	213-875-2656
Skirpan Lighting Control Co/1100 W Chestnut St, Burbank, CA	213-840-7000
Tech Camera/6370 Santa Monica Blvd, Hollywood, CA	213-466-3238
Wallace Lighting/6970 Varna Ave, Van Nuys, CA	213-764-1047
Young Generations/8517 Geyser Ave, Northridge, CA	213-873-5135

Studio Rentals

New York City

3G Stages Inc/236 W 61st St	212-247-3130
American Museum of the Moving Image/31-12 36th St	718-784-4520
Antonio/Stephen Ad Photo/45 E 20th St	212-674-2350
Boken Inc/513 W 54th St	212-581-5507
C & C Visual/12 W 27th St 7th Fl	212-684-3830
Camera Mart Inc/456 W 55th St	212-757-6977
Cine Studio/241 W 54th St	212-581-1916
Codalight Rental Studios/151 W 19th St	212-206-9333
Contact Studios/165 W 47th St	212-354-6400
Control Film Service/321 W 44th St	212-245-1574

DeFilippo/207 E 37th St	212-986-5444
Duggal Color Projects/9 W 20th St	212-242-7000
Farkas Films Inc/385 Third Ave	212-679-8212
Gruszczynski Studio/821 Broadway	212-673-1243
Horvath & Assoc Studios/95 Chambers	212-741-0300
Matrix Studios Inc/727 Eleventh Ave	212-265-8500
Mothers Sound Stages/210 E 5th St	212-260-2050
National Video Industries/15 W 17th St	212-691-1300
New York Flash Rental/156 Fifth Ave	212-741-1165
Ninth Floor Studio/1200 Broadway	212-679-5537
North American Video/423 E 90th St	212-369-2552
North Light Studios/122 W 26th St	212-989-5498
Osonitsch, Robert/112 Fourth Ave	212-533-1920
PDN Studio/167 Third Ave	212-677-8418
Phoenix State Ltd/537 W 59th St	212-581-7721
Photo-Tekniques/119 Fifth Ave	212-254-2545
Production Center/221 W 26th St	212-675-2211
Professional Photo Supply/141 W 20th St	212-924-1200
Reeves Teletape Corp/304 E 44th St	212-573-8888
Rotem Studio/259 W 30th St	212-947-9455
Schnoodle Studios/54 Bleecker St	212-431-7788
Silva-Cone Studios/260 W 36th St	212-279-0900
Stage 54 West/429 W 54th St	212-757-6977
Stages 1&2 West/460 W 54th St	212-757-6977
Studio 35/35 W 31st St	212-947-0898
Studio 39/144 E 39th St	212-685-1771
Studio Twenty/6 W 20th St	212-675-8067
The 95th St Studio/206 E 95th St	212-831-1946
Vagnoni, A Devlin Productions/150 W 55th St	212-582-5572
Yellowbox/47 E 34th St	212-532-4010

Northeast

Allscope Inc/PO Box 4060, Princeton, NJ	609-799-4200
Bay State Film Productions Inc/35 Springfield St, Agawam, MA	413-786-4454
Century III/651 Beacon St, Boston, MA	617-267-6400
Color Leasing Studio/330 Rt 46 East, Fairfield, NJ	201-575-1118
D4 Film Studios Inc/109 Highland Ave, Needham, MA	617-444-0226
Penrose Productions/4 Sandalwood Dr, Livingston, NJ	201-992-4264
Pike Productions Inc/47 Galen St, Watertown, MA	617-924-5000
September Productions Inc/171 Newbury St, Boston, MA	617-262-6090
Television Productions & Services/55 Chapel St, Newton, MA	617-965-1626
Ultra Photo Works/468 Commercial Ave, Palisades Pk, NJ	201-592-7730
Videocom Inc/502 Sprague St, Dedham, MA	617-329-4080
WGGB-TV/PO Box 3633, Springfield, MA	413-785-1911
WLNE-TV/430 County St, New Bedford, MA	617-993-2651

Southeast

Enter Space/20 14th St NW, Atlanta, GA	404-885-1139
The Great Southern Stage/15221 NE 21st Ave, North Miami Beach, FL	305-947-0430
Williamson Photography Inc/9511 Colonial Dr, Miami, FL	305-255-6400

Midwest

Emerich Style & Design/PO Box 14523, Chicago, IL	312-871-4659
Gard, Ron/2600 N Racine, Chicago, IL	312-975-6523
Hanes, Jim/1930 N Orchard, Chicago, IL	312-944-6554
Lewis, Tom/2511 Brumley Dr, Flossmoor, IL	312-799-1156
Rainey, Pat/4031 N Hamlin Ave, Chicago, IL	312-463-0281
Sosin, Bill/415 W Superior St, Chicago, IL	312-751-0974
Stratford Studios Inc/2857 E Grand Blvd, Detroit, MI	313-875-6617
The Production Center/151 Victor Ave, Highland Park, MI	313-868-6600
Zawaki, Andy & Jake/1830 W Cermak, Chicago, IL	312-422-1546

Southwest

AIE Studios/3905 Braxton, Houston, TX	713-781-2110
Arizona Cine Equipment/2125 E 20th St, Tucson, AZ	602-623-8268
Hayes Productions Inc/710 S Bowie, San Antonio, TX	512-224-9565
MFC Film Productions Inc/5915 Star Ln, Houston, TX	713-781-7703

Pearlman Productions Inc/2506 South Blvd, Houston, TX	713-523-3601
Pinnacle Studios/2410 Farrington St, Dallas, TX	514-637-2748
Stokes, Bill Assoc/5642 Dyer, Dallas, TX	214-363-0161
Tecfilms Inc/2856 Fort Worth Ave, Dallas, TX	214-339-2217

West Coast

39 East Walnut/39 E Walnut St, Pasadena, CA	818-584-4090
Blakeman, Bob Studios/710 S Santa Fe, Los Angeles, CA	213-624-6662
Carthay Studio/5907 W Pico Blvd, Los Angeles, CA	213-938-2101
Chris-Craft Video Tape/915 N LaBrea, Los Angeles, CA	213-850-2236
Cine-Rent West Inc/991 Tennessee St, San Francisco, CA	415-864-4644
Cine-Video/948 N Cahuenga Blvd, Los Angeles, CA	213-464-6200
Columbia Pictures/Columbia Plaza, Burbank, CA	818-954-6000
Design Arts Studios/1128 N Las Palmas, Hollywood, CA	213-464-9118
Disney, Walt Productions/500 S Buena Vista St, Burbank, CA	818-840-1000
Dominick/833 N LaBrea Ave, Los Angeles, CA	213-934-3033
Eliot, Josh Studio/706 W Pico Blvd, Los Angeles, CA	213-742-0367
Goldwyn, Samuel Studios/1041 N Formosa Ave, Los Angeles, CA	213-650-2500
Great American Cinema Co/10711 Wellworth Ave, Los Angeles, CA	213-475-0937
Hill, Dennis Studio/20 N Raymond Ave #14, Pasadena, CA	818-795-2589
Hollywood National Studios/6605 Eleanor Ave, Hollywood, CA	213-467-6272
Hollywood Stage/6650 Santa Monica Blvd, Los Angeles, CA	213-466-4393
Kelley, Tom Studios/8525 Santa Monica Blvd, Los Angeles, CA	213-657-1780
Kings Point Corporation/9336 W Washington, Culver City, CA	213-836-5537
Lewin, Elyse/820 N Fairfax Ave, Los Angeles, CA	213-655-4214
Liles, Harry Productions Inc/1060 N Lillian Way, Los Angeles, CA	213-466-1612
MGM Studios/10202 W Washington, Culver City, CA	213-836-3000
MPI Studios/1714 N Wilton Pl, Los Angeles, CA	213-462-6342
Norwood, David/4040 Del Rey Ave #7, Marina Del Rey, CA	213-827-2020
Paramount/5555 Melrose, Los Angeles, CA	213-468-5000
Raleigh Studio/650 N Bronson Ave, Los Angeles, CA	213-466-7778
Solaris T V Studios/2525 Ocean Park Blvd, Santa Monica, CA	213-450-6227
Studio AV/1227 First Ave S, Seattle, WA	206-292-9931
Studio Center CBS/4024 Radford Ave, Studio City, CA	818-760-5000
Studio Resources/1915 University Ave, Palo Alto, CA	415-321-8763
Sunset/Gower Studio/1438 N Gower, Los Angeles, CA	213-467-1001
Superstage/5724 Santa Monica Blvd, Los Angeles, CA	213-464-0296
Team Production Co Inc/4133 Lankershim Blvd, North Hollywood, CA	818-506-5700
Television Center Studios/846 N Cahuenga Blvd, Los Angeles, CA	213-462-5111
The Videography Studios/8471 Universal Plaza, Universal City, CA	213-204-2000
Trans-American Video/1541 Vine St, Los Angeles, CA	213-466-2141
Twentieth Century Fox/10201 W Pico Blvd, Los Angeles, CA	213-277-2211
UPA Pictures/4440 Lakeside Dr, Burbank, CA	213-842-7171
Universal City Studios/Universal Studios, Universal City, CA	213-985-4321
Vine Street Video Center/1224 Vine St, Pasadena, CA	213-462-1099
Warner Brothers/4000 Warner Blvd, Burbank, CA	213-843-6000
Wolin/Semple Studio/520 N Western Ave, Los Angeles, CA	213-463-2109

Animators

New York City

A P A/230 W 10th St	212-929-9436
ALZ Productions/11 Waverly Pl	212-473-7620
Abacus Productions Inc/475 Fifth Ave	212-532-6677
Ani-Live Film Service Inc/45 W 45th St	212-819-0700
Animated Productions Inc/1600 Broadway	212-265-2942
Animation Camera Workshop/49 W 24th St	212-807-6450
Animation Center Inc/15 W 46th St	212-869-0123
Animation Service Center/293 W 4th St	212-924-3937
Animation Services Inc/221 W 57th St 11th Fl	212-333-5656
Animex Inc/1540 Broadway	212-575-9494

Production/Support Services

Continued

Please send us your additions and updates.

Animus Films/15 W 44th St	212-391-8716
Avekta Productions Inc/164 Madison Ave	212-686-4550
Backle, RJ Prod/321 W 44th St	212-582-8270
Bakst, Edward/160 W 96th St	212-666-2579
Beckerman, Howard/45 W 45th St #300	212-869-0595
Blechman, R O/2 W 47th St	212-869-1630
Broadcast Arts Inc/632 Broadway	212-254-5910
Cel-Art Productions Inc/20 E 49th St	212-751-7515
Charisma Communications/32 E 57th St	212-832-3020
Charlex Inc/2 W 45th St	212-719-4600
Cinema Concepts/321 W 44th St	212-541-9220
Clark, Ian/229 E 96th St	212-289-0998
Computer Graphics Lab/405 Lexington Ave	212-557-5130
D & R Productions Inc/6 E 39th St	212-532-5303
DaSilva, Raul/137 E 38th St	212-696-1657
Dale Cameragraphics Inc/12 W 27th St	212-696-9440
Darino Films/222 Park Ave S	212-228-4024
Devlin Productions Inc/150 W 55th St	212-582-5572
Diamond & Diaferia/12 E 44th St	212-986-8500
Digital Effects Inc/321 W 44 St	212-581-7760
Dolphin Computer Animation/140 E 80th St	212-628-5930
Doros Animation Inc/475 Fifth Ave	212-684-5043
Elinor Bunin Productions Inc/30 E 60th St	212-688-0759
Fandango Productions Inc/15 W 38th St	212-382-1813
Feigenbaum Productions Inc/25 W 43rd St # 220	212-840-3744
Film Opticals/144 E 44th St	212-697-4744
Film Planning Assoc/38 E 20th	212-260-7140
Friedman, Harold Consortium/420 Lexington Ave	212-697-0858
Gati, John/881 Seventh Ave #832	212-582-9060
Granato Animation Photography/15 W 46th St	212-869-3231
Graphic Motion Group Ltd/16 W 46th St	212-354-4343
Greenberg, R Assoc/240 Madison Ave	212-689-7886
Grossman, Robert/19 Crosby St	212-925-1965
High-Res Solutions Inc/10 Park Ave #3E	212-684-1397
Howard Graphics/36 W 25th St	212-929-2121
I F Studios/15 W 38th St	212-697-6805
ICON Communications/717 Lexington Ave	212-688-5155
Image Factory Inc/18 E 53rd St	212-759-9363
International Production Center/514 W 57th St	212-582-6530
J C Productions/16 W 46th St	212-575-9611
Kim & Gifford Productions Inc/548 E 87th St	212-986-2826
Kimmelman, Phil & Assoc Inc/50 W 40th St	212-944-7766
Kurtz & Friends/130 E 18th St	212-777-3258
Leo Animation Camera Service/25 W 43rd St	212-997-1840
Lieberman, Jerry/76 Laight St	212-431-3452
Locomo Productions/875 West End Ave	212-222-4833
Marz Productions Inc/118 E 25th St	212-477-3900
Metropolis Graphics/28 E 4th St	212-677-0630
Motion Picker Studio/416 Ocean Ave	718-856-2763
Murphy, Neil/208 W 23rd St	212-691-5730
Musicvision, Inc/185 E 85th St	212-860-4420
New York Siggraph/451 W 54th St	212-582-9223
Omnibus Computer Graphics/508 W 57th St	212-975-9050
Ovation Films/49 W 24th St	212-675-4700
Paganelli, Albert/21 W 46th St	212-719-4105
Perpetual Animation/17 W 45th St	212-840-2888
Polestar Films & Assoc Arts/870 Seventh Ave	212-586-6333
Rankin/Bass Productions/1 E 53rd St	212-759-7721
Rembrandt Films/59 E 54th St	212-758-1024
Robinson, Keith Prod Inc/200 E 21st St	212-533-9078
Seeger, Hal/45 W 45th St	212-575-8900
Shadow Light Prod, Inc/12 W 27th St 7th Fl	212-689-7511
Singer, Rebecca Studio Inc/111 W 57th St	212-944-0466
Stanart Studios/1650 Broadway	212-586-0445
Stark, Philip/245 W 29th St 15th Fl	212-868-5555
Sunflower Films/15 W 46th St	212-869-0123
Telemated Motion Pictures/PO Box 176	212-475-8050
The Fantastic Animation Machine/12 E 46th St	212-697-2525
Today Video, Inc/45 W 45th St	212-391-1020
Triology Design/25 W 45th St	212-382-3592
Videart Inc/39 W 38th St	212-840-2163
Video Works/24 W 40th St	212-869-2500
Weiss, Frank Studio/66 E 7th St	212-477-1032
World Effects Inc/20 E 46th St	212-687-7070
Zanders Animation Parlour/18 E 41st St	212-725-1331

Northeast

Aviation Simulations International Inc/Box 358, Huntington, NY	516-271-6476
Comm Corps Inc/711 4th St NW, Washington, DC	202-638-6550
Consolidated Visual Center/2529 Kenilworth Ave, Tuxedo, MD	301-772-7300
Felix, Luisa/180 12th St, Jersey City, NJ	201-653-1500
Hughes, Gary Inc/PO Box, Cabin John, MD	301-229-1100
Penpoint Prod Svc/331 Newbury St, Boston, MA	617-266-1331
Pilgrim Film Service/2504 50th Ave, Hyattsville, MD	301-773-7072
Symmetry T/A/13813 Willoughby Road, Upper Marlboro, MD	301-627-5050
Synthavision-Magi/3 Westchester Plaza, Elmsford, NY	212-733-1300
The Animators/247 Ft Pitt Blvd, Pittsburgh, PA	412-391-2550
West End Film Inc/2121 Newport Pl NW, Washington, DC	202-331-8078

Southeast

Bajus-Jones Film Corp/401 W Peachtree St #1720, Atlanta, GA	404-221-0700
Cinetron Computer Systems Inc/6700 IH 85 North, Norcross, GA	404-448-9463

Midwest

AGS & R Studios/425 N Michigan Ave, Chicago, IL	312-836-4500
Associated Audio-Visual Corp/2821 Central St, Evanston, IL	312-866-6780
Bajus-Jones Film Corp/203 N Wabash, Chicago, IL	312-332-6041
Boyer Studio/1324 Greenleaf, Evanston, IL	312-491-6363
Coast Prod/505 N Lake Shore Dr, Chicago, IL	312-222-1857
Filmack Studios Inc/1327 S Wabash, Chicago, IL	312-427-3395
Freese & Friends Inc/1429 N Wells, Chicago, IL	312-642-4475
Goldsholl Assoc/420 Frontage Rd, Northfield, IL	312-446-8300
Goodrich Animation/405 N Wabash, Chicago, IL	312-329-1344
Kayem Animation Services/100 E Ohio, Chicago, IL	312-664-7733
Kinetics/444 N Wabash, Chicago, IL	312-644-2767
Optimation Inc/9055 N 51st St, Brown Deer, WI	414-355-4500
Pilot Prod/1819 Ridge Ave, Evanston, IL	312-328-3700
Quicksilver Assoc Inc/16 W Ontario, Chicago, IL	312-943-7622
Ritter Waxberg & Assoc/200 E Ontario, Chicago, IL	312-664-3934
Simott & Associates/676 N La Salle, Chicago, IL	312-440-1875
The Beach Productions Ltd/1960 N Seminary, Chicago, IL	312-281-4500

Southwest

Graphic Art Studio/5550 S Lewis Ave, Tulsa, OK	918-743-3915
Media Visions Inc/2716 Bissonnet #408, Houston, TX	713-521-0626

Rocky Mountain

Phillips, Stan & Assoc/865 Delaware, Denver, CO	303-595-9911

West Coast

Abel, Bob & Assoc/953 N Highland Ave, Los Angeles, CA	213-462-8100
Animation Filmakers Corp/7000 Romaine St, Hollywood, CA	213-851-5526
Animedia Productions Inc/10200 Riverside Dr, North Hollywood, CA	213-851-4777
Bass, Saul/Herb Yeager/7039 Sunset Blvd, Hollywood, CA	213-466-9701
Bosustow Entertainment/1649 11th St, Santa Monica, CA	213-394-0218
Cinema Research Corp/6860 Lexington Ave, Hollywood, CA	213-461-3235
Clampett, Bob Prod/729 Seward St, Hollywood, CA	213-466-0264
Cornerstone Productions/5915 Cantelope Ave, Van Nuys, CA	213-994-0007
Court Productions/1030 N Cole, Hollywood, CA	213-467-5900
Craig, Fred Productions/932 S Pine, San Gabriel, CA	213-287-6479
Creative Film Arts/7026 Santa Monica Blvd, Hollywood, CA	213-466-5111
DePatie-Freleng Enterprises/16400 Ventura Blvd #312, Encino, CA	818-906-3375
Duck Soup Productions Inc/1026 Montana Ave, Santa Monica, CA	213-451-0771

Energy Productions/846 N Cahuenga Blvd, Los Angeles, CA	213-462-3310
Excelsior Animated Moving Pictures/749 N LaBrea, Hollywood, CA	213-938-2335
Filmcore/849 N Seward, Hollywood, CA	213-464-7303
Filmfair/10900 Ventura Blvd, Studio City, CA	213-877-3191
Gallerie International Films Ltd/11320 W Magnolia Blvd, Hollywood, CA	213-760-2040
Hanna-Barbera/3400 W Cahuenga, Hollywood, CA	213-466-1371
Jacques, Jean-Guy & Assoc/633 N LaBrea Ave, Hollywood, CA	213-936-7177
Kurtz & Friends/2312 W Olive Ave, Burbank, CA	213-461-8188
Littlejohn, William Prod Inc/23425 Malibu Colony Dr, Malibu, CA	213-456-8620
Lumeni Productions/1727 N Ivar, Hollywood, CA	213-462-2110
Marks Communication/5550 Wilshire Blvd, Los Angeles, CA	213-464-6302
Melendez, Bill Prod Inc/439 N Larchmont Blvd, Los Angeles, CA	213-463-4101
Murakami Wolf Swenson Films Inc/1463 Tamarind Ave, Hollywood, CA	213-462-6474
New Hollywood Inc/1302 N Cahuenga Blvd, Hollywood, CA	213-466-3686
Pantomime Pictures Inc/12144 Riverside Dr, North Hollywood, CA	818-980-5555
Pegboard Productions/1310 N Cahuenga Blvd, Hollywood, CA	818-353-4991
Quartet Films Inc/5631 Hollywood Blvd, Hollywood, CA	213-464-9225
R & B EFX/1802 Victory Blvd, Glendale, CA	818-956-8406
Raintree Productions Ltd/666 N Robertson Blvd, Hollywood, CA	213-652-8330
S & A Graphics/3350 Barham Blvd, Los Angeles, CA	213-874-2301
Spungbuggy Works Inc/8506 Sunset Blvd, Hollywood, CA	213-657-8070
Sullivan & Associates/3377 Barham Blvd, Los Angeles, CA	213-874-2301
Sunwest Productions Inc/1021 N McCadden Pl, Hollywood, CA	213-461-2957
Title House/738 Cahuenga Blvd, Los Angeles, CA	213-469-8171
Triplane Film & Graphics Inc/328 1/2 N Sycamore Ave, Los Angeles, CA	213-937-1320
U P A Pictures Inc/875 Century Park East, Los Angeles, CA	213-556-3800
Williams, Richard Animation/5631 Hollywood Blvd, Los Angeles, CA	213-461-4344

Models & Talent

New York City

Abrams Artists/420 Madison Ave	212-935-8980
Act 48 Mgt Inc/1501 Broadway #1713	212-354-4250
Adams, Bret/448 W 44th St	212-246-0428
Agency for Performing Arts/888 Seventh Ave	212-582-1500
Agents for the Arts/1650 Broadway	212-247-3220
Alexander, Willard/660 Madison Ave	212-751-7070
Amato, Michael Theatrical Entrps/1650 Broadway	212-247-4456
Ambrose Co/1466 Broadway	212-921-0230
American Intl Talent/166 W 125th St	212-663-4626
American Talent Inc/888 Seventh Ave	212-977-2300
Anderson, Beverly/1472 Broadway	212-944-7773
Associated Booking/1995 Broadway	212-874-2400
Associated Talent Agency/41 E 11th St	212-674-4242
Astor, Richard/1697 Broadway	212-581-1970
Avantege Model Management/205 E 42nd St #1303	212-687-9890
Baldwin Scully Inc/501 Fifth Ave	212-922-1330
Barbizon Agency/3 E 54th St	212-371-3617
Barbizon Agency of Rego Park/95-20 63rd	718-275-2100
Barry Agency/165 W 46th St	212-869-9310
Bauman & Hiller/250 W 57th St	212-757-0098
Beilin, Peter/230 Park Ave	212-949-9119
Big Beauties Unlimited/159 Madison Ave	212-685-1270
Bloom, J Michael/400 Madison Ave	212-832-6900
Brifit Models/236 E 46th St 4th Fl	212-949-6262
Buchwald, Don & Assoc Inc/10 E 44th St	212-867-1070
Cataldi, Richard Agency/180 Seventh Ave	212-741-7450

Celebrity Lookalikes/235 E 31st St	212-532-7676
Click Model Management/881 Seventh Ave #1013	212-245-4306
Coleman-Rosenberg/667 Madison Ave	212-838-0734
Columbia Artists/165 W 57th St	212-397-6900
Cunningham, W D/919 Third Ave	212-832-2700
DMI Talent Assoc/250 W 57th St	212-246-4650
DeVore, Ophelia/1697 Broadway	212-586-2144
Deacy, Jane Inc/300 E 75th St	212-752-4865
Diamond Artists/119 W 57th St	212-247-3025
Dolan, Gloria Management Ltd/850 Seventh Ave	212-696-1850
Draper, Stephen Agency/37 W 57th St	212-421-5780
Eisen, Dulcina Assoc/154 E 61st St	212-355-6617
Elite Model Management Corp/150 E 58th St	212-935-4500
Faces Model Management/567 Third Ave	212-661-1515
Fields, Marje/165 W 46th St	212-764-5740
Ford Models Inc/344 E 59th St	212-753-6500
Foster Fell Agency/26 W 38th St	212-944-8520
Funny Face/440 E 62nd St	212-752-6090
Gage Group Inc/1650 Broadway	212-541-5250
Greco, Maria & Assoc/888 Eighth Ave	212-757-0681
HV Models/305 Madison Ave	212-751-3005
Hadley, Peggy Ent/250 W 57th St	212-246-2166
Harth, Ellen Inc/149 Madison Ave	212-686-5600
Hartig, Michael Agency Ltd/114 E 28th St	212-684-0010
Henderson-Hogan/200 W 57th St	212-765-5190
Henry, June/175 Fifth Ave	212-475-5130
Hesseltine Baker Assocs/165 W 46th St	212-921-4460
Hunt, Diana Management/44 W 44th St	212-391-4971
Hutto Management Inc/405 W 23rd St	212-807-1234
International Creative Management/40 W 57th St	212-556-5600
International Legends/40 E 34th St	212-684-4600
International Model Agency/232 Madison Ave	212-686-9053
Jacobsen-Wilder Inc/419 Park Ave So	212-686-6100
Jan J Agency/224 E 46th St	212-490-1875
Jordan, Joe Talent Agency/200 W 57th St	212-582-9003
KMA Associates/303 W 42nd St	212-581-4610
Kahn, Jerry Inc/853 Seventh Ave	212-245-7317
Kay Models/328 E 61st St	212-308-9560
Kennedy Artists/237 W 11th St	212-675-3944
Kid, Bonnie Agency/25 W 36th St	212-563-2141
King, Archer/1440 Broadway	212-764-3905
Kirk, Roseanne/161 W 54th St	212-888-6711
Kolmar-Luth Entertainment Inc/1501 Broadway	212-730-9500
Kroll, Lucy/390 West End Ave	212-877-0556
L B H Assoc/1 Lincoln Plaza	212-787-2609
L'Image Model Management Inc/114 E 32nd St	212-725-2424
Larner, Lionel Ltd/850 Seventh Ave	212-246-3105
Leach, Dennis/160 Fifth Ave	212-691-3450
Leaverton, Gary Inc/1650 Broadway	212-541-9640
Leigh, Sanford Entrprs Ltd/440 E 62nd St	212-752-4450
Leighton, Jan/205 W 57th St	212-757-5242
Lenny, Jack Assoc/140 W 58th St #1B	212-582-0270
Lewis, Lester Assoc/110 W 40th St	212-921-8370
M E W Company/370 Lexington Ave	212-889-7272
MMG Ent/Marcia's Kids/250 W 57th St	212-246-4360
Mannequin Fashion Models Inc/40 E 34th St	212-684-5432
Martinelli Attractions/888 Eighth Ave	212-586-0963
Matama Talent & Models/30 W 90th St	212-580-2236
McDearmon, Harold/45 W 139th St	212-283-1005
McDermott, Marge/216 E 39th St	212-889-1583
McDonald/ Richards/235 Park Ave S	212-475-5401
Models Models Inc/37 E 28th St #506	212-889-8233
Models Service Agency/1457 Broadway	212-944-8896
Models Talent Int'l/1140 Broadway	212-684-3343
Morris, William Agency/1350 Sixth Ave	212-586-5100
New York Production Studio/250 W 57th St	212-765-3433
Nolan, Philip/184 Fifth Ave	212-243-8900
Oppenheim-Christie/565 Fifth Ave	212-661-4330
Oscard, Fifi/19 W 44th St	212-764-1100
Ostertag, Barna Agency/501 Fifth Ave	212-697-6339
Our Agency/19 W 34th St #700	212-736-9582
Packwood, Harry Talent Ltd/250 W 57th St	212-586-8900

Please send us your additions and updates.

Palmer, Dorothy/250 W 57th St	212-765-4280
Perkins Models/1697 Broadway	212-582-9511
Petite Model Management/123 E 54th St #9A	212-759-9304
Pfeffer & Roelfs Inc/850 Seventh Ave	212-315-2230
Plus Models/49 W 37th St	212-997-1785
PlusModel Model Management Ltd/49 W 37th St	212-997-1785
Powers, James Inc/12 E 41st St	212-686-9066
Prelly People & Co/296 Fifth Ave	212-714-2060
Premier Talent Assoc/3 E 54th St	212-758-4900
Prestige Models/80 W 40th St	212-382-1700
Rogers, Wallace Inc/160 E 56th St	212-755-1464
Roos, Gilla Ltd/555 Madison Ave	212-758-5480
Rosen, Lewis Maxwell/1650 Broadway	212-582-6762
Rubenstein, Bernard/215 Park Ave So	212-460-9800
Ryan, Charles Agency/200 W 57th St	212-245-2225
STE Representation/888 Seventh Ave	212-246-1030
Sanders, Honey Agency Ltd/229 W 42nd St	212-947-5555
Schuller, William Agency/1276 Fifth Ave	212-532-6005
Silver, Monty Agency/200 W 57th St	212-765-4040
Smith, Friedman/850 Seventh Ave	212-581-4490
Stars/360 E 65th St #17H	212-988-1400
Stein, Lillian/1501 Broadway	212-840-8299
Stewart Artists Corp/215 E 81st St	212-249-5540
Stroud Management/119 W 57th St	212-688-0226
Summa/38 W 32nd St	212-947-6155
Szold Models/644 Broadway	212-777-4998
Talent Reps Inc/20 E 53rd St	212-752-1835
Tatinas Models & Fitters Assoc/1328 Broadway	212-947-5797
The Lantz Office/888 Seventh Ave	212-586-0200
The Starkman Agency/1501 Broadway	212-921-9191
Theater Now Inc/1515 Broadway	212-840-4400
Thomas, Michael Agency/22 E 60th St	212-755-2616
Total Look/404 Riverside Dr	212-662-1029
Tranum Robertson Hughes Inc/2 Dag Hammarskjold Plaza	212-371-7500
Triad Artists/888 Seventh Ave	212-489-8100
Troy, Gloria/1790 Broadway	212-582-0260
Universal Attractions/218 W 57th St	212-582-7575
Universal Talent/505 5th Ave	212-661-3896
Van Der Veer People Inc/225 E 59th St #A	212-688-2880
Waters, Bob Agency/510 Madison Ave	212-593-0543
Wilhelmina Models/9 E 37th St	212-532-6800
Witt, Peter Assoc Inc/215 E 79th St	212-861-3120
Wright, Ann Assoc/136 E 57th St	212-832-0110
Zoli/146 E 56th St	212-758-5959

Northeast

Cameo Models/392 Boylston St, Boston, MA	617-536-6004
Carnegie Talent Agency/300 Northern Blvd, Great Neck, NY	516-487-2260
Conover, Joyce Agency/33 Gallowae, Westfield, NJ	201-232-0908
Copley 7 Models & Talent/29 Newbury St, Boston, MA	617-267-4444
Hart Model Agency/137 Newbury St, Boston, MA	617-262-1740
Johnston Model Agency/32 Field Point Rd, Greenwich, CT	203-622-1137
National Talent Assoc/40 Railroad Ave, Valley Stream, NY	516-825-8707
Rocco, Joseph Agency/Public Ledger Bldg, Philadelphia, PA	215-923-8790
Somers, Jo/29 Newbury St, Boston, MA	617-267-4444
The Ford Model Shop/176 Newbury St, Boston, MA	617-266-6939
Trone, Larry/19-A Dean St, New Castle, DE	302-328-8399

Southeast

A del Corral Model & Talent Agency/5830 Argonne Blvd, New Orleans, LA	504-482-8963
Act 1 Casting Agency/1460 Brickell Ave, Miami, FL	305-371-1371
Amaro Agency/1617 Smith St, Orange Park, FL	904-264-0771
Artists Representatives of New Orleans/1012 Philip, New Orleans, LA	504-524-4683
Atlanta Models & Talent Inc/3030 Peachtree Rd NW, Atlanta, GA	404-261-9627
Birmingham Models & Talent/1023 20th St, Birmingham, AL	205-252-8533
Brown, Bob Marionettes/1415 S Queen St, Arlington, VA	703-920-1040
Brown, Jay Theatrical Agency Inc/221 W Waters Ave, Tampa, FL	813-933-2456

Bruce Enterprises/1022 16th Ave S, Nashville, TN	615-255-5711
Burns, Dot Model & Talent Agcy/478 Severn St, Tampa, FL	813-251-5882
Byrd, Russ Assoc/9450 Koger Blvd, St Petersburg, FL	813-586-1504
Carolina Talent/1347 Harding Pl, Charlotte, NC	704-332-3218
Cassandra Models Agency/635 N Hyer St, Orlando, FL	305-423-7872
Central Casting of FL/PO Box 7154, Ft Lauderdale, FL	305-379-7526
Chez Agency/922 W Peachtree St, Atlanta, GA	404-873-1215
Dassinger, Peter International Modeling/1018 Royal, New Orleans, LA	504-525-8382
Directions Talent Agency/400-C State St Station, Greensboro, NC	919-373-0955
Dodd, Barbara Studios/3508 Central Ave, Nashville, TN	615-385-0740
Faces, Ltd/2915 Frankfort Ave, Louisville, KY	502-893-8840
Falcon, Travis Modeling Agency/17070 Collins Ave, Miami, FL	305-947-7957
Flair Models/PO Box 373, Nashville, TN	615-361-3737
Florida Talent Agency/2631 E Oakland Pk, Ft Lauderdale, FL	305-565-3552
House of Talent of Cain & Sons/996 Lindridge Dr NE, Atlanta, GA	404-261-5543
Irene Marie Models/3212 S Federal Hwy, Ft Lauderdale, FL	305-522-3262
Jo-Susan Modeling & Finishing School/3415 West End Ave, Nashville, TN	615-383-5850
Lewis, Millie Modeling School/10 Calendar Ct #A, Forest Acres, SC	803-782-7338
Lewis, Millie Modeling School/880 S Pleasantburg Dr, Greenville, SC	803-271-4402
Mar Bea Talent Agency/923 Crandon Blvd, Key Biscayne, FL	305-361-1144
Marilyns Modeling Agency/3800 W Wendover, Greensboro, NC	919-292-5950
McQuerter, James/4518 S Cortez, Tampa, FL	813-839-8335
Parker, Sarah/425 S Olive Ave, West Palm Beach, FL	305-659-2833
Polan, Marian Talent Agency/PO Box 7154, Ft Lauderdale, FL	305-525-8351
Pommier, Michele/7520 Red Rd, Miami, FL	305-667-8710
Powers, John Robert School/828 SE 4th St, Fort Lauderdale, FL	305-467-2838
Professional Models Guild & Workshop/210 Providence Rd, Charlotte, NC	704-377-9299
Remington Models & Talent/2480 E Commercial Blvd PH, Ft Lauderdale, FL	305-944-6608
Rose, Sheila/8218 NW 8th St, Plantation, FL	305-473-9747
Serendipity/3130 Maples Dr NE #19, Atlanta, GA	404-237-4040
Signature Talent Inc/PO Box 221086, Charlotte, NC	704-542-0034
Sovereign Model & Talent/11111 Biscayne Blvd, Miami, FL	305-899-0280
Spivia, Ed/PO Box 38097, Atlanta, GA	404-292-6240
Stevens, Patricia Modeling Agency/3312 Piedmont Rd, Atlanta, GA	404-261-3330
Talent & Model Land, Inc/1501 12th Ave S, Nashville, TN	615-385-2723
Talent Enterprises Inc/3338 N Federal Way, Ft Lauderdale, FL	305-949-6099
Talent Management of VA/2940 N Lynnhaven Rd, Virginia Beach, VA	804-486-5550
The Agency South/1501 Sunset Dr, Coral Gables, FL	305-667-6746
The Casting Directors Inc/1524 NE 147th St, North Miami, FL	305-944-8559
The Talent Shop Inc/3210 Peachtree Rd NE, Atlanta, GA	404-261-0770
Theatrics Etcetera/PO Box 11862, Memphis, TN	901-728-7454
Thompson, Jan Agency/1708 Scott Ave, Charlotte, NC	704-377-5987
Top Billing Inc/PO Box 121089, Nashville, TN	615-327-1133
Tracey Agency Inc/PO Box 12405, Richmond, VA	804-358-4004

Midwest

A-Plus Talent Agency Corp/666 N Lakeshore Dr, Chicago, IL	312-642-8151
Advertisers Casting Service/15 Kercheval Ave, Grosse Point Farms, MI	313-881-1135
Affiliated Talent & Casting Service/28860 Southfield Rd #100, Southfield, MI	313-559-3110
Arlene Willson Agency/9205 W Center St, Milwaukee, WI	414-259-1611
Creative Casting Inc/430 Oak Grove, Minneapolis, MN	612-871-7866
David & Lee Model Management/70 W Hubbard, Chicago, IL	312-661-0500
Gem Enterprises/5100 Eden Ave, Minneapolis, MN	612-927-8000
Hamilton, Shirley Inc/620 N Michigan Ave, Chicago, IL	312-644-0300
Lee, David Models/70 W Hubbard, Chicago, IL	312-661-0500
Limelight Assoc Inc/3460 Davis Lane, Cincinnati, OH	513-631-8276
Marx, Dick & Assoc Inc/101 E Ontario St, Chicago, IL	312-440-7300

Production/Support Services

Continued

Please send us your additions and updates.

Monza Talent Agency/1001 Westport Rd, Kansas City, MO — 816-931-0222
Moore, Eleanor Agency/1610 W Lake St, Minneapolis, MN — 612-827-3823
National Talent Assoc/3525 Patterson Ave, Chicago, IL — 312-539-8575
New Faces Models & Talent Inc/310 Groveland Ave,
Minneapolis, MN — 612-871-6000
Pastiche Models Inc/161 Ottawa NW #300K, Grand Rapids,
MI — 616-451-2181
Powers, John Robert/5900 Roche Dr, Columbus, OH — 614-846-1047
SR Talent Pool/206 S 44th St, Omaha, NE — 402-553-1164
Schucart, Norman Ent/1417 Green Bay Rd, Highland Park, IL — 312-433-1113
Sharkey Career Schools Inc/1299-H Lyons Rd Governours Sq
Centerville, , OH — 513-434-4461
Station 12-Producers Express/1759 Woodgrove Ln,
Bloomfield Hills, MI — 313-855-1188
Talent & Residuals Inc/303 E Ohio St, Chicago, IL — 312-943-7500
Talent Phone Productions/612 N Michagan Ave, Chicago, IL — 312-664-5757
The Model Shop/415 N State St, Chicago, IL — 312-822-9663
Verblen, Carol Casting Svc/2408 N Burling, Chicago, IL — 312-348-0047
White House Studios/9167 Robinson, Kansas City, MO — 913-341-8036

Southwest

ARCA/ Freelance Talent/PO Box 5686, Little Rock, AR — 501-224-1111
Aaron, Vicki/2017 Butterfield, Grand Prairie, TX — 214-641-8539
Accent Inc/6051 N Brookline, Oklahoma City, OK — 405-843-1303
Actors Clearinghouse/501 N IH 35, Austin, TX — 512-476-3412
Ball, Bobby Agency/808 E Osborn, Phoenix, AZ — 602-264-5007
Barbizon School & Agency/1647-A W Bethany Home Rd,
Phoenix, AZ — 602-249-2950
Bennett, Don Agency/4630 Deepdale, Corpus Christi, TX — 512-854-4871
Blair, Tanya Agency/3000 Carlisle St, Dallas, TX — 214-748-8353
Creme de la Creme/5643 N Pennsylvania, Oklahoma City, OK — 405-721-5316
Dawson, Kim Agency/PO Box 585060, Dallas, TX — 214-638-2414
Ferguson Modeling Agency/1100 W 34th St, Little Rock, AR — 501-375-3519
Flair-Career Fashion & Modeling/11200 Menaul Rd,
Albuquerque, NM — 505-296-5571
Fosi's Talent Agency/2777 N Campbell Ave #209, Tucson, AZ — 602-795-3534
Fullerton, Jo Ann/923 W Britton Rd, Oklahoma City, OK — 405-848-4839
Hall, K Agency/503 W 15th St, Austin, TX — 512-476-7523
Harrison-Gers Modeling Agency/1707 Wilshire Blvd NW,
Oklahoma City, OK — 405-840-4515
Kyle & Mathews/5250 Gulfton #3-A, Houston, TX —
Layman, Linda Agency/3546 E 51st St, Tulsa, OK — 918-744-0888
Mannequin Modeling Agency/204 E Oakview, San Antonio, TX — 512-231-4540
Melancon, Joseph Studios/2934 Elm, Dallas, TX — 214-742-2982
Models and Talent of Tulsa/4528 S Sheridan Rd, Tulsa, OK — 918-664-5340
Models of Houston Placement Agency/7676 Woodway,
Houston, TX — 713-789-4973
New Faces Inc/5108-B N 7th St, Phoenix, AZ — 602-279-3200
Norton Agency/3900 Lemon Ave, Dallas, TX — 214-528-9960
Plaza Three Talent Agency/4343 N 16th St, Phoenix, AZ — 602-264-9703
Powers, John Robert Agency/3005 S University Dr, Fort
Worth, TX — 817-923-7305
Shaw, Ben Modeling Studios/4801 Woodway, Houston, TX — 713-850-0413
Southern Arizona Casting Co/2777 N Campbell Ave #209,
Tucson, AZ — 602-795-3534
Strawn, Libby/3612 Foxcroft Rd, Little Rock, AR — 501-227-5874
The Mad Hatter/7349 Ashcroft Rd, Houston, TX — 713-995-9090
The Texas Cowgirls Inc/4300 N Central #109C, Dallas, TX — 214-696-4176
Wyse, Joy Agency/2600 Stemmons, Dallas, TX — 214-638-8999

Rocky Mountain

Aspen/Vannoy Talent/PO Box 8124, Aspen, CO — 303-771-7500
Colorado Springs/Vannoy Talent/223 N Wahsatch, Colorado
Springs, CO — 303-636-2400
Denver/ Vannoy Talent/7400 E Caley Ave, Engelwood, CO — 303-771-6555
Illinois Talent/2664 S Krameria, Denver, CO — 303-757-8675
Mack, Jess Agency/111 Las Vegas Blvd S, Las Vegas, NV — 702-382-2193
Morris, Bobby Agency/1629 E Sahara Ave, Las Vegas, NV — 702-733-7575
Universal Models/953 E Sahara, Las Vegas, NV — 702-732-2499

West Coast

Adrian, William Agency/520 S Lake Ave, Pasadena, CA — 213-681-5750
Anthony's , Tom Precision Driving/1231 N Harper, Hollywood,
CA — 213-462-2301
Artists Management Agency/2232 Fifth Ave, San Diego, CA — 619-233-6655
Barbizon Modeling & Talent Agy/15477 Ventura Blvd, Sherman
Oaks, CA — 213-995-8238
Barbizon School of Modeling/452 Fashion Valley East, San
Diego, CA — 714-296-6366
Blanchard, Nina/1717 N Highland Ave, Hollywood, CA — 213-462-7274
Brebner Agency/185 Berry St, San Francisco, CA — 415-495-6700
Celebrity Look-Alikes/9000 Sunset Blvd #407, W Hollywood,
CA — 213-273-5566
Character Actors/935 NW 19th Ave, Portland, OR — 503-223-1931
Commercials Unlimited/7461 Beverly Blvd, Los Angeles, CA — 213-937-2220
Crosby, Mary Talent Agency/2130 Fourth Ave, San Diego, CA — 714-234-7911
Cunningham, William D/261 S Robertson, Beverly Hills, CA — 213-855-0200
Demeter and Reed Ltd/70 Zoe #200, San Francisco, CA — 415-777-1337
Drake, Bob/3878-A Fredonia Dr, Hollywood, CA — 213-851-4404
Franklin, Bob Broadcast Talent/10325 NE Hancock, Portland,
OR — 503-253-1655
Frazer-Nicklin Agency/4300 Stevens Creek Blvd, San Jose, CA — 408-554-1055
Garrick, Dale Intern'l Agency/8831 Sunset Blvd, Los Angeles,
CA — 213-657-2661
Grimme Agency/207 Powell St, San Francisco, CA — 415-392-9175
Hansen, Carolyn Agency/1516 6th Ave, Seattle, WA — 206-622-4700
International Creative Management/8899 Beverly Blvd, Los
Angeles, CA — 213-550-4000
Kelman, Toni Agency/8961 Sunset Blvd, Los Angeles, CA — 213-851-8822
L'Agence Models/100 N Winchester Blvd #370, San Jose, CA — 408-985-2993
Leonetti, Ltd/6526 Sunset Blvd, Los Angeles, CA — 213-462-2345
Liebes School of Modeling Inc/45 Willow Lane, Sausalito, CA — 415-331-5383
Longenecker, Robert Agency/11500 Olympic Blvd, Los
Angeles, CA — 213-477-0039
Media Talent Center/4315 NE Tillamook, Portland, OR — 503-281-2020
Model Management Inc/1400 Castro St, San Francisco, CA — 415-282-8855
Neuman, Allan/825 W 16th St, Newport Beach, CA — 714-548-8800
Pacific Artists, Ltd/515 N La Cienaga, Los Angeles, CA — 213-657-5990
Playboy Model Agency/8560 Sunset Blvd, Los Angeles, CA — 213-659-4080
Powers, John Robert/1610 6th Ave, Seattle, WA — 206-624-2495
Remington Models & Talent/924 Westwood Blvd #545, Los
Angeles, CA — 213-552-3012
Schwartz, Don Agency/8721 Sunset Blvd, Los Angeles, CA — 213-657-8910
Seattle Models Guild/1610 6th Ave, Seattle, WA — 206-622-1406
Shaw, Glen Agency/3330 Barham Blvd, Los Angeles, CA — 213-851-6262
Smith, Ron's Celebrity Look-Alikes/9000 Sunset Blvd,
Hollywood, CA — 213-273-5566
Sohbi's Talent Agency/1750 Kalakaua Ave #116, Honolulu, HI — 808-946-6614
Stern, Charles Agency/9220 Sunset Blvd, Los Angeles, CA — 213-273-6890
Studio Seven/261 E Rowland Ave, Covina, CA — 213-331-6351
Stunts Unlimited/3518 Cahuenga Blvd W, Los Angeles, CA — 213-874-0050
TOPS Talent Agency/404 Piikoi St, Honolulu, HI — 808-537-6647
Tanner, Herb & Assoc/6640 W Sunset Blvd, Los Angeles, CA — 213-466-6191
Wormser Heldford & Joseph/1717 N Highland #414, Los
Angeles, CA — 213-466-9111

Casting

New York City

BCI Casting/1500 Broadway — 212-221-1583
Brinker, Jane/51 W 16th St — 212-924-3322
Brown, Deborah Casting/250 W 57th St — 212-581-0404
Burton, Kate/271 Madison Ave — 212-243-6114
C & C Productions/445 E 80th St — 212-472-3700
Carter, Kit & Assoc/160 W 95th St — 212-864-3147
Cast Away Casting Service/14 Sutton Pl S — 212-755-0960
Central Casting Corp of NY/200 W 54th St — 212-582-4933

Production/Support Services

Continued

Please send us your additions and updates.

Cereghetti Casting/119 W 57th St	212-307-6081
Claire Casting/118 E 28th St	212-889-8844
Complete Casting/240 W 44th St	212-382-3835
Contemporary Casting Ltd/41 E 57th St	212-838-1818
Davidson/Frank Photo-Stylists/209 W 86th St #701	212-799-2651
DeSeta, Donna Casting/424 W 33rd St	212-239-0988
Deron, Johnny/30-63 32nd St	718-728-5326
Digiaimo, Lou/PO Box 5296	212-691-6073
Fay, Sylvia/71 Park Ave	212-889-2626
Feuer & Ritzer Casting Assoc/1650 Broadway	212-765-5580
Greco, Maria Casting/888 Eighth Ave	212-757-0681
Herman & Lipson Casting, Inc/114 E 25th St	212-777-7070
Howard, Stewart Assoc/215 Park Ave So	212-477-2323
Hughes/Moss Assoc/311 W 42nd St	212-307-6690
Iredale/ Burton Ltd/271 Madison Ave	212-889-7722
Jacobs, Judith/336 E 81st St	212-744-3758
Johnson/Liff/1501 Broadway	212-391-2680
Kressel, Lynn Casting/111 W 57th St	212-581-6990
L 2 Casting, Inc/4 W 83rd St	212-496-9444
McCorkle-Sturtevant Casting Ltd/240 W 44th St	212-888-9160
Navarro-Bertoni Casting Ltd/25 Central Park West	212-765-4251
Reed/Sweeney/Reed Inc/1780 Broadway	212-265-8541
Reiner, Mark Contemporary Casting/16 W 46th St	212-838-1818
Schneider Studio/119 W 57th St	212-265-1223
Shapiro, Barbara Casting/111 W 57th St	212-582-8228
Shulman/Pasciuto, Inc/1457 Broadway #308	212-944-6420
Silver, Stan/108 E 16th St	212-477-5900
Todd, Joy/250 W 57th St	212-765-1212
Weber, Joy Casting/250 W 57th St #1925	212-245-5220
Wollin, Marji/233 E 69th St	212-472-2528
Woodman, Elizabeth Roberts/222 E 44th St	212-972-1900

Northeast

Baker, Ann Casting/6 Wheeler Rd, Newton, MA	617-964-3038
Booking Agent Lic/860 Floral Ave, Union, NJ	201-353-1595
Central Casting/623 Pennsylvania Ave SE, Washington, DC	202-547-6300
Dilworth, Francis/496 Kinderkamack Rd, Oradell, NJ	201-265-4020
Holt/Belajac & Assoc Inc/The Bigelow #1924, Pittsburgh, PA	412-391-1005
Lawrence, Joanna Agency/82 Patrick Rd, Westport, CT	203-226-7239
Panache/3214 N St NW, Washington, DC	202-333-4240
Producers Audition Hotline/18156 Darnell Dr, Olney, MD	301-924-4327

Southeast

Central Casting/PO Box 7154, Ft Lauderdale, FL	305-379-7526
DiPrima, Barbara Casting/2951 So Bayshore Dr, Coconut Grove, FL	305-445-7630
Elite Artists, Inc/785 Crossover, Memphis, TN	901-761-1046
Manning, Maureen/1283 Cedar Hts Dr, Stone Mt, GA	404-296-1520
Taylor Royal Casting/2308 South Rd, Baltimore, MD	301-466-5959

Midwest

Station 12 Producers Express Inc/1759 Woodgrove Ln, Bloomfield Hills, MI	313-855-1188

Southwest

Abramson, Shirley/321 Valley Cove, Garland, TX	214-272-3400
Austin Actors Clearinghouse/501 North 1H 35, Austin, TX	512-476-3412
Blair, Tanya Agency/Artists Managers/3000 Carlisle #101, Dallas, TX	214-748-8353
Chason, Gary & Assoc/5645 Hillcroft St, Houston, TX	713-789-4003
Greer, Lucy & Assoc Casting/600 Shadywood Ln, Richardson, TX	214-231-2086
Jr Black Acad of Arts & Letters/723 S Peak St, Dallas, Tx75223	214-526-1237
KD Studio/2600 Stemons #147, Dallas, TX	214-638-0484
Kegley, Liz/Shari Rhodes/2021 Southgate, Houston, TX	713-522-5066
Kegley, Liz/Shari Rhodes/5737 Everglade, Dallas, TX	214-475-2353
Kent, Rody/5338 Vanderbilt Ave, Dallas, TX	214-827-3418
New Visions/Box 14 Whipple Station, Prescott, AZ	602-445-3382
Schermerhorn, Jo Ann/PO Box 2672, Conroe, TX	409-273-2569

Rocky Mountain

Aspen/Vannoy Talent/PO Box 8124, Aspen, CO	303-771-7500
Colorado Springs/Vannoy Talent/223 N Wahsatch, Colorado Springs, CO	303-636-2400
Denver/ Vannoy Talent/7400 E Caley Ave, Engelwood, CO	303-771-6555

West Coast

Abrams-Rubaloff & Associates/9012 Beverly Blvd, Los Angeles, CA	213-273-5711
Associated Talent International/9744 Wilshire Blvd, Los Angeles, CA	213-271-4662
BCI Casting/5134 Valley, Los Angeles, CA	213-222-0366
C H N International/7428 Santa Monica Blvd, Los Angeles, CA	213-874-8252
Celebrity Look-Alikes/9000 Sunset Blvd #407, West Hollywood, CA	213-273-5566
Commercials Unlimited/7461 Beverly Blvd, Los Angeles, CA	213-937-2220
Creative Artists Agency Inc/1888 Century Park E, Los Angeles, CA	213-277-4545
Cunningham, William & Assocs/261 S Robertson Blvd, Beverly Hills, CA	213-855-0200
Davis, Mary Webb/515 N LaCienega, Los Angeles, CA	213-652-6850
Garrick, Dale Internat'l Agency/8831 Sunset Blvd #402, Los Angeles, CA	213-657-2661
Hecht, Beverly Agency/8949 Sunset Blvd #203, Los Angeles, CA	213-278-3544
Kelman, Toni Agency/8961 Sunset Blvd, Los Angeles, CA	213-851-8822
Leonetti, Caroline Ltd/6526 Sunset Blvd, Los Angeles, CA	213-462-2345
Lien, Michael Casting/7461 Beverly Blvd, Los Angeles, CA	213-550-7381
Loo, Bessi Agency/8235 Santa Monica, W Hollywood, CA	213-650-1300
Mangum, John Agency/8831 Sunset Blvd, Los Angeles, CA	213-659-7230
Morris, William Agency/151 El Camino Dr, Beverly Hills, CA	213-274-7451
Pacific Artists Limited/515 N LaCienega Blvd, Los Angeles, CA	213-657-5990
REB-Sunset International/6912 Hollywood Blvd, Hollywood, CA	213-464-4440
Rose, Jack/6430 Sunset Blvd #1203, Los Angeles, CA	213-463-7300
Schaeffer, Peggy Agency/10850 Riverside Dr, North Hollywood, CA	818-985-5547
Schwartz, Don & Assoc/8721 Sunset Blvd, Los Angeles, CA	213-657-8910
Stern, Charles H Agency/9220 Sunset Blvd, Los Angeles, CA	213-273-6890
Sutton Barth & Venari/8322 Beverly Blvd, Los Angeles, CA	213-653-8322
Tannen, Herb & Assoc/6640 Sunset Blvd #203, Los Angeles, CA	213-466-6191
Wilhelmina/West/1800 Centyry Park E #504, Century City, CA	213-553-9525
Wormser Heldford & Joseph/1717 N Highland #414, Hollywood, CA	213-466-9111
Wright, Ann Assoc/8422 Melrose Place, Los Angeles, CA	213-655-5040

Animals

New York City

All Tame Animals/37 W 57th St	212-752-5885
Animals for Advertising/310 W 55th St	212-245-2590
Berloni Theatrical Animals/314 W 57th St Box 37	212-974-0922
Canine Academy of Ivan Kovach/3725 Lyme Ave	718-682-6770
Captain Haggertys Theatrical Dogs/1748 First Ave	212-410-7400
Chateau Theatrical Animals/608 W 48th St	212-246-0520
Claremont Riding Academy/175 W 89th St	212-724-5100
Dawn Animal Agency/160 W 46th St	212-575-9396
Mr Lucky Dog Training School Inc/27 Crescent St	718-827-2792

Northeast

American Driving Society/PO Box 1852, Lakeville, CT	203-435-0307
Animal Actors Inc/Box 221, RD 3, Washington, NJ	201-689-7539

Production/Support Services

Continued

Please send us your additions and updates.

Davis, Greg/Box 159T, RD 2, Greenville, NY	518-966-8229
Long Island Game Farm & Zoo/Chapman Blvd, Manorville, NY	516-727-7443
Parrots of the World/239 Sunrise Hwy, Rockville Center, NY	212-343-4141

Southeast

Dog Training by Bob Maida/7605 Old Centerville Rd, Manassas, VA	713-631-2125
Studio Animal Rentals/170 W 64th St, Hialeah, FL	305-558-4160

Midwest

Plainsmen Zoo/Rt 4, Box 151, Elgin, IL	312-697-0062

Southwest

Bettis, Ann J/Rt 1-A Box 21-B, Dripping Springs, TX	512-264-1952
Dallas Zoo in Marsalis Park/621 E Clarendon, Dallas, TX	214-946-5155
Estes, Bob Rodeos/PO Box 962, Baird, TX	915-854-1037
Fort Worth Zoological Park/2727 Zoological Park Dr., Fort Worth, TX	817-870-7050
International Wildlife Park/601 Wildlife Parkway, Grand Prairie, TX	214-263-2203
Newsom's Varmints N' Things/13015 Kaltenbrun, Houston, TX	713-931-0676
Scott, Kelly Buggy & Wagon Rentals/Box 442, Bandera, TX	512-796-3737
Taylor, Peggy Talent Inc/6311 N O'Connor 3 Dallas Comm, Irving, TX	214-869-1515
Y O Ranch/Dept AS, Mountain Home, TX	512-640-3222

Rocky Mountain

Denver/ Vannoy Talent/7400 E Caley Ave, Engelwood, CO	303-771-6555

West Coast

American Animal Enterprises/PO Box 337, Littlerock, CA	805-944-3011
Animal Action/PO Box 824, Arleta, CA	818-767-3003
Animal Actors of Hollywood/864 Carlisle Rd, Thousand Oaks, CA	805-495-2122
Birds and Animals/25191 Riverdell Dr, El Toro, CA	714-830-7845
Casa De Pets/11814 Ventura Blvd, Studio City, CA	818-761-3651
Di Sesso's, Moe Trained Wildlife/24233 Old Road, Newhall, CA	805-255-7969
Frank Inn Inc/12265 Branford St, Sun Valley, CA	818-896-8188
Gentle Jungle/3815 W Olive Ave, Burbank, CA	818-841-5300
Griffin, Gus/11281 Sheldon St, Sun Valley, CA	818-767-6647
Martin, Steve Working Wildlife/PO Box 65, Acton, CA	805-268-0788
Pyramid Bird/1407 W Magnolia, Burbank, CA	818-843-5505
Schumacher Animal Rentals/14453 Cavette Pl, Baldwin Park, CA	818-338-4614
The American Mongrel/PO Box 2406, Lancaster, CA	805-942-7550
The Blair Bunch/7561 Woodman Pl, Van Nuys, CA	213-994-1136
The Stansbury Company/9304 Santa Monica Blvd, Beverly Hills, CA	213-273-1138
Weatherwax, Robert/16133 Soledad Canyon Rd, Canyon Country, CA	805-252-6907

Hair & Make-Up

New York City

Abrams, Ron/126 W 75th St	212-580-0705
Baeder, D & Sehven, A/135 E 26th St	212-532-4571
Barba, Olga/201 E 16th St	212-420-8611
Barron, Lynn/135 E 26th St	212-532-4571
Beauty Booking/130 W 57th St	212-977-7157
Blake, Marion/130 W 57th St	212-977-7157
Boles, Brad/New York	212-724-2800
Boushelle/444 E 82nd St	212-861-7225
Braithwaite, Jordan/130 W 57th St	212-977-7157

Hammond, Claire/440 E 57th St	212-838-0712
Imre, Edith Beauty Salon/8 W 56th St	212-758-0233
Jenrette, Pamela/300 Mercer St	212-673-4748
Keller, Bruce Clyde/422 E 58th St	212-593-3816
Lane, Judy/444 E 82nd St	212-861-7225
Multiple Artists/42 E 23 St	212-473-8020
Narvaez, Robin/360 E 55th St	212-371-6378
Richardson, John Ltd/119 E 64th St	212-772-1874
Stessin, Warren Scott/New York	212-243-3319
Tamblyn, Thom Inc/240 E 27th St	212-683-4514
Weithorn, Rochelle/431 E 73rd St	212-472-8668

Northeast

E-Fex/623 Pennsylvania Ave SE, Washington, DC	202-543-1241
Rothman, Ginger/1915 Lyttonsville Rd, Silver Spring, MD	301-565-2020

Southeast

Irene Marie Models/3212 S Federal Hwy, Ft Lauderdale, FL	305-522-3262
Parker, Julie Hill/PO Box 19033, Jacksonville, FL	904-724-8483

Midwest

Adams, Jerry Hair Salon/1123 W Webster, Chicago, IL	312-327-1130
Alderman, Frederic/Rt 2 Box 205, Mundelein, IL	312-438-2925
Bobak, Ilona/300 N State, Chicago, IL	312-321-1679
Camylle/112 E Oak, Chicago, IL	312-943-1120
Cheveux/908 W Armitage, Chicago, IL	312-935-5212
Collins Chicago, Inc/67 E Oak, Chicago, IL	312-266-6662
Emerich, Bill/PO Box 14523, Chicago, IL	312-871-4659
International Guild of Make-Up/6970 N Sheridan, Chicago, IL	312-761-8500
Okains Costume & Theater/2713 W Jefferson, Joliet, IL	815-741-9303
Sguardo, Che/716 N Wells St, Chicago, IL	312-440-1616
Simmons, Sid Inc/2 E Oak, Chicago, IL	312-943-2333
Wawiorka, Karen/Chicago, IL, 312-642-4219	

Southwest

Dawson, Kim Agency/PO Box 585060, Dallas, TX	214-638-2414

Rocky Mountain

DeRose, Mary Fran/4430 W 30th Ave, Denver, CO	303-422-2152

West Coast

Andre, Maurice/9426 Santa Monica Blvd, Beverly Hills, CA	213-274-4562
Antovniov/11908 Ventura Blvd, Studio City, CA	818-763-0671
Armando's/607 No Huntley Dr, W Hollywood, CA	213-657-5160
Bourget, Lorraine/559 Muskingum Pl, Pacific Palisades, CA	213-454-3739
Cassandre 2000/18386 Ventura Blvd, Tarzana, CA	818-881-8400
Cloutier Inc/704 N Gardner, Los Angeles, CA	213-655-1263
Craig, Kenneth/13211 Ventura Blvd, Studio City, CA	818-995-8717
Design Pool/11936 Darlington Ave #303, Los Angeles, CA	213-826-1551
Francisco/PO Box 49995, Los Angeles, CA	213-826-3591
Frier, George/, , CA	213-393-0576
Gavilan/139 S Kings Rd, Los Angeles, CA	213-655-4452
Geiger, Pamela/, , CA	213-274-5737
HMS/1541 Harvard St #A, Santa Monica, CA	213-828-2080
Hamilton, Bryan J/909 N Westbourne Dr, Los Angeles, CA	213-654-9006
Hirst, William/15130 Ventura Blvd, Sherman Oaks, CA	818-501-0993
Johns, Arthur/8661 Sunset Blvd, Hollywood, CA	213-855-9306
Ray, David Frank/15 Wave Crest, Venice, CA	213-392-5640
Samuel, Martin/6138 W 6th, Los Angeles, CA	213-930-0794
Serena, Eric/840 N Larabee, Bldg 4, W Hollywood, CA	213-652-4267
Studio Seven/261 E Rowland Ave, Covina, CA	213-331-6351
Total You Salon/1647 Los Angeles Ave, Simi, CA	805-526-4189
Towsend, Jeanne/433 N Camden Dr, Beverly Hills, CA	213-851-7044
Welsh, Franklyn/704 N LaCienega Blvd, Los Angeles, CA	213-656-8195

Production/Support Services

Continued

Please send us your additions and updates.

Hair

New York City

Albert-Carter/Hotel St Moritz	212-688-2045
Benjamin Salon/104 Washington Pl	212-255-3330
Caruso, Julius/22 E 62nd St	212-751-6240
Daines, David Salon Hair Styling/833 Madison Ave	212-535-1563
George V Hair Stylist/501 Fifth Ave	212-687-9097
Moda 700/700 Madison Ave	212-935-9188
Monsieur Marc Inc/22 E 65th St	212-861-0700
Peter's Beauty Home/149 W 57th St	212-247-2934
Pierro, John/130 W 57th St	212-977-7157

Northeast

Brocklebank, Tom/249 Emily Ave, Elmont, NY	516-775-5356

Southeast

Yellow Strawberry/107 E Las Olas Blvd, Ft Lauderdale, FL	305-463-4343

Midwest

Rodriguez, Ann/1123 W Webster, Chicago, IL	312-327-1130

Southwest

Southern Hair Designs/3563 Far West Blvd, Austin, TX	512-346-1734

Rocky Mountain

City Lights Hair Designs/2845 Wyandote, Denver, CO	303-458-0131
Zee for Hair/316 E Hopkins, Aspen, CO	303-925-4434

West Coast

Anatra, M Haircutters/530 No LaCienega, Los Angeles, CA	213-657-1495
Barronson Hair/11908 Ventura, Studio City, CA	818-763-4337
Beck, Shirley/, , CA	213-763-2930
Edwards, Allen/455 N Rodeo Dr, Beverly Hills, CA	213-274-8575
Ely, Shannon/616 Victoria, Venice, CA	213-392-5832
Fisher, Jim/c/o Rumours, 9014 Melrose, Los Angeles, CA	213-550-5946
Francisco/PO Box 49995, Los Angeles, CA	213-826-3591
Grieve, Ginger/, , CA	818-347-2947
Gurasich, Lynda/, , CA	818-981-6719
HMS/1541 Harvard St #A, Santa Monica, CA	213-828-2080
Hjerpe, Warren/9018 Beverly Blvd, Los Angeles, CA	213-550-5946
Iverson, Betty/, , CA	213-462-2301
John, Michael Salon/414 N Camden Dr, Beverly Hills, CA	213-278-8333
Kemp, Lola/, , CA	213-293-8710
Lorenz, Barbara/, , CA	213-657-0028
Malone, John/, , CA	213-246-1649
Menage a Trois/8822 Burton Way, Beverly Hills, CA	213-278-4431
Miller, Patty/, , CA	818-843-5208
Morrissey, Jimie/, , CA	213-657-4318
Payne, Allen/, , CA	213-395-5259
Phillips, Marilyn/, , CA	213-923-6996
Sami/1230 N Horn Ave #525, Los Angeles, CA	213-652-5816
Sassoon, Vidal Inc/2049 Century Park E #3800, Los Angeles, CA	213-553-6100
The Hair Conspiracy/11923 Ventura Blvd, Studio City, CA	818-985-1126
Trainoff, Linda/, , CA	818-769-0373
Vecchio, Faith/, , CA	818-345-6152

Make-Up

New York City

Adams, Richard/130 W 57th St	212-977-7157
Armand/147 W 35th St	212-947-2186
Bertoli, Michele/264 Fifth Ave	212-684-2480
Bonzignor's Cosmetics/110 Fulton	212-267-1108
Lawrence, Rose/444 E 82nd St	212-861-7225
Make-Up Center Ltd/150 W 55th St	212-977-9494
Oakley, Sara/New York	212-749-5912
Richardson, John Ltd/119 E 64th St	212-772-1874
Ross, Rose Cosmetics/16 W 55th St	212-586-2590
Sartin, Janet of Park Ave Ltd/480 Park Ave	212-751-5858
Stage Light Cosmetics Ltd/630 Ninth Ave	212-757-4851
Suzanne de Paris/509 Madison Ave	212-838-4024

Northeast

Damaskos-Zilber, Zoe/78 Waltham St #4, Boston, MA	617-628-6583
Douglas, Rodney N/473 Avon Ave #3, Newark, NJ	201-375-2979
Fiorina, Frank/2400 Hudson Terr #5A, Fort Lee, NJ	212-242-3900
Gilmore, Robert Assoc Inc/990 Washington St, Dedham, MA	617-329-6633
Meth, Miriam/96 Greenwood Ln, White Plains, NY	212-787-5400
Minassian, Amie/62-75 Austin St, Rego Park, NY	212-446-8048
Phillipe, Louise Miller/22 Chestnut Pl, Brookline, MA	617-566-3608
Phillipe, Robert/22 Chestnut Pl, Brookline, MA	617-566-3608
Something Special/1601 Walter Reed Dr S, Arlington, VA	703-892-0551
Tyson, Karen/344 E 85th St #6D, New York, NY	212-517-3508
Zack, Sandra/94 Orient Ave, East Boston, MA	617-567-7581

Southeast

Star Styled of Miami/475 NW 42nd Ave, Miami, FL	305-541-2424
Star Styled of Tampa/4235 Henderson Blvd, Tampa, FL	813-872-8706

Southwest

ABC Theatrical Rental & Sales/825 N 7th St, Phoenix, AZ	602-258-5265
Chelsea Cutters/One Chelsea Pl, Houston, TX	713-529-4813
Copeland, Tom/502 West Grady, Austin, TX	512-835-0208
Corey, Irene/4147 Herschel Ave, Dallas, TX	214-528-4836
Dobes, Pat/1826 Nocturne, Houston, TX	713-465-8102
Ingram, Marilyn Wyrick/10545 Chesterton Drive, Dallas, TX	214-349-2113
Stamm, Louis M/721 Edgehill Dr, Hurst, TX	817-268-5037

Rocky Mountain

Moen, Brenda/, , CO	303-871-9506
Moon Sun Emporium/2019 Broadway, Boulder, CO	303-443-6851

West Coast

Astier, Guy/11936 Darlington Ave #303, Los Angeles, CA	213-826-1551
Blackman, Charles F/12751 Addison, N Hollwyood, CA	818-761-2177
Blackman, Gloria/12751 Addison, N Hollwyood, CA	818-761-2177
Case, Tom/5150 Woodley, Encino, CA	818-788-5268
Cooper, David/3616 Effie, Los Angeles, CA	213-660-7326
Cosmetic Connection/9484 Dayton Way, Beverly Hills, CA	213-550-6242
D'Ifray, T J/468 N Bedford Dr, Beverly Hills, CA	213-274-6776
Dawn, Wes/11113 Hortense St, N Hollywood, CA	818-761-7517
Fradkin, Joanne c/o Pigments/8822 Burton Way, Beverly Hills, CA	213-858-7038
Francisco/PO Box 49995, Los Angeles, CA	213-826-3591
Freed, Gordon/, , CA	818-360-9473
Geike, Ziggy/, , CA	818-789-1465
Henrriksen, Ole/8601 W Sunset Blvd, Los Angeles, CA	213-854-7700
Howell, Deborah/291 S Martel Ave, Los Angeles, CA	213-655-1263
Koelle, c/o Pigments/8822 Burton Way, Beverly Hills, CA	213-668-1690

Production/Support Services

Continued

Please send us your additions and updates.

Kruse, Lee C/, , CA	818-894-5408
Laurent, c/o Menage a Trois/8822 Burton Way, Beverly Hills, CA	213-278-4430
Logan, Kathryn/, , CA	818-988-7038
Malone, John E/, , CA	818-247-5160
Manges, Delanie (Dee)/, , CA	818-763-3311
Maniscalco, Ann S/, , CA	818-894-5408
Menage a Trois/8822 Burton Way, Beverly Hills, CA	213-278-4431
Minch, Michelle/339 S Detroit St, Los Angeles, CA	213-484-9648
Natasha/4221 1/2 Avocado St, Los Angeles, CA	213-663-1477
Nielsen, Jim/, , CA	213-461-2168
Nye, Dana/, , CA	213-477-0443
Odessa/1448 1/2 N Fuller Ave, W Hollywood, CA	213-876-5779
Palmieri, Dante/, , CA	213-396-6020
Penelope/, ,	213-654-6747
Pigments/8822 Burton Way, Beverly Hills, CA	213-858-7038
Romero, Bob/5030 Stern Ave, Sherman Oaks, CA	818-891-3338
Rumours/9014 Melrose, W Hollywood, CA	213-550-5946
Sanders, Nadia/, , CA	213-465-2009
Shulman, Sheryl Leigh/, , CA	818-760-0101
Sidell, Bob/, ,	818-360-0794
Striepke, Danny/4800 #C Villa Marina, Marina Del Rey, CA	213-823-5957
Tuttle, William/, ,	213-454-2355
Tyler, Diane/, ,	415-381-5067
Warren, Dodie/, ,	818-763-3172
Westmore, Michael/, ,	818-763-3158
Westmore, Monty/, ,	818-762-2094
Winston, Stan/, ,	818-886-0630
Wolf, Barbara/, , CA	213-466-4660

Stylists

New York City

Baldassano, Irene/16 W 16th St	212-255-8567
Bandiero, Paul/PO Box 121 FDR Station	212-586-3700
Barritt, Randi Stylist/240 W 15th St	212-255-5333
Batteau, Sharon/130 W 57th St	212-977-7157
Beauty Bookings/130 W 57th St	212-977-7157
Benner, Dyne (Food)/311 E 60th St	212-688-7571
Berman, Benicia/399 E 72nd St	212-737-9627
Bromberg, Florence/350 Third Ave	212-255-4033
Cheverton, Linda/150 9th Avenue	212-691-0881
Chin, Fay/67 Vestry St	212-219-8770
Cohen, Susan/233 E 54th St	212-755-3157
D'Arcy, Timothy/43 W 85th St	212-580-8804
Davidson/Frank Photo-Stylists/209 W 86th St #701	212-799-2651
DeJesu, Joanna (Food)/101 W 23rd St	212-255-3895
Eller, Ann/7816 Third Ave	718-238-5454
Final Touch/55-11	718-435-6800
Galante, Kathy/9 W 31st St	212-239-0412
George, Georgia A/404 E 55th St	212-759-4131
Goldberg, Hal/11 Fifth Ave	212-982-7588
Greene, Jan/200 E 17th St	212-233-8989
Herman, Joan/15 W 84th St	212-724-3287
Joffe, Carole Reiff/233 E 34th St	212-725-4928
Klein, Mary Ellen/330 E 33rd St	212-683-6351
Lakin, Gaye/345 E 81st St	212-861-1892
Levin, Laurie/55 Perry St	212-242-2611
Lopes, Sandra/444 E 82nd St	212-249-8706
Magidson, Peggy/182 Amity St	212-508-7604
Manetti, Palmer/336 E 53rd St	212-758-3859
McCabe, Christine/200 W 79th St	212-799-4121
Meshejian, Zabel/125 Washington Pl	212-242-2459
Meyers, Pat/436 W 20th St	212-620-0069
Minch, Deborah Lee/175 W 87th St	212-873-7915
Nagle, Patsy/242 E 38th St	212-682-0364
Orefice, Jeanette/Brooklyn	718-643-8266
Ouellette, Dawn/336 E 30th St	212-799-9190

Peacock, Linda/118 W 88th St	212-580-1422
Reilly, Veronica/60 Gramercy Park N	212-840-1234
Sampson, Linda/431 W Broadway	212-925-6821
Scherman, Joan/450 W 24th St	212-620-0475
Schoenberg, Marv/878 West End Ave #10A	212-663-1418
Seymour, Celeste/130 E 75th St	212-744-3545
Sheffy, Nina/838 West End Ave	212-662-0709
Slote, Ina/7 Park Ave	212-679-4584
Smith, Rose/400 E 56th St #19D	212-758-8711
Specht, Meredith/166 E 61st St	212-832-0750
Weithorn, Rochelle/431 E 73rd St	212-472-8668
West, Susan/59 E 7th St	212-982-8228

Northeast

Bailey Designs/110 Williams St, Malden, MA	617-321-4448
Baldwin, Katherine/109 Commonwealth Ave, Boston, MA	617-267-0508
Carafoli, John (Food)/1 Hawes Rd, Sagamore Beach, MA	617-888-1557
E-Fex/623 Pennsylvania Ave SE, Washington, DC	202-543-1241
Gold, Judy/40 Sulgrave Rd, Scarsdale, NY	914-723-5036
Maggio, Marlene - Aura Prdtns/Brook Hill Ln Ste 5E, Rochester, NY	716-381-8053
Rosemary's Cakes Inc/299 Rutland Ave, Teaneck, NJ	201-833-2417
Rothman, Ginger/1915 Lyttonsville Rd, Silver Spring, MD	301-565-2020
Rubin, L A/359 Harvard St #2, Cambridge, MA	617-576-1808

Southeast

Foodworks/1541 Colonial Ter, Arlington, VA	703-524-2606
Gaffney, Janet D/464 W Wesley N W, Atlanta, GA	404-355-7556
Kupersmith, Tony/320 N Highland Ave NE, Atlanta, GA	404-577-5319
Parker, Julie Hill/PO Box 19033, Jacksonville, FL	904-724-8483
Polvay, Marina Assoc/9250 NE 10th Ct, Miami Shores, FL	305-759-4375
Stern, Ellen (Food)/13501 S Biscane River Dr, Miami, FL	305-681-0090
Torres, Martha/927 Third St, New Orleans, LA	504-895-6570

Midwest

Alan, Jean/1032 W Altgeld, Chicago, IL	312-929-9768
Carlson, Susan/255 Linden Park Pl, Highland Park, IL	312-433-2466
Carter, Karen/3323 N Kenmore, Chicago, IL	312-935-2901
Chevaux Ltd/908 W Armitage, Chicago, IL	312-935-5212
Ellison, Faye/3406 Harriet Ave S, Minneapolis, MN	612-822-7954
Emruh Style Design/714 W Fullerton, Chicago, IL	312-871-4659
Erickson, Emily/2954 No Racine, Chicago, IL	312-281-4899
Heller, Nancy/1142 W Diversey, Chicago, IL	312-549-4486
Lapin, Kathy Santis/925 Spring Hill Dr, Northbrook, IL	312-272-7487
Mary, Wendy/719 W Wrightwood, Chicago, IL	312-871-5476
Pace, Leslie/6342 N Sheridan, Chicago, IL	312-761-2480
Perry, Lee Ann/1615 No Clybourne, Chicago, IL	312-649-1815
Rabert, Bonnie/2230 W Pratt, Chicago, IL	312-743-7755
Sager, Sue/875 N Michigan, Chicago, IL	312-642-3789
Seeker, Christopher/100 E Walton #21D, Chicago, IL	312-944-4311
Shaver, Betsy/3714 N Racine, Chicago, IL	312-327-5615
Style Vasilak and Nebel/314 W Institute Pl, Chicago, IL	312-280-8516
The Set-up & Co/1049 E Michigan St, Indianapolis, IN	317-635-2323
Weber-Mack, Kathleen/2119 Lincoln, Evanston, IL	312-869-7794

Southwest

Bishop, Cindy/6101 Charlotte, Houston, TX	713-666-7224
Janet-Nelson/PO Box 143, Tempe, AZ	602-968-3771
Taylor, John Michael/2 Dallas Commun Complex #, Irving, TX	214-823-1333
Thomas, Jan/5651 East Side Ave, Dallas, TX	214-823-1955

Rocky Mountain

DeRose, Mary Fran/4430 W 30th Ave, Denver, CO	303-422-2152

West Coast

Akimbo Prod/801 Westbourne, W Hollywood, CA	213-657-4657

Production/Support Services

Continued

Please send us your additions and updates.

Alaimo, Doris/8800 Wonderland Ave, Los Angeles, CA	213-851-7044
Allen, Jamie R/, Los Angeles, CA	213-655-9351
Altbaum, Patti/244-CS Lasky Dr, Beverly Hills, CA	213-553-6269
Azzara, Marilyn/3165 Ellington Drive, Los Angeles, CA	213-851-0531
Castaldi, Debbie/10518 Wilshire Blvd #25, Los Angeles, CA	213-475-4312
Chinamoon/642 S Burnside Ave #6, Los Angeles, CA	213-937-8251
Corwin-Hankin, Aleka/1936 Cerro Gordo, Los Angeles, CA	213-665-7953
Craig, Kenneth/13211 Ventura Blvd, Studio City, CA	818-995-8717
Davis, Rommie/4414 La Venta Dr, West Lake Village, CA	818-906-1455
Design Pool/11936 Darlington Ave #303, Los Angeles, CA	213-826-1551
Evonne/, , CA	213-275-1658
Flating, Janice/8113 1/2 Melrose Ave, Los Angeles, CA	213-653-1800
Frank, Tobi/1269 N Hayworth, Los Angeles, CA	213-552-7921
Gaffin, Lauri/1123-12th St, Santa Monica, CA	213-451-2045
Governor, Judy/963 North Point, San Francisco, CA	415-861-5733
Graham, Victory/24 Ave 26, Venice, CA	213-934-0990
Granas, Marilyn/200 N Almont Dr, Beverly Hills, CA	213-278-3773
Griswald, Sandra/963 North Point, San Francisco, CA	415-775-4272
HMS/1541 Harvard St #A, Santa Monica, CA	213-828-2080
Hamilton, Bryan J/1269 N Hayworth, Los Angeles, CA	213-654-9006
Hewett, Julie/7551 Melrose Ave, Los Angeles, CA	213-651-5172
Hirsch, Lauren/858 Devon, Los Angeles, CA	213-271-7052
Howell, Deborah/219 S Martel Ave, Los Angeles, CA	213-655-1263
James, Elizabeth/5320 Bellingham Ave, N Hollywood, CA	213-761-5718
Kimball, Lynnda/133 S Peck Dr, Beverly Hills, CA	213-461-6303
King, Max/308 N Sycamore Ave, Los Angeles, CA	213-938-0108
Lawson, Karen/6836 Lexington Ave, Hollywood, CA	213-464-5770
Lynch, Jody/19130 Pacific Coast Hwy, Malibu, CA	213-456-2383
Material Eyes/501 Pacific Ave, San Francisco, CA	415-362-8143
Miller, Freyda/1412 Warner Ave, Los Angeles, CA	213-474-5034
Minot, Abby/53 Canyon Rd, Berkeley, CA	415-841-9600
Moore, Francie/842 1/2 N Orange Dr, Los Angeles, CA	213-462-5404
Morrow, Suzanne/26333 Silver Spur, Palos Verdes, CA	213-378-2909
Neal, Robin Lynn/3105 Durand, Hollywood, CA	213-465-6037
Olsen, Eileen/1619 N Beverly Dr, Beverly Hills, CA	213-273-4496
Parshall, Mary Ann/19850 Pacific Coast Hwy, Malibu, CA	213-456-8303
Prindle, Judy Peck/6057 Melrose Ave, Los Angeles, CA	213-650-0962
Russo, Leslie/377 10th, Santa Monica, CA	213-395-8461
Shatsy/9008 Harratt St, Hollywood, CA	213-275-2413
Skinner, Jeanette/1622 Moulton Pkwy #A, Tustin, CA	714-730-5793
Skinner, Randy/920 S Wooster St, Los Angeles, CA	213-659-2936
Skuro, Bryna/134-B San Vicente Blvd, Santa Monica, CA	213-394-2430
Sloane, Hilary/6351 Ranchito, Van Nuys, CA	213-855-1010
Surkin, Helen/2100 N Beachwood Dr, Los Angeles, CA	213-464-6847
Thomas, Lisa/9029 Rangely Ave, W Hollywood, CA	213-858-6903
Townsend, Jeanne/433 N Camden Dr, Beverly Hills, CA	213-851-7044
Tucker, Joan/1402 N Fuller St, Los Angeles, CA	213-876-3417
Tyre, Susan/, , CA	213-877-3884
Valade/, , CA	213-659-7621
Weinberg & James Foodstyle/3888 Woodcliff Rd, Sherman Oaks, CA	213-274-2383
Weiss, Sheri/2170 N Beverly Glen, Los Angeles, CA	213-470-1650

Costumes

New York City

AM Costume Wear/135-18 Northern Blvd	718-358-8108
Academy Clothes Inc/1703 Broadway	212-765-1440
Austin Ltd/140 E 55th St	212-752-7903
Capezio Dance Theater Shop/755 Seventh Ave	212-245-2130
Chenko Studio/167 W 46th St	212-944-0215
David's Outfitters Inc/36 W 20th St	212-691-7388
Eaves-Brookes Costume/21-07 41st Ave	718-729-1010
G Bank's Theatrical & Custom/320 W 48th St	212-586-6476
Grace Costumes Inc/254 W 54th St	212-586-0260
Herbert Danceware Co/902 Broadway	212-677-7606
Huey, Camilla/145 W 58th St #2C	212-459-9716
Ian's Boutique Inc/1151-A Second Ave	212-838-3969

Karinska/16 W 61st St	212-247-3341
Kulyk/72 E 7th St	212-674-0414
Lane Costume Co/234 Fifth Ave	212-684-4721
Martin, Alice Manougian/239 E 58th St	212-688-0117
Meyer, Jimmy & Co/428 W 44th St	212-765-8079
Michael-Jon Costumes Inc/39 W 19th St	212-741-3440
Mincou, Christine/405 E 63rd St	212-838-3881
Purcell, Elizabeth/105 Sullivan St	212-925-1962
Rubie's Costume Co/1 Rubie Plaza	718-846-1008
Sampler Vintage Clothes/455 W 43rd St	212-757-8168
Stivanello Costume Co Inc/66-38 Clinton Ave	718-651-7715
Tint, Francine/1 University Pl	212-475-3366
Universal Costume Co Inc/1540 Broadway	212-575-8570
Weiss & Mahoney Inc/142 Fifth Ave	212-675-1915
Winston, Mary Ellen/11 E 68th St	212-879-0766
Ynocencio, Jo/302 E 88th St	212-348-5332

Northeast

At-A-Glance Rentals/712 Main, Boonton, NJ	201-335-1488
Baldwin, Katharine/109 Commonwealth Ave, Boston, MA	617-267-0508
Barris, Alfred Wig Maker/10 E Sirtsink Dr, Pt Washington, NY	516-883-9061
Costume Armour Inc/Shore Rd Box 325, Cornwall on Hudson, NY	914-534-9120
Douglas, Rodney N/473 Avon Ave #3, Newark, NJ	201-375-2979
House of Costumes Ltd/166 Jericho Tpk, Mineola, NY	516-294-0170
Penrose Productions/4 Sandalwood Dr, Livingston, NJ	201-992-4264
Strutters/11 Paul Sullivan Way, Boston, MA	617-423-9299
Westchester Costume Rentals/540 Nepperhan Ave, Yonkers, NY	914-963-1333

Southeast

ABC Costume/185 NE 59th St, Miami, FL	305-757-3492
Atlantic Costume Co/2089 Monroe Dr, Atlanta, GA	404-874-7511
Carol, Lee Inc/2145 NW 2nd Ave, Miami, FL	305-573-1759
Fun Stop Shop/1601 Biscyne Blvd Omni Int F27, Miami, FL	305-358-2003
Goddard, Lynn Prod Svcs/712 Pelican Ave, New Orleans, LA	504-367-0348
Poinciana Sales/2252 W Flagler St, Miami, FL	305-642-3441
Star Styled/475 NW 42nd Ave, Miami, FL	305-649-3030

Midwest

Advance Theatrical Co/1900 N Narragansett, Chicago, IL	312-889-7700
Backstage Enterprises/1525 Ellinwood, Des Plaines, IL	312-692-6159
Be Something Studio/5533 N Forest Glen, Chicago, IL	312-685-6717
Broadway Costumes Inc/932 W Washington, Chicago, IL	312-829-6400
Brune, Paul/6330 N Indian Rd, Chicago, IL	312-763-1117
Center Stage/Fox Valley Shopping Cntr, Aurora, IL	312-851-9191
Chicago Costume Co Inc/1120 W Fullerton, Chicago, IL	312-528-1264
Ennis, Susan/2961 N Lincoln Ave, Chicago, IL	312-525-7483
Kaufman Costumes/5117 N Western, Chicago, IL	312-561-7529
Magical Mystery Tour, Ltd/6010 Dempster, Morton Grove, IL	312-966-5090
Okains Costume & Theater/2713 W Jefferson, Joliet, IL	815-741-9303
Stechman's Creations/1920 Koehler, Des Plaines, IL	312-827-9045
Taylor, Corinna/1700B W Granville, Chicago, IL	312-472-6550
The Set-up & Co/1049 E Michigan St, Indianapolis, IN	317-635-2323
Toy Gallery/1640 N Wells, Chicago, IL	312-944-4323

Southwest

ABC Theatrical Rental & Sales/825 N 7th St, Phoenix, AZ	602-258-5265
Abel, Joyce/Rt 1 Box 165, San Marcos, TX	512-392-5659
Campioni, Frederick/1920 Broken Oak, San Antonio, TX	512-342-7780
Corey, Irene/4147 Herschel Ave, Dallas, TX	214-528-4836
Incredible Productions/3327 Wylie Dr, Dallas, TX	214-350-3633
Lucy Greer & Assoc. Casting/600 Shadywood Ln, Richardson, TX	214-231-2086
Moreau, Suzanne/1007-B West 22nd St, Austin, TX	512-477-1532
Nicholson, Christine/c/o Lola Sprouse, Carrollton, TX	214-245-0926
Old Time Teenies Vintage Clothing/1126 W 6th St, Austin, TX	512-477-2022
Second Childhood/900 W 18th St, Austin, TX	512-472-9696

Production/Support Services

Continued

Please send us your additions and updates.

Starline Costume Products/1286 Bandera Rd, San Antonio, TX — 512-435-3535
Thomas, Joan S/6904 Spanky Branch Court, Dallas, TX — 214-931-1900
Welch, Virginia/3707 Manchaca Rd #138, Austin, TX — 512-447-1240

Rocky Mountain

And Sew On-Jila/2017 Broadway, Boulder, CO — 303-442-0130
Raggedy Ann Clothing & Costume/1213 E Evans Ave, Denver, CO — 303-733-7937

West Coast

Aardvark/7579 Melrose Ave, Los Angeles, CA — 213-655-6769
Adele's of Hollywood/5059 Hollywood Blvd, Hollywood, CA — 213-663-2231
American Costume Corp/12980 Raymer, N Hollywood, CA — 818-764-2239
Auntie Mame/1102 S La Cienega Blvd, Los Angeles, CA — 213-652-8430
Boserup House of Canes/1636 Westwood Blvd, W Los Angeles, CA — 213-474-2577
CBS Wardrobe Dept/7800 Beverly Blvd, Los Angeles, CA — 213-852-2345
California Surplus Mart/6263 Santa Monica Blvd, Los Angeles, CA — 213-465-5525
Capezio Dancewear/1777 Vine St, Hollywood, CA — 213-465-3744
Courtney, Elizabeth/8636 Melrose Ave, Los Angeles, CA — 213-657-4361
Crystal Palace (Sales)/8457 Melrose Ave, Hollywood, CA — 818-761-1870
Design Studio/6685-7 Sunset Blvd, Hollywood, CA — 213-469-3661
E C 2 Costumes/431 S Fairfax, Los Angeles, CA — 213-934-1131
Fantasy Costume/4310 San Fernando Rd, Glendale, CA — 213-245-7367
International Costume Co/1269 Sartori, Torrance, CA — 213-320-6392
Kings Western Wear/6455 Van Nuys Blvd, Van Nuys, CA — 818-785-2586
Krofft Entertainment/7200 Vineland Ave, Sun Valley, CA — 213-875-0324
LA Uniform Exchange/5239 Melrose Ave, Los Angeles, CA — 213-469-3965
MGM/UA Studios Wardrobe Dept/10202 W Washington Blvd, Culver City, CA — 213-558-5600
Military Antiques & War Museum/208 Santa Monica Ave, Santa Monica, CA — 213-393-1180
Minot, Abby/53 Canyon Rd, Berkeley, CA — 415-841-9600
Nudies Rodeo Tailor/5015 Lanskershim Blvd, N Hollywood, CA — 818-762-3105
Palace Costume/835 N Fairfax, Los Angeles, CA — 213-651-5458
Paramount Studios Wardrobe Dept/5555 Melrose Ave, Hollywood, CA — 213-468-5288
Peabodys/1102 1/2 S La Cienega Blvd, Los Angeles, CA — 213-352-3810
Piller's, Jerry/8163 Santa Monica Blvd, Hollywood, CA — 213-654-3038
The Burbank Studios Wardrobe Dept/4000 Warner Blvd, Burbank, CA — 818-954-1218
Tuxedo Center/7360 Sunset Blvd, Los Angeles, CA — 213-874-4200
Valu Shoe Mart/5637 Santa Monica Blvd, Los Angeles, CA — 213-469-8560
Western Costume Co/5335 Melrose Ave, Los Angeles, CA — 213-469-1451

Props

New York City

Abet Rent-A-Fur/307 Seventh Ave — 212-989-5757
Abstracta Structures Inc/347 Fifth Ave — 212-532-3710
Ace Galleries/91 University Pl — 212-991-4536
Adirondack Direct/219 E 42nd St — 212-687-8555
Alice's Antiques/552 Columbus Ave — 212-874-3400
Alpha-Pavia Bookbinding Co Inc/55 W 21st St — 212-929-5430
Archer Surgical Supplies Inc/544 W 27th St — 212-695-5553
Artisan's Studio/232 Atlantic Ave — 718-855-2796
Artistic Neon by Gasper/75-49 61st St — 718-821-1550
Arts & Crafters/175 Johnson St — 718-875-8151
Arts & Flowers/234 W 56th St — 212-247-7610
Associated Theatrical Designer/220 W 71st St — 212-362-2648
Austin Display/139 W 19th St — 212-924-6261
Baird, Bill Marionettes/41 Union Square — 212-989-9840
Baker, Alex/30 W 69th St — 212-799-2069
Bill's Flower Mart/816 Ave of the Americas — 212-889-8154
Brandon Memorabilia/222 E 51st St — 212-691-9776

Breitrose, Mark/156 Fifth Ave — 212-242-7825
Brooklyn Model Works/60 Washington Ave — 718-834-1944
California Artificial Flower Co/225 Fifth Ave — 212-679-7774
Carroll Musical Instrument Svc/351 W 41st St — 212-868-4120
Chateau Stables Inc/608 W 48th St — 212-246-0520
Churchill/Winchester Furn Rental/44 E 32nd St — 212-535-3400
Constructive Display/142 W 26th St — 212-675-7320
Cooper Film Cars/132 Perry St — 212-929-3909
Cycle Service Center Inc/74 Sixth Ave — 212-925-5900
Doherty Studios/252 W 46th St — 212-840-6219
Eclectic Properties Inc/204 W 84th St — 212-799-8963
Encore Studio/410 W 47th St — 212-246-5237
Florenco Foliage Systems Inc/30-28 Starr Ave — 718-729-6600
Furs, Valerie/150 W 30th St — 212-947-2020
Golden Equipment Co Inc/422 Madison Ave — 212-838-3776
Gordon Novelty Co/933 Broadway — 212-254-8616
Gossard & Assocs Inc/801 E 134th St — 212-665-9194
Gothic Color Co Inc/727 Washington St — 212-929-7493
Guccione/333 W 39th St — 212-279-3602
Harra, John Wood & Supply Co/39 W 19th St, 11th Fl — 212-741-0290
Harrison/Erickson/95 Fifth Ave — 212-929-5700
Jeffers, Kathy-Modelmaking/106 E 19th St 12th Fl — 212-475-1756
Joyce, Robert Studio Ltd/321 W 44th St #404 — 212-586-5041
Kaplan, Howard/35 E 10th St — 212-674-1000
Karpen, Ben/212 E 51st St — 212-755-3450
Kempler, George J/160 Fifth Ave — 212-989-1180
Kenmore Furniture Co Inc/156 E 33rd St — 212-683-1888
Mallie, Dale & Co/35-30 38th St — 718-706-1234
Manhattan Model Shop/40 Great Jones St — 212-473-6312
Maniatis, Michael Inc/48 W 22nd St — 212-620-0398
Manwaring Studio/232 Atlantic Ave — 718-855-2796
Marc Modell Associates/430 W 54th St — 212-541-9676
Mason's Tennis Mart/911 Seventh Ave — 212-757-5374
Matty's Studio Sales/543 W 35th St — 212-757-6246
McConnell & Borow Inc/10 E 23rd St — 212-254-1486
Mendez, Raymond A/220 W 98th St #12B — 212-864-4689
Messmore & Damon Inc/530 W 28th St — 212-594-8070
Metro Scenery Studio Inc/215-31 99th Ave — 718-464-6328
Modern Miltex Corp/280 E 134th St — 212-585-6000
Morozko, Bruce/41 White St — 212-226-8832
Movie Cars/825 Madison Ave — 212-288-6000
Newell Art Galleries Inc/425 E 53rd St — 212-758-1970
Nostalgia Alley Antiques/547 W 27th St — 212-695-6578
Novel Pinball Co/593 Tenth Ave — 212-736-3868
Plant Specialists Inc/524 W 34th St — 212-279-1500
Plastic Works!/2107 Broadway @ 73rd — 212-362-1000
Plexability Ltd/200 Lexington Ave — 212-679-7826
Porter-Rayvid/155 Attorney — 212-460-5050
Portobello Road Antiques Ltd/370 Columbus Ave — 212-724-2300
Props and Displays/132 W 18th St — 212-620-3840
Props for Today/15 W 20th St — 212-206-0330
Ray Beauty Supply Co Inc/721 Eighth Ave — 212-757-0175
Ridge, John Russell/531 Hudson St — 212-929-3410
Say It In Neon/434 Hudson St — 212-691-7977
Simon's Dir of Theatrical Mat/27 W 24th St — 212-255-2872
Smith & Watson/305 E 63rd St — 212-355-5615
Smith, David/New York — 212-730-1188
Solco Plumbing Suplies & Bathtubs/209 W 18th St — 212-243-2569
Special Effects/40 W 39th St — 212-869-8636
Starbuck Studio - Acrylic props/162 W 21st St — 212-807-7299
State Supply Equipment Co Inc/68 Thomas St — 212-233-0474
The Manhattan Model Shop/40 Great Jones St — 212-473-6312
The Place for Antiques/993 Second Ave — 212-475-6596
The Prop House Inc/76 Ninth Ave — 212-691-9099
The Prop Shop/26 College Pl — 718-522-4606
Theater Technology Inc/37 W 20th St — 212-929-5380
Times Square Theatrical & Studio/318 W 47th St — 212-245-4155
Uncle Sam's Umbrella/161 W 57th St — 212-582-1976
Whole Art Inc/259 W 30th St — 212-868-0978
Wizardworks/67 Atlantic Ave — 718-349-5252
Zakarian, Robert Prop Shop Inc/26 College Pl — 718-522-4606
Zeller, Gary & Assoc/Special Effects/40 W 39th St — 212-869-8636

Production/Support Services

Continued

Please send us your additions and updates.

Northeast

Antique Bicycle Props Service/113 Woodland Ave, Montvale, NJ	201-391-8780
Atlas Scenic Studios Ltd/46 Brokfield Ave, Bridgeport, CT	203-334-2130
Baily Designs/110 Williams St, Malden, MA	617-321-4448
Baldwin, Katherine/109 Commonwealth Ave, Boston, MA	617-267-0508
Bestek Theatrical Productions/218 Hoffman, Babylon, NY	516-225-0707
Cadillac Convertible Owners/, Thiells, NY	914-947-1109
Dewart, Tim Assoc/83 Old Standley St, Beverly, MA	617-922-9229
Geiger, Ed/12 Church St, Middletown, NJ	201-671-1707
Hart Scenic Studio/35-41 Dempsey Ave, Edgewater, NJ	212-947-7264
L I Auto Museum/Museum Square, South Hampton, NY	516-283-1880
Master & Talent Inc/1139 Foam Place, Far Rockaway, NY	516-239-7719
Model Sonics/272 Ave F, Bayonne, NJ	201-436-6721
Newbery, Tomas/Ridge Rd, Glen Cove, NY	516-759-0880
Pennington Inc/72 Edmund St, Edison, NJ	201-985-9090
Rindner, Jack N Assoc/112 Water St, Tinton Falls, NJ	201-542-3548
Shuller, Judy/POB 1168, Kennett, PA	
Stewart, Chas H Co/6 Clarendon Ave, Sommerville, MA	617-625-2407
Strutters/11 Paul Sullivan Way, Boston, MA	617-423-9299

Southeast

Alderman Company/325 Model Farm Rd, High Point, NC	919-889-6121
Arawak Marine/PO Box 7362, St Thomas, VI	809-775-1858
Charisma Prod Services/PO Box 19033, Jacksonville, FL	904-724-8483
Crigler, MB/Smooth As Glass Prod Svcs/607 Bass St, Nashville, TN	615-254-6061
Dangar, Jack/3640 Ridge Rd, Smyrna, GA	404-434-3640
Dunwright Productions/15281 NE 21st Ave, N Miami Beach, FL	305-944-2464
Enter Space/20 14th St NW, Atlanta, GA	404-885-1139
Kupersmith, Tony/320 N Highland Ave NE, Atlanta, GA	404-577-5319
Manning, Maureen/1283 Cedar Heights Dr, Stone Mountain, GA	404-296-1520
Miller, Lee/Rte 1, Box 98, Lumpkin, GA	912-838-4959
Player, Joanne/3403 Orchard St, Hapeville, GA	404-767-5542
S C Educational TV/2712 Millwood Ave, Columbia, SC	803-758-7284
Smith, Roscoe/15 Baltimore Pl NW, Atlanta, GA	404-252-3540
Sugar Creek Studio Inc/16 Young St, Atlanta, GA	404-522-3270
Sunshine Scenic Studios/1370 4th St, Sarasota, FL	813-366-8848
Winslow, Geoffrey C/1027 North Ave, Atlanta, GA	404-522-1669

Midwest

Advance Theatrical/125 N Wabash, Chicago, IL	312-889-7700
Becker Studios Inc/2824 W Taylor, Chicago, IL	312-722-4040
Bregstone Assoc/440 S Wabash, Chicago, IL	312-939-5130
Cadillac Plastic/1924 N Paulina, Chicago, IL	312-342-9200
Carpenter, Brent Studio/314 W Institute Pl, Chicago, IL	312-787-1774
Center Stage/Fox Valley Shopping Cntr, Aurora, IL	312-851-9191
Chanco Ltd/3131 West Grand Ave, Chicago, IL	312-638-0363
Chicago Scenic Studios Inc/2217 W Belmont Ave, Chicago, IL	312-477-8362
Hartman Furniture & Carpet Co/220 W Kinzie, Chicago, IL	312-664-2800
Hollywood Stage Lighting/5850 N Broadway, Chicago, IL	312-869-3340
House of Drane/410 N Ashland Ave, Chicago, IL	312-829-8686
Merrick Models Ltd/1426 W Fullerton, Chicago, IL	312-281-7787
Okains Costume & Theater/2713 W Jefferson, Joliet, IL	815-741-9303
Scroungers Inc/351 Lyndale Ave S, Minneapolis, MN	612-823-2340
Starr, Steve Studios/2654 N Clark St, Chicago, IL	312-525-6530
Studio Specialties/409 W Huron, Chicago, IL	312-337-5131
The Emporium/1551 N Wells, Chicago, IL	312-337-7126
The Model Shop/415 N State St, Chicago, IL	312-822-9663
The Set-up & Co/1049 E Michigan St, Indianapolis, IN	317-635-2323
White House Studios/9167 Robinson, Kansas City, MO	913-341-8036

Southwest

Desert Wren Designs, Inc/7340 Scottsdale Mall, Scottsdale, AZ	602-941-5056
Doerr, Dean/11321 Greystone, Oklahoma City, OK	405-751-0313
Eats/PO Box 52, Tempe, AZ	602-966-7459
Janet-Nelson/PO Box 143, Tempe, AZ	602-968-3771
Marty, Jack/2225 South First, Garland, TX	214-840-8708
Melancon, Joseph Studios/2934 Elm, Dallas, TX	214-742-2982
Southern Importers/4825 San Jacinto, Houston, TX	713-524-8236
Young Film Productions/PO Box 50105, Tucson, AZ	602-623-5961

West Coast

A & A Special Effects/7021 Havenhurst St, Van Nuys, CA	818-782-6558
Abbe Rents/600 S Normandie, Los Angeles, CA	213-384-5292
Aldik Artificial Flowers Co/7651 Sepulveda Blvd, Van Nuys, CA	213-988-5970
Allen, Walter Plant Rentals/5500 Melrose Ave, Hollywood, CA	213-469-3621
Altbaum, Patti/244-CS Lasky Dr, Beverly Hills, CA	213-553-6269
Anabel's Diversified Services/PO Box 532, Pacific Palisades, CA	213-454-1566
Antiquarian Traders/8483 Melrose Ave, Los Angeles, CA	213-658-6394
Arnelle Sales Co Prop House/7926 Beverly Blvd, Los Angeles, CA	213-930-2900
Asia Plant Rentals/1215 225th St, Torrance, CA	818-775-1811
Astrovision, Inc/7240 Valjean Ave, Van Nuys, CA	818-989-5222
Backings, c/o 20th Century Fox/10201 W Pico Blvd, Los Angeles, CA	213-277-0522
Baronian Manufacturing Co/1865 Farm Bureau Rd, Concord, CA	415-671-7199
Barris Kustom Inc/10811 Riverside Dr, N Hollywood, CA	213-877-2352
Barton Surrey Svc/518 Fairview Ave, Arcadia, CA	818-447-6693
Beverly Hills Fountain Center/7856 Santa Monica Blvd, Hollywood, CA	
Bischoff's/449 S San Fernando Blvd, Burbank, CA	213-843-7561
Boserup House of Canes/1636 Westwood Blvd, W Los Angeles, CA	213-474-2577
Brown, Mel Furniture/5840 S Figueroa St, Los Angeles, CA	213-778-4444
Buccaneer Cruises/Berth 76W-33 Ports O'Call, San Pedro, CA	213-548-1085
Cinema Float/447 N Newport Blvd, Newport Beach, CA	714-675-8888
Cinema Mercantile Co/5857 Santa Monica Blvd, Hollywood, CA	213-466-8201
Cinema Props Co/5840 Santa Monica Blvd, Hollywood, CA	213-466-8201
City Lights/404 S Figueroa, Los Angeles, CA	213-680-9876
Colors of the Wind/2900 Main St, Santa Monica, CA	213-399-8044
Corham Artifical Flowers/11800 Olympic Blvd, Los Angeles, CA	213-479-1166
Custom Neon/3804 Beverly Blvd, Los Angeles, CA	213-386-7945
D'Andrea Glass Etchings/3671 Tacoma Ave, Los Angeles, CA	213-223-7940
Decorative Paper Productions/1818 W 6th St, Los Angeles, CA	213-484-1080
Deutsch Inc/426 S Robertson Blvd, Los Angeles, CA	213-273-4949
Ellis Mercantile Co/169 N LaBrea Ave, Los Angeles, CA	213-933-7334
Featherock Inc/20219 Bohama St, Chatsworth, CA	818-882-3888
First Street Furniture Store/1123 N Bronson Ave, Los Angeles, CA	213-462-6306
Flower Fashions/9960 Santa Monica Blvd, Beverly Hills, CA	213-272-6063
Games Unlimited/8924 Lindblade, Los Angeles, CA	213-836-8920
Golden West Billiard Supply/21260 Deering Court, Canoga Park, CA	213-877-4100
Grand American Fare/3008 Main St, Santa Monica, CA	213-450-4900
Haltzman Office Furniture/1417 S Figueroa, Los Angeles, CA	213-749-7021
Hawaii Design Create/1750 Kalakaua Ave #116, Honolulu, HI	808-235-2262
Hollywood Toys/6562 Hollywood Blvd, Los Angeles, CA	213-465-3119
House of Props Inc/1117 N Gower St, Hollywood, CA	213-463-3166
Hume, Alex R/1527 W Magnolia, Burbank, CA	213-849-1614
Independent Studio Svcs/11907 Wicks St, Sun Valley, CA	213-764-0840
Iwasaki Images/19330 Van Ness Ave, Torrance, CA	213-533-5986
Jackson Shrub Supply/9500 Columbus Ave, Sepulveda, CA	213-893-6939
Johnson, Ray M Studio/5555 Sunset Blvd, Hollywood, CA	213-465-4108
Krofft Enterprise/1040 Las Palmas, Hollywood, CA	213-467-3125
Laughing Cat Design Co/723 1/2 N La Cienega Blvd, Los Angeles, CA	213-854-0135
Living Interiors/7273 Santa Monica Blvd, Los Angeles, CA	213-874-7815
MGM Studios Prop Dept/10202 W Washington Blvd, Culver City, CA	213-836-3000
Macduff Flying Circus/5527 Saigon St, Lancaster, CA	805-942-5406
Malibu Florists/21337 Pacific Coast Hwy, Malibu, CA	213-456-2014
Marvin, Lennie Entrprs Ltd/1105 N Hollywood Way, Burbank, CA	818-841-5882

McDermott, Kate/1114 S Point View, Los Angeles, CA	213-935-4101
Modelmakers/216 Townsend St, San Francisco, CA	415-495-5111
Mole-Richardson/937 N Sycamore Ave, Hollywood, CA	213-851-0111
Moskatels/733 S San Julian St, Los Angeles, CA	213-627-1631
Motion Picture Marine/616 Venice Blvd, Marina del Rey, CA	213-822-1100
Music Center/5616 Santa Monica Blvd, Hollywood, CA	213-469-8143
Omega Cinema Props/5857 Santa Monica Blvd, Los Angeles, CA	213-466-8201
Omega Studio Rentals/5757 Santa Monica Blvd, Hollywood, CA	213-466-8201
Pacific Palisades Florists/15244 Sunset Blvd, Pacific Palisades, CA	213-454-0337
Paramount Studios Prop Dept/5555 Melrose Ave, Los Angeles, CA	213-468-5000
Photo Productions/400 Montgomery St, San Francisco, CA	415-392-5985
Post, Don Studios/8211 Lankershim Blvd, N Hollywood, CA	818-768-0811
Producers Studio/650 N Bronson Ave, Los Angeles, CA	213-466-7778
Professional Scenery Inc/7311 Radford Ave, N Hollywood, CA	213-875-1910
Prop City/9336 W Washington, Culver City, CA	213-559-7022
Prop Service West/918 N Orange Dr, Los Angeles, CA	213-461-3371
Rent-A-Mink/6738 Sunset Blvd, Hollywood, CA	213-467-7879
Roschu/6514 Santa Monica Blvd, Hollywood, CA	213-469-2749
Rouzer, Danny Studio/7022 Melrose Ave, Hollywood, CA	213-936-2494
Scale Model Co/4613 W Rosecrans Ave, Los Angeles, CA	213-679-1436
School Days Equipment Co/973 N Main St, Los Angeles, CA	213-223-3474
Silvestri Studios/1733 W Cordova St, Los Angeles, CA	213-735-1481
Snakes/6100 Laurel Canyon Blvd, North Hollywood, CA	213-985-7777
Special Effects Unlimited/752 N Cahuenga Blvd, Hollywood, CA	213-466-3361
Spellman Desk Co/6159 Santa Monica Blvd, Hollywood, CA	213-467-0628
Stage Right/Box 2265, Canyon Country, CA	805-251-4342
Star Sporting Goods/1645 N Highland Ave, Hollywood, CA	213-469-3531
Stembridge Gun Rentals/431 Magnolia, Glendale, CA	818-246-4833
Studio Specialties/3013 Gilroy St, Los Angeles, CA	213-480-3101
Stunts Unlimited/3518 Cahuenga Blvd W, Los Angeles, CA	213-874-0050
Surf, Val/4807 Whitsett, N Hollywood, CA	818-769-6977
The Burbank Studios Prop Dept/4000 Warner Blvd, Burbank, CA	818-954-6000
The Hand Prop Room/5700 Venice Blvd, Los Angeles, CA	213-931-1534
The High Wheelers Inc/109 S Hidalgo, Alhambra, CA	213-576-8648
The Plantation/38 Arena St, El Segundo, CA	213-322-7877
Transparent Productions/3410 S Lacienaga Blvd, Los Angeles, CA	213-938-3821
Tri-Tronex Inc/2921 W Alameda Ave, Burbank, CA	213-849-6115
Tropizon Plant Rentals/1401 Pebble Vale, Monterey Park, CA	213-269-2010
UPA Pictures/4440 Lakeside Dr, Burbank, CA	213-556-3800
Western Costume Company/5335 Melrose Ave, Hollywood, CA	213-469-1451
Wizards Inc/8333 Lahui, Northridge, CA	818-368-8974

Locations

New York City

Act Travel/310 Madison Ave	212-697-9550
Ayoub, Jimmy/132 E 16th St	212-598-4467
C & C Productions/445 E 80th St	212-472-3700
Carmichael-Moore, Bob Inc/PO Box 5	212-255-0465
Cinema Galleries/517 W 35th St 1st Fl	212-627-1222
Dancerschool/400 Lafayette St	212-260-0453
Davidson/Frank Photo-Stylists/209 W 86th St #701	212-799-2651
Howell, T J Interiors/301 E 38th St	212-532-6267
Juckes, Geoff/295 Bennett Ave	212-567-5676
Kopro, Ken/206 E 6th St	212-677-1798
Leach, Ed Inc/160 Fifth Ave	212-691-3450
Location Connection/31 E 31st St	212-684-1888
Location Locators/225 E 63rd St	212-832-1866
Loft Locations/50 White St	212-966-6408
Marks, Arthur/140 E 40th St	212-685-2761

Myriad Communications, Inc/208 W 30th St	212-564-4340
NY State Film Commission/230 Park Ave #834	212-309-0540
Ruekberg, Brad/3211 Ave I #5H	718-377-3506
Terrestris/409 E 60th St	212-758-8181
The Perfect Place Ltd/182 Amity St	718-570-6252
This Must Be The Place/2119 Albermarle Terrace	718-282-3454
Unger, Captain Howard/80 Beach Rd	718-639-3578
Wolfson, Paula/227 W 10th St	212-741-3048

Northeast

C-M Associates/268 New Mark, Rockville, MD	301-340-7070
Cinemagraphics/100 Massachusetts Ave, Boston, MA	617-266-2200
Connecticut State Travel Office/210 Washington St, Hartford, CT	203-566-3383
Cooper Productions/175 Walnut St, Brookline, MA	617-738-7278
Delaware State Travel Service/99 Kings Highway, Dover, DE	302-736-4254
Dobush, Jim/148 W Mountain, Ridgefield, CT	203-431-3718
E-Fex/623 Pennsylvania Ave SE, Washington, DC	202-543-1241
Film Services of WV Library Comm/1900 Washington St E, Charleston, WV	304-348-3977
Florentine Films, Inc/25 Main St, Northampton, MA	413-584-0816
Forma, Belle/433 Claflin Ave, Mamaroneck, NY	914-698-2598
Gilmore, Robert Assoc Inc/990 Washington St, Dedham, MA	617-329-6633
Girl/Scout Locations/One Hillside Ave, Port Washington, NY	516-883-8409
Great Locations/97 Windsor Road, Tenafly, NJ	201-567-1455
Hackerman, Nancy Prod Inc/6 East Eager St, Baltimore, MD	301-685-2727
Hampton Locations/109 Hill Street, South Hampton, NY	516-283-2160
Jurgielewicz, Annie/PO Box 422, Cambridge, MA	617-628-1141
Krause, Janet L/43 Linnaean St #26, Cambridge, MA	617-492-3223
Lewis, Jay/87 Ripley St, Newton Center, MA	617-332-1516
Location Scouting Service/153 Sidney St, Oyster Bay, NY	516-922-1759
Location Services/30 Rockledge Rd, W Redding , CT	203-938-3227
Location Unlimited/24 Briarcliff, Tenafly, NJ	201-567-2809
Locations-Productions/, Boston, MA	617-423-9793
Maine State Development Office/193 State St, Augusta, ME	207-289-2656
Maryland Film Commission/45 Talvert, Annapolis, MD	301-269-3577
Massachusetts State Film Bureau/100 Cambridge St, Boston, MA	617-727-3330
McGlynn, Jack/34 Buffum St, Salem, MA	617-745-8764
NJ State Motion Pic Dev/Gateway One, Newark, NJ	201-648-6279
Nassau Farmer's Market/600 Hicksville Rd, Bethpage, NY	516-931-2046
New Hampshire Vacation Travel/PO Box 856, Concord, NH	603-271-2666
Nozik, Michael/9 Cutler Ave, Cambridge, MA	617-783-4315
Pennington Inc/72 Edmund St, Edison, NJ	201-985-9090
Pennsylvania Film Bureau/461 Forum Bldg, Harrisburg, PA	717-787-5333
Penrose Productions/4 Sandalwood Dr, Livingston, NJ	201-992-4264
PhotoSonics/1116 N Hudson St, Arlington, VA	703-522-1116
Proteus Location Services/9217 Baltimore Blvd, College Park, MD	301-441-2928
RenRose Locations, Ltd/4 Sandalwood Dr, Livingston, NJ	201-992-4264
Rhode Island State Tourist Division/7 Jackson Walkway, Providence, RI	401-277-2601
Strawberries Finders Service/Buck County, Reigelsville, PA	215-346-8000
Terry, Karen/131 Boxwood Dr, Kings Park, NY	516-724-3964
The Hermitage/PO Box 4, Yorktown Heights, NY	914-632-5315
The Location Hunter/16 Iselin Terr, Larchmont, NY	914-834-2181
Upstate Production Services, Inc/277 Alexander St #510, Rochester, NY	716-546-5417
Verange, Joe - Century III/545 Boylston St, Boston, MA	617-267-9800
Vermont State Travel Division/134 State, Montpelier, VT	802-828-3236
Washington DC Public Space Committee/415 12th St, N W Washington, DC	202-629-4084

Southeast

Alabama State Film Commission/340 North Hull St, Montgomery, AL	800-633-5898
Baker, Sherry/1823 Indiana Ave, Atlanta, GA	404-373-6666
Bruns, Ken & Gayle/7810 SW 48th Court, Miami, FL	305-666-2928

Charisma Prod Services/PO Box 19033, Jacksonville, FL	904-724-8483
Crigler, MB/Smooth As Glass Prod Svcs/607 Bass St, Nashville, TN	615-254-6061
Dangar, Jack/3640 Ridge Rd, Smyrna, GA	404-434-3640
Darracott, David/1324 Briarcliff Rd #5, Atlanta, GA	404-872-0219
Fl State Motion Picture/TV Svcs/107 W Gaines St, Tallahassee, FL	904-487-1100
Georgia State Film Office/PO Box 1776, Atlanta, GA	404-656-3591
Harris, George/2875 Mabry Lane NE, Atlanta, GA	404-231-0116
Irene Marie/3212 S Federal Hwy, Ft Lauderdale, FL	305-522-3262
Kentucky Film Comm/Berry Hill Mansion/Louisville, Frankfort, KY	502-564-3456
Kupersmith, Tony/320 N Highland Ave NE, Atlanta, GA	404-577-5319
Locations Extraordinaire/6794 Giralda Cir, Boca Raton, FL	305-487-5050
McDonald, Stew/6905 N Coolidge Ave, Tampa, FL	813-886-3773
Miller, Lee/Rte 1, Box 98, Lumpkin, GA	912-838-4959
Mississippi State Film Commission/PO Box 849, Jackson, MS	601-359-3449
Natchez Film Comm/Liberty Pk Hwy, Hwy 16, Natchez, MS	601-446-6345
North Carolina Film Comm/430 N Salisbury St, Raleigh, NC	919-733-9900
Player, Joanne/3403 Orchard St, Hapeville, GA	404-767-5542
Reel Wheels/2267 NE 164th St, Miami, FL	305-947-9304
Remington Models & Talent/2480 E Commercial Blvd PH, Ft Lauderdale, FL	305-566-5420
Rose, Sheila/8218 NW 8th St, Plantation, FL	305-473-9747
South Florida Location Finders/7621 SW 59th Court, S Miami, FL	305-445-0739
TN State Econ & Comm Dev/1007 Andrew Jackson Bldg, Nashville, TN	615-741-1888
Tennessee Film Comm/James Polk Off Bldg, Nashville, TN	615-741-3456
USVI Film Promotion Office/St Thomas, VI,	809-774-1331
Virginia Division of Tourism/202 North 9th St, Richmond, VA	804-786-2051

Midwest

A-Stock Photo Finder/1030 N State St, Chicago, IL	312-645-0611
Illinois State Film Office/100 W Randolph #3-400, Chicago, IL	312-793-3600
Indiana State Tourism Development/1 N Capital, Indianapolis, IN	317-232-8860
Iowa State Development Commission/600 E Court Ave #A, Des Moines, IA	515-281-3251
Kansas State Dept-Econ Div/503 Kansas Ave, Topeka, KS	913-296-3481
Location Services Film & Video/417 S 3rd St, Minneapolis, MN	612-338-3359
Manya Nogg Co/9773 Lafayette Plaza, Omaha, NB	402-397-8887
Michigan State Travel Bureau/PO Box 30226, Lansing, MI	517-373-0670
Minnesota State Tourism Division/419 N Robert, St Paul, MN	612-296-5029
Missouri State Tourism Commission/301 W High St, Jefferson City, MO	314-751-3051
ND State Business & Industrial/Liberty Memorial Bldg, Bismarck, ND	701-224-2810
Ohio Film Bureau/30 E Broad St, Columbus, OH	614-466-2284
Station 12 Producers Express/1759 Woodgrove Ln, Southfield, MI	313-569-7707
Stock Market/4211 Flora Place, St Louis, MO	314-773-2298

Southwest

Alamo Village/PO Box 528, Brackettville, TX	512-563-2580
Arizona Land Co/PO Box 63441, Phoenix, AZ	602-956-5552
Arkansas State Dept of Economics/#1 Capital Mall, Little Rock, AR	501-371-1121
Blair, Tanya Agency/3000 Carlisle, Dallas, TX	214-748-8353
Cinema America/Box 56566, Houston, TX	713-780-8819
Dawson, Kim Agency/PO Box 585060, Dallas, TX	214-638-2414
Duncan, S Wade/PO Box 140273, Dallas, TX	214-828-1367
El Paso Film Liaison/5 Civic Center Plaza, El Paso, TX	915-544-3650
Epic Film Productions/1203 W 44th St, Austin, TX	512-452-9461
Fashion Consultants/262 Camelot Center, Richardson, TX	214-234-4006
Flach, Bob/3513 Norma, Garland, TX	214-272-8431
Fowlkes, Rebecca W/412 Canterbury Hill, San Antonio, TX	512-826-4142
Grapevine Productions/3214-A Hemlock Avenue, Austin, TX	512-472-0894
Greenblatt, Linda/6722 Waggoner, Dallas, TX	214-691-6552
Griffin, Gary Productions/12667 Memorial Dr #4, Houston, TX	713-465-9017

Kessel, Mark/3631 Granada, Dallas, TX	214-526-0415
MacLean, John/10017 Woodgrove, Dallas, TX	214-343-0181
Maloy, Buz/Rt 1 Box 155, Kyle, TX	512-398-3148
Maloy, John W/718 W 35th St, Austin, TX	512-453-9660
McLaughlin, Ed M/3512 Rashti Court, Ft Worth, TX	817-927-2310
Murray Getz Commer & Indust Phot/2310 Genessee, Houston, TX	713-526-4451
Nichols, Beverly & Skipper Richardson/6043 Vanderbilt Ave, Dallas, TX	214-349-3171
OK State Tourism-Rec Dept/500 Will Rogers Bldg, Oklahoma City, OK	405-521-3981
Oklahoma Film Comm/500 Will Rogers Bldg, Oklahoma City, OK	405-521-3525
Putman, Eva M/202 Dover, Richardson, TX	214-783-9616
Ranchland - Circle R/Rt 3, Box 229, Roanoke, TX	817-430-1561
Ray, Al/2304 Houston Street, San Angelo, TX	915-949-2716
Ray, Rudolph/2231 Freeland Avenue, San Angelo, TX	915-949-6784
Reinninger, Laurence H/501 North IH 35, Austin, TX	512-478-8593
San Antonio Zoo & Aquar/3903 N St Marys, San Antonio, TX	512-734-7184
Senn, Loyd C/PO Box 6060, Lubbock, TX	806-792-2000
Summers, Judy/1504 Harvard, Houston, TX	713-661-1440
TBK Talent Enterprises/5255 McCullough, San Antonio, TX	512-822-0508
Taylor, Peggy Talent/6311 N O'Connor 3 Dallas Comm, Irving, TX	214-869-1515
Texas Film Commission/PO Box 12428 Capitol Station, Austin, TX	512-475-3785
Texas Pacific Film Video, Inc/501 North IH 35, Austin, TX	512-478-8585
Texas World Entrtnmnt/8133 Chadbourne Road, Dallas, TX	214-358-0857
Tucson Film Comm/Ofc of Mayor Box 27370, Tucson, AZ	602-791-4000
Wild West Stunt Company/Box T-789, Stephenville, TX	817-965-4342
Young Film Productions/PO Box 50105, Tucson, AZ	602-623-5961
Zimmerman and Associates, Inc/411 Bonham, San Antonio, TX	512-225-6708
Zuniga, Tony/2616 North Flores #2, San Antonio, TX	512-227-9660

Rocky Mountain

Montana Film Office/1424 Ninth Ave, Helena, MT	406-449-2654
Wyoming Film Comm/IH 25 & College Dr #51, Cheyenne, WY	307-777-7851

West Coast

California Film Office/6922 Hollywood Blvd, Hollywood, CA	213-736-2465
Daniels, Karil, Point of View Prod/2477 Folsom St, San Francisco, CA	415-821-0435
Design Art Studios/1128 N Las Palmas, Hollywood, CA	213-464-9118
Excor Travel/1750 Kalakaua Ave #116, Honolulu, HI	808-946-6614
Film Permits Unlimited/8058 Allott Ave, Van Nuys, CA	213-997-6197
Herod, Thomas Jr/PO Box 2534, Hollywood, CA	213-353-0911
Juckes, Geoff/3185 Durand Dr, Hollywood, CA	213-465-6604
Location Enterprises Inc/6725 Sunset Blvd, Los Angeles, CA	213-469-3141
Mindseye/767 Northpoint, San Francisco, CA	415-441-4578
Minot, Abby/53 Canyon Rd, Berkeley, CA	415-841-9600
Newhall Ranch/23823 Valencia, Valencia, CA	818-362-1515
Pacific Production & Location Svc/424 Nahua St, Honolulu, HI	808-926-6188
San Francisco Conv/Visitors Bur/1390 Market St #260, San Francisco, CA	415-626-5500
The Location Co/8646 Wilshire Blvd, Beverly Hills, CA	213-855-7075

Sets

New York City

Abstracta Structures/347 Fifth Ave	212-532-3710
Alcamo Marble Works/541 W 22nd St	212-255-5224
Baker, Alex/30 W 69th St	212-799-2069
Coulson, Len/717 Lexington Ave	212-688-5155
Dynamic Interiors/760 McDonald Ave	718-435-6326
Golden Office Interiors/574 Fifth Ave	212-719-5150
LaFerla, Sandro/108 W 25th St	212-620-0693

Production/Support Services

Continued

Please send us your additions and updates.

Lincoln Scenic Studio/560 W 34th St	212-244-2700
Moroxko, Bruce/41 White St	212-226-8832
Nelson, Jane/21 Howard St	212-431-4642
Oliphant, Sarah/38 Cooper Square	212-741-1233
Plexability Ltd/200 Lexington Ave	212-679-7826
Set Shop/3 W 20 St	212-929-4845
Siciliano, Frank/125 Fifth Ave	212-620-4075
Stage Scenery/155 Attorney St	212-460-5050
Theater Technology Inc/37 W 20th St	212-929-5380
Unique Surfaces/28 W 27th St	212-696-9229
Variety Scenic Studio/25-19 Borden Ave	718-392-4747
Yurkiw, Mark/568 Broadway	212-243-0928

Northeast

Davidson, Peter/144 Moody St, Waltham, MA	617-899-3239
Foothills Theater Company/PO Box 236, Worcester, MA	617-754-0546
Penrose Productions/4 Sandalwood Dr, Livingston, NJ	201-992-4264
The Focarino Studio/31 Deep Six Dr, East Hampton, NY	516-324-7637
Trapp, Patricia/42 Stanton Rd, Brookline, MA	617-734-9321
Videocom, Inc/502 Sprague St, Dedham, MA	617-329-4080
White Oak Design/PO Box 1164, Marblehead, MA	617-426-7171

Southeast

Crigler, MB/Smooth As Glass Prod Svcs/607 Bass St, Nashville, TN	615-254-6061
Enter Space/20 14th St NW, Atlanta, GA	404-885-1139
Kupersmith, Tony/320 N Highland Ave NE, Atlanta, GA	404-577-5319
Sugar Creek Scenic Studio, Inc/465 Bishop St, Atlanta, GA	404-351-9404
The Great Southern Stage/15221 NE 21 Ave, N Miami Beach, FL	305-947-0430

Midwest

Backdrop Solution/311 N Desplaines Ave #607, Chicago, IL	312-993-0494
Becker Studio/2824 W Taylor, Chicago, IL	312-722-4040
Centerwood Cabinets/3700 Main St NE, Blaine, MN	612-786-2094
Chicago Scenic Studios Inc/213 N Morgan, Chicago, IL	312-942-1483
Dimension Works/4130 W Belmont, Chicago, IL	312-545-2233
Douglas Design/2165 Lakeside Ave, Cleveland, OH	216-621-2558
Grand Stage Lighting Co/630 W Lake, Chicago, IL	312-332-5611
Morrison, Tamara/1225 Morse, Chicago, IL	312-864-0954
The Set-up & Co/1049 E Michigan St, Indianapolis, IN	317-635-2323

Southwest

Country Roads/701 Ave B, Del Rio, TX	512-775-7991
Crabb, Ken/3066 Ponder Pl, Dallas, TX	214-352-0581
Dallas Stage Lighting & Equipment/1818 Chestnut, Dallas, TX	214-428-1818
Dallas Stage Scenery Co, Inc/3917 Willow St, Dallas, TX	214-821-0002
Dunn, Glenn E/7412 Sherwood Rd, Austin, TX	512-441-0377
Edleson, Louis/6568 Lake Circle, Dallas, TX	214-823-7180
Eschberger, Jerry/6401 South Meadows, Austin, TX	512-447-4795
Freeman Design & Display Co/2233 Irving Blvd, Dallas, TX	214-638-8800
H & H Special Effects/2919 Chisholm Trail, San Antonio, TX	512-826-8214
Houston Stage Equipment/2301 Dumble, Houston, TX	713-926-4441
Reed, Bill Decorations/333 First Ave, Dallas, TX	214-823-3154
Texas Scenic Co Inc/5423 Jackwood Dr, San Antonio, TX	512-684-0091
Texas Set Design/3103 Oak Lane, Dallas, TX	214-426-5511

Rocky Mountain

Love, Elisa/1035 Walnut, Boulder, CO	303-442-4877

West Coast

Grosh, R L & Sons Scenic Studio/4144 Sunset Blvd, Los Angeles, CA	213-662-1134
Act Design & Execution/PO Box 5054, Sherman Oaks, CA	818-788-4219
American Scenery/18555 Eddy St, Northridge, CA	818-886-1585
Backings, J C/10201 W Pico Blvd, Los Angeles, CA	213-277-0522
CBS Special Effects/7800 Beverly Blvd, Los Angeles, CA	213-852-2345
Carthay Set Services/5176 Santa Monica Blvd, Hollywood, CA	213-469-5618
Carthay Studio/5907 W Pico, Los Angeles, CA	213-938-2101
Cloutier Inc/704 N Gardner, Los Angeles, CA	213-655-1263
Erecter Set Inc/1150 S LaBrea, Hollywood, CA	213-938-4762
Grosh, RL & Sons/4144 Sunset Blvd, Los Angeles, CA	213-662-1134
Hawaii Design Create/1750 Kalakaua Ave #116, Honolulu, HI	808-235-2262
Hollywood Scenery/6605 Elenor Ave, Hollywood, CA	213-467-6272
Hollywood Stage/6650 Santa Monica Blvd, Los Angeles, CA	213-466-4393
Krofft Entrprs/1040 Las Palmas, Hollywood, CA	213-467-3125
Pacific Studios/8315 Melrose Ave, Los Angeles, CA	213-653-3093
Producers Studio/650 N Bronson Ave, Los Angeles, CA	213-466-3111
RJ Show Time/1011 Gower St, Hollywood, CA	213-467-2127
Shafton Inc/5500 Cleon Ave, N Hollywood, CA	818-985-5025
Superstage/5724 Santa Monica Blvd, Los Angeles, CA	213-464-0296
Triangle Scenery/1215 Bates Ave, Los Angeles, CA	213-661-1262

Index Illustrators, Graphic Designers & Photographers

Continued on next page.

Index Illustrators, Graphic Designers & Photographers

Continued from previous page.